BURKE'S GUIDE TO COUNTRY HOUSES

Coole Park

Here, traveller, scholar, poet, take your stand
When all those rooms and passages are gone,
When nettles wave upon a shapeless mound
And saplings root among the broken stone . . .

W. B. YEATS *1929*

Frontispiece: *Galgorm Castle*

BURKE'S SERIES
Founded by John Burke 1826
Editor Hugh Montgomery-Massingberd

BURKE'S GUIDE TO COUNTRY HOUSES

VOLUME I · IRELAND

Mark Bence-Jones

LONDON
BURKE'S PEERAGE LTD
MCMLXXVIII

Dedicated to the memory of my cousin Roly Price-Jones,
whose love of country houses was as great as mine
and whose knowledge of them was greater

PUBLISHERS' NOTE
Every care was taken to check the information supplied for this edition
but the Author and Publishers cannot accept responsibility for mis-statements,
omissions or other inaccuracies which may appear in this work

ISBN 0 85011 026 2

This book has been set in Imprint by
Typesetting Services Ltd, of Glasgow, Scotland,
printed and bound by Robert MacLehose & Co Ltd, of Glasgow,
for the Publishers, Burke's Peerage Ltd
(Registered Office: 42 Curzon Street, London W1.
Publishing Offices: 56 Walton Street, London SW3, England)

First published 1978
Reprinted 1980

Book Designer: Humphrey Stone
(The Compton Press Ltd, Tisbury, Wiltshire, England)

Contents

Editor's Preface

THE COUNTRY houses of the British Isles are a magnificent heritage which constitute the greatest and, blending comfort with elegance, most representative contribution made by these islands to world culture. Previous books on the subject, however, have seldom strayed from the well-worn paths leading to stately homes we now know quite enough about. These important buildings will probably be preserved whatever political system is in force. It is the "illustrious obscure" houses that are the special glory of the British Isles and their disappearance is destroying the fabric of history. When going around, one sees a country house over, or through, a wall or hedge; one's curiosity is aroused. Looking it up in a guide-book, the chances are that one will either not find it or be given a brief dismissive piece on its lack of architectural distinction; it is a safe bet that, in any event, one will not be told about the family associated with the house. The architectural purists who ignore the family connexion miss the point: it is the families who have created these houses, have built up their collections, have indulged varied tastes, to which pseudo-aesthetes might take exception, and have achieved unique atmospheres. It is indeed the families—in the ever-decreasing cases where they are still *in situ*—who are unquestionably the best custodians to preserve this heritage. As Professor Mark Girouard said of one country house: "Agreeable architecture, interesting family still has original furniture, fittings and family papers—cumulatively an important house."

In April 1972, we announced a major new series of books which would cover the country houses of the British Isles, *Burke's Guide to Country Houses*, running to eight volumes. Although mainly associated with genealogy and heraldry since its foundation in 1826, *Burke's* could claim that this architectural innovation was not without precedent: Sir Bernard Burke's *Visitation of Seats and Arms of the Noblemen and Gentlemen of Great Britain and Ireland* (1852/53 and 1854/55) is the ancestor of the present series and we have actually used some of its illustrations in this first volume. The declared aim of *Burke's Guide to Country Houses* was to be comprehensive on an unprecedented scale, covering the field of important and "illustrious obscure" houses, standing and demolished, more extensively than had ever been done before. *Burke's* is in a singular position to break new ground in stressing the family connexions of the "seats": a remarkably high percentage of the families who have owned country houses are featured in one of *Burke's* genealogical publications.

"What is a country house?" is a difficult question to answer properly and one is tempted to leave the answer to people's commonsense. In this series, architectural merit is not a criterion, and perhaps "a house with social-cum-architectural pretensions to being the country seat of a landed family" may serve as a reply. Town houses are not to be found in this book however important they are architecturally. Some of the houses which do appear are in fact situated in towns, such as DAMER HOUSE; but they qualify since they were the seats of families who owned landed estates in the neighbourhood, rather than mere town houses which were only occupied occasionally. In the same way, Bishop's Palaces in towns are deemed to qualify because they were not just town residences but the permanent seats of Bishops. The book is not entirely rigid in scope; thus it includes some houses in the outskirts of major towns of the kind formerly known as "villas", and also a few rectories and marine residences.

Each volume in *Burke's Guide to Country Houses* was planned as an alphabetical dictionary of houses, with individual entries comprising an architectural description and commentary, a brief history of the property and its devolution, and any anecdotes and notes of interest concerning the family, the interior, the gardens, park, opening arrangements, etc. Illustrations would accompany the entry in as many instances as possible.

Our main genealogical production of the mid-1970s was *Burke's Irish Family Records* and the collection of so much Irish material was a strong factor in deciding to devote the first volume of *Burke's Guide to Country Houses* to Ireland. Other factors included the comparative shortage of books already published on Irish country houses—certainly none had approached our project in comprehensiveness—and the Irish ancestry of the Burke family and of the current Editor of *Burke's*.

As well as houses owned at one stage or another by families whose histories appear in *Burke's Peerage & Baronetage, Burke's Irish Family Records* and the old *Burke's Landed Gentry of Ireland*, all other properties of significance find a place amongst the 2,000 entries in the pages that follow. These entries were chosen without any limitations, including every style and covering the spectrum of Irish domestic architecture, regardless of architectural merit; with as many entries as could be fitted in for houses which have gone in the past century.

To undertake this great task we commissioned Mark Bence-Jones, whose architectural scholarship is enlivened by his encyclopaedic knowledge of Irish social history and a fund of amusing anecdotes. Mr Bence-Jones has been an expert on Irish country houses for many years and has been a regular contributor to *Country Life*, the *Irish Times* and the *Irish Georgian Society Bulletin* on the subject. Apart from being the author of *Palaces of the Raj, Clive of India, The Cavaliers* and three novels, he has written a perceptive anatomy of Ireland, *The Remarkable Irish*. He has been a regular contributor to *Burke's* for twenty years and was Consultant Editor of *Burke's Irish Family Records*.

This is Mr Bence-Jones's book: he has written the text and assembled over 1,300 pictures. As a single-handed effort put together in a short time, it is, in our view, a tremendous and almost incredible achievement. Mr Bence-Jones, however, has asked us to point out the limitations of such an ambitious individual undertaking. In spite of its 2,000 entries, the book is not complete—one doubts that it could have been so, even if a team of researchers had worked over a much longer period—and inevitably the scholarship is uneven; knowledge of a demolished house is often limited to one single old photograph. The relevant records are scarce to a degree and many families are completely lacking in information about their houses. Even if there had been more time available for research, it does not alter the fact that the families, on the whole, are not a fruitful source in the best of circumstances. The age of the amateur architectural historian copying out his hostess's mythological version of the house's history is gone: the modern professional finds his material in the muniments room, rather than in the drawing room.

The photographs in the book are very varied in quality. In numerous cases there was no other choice available; in others, it was a major *coup* to find an illustration at all. The ARCHITECTURAL GLOSSARY refers to photographs in the book which provide helpful illustrations of points. Some of the photographs, showing people, horses and early motor-cars, have a nostalgic appeal evoking a vanished way of life. These, and the many delightful anecdotes, add to the book's worth as a document of social, as well as architectural, history.

It should be explained that the references in parentheses at the beginning of the large majority of entries are to the histories of the families, who own or have owned the house, in a *Burke's* publication. A note at the end of the SELECT BIBLIOGRAPHY elucidates the codes used. Family names of Peers are given before the title, with the rank after the title, *viz* "D"(uke), "M"(arquess), "E"(arl), "V"(iscount), "B"(aron); in the case of a house being owned by a collateral member of a *Peerage* family, "*sub*" is inserted between the family name and the title.

We thank all those who gave help on this book and the owners of houses for their kind co-operation. In gratitude to the owners, we must remind the reader that the majority of Irish country houses are *not* open to the public: details of such houses as are open, appear in VISITING IRISH HOUSES on page xxx . We are pleased to endorse the AUTHOR'S ACKNOWLEDGMENTS (which follow) and in particular we express our gratitude to the principal Irish architectural historians, Desmond Guinness, the Knight of Glin, Maurice Craig, Edward McParland, C. E. B. Brett, *et al.* Humphrey Stone, of The Compton Press, designed and laid out the book with assistance from Jonathan Tetley, the artist, and Elaine Hunter; John Montgomery-Massingberd read the proofs; Denys Baker drew the map endpapers; and our erstwhile editorial staff, Charles Kidd, Suzanna Osman Jones and Camilla Binny were as helpful as only they could be.

Finally, the publication of this book comes at a critical time for Irish country houses. A horrifying number of entries end with bleak statements such as "Sold 197 . . ."; "now derelict . . ."; ". . . its future is uncertain". This is therefore valuable as a permanent record of what has already been lost and of what will go unless the capital taxation in Ireland is reformed as a matter of urgency. Mr Bence-Jones's INTRODUCTION is essential reading for all who care about the future of "Heritage Houses", as they are described in a masterly report *The Dissolution of the Irish Country House*, recently submitted to the Irish Government by a working party of An Taisce (the National Trust for Ireland). This is an absolutely fascinating and brilliantly argued document which assesses the present situation in analytical detail and predicts the demise of country houses under capital taxes, unless the report's excellent practical proposals are adopted to avert this disaster.

HUGH MONTGOMERY-MASSINGBERD
Editor *Burke's* Series
Wiltshire
October 1977

Author's Acknowledgments

IN WRITING this book, I was greatly helped by the kindness and generosity of others working in the same field. Dr Maurice Craig patiently allowed me to question him time and again on houses about which I was uncertain. I also owe him a debt of gratitude for his masterly *Classic Irish Houses of the Middle Size*, and for the unpublished reports which he and Mr William Garner are compiling for An Foras Forbartha. The value of these reports to me was equalled only by that of the wholly admirable *Lists and Surveys* produced by the Ulster Architectural Heritage Society. For the information in these *Lists and Surveys* alone, my debt to the Ulster Architectural Heritage Society would be great; but the Society has also most generously allowed me to reproduce many of the photographs in its publications. And for full measure, Mr C. E. B. Brett and Mr Hugh Dixon went to great pains to help me with various houses outside the scope of the Lists and Surveys which the Society has already published.

The Knight of Glin, like Dr Craig, provided me with the answer to many queries; he gave me the freedom of his photographic archive at Glin—which has since been deposited in the newly-established National Trust Archive in Dublin—and he volunteered, without any solicitation on my part, to undertake the daunting task of reading through my script; making corrections and valuable additions to the text. Mr Edward McParland was no less helpful, giving me the full benefit of his knowledge, his archive and his photographs; as well as making useful suggestions for the BIBLIOGRAPHY. Hon Desmond Guinness also helped me both with information and photographs, and allowed me to make full use of the photographic archive of the Irish Georgian Society.

Among those whom I would particularly like to thank for their help, Mr Daniel and Mr Sylvester Gillman occupy a special place. Not only have I been able to take full advantage of their encyclopaedic knowledge of Irish country houses; but their unparalleled collection of photographs, postcards and prints has provided me with a large number of my illustrations; many of them of houses which have long disappeared and of which, to my knowledge, no other pictures exist. A list of credits for individual illustrations follows; but I feel I must give special thanks to some of the many people who have provided me with photographs. To Rev Father Patrick Doyle, SJ, Jesuit Provincial, and Rev Father John Guiney, SJ, for allowing me to use photographs taken by the late Father Frank Browne, SJ. To Mr Fergus Pyle, Editor of the *Irish Times*, for allowing me to use photographs which were taken some years ago by the *Irish Times* to illustrate my articles in that newspaper. To Mr William Garner and An Foras Forbartha for allowing me to use some of the photographs which he has taken. To Mr Hugh Doran, Mr George Gossip and Dr Rolf Loeber, who have also been most generous in allowing me to use their photographs. To Bord Fáilte, to the National Parks and Monuments Branch, Office of Public Works, to the Historic Monuments and Buildings Branch, Northern Ireland, and to the Northern Ireland National Trust. To Mr R. F. Thompson, Art Editor of *Country Life*, and to Mrs Cunliffe-Lister, for allowing me to use photographs from the *Country Life* files and for their help. To Mr Nicholas Sheaff, Archive Director of The National Trust Archive, which has recently been established by An Taisce at 63 Merrion Square, Dublin. This is a collection of photographs and drawings providing a visual record of Irish architecture; something which was long needed, and which at last makes up for the lack of an Irish equivalent of the National Monuments Record in Britain and the drawings collection of the Royal Institute of British Architects. The extensive photographic archive built up by Hon Desmond Guinness and the Knight of Glin is now deposited in the National Trust Archive, together with other collections. Anyone owning photographs or drawings of Irish country houses or other buildings who does not know what to do with them would be well advised to present or loan them to the Archive; not only would they be well looked after, but they would be of real service to architectural scholarship and the cause of preservation. Before leaving the subject of illustrations, I would like to express my thanks to Mr James Byrne for all the help he has given me in the processing and selection of the photographs in this book which I have taken myself.

Just as in the matter of illustrations, there are people deserving of a better acknowledgment than a mere inclusion in the list of credits, so are there certain publications which were of such help to me that to include them in the BIBLIOGRAPHY does not seem enough. I have already mentioned Dr Craig's *Classic Irish Houses of the Middle Size* and the *Lists and Surveys* of the Ulster Architectural Heritage Society. To these I must add the *Bulletin* of the Irish Georgian Society, *Irish Houses and Castles* by Desmond Guinness and William Ryan, *Ireland Observed* by Maurice Craig and the Knight of Glin, *The Houses of Ireland* by Brian de Breffny and Rosemary ffolliott, and the articles on Irish Country Houses in *Country Life*: in particular those by John Cornforth, Mark Girouard and Alistair Rowan.

I would like to say a special word of thanks to the staff of the National Library, Dublin; and I would also like to acknowledge the help of the following: Mr Martyn Anglesea, the Earl of Arran, the Earl Belmore, Rev Martin Coen, Commandant Cornelius Costello, Miss Anne Crookshank, Lt-Col Hubert Gallwey, Mr Aquin Henley, Miss Mary Keegan, the Lord Kilmaine, Mr Charles Lysaght, Mr Henry McDowell, Mr Gerald McSweeney, Mr Gordon St George Mark, Captain Peter Montgomery, Mr Edward More O'Ferrall, Mr Nicholas Nicholson, Professor Maurice O'Connell, Miss Josephine O'Conor, Mr Padraig O Maidin, Mr Leslie Roberts, Mr George Stacpoole, Mr David Synnott, Major Pierce Synnott, Major-General E. A. E.

Tremlett and Mr Jeremy Williams.

Many of the people I have mentioned gave me hospitality as well as helping me with this book. Unfortunately, space does not permit me to mention all those other people whose hospitality not only facilitated my task of visiting and photographing country houses all over Ireland, but made it a pleasure. Again, I must plead shortage of space for saying no more than a general "thank you" to all those who sent me information on houses in, or formerly in, their families and photographs of them; and to the owners of the houses which I visited in connexion with this book, who almost invariably offered me hospitality as well as allowing me to see and photograph their houses. I much regret that, in the time available to me, I was only able to visit a limited number of those houses still in private occupation with which I was not already familiar. With the others, I had to make do with quick exterior glimpses, photographs or descriptions which I knew to be reliable. This will inevitably mean that I have missed various points of interest in my descriptions of some of these houses; I can only offer my apologies, and say that if I had set out to visit all the Irish country houses to which I had not yet been, this book would still be unwritten many years hence.

Finally, I must express my deep gratitude to Mr Hugh Montgomery-Massingberd, the instigator of this and of so many other *Burke* projects, for his constant help and encouragement.

Credits for Illustrations

Where there is more than one source on a page, the credits start with the picture furthest to the left and nearest the top of the page and work down each column (a, b, c, d, e, etc).

Gen Sir John Anderson, page 23*b*; Armagh County Museum, 66*d*; G. H. Armstrong-Lushington-Tulloch, 257*e*; Walter Armytage, 172*f*, 212*d*; the Earl of Arran, 69*a*; Major A. G. Atkinson, 55*f*, 194*b*; Miss Clare Bancroft, 122*b*; John Bayly, 16*b*, 100*e*; Mark Bence-Jones, 2*def*, 5*af*, 6*cd*, 8*d*, 9*d*, 10*cd*, 11*d*, 14*cd*, 15*b*, 16*a*, 17*abcd*, 18*b*, 20*bcd*, 21*b*, 22*cde*, 23*c*, 24*ac*, 25*cfg*, 27*ce*, 32*bc*, 34*fg*, 36*b*, 39*a*, 40*e*, 43*a*, 45*ab*, 47*bd*, 48*bcd*, 50*e*, 54*d*, 56*c*, 61*b*, 66*c*, 67*ac*, 69*bc*, 71*cd*, 73*ab*, 76*b*, 78*c*, 83*ab*, 84*ad*, 85*f*, 86*a*, 87*a*, 88*abc*, 89*c*, 90*b*, 92*a*, 94*b*, 95*d*, 96*ab*, 97*b*, 98*c*, 99*a*, 100*cd*, 101*b*, 102*b*, 107*c*, 109*f*, 111*b*, 114*e*, 115*c*, 119*c*, 120*ab*, 121*ab*, 123*d*, 128*a*, 129*de*, 136*c*, 137*be*, 140*abd*, 141*ac*, 143*g*, 150*ce*, 151*e*, 152*efg*, 154*abc*, 164*c*, 165*ae*, 166*cdef*, 167*a*, 169*ae*, 170*ade*, 171*a*, 172*e*, 174*bd*, 175*b*, 179*ad*, 182*e*, 183*c*, 184*cd*, 187*cd*, 188, 191*be*, 193*de*, 194*a*, 201*bd*, 206*de*, 208*e*, 209*a*, 213*abc*, 215*a*, 218*abc*, 219*ae*, 220*c*, 222*c*, 225*a*, 229*ef*, 230*b*, 231*bc*, 243*a*, 246*a*, 256*aef*, 267*c*, 268*ce*, 269*a*, 273*b*, 275*a*, 278*c*, 283*a*, 284*ce*, 285*bd*, 286*ac*, 287*d*; J. R. Beresford-Ash, 12*d*; Peter Bishop, 82*cdefg*, 111*gh*, 112*abc*, 257*abcd*, 272*bc*; Lt-Col J. M. Blakiston-Houston, 39*e*; W. A. N. MacGeough Bond, 12*b*; Bord Fáilte, 14*a*, 49*d*, 53*b*, 57*b*, 60*c*, 61*a*, 89*d*, 121*c*, 160*ac*, 161*ac*, 167*b*, 180*a*, 184*a*, 190*c*, 220*b*, 221*c*, 234*c*, 235*b*, 242*c*, 283*df*; C. E. B. Brett, 99*d*; the late Rev Frank Browne, SJ, 7*abc*, 31*bcde*, 34*ab*, 42*abcd*, 45*de*, 46*ab*,

47*c*, 48*g*, 49*a*, 71*egh*, 76*abde*, 77*abcde*, 100*b*, 120*cdefg*, 128*efg*, 129*ab*, 143*abcdef*, 151*abdfghi*, 155*bcde*, 156*abd*, 171*f*, 172*abcd*, 176*bde*, 179*ce*, 199*abde*, 200*a*, 201*cef*, 210*abc*, 212*c*, 239*ef*, 244*abcde*, 259*bcde*; Major W. S. Brownlow, 30*a*; Gerard Camplisson, 11*c*, 253*a*; Major Paul Cassidi, 137*a*; A. A. M. Clark, 4*a*; Lt-Col R. L. Clarke, 145*c*; Rev Martin Coen, 2*c*, 175*g*; the late Judge H. L. Conner, 217*f*; Miss M. C. Considine, 101*a*; Brig. E. C. Cooke-Collis, 64*e*; E. W. R. Cookman, 208*a*; *Cork Examiner*, 186*b*, 276*a*; Cmdt Cornelius Costello, 114*d*; *Country Life*, 21*c*, 36*de*, 37*c*, 55*bd*, 60*bd*, 97*c*, 98*b*, 111*cd*, 156*ce*, 173*ab*, 181*bd*, 238*de*, 239*a*, 250*bc*, 275*b*; Courtauld Institute of Art, 33*ab*, 56*a*, 74*d*, 88*d*, 134*a*; Lt-Col K. B. L. Davidson, 119*b*, 128*b*; S. K. Davies, 171*e*; R. L. Dean, 101*e*; R. G. F. de Stacpoole, 213*e*, 274*a*; Detroit Institute of Arts, 122*c*; Hugh Doran, 5*de*, 8*abc*, 18*cd*, 27*d*, 35*a*, 37*ab*, 39*bc*, 56*d*, 82*b*, 89*a*, 181*c*, 189*de*, 195*acd*, 196*bc*, 197, 214*ab*, 223*ac*, 224, 231*d*, 232*a*, 234*b*, 235*a*, 245*d*, 251*a*, 258*c*, 259*a*, 262*a*, 283*e*, 284*ab*; Austin Dunphy, 12*e*, 131*bc*, 132*a*; Sir Ivan Ewart, Bt, 103*ab*; C. Gordon Falloon, 206*c*; Mark Fiennes, 28*c*, 228*b*; Foras Forbartha and William Garner, 4*a*, 60*a*, 107*ab*, 112*g*, 141*d*, 158*a*, 170*bc*, 190*de*, 194*f*, 208*b*, 211*b*, 228*c*, 237*c*, 245*ef*, 261*c*, 288; Lt-Col H. D. Gallwey, 123*a*, 219*b*; the Dowager Lady Garvagh, 132*cd*; Col A.

W. Gason, 177*a*; Jonathan M. Gibson, 80*bcdef*, 120*hi*, 139*abc*; Gillman Collection, 20*ae*, 36*f*, 48*e*, 50*d*, 54*a*, 61*d*, 64*cd*, 85*b*, 87*c*, 90*a*, 91*b*, 92*e*, 93*a*, 112*f*, 119*d*, 123*c*, 130*d*, 142*c*, 152*abd*, 163*g*, 165*h*, 166*a*, 168*e*, 172*gh*, 174, 175*c*, 176*a*, 177*b*, 192*bcd*, 193*c*, 200*c*, 211*cd*, 212*a*, 217*de*, 227*b*, 240*cde*, 241*a*, 251*b*, 252, 255*d*, 256*g*, 268*f*, 269*b*, 285*c*; the Knight of Glin, 54*b*, 80*a*; George Gossip, 3*cde*, 7*d*, 19*a*, 21*d*, 25*a*, 28*a*, 53*d*, 64*b*, 66*ab*, 67*b*, 73*f*, 96*be*, 114*c*, 118*c*, 122*a*, 145*efg*, 157, 159*b*, 176*c*, 183*a*, 191*cd*, 194*cg*, 198*a*, 212*b*, 215*d*, 216*b*, 233*c*, 247*d*, 276*b*, 280; Green Studio, 232*ef*; D. F. Greer, 241*c*; Lt-Col Terence Grove-White, 164*a*, 243*c*; Charles Harman, 95*c*; Harrison family, 70*a*; J. & S. Harsch, 154*c*, 229*c*; Col W. Harvey-Kelly, 87*b*; Mrs Patricia Hawker, 25*b*; Cmdr C. A. Herdman, 260*b*; W/Cmdr J. S. Higginson, 29*c*; Historic Monuments and Buildings Branch, Northern Ireland, 22*ab*, 54*e*, 55*a*, 59, 125*ab*, 133*efg*, 147*abde*; H. E. Hodgson, 205*d*; Robert Hull, 182*d*; Irish Georgian Society, 1*a*, 76*cf*, 99*bc*, 196*a*, 242*d*, 248*cd*; *Irish Times*, 17*ef*, 23*de*, 26*ce*, 27*ab*, 44*bcde*, 58*bc*, 63*ab*, 67*de*, 68*bc*, 86*cdef*, 105*de*, 106*abcd*, 109*bcd*, 115*de*, 119*de*, 124*ab*, 126*a*, 127, 131*ad*, 140*c*, 144, 145*d*, 148, 175*de*, 181*a*, 194*de*, 199*c*, 200*b*, 202, 219*d*, 240*ab*, 262*bc*, 263*cde*, 265*bc*, 266*a*, 267*b*, 277*g*, 278*ab*; W. H. P. Jervois, 46*ef*; Robert Kellock, 73*d*; Mrs. W. D. O. Kemmis, 16*c*; the Lord Kilmaine, 133*a*, 222*b*; Knight, Frank & Rutley, 91*ac*; Maurice A. Knox, 74*e*; Sam Lambert, 81*d*; Prof C. J. P. La Touche (and National Trust Archive), 203*ab*; Dr Rolf Loeber, 19*c*, 31*f*, 55*c*, 85*d*, 100*a*, 133*c*, 146*a*, 166*b*, 182*a*, 215*b*, 229*a*, 232*b*, 238*c*, 241*d*, 242*b*, 254*af*, 255*ef*, 264*c*; Miss Margaret L. Longfield, 165*bc*; McCalmont family, 203*e*; the Madam McGillyguddy, 241*b*; Dr Edward MacLysaght, 150*b*, 237*a*; Edward McParland, 33*cdef*, 98*a*, 129*c*, 145*ab*, 149*cd*, 150*a*, 227*c*, 228*a*; Gerald McSweeney, 62*d*; Ian B. Madden, 153*c*; Major J. W. R. Madden, 153*c*; Brig W. M. T. Magan, 174*a*; Mrs S. Mannion, 125*c*; Gordon St George Mark, 9*b*, 94*d*, 165*f*, 205*e*, 27*gb*; Christine Martinoni, 111*ef*, 135*b*, 139*d*; Patrick Montague-Smith, 222*d*; Edward More O'Ferrall, 30*e*, 87*d*, 146*b*, 185*a*, 192*a*, 213*d*, 285*a*; the late Mrs M. Archdale Morris, 87*e*; Miss Sheila A. Murphy, 206*b*; the Lord Muskerry (and National Trust Archive), 263*ab*; Mrs. Rupert Nash, 89*e*, 123*b*, 267*a*; National Library of Ireland (Lawrence Collection), 1*b*, 2*ab*, 3*a*, 4*c*, 5*bc*, 6*b*, 7*e*, 8*ef*, 9*a*, 10*a*, 11*a*, 13*abcd*, 15*c*, 21*a*, 22*f*, 23*f*, 24*bd*, 26*bd*, 30*fg*, 32*de*, 35*bc*, 36*ac*, 38*bcd*, 39*df*, 40*d*, 43*cd*, 44*a*, 45*c*, 47*a*, 49*bc*, 50*ab*, 51*b*, 52*a*,

53*cf*, 54*cf*, 55*e*, 58*a*, 61*c*, 62*bce*, 63*cde*, 64*a*, 67*f*, 68*a*, 70*c*, 71*f*, 72*ac*, 74*c*, 77*f*, 78*b*, 79*abd*, 81*bc*, 82*a*, 83*be*, 84*c*, 85*a*, 89*b*, 90*d*, 92*c*, 93*c*, 95*a*, 97*b*, 101*cd*, 102*a*, 103*c*, 104, 105*ab*, 106*g*, 108, 110*b*, 111*a*, 113*bcde*, 114*ab*, 116*a*, 118*abd*, 121*d*, 126*c*, 128*cd*, 130*ab*, 132*b*, 134*b*, 135*cefg*, 136*ab*, 137*c*, 138*c*, 142*a*, 146*c*, 147*f*, 149*ab*, 150*d*, 153*ab*, 155*a*, 159*a*, 160*bc*, 162*cd*, 163*abe*, 168*abcd*, 169*cd*, 171*cd*, 174*ce*, 177*cd*, 178*abd*, 179*b*, 180*b*, 182*b*, 183*c*, 185*c*, 187*a*, 189*a*, 192*ef*, 205*a*, 207, 210*d*, 212*ef*, 214*c*, 215*c*, 218*d*, 219*c*, 221*ab*, 223*b*, 225*bc*, 226*a*, 227*a*, 228*e*, 231*a*, 233*ade*, 234*a*, 236*bc*, 237*b*, 239*bd*, 243*d*, 246*b*, 247*e*, 248*ab*, 249*abcd*, 253*b*, 254*de*, 255*ab*, 260*c*, 266*bc*, 270*bc*, 271*ab*, 274*d*, 275*a*, 277*bf*, 282*c*, 283*b*, 286*b*, 287*abc*; National Parks and Monuments Branch, Office of Public Works, 14*b*, 32*a*, 50*c*, 10*gh*, 117*c*, 141*b*, 190*b*, 273*c*; National Trust, 35*d*; National Trust, Committee for Northern Ireland, 11*bc*, 65*abc*, 79*c*, 102*b*, 217*abc*; National Trust Archive, 8*gh*, 208*d*, 263*ab*, 282*b*; J. W. Nicholson, 30*c*; Nicholas Nicholson, 52*bcd*, 53*a*, 69*de*, 75*a*, 93*b*, 189*b*, 238*b*, 243*b*, 264*b*, 268*ab*, 272*de*; Prof Maurice O'Connell, 26*a*, 27*f*, 85*c*, 113*f*, 116*c*, 137*d*, 200*d*, 236*a*, 242*c*, 283*c*; Miss Josephine O'Conor, 74*f*, 85*e*, 86*b*, 115*ab*, 191*a*, 250*ab*, 261*a*; Major N. R. Ogle, 117*de*; F. C. O'Hara, 91*f*; A. J. Ormsby, 18*a*; Thomas M. Ormsby, 206*a*; the late Capt R. J. O. Otway-Ruthven, 74*b*; Francis Pollen, 163*cd*; Sir Richard Proby, Bt, 265*a*; Major G. N. Proctor, 277*c*; Peter Reid, 205*b*, 211*c*; Leslie Roberts, 47*ef*, 48*a*, 216*a*; Patrick Rossmore, 29*ab*, 112*h*, 117*ab*; Royal Irish Academy, 274*f*; Major R. F. Ruttledge, 44*g*; Charles Scott, 48*f*, 187*b*, 254*c*, 272*a*, 277*de*; Ian Sherriff, 154*d*; George Stacpoole, 186*a*, 230*d*; Gordon D. Stannus, 30*d*, 119*e*; W. B. Stevenson, 13*e*, 178*c*; Humphrey Stone, 200*d*, 201*a*; G/Capt Rudolph Taaffe, 158*b*, 216*b*; Mrs J. Stewart Thompson, 40*abc*; M. Thompson-Butler-Lloyd, 185*d*, 189*c*; N. R. E. Travers, 273*a*; Major-Gen E. A. E. Tremlett, 9*c*, 229*b*; Ulster Architectural Heritage Society, 25*d*, 30*b*, 34*cd*, 37*de*, 40*f*, 78*a*, 83*a*, 88*e*, 92*d*, 93*d*, 95*b*, 107*d*, 112*d*, 113*a*, 114*f*, 116*bd*, 235*d*, 138*d*, 152*l*, 182*c*, 184*b*, 185*b*, 209*cd*, 232*g*, 233*b*, 240*c*, 244*f*, 245*c*, 256*bcd*, 264*a*, 266*d*, 274*c*, 282*a*; Ulster Museum, 66*e*, 94*a*, 208*c*, 258*ab*; Patrick D. Verschoyle, 270*d*; Miss Pats Vigors, 260*a*; Mrs F. Villiers-Stuart, 109*aef*; Miss Christabel Ward, 147*c*, 266*b*; Mrs R. Wells, 142*b*; John Westby, 245*ab*; J. M. Wilson-Wright, 90*c*.

Page i, picture of Coole Park reproduced by kind permission of Colin Smythe.

Select Bibliography

Ball, Dr Francis Elrington: *A History of the County of Dublin*, 6 vols (Dublin, 1902–1920).

Bell, G. P.: *See* under ULSTER ARCHITECTURAL HERITAGE SOCIETY.

Bence-Jones, Mark: Articles in *Country Life*: "An Archbishop's Palladian Palace" [Cashel Palace], 31 Aug 1972; "Building Dreams of a Viceroy" [Clandeboye], 1/8 Oct 1970; Dromore Castle, 12 Nov 1964; Mitchelstown Castle, 18 April 1963; "A Suitably Celtic Twilight" and "Ravages of Time and Neglect" [Lost Irish Country Houses], 23/30 May 1974; Thomastown Castle, 2 Oct 1969.

Bence-Jones, Mark: "The Empty Grandeurs of Ardo", *Country Life Annual* (1968).

Bence-Jones, Mark: Lissadell, *Ireland of the Welcomes* (Nov-Dec 1970).

Bence-Jones, Mark: Articles in *Irish Times*, "People and Houses" series: Ballinamona Park, 25 Oct 1968; Ballynatray, 19 March 1963; Blessingbourne, 18 June 1963; Carrigglas Manor, 21 Jan 1964; Castle Blunden, 27 Aug 1966; Castle ffrench, 18 Jan 1969; Doneraile Court, 26 March 1963; Dromana, 13 Sept 1968; Dunkathel, 30 April 1963; Farnham, 12 Sept 1964; Florence Court, 11 June 1963; Fota, 7 May 1963; Gardenmorris, 6 Aug 1966; Glenville Park, 16 April 1963; Gosford Castle, 4 Sept 1963; Gurteen le Poer, 24 Dec 1968; Mallow Castle, 12 March 1963; Markree Castle, 1 Oct 1963; Rathkenny, 5 Nov 1963; Springhill, 2 July 1963; Strokestown Park, 22 Aug 1968; Tullynally Castle, 14 Jan 1964.

Bence-Jones, Mark: *See* also under IRISH GEORGIAN SOCIETY.

Betjeman, John: "Francis Johnston, Irish Architect", *The Pavilion* (London, 1946).

Bowen, Elizabeth: *Bowen's Court* (London, 1942).

Boylan, Lena: *The Early History of Castletown* (Dublin, 1967).

Boylan, Lena: *See* also under IRISH GEORGIAN SOCIETY.

Brett, C. E. B.: *Buildings of Belfast* (London, 1967).

Brett, C.E.B.: *See* also under ULSTER ARCHITECTURAL HERITAGE SOCIETY.

Brewer, James Norris: *The Beauties of Ireland*, 2 vols

(London, 1825–26).

Browne, Rev Frank, SJ, and others: Articles in *Irish Tatler and Sketch*, "Historic Irish Residences" series: Abbey Leix, May 1950; Adare Manor, March/April 1950; American Legation, Oct 1949; Áras an Uachtaráin, Dec 1948; Bantry House, March 1947; Barmeath Castle, April 1947; Beaulieu, Feb 1950; Birr Castle, Feb 1948; Borris House, Nov 1949; Castle Leslie, Jan 1950; Castletown, Oct 1947; Clonalis, Jan/Feb 1951; Curraghmore, March 1948; Dromoland Castle, Feb/March 1949; Dunsany Castle, Dec 1951; Fota, Nov 1950; French Park, Jan 1949; Glin Castle, Dec 1949; Gormanston Castle, May 1947; Gurteen le Poer, Nov 1947; Headfort, Oct 1948; Howth Castle, April/May 1948; Killeen Castle, Oct 1950; Killruddery, Dec 1947; Knocklofty, April 1949; Lismore Castle, Dec 1952/Jan 1953; Malahide Castle, Jan 1948; Mallow Castle, May 1949; Rockingham, Nov 1948; Shelton Abbey, Jan 1947; Stradbally Hall, Feb 1947; Strokestown Park, Jan 1954.

Burgoyne, C.: Kilmurry, *Irish Tatler and Sketch* (Feb 1952).

Burke, (Sir) Bernard: *A Visitation of Seats and Arms of the Noblemen and Gentlemen of Great Britain and Ireland*, 2 vols (London, 1852–53); 2nd Series, 2 vols (London, 1854–55).

Colvin, Howard & Craig, Maurice: *Architectural Drawings in the Library of Elton Hall, by Sir John Vanbrugh and Sir Edward Lovett Pearce* (Oxford, for the Roxburghe Club, 1964).

Colvin, Howard & Harris, John (editors): *The Country Seat, Studies . . . presented to Sir John Summerson* (London, 1970).

Cornforth, John: Articles in *Country Life*: Adare Manor, 15/22/29 May 1969; Dunsany Castle, 27 May/3 June 1971; "Genesis of Headfort", 5 April 1973; "Malahide and After", 14 July 1977; Mount Kennedy, 28 Oct/11 Nov 1965; Rathbeale Hall, 24 Aug 1972; Russborough, 5/12/19 Dec 1963; St Columb's, 22 May 1975.

Cornforth, John: *See* also under CRAIG, Maurice; GLIN, Knight of; TIERNEY, Mark.

Cosby, Major E. A. S.: Stradbally Hall, *Irish Tatler and Sketch* (April 1951).

Cosgrave, E. Macdowel: *Dublin and co Dublin in the 20th Century* (Brighton and London, 1908).

Country Life: Castletown, co Kilkenny, 7/14 Sept 1918.

Country Life: *See* also under BENCE-JONES, Mark; CORNFORTH, John; CRAIG, Maurice; DIXON, Hugh; GIROUARD, Mark; GLIN, Knight of; GREEN, E.R.R.; HUSSEY, Christopher; McPARLAND, Edward; RANKIN, Peter; ROWAN, A.J.; WEAVER, Lawrence.

County Down Archaeological Survey (Belfast, HMSO, 1966).

Craig, Maurice: *Classic Irish Houses of the Middle Size* (London and New York, 1976).

Craig, Maurice: Articles in *Country Life*: Bellamont Forest, 21/28 May 1964; "Some Smaller Irish Houses", 8 July 1949; (with Knight of Glin & John Cornforth) Castletown, 27 March/3/10 April 1969.

Craig, Maurice: *Portumna Castle* (Dublin, 1976).

Craig, Maurice & Glin, Knight of: *Catalogue of Exhibition of Irish Architectural Drawings* (Dublin, Belfast and London (RIBA), 1965).

Craig, Maurice & Glin, Knight of: *Ireland Observed: A Handbook to the Buildings and Antiquities* (Cork, 1970).

Craig, Maurice: *See* also under COLVIN, Howard; IRISH GEORGIAN SOCIETY.

Croft-Murray, Edward: *Decorative Painting in England 1537–1837* (London, 1962–70). [Vol II contains useful Irish material.]

Crookshank, Anne (with Desmond Guinness, James White & Knight of Glin): *Catalogue of Irish Houses and Landscapes Exhibition* (Belfast (Ulster Museum) and Dublin, 1963).

Crookshank, Anne: *See* also under IRISH GEORGIAN SOCIETY.

Curran, C. P.: *See* under IRISH GEORGIAN SOCIETY.

Davis, Terence: *See* under IRISH GEORGIAN SOCIETY.

de Breffny, Brian & ffolliott, Rosemary: *The Houses of Ireland* (London, 1975).

de Breffny, Brian: *Castles of Ireland* (London, 1977).

Dickinson, P. L.: *See* under SADLEIR, T. U.

Dixon, Hugh: *An Introduction to Ulster Architecture* (Belfast (UAHS), 1975).

Dixon, Hugh: *Catalogue of Ulster Architecture Exhibition* (Belfast (UAHS), 1972).

Dixon, Hugh & Rowan, A. J.: "The Architecture of Thomas Turner", *Country Life*, 24 May 1973.

Dixon, Hugh: *See* also under ULSTER ARCHITECTURAL HERITAGE SOCIETY.

Duignan, Michael V.: *See* under KILLANIN, Lord.

Dunleath, Lady: *See* under ULSTER ARCHITECTURAL HERITAGE SOCIETY.

Dunlop, D.: *Life of W. J. Barre* (Belfast, 1868).

Ellison, Canon C. C.: *See* under IRISH GEORGIAN SOCIETY.

Elmes, Rosalind: *Catalogue of Irish Topographical Prints and Original Drawings*, new edn revised and enlarged by Michael Hewson (Dublin, 1975).

English, N. W.: Articles in *The Irish Ancestor*: "Some Country Houses near Athlone", 1, 1973; "Some Lost Country Houses near Athlone", 2, 1974.

Enniskillen, Countess of: *Florence Court, My Irish Home* (Monaghan, 1972).

ffolliott, Rosemary: Articles in *The Irish Ancestor*: "Houses in Ireland in the 17th Century", 1, 1974; "Some Lesser Known Country Houses in Munster and Leinster", 1, 1971.

ffolliott, Rosemary: *See* also under DE BREFFNY, Brian.

FitzGerald, Brian: Articles in *Country Life*: Carton, 7/14 Nov 1936; Russborough, 23/30 Jan 1937.

FitzGerald, Rosemary: *See* under IRISH GEORGIAN SOCIETY.

FitzGibbon, Constantine: *See* under IRISH GEORGIAN SOCIETY.

Georgian Society Records of Eighteenth Century Domestic Architecture and Decoration in Dublin, 5 vols (Dublin, 1909–13).

Georgian Society: *See* IRISH GEORGIAN SOCIETY.

Gibbon, Monk: Russborough, *Great Houses of Europe* (ed. Sacheverell Sitwell) (London, 1961).

Girouard, Mark: Articles in *Country Life*: Beaulieu, 15/22 Jan 1959; Belvedere, 22/29 June 1961; Birr Castle, 25 Feb/4/11 March 1965; Castleward, 23/30 Nov 1961; Charleville Forest, 27 Sept 1962; Clontra, 29 May 1975; Curraghmore, 7/14/21 Feb 1963; Glin Castle, 27 Feb/5 March 1964; Humewood Castle, 9/16 May 1968; Lismore Castle, 6/13 Aug 1964; "Model House in an Ancient Tower" [Dunguaire Castle], 28 March 1963; "Modernising an Irish Country House" and "Comforts for a Victorian Household" [Tullynally Castle], 23/30 Dec 1971; Mount Ievers, 8 Nov 1962; Westport House, 29 April/6 May 1965; Whitfield Court, 7 Sept 1967.

Girvan, Donald: *See* under ULSTER ARCHITECTURAL HERITAGE

SOCIETY.

Glin, Knight of: "Nathaniel Clements and Some Eighteenth Century Irish Houses", *Apollo* (Oct 1966).

Glin, Knight of: Luggala, *House and Garden* (May 1965).

Glin, Knight of: Articles in *Country Life*: "A Baroque Palladian in Ireland" [the Architecture of Davis Duckart], 28 Sept/5 Oct 1967; (with John Cornforth) Killruddery, 14/21 July 1977.

Glin, Knight of: *See* also under CRAIG, Maurice; CROOKSHANK, Anne; IRISH GEORGIAN SOCIETY; MALINS, Edward.

Green, E. R. R.: Downhill Castle, *Country Life*, 6 Jan 1950.

Griffin, David J.: *See* under IRISH GEORGIAN SOCIETY.

Grove White, James: *Historical and Topographical Notes on . . .* [numerous localities in the baronies of North co Cork], 4 vols (Cork, 1905–25).

Guinness, Desmond: *The Irish House* (Dublin, 1975).

Guinness, Desmond & Ryan, William: *Irish Houses and Castles* (London, 1971).

Guinness, Desmond & Sadler, J. J.: *The Palladian Style in England, Ireland and America* (London, 1976).

Guinness, Desmond: *See* under CROOKSHANK, Anne; IRISH GEORGIAN SOCIETY.

Gwynn, Denis: Shanbally Castle, *Irish Tatler and Sketch* (Nov 1957).

Harris, John: *Headfort House and Robert Adam: Drawings from the Collection of Mr & Mrs Paul Mellon* (London (RIBA), 1973).

Harris, John: *Sir William Chambers* (London, 1970).

Harris, John: *See* also under COLVIN, Howard; IRISH GEORGIAN SOCIETY.

Hayes, Richard J.: *Manuscript Sources for the History of Irish Civilization* (Boston, USA, 1965).

Hewson, Michael: *See* under ELMES, Rosalind.

Hodges, Rev Richard J.: *Cork and County Cork in the Twentieth Century* (Brighton, 1911).

Horner, Arnold: *See* under IRISH GEORGIAN SOCIETY.

Hussey, Christopher: Articles in *Country Life*: Caledon, 27 Feb/6 March 1937; Castlecoole, 19/26 Dec 1936; Castletown, 15/22 Aug 1936; Howth Castle, 6/13 Sept 1930; Lambay, 20/27 July 1929; Lucan House, 31 Jan 1947; Malahide Castle, 18/25 April 1947; Powerscourt, 6/13/20 Dec 1946; Townley Hall, 23/30 July 1948; (with G. C. Taylor) Headfort, 21/28 March/4 April 1936; (with G. C. Taylor) Mount Stewart, 5/12 Oct 1935.

Ide, John J.: *Some Examples of Irish Country Houses of the Georgian Period* (New York, 1959).

Irish Builder (1859 onwards).

Irish Georgian Society Bulletin (1958 onwards): Articles by Mark Bence-Jones, Lena Boylan, Maurice Craig, Anne Crookshank, C. P. Curran, Terence Davis, Canon C. C. Ellison, Rosemary FitzGerald, Constantine FitzGibbon, Knight of Glin, David J. Griffin, Desmond Guinness, John Harris, Arnold Horner, Rolf Loeber, R. J. McKinstry, Edward McParland, Edward Malins, Gordon St George Mark, John O'Connell, T. G. F. Paterson, A. J. Rowan, Michael Wynne, etc.

Irish Tatler and Sketch: Miscellaneous articles: Blarney Castle, May 1955; Gaybrook, June 1951; Glananea, Nov 1952; The Island, Waterford, Dec 1961; Lucan House, Dec 1954; Rockfleet, May 1954; St Mary's Abbey, July 1951.

Jope, E. M. (editor): *Studies in Building History in Memory of B. H. St J. O'Neil* [Articles by H. G. Leask & D. M. Waterman] (London, 1961).

Killanin, Lord & Duignan, Michael V.: *The Shell Guide to Ireland*, 2nd edn (London, 1967).

Leask, H. G.: *Irish Castles and Castellated Houses*, 2nd edn (Dundalk, 1951).

Lenox-Conyngham, Mina: *An Old Ulster Home* [Springhill] . . . (Dundalk, 1946).

Lewis, Samuel: *Topographical Dictionary of Ireland*, 2 vols (London, 1837).

Loeber, Rolf: *See* under IRISH GEORGIAN SOCIETY.

MacGowan, Gearoid: Castle MacGarrett, *Irish Tatler and Sketch* (Aug/Sept 1956).

McKinstry, R. J. & Rankin, Peter: *Neo-Classicism in Ulster* [Catalogue of joint exhibition with the Arts Council of Northern Ireland] (Belfast (UAHS), 1973).

McKinstry, R. J.: *See* also under IRISH GEORGIAN SOCIETY.

MacLysaght, Edward: *Irish Life in the Seventeenth Century*, 2nd, revised and enlarged edn (Cork, 1950).

MacMahon, Ella: Chapters on Kilkenny Castle, Lismore Castle and Malahide Castle, *Historic Houses of the United Kingdom* (London, 1892).

McParland, Edward: Articles in *Country Life*: Ballyfin, 13/20 Sept 1973; Emo Court, 23/30 May 1974; "Sir Richard Morrison's Country Houses", 24/31 May 1973.

McParland, Edward: *See* also under IRISH GEORGIAN SOCIETY.

Malins, Edward & Glin, Knight of: *Lost Demesnes: Irish Landscape Gardening 1660–1845* (London, 1976).

Mark, Gordon St George: *See* under IRISH GEORGIAN SOCIETY.

Matthew, Sir Robert: *See* under ULSTER ARCHITECTURAL HERITAGE SOCIETY.

Maxwell, Constantia: *Country and Town in Ireland under the Georges* (Dundalk, 1949).

Milton, Thomas: *A Collection of select views from different seats of the nobility and gentry in . . . Ireland* (London, 1783–93; partly reprinted by the Irish Georgian Society, Dublin, 1963).

Morris, Rev F. O.: *A Series of Picturesque Views of Seats of the Noblemen and Gentlemen of Great Britain and Ireland*, 6 vols (London, 1866–80).

Morrison, J.: "Life of the late William Vitruvius Morrison", *Weale's Quarterly Papers on Architecture* I (1843), Part I, Paper III.

Morrison, (Sir) Richard: *Useful and Ornamental Designs in Architecture . . . Peculiarly Adapted for Execution* (Dublin, 1793).

National Trust Guidebooks: Ardress, 1962; Castlecoole; Castleward; Downhill and the Mussenden Temple, 1968; Springhill; The Temple of the Winds, Mount Stewart, 1966.

Neale, J. P.: *Views of the Seats of Noblemen and Gentlemen in England, Wales, Scotland and Ireland*, 6 vols (London, 1818–23); 2nd Series, 5 vols (London, 1824–29).

O'Connell, John: *See* under IRISH GEORGIAN SOCIETY.

O'Farrell, M.: Sopwell Hall, *Irish Tatler and Sketch* (April 1955).

O'Flanagan, J. R.: *The Blackwater in Munster* (London, 1844).

O'Higgins, Kay: Articles in *Irish Tatler and Sketch*: Bermingham House, June 1955; Carton, Dec 1955/Jan/Feb 1956; Castletown, May/June/July 1956; Kilkea Castle, Aug/Sept 1957; Luttrellstown Castle, Oct/Nov 1956; Mount Juliet, Dec 1957/Jan 1958; Powerscourt, Dec 1956/Jan/Feb 1957; Russborough, Aug/Sept-Oct

1955; Slane Castle, Nov 1955.

O'Lochlainn, C.: "Francis Johnston; Architect", *The Irish Book Lover* (May 1942).

O'Mahony, Eoin: "Castletown Cox", *Forgnán* (Sept/Oct 1962).

O'Neill, Madeleine Clarke: Áras an Uachtaráin, *Irish Tatler and Sketch* (Sept 1958).

Oram, R.: *See* under ULSTER ARCHITECTURAL HERITAGE SOCIETY.

Paterson, T. G. F.: *See* under IRISH GEORGIAN SOCIETY.

Payne, Rev John: *Twelve Designs for Country Houses* (Dublin, 1757).

Rankin, Peter: *Irish Building Ventures of the Earl Bishop of Derry* (Belfast (UAHS), 1972, reprinted 1973).

Rankin, Peter: Downhill, *Country Life*, 8/15 July 1971.

Rankin, Peter: *See* also under MCKINSTRY, R. J.; ULSTER ARCHITECTURAL HERITAGE SOCIETY.

Rowan, A. J.: Articles in *Country Life*: Ballywalter Park, 2/9 March 1967; Killyleagh Castle, 19/26 March 1970; "Ulster's Architectural Identity", 27 May 1971.

Rowan, A. J.: *See* also under DIXON, Hugh; IRISH GEORGIAN SOCIETY; ULSTER ARCHITECTURAL HERITAGE SOCIETY.

Ryan, William: *See* under GUINNESS, Desmond.

Sadleir, T. U. & Dickinson, P. L.: *Georgian Mansions in Ireland* (Dublin, 1915).

Sadler, J. T.: *See* under GUINNESS, Desmond.

Shelswell-White, Geoffrey: "The Story of Bantry House", *Irish Tatler and Sketch* (May 1951).

Sitwell, Sacheverell: *British Architects and Craftsmen* (London, 1945).

Smith, Charles: *The Antient and Present State of the County and City of Cork* (Dublin, 1750).

Smith, Charles: *The Antient and Present State of the County and City of Waterford* (Dublin, 1746).

Taylor, G. C.: *See* under HUSSEY, Christopher.

Tierney, Mark & Cornforth, John: Glenstal Castle, *Country Life*, 3 Oct 1974.

Tighe, Joan: Articles in *Irish Tatler and Sketch*: Ballynegall, May 1962; Bellamont Forest, Nov 1962; Castleward, Aug 1961; Florence Court, Dec 1961; Lyons, March 1962; Moore Abbey, Sept 1962.

Ulster Architectural Heritage Society (Belfast (UAHS), 1969 onwards): *Lists and Surveys* by G. P. Bell, C. E. B. Brett,

Hugh Dixon, Lady Dunleath, Donald Girvan, Sir Robert Matthew, R. Oram, Peter Rankin, A. J. Rowan, etc.

Watkin, David: *C. R. Cockerell* (London, 1976).

Weaver, Lawrence: Heywood, *Country Life* (4/11 Jan 1919).

White, James: *See* under CROOKSHANK, Anne.

White, Terence de Vere: Articles in *Irish Times*, "People and Houses" series: Altidore Castle, 15 Jan 1963; Ballina Park, 1 Jan 1963; Charleville, 8 Jan 1963; Leixlip Castle, 5 Feb 1963; Mount Kennedy, 22 Jan 1963.

Wicklow, Earl of: Shelton Abbey, *Irish Tatler and Sketch* (March 1951).

Wilson, William: *The Post-chaise Companion*, 3rd edn (Dublin, 1803).

Wright, G. N.: *Ireland Illustrated* (London, 1831).

Wynne, Michael: *See* under IRISH GEORGIAN SOCIETY.

Young, Robert M.: *Belfast and the Province of Ulster in the 20th Century* (Brighton, 1909).

BURKE'S SERIES

A full Bibliography of *Burke's* is given in *Burke's Family Index* (1976). The following abbreviations have been used for references to *Burke's* books in this work:

PB	*Burke's Peerage and Baronetage*, 105 edns (1826 onwards) [a reference to plain "PB" in the text, indicates that the family history appears in the current (105th) edn; references to previous edns have dates of publication].
DEP	*Burke's Dormant and Extinct Peerages*, 5 edns (1831-83).
EDB	*Burke's Extinct and Dormant Baronetcies*, 2 edns (1838, 1841).
LG	*Burke's Landed Gentry*, 18 edns (1833/37 onwards).
LGI	*Burke's Landed Gentry of Ireland*, 4 edns (1899, 1904, 1912 and 1958).
IFR	*Burke's Irish Family Records* (1976).
GRF	*Burke's Guide to The Royal Family* (1973).
PFUSA	*Burke's Presidential Families of USA* (1975).
RFW	*Burke's Royal Families of the World*, Vol I (1977).
VSA	*Burke's Visitation of Seats and Arms . . .* (*see above*).
AA	*Burke's Authorized Arms* (1860).

Architectural Glossary

MOST OF the descriptions of houses in this book mention how many *storeys* a particular house is—or was—in height, and how many *bays* in length. Basements are not included in the number of storeys, but are mentioned in addition to them. In this respect, it should be pointed out that a basement can be entirely above ground level (*see* SANTRY COURT); what makes it a basement is the fact that it is considerably lower than the storey above it; it is also likely to be treated with *rustication* or *channelling* (*qqv*). An attic, if it is in the roof-space of a house, lit by gables or dormers, is also men-

tioned in addition to the number of storeys. An attic in the strict architectural sense—that is, a top storey situated above the *cornice* (*qv*), is, however, counted as a storey; though usually with some qualification such as "top storey treated as an attic, above the cornice" (*see* CASTLEBORO).

A *bay* is a vertical division of the exterior of a building, marked by a single tier of windows in its centre. Thus the number of bays in a facade is usually the same as the number of windows in each storey; in a facade of 5 bays, each storey has 5 windows (*see* DONARD). There are, however, facades in which some of the bays contain 2 or more narrower windows in each storey in place of a single window of whatever width is the norm: thus the wing to the right of the main block of PILTOWN HOUSE (*qv*) is of 3 bays, with 2 windows in each storey of the 2 right hand bays. The main block of Piltown serves to demonstrate how the bays which make up a facade can vary in width: it is of 5 bays, but the bay in the centre—which is also an example of a *breakfront* (*qv*)—is wider than the 2 bays on either side of it, and contains a window which is wider than the norm, of the type known as a *Wyatt window* (*qv*).

Because of this use of the word *bay* to denote a division, the word is never used in this book to mean a *bay window*, which is always described as a *bow*, curved or 3 sided as the case may be. For simplicity's sake, all polygonal bows are described as "3 sided", including those which are, strictly speaking, 5 sided, having 2 short faces at right angles to the facade as well as the central face and the 2 canted faces; and which are sometimes known as "half-octagons".

Acanthus Decoration based on the leaf of the acanthus plant, which forms part of the *Corinthian* capital. [*See* BALLIN-LOUGH CASTLE]

Acroteria Ornamented blocks of stone resting on an *entablature* or *pediment*; a characteristic of Grecian-Revival architecture. [*See* NEWBLISS HOUSE]

Aedicule The framing of a window or other opening with columns and a *pediment* or *entablature*. [*See* BALLYWALTER PARK]

Antis, in A term used to describe a *portico* which is wholly or partly recessed in the body of the building. [*See* SEA-FIELD, co Dublin]

Architrave Strictly speaking, the lowest member of the Classical *entablature*; used loosely to denote the moulded frame of a door or window opening.

Ashlar Squared cut stone in regular courses.

Astragal Strictly speaking, a narrow semi-circular moulding; used loosely to denote the glazing bars in a Georgian sash window.

Banded column A column of which the shaft is interrupted with stone bands.

Bargeboard A wooden board, often ornamented, along the slope of the gable of an *eaved roof*, hiding the ends of the roof timbers. [*See* OLD COURT, co Down]

Barrel Vault A curved vault, found in both Medieval and Classical architecture. [*See* ARDBRACCAN]

Bartizan A turret corbelled out from a wall. [*See* BALLY-GALLY CASTLE]

Baseless Pediment A *pediment* in which the base moulding is omitted. [*See* BELLARENA]

Batty Langley Gothic The earliest form of Georgian-Gothic, as popularized by the English architectural writer, Batty Langley (1696–1751).

Belvedere A *loggia* on the tower of a house. [*See* KILLASHEE]

Blind window, arch A window, arch or other opening which is filled in.

Blocked column/pilaster A column or pilaster of which the shaft is interrupted with square blocks. [*See* NEWBROOK]

Blocking The use of alternating large and small blocks of stone, or of intermittent large blocks, in a doorcase, window surround or similar feature. Also known as *rustication*. [*See Gibbsian doorcase/surround*]

Bolection moulding A broad curved moulding characteristic

of late C17 and early C18 interiors; used in chimneypieces and also on panelling. [*See* FRENCH PARK]

Bossi chimneypiece A late C18 marble chimneypiece by, or in the style of, the Italian craftsman, Pietro Bossi; characterized by delicate inlaid ornament in coloured marbles against a white ground. [*See* SPRINGFIELD CASTLE]

Breakfront A slight projection in the centre of a facade, rising through its full height and usually extending for 3 bays, but sometimes for more bays or less. [*See* CROSS-HAVEN HOUSE]

Broken pediment A pediment with a gap in its centre. [*See* CASTLE MARTYR]

Bucrania Sculptured ox-skulls, used as ornaments in the *metopes* of a *Doric frieze*. [*See* LYONS]

Camber-headed window A window of which the head is in the form of a shallow convex curve. [*See* PLATTEN HALL]

Cantilevered staircase A stone staircase in which the treads are monolithic and fixed at one end only. [*See* CASTLETOWN, co Kildare]

Caryatid A sculptured female figure used to support an entablature. [*See* GORMANSTON CASTLE]

Channelling Decoration of the outside of a building with horizontal grooves; a treatment usually confined to the basement or lower part of the building. [*See Rustication*]

Claire-voie A wrought-iron screen.

Clerestory A row of windows in the upper part of a hall or other room which rises through several storeys.

Coade stone An artificial cast stone of fine quality, invented in 1770s by Mrs Eleanor Coade and made by the Coade factory in London; widely used in the late-Georgian period for plaques, reliefs, capitals and other ornamentation. [*See* EMO COURT]

Coffering Recessed panels in a ceiling or dome. [*See* BELLA-MONT FOREST]

Composite Order An Order used originally by the Romans, having a capital which is partly *Ionic* and partly *Corinthian*. [*See* GOWRAN CASTLE]

Console bracket A scrolled bracket carrying an *entablature*, window surround or other member. [*See* MOORE HALL]

Corbel A block of stone projecting from a wall, supporting the beam of a roof or any other member; often ornamented.

Corinthian Order The third Order of Classical architecture. [*See* CASTLETOWN, co Kilkenny]

Cornice Strictly speaking, the crowning or upper projecting part of the Classical *entablature*; used to denote any projecting moulding along the top of a building, and in the angle between the walls and the ceiling of a room.

Crocket Projecting carved foliage, used to decorate *pinnacles* and similar features in Gothic or Gothic-Revival architecture.

Curved sweeps The curving walls or corridors joining the centre block of a Palladian house to the wings or pavilions. Also known as *quadrant walls*. [*See* RATHBEALE HALL]

Dado The lower part of the walls of a room, when treated differently from the area above.

Dentil cornice A *cornice* with tooth-like ornamentation. [*See* EDGEWORTHSTOWN HOUSE]

Die A raised rectangular block in the centre of the roof parapet of a house, or in the centre of the *portico* or porch [*See* MOORE HALL]

Diocletian window A semi-circular window divided vertically into 3 lights. [*See* BEAU PARC]

Doric Order The first and simplest Order of Grecian architecture. [*See* BALLIN TEMPLE]

Eaved roof A roof of which the eaves overhang the walls of the house. [*See* GLYNCH HOUSE]

Engaged columns Columns attached to, or partly sunk in, the wall of a building. [*See* CASTLEWARD]

Entablature A horizontal member, properly consisting of an *architrave*, *frieze* and *cornice*, supported on columns, or on a wall, with or without columns or *pilasters*. [*See* OLDTOWN]

Fenestration The arrangement of windows in a facade.

Festoon A carved ornament in the form of a garland of fruit and flowers; also known as a *swag*. [*See* RUSSBOROUGH]

Finial The top of a pinnacle or similar feature. [*See* COOLBAWN]

Floating pediment A *pediment* which is based neither on a *breakfront*, nor on columns or *pilasters*. [*See* BELLARENA]

Fluting Vertical channelling on the shaft of a column or *pilaster*. [*See* CASTLETOWN, co Kilkenny]

Framing bands Projecting bands, vertical and horizontal, framing a facade or certain bays of a facade. [*See* PILTOWN HOUSE]

Fretted ceiling A ceiling divided by criss-cross mouldings, a characteristic of Tudor and Tudor-Revival architecture. [*See* KILCORNAN]

Frieze Strictly speaking, the middle part of an *entablature* in Classical architecture; used also to denote a band of ornament running round a room immediately below the ceiling. [*See* OAK PARK, co Carlow]

Giant portico/columns/pilasters/order A *portico*, columns or *pilasters*, rising through 2 or more storeys of a building. [*See* CASTLECOOLE]

Gibbsian doorcase/surround A type of doorcase or surround made popular by the British architect, James Gibbs (1682–1754), characterized by alternating large and small blocks of stone or intermittent large blocks and a head composed of 5 *voussoirs* and a *pediment* or *entablature*. [*See* DROMANA]

Herm [*See* Term]

Hood moulding A projecting moulding over the heads of windows and doorways in Gothic, Tudor, Gothic-Revival and Tudor-Revival architecture. [*See* LOUGH RYNN] *Hood mouldings* also occur in some plain late-Georgian Irish country houses. [*See* STEPHENSTOWN]

Imperial staircase A bifurcating staircase—consisting of a single lower ramp, dividing into 2 upper ramps—on a grand scale. [*See* ROCKINGHAM]

Ionic Order The second Order of Classical architecture. [*See* CASTLECOOLE]

Irish battlements Stepped battlements, characteristic of Irish architecture from C15 onwards. [*See* CASTLETOWN CASTLE, co Louth] Used also in C19 castellated buildings. [*See* DERRYNANE]

Keyhole pattern A geometrical pattern of vertical and horizontal straight lines, used in Classical decoration. [*See* OAK PARK, co Carlow]

Lancet window A sharply pointed Gothic window. [*See* BARNANE]

Lantern A raised section of a roof, with windows all round, lighting a room below.

Lunette A semi-circular window, opening or recess. [*See* FURNESS]

Machicolation A corbelled gallery on the walls and towers of a castle, from which missiles, boiling oil, etc, could be thrown down. A feature frequently reproduced in C19 castles. [*See* CHARLEVILLE FOREST]

Machicoulis A small projection on the wall of a castle, commanding a doorway or an angle. [*See* LOUGHMOE COURT]

Mansard roof A steep roof with a double slope, named after the French architect Francois Mansart (1598–1666). [*See* BALYNA]

Metopes The spaces between the *triglyphs* in a *Doric frieze*; often ornamented with Classical reliefs. [*See* NEW HALL]

Mezzanine A low "half" storey between 2 higher ones. [*See* KILSHANNIG]

Modillion cornice The *cornice* of the *Corinthian Order*, made up of *modillions*, or ornamented brackets. Frequently used as the *cornice* of a ceiling. [*See* SPRINGHILL]

Mullioned window A window divided into lights by vertical bars of stone or timber; found in Gothic and Tudor architecture. [*See* CARRICK-ON-SUIR] Also common in Gothic-Revival and Tudor-Revival architecture. [*See* DUNLECKNEY MANOR]

Mutules The projecting blocks in a *Doric cornice*. [*See* NEW HALL]

Oculus A round window, also known as an *oeil-de-boeuf*. [*See* FRYBROOK]

Oeil-de-boeuf [*See* Oculus]

Ogee A window head or arch made up of convex and concave curves; found in Gothic and Gothic-Revival architecture. [*See* GREY ABBEY]

Oriel A large projecting window in Gothic, Tudor, Gothic-Revival and Tudor-Revival architecture; sometimes rising through 2 or more storeys, sometimes in an upper storey only and carried on *corbelling*. [*See* DUNLECKNEY MANOR]

Overlapping wings Wings projecting forward on either side of the centre block of a house, and overlapping it by the thickness of one wall which is common to both centre block and wing. [*See* WARINGSTOWN HOUSE]

Pediment Originally the low-pitched triangular gable of the roof of a Classical temple, and of the roof of a *portico*; used as an ornamental feature, generally in the centre of a facade, without any structural purpose. [*See* CROSSHAVEN HOUSE]

Pendentives The triangular curving surfaces below the domed ceiling of a rectangular room. [*See* CASTLEGAR]

Perpendicular window A large tracery window derived from English Gothic architecture of C15 and C16. [*See* DROMORE CASTLE, co Kerry]

Perron A platform approached by outside steps in front of the entrance door of a house, when the entrance is raised on a high basement. [*See* DESART COURT]

Piano Nobile The storey in which the principal reception rooms of a house are situated, when it is raised on a high basement or is at 1st-floor level.

Pier A vertical supporting member, other than a column. [*See* KILMURRY, co Cork]

Pilaster A flat pillar projecting from a wall, usually with a capital of one of the principal Orders of architecture. [*See* CASTLETOWN, co Kilkenny]

Pinnacle A small turret-like projection in Gothic, Tudor, Gothic-Revival and Tudor-Revival architecture. [*See* KILRONAN CASTLE] Also the point of a buttress. [*See* SHELTON ABBEY]

Polychromy, structural The use of different coloured stone, or stone and brick, for the various parts of the wall of a house; a favourite device with architects of the High Victorian period. [*See* BENBURB MANOR]

Porch oriel An *oriel* above the entrance door of a Tudor or Tudor-Revival house. [*See* CARRICK-ON-SUIR; CARRIGGLAS MANOR]

Porte-cochère A *portico* wide enough for carriages to drive beneath it. [*See* PORTGLENONE]

Portico An open porch consisting of a *pediment* or *entablature* carried on columns. [*See* CASTLECOOLE]

Quadrant walls [*See Curved sweeps*]

Quatrefoil window A window in the shape of a 4 leafed clover; found in Gothic and Gothic-Revival architecture. [*See* DERRYMORE HOUSE]

Quoins The slightly projecting dressed stones at the corners of a building, usually laid so as to have faces that are alternately large and small, and serving as an architectural feature; used also to give emphasis to certain bays of a facade. [*See* FLORENCE COURT]

Reeding The decoration of a surface with narrow convex mouldings parallel and close together.

Relieving arch A blind arch above a window. [*See* BRAGANZA]

Rendering The covering of the external face of a building with cement, plaster etc.

Rubble Rough unhewn stones used for building.

Rustication The use of stone blocks with recessed joints and often with rough or specially treated faces; a treatment generally confined to the basement or the lower part of a building. [*See* CASTLEWARD]

Scagliola An artificial marble made out of marble chips, cement and plaster.

Screen In Gothic or Tudor architecture, a partition of wood, often elaborately carved, at one end of a hall or chapel. In Classical architecture, 2 or more columns dividing one end of a room from the rest of it; usually reflected by a *pilaster* of the same Order on the wall at either side. [*See* LUCAN HOUSE]

Scroll pediment A *broken pediment* in which the sloping members are shaped like scrolls. [*See* DAMER HOUSE]

Segmental pediment A *pediment* in the shape of a segment of a circle. [*See* PLATTEN HALL]

Shouldered architrave/doorcase A door or window surround with projections at the upper and sometimes also the lower corners; characteristic of c18 houses. [*See* FLORENCE COURT]

Soanian In the manner of the English architect, Sir John Soane (1753–1837), who is noted for his restrained but highly original neo-Classicism and his spatial effects.

Soffit The underside of an arch or any other member. [*See* CASTLEGAR]

Spandrels The triangular spaces on either side of an arch. [*See* CASTLE LESLIE]

Sprocketed roof A roof with a slight concave curve. [*See* BONNETTSTOWN]

Strapwork Ornamentation composed of curving interlacing bands, characteristic of Elizabethan and Jacobean architecture. [*See* PORTUMNA CASTLE] Also common in Elizabethan-Revival and Jacobean-Revival architecture. [*See* BANGOR CASTLE]

String course A prominent horizontal band of masonry. [*See* CUBA COURT]

Strip pilaster A plain *pilaster*, without a capital. [*See* KILMORE: SEE HOUSE]

Swag [*See Festoon*]

Sweeps, curved [*See Curved sweeps*]

Term A tapering pedestal supporting a bust, or merging into a sculptured figure, used ornamentally, particularly at the sides of chimneypieces. Roughly similar to a *herm*.

Tower of the Winds Order A modified *Corinthian* order, derived from the Tower of the Winds in Athens. [*See* MOUNT STEWART]

Transom A horizontal *mullion* in a window.

Trefoil window, trefoil-headed window A Gothic window shaped like, or with a head in the form of, a three-leafed clover. [*See* GLENBEIGH TOWERS]

Triglyphs The channelled projections in a Doric *frieze*. [*See* NEW HALL]

Tripod A Classical tripod, used as ornament. [*See* LYONS]

Tuscan Order A simplified *Doric Order*. [*See* BRAGANZA]

Tympanum The triangular space within the mouldings of a *pediment*, often ornamented and containing armorial bearings, etc. [*See* BURNHAM HOUSE]

Venetian doorway A doorway based on a *Venetian window*. [*See* COOPERSHILL]

Venetian window A window with three openings, that in the centre being round-headed and wider than those on either side; a very familiar feature of Palladian architecture. [*See* BEAU PARC]

Vermiculation The treatment of stone blocks to give a worm-like texture. [*See* EGLINTON: MANOR HOUSE]

Volute A scroll derived from the scroll in the *Ionic* capital.

Voussoirs The wedge-shaped blocks forming an arch; sometimes given prominence by being proud of the surrounding masonry, or by being of a different coloured stone or brick. [*See* CAHIRMOYLE]

Weather-slating The covering of the external walls of a house with slates; a treatment often met with in the south and south-west of Ireland. [*See* SALISBURY]

Wyatt window A rectangular triple window very common in late-Georgian domestic architecture, named after the English architect, James Wyatt (1747–1813). [*See* FRANKVILLE HOUSE]

Introduction

OF THE 2,000 or so Irish country houses described in this book, few date from earlier than the 15th century; though house-agents usually claim that the castle in Ireland which they are offering is "XII Century Norman" (the Roman numerals being doubtless intended to convey an even greater sense of antiquity). Plenty of houses occupy very ancient sites; but apart from foundations, and perhaps the odd piece of masonry, nothing now survives of what was there in the Middle Ages. Among the exceptions are the round towers at Kilkenny Castle, at Leixlip Castle, co Kildare, and at Killyleagh Castle, co Down, which are certainly 13th century and could very possibly be 12th century; the Celtic-Romanesque arch at Lismore Castle, co Waterford; and the medieval core of castles such as Howth, Malahide and Dunsany, which, like Leixlip, are in the Pale, the enclave round Dublin held throughout the Middle Ages by the English Crown. Each of the castles just mentioned could qualify for the title of "the oldest inhabited castle in Ireland"—another favourite house-agents' claim—but the one which seems most to deserve it is Malahide; not on account of its early medieval masonry, but because of its late 15th century great hall, the only medieval hall in Ireland to have survived relatively unchanged and in domestic use until recently. Some of the other castles may have older walls than those of Malahide, but none can boast of a medieval room like the Malahide hall; having been extensively rebuilt at subsequent periods, as indeed most of Malahide has been. In fact, all the castles just mentioned are of as much or even greater interest on account of their later architecture than for what they have to show of the architecture of the Middle Ages: Howth, Dunsany, Leixlip and Malahide for their splendid 18th century interiors; Kilkenny for its early 18th century Classical gateway and its Victorian-Gothic gallery; Lismore for its Jacobean ranges and its remodelling by that early-Victorian genius, Sir Joseph Paxton.

The best surviving examples of medieval domestic architecture are to be found among the castles which are no longer inhabited. Space permits the inclusion of only the most important of them in this book: the ruined or partly ruined castles of Askeaton and Newcastle West,

with their magnificent 15th century halls; the intact, but long-deserted castle of Cahir; the world-famous Blarney Castle and the recently restored Bunratty. These castles, however, are by no means typical. Blarney and Bunratty were the seats of Sovereign Princes, the MacCarthys and the O'Briens of Thomond; Askeaton and Newcastle West of the Desmonds, the greatest nobles of the realm; Cahir of a branch of the other great noble house of Butler.

Most Irish castles, of the 15th, 16th and early 17th centuries were simple "tower-houses", rather like the pele towers of the Scottish borders. These towers can be seen all over the Irish countryside; the majority of them deserted, and in varying stages of ruin, having been abandoned after the mid-17th century wars, or during the two centuries that followed. Some of them, however, continued to be lived in, and were generally enlarged in the late 17th or 18th centuries by the addition of a domestic wing. The tower house with a later wing attached is in fact the most usual form of "old"—as distinct from 19th century—Irish castle. Sometimes the wing is in a plain Georgian style, like that at Ballymore Castle, co Galway, or the ranges added to the medieval Smarmore Castle, co Louth; often it has been castellated in the 19th century, as at Castle Widenham, co Cork. Usually the later building is lower than the tower, which stands prominently at one end of it, or behind it; but in some cases the later buildings and the tower are all of the same height; such as at Louth Hall, co Louth, where they are given unity by a continuous skyline of 19th century battlements. At Ballinakill, co Waterford, the tower has been completely built into the 18th century house and its presence is not noticeable from the outside. At the opposite end of the scale are those houses which are built alongside old towers, but not actually joined to them, like Creagh Castle, co Cork. Often the tower, while not actually abutting on the house, forms part of the adjoining offices as at Rosegarland and Butlerstown Castle, both in co Wexford.

Almost every Irish country house dating from before the middle of the 17th century was a castle of some kind or another. The 10th Earl of Ormonde's Elizabethan manor house at Carrick-on-Suir, co Tipperary, had the protection of the 15th century castle standing behind it. Sir Basil Brooke's Jacobean house at Donegal was built onto an old keep of the O'Donnells. Myrtle Grove, co Cork, where, according to tradition, Sir Walter Raleigh lived, is unique in being an entirely unfortified late 16th century manor house; but it was built within the walls of the town of Youghal.

Towards the end of the 16th century and in the early 17th century, however, a new type of castle evolved, the semi-fortified house. It was gabled, usually symmetrical, with regularly-disposed mullioned windows; in fact, rather like the plainer, taller and more severe Elizabethan and Jacobean houses in the north and west of England; but it was nevertheless designed to repel an attack, and had defensive galleries and loops and was usually surrounded by a fortified outer wall. The semi-fortified houses, which continued to bear the designation of "castle", are particularly associated with the English settlers; yet some of the best examples of them, such as Portumna and Glinsk castles in co Galway, Burntcourt, co Tipperary, and Monkstown Castle, co Cork, were built by old Norman-Irish families. As a group, they fared badly. The majority of them were destroyed in the 1641 Rising and in the wars that followed. Portumna, the finest of them, seat of the Burkes, Earls of Clanricarde, survived the 17th century wars only to be accidentally burnt in 1826. Monkstown Castle, co Cork, one of the very few to have survived intact to the present day is now more or less derelict.

Ulster had its own particular version of the semi-fortified house, the "Plantation Castle", which looked more Scottish than English, with round towers and pointed roofs; like Ballygally Castle, co Antrim, the most perfect surviving example, which might have come straight from the lowlands of Scotland. Just as the semi-fortified houses in the rest of Ireland are particularly associated with the English, so are the Plantation Castles in Ulster naturally associated with the Scots; yet some of them, such as Castle Upton, co Antrim, were built by English settlers; while at least one of them, the original Shane's Castle, also in co Antrim, was built by Shane McBrian O'Neill, a scion of the ancient Irish Royal House who was allowed to keep part of his ancestral lands after the Plantation.

Unique among the Irish country houses of the first half of the 17th century was the palace near Naas, in co Kildare—now a ruin known by the rather undignified name of Jigginstown—built about 1636 by the Lord-Deputy, Thomas, Viscount Wentworth, afterwards Earl of Strafford. This was in every sense a prodigy house: in its vast size, in being entirely unfortified, in being of brick instead of stone; in being the only Irish house built in the reign of Charles I of which the architecture could be called Carolean. It is said to have been designed by John Allen, a Dutch merchant who settled in Ireland and "being skilful in architecture was esteemed and consulted by the most eminent of the nobility in their buildings". It is thus the first Irish country house to be attributed to an architect whose name is known. The Dutchman, Allen, whose descendants became rich and themselves joined the Irish nobility, with Stillorgan House, co Dublin, as their seat, is thus the first known Irish country house architect. The popular myth by which almost every late 17th and early 18th century Irish house of consequence is attributed to an anonymous "Dutch architect" may well have originated with him. Apart from a shadowy late 17th century figure named Leuventhen, there is no evidence of any Dutch architect after Allen; the memory of him, however, could well have given rise to the belief that all country house achitects were of necessity Dutch.

The presence of "Dutch" or curvilinear gables in a number of late 17th and early 18th century Irish country houses—Rich Hill, co Armagh, Waringstown, co Down and Palace Anne, co Cork, for example—contributes to this Dutch myth, though the curvilinear gable is, after all, a familiar feature of 17th century English architecture. With or without gables, the more important Irish country houses of the period between the Restoration and the 1720s were, in fact, very English in character; though they naturally tended to be old-fashioned—thus Stackallan House, co Meath, built in 1716, and the house which the 3rd Viscount Kenmare built at Killarney about 1726, could be mistaken for English country houses of the 1670s and 80s. They had that sense of comfortable well-being of the middle-sized English country houses of the reign of Charles II: dignified but unpretentious facades with many windows grouped rather closely together, recessed centres and pedimented doorcases; high-pitched roofs on sturdy timber cornices; panelled interiors with bolection mouldings and perhaps carved pilasters. Though some of them, such as Burton, co Cork, were surrounded by defensive walls, they were in other respects unfortified. With one or two exceptions, notably the palace which the Great Duke of Ormonde built at Dunmore, near Kilkenny, these houses were of moderate size: in fact small enough to be manageable even at the present time. Yet those of them which survived the Williamite War and the 18th and early 19th century rebuildings have been particularly unlucky. Palace Anne and Eyrecourt Castle, co Galway, have been allowed to fall into ruin; Kilmacurragh, co Wicklow, is now in an advanced state of decay; Platten Hall, co Meath and Anngrove, co Cork, were demolished in the 1950s. Now, in the Irish Republic, Beaulieu, co Louth, stands alone as a house dating from the second half of the 17th century which keeps its original character and is still the home of the descendants of the family who built it.

If few enough of the more important late 17th century houses remain, the smaller ones have fared even worse. Most of them were demolished and replaced by 18th century houses. Some have been abandoned and are now ruins. Others still exist but have been so engulfed by later additions as to be unrecognizable. The Irish gentry, when enlarging a small house, were less inclined to build wings onto it as to add a new front, so that the original house became back premises. Often the process was repeated at a later date again, so that a house with a late-Georgian front has two earlier houses buried in its "tail". Unfortunately the earlier—or earliest—house seldom retains any of its original features, so that there is nothing but guesswork or family tradition to tell us when it was built. Owners of houses of this kind are apt to suppose that the tail is 17th century and that the Georgian front dates from about 1750; whereas the front is as often as not more like 1800, so that the tail is also probably half-a-century later than what it is imagined to be.

The architectural fashions of early 18th century England—the monumental Classicism of Vanbrugh and Hawksmoor, the Palladianism of Lord Burlington and his circle—are generally regarded as having been introduced into Ireland towards the end of the 1720s by the brilliant young Irish architect, Sir Edward Lovett Pearce. They were not, however, entirely unknown in Ireland before Pearce's time; as is witnessed by the 2nd Duke of Ormonde's sophisticated Classical gateway at Kilkenny Castle, and Thomas Burgh's Palladian house at Oldtown, co Kildare, both of which were built about 1709. But while these were isolated phenomena, Pearce, during his all too short career, brought about a revolution in the architectural taste of the Irish aristocracy.

Pearce's country house *oeuvre* is small enough, and much of it is undocumented, though it can with certainty be attributed to him. It included Bellamont Forest, co Cavan, Cashel Palace, co Tipperary, Summerhill, co Meath, Desart Court, co Kilkenny and the colonnades and wings of Castletown, co Kildare, of which the centre block was designed by the Italian, Alessandro Galilei. But his influence lived on after his premature death in 1733 in the houses designed by his assistants, particularly those by Richard Castle, who succeeded to his practice. Castle, though he was a German, was influenced more by current English architectural fashions—notably by the designs of James Gibbs —than by the light-hearted architecture of his native land. But while he was certainly less talented than Pearce, he does not deserve his reputation for heaviness. He tends to be associated with his rather dull rebuilding of Carton, simply because this was the seat of Ireland's premier peer, the 19th Earl of Kildare,

father of the 1st Duke of Leinster; people forget that he was also the architect of Russborough, co Wicklow, regarded by many as the most beautiful house in Ireland; and of the magnificent but by no means overwhelming entrance front of Powerscourt, in the same county.

Pearce was Vanbrugh's first cousin once removed and one can see a certain Vanbrughian influence in Summerhill, the most dramatic of all the great 18th century Irish country houses, which is attributed to him in collaboration with Castle; but while a sense of drama is seldom absent from houses of the Pearce-Castle school—nor, indeed from 18th century Irish country house architecture as a whole—there is never the portentous grandeur of Vanbrugh, or of the more heavy-handed English Palladians, such as Henry Flitcroft. To a certain extent this is due to the fact that there were no 18th century Irish country houses as large as the more important houses of contemporary England; but the nobility and gentry of mid-18th century Ireland seem on the whole to have had an aversion to the feature which, more than any other, gives the palaces of the great English Whig magnates their pomp: the giant portico. This was always an expensive feature; but it may also have been regarded as unsuitable to the Irish climate. We now tend to think of a portico in terms of its 19th century function: as a porch under which guests arriving in their best clothes can shelter from the rain. The giant portico of English Palladian architecture is, however, more suited to fine weather than to wet. One sits under it on a sunny day and sees the blue sky framed by its columns; it prevents the stuffs in the rooms beneath it from becoming faded. But on a wet day it drips depressingly with rain and makes the rooms beneath it dark; while since it is raised on a basement, the arriving guest has to ascend a long flight of slippery steps before gaining its shelter. Besides, in the middle of the 18th century, when roads were still extremely bad, guests tended to arrive at a country house travel-stained, for a long stay, rather than in their finery for an afternoon or evening visit.

Surprisingly enough, the pediment carried on a giant order of pilasters or half-columns, which in England and elsewhere was the usual substitute for the portico as a central feature, was also not popular in 18th century Ireland. Castle used it with great success at Powerscourt; and it also occurs at Castle Ward, co Down, which, significantly, is thought to be by an English architect. Castle's central feature at Russborough, like Pearce's portico at Bellamont Forest, does not, strictly speaking, incorporate a giant order, since it is only carried through the principal storey; the upper storey being treated as an attic.

The Palladianism introduced into Ireland by Pearce and Castle was thus a toned-down version of that on the other side of the Irish sea; it might have been deliberately or subconsciously modified to suit the soft Irish light. The centre of a facade was given emphasis by a pediment only, such as at Carton; by superimposed pilasters, as at Desart or Castle's Ballyhaise, co Cavan; by a subtle grouping of windows and other elements. Castle made great use of oculi and niches, as at Hazlewood, co Sligo. He also favoured the tripartite doorway with a pediment extending over the door and flanking windows, which he used at Westport House, co Mayo; and which also occurs at Hazlewood and at Ledwithstown, co Longford, a delightful small house thought to be by him. The Venetian window, that favourite feature of the English Palladians, was frequently used to emphasize the centre of a facade, or the sides, such as at Cashel Palace; it was also used in conjunction with the semicircular Diocletian window, as at Belvedere, co Westmeath. From the time of Castle until almost the end of the 18th century, Irish country house architecture was to be characterized by this grouping of minor elements rather than by the use of a single major theme, such as a giant portico.

As well as introducing Palladian—or reputedly Palladian—elements into the elevations of their country houses, Pearce and Castle favoured the Palladian plan of a centre block joined to subordinate wings by straight or curving links. This plan was fashionable in Ireland far longer than it was in England; it even appears in certain houses built after 1800, notably Castleboro, co Wexford, which dates from as late as about 1840. It was used not only for the great mansions, the Castletowns, Russboroughs and Powerscourts, but for medium-sized houses like Monksgrange, co Wexford and Burtown, co Kildare, as well; and also for small houses such as Kilcarty, co Meath and Factory Hill, co Cork. To join the centre block to the wings, corridors or screen walls became more popular than the arcades and colonnades favoured by Palladio and his 18th century English disciples; the colonnade, like the giant portico, was clearly beyond the means of most of the Irish nobility and gentry and only occurs in the houses of the very rich, such as Castletown and Russborough. But if the Irish departed from Palladio in this respect, they came closer to him than the English in their use of the wings, which almost invariably served as stables or offices rather than containing additional reception rooms, as is so often the case in England. With smaller houses, such as Kilcarty, they frequently followed Palladio's precepts even further and produced architectural groupings that comprised not just the house and the offices, but also the farm buildings.

While so many 18th century Irish country houses are thus wide-spreading, there are just as many which are compact and tall; vertical, so to speak, rather than horizontal. What is generally regarded as the most typical Irish house, the three-storey Georgian block, almost as high as it is long with five or seven bays in its principal front, can be said to have originated with Mount Ievers, co Clare, which dates from the 1730s and was designed by John Rothery assisted by members of his family. The Rotherys were a rather shadowy family of architects practising in the south and west of Ireland, away from the influence of Pearce and Castle; it has been suggested that they got their inspiration for Mount Ievers from the 17th century design of Chevening, in Kent—now the country home of The Prince of Wales. Whether or not this so, the tall Irish house certainly has an ancestry going back before the introduction of Palladianism; and yet it was still extremely popular after Palladianism had gone out of fashion. Bowen's Court, co Cork, which is attributed to Isaac Rothery and which had much of Mount Ievers's dreamlike, melancholy beauty, was built between 1766 and 1776. Coolmore, another tall house in the same county, dates from 1788; and there are plenty of houses of this kind which were built a decade or even two decades later. Professor Girouard sees these houses as "the Georgian equivalent of the tower-houses in which Irish and Anglo-Irish alike lived until the seventeenth century—re-phrasing, in classical form, something that appealed to the Irish or Anglo-Irish character".

One tends to think of the tall Irish houses as severely simple, which is certainly true of Mount Ievers and Bowen's Court and of the majority of those built towards the end of the 18th century. But some of them, mostly dating from the middle of the century, have more elaborate facades. Florence Court, co Fermanagh, which was built as a tall block though it later became widespreading by the addition of arcades and pavilions, has a front heavily enriched with rustications, balustrades, pedimented niches and other features. Then there is a group of houses by, or attributed to, Francis Bindon, who dominated the Irish architectural scene after Castle's death in 1751: Raford, co Galway, Coopershill, co Sligo, Drewstown, co Meath, Woodstock, co Kilkenny (the latter, like Florence Court, subsequently extended by the addition of wings.) The front of each of these houses has a centre emphasized by the use of Venetian or Diocletian windows, niches, oculi and other motifs; often somewhat clumsily handled, for Bindon, despite his prominence as an architect and his large output, was only an amateur; a talented and well-connected member of the co Clare landed gentry who was also a successful portrait painter.

It is remarkable how no professional was forthcoming to take Castle's place; for the other most influential Irish architect of the third quarter of the 18th century was also an amateur. This was Nathaniel Clements, who became rich as a banker, as one of the developers of Georgian Dublin and through holding the lucrative post of Vice-Treasurer of Ireland; and who was a force in the political as well as the architectural world, an MP, a Privy Councillor and father of the 1st Earl of Leitrim. The houses of Clements and his school, which include Beau Parc, co Meath, Newberry Hall and Lodge Park, co Kildare, Colganstown co Dublin and Clements's own house in Phoenix Park, now known as Áras an Uachtaráin and the official residence of the President of Ireland, are characterized by the use of elements from the contemporary English pattern books —notably those of James Gibbs and Isaac Ware—which are combined more felicitously than the elements of Bindon's facades; the particular Clements hallmarks being the central Diocletian window and the pedimented tripartite doorcase with engaged columns. Whereas most of the Bindon houses are tall blocks, Clements favoured the wide-spreading Palladian layout. One wonders whether the places of origin of the two architects had anything to do with their preferences in this respect; Bindon, though influenced by Pearce, may also have been in touch with the Rotherys and familiar with Mount Ievers, coming as he did from co Clare; whereas Clements, whose home county was Cavan, would have been influenced by Pearce alone.

Though the wide-spreading Palladian house and the tall block constitute the two most important groups of 18th century Irish country houses, there are as many or more houses which do not fit into either of these categories. There are the two storey houses without wings, ranging from mansions like Bellevue, co Wicklow, the earlier part of Curragh Chase, co Limerick, Syngefield, Offaly, and Dangan Castle, co Meath, the boyhood home of the great Duke of Wellington, down to the unassuming five and three bay houses of the lesser gentry; such as Derk, co Limerick and Derryvoulin, co Galway; one can list them without end. There are the bow-fronted houses, with one bow or two, curved or three-sided: Gill Hall, co Down, Abbeville, co Dublin, Rockforest, co Cork. There are the bow-ended houses, of which the progenitor is probably Castle's superb villa on Lough Ennel in co Westmeath, Belvedere. There are houses with wings joined directly to the centre block, rather than by corridors or screen walls in the Palladian manner; sometimes the centre block is a storey higher than the wings, as at Mount Druid, co Roscommon and Inch, co Dublin; sometimes both the centre and the wings are of the same height. There is that small and freakish group of houses with central attic-towers, headed by Gola, co Monaghan.

As well as grouping houses according to their shape and style, one can divide them into the "architectural" and the "plain". Naturally, a higher proportion of the larger houses are architectural, though there are plain houses among them: Moore Park, co Cork, seat of the Earls Mount Cashell, for example, or Headfort, co Meath, which is outwardly plain despite its lavish interior. And Ireland is also surprisingly rich in quite small houses of the highest architectural quality; contrary to the popular myth that there is nothing in Ireland to compare with the attractive "middling" houses of England. In fact, if one regards the houses as classical architecture rather than merely as examples of pleasant vernacular building, it would be true to say that Ireland is better endowed than England in this respect; for whereas the smaller English classic house is usually provincial—that is, it betrays its designer's imperfect understanding of the classical idiom by some obvious architectural solecism—provincialism is often absent from its Irish counterpart. The classical idiom seems to have become second nature to the 18th and early 19th century Irish; even to local builders working for the minor gentry or for tradesmen or prosperous farmers. It was more than just being able to interpret classical elements correctly; it was, in the words of Dr Maurice Craig,

> that the designers and craftsmen of the period were so deeply imbued with the language of classicism, and that it answered so well to their everyday needs, that they used it unselfconsciously and felt no need to be scurrying off continually to look things up in pattern-books.

Examples of smaller "architectural" houses include Bonnettstown Hall, co Kilkenny, Summer Hill, co Mayo, Monart, co Wexford and Dysert, co Westmeath. Dysert is one of the many smaller Irish houses which has a symmetrical interior plan. This is another instance where the smaller 18th century Irish country house is often superior to its English counterpart. In England, all too frequently, classicism goes no further than the facade; the rooms which lie behind it are low, of dull proportions and haphazardly arranged. But the interiors of quite humble Irish houses reflect the exteriors in the best classical way; ceilings are high, rooms well proportioned; there are good spatial effects.

Good proportions and handsome joinery—shouldered doorcases, stairs with robust turned balusters—were generally all that the lesser gentry could afford to give dignity and elegance to the interiors of their houses. Plasterwork, apart from plain cornices and friezes, was generally beyond their means; though one sometimes finds simple stucco decoration in quite small houses, such as Summer Hill, co Mayo. It is, however, in the houses of the nobility and the richer commoners that the more elaborate plasterwork is to be found. The earliest stucco ceilings in Irish country houses are of the compartmented type, with circles or ovals of foliage and flowers; there are examples at Beaulieu, co Louth, and a more sophisticated coffered ceiling designed by Pearce and dating from about 1730 at Bellamont Forest, co Cavan. A few years later there was a revolution in Irish plasterwork caused by the arrival of the Italian stuccodores, the brothers Paul and Philip Francini, who introduced the full-bloodedness of the baroque, with human figures, swags and trophies in high relief. Their first Irish patron appears to have been Dr Jemmet Browne, Protestant Bishop of Cork, who commissioned them about 1734 to decorate the walls and ceilings of the dining room of his plain and comparatively modest family home in co Cork, Riverstown House, with classical figures. In 1739, they executed the wonderful ceiling of the saloon at Carton, representing "the Courtship of the Gods". During the next three decades, they worked in many Irish houses, including Castletown, co Kildare, Kilshannig, co Cork and, almost certainly, Russborough, giving rise to the legend of the "Italian Plasterers" which proved no less persistent than the myth of the "Dutch Architect"; to this day, there are those who attribute all forms of decorative plasterwork, whether of the 18th, 19th or 20th centuries, to "Italians". In fact, Irish craftsmen quickly learnt the art of the Francini and went from the baroque into the gay exuberance of the rococo. The outstanding Irish stuccodore of the mid-18th century was Robert West, whose work is characterized by lively and naturalistic birds. There is a ceiling of about 1760 at Montalto, co Down, attributed to West; while the vigorous plasterwork at Florence Court is very much in his manner, as is the ceiling of the splendid double cube room at Castle Martyr, co Cork. Perhaps the most beautiful ceilings of all are the kind in which figures emerge from clouds, giving a wonderful half-tone effect; like the ceilings at Belvedere, and those which formerly existed at Summerhill, co Meath.

The neo-Classical style of plasterwork, characterized by its delicacy and by the use of motifs copied from the recently-discovered paintings at Pompeii and Herculaneum, which was made fashionable in Britain by Robert Adam and James Wyatt, first appeared in Ireland in the 1770s. Within a decade or so, it had ousted the rococo. This is to be regretted; for while neo-Classical decoration has a beauty and elegance of its own, it lacks the spontaneous vigour of the plasterwork of the Francini and West and their followers; being all cast from moulds, whereas the baroque and rococo plasterwork was modelled *in situ;* so that every figure and bird tended to have a different expression.

Adam himself has been invested with the same immortality as the "Italian Plasterers" and the "Dutch Architect"; plasterwork not attributed to the mythical "Italians" is popularly attributed to him; one would have suspected people of thinking of him as the Father of Plasterwork just as his namesake is the Father of Mankind, except that he is all too often referred to erroneously as "Adams". In fact, there are only two Irish houses containing his work: Headfort, co Meath, for which he designed a splendid series of rooms, and Castle Upton, co Antrim, which he remodelled in his "Castle Style", adding magnificent battlemented stables. A somewhat larger number of Irish country houses contain rooms by Wyatt, notably Curraghmore, co Waterford and Abbeyleix, co Leix; but the great majority of the neo-Classical or "Adamesque" interiors in Ireland are by Irish craftsmen, who learnt the neo-Classical idiom as rapidly as their fathers and grandfathers had mastered the rococo. Chief among the Irish stuccodores of the period was Michael Stapleton, known as the "Dublin Adam", though in fact he evolved a very distinctive style of his own; among the country houses where he worked, or is thought to have worked, are Lucan, co Dublin and Furness, co Kildare. The fact that neo-Classical plasterwork was cast from moulds meant that it could, so to speak, be mass-produced and was thus within the means of the smaller gentry, who had been unable to afford the cost of getting proficient stuccodores to work in their houses. There was neo-Classical decoration for every purse. The very rich could have rooms in which the walls were ornamented as well as the ceilings, like the exquisite dining room at Heywood, co Leix, now, alas, no more; and they could complement the plasterwork with painted panels and medallions, as at Rathfarnham Castle, co Dublin. The moderately affluent could afford somewhat less elaborate ceilings, like that at Castle Blunden, co Kilkenny. Those of more slender means contented themselves with neo-Classical friezes, leaving the flat of their ceilings plain.

The change from rococo plasterwork to neo-Classical coincided with the rise of a new generation of architects in Ireland. Bindon died in 1765, Clements in 1777. The Sardinian, Davis Duckart, who is generally regarded as the last of the Palladians and gave Ireland one of the most beautiful of all her Palladian houses, "the other" Castletown, in co Kilkenny, disappears from the scene after 1774, though his death does not seem to have occurred for another ten years. In the 1780s, the two stars were both Englishmen, Thomas Cooley and James Gandon, who were patronized by rival factions of the nobility. Cooley had connexions with Wyatt, whose design for Mount Kennedy, co Wicklow, he modified and executed. Mount Kennedy, which was completed in 1784, is something of a "key" house; a forerunner of the compact free-standing "villa" which became increasingly popular during the next half century. Its plan—with a curved bow in the centre of its garden front, containing an oval room—is very similar to that of Lucan House, co Dublin, in which Wyatt also had a hand; it also resembles that of Caledon, co Tyrone, which Cooley himself designed. In a more elongated form, it is the plan of Castle Bernard, co Cork; and there is a still larger castellated version of it at Slane Castle, co Meath, by Wyatt and Francis Johnston, who was Cooley's assistant and took over his practice after his premature death in 1784. Johnston, who made use of this plan in a simplified form for Ballycurry, co Wicklow, a house which he designed after 1800, set fashionable Irish domestic architecture firmly on the the neo-Classical path. Whereas Mount Kennedy and Lucan, though neo-Classical within, were Palladian outside, Johnston's elevations have a Grecian austerity which is nowhere more evident than at Townley Hall, co Louth, his Classical masterpiece, designed in 1794.

Francis Johnston's less well-known brother, Richard, was also an exponent of the neo-Classical, and produced the original design for Castlecoole, co Fermanagh, on which Wyatt based the design that was executed. Though it has a Palladian plan, Castlecoole, built in the 1790s, is one of the most perfect examples in Ireland of late 18th century Hellenism. It is also one of the most monumental and palatial of all Irish houses; and has the full panoply of giant porticoes and colonnades. The giant portico, in its neo-Classical rather than its Palladian form, can be said to have made its Irish debut at this time; for it also features in a great house by Gandon, Emo Court, co Leix. Emo, which consists of a single rectangular block with a raised attic at either end, is perhaps even more monumental than Castlecoole, though not quite as large; it is the domestic counterpart of Gandon's most famous public building, the Dublin Custom House.

Houses like Castlecoole and Emo were far beyond the means of most of the Irish nobility and gentry; indeed, the cost of completing Emo, which was still unfinished when its builder, the 1st Earl of Portarlington, died in 1798, proved almost too much for the next two generations of the Portarlington family. And the villas and cheaper neo-Classical houses did not really become popular until after the turn of the century. The great majority of houses built during the 1780s and 1790s differed only in certain minor respects from those built during the two previous decades. Windows were larger, glazing bars thinner. Bows were more popular, so were fanlights; which became increasingly large, resembling fanlights of contemporary Dublin; even to having delicate leaded glazing instead of wooden astragals, as at Davidstown, co Kildare.

The end of the 18th century was marked by the passing of the Act of Union between Ireland and Britain. Though in most ways the Union was a disaster for Ireland, it actually caused an increase in country house building. The popular belief that half the Irish nobility and gentry disappeared to England after the Union is not true. Certainly the nobility and gentry deserted Dublin when it was no longer the seat of the Irish Parliament; but this meant that they henceforth spent more time on their Irish estates. Of all those who, before the Union, had kept Dublin houses and cut a dash in Dublin society, only a few were rich and well-connected enough to live in the same way in London. The others said good-bye to town life and made do with the country; spending the money which they had hitherto spent in Dublin, on rebuilding and improving their country houses. Those of them who had owned Parliamentary boroughs in the Irish Parliament and been therefore compensated for their loss by the Government had even more money to spend on building. In many cases, country houses were built on estates where previously no country house had existed; or where the earlier house or castle had long been in ruins; or again, where there had formerly been only a "cottage" to accommodate the owner on his brief and infrequent visits. The absentee landlord, that villain of 19th century Irish agrarian history, did not, as is popularly supposed, leave his ancestral home in Ireland for the bright lights of London; for he usually had no ancestral home to leave, but just a certain number of acres from which he drew rents and which he could only visit by staying with his agent or at the hotel in the nearest town. During the course of the 19th century, many of these landlords built houses for themselves on their estates and ceased to be absentees—among them, incidentally, the great-grandfather of the present writer and his kinsman, the great-grandfather of the current Editor of *Burke's* Series.

In the years immediately after the Union, the Irish architectural scene was dominated by Francis Johnston; the first time, since the death of Pearce, that an Irishman who was a professional architect had occupied this position. Johnston soon had a formidable rival in Richard (afterwards Sir Richard) Morrison, also an Irishman and highly professional, who started his career under the influence of Gandon. Morrison's Classical houses are much less austere than those of Johnston; in fact his early designs were decidedly Palladian. He first made his name in the country house field with his villas; comfortable and compact houses like Bearforest, co Cork and Kilpeacon, co Limerick, which were intended to combine "simplicity and elegance"; some of them being on quite a large scale, such as Castlegar, co Galway. Morrison's villas are notable for what Mr Edward McParland calls "a vigorous type of modelling, both internally and externally". Outside, they have curved bows and semi-circular porches, fronted with pillars; windows and doors set in arched recesses.

Inside, there are columnar apses, vaulted ceilings, impressive central staircase halls. His interiors are richly decorated; not in the delicate Adamesque manner, but with a more robust plasterwork which, in its use of large swags, trophies, birds and other motifs, seems to hark back to the rococo, though the general effect is neo-Classical. This is particularly true of some of Morrison's later Classical interiors, such as those at Fota Island, co Cork; and in the Classical interiors designed by his son, William Vitruvius, who joined him in his practice about 1810.

As a designer of villas, Richard Morrison was concerned with simplicity and making the most of a restricted space, yet when the opportunity arose, he could, so to speak, pull out the stops and design a neo-Classical house in the grand manner; like Ballyfin, co Leix; which, with its giant portico and its magnificent interior, is as palatial as any house of its time. William Vitruvius could also produce this large-scale Classical splendour; as he did at Oak Park, co Carlow and in his remodelling of Barons Court, co Tyrone.

Though the Morrisons were essentially Classical architects, they could, when required, turn their hand to the Gothic; as indeed could Johnston. The Gothic taste, which was the architectural expression of the Romantic Movement, first made its appearance in Irish domestic architecture in the 1760s, with Moore Abbey, co Kildare and the Gothic front of Castleward, co Down; but it was not really fashionable until immediately after the Union, when Gothic castles suddenly became all the rage. Their popularity with the Irish nobility and gentry can be ascribed to various reasons. They were thought to be more in keeping with the rugged and dramatic Irish scenery—which the Romantic Movement had taught people to appreciate—than Classical houses. Then there was the fact that so many Irish houses—particularly those of the more ancient families—incorporated an old tower-house, or had the ruin of one in their grounds, and consequently bore the designation of "castle". The owners of these houses imagined that by decking them out with battlements and turrets they were restoring them to their medieval splendour; while those who built castles from scratch, or turned houses of more recent origin into castles, felt that by so doing they were giving an air of antiquity to their homes—and also to their pedigrees. They would doubtless be gratified to know that their castles—or the ruins of them—are now often believed by the local people to be genuinely medieval; even though the architectural experts of a generation or two ago dismissed them as "shams". Present-day architectural historians no longer make the mistake of comparing them disparagingly with real medieval castles, but regard them as architecture in their own right. Many see them as having an affinity with the rococo; Mr Desmond Guinness considers that, like the rococo, they were a truer expression of the "native exuberance" of the Irish than the restraint and uniformity of neo-Classicism.

There is certainly something rococo about the sugary plaster fan vaulted ceilings in some of the best-appointed of the castles, such as Charleville Forest, Offaly. Charleville, by Johnston, is perhaps the most successful early 19th century Irish castle. It was built from scratch, whereas another of Johnston's castles, Markree, in co Sligo, was a conversion of a Georgian house; while at Killeen, co Meath, Johnston built a romantic castle round the medieval stronghold of the Plunketts, Earls of Fingall. The Morrison's castles are nearly all of them "conversion jobs"—like Castle Freke, co Cork and Ballyheigue Castle, co Kerry, where Gothic cloaks were thrown over plain Georgian houses—and perhaps for this reason they tend to be rather thin. The gentlemen of more moderate means, who could not afford a cloak tailored by the Morrisons or by one of the other fashionable architects, had one run up by a local builder; the somewhat amateurish array of turrets and battlements which transformed a square Georgian house into a castle at Drishane, co Cork, is clearly of this sort. Many were content with just a few battlements: like Daniel O'Connell, "The Liberator", whose additions to his ancestral home, Derrynane in co Kerry, included a very simple castellated block; probably to please his romantically-minded wife.

As a sign of the boom in country house building in the half-century between the Union and the Great Famine, there is the multiplicity of architects who enjoyed a country house practice in Ireland during this period. In addition to the Morrisons and Johnston, whose practice was inherited by his nephew, William Murray, there was the Darley dynasty, John B. Keane and William Farrell. There were the Hargrave and Deane dynasties in Cork; there were the Pain brothers in Cork and Limerick; there were the Robertsons in Kilkenny; there was Thomas A. Cobden in Carlow; there was William Tinsley in Clonmel. Most of these architects, if not all of them, were equally competent in Classical and Gothic, as well as in the other styles which became popular during the period: Tudor-Revival, Elizabethan-Revival, Tudor-Gothic, Cottage-Gothic, Italianate. Thus the Morrisons, in addition to their Classical houses and castles, produced houses in Tudor-Revival and also the most successful Elizabethan-Revival mansion in Ireland, Killruddery, co Wicklow. Keane designed the Italianate Edermine, co Wexford, as well as the Tudor-Gothic Camlin, co Donegal. Cobden was the architect of the restrained Grecian Clobemon Hall, co Wexford as well of that Gothic extravaganza, Duckett's Grove, co Carlow. On the other hand, it was natural that some of these architects should have had their preferences and specialities. Murray followed Johnston's Classical austerity, as did Farrell, whose practice, like Murray's, was largely in Ulster, which was also Johnston's home province; so that very many early 19th century Ulster houses are in a restrained Classical style; ranging from The Argory, co Armagh, by architects named Williamson who had worked under Johnston, to Farrell's Colebrooke, co Fermanagh and Rathkenny, co Cavan; from Cornacassa, co Monaghan to Seaforde, co Down, which is thought to be by an English architect, Peter Frederick Robinson. One would be tempted to assume that this style appealed to the temperament of Ulstermen of Lowland-Scots blood, whose Scottish kinsmen were at the same time making Edinburgh into a "modern Athens"; though, as it happens, most of the houses just mentioned were built for families of English descent. The Pain Brothers are particularly remembered for their castles, which included the enormous Mitchelstown, co Cork, built for that larger-than-life character, "Big George", Earl of Kingston; and Dromoland, co Clare, seat of the Royal House of O'Brien. The Pains, who were English, settled in Ireland after being sent over by John Nash to supervise the building of Lough Cutra Castle, co Galway, one of the four Irish castles which he designed. Nash was also the architect of a large Irish Classical house, Rockingham, co Roscommon; and he produced a design for a notable villa in the Cottage Gothic style, Gracefield Lodge, co Leix; which, however, was modified and cut down by William Robertson, of Kilkenny, who carried out the building. As well as Nash, there were several prominent British architects of the first half of the 19th century with one or more Irish country houses to their credit; including C. R. Cockerell, Thomas Rickman, George Papworth, Francis Goodwin, Edward Blore, William Burn and William Playfair.

The output of all these architects, however, is greatly surpassed by the number of houses of unknown authorship that date from the first half of the 19th century; most of them in a style closer to that of the simpler houses of the late 18th century than to any of the fashionable styles enumerated above. Such houses can only be described as "late-Georgian", though many of them were built in the reign of William IV or the first years of Victoria; indeed, much of what is now regarded as "Georgian Ireland" dates from the 1830s and 1840s. To mention a few random examples, there is Ampertain, co Derry, Ballinafad, co Mayo, Donard, co Wicklow, Graiguenoe Park, co Tipperary, and Woodlands, co Waterford. Of the five houses just mentioned, no two are the same; yet they have features in common. They are all two-storeyed; the three-storey block having gone almost completely out of fashion by the end of the first decade of the century. Three out of the five have roofs with overhanging eaves. Three out out of the five have porches or single-storey porticos—another, Ballinafad, also has a porch, but this is clearly a later addition. In the first half of the 19th century, porches and porticos were as ubiquitous as they were rare in the 18th century; probably on account of the improvement in the roads, which enabled people to come visiting in their carriages, wearing their best clothes. Numerous 18th century houses were given porches or single-storey porticos during this period. As well as being practical, a portico —or a porch fronted with columns—gave a stylish neo-Classical air to an old-fashioned house. At Benekerry, co Carlow, a porch prolonged on either side by a Grecian colonnade was added to a house dating from about 1700. The Classically-minded owner of a plain 18th century house with more money to spend could have a Classical cloak—or perhaps it would be more correct to say toga— thrown over it, like that which Murray threw over Roxborough, the Earl of Charlemont's house in co Tyrone. Other 18th century houses were given neo-Classical wings, such as those added to Kilmurry, co Kilkenny, by Charles Kendal Bushe, "the Incorruptible". Towards the end of the period, houses which were enlarged and revamped in this way tended to be given an Italianate rather than a neo-Classical character.

That terrible calamity, the Great Famine of 1847, was a disaster for the landlords as well as for the tenantry. Many country houses and estates were sold up during the years that followed; some of them compulsorily, by order of the Encumbered Estates Court. A certain number of houses, including Ballynahinch Castle, co Galway, ancestral home of the unfortunate Mary Laetitia Martin, "Princess of Connemara", found new well-to-do owners who maintained them as well as they had been maintained before; but others passed into the possession of farmers, who neglected them. Others again, like the beautiful early 18th century Palace Anne, co Cork, were abandoned altogether and fell into ruin. Those of the nobility and gentry who managed to keep their estates had little money to spare for building; so that the number of Irish country houses built or rebuilt in the second half of the 19th century is very low by comparison with the first half of the century. It would have been lower still but for certain new factors which encouraged the building of country houses. The Famine itself caused some of the richer and more philanthropic landlords to build or rebuild country houses in order to give employment; like the two young Oliver-Gascoigne sisters, who though comfortably established at their country house in Yorkshire, rebuilt Castle Oliver, the family seat in co Limerick, as a vast baronial mansion. Then there was the advent of railways, which opened up the remoter parts of the country; encouraging absentee landlords who owned estates in these parts to build houses on them. And while Ireland as a whole was not much affected by the Industrial Revolution, there were, nevertheless, a certain number of Irish country houses built as a result of Victorian industrial prosperity. Most of these, of course, are near Belfast, the only Irish city to compare with the great industrial centres of Victorian Britain; one of the finest of them being Ballywalter Park, co Down, a splendid Italianate palazzo built for the linen magnate Andrew Mulholland, father of the 1st Lord Dunleath. Elsewhere in Ireland, there were the mansions built for various members of the even richer brewing family of Guinness: St Anne's and Farmleigh near Dublin, Ashford Castle, co Galway. And there were a few houses built by wealthy British businessmen who fell in love with Ireland and bought Irish estates: like Mitchell Henry, builder of that much-photographed Victorian castle in Connemara, Kylemore.

The Famine is of significance in the history of Irish domestic architecture not only because it put an end to the boom in country house building of the first half of the 19th century; but also because it made the change from Georgian to Victorian more abrupt than would otherwise have been the case. Had it not occured, there is no reason why the more conservative Irish gentry should not have gone on building pleasant late-Georgian houses well into the middle of Victoria's reign. But the Famine hit the smaller gentry even worse than it hit the richer families; so that the sort of people who would have built late-Georgian houses virtually ceased to build altogether. Henceforth, country house building was largely confined to the richer and more sophisticated families, who naturally wished to be fashionable and therefore built houses that were definitely Victorian.

The building slump following the Famine, which put many Irish architects out of business—including William Tinsley, who emigrated to the United States—happened just about the time when many of the architectural luminaries of the previous half-century were disappearing from the scene through death or retirement; notably the veteran Sir Richard Morrison, who died in 1849, his son, William Vitruvius, having predeceased him in 1838. So there was something of a clean sweep of Irish architects round about 1850, leaving the field open to a new generation of architects who were definitely Victorian. Chief among them was Charles (afterwards Sir Charles) Lanyon, who, significantly, was based not in Dublin but in Belfast; though his practice was by no means confined to Ulster. One can observe the transition from Georgian to Victorian in Lanyon's early career. His first major country house, Drenagh, co Derry, built in 1837, is late-Georgian; but Dunderave, co Antrim, which he designed ten years later, is Victorian; the first and one of the finest of the Italianate *palazzi*

which were to be his speciality and of which Ballywalter is the other outstanding example. A few years later again, in 1854, Lanyon took as his partner a younger man, William Henry Lynn, who was not just a Victorian but a High Victorian; specializing in a somewhat dour and angular Gothic and Baronial. Lynn's High Victorian country houses, such as Benburb Manor, co Tyrone, with its polychrome elevations of brick and stone, are among the few examples of this *genre* in Ireland; others being the Ruskinian-Gothic houses of a later member of the Deane dynasty, Sir Thomas Newenham Deane, such as the second Portumna Castle in co Galway. On the whole, High Victorianism—which is not so much a style as a mood, in which the earnestness is paradoxically mixed with a roguish frivolity in the handling of elements taken from the styles of earlier periods—did not seem to catch on in Ireland, not, at any rate, in country house architecture. It doubtless did not suit the native temperament; while the fact that the two brilliant young men of High Victorianism, Deane's partner, Benjamin Woodward and the Northerner, William J. Barre—whose Clanwilliam House, in the suburbs of Belfast, is such a classic of its kind that it has been included in this book, though it is not, strictly speaking, a country house—both died young, may also have had something to do with it. With the exception of Lynn and of Sir Thomas Newenham Deane, none of the other architects who designed Irish country houses in the second half of the 19th century was a High Victorian of the stamp of Woodward and Barre; they were more in the manner of Lanyon, carrying on the easy-going eclectic tradition of the Morrisons in a Victorian rather than a Georgian manner. Thus John McCurdy, almost at the same time he designed the High Victorian Gothic Knocktopher Abbey, in co Kilkenny, produced the comfortable Italianate Leyrath, in the same county, which has what Elizabeth Bowen calls the "sort of late-flowering Classicism" of his best-known urban building, the Shelbourne Hotel in Dublin. James Franklin Fuller, the most prolific Irish country house architect of the later decades of the century, designed the severely Baronial Ashford Castle as well as the richly Italianate St Anne's, both for the same client, Arthur Guinness, Lord Ardilaun. George Ashlin, another prolific architect of the period, also had a hand in St Anne's, though he was the son-in-law of A. W. Pugin and specialized in Gothic churches.

The Italianate style favoured by Lord Ardilaun at St Anne's—symmetrical or nearly symmetrical, little different from the Italianate of the 1840s and 1850s—was uniformly popular in Ireland throughout the second half of the 19th century; not just for large mansions like St Anne's but also for medium-sized houses such as Ballywhite, co Down and Balyna, co Kildare and for quite small houses like Belfort, co Cork. In its simpler manifestations, it was more or less indistinguishable from another popular style, which can be described as a Victorian version of late-Georgian. As an example of a large mansion in this style, there is another Guinness house, Farmleigh, co Dublin; as an example of a house of more moderate size, Sandham Symes's Glenville Park in co Cork.

It can be taken as a sign of how the 18th century Classical tradition was still alive among the Victorian Irish gentry that these styles should have remained more popular than those deriving from the Gothic like the Tudor- or Elizabethan-Revival, which, having been very much in vogue before the Famine, seemed to go out of favour later in the century, just at the time when they were at their most popular in England. Significantly, the two most notable late 19th century Tudor-Revival country houses in Ireland, the vast red-brick Killarney House and the smaller and more attractive Blessingbourne, in co Tyrone, were designed by English architects, George Devey and F. Pepys Cockerell. There are, however, a number of houses where Tudor-Revival is combined with Baronial to make a castle, as at Gurteen-le-Poer, co Waterford and Lough Eske, co Donegal. The Victorian Irish still had that penchant for castles which had produced such a flowering of turrets and battlements in the late-Georgian period. As well as Ashford, Kylemore and Lough Eske, the castles built in Ireland in the second half of the 19th century include the new Belfast Castle and Ballymena Castle, also in co Antrim, both of them Scottish-Baronial and by Lynn; the dramatic Glenveagh Castle in co Donegal; Dunboy Castle, co Cork, Humewood, co Wicklow, Dromore Castle, co Limerick and Glenbeigh Towers, co Kerry. The last four are among the most architecturally interesting of all Victorian country houses, not just in Ireland but in the British Isles as a whole. Humewood was designed by that eccentric English architect, William White; Dromore by another unusual Englishman, Edward William Godwin. Both White and Godwin became embroiled in unfortunate quarrels with their Irish clients, which may have discouraged other English architects of the time from accepting Irish country house commissions—indeed, Godwin, in an oft-quoted remark, positively exhorted English architects to refuse them. Certainly, the leading English country house architects of the later 19th century are not represented in Ireland in the way that C. R. Cockerell, Blore and other architects of the earlier period are. In particular, the school of Norman Shaw and Philip Webb, which so influenced English country house taste in the late-Victorian and Edwardian periods, is hardly represented at all. Before it was burnt, Palmerston, co Kildare, was perhaps the only full-blown example of Shaw's Queen Anne Revival style, which was

so popular in England. There are naturally more examples of the other style which Shaw made popular, the "quaint" half-timbered; such as Sion House, co Tyrone and Clonmeen, co Cork; but even these are quite rare. Hollybrook, co Cork, by a little-known Scottish architect, R. S. Balfour, is also under the influence of Shaw and Webb, though in a somewhat different style again.

Hollybrook, built in 1903–1904, is one of the few Irish country houses of the Edwardian period; others include the Romanesque Spiddal House, co Galway, the Tudor-Baronial Ardmulchan Castle, co Meath and the ornate would-be Classical Herbertstown, also in co Meath, which though built six years after King Edward's death can definitely be counted as Edwardian. Ireland possesses no Classical house by the greatest English country house architect of this period, Sir Edwin Lutyens; though Lutyens has a place in the history of Irish country house architecture with his enchanting remodelling of the old castle on Lambay Island, off the Dublin coast, his no less successful work at Howth Castle, and his garden at Heywood, co Leix.

The scarcity of Edwardian country houses was largely due to the fact that the agricultural depression of the 1880s and the consequent agrarian troubles had left the Irish nobility and gentry even worse off than they had been in the years following the Famine; though those of them who sold their tenanted land under the terms of the Wyndham Act of 1903 enjoyed a temporary affluence. Then there was the uncertain political situation which did not greatly encourage building. The controversy over Home Rule was followed by the struggle for independence which lasted from 1919 to 1921, and which was followed closely by the Civil War of 1922–23. During those troubled years, a number of Irish country houses were burnt; though not nearly as many as is popularly supposed. According to a list published at the time, which clearly exaggerates the number of burnings, the figure for the Civil War period is about 35. Even allowing for as many houses again to have been burnt during the 1919–21 period—whereas, in fact, the burnings then were fewer—the total would only be something like 70, at a time when there would have been at least 2,000 country houses in Ireland. Of the houses burnt, a surprisingly large number were subsequently rebuilt; some of them exactly as they were before, except that the interior plasterwork was seldom reinstated; others, like Castle Hacket, co Galway and Springfield Castle, co Limerick, on a reduced scale. In other cases again, new houses were built in the characteristic style of the 1920s; such as Glenmona House, co Antrim, which is by Clough (now Sir Clough) Williams-Ellis.

Encouraging the belief that almost every Irish country house was "burnt in the Troubles", the ruined country house is an all-too-frequent sight in Ireland, particularly in the western counties. In fact, the great majority of these ruined houses were not burnt but either dismantled or allowed to fall down. Most of them were sold by their original owners some time after the end of World War I; the people who bought them were usually interested only in the land which went with them, and either demolished them immediately in order to save rates, or so neglected them that they fell into ruin. The number of Irish country houses which have thus been lost greatly exceeds the number of those which still exist as ruins; for as often as not the ruin of a demolished house is cleared away so that no trace of it remains.

The disturbed state of the country at the time of the struggle for independence caused some people to sell their ancestral homes; while others sold up because they did not wish to live in an Ireland that was not part of the United Kingdom. On the whole, however, people sold their houses for the obvious reason that they could no longer afford to live in them. The Irish landowning class, which had suffered a steady decline in prosperity since the Famine, was finally ruined by the Wyndham Act and the subsequent Land Acts; though at the time they were regarded as advantageous to landlords as well as to tenants. As a result of these Acts, all land let to tenants was acquired by the Government, and then sold to the tenants who paid for it by easy instalments. The landlord, who had formerly owned several thousand acres, was left with his house and the "demesne" surrounding it and little else; on an average about 200 or 300 acres, including unproductive woodland and waste; often much less. Even today, when, thanks to the Common Market, Irish farming is better than it has been at any other time in the present century, this is not really enough land to support a country house. As for the money which the Government paid the landlords for their tenanted land, this, though regarded as quite generous at the time, when Irish landed estates brought poor returns, was nothing like what the land became subsequently worth, or what it had been worth before the Famine. And while land, whatever its present value may be, is always there, money has a habit of running away. This, alas, was particularly true of the money paid to the landlords under the Land Acts; it tended to be badly invested, or spent as income when it should have been treated as capital. So whereas the average English country house may still be supported by at least a thousand acres—worth at the present time over a million sterling—the average Irish country house is endowed with only a fraction of this amount.

So from the early 1920s onwards, the history of the Irish country house was one of continual sellings-up and pullings down. Then, during the 1960s and early '70s,

the situation began to look much brighter. With the improvement in farming and land values, those of the original families who still kept their houses found themselves in a better position to maintain them.

With the increase in tourism there was the hope that costs might be offset by opening houses to the public; though this is still a very doubtful financial proposition and in the Irish Republic the Government as yet allows no tax concessions for the opening of houses such as are allowed in Britain and elsewhere.

Thanks largely to the work of the Irish Georgian Society and the Ulster Architectural Heritage Society, as well as of such organizations as the Northern Ireland National Trust and An Taisce, there was a growing interest in Irish country house architecture, abroad as well as in Ireland itself; so that it became easier to find sympathetic buyers for houses which needed saving. Houses which previously had been considered beyond repair were restored; including Kilbrittain Castle, co Cork, which had long been a burnt-out ruin. Several houses which had been used as institutions reverted to private occupation; notably Emo Court, which has come into its own in a way that it never did in the past. The interest in architecture also led to the building of new country houses—something which had been almost unknown in Ireland since the 1920s. Among the more distinguished houses built in recent years are Martinstown, co Limerick, by the English architect, Mrs Baker-Baker, Garretstown, co Meath, by Mr Austin Dunphy, and the new Mount Coote, co Limerick, by Mr Donal O'Neill-Flanagan, all of them in the Classical style; and Greenmount, co Limerick, also by Mr O'Neill-Flanagan, which is externally plain, with modern steel-framed windows, but has an interior of the grandest Classical proportions.

The somewhat hopeful climate of the 1960s and early 1970s has given way to a mood of unrelieved pessimism owing to the introduction of capital taxes in the Irish Republic; which came just at a time when maintenance costs were rocketing owing to the inflation following the fuel crisis of 1973. Most country house owners are obliged to spend capital in order to maintain their houses; so for many of them it is the last straw to have inroads made into their capital by the tax collector. Since 1975, an alarming number of houses have been sold, including some of the first importance; such as Fota Island, co Cork, Malahide Castle, co Dublin, Castletown, co Kilkenny and Carton, co Kildare—the latter being one of the houses which in recent years had been open to the public. Unless the situation changes yet again, it seems all too likely that in a very few years time there will be no major Irish country houses left in private occupation.

In the past, there were people in Ireland who positively disliked country houses, regarding them as "monuments of landlordism and oppression"; though, as has already been pointed out, the presence of a country house generally meant that the landlord was at least not an absentee. There was the belief that landlords raised their tenants' rents in order to pay for larger and grander houses than they could afford. In fact, the expenditure of the Irish nobility and gentry on building was surprisingly moderate in relation to the income which they enjoyed; houses seldom cost more than two years' income, often a good deal less. There is a myth that Irish country houses are on the whole bigger than those in England, whereas the truth is the very opposite. Starting with Carton and Barons Court, the seats of the two Irish Dukes of Leinster and Abercorn, which are small by English ducal standards, one finds that the Irish nobleman or gentleman almost invariably had a smaller house than his English counterpart.

Active dislike of country houses gave way to apathy regarding their fate. Now, the public is on the whole anxious that they should be preserved; but public opinion is usually satisfied by the preservation of the fabric of the house alone; there is all too little concern about the dispersal of the contents and the spoiling of the surroundings and the fact that a house invariably loses its character if it is used for any purpose other than that for which it was built. A country house is not just a building, but a work of art in which the house itself, its contents and its setting each forms an essential part. For conservation to be really satisfactory, all three must be preserved together in their original form; and if possible, the house must continue to be lived in; for it loses much if it ceases to be a family home, even if it is carefully and lovingly preserved with its contents intact and its surroundings unspoiled. The owners of country houses should thus be given every help and encouragement by the State; for in their hands the nation's heritage of houses will be maintained not only in the best possible way, but also in the cheapest. Cheapest in that it is obviously preferable for the cost of maintaining them to be met by private individuals than by the taxpayer; and cheapest also in that it is a fact that a private individual can maintain a country house for less money than an organization like the British or Northern Ireland National Trust; just as a body such as the National Trust can do for so less money than the State. In the Irish Republic, where there is still no organization comparable to the National Trust—An Taisce as yet lacks the resources and tax concessions to enable it to maintain country houses as its British counterpart does—almost all the conservation and preservation of country houses has been carried out by private individuals. The fact that Castletown, co Kildare, the largest and most important of the great 18th century houses, has been saved from possible destruction and is now well maintained, suitably furnished and open to the public, is largely thanks to the courage and hard work of a private individual, Mr Desmond Guinness, who bought it and made it the headquarters of the Irish Georgian Society, of which he is the founder.

The owners of country houses therefore deserve the gratitude of the public, for they are maintaining, at their own expense, a national heritage and a tourist attraction. Though only a small number of Irish houses are open to the public in the way that country houses are in England—and for most country house owners in Ireland, opening to the public is not only totally uneconomic but just not feasible—houses of architectural interest are often shown to the members of societies such as the Irish Georgian Society, the Ulster Architectural Heritage Society, An Taisce and the Cork Preservation Society. There are also tours of Irish country houses and gardens organized by foreign conservation and architectural enthusiasts. Like the many foreign members of the Irish Georgian Society; these groups provide good custom for hotels, restaurants and shops; whereas the owners of the houses which they come to see usually expect no financial reward for admitting them. Country houses—and this applies to all of them, not just to those of architectural interest—also have a tourist potential in that their owners usually have friends from abroad to stay, who combine a visit to them with a tour of another part of the country, staying in hotels. If these people had no country houses to attract their friends to Ireland, they would not come at all.

The country houses of no particular architectural merit are thus also worthy of preservation. They have their own charm and character and the patina of age; while their contents, even if not of much interest to the connoisseur of art, is almost always fascinating to the social historian. One can also truthfully say that they have no counterpart anywhere else in Europe. It would be a mistake, however, to suppose that only these humbler houses, with their lack of architectural pretensions and their homely clutter of photographs and assorted objects, are truly Irish. The grander mansions which survive with their splendid contents intact are just as much a true part of Ireland; while at the same time comparing favourably with the great architecture of other European nations.

Visiting Irish Houses

OF THE Irish country houses still in private occupation, the great majority are *not* open to the public; for reasons that have been discussed in the INTRODUCTION.

HISTORIC IRISH TOURIST HOUSES & GARDENS ASSOCIATION LIST OF HOUSES

There are, however, a few that are open regularly to visitors during the summer months, in the way that houses are open in Britain and on the Continent. Most of these are listed—together with details of opening times, admission charges and catering arrangements where available—in a leaflet issued by HITHA (HISTORIC IRISH TOURIST HOUSES & GARDENS ASSOCIATION, *3A Castle Street, Dalkey, co Dublin*). The 1977 list includes ADARE MANOR, *co Limerick*; ARDRESS, *co Armagh*; BANTRY HOUSE, *co Cork*; BULLOCK CASTLE, *co Dublin*; BUN-RATTY CASTLE, *co Clare*; CASTLECOOLE, *co Fermanagh*; CASTLE MATRIX, *co Limerick*; CASTLETOWN, *co Kildare*; CASTLEWARD, *co Down*; CLOGHAN CASTLE, *Offaly*; CLONALIS, *co Roscommon*; DUNGUAIRE CASTLE, *co Galway*; FLORENCE COURT, *co Fermanagh*; KNOPPOGUE CASTLE, *co Clare*; LISSADELL, *co Sligo*; MALAHIDE CASTLE, *co Dublin*; MOUNT STEWART, *co Down*; MUCKRUSS, *co Kerry*; RIVERSTOWN HOUSE, *co Cork*; SPRING-HILL, *co Derry*; TULLYNALLY CASTLE, *co Westmeath* and WESTPORT HOUSE, *co Mayo*. Of these houses, Adare, Bantry, Clonalis, Lissadell, Tullynally and Westport are still owned by the families to whom they have always belonged. The houses in Northern Ireland—Ardress, Castlecoole, Castle-ward, Florence Court, Mount Stewart and Springhill—are all in the care of the National Trust; though some of them, such as Florence Court, are still occupied by their original families. Full information on them can be obtained from THE NATIONAL TRUST (*Rowallane House, Saintfield, Bally-nahinch, co Down*). If one becomes a member of the Trust, one has the privilege of free admission to all these houses.

Of the remaining houses in the HITHA list, some are owned by private individuals, such as Cloghan Castle—an old tower-house with a later wing, not included in this book—which has been restored and furnished by its present owner, Mr Brian Donovan Thompson. Others belong to organizations, private or public. Castletown is the head-quarters of the Irish Georgian Society; Malahide, which was sold a couple of years ago by its original owners, the Talbot family, to Dublin County Council, has recently been opened to the public by Dublin Tourism. It contains some fine furniture and a splendid collection of historical portraits, lent by the National Gallery. Some of the portraits have always been in the Castle, as well as much of the furniture; having been bought by the Gallery and Dublin Tourism at the auction.

GARDENS

HITHA also lists a number of notable gardens open to the public, where the houses, though not themselves open, can be seen from the outside. These include the gardens of ABBEY LEIX, *co Leix*; BIRR CASTLE, *Offaly*; DERREEN, *co Kerry*; HOWTH CASTLE, *co Dublin*; LISMORE CASTLE, *co Waterford*; MOUNT USHER, *co Wicklow* and ROWALLANE, *co Down*; as well as the famous garden of POWERSCOURT, *co Wicklow*, where the house was most tragically gutted by fire in 1974. Then there is the Mussenden Temple, DOWNHILL, *co Derry*, which is in the care of the National Trust; and where the great house is, like Powerscourt, a shell. Another National Trust property listed is DERRYMORE HOUSE, *co Armagh*, which is open by arrangement. At the opposite corner of Ireland, GLIN CASTLE, *co Limerick*, is also open by appointment, to groups. The casual visitor can see the delightful Georgian Gothic gate lodges, one of which now serves as an eating house and a craft shop; and a good view of the castle itself may be had from the main road.

OTHER CASTLES, HOUSES AND DEMESNES OPEN

There are a few houses and gardens open to the public which are not listed by HITHA. Most of these are owned by the Commissioners for Public Works; there is KILKENNY CASTLE, which is still only partly restored, but where a few rooms have been completed and furnished; DERRYNANE, *co Kerry*, which also contains furniture and family portraits; the ex-quisite Casino at MARINO, *co Dublin*; and THE CASTLE, CARRICK-ON-SUIR, *co Tipperary*, which is unfurnished and still in the process of restoration. To these one could add CAHIR CASTLE, *co Tipperary*, which comes on the borderline between country house and ancient monument, like the world-famous BLARNEY CASTLE, *co Cork*, which is privately owned and included in the HITHA list. There are numer-ous other old castles owned by the Commissioners for Pub-lic Works in the Irish Republic and the Historic Buildings Branch in Northern Ireland, which can be visited by the public. Some of them are described in this book, though the majority are outside its scope. They are mostly well sign-posted, though some of them are approached along very rough lanes, so that the visitor would be well advised to leave his or her car on the main road and proceed on foot.

Very different from these old castles is JOHNSTOWN CASTLE, *co Wexford*, an impressive 19th century castellated mansion, which now belongs to the nation and is used as an agricul-tural research centre. The exterior of the castle can be seen by the public who are admitted to the splendid gardens and grounds. In Northern Ireland, there are several country houses owned by the State or the local authorities where the grounds are regularly open to the public. These include

BELFAST CASTLE, where the house itself is open though no no longer furnished as a country house; BROWNLOW HOUSE, *Lurgan, co Armagh* and CASTLEWELLAN, *co Down*, where the demesne is a forest park. A few miles from Castlewellan is TOLLYMORE, also now a forest park and open to the public; the house here has gone, but the demesne still boasts of a remarkable series of follies. Two great demesnes in the Irish Republic have become forest parks: CURRAGH CHASE, *co Limerick*, where the ruined house is well maintained as a show place; and DONERAILE COURT, *co Cork*, where the house is being restored by the Irish Georgian Society and will, it is hoped, be open to the public some time in the future. The Georgian Society is also restoring DAMER HOUSE, *Roscrea, co Tipperary*, the outside of which can be seen by visitors to the castle at Roscrea. With its very limited funds, and many other commitments, the Georgian Society has shown great courage in undertaking the restoration of these two large houses, both of which had fallen into disrepair when the Society took them over; the work on them is of necessity slow. A house which is likely to be open to the public at an earlier date than either Doneraile Court or Damer House is FOTA, *co Cork*, where repairs are at present being carried out by its new owners, University College, Cork. Conservation work is also in progress in the famous gardens and arboretum, which will likewise be open to the public.

SOCIETY TOURS

Tours of country houses and gardens not normally open to the public are arranged during the summer months by the IRISH GEORGIAN SOCIETY (*Castletown, Celbridge, co Kildare*), the ULSTER ARCHITECTURAL HERITAGE SOCIETY (*181a Stranmillis Road, Belfast 9*), AN TAISCE, the National Trust for Ireland (*41 Percy Place, Dublin 4*), the NORTHERN IRELAND NATIONAL TRUST (address as above) and the CORK PRESERVATION SOCIETY (*Trafalgar House, Montenotte, Cork*). Country house enthusiasts are strongly recommended to join one or more of these organizations, all of which welcome foreign members; the subscription rates are extremely modest, and the charges for going on their outings are generally less than what it would cost to visit an equivalent number of houses open to the public in the ordinary way. It should be added that these charges are to cover the cost of organizing the outings and to benefit the society which organizes them; no money goes to the owners of the houses visited, who receive the visiting groups as their guests, usually showing them round themselves and sometimes even entertaining them to tea or drinks. Since many of the houses visited are of only moderate size, the numbers of those taking part in these outings have to be strictly limited. Prospective visitors to Ireland should therefore join whichever society or societies they choose several months before setting out on their trip; so as to receive information on forthcoming outings in time to book places in them.

HOTELS AND GUEST HOUSES

The tourist in Ireland, if he chooses his sleeping, eating and drinking places with care, can see a wide variety of country house architecture; for many country houses are now hotels, guest houses and restaurants. Some houses which are still owned and occupied by the families who have always lived in them are open to guests; these include MOUNT IEVERS, *co Clare*; MOUNT LOFTUS, *co Kilkenny* and TURLOUGH PARK, *co Mayo*. Houses such as these naturally contain their original furnishings and pictures and have the authentic country house atmosphere; though there are other country houses now run as hotels and guest houses which are also furnished in keeping with their architecture and have much of the atmosphere of a country house in private occupation. These include LONGFIELD, *co Tipperary* and ROUNDWOOD, *co Leix*, both owned by the Irish Georgian Society and restored under the Society's auspices; BARGY CASTLE, *co Wexford*; BALLYMACMOY and BALLYMALOE, both in *co Cork*, and CASHEL PALACE, *co Tipperary*. It would be outside the scope of this book to give a full list of country houses run as hotels, guest houses and restaurants, but to mention a few more, there is ACLARE HOUSE, *co Meath*; ASHFORD CASTLE, *co Galway*; BALLYGALLY CASTLE, *co Antrim*; BALLYNAHINCH CASTLE, *co Galway*; BALLYSEEDY, *co Kerry*; BREAGHWY, *co Mayo*; CABRA CASTLE, *co Cavan*; THE CASTLE, CASTLEBELLINGHAM, *co Louth*; CURRAREVAGH, *co Galway*; DROMOLAND CASTLE, *co Clare*; GLENGARRIFF CASTLE, *co Cork*; KILKEA CASTLE, *co Kildare*; KILLINEY CASTLE, *co Dublin*; and LONGUEVILLE, *co Cork*. Visitors to Ireland are advised to obtain lists from the IRISH TOURIST BOARD (*Baggot Street Bridge, Dublin 2*) and the NORTHERN IRELAND TOURIST BOARD (*River House, High Street, Belfast 1*).

INSTITUTIONS

In addition to the Irish country houses which are hotels and guest houses, there are those which are now institutions, mostly run by religious orders. Generally there is no objection to visitors driving up to these houses to view them from the outside; often the people in charge of them will show visitors the principal rooms. Knowing, however, how hard-pressed the staff of institutions are these days, one would urge country house enthusiasts not to ask to see the inside of a house in institutional use unless it contains rooms of outstanding architectural importance; while a telephone call beforehand to the Superior or Bursar is not only courteous but will ensure that the visitor will not arrive at a time when all the staff are busy.

RUINS

Finally, the country house enthusiast in Ireland can see a great deal of country house architecture by seeking out houses which are now ruins. This is an occupation which has an element of adventure, expectation and surprise. One comes to a broken-down demesne wall, looks for an entrance or a gap (a "vacancy", to use the Irish expression), follows a rutted and grass-grown avenue (if one is wise, one will leave one's car outside and walk). One may be obliged to negotiate fences and ditches and to cross a couple of fields. And then the ruined house looms up; perhaps so shrouded in ivy that none of its features is recognizable; perhaps with details showing: a crumbling portico which could be part of a picture by Pannini or Piranesi, towers and battlements that might have inspired a poem by John Betjeman.

Having found one's ruin, one would be well advised to contemplate it from a respectful distance, while indulging in thoughts of nostalgia and pleasant melancholy (or partaking of a picnic of Limerick ham, soda bread, Irish cheese and Guinness such as Mr Henry McDowell thoughtfully suggests in his essay in *Burke's Introduction to Irish Ancestry*). To go too close to a ruin with which one is unfamiliar, or to venture within its walls, is to court falling plaster on one's head and unexpected cellars opening up beneath one's feet. To those who do not set much store by their own safety, it should be pointed out that if an accident were to occur, the ruin in question would almost certainly be bulldozed as being "dangerous"; so that in the interests of preservation, as well as in their own interests, country house enthusiasts should treat ruins with respect. So great is the popular belief in the danger of ruins that almost all ruined country houses are constantly at risk; their owners—whether private individuals or public bodies—are apt to bulldoze them at short notice, without anybody knowing that they have gone. For this reason, it has seldom been possible in this book to state with any certainty whether a house which has been dismantled, demolished or burnt still stands as a ruin or has vanished altogether. The preservation of country house ruins is a problem which should be considered along with that of the preservation of houses still intact; many of them are just as worthy of preservation as the ruined abbeys, castles and churches of an earlier period.

A

Abbeville, Malahide, co Dublin (BERES-FORD, *sub* WATERFORD, M/PB; COOPER/IFR; CUSACK/IFR). A house built for Rt Hon John Beresford, Taster of the Wines in the Port of Dublin, brother of the 1st Marquess of Waterford and one of the most powerful men in Ireland at the end of C18; its name commemorating the fact that Beresford's 1st wife came from Abbeville in Northern France. Of 2 storeys over a basement; front of 7 bays between 2 wide curved bows prolonged by single-storey 1 bay wings, each with a fanlighted triple window and an urn on a die. Pilastered entrance doorway. Good drawing room with alcove, ceiling of Adamesque plasterwork and husk decoration on walls, incorporating circular painted medallions. Sold 1815 to the antiquarian, Austin Cooper, FSA; re-sold after his death 1830. Bought by Prof James William Cusack, Surgeon-in-Ordinary to Queen Victoria in Ireland; remained in the Cusack family until sold by Major R. S. O. Cusack in the present century. Subsequently owned by Mr A. P. Reynolds; now the home of Mr Charles Haughey, TD.

Abbeylands, Whiteabbey, co Antrim (MCCALMONT/IFR). A 2 storey Victorian house, vaguely Italianate, but with mullioned windows in the centre of its symmetrical front. Shallow curved bows on either side of front; single storey Ionic porch; narrow pedimented attic storey, with 3 narrow windows, in centre. Balustraded roof parapet.

Abbey Leix, co Leix (VESEY, DE VESCI, V/PB). A 3 storey late C18 block, built from 1773 onwards by Thomas Vesey, 2nd Lord Knapton and afterwards 1st Viscount de Vesci, with some interiors designed by James Wyatt. 7 bay entrance front, with 3 bay pedimented breakfront; frontispiece of coupled Doric columns and entablature around entrance door. 5 bay garden front with 3 bay breakfront. In C19 the elevations were made more ornate with a balustraded roof parapet, entablatures over the windows, balconies and other features. A large conservatory was also added at one side of the house, which was blown away by the "Great Wind" of 1902 and replaced by a wing containing a new dining room. The principal rooms in the main block have ceilings and, in the old dining room, walls decorated with Wyatt plasterwork. The hall has a screen of fluted Ionic columns; the drawing room is hung with a C19 blue wallpaper. The demesne contains some magnificent trees, including oaks which are part of a primeval forest. A formal garden with terraces and ironwork balustrades was laid out by Lady Emma Herbert, who married 3rd Viscount 1839; inspired by the garden of her Russian grandfather, Count Simon Woronzow, at Alupka, near Yalta, in the Crimea. Towards the end of C19, in the time of 4th Viscount, whose wife was Lady Evelyn Charteris, daughter of 10th Earl of Wemyss, Abbey Leix was the Irish outpost of the "Souls". The garden is now open to the public.

Abbeyville, Ballymote, co Sligo (PHIBBS/LGI1912). A 2 storey house built between 2 fortified towers 1716 by William Phibbs. Sold 1810 to Richard Fleming, who modernized and altered the house 1816. Sold by the Flemings *ca* 1880; eventually fell into ruins.

Abbotstown (also known as **Sheephill**), **Castleknock, co Dublin** (HAMILTON, HOLM PATRICK, B/PB). A 2 storey house, added to at various times, but of predominantly early to mid-C19 aspect. 5 bay entrance front, the centre bay breaking forward with a triple window above a projecting pilastered porch. Similar side elevation, with single-storey pillared bow instead of porch; prolonged by curved bow of full height. Parapeted roof; entablatures on console brackets over triple windows and other embellishments.

Aberdelghy, Lambeg, co Antrim (RICHARDSON/LGI1912). An irregular 2 storey house of mid-C19 aspect; shallow gables with bargeboards; hood mouldings over windows. A seat of Alexander Airth Richardson, son of Jonathan Richardson, MP, of Lambeg, and his wife, Margaret Airth.

Aclare House, Drumconrath, co Meath (SINGLETON/LGI1912; LINDSAY, *sub* CRAWFORD, E/PB). An almost Italianate house built 1840 for H. C. Singleton; 2 storey and faced with ashlar. 3 bay entrance front, projecting central bay with pediment and Wyatt window above Grecian Doric portico; 3 bay side with slightly projecting end bay. Office wing set back, fronted by graceful conservatory with curving ends and roof. Inner hall ceiling supported on carved wood brackets; upstairs landing screened from central top-lit space by arcade supported on Tuscan columns. Opened as an hotel *ca* 1950 by its then owner, Mr D. E. T. Lindsay; it has since been sold, but is still run as an hotel.

Abbey Leix

Adare Manor

Adare Manor, Adare, co Limerick (WYNDHAM-QUIN, DUNRAVEN, E/PB). Originally a 2 storey 7 bay early C18 house with a 3 bay pedimented breakfront and a high-pitched roof on a bracket cornice; probably built *ca* 1720–30 by Valentine Quin, grandfather of 1st Earl of Dunraven. From 1832

Adare Manor: Hall

Adare Manor: Gallery

onwards 2nd Earl, whose wife was the wealthy heiress of the Wyndhams of Dunraven, Glamorganshire, and who was prevented by gout from shooting and fishing, began rebuilding the house in the Tudor-Revival style as a way of occupying himself; continuing to live in the old house while the new buildings went up gradually behind it; only moving out of it about 10 years later when it was engulfed by the new work and demolished. To a certain extent Lord and Lady Dunraven acted as their own architects, helped by a master mason named James Conolly; and making as much use as they could of local craftsmen, notably a talented carver. At the same time, however, they employed a professional architect, James Pain; and in 1846, when the house was three-quarters built, they commissioned A. W. Pugin to design some of the interior features of the great hall. Finally, between 1850 and 1862, after the death of 2nd Earl, his son, the 3rd Earl, a distinguished Irish archaeologist, completed the house by building the principal garden front, to the design of P. C. Hardwick. The house, as completed, is a picturesque and impressive grey stone pile, composed of various elements that are rather loosely tied together; some of them close copies of Tudor originals in England; thus the turreted entrance tower, which stands rather incongruously at one corner of the front instead of in the middle, is a copy of the entrance to the Cloister Court at Eton. The detail, however, is of excellent quality; and the whole great building is full of interest, and abounds in those historical allusions which so appealed to early-Victorians of the stamp of the 2nd Earl, his wife and his son. As might be expected, Hardwick's front is more architecturally correct than the earlier parts of the house, but less inspired; a rather heavy 3 storey asymmetrical composition of oriels and mullioned windows, relieved by a Gothic cloister at one end and dominated by an Irish-battlemented tower with a truncated pyramidal roof, surmounted by High-Victorian decorative iron

cresting. The entrance hall has doorways of grey marble carved in the Irish-Romanesque style; the ceiling is timbered, the doors are covered in golden Spanish leather. The great hall beyond, for which Pugin provided designs, is a room of vast size and height; divided down the middle by a screen of giant Gothic arches of stone, and with similar arches in front of the staircase, so that there are Gothic vistas in all directions. A carved oak minstrels' gallery runs along one side; originally there was also an organ-loft. From the landing of the stairs, a vaulted passage constitutes the next stage in the romantic and devious approach to the grandest room in the house, the long gallery, which was built before the great hall, in 1830s; it is 132 feet long and 26 feet high with a timbered roof; along the walls are carved C17 Flemish choir stalls and there is a great deal of other woodcarving, including C15 carved panelling in the door. The other principal reception rooms are in Hardwick's garden front; they have ceilings of Tudor-Revival plasterwork and elaborately carved marble chimneypieces; that in the drawing room having been designed by Pugin. The house stands close to the River Maigue surrounded by a splendid demesne in which there is a Desmond castle, and a ruined medieval Franciscan friary; one of 3 medieval monastic buildings at Adare, the other 2 having been restored as the Catholic and Protestant churches. Adare Manor is now open to the public.

Adelphi, Corofin, co Clare (FITZGERALD/LGI1863; BLOOD/IFR). An early C19 house of 1 storey in the front and 2 storeys at the back. 5 bay front with Wyatt windows; end bow; wide-eaved roof. Behind the house is an old ruined tower.

Aggard, Craughwell, co Galway (LAMBERT/IFR). A house of mid to late C18 appearance of 2 storeys over a high basement. Front of 1 bay on either side of a central 3 sided bow incorporating a fanlighted doorcase with rustications, pylons and a keystone surmounted by a pedestal.

Aggard

Aghaboe, Ballybrophy, co Leix. A 2 storey 7 bay house with a pedimented and fanlighted doorcase, probably dating from 1st half of C18; formerly linked to 2 flanking wings, one of which has disappeared; the surviving wing being in fact a small late C17 house with plaster panelling in its interior.

Aghada House, Aghada, co Cork. A late-Georgian house by the elder Abraham Hargrave, built for John Roche between 1791 and *ca* 1808.

Aghade Lodge

Aghade Lodge, Tullow, co Carlow (ROCHE, Bt/PB; BROWNE/IFR). A 2 storey gabled Victorian house on the River Slaney, with an overhanging roof and bargeboards.

Aghadoe House

Aghadoe House, Killarney, co Kerry (WINN, HEADLEY, B/PB). A Victorian house of red sandstone ashlar with limestone facings, consisting of an irregular 2 storey main block that goes in and out a great deal, and a 3 storey office wing. Vast round-headed plate glass windows on ground floor of main block, either single or grouped in threes, separated by slender mullions. Much narrower mullioned windows with round-headed lights above, and in the wing; mostly two-light, and in one case, five-light. Limestone porch with 3 arches and balustrade. Burnt 1922 and subsequently rebuilt, when the eaves of the roof were made to overhang much more than they did previously. Now a youth hostel.

Aghamarta Castle, Carrigaline, co Cork (O'GRADY/LGI1912; CLARKE/IFR). An irregular 2 storey C19 house faced in cement, with an enclosed porch fronted by Doric columns

Aghern

and some dormer-gables. The house stands in a fine position overlooking the Owenboy estuary; there is a ruined castle in the grounds.

Aghern, Conna, co Cork (BOWLES/LGI-1912; KINAHAN/IFR; HARE, *sub* LISTOWEL, E/PB). A simple 2 storey late Georgian house built alongside an old Desmond castle on the northern bank of the River Bride. The principal front has a central semi-circular bow with a single bay on either side of it; the long adjoining front facing the river has irregular fenestration and a shallow bow window which is a later addition. The house was inherited 1923 by Grace (*née* Hudson-Kinahan), widow of Spotswood Bowles, who left it to her sister, Ellen, widow of Capt H. V. Hare; by whose son, Cmdr R. G. W. Hare, it has been sold.

Ahanesk, Midleton, co Cork (JACKSON/LGI1894; SADLEIR-JACKSON, *sub* TRENCH/IFR; LOMER, *sub* STAFFORD-KING-HARMAN, Bt/PB). A plain, rambling, predominantly C19 house, with a rectangular oriel on 1 wing; overlooking a backwater of Cork Harbour. Large, characteristically Edwardian hall, with a low, heavily-embossed ceiling and a straight enclosed staircase rising from one side of it down which, in the late-Victorian and Edwardian period, the dashing Mrs Sadleir-Jackson (the first lady in co Cork to ride astride) is said to have been in the habit of sliding on a tray, wearing pink tights, to entertain her guests. Other reception rooms with higher ceilings. For some years after World War II, Ahanesk was the home of Major & Mrs Robert Lomer.

Aherlow Castle

Aherlow Castle, Bansha, co Tipperary (MOORE/IFR). A small late C19 "pasteboard" castle in the Glen of Aherlow, built by the Moore family, of Mooresfort (*qv*). Polygonal tower, with dummy loops; square tower. Recently demolished.

Ahern, co Cork (*see* AGHERN).

Allenton, Tallaght, co Dublin. An attractive little 2 storey 5 bay early C18 house with a pedimented 3 bay breakfront and a fanlighted, pedimented and rusticated doorcase. Lunette window in pediment. Originally weather-slated. Given its present name after it was built by Sir Timothy Allen, who acquired it in *ca* mid-C18. In 1814 the residence of George F. Murphy; in 1837, of F. R. Cotton. Now threatened with demolition.

Altadore Castle, co Wicklow (*see* ALTI-DORE CASTLE).

Altamira, Liscarroll, co Cork (PURCELL/LGI1912). A plain, 3 storey Georgian block, 3 bay entrance front, 4 bay front adjoining; entrance doorway of rather urban style with a large fanlight extending over the door and 2 sidelights.

Altamont, Kilbride, co Carlow (ST GEORGE/IFR; BORRER, *sub* ORLEBAR/LGI1952; WATSON/IFR). Main block of *ca* 1760, incorporating earlier house, with 3 sided bow in centre and 2 bays on either side, high-pitched roof and odd Gothic cresting; gabled C19 Gothic wings added 1870.

Altavilla

Altavilla, Rathkeale, co Limerick (BATE-MAN/LGI1912; GREENALL, DARESBURY, B/PB). A house built *ca* 1745-46 by John Bateman, undoubtedly to the design of Francis Bindon; consisting of a centre block of 3 storeys over a basement joined by screen walls to 2 storey flanking wings enclosing courts. Centre block with 6 bay entrance front, 2 bay breakfront, tripartite pedimented and rusticated doorcase; wings with 2 modified Venetian windows, having niches in their centre section, in the upper storey; straight screen walls with rusticated doors flanked by niches. Garden front of centre block with 2 bays on either side of a niche and oculus; quadrant walls on this side joining centre block to wings, showing (as the Knight of Glin has pointed out) the influence of Vanbrugh. Its pedimented interior doors and fielded panelling were burnt. The house became a ruin but has now been restored by 2nd and present Lord Daresbury, though without the top storey.

Altidore Castle

Altidore Castle, Kilpedder, co Wicklow (DOPPING-HEPENSTAL/LGI1958; MAINWAR-ING-BURTON/IFR; EMMET/IFR). A charming late Georgian "toy fort", with 4 octagonal corner turrets; of 2 storeys on the entrance side and 3 on the other sides, where the ground falls away. Despite the battlements on the turrets, the house is more Classical than Gothic; it is symmetrical and has a

Altidore Castle: Dining Room

Altidore Castle: Medallion

central Venetian window over a pillared porch. The interior makes even fewer concessions to medievalism: there are fine C18 marble chimneypieces, medallions with Classical figures on the walls of the dining room and a staircase similar to those in numerous Irish C18 houses, of stout but elegant joinery with a scrolled end to its balusters. Altidore originally belonged to a family named Blachford. It was acquired by the Hepenstals early in C19; subsequent owners included Percy Burton, who may have been attracted to it by its superficial resemblance to the Jacobean Lulworth Castle in Dorset, where he had been land agent. Since 1945 it has been the home of the Emmet family, who are descended from Thomas Addis Emmet, a leader of the United Irishmen and brother of Robert Emmet, "The Patriot".

Ampertain House

Ampertain House, Upperlands, co Derry (CLARK/IFR). The most important of several country houses in the neighbourhood built by members of the Clark family, whose linen mills, which gave rise to the nearby "linen village" of Upperlands, are still basically situated in the yard of one of these country houses, driven by water power. A plain late-Georgian type house built *post* 1821 by Alexander Clark. 2 storeys over a high basement, 5 bay front; shallow projecting porch, with fanlighted doorway set in arched recess. Eaved roof on bracket cornice. The front prolonged by a 2 storey 3 bay wing of similar style, set back; added 1915. At the other end, a Victorian conservatory on a high plinth.

Anaverna, Dundalk, co Louth (LENOX-CONYNGHAM/IFR). A plain late-Georgian house built *ca* 1807 for Baron McClelland to the design of an architect named Gallier, who afterwards designed many buildings in New Orleans, USA. 5 bays, 3 bay breakfront centre; fanlighted doorway; windows of upper storey set under relieving arches. Owned by the Thompson family 1831–1915; bought by E. F. Lenox-Conyngham 1916.

Ancketill's Grove

Ancketill's Grove (or **Anketell Grove**), **Emyvale, co Monaghan** (ANCKETILL/IFR). Capt Oliver Ancketill built 1st Ancketill's Grove *ca* 1640, on low ground. His grandson, Oliver, rebuilt the house on higher ground at the head of the once-famous copper beech avenue. This house was demolished 1781 and a 3rd house built on another site again: a 2 storey 5 bay gable-ended main block with a small pediment, joined by curved sweeps to single-storey 2

Annaghmore, co Sligo

bay wings. Georgian Gothic windows in the wings; a door with a good keystone between 2 round-headed windows in each of the sweeps. The house was extensively remodelled *ca* 1840; its most freakish feature, an Italianate campanile sprouting from the centre of the main block, would appear to date from this time; though there may always have been a central attic-tower, following the precedent of Gola (*qv*), in the same county. The additions of 1840 included a porch and a new staircase; while at the same time the principal rooms were given ceilings of carved woodwork. Sold 1920.

Annagh, Riverstown, co Tipperary (MINCHIN/IFR). An attractive late-Georgian villa which became the seat of the Annagh branch of the Minchin family when they left Annagh Castle.

Annaghdown House, Corrandulla, co Galway (BLAKE, *sub* O'BRIEN-TWOHIG/LGI 1958). A pleasant Georgian house on the eastern shore of Lough Corrib. The seat of a branch of the Blake family.

Annaghlee, Cootehill, co Cavan. A distinguished mid-C18 red-brick house attributed to Richard Castle. 2 storeys over basement, curved bow in centre of front, with 1 bay on either side of it; 3 sided bow

in centre of rear elevation. Bow-fronted hall with apse at inner end; staircase in inner hall, extending into bow at rear. In 1814, the residence of Michael Murphy. Now almost completely destroyed.

Annaghmore, Tullamore, Offaly (FOX/LGI1912). A house with a fine neo-Classical bifurcating staircase. Much altered externally.

Annaghmore, Collooney, co Sligo (O'HARA/IFR). A house of *ca* 1820, consisting of a 2 storey 3 bay centre with a single-storey Ionic portico and single-storey 2 bay wings, greatly enlarged *ca* 1860–70 by C. W. O'Hara to the design of James Franklin Fuller; the additions being in the same late-Georgian style as the original house. The wings were raised a storey and extended back so that the house had a side elevation as high as the front and as long, or longer; consisting of 1 bay, a curved bow, 3 further bays and a three-sided bow. At the same time, the fenestration of the original centre was altered, paired windows being inserted into the two outer bays instead of the original single window above a Wyatt window. All the ground floor windows except for those in the three-sided bow have plain entablatures over them. Parapeted roof. Short area balustrade on either side of centre. Curved staircase behind entrance hall. Doorcases with reeded architraves and rosettes.

Annaghs Castle, Glenmore, co Kilkenny. A square 2 storey house of 1797; 5 bay front, fanlighted tripartite doorway with Composite columns; 4 bay side. Balustraded roof. Very delicate plasterwork in the style of Patrick Osborne in the hall. Later plasterwork in other rooms. In later C19, a residence of the Sweetman family.

Anna Liffey House, Lucan, co Dublin (SHACKLETON, B/PB). A Georgian mill-house by the side of the River Liffey, with a noted garden. The home of the Shackleton family, cousins of Sir Ernest Shackleton, the explorer.

Annemount, Glounthaune, co Cork (FALKINER, Bt/PB; CUMMINS/IFR; BEAMISH/ IFR; GILLMAN/IFR; MURPHY/IFR; BENCE-JONES/IFR). A 2 storey house in a magnificent situation overlooking Lough Mahon and the upper reaches of Cork Harbour; built in late C18 by Sir Riggs Falkiner, 1st Bt, who named it in honour of his second wife; enlarged and remodelled *ca* 1883 to the design of George Ashlin for John Murphy, MFH of the United Hunt, who first discovered the house when the fox which he was hunting led him here. As remodelled, the house was faced in cement, with entablatures over the windows; a projecting 2 storey porch, with a pediment and pilasters in its upper storey, was added in the centre of the front, with a single-storey three-sided pilastered bow on either side of it.

Annemount

The front was extended at one end by the addition of a 2 storey wing of the same height and in the same style, with a 3rd single-storey bow and an Italianate campanile tower. Impressive 2 storey hall, with staircase and gallery of oak and pitch-pine; ceiling of coloured C19 plasterwork. Coloured C19 plasterwork also in drawing room and dining room, and richly ornamented pilasters; flat of drawing room ceiling covered with embossed gilt paper; moulded entablatures over doors; fine late-Georgian chimneypiece of white marble in drawing room, with Classical head in medallion, flowers, foliage and trophies. Bought 1945 by Col Philip Bence-Jones; destroyed by fire 1948, when a mild sensation was caused by the fact that a statue of the Madonna in the small oratory upstairs was untouched by the flames. The ruin was subsequently demolished.

Anner Castle (formerly **Ballinahy**), **Clonmel, co Tipperary** (MANDEVILLE/IFR). An impressive C19 castle of random ashlar, built in 1860s by Rev N. H. Mandeville to the design of a Cork architect, William Atkins; incorporating the old square castle of the Mandeville family which had up to then been known as Ballinahy, but which was renamed Anner Castle after being enlarged and transformed. Impressive entrance front with twin octagonal battlemented and machicolated towers. Burnt 1926 and only the front part rebuilt.

Annerville

Annerville, Clonmel, co Tipperary (RIALL/LGI1958). A 2 storey Victorian house with a roof carried on a bracket cornice; entrance front with 2 storey porch between 2 single storey 3 sided balustraded bows; and in the upper storey, 2 Venetian windows.

Annesbrook

Annesbrook, Duleek, co Meath (SMITH/ LGI1912). A 2 storey 3 bay Georgian house with ground floor windows set under relieving arches and a large rusticated and fanlighted doorway; to which an impressive

Annesbrook: ceiling of "Banqueting Room"

pedimented portico of 4 fluted Ionic columns and a single-storey wing containing a charming Georgian-Gothic "banqueting room" were added early in C19 by Henry Smith. According to the story, he made these additions 1821, for when George IV came over to dine with him while staying with Lady Conyngham at Slane Castle (*qv*); the monarch, however, never saw the banqueting room, preferring to dine out of doors.

Annes Grove

Annes Grove (formerly **Ballyhemock** or **Ballyhimmock**), **Castletownroche, co Cork** (GROVE ANNESLEY/IFR and *sub* ANNESLEY, E/PB). An early C19 house of 2 storeys over a basement, built by Lt-Gen Hon Arthur Grove Annesley, who inherited the estate from his aunt by marriage, the heiress of the Grove family, who owned it previously. 7 bay entrance front; wooden porch with engaged Doric columns and entablature and sidelights with curved astragals; eaved roof. Irregular garden front facing the River Awbeg, in which, owing to the ground falling away, the basement forms an extra storey. Flanking the garden front are two stable courts. Walled garden with C18 "mount"; famous river garden of great extent, laid out and planted by R.A. Grove Annesley between *ca* 1900 and his death in 1966, and continued by his son, the late E.P. Grove Annesley. Castellated entrance gateway at one end of the demesne.

Annestown, co Waterford (PALLISER, *sub* GALLOWAY/IFR). A rambling 3 storey house at right angles to the village street of Annestown, which is in fact 2 houses joined together. The main front of the house faces the sea; but it has a gable-end actually on the street. Low-ceilinged but spacious rooms; long drawing room divided by an arch with simple Victorian plasterwork; large library approached along a passage. Owned at beginning of C19 by Henry St George Cole; bought *ca* 1830 by the Palliser family, from whom it was inherited by the Galloways.

Anner Castle

Anngrove

Anngrove (formerly **Ballinsperrig**), **Carrigtwohill, co Cork** (COTTER, Bt/PB; BARRY/IFR; GUBBINS/LG1937Supp). A remarkable late C17 house rather like a French manor house; built by Sir James Cotter, MP, a staunch adherent of Charles II who, in 1664, went to Switzerland with two companions and shot the fugitive Regicide, John Lisle. The house consisted of a rather high 2 storey 5 bay centre with boldly projecting square corner towers of 1 bay each. The towers were also 2 storey and their cornice was at the same level as that of the centre; but they had pyramidal roofs which were slightly lower than the high-pitched roof of the main block. The cornice was well-moulded, and there was a prominent string course between the two storeys, continuing round the towers. The doorcase had an entablature. One of the rooms originally contained a "velvet bed with hangings and gold brocade" which was said to have belonged to Charles I and to have been given to Sir James Cotter by Queen Henrietta Maria "as a mark of her royal favour and thanks" for having led the successful action against Lisle. James II is traditionally supposed to have stayed a night in the house and to have slept in this bed. The lands on which the house was built were leased from the Barrys, Earls of Barrymore; some time *post* 1720, the widow of Sir James Cotter's son sold the reversion of the lease to the 4th Earl and the Cotter family seat was henceforth Rockforest (*qv*). The 5th Earl of Barrymore, as Viscount Buttevant, lived for a period at Anngrove; but it was afterwards let. Charles I's bed, which the Cotters had left behind, was removed to Castle Lyons (*qv*), the principal Barrymore seat, where it was burnt in the fire of 1771. Towards the end of C18, or in early C19, Anngrove passed to the Wise family, from whom it was inherited, later in C19, by the Gubbins family. The house was still standing in *ca* 1950s; but it had been demolished by *ca* 1965.

Antrim Castle, co Antrim (SKEFFINGTON, MASSEREENE AND FERRARD, V/PB). A castle by the side of the Sixmilewater, just above where it flows into Lough Neagh, built originally 1613 by the important English settler, Sir Hugh Clotworthy, and enlarged 1662 by his son, 1st Viscount Massereene. The castle was rebuilt 1813 as a solid 3 storey Georgian-Gothic castellated mansion, designed by John Bowden, of Dublin, faced in Roman cement of a pleasant orange colour; the original Carolean doorway of the castle, a tremendous affair of Ionic pilasters, heraldry, festoons and a head of Charles I, being re-erected as the central feature of the entrance front, below a battlemented pediment. Apart from this, and tower-like projections at the corners, with

Antrim Castle

Antrim Castle: Carolean doorway

Antrim Castle: Canal

slender round angle turrets and shallow pyramidal roofs, the elevations were plain; the entrance front being of 4 bays between the projections, and the long adjoining front of 11 bays. Mullioned oriels and a tall octagonal turret of ashlar were added to the long front in 1887, when the castle was further enlarged. Remarkable C17 formal garden, unique in Ulster, its only surviving counterpart in Ireland being at Killruddery, co Wicklow (*qv*). Long canal, bordered with tall hedges, and another canal at right angles to it, making a "T" shape; old trees, dark masses of yew and walls of rose-

coloured brick. Mount, with spiral path, originally the *motte* of a Norman castle. Imposing Jacobean-Revival outbuildings of coursed rubble basalt with sandstone dressings; built *ca* 1840. Entrance gateway to the demesne with octagonal turrets. Antrim Castle was burnt 1922.

Áras an Uachtaráin (formerly **Viceregal Lodge,** and before that, **Phoenix Lodge**), **Phoenix Park, Dublin** (CLEMENTS, *sub* LUCAS-CLEMENTS/IFR). A house originally designed and built for himself 1751–52 by Rt Hon Nathaniel Clements, MP, the banker, politician, developer of C18 Dublin and amateur architect, in its own demesne within the Phoenix Park, the former Royal deer-park of which he was Ranger and Master of the Game. As built by Clements, it was of brick, consisting of a 2 storey 5 bay centre block with a mezzanine on its entrance front, joined by curved sweeps to single-storey wings; the entrance front of the centre block having a tripartite doorway surmounted by a Diocletian window. In 1782 Clements's son, Robert, afterwards 1st Earl of Leitrim, sold the house to the Government as an "occasional residence" for the Lord-Lieutenant, or Viceroy, and it thus came to be known as Viceregal Lodge; in the following century the Viceroys tended to live here for most of the year, only moving into Dublin Castle for the few weeks of the "Viceregal Season" in the winter. After being bought by the Government, the house was altered and enlarged at various times; notably by Michael Stapleton—who was an architect as well as a stuccodore—Robert Woodgate and Francis Johnston. An extra storey was added to the wings; the entrance front was given a single-storey Doric portico 1808. In 1815 Johnston extended the garden front by 5 bays on either side, the 2 end bays projecting forwards; and in the centre of this front he added the pedimented portico of 4 giant Ionic columns which is the house's most familiar feature. Finally, a new wing was added at one end of the garden front for Queen Victoria's visit 1849. Despite the additions and alterations, the interior of the centre of the house remains much as it was in Clements's time. The hall is the hall of his house, and therefore not large; though its coffered barrel-vaulted ceiling and screen of fluted Doric columns

Áras an Uachtaráin

date from the beginning of C19. The stair-case, in a separate hall on one side, is also on a small scale. In the centre of the garden front are 3 reception rooms of Clements's house; a large drawing room which keeps its original 1751 ceiling of elaborate rococo plasterwork in compartments, with a smaller room on either side; one of which has a coved ceiling with original mid-C18 plaster-work of an *Aesop's Fables* theme. One of Johnston's extensions to the garden front contains a large early-Victorian state draw-ing room or ballroom and a large dining room beyond. With the establishment of the Irish Free State, the house became the residence of the Governor-General; and since 1937, it has been the residence of the President of Ireland; and known as *Áras an Uachtaráin*—"The House of the Presi-dent". During the incumbency of President Sean T. O'Kelly, a wonderful mid-C18 plasterwork ceiling representing "Jupiter and the Four Elements", with figures half covered in clouds, was brought from Mespil House, Dublin, which was then being demolished, and installed in the President's reception room, one of 2 smaller rooms in the garden front of the original house; the other, which has the *Aesop's Fables* ceiling, being used as a small dining room and for meetings of the Council of State. (The Mespil House ceiling was brought here at the instigation of Dr C. P. Curran, who was also instrumental in having casts made of the plasterwork by the Francini at Rivers-town House, co Cork (*qv*) which then seemed in danger; and which have been installed in the ballroom and in the adjoin-ing corridor. Since the beginning of the present century, the house has been occu-pied by the following VICEROYS (all PB): 5th Earl Cadogan; 2nd Earl of Dudley; 7th Earl (afterwards 1st Marquess) of Aber-deen; 2nd Lord (afterwards 1st Viscount) Wimborne; 1st Viscount French (after-wards 1st Earl of Ypres); 1st Viscount FitzAlan of Derwent (son of 14th Duke of Norfolk). GOVERNORS-GENERAL (both IFR): Timothy Healy; James MacNeill. PRESI-DENTS (all IFR, save for O'Kelly and Hillery): Douglas Hyde; Sean T. O'Kelly; Eamon De Valera; Erskine Childers; Cearbhall Ó Dálaigh; Patrick Hillery.

Arbutus Lodge, Montenotte, Cork, co Cork. A 2 storey mid-C19 Italianate house with Romanesque overtones. Modillion cornice; porch at end of house with Roman-

Áras an Uachtaráin: Hall

Áras an Uachtaráin: Drawing Room

esque columns. Ballroom with Corinthian columns at one side. Formerly the home of the Kearney family. Now an hotel.

Arch Hall

Arch Hall, Wilkinstown, co Meath (GAR-NETT/LGI1912). A 3 storey early C18 house attributed, as is the arch in the garden, to Sir Edward Lovett Pearce. Curved bow in centre of front, doorway with pediment and blocking; curved ends, with round-headed windows. Top storey treated as an attic. In C19, the house was given a high-pitched roof on a bracket cornice; the curved ends being given conical roofs, so that they looked like the round towers of a French château. Also in C19, the windows in the attic storey were replaced by rather strange Romanesque windows in pairs. Now a ruin.

Archerstown, Thurles, co Tipperary (LANGLEY/IFR). A plain 2 storey 3 bay high-roofed Georgian house. Wing with Wyatt windows.

Ardagh House, Ardagh, co Longford (FETHERSTON, Bt/PB1923). An irregular 2 storey house of predominantly early to mid C19 appearance. Eaved roof on bracket cornice; porch and corridor with pilasters. Now a domestic science college.

Ardamine

Ardamine, Gorey, co Wexford (RICH-ARDS/LGI1912). An early to mid-C19 house of 2 storeys over a basement, consisting of 2 contiguous blocks one slightly higher than the other. Eaved roofs on bracket cornices; wide projecting porch, partly open, with Doric columns, partly enclosed, with pilasters; single storey curved bow. Giant corner pilasters on both blocks. Balustraded area.

Ardavilling, Cloyne, co Cork (LITTON/LGI1912; BECKFORD, *sub* NUTTING, Bt/PB). A mildly Tudor-Revival C19 house, gabled and with a mullioned bow. The seat of the Litton family; in the present century, of a branch of the Stacpoole family. Owned for some years after World War II by Lt-Col & Mrs F. J. Beckford.

Ardbraccan, Navan, co Meath. The Palace of the (C of I) Bishops of Meath, on the site of the old castle where the Bishops lived from C14. Bishop Evans left money for the building of a new house here early in C18; his successor, Bishop Henry Downes, came here with Dean Swift to lay out the ground; but it was not until the time of the next Bishop again, Arthur Price, that the house was begun *ca* 1734, to the design of Richard Castle. When the two 2 storey 5 bay wings of what was to be a Palladian mansion had been completed, Price was elevated to the Archdiocese of Cashel. For the next 30 years, the subsequent Bishops did nothing about building the centre block, but lived in one of the wings, using the other for guests. It was not until early 1770s that Bishop Henry Maxwell, a younger son

Ardbraccan: Entrance Front

of 1st Lord Farnham, decided to complete the house; he is said to have boasted that he would build a palace so grand that no scholar or tutor would dare live in it. He obtained designs from Thomas Cooley and also from one of his own clergy, Rev Daniel Beaufort, Rector of Navan, who was a talented amateur architect. Both of them were, to a certain extent, under the influence of James Wyatt, who produced a sketch of the garden front. The centre block, which was eventually begun 1776 and took several years to build, is a simple and dignified grey stone house of 2 storeys and 7 bays, with an Ionic doorcase; it harmonizes well with Castle's wings, to which it is joined by

Ardbraccan: Garden Front

Ardbraccan: Entrance Vestibule

curved sweeps with niches. The garden front, also of 7 bays, has a 3 bay central breakfront in which the ground floor windows are set in a blind arcade. The restrained neo-Classical interior plasterwork is said to have been designed by Wyatt, though Beaufort was asked by Bishop Maxwell to design a ceiling for the entrance vestibule 1780. This is a narrow room with

a barrel-vaulted ceiling of shallow hexagonal coffering; a door under a large and elegant internal fanlight at its inner end opens into the main hall or saloon in the middle of the garden front, which has a cornice of mutules and elliptical panels above the doors. The principal and secondary stairs lie on either side of this saloon, which also communicates with the drawing room and dining room in the entrance front, on either side of the vestibule. Despite Bishop Maxwell's hope that the grandeurs of Ardbraccan would discourage scholars and tutors from aspiring to the Diocese, his successor was Thomas O'Beirne who had started life as a humble schoolmaster; but who none the less carried out improvements to the outbuildings, advised by Beaufort. The more aristocratic Bishop Nathaniel Alexander carried out grander improvements to the outbuildings in 1820s and 1830s. The handsome farm and stable yards are joined by a tunnel under the garden terrace.

Ardbrack House

Ardbrack House, Kinsale, co Cork (LUCAS/IFR). An attractive 2 storey 5 bay weather-slated late-Georgian house. Camberheaded windows; pedimented and fanlighted doorcase.

Ardcandrisk

Ardcandrisk, nr Wexford, co Wexford (GROGAN-MORGAN/LG1863; DEANE, MUSKERRY, B/PB). A 2 storey Regency villa composed of 3 polygons of different sizes. Eaved roofs; Wyatt windows at one end. Tall blind panels on narrow faces of polygons.

Ardee House, co Louth (RUXTON/LG11912 and *sub* FITZHERBERT/IFR). A 3 storey, 7 bay C18 house of red brick. Small porch with pilasters, pediment and fanlight. Now a hospital.

Ardfert Abbey, Ardfert, co Kerry (CROSBIE/IFR). A house originally built towards the end of C17 by Sir Thomas Crosbie, MP; "modernized" 1720 by Maurice Crosbie,

Ardfert Abbey

1st Lord Branden, and again altered *ca* 1830, though keeping its original character. 2 storey main block with 7 bay front, the 2 outer bays on either side breaking forwards and framed by quoins; pedimented centre, in which a single triple window was substituted at some period—presumably during the alterations of *ca* 1830—for the 3 first-floor bays. Plain rectangular doorcase; high eaved roof on modillion cornice. The front was prolonged by lower 2 storey wings, which, having started in the same plane as the front of the main block, ran forwards at right angles to it, forming an open forecourt, and then turned outwards and extended for a considerable way on either side. Irregular wing at back of house. Panelled hall decorated with figures painted in monochrome on the panels. Early C18 staircase and gallery of good joinery; Corinthian newels; handrail curving upwards; panelling on landing with Corinthian pilasters; modillion cornice. Large drawing room with compartmented plasterwork in ceiling, in which hung the full-length Reynolds portrait of Lady Glandore. Caryatid chimneypiece in one room. Early formal layout; sunken parterre, yew alleys, trees "cut into an arcade"; avenues of beech, lime and elm. Ruined Franciscan friary in grounds. To Caroline, Countess of Portarlington, who stayed here 1785, Ardfert was "an old-fashioned place in a very bleak country . . .

Ardfert Abbey: Hall

Ardfert Abbey: Hall

Ardfinnan Castle

small low rooms, wainscoted, and the drawing room perfectly antique". However, she admired the dressing room which her hostess, Diana (*née* Sackville), wife of John Crosbie, 2nd Earl of Glandore—a young woman of fashionable tastes whose fondness for gaming and slowness in paying her debts earned her the nickname of "Owen Glendower" ("Owing Glandore")—had done up for herself; and described it at length in a letter to her sister. "It is hung with white paper, to which she has made a border of pink silk, with white and gold flowers stuck upon it, and hung the room with all Mr Bunbury's beautiful prints; the window curtains are pale pink linen with white silk fringe, the chairs pink linen with a border painted on paper, cut out and stuck on gauze, and then tacked onto the linen". Ardfert eventually passed to Rev John Talbot (*see* MOUNT TALBOT), son of 2nd Earl of Glandore's sister, who assumed the additional surname of Crosbie. It was sold in the present century by J. B. Talbot-Crosbie. Nothing now remains of the house, but there are still some relics of the formal garden.

Ardfinnan Castle, Ardfinnan, co Tipperary (PRENDERGAST/LG1937Supp). An old tower-house above the River Suir, with a 3 storey gable-ended Georgian wing and also a 3 storey battlemented tower added in C19, when the gable of the Georgian wing was stepped and the old tower was given impressive Irish battlements.

Ardfry, Oranmore, co Galway (BLAKE/IFR). A long, 2 storey house probably of *ca* 1770 on a peninsula jutting out into Galway Bay where previously there had been a castle which, during the Civil War, Sir Richard Blake garrisoned in the service of Charles I. Principal front of 9 bays with a central pediment and a higher, pyramidal-roofed, pavilion at either end. On the front face of each pavilion is a 2 storey curved bow roofed with a shallow half-dome. Hall

with alcoves supported by pairs of columns embedded in the wall. Dorothea Herbert and a cousin called here in 1784 during the

Ardfry in 3 stages: more or less intact; ruinous; and re-roofed and re-windowed for Mackintosh Man

celebrations for the wedding of Joseph Blake, afterwards 1st Lord Wallscourt, to a daughter of the Earl of Louth; when an unfortunate incident was caused by the cousin's dog (to which he was in the habit of feeding "Ripe Peaches and apricots") "dirtying the Room and Lord Louth's blindly stepping into it". At the time of 3rd Lord Wallscourt's marriage to the beautiful Bessie Lock 1822, the house had been empty for some years and was very dilapidated; at first they thought it was beyond repair, but then they decided to restore it; the work was completed by 1826. It was probably then that the house was given its few mild Gothic touches: a pointed entrance doorway with pinnacles beneath a quatrefoil window; battlements on the end pavilions; and a Gothic conservatory with stone piers. The rather strange 4 storey block at the back of the house which has hood mouldings over its small windows may either have been built, or re-faced, at this time. The 3rd Lord Wallscourt, a man of exceptional strength and often very violent, liked walking about the house naked; his wife persuaded him to carry a cowbell when he was in this state so as to warn the maidservants of his approach. In the early years of the present century, the 2nd wife of 4th Lord Wallscourt sold the lead off the roof to pay her gambling debts; so that the house gradually fell into ruin. It was recently re-roofed and re-windowed so as to be used for the film *Mackintosh Man*; now, with the film-property roof a skeleton and the windows falling out, the house seems like the ghost of what it was in an earlier stage of its decay.

Ardgillan Castle, Balbriggan, co Dublin (TAYLOUR, *sub* HEADFORT, M/PB). A C18 house consisting of a 2 storey bow-fronted centre with single-storey overlapping wings, mildly castellated either towards the end of the C18 or early in the C19. The central bow has been made into a round tower by raising it a storey and giving it a skyline of Irish battlements; the main roof parapet has been crenellated and the windows given hood mouldings. Over each of the wings was thrown, literally speaking, a Gothic cloak of battlements and pointed arches; below which the original facade, with its quoins and rectangular sash windows, shows in all its Classical nakedness. Battlemented ranges and an octagon tower were added on the other side of the house.

Ardglass Castle

Ardo

Ardo

Ardglass Castle (also known as **The Newark**), **Ardglass, co Down** (FITZ-GERALD, *sub* LEINSTER, D/PB; BEAUCLERK, *sub* ST ALBANS, D/PB). Originally a row of C15 warehouses by the harbour, protected by 3 towers standing alongside it. Made into a castellated house at the end of C18 by Lord Charles FitzGerald, 1st and last Lord Lecale; also lived in by his mother, Emily, Duchess of Leinster, and her second husband, William Ogilvie, a Scot who had been tutor to her more famous son, Lord Edward FitzGerald, and who subsequently developed Ardglass as a fashionable seaside resort. The old warehouses were given battlements, regularly-disposed windows with Georgian Gothic astragals and a fanlighted doorway; the interior was decorated with plasterwork of the period, one room having a frieze with olive sprays and a repeated bust, which might perhaps be of Lord Edward. Ardglass Castle was eventually inherited by William Ogilvie's daughter by a former marriage, who was the wife of Charles Beauclerk, a great-grandson of 1st Duke of St Albans. In the later C19, some of the Georgian astragals were replaced by heavy window-frames, and a porch, rather like a miniature truncated version of the canopy of the Albert Memorial, was added to one front. The castle became a golf club 1911.

Ardigon, Killyleagh, co Down (HERON/IFR). A solid Georgian block.

Ardkeen, Waterford, co Waterford. A 2 storey early to mid-C19 house with a 5 bay front and a single-storey Doric portico. Built by a member of the Quaker family of Malcolmson, who founded the great cotton mills at Portlaw in early C19. Afterwards owned by the de Bromhead family. Now a hospital.

Ardmore, Passage West, co Cork (ROBERTS/IFR). A 3 storey 5 bay Georgian house with 2 storey 3 sided bows on its front, which is prolonged by an arch on either side leading into the yard behind.

Ardmore Place, Bray, co Wicklow (PAGET/LG1972; CARLETON-PAGET, *sub* CARLETON/IFR). A plain 2 storey C19 house, with an eaved roof and 3 sided bows on adjoining fronts.

Ardmulchan, Beauparc, co Meath (TAAFFE/IFR; GALVIN, *sub* LAW/IFR). Originally a house of the Taaffe family; bought 1904 by Mrs F. G. Fletcher (later Mrs R. W. McGrath), who replaced it by an Edwardian mansion to the design of Sidney, Mitchell & Wilson, of Edinburgh; mostly in the plain, gabled and mullioned Tudor manor house style, but with a large Baronial tower, and an English Renaissance doorway: an elaborate confection of coupled Doric columns, a Doric frieze, scroll pediments and heraldic beasts. In recent years, it was the home of Mr & Mrs Riddell-Martin; it is now the home of Mr & Mrs Séan Galvin.

Ardmulchan

Ardnalee, Carrigrohane, co Cork (COL-LINS/LGI1912; ALDWORTH/IFR; DALY, *sub* VILLIERS-STUART/IFR). A 2 storey house built by a member of the Morgan family 1832. 5 bay principal front, overlooking the River Lee; fanlighted entrance door beneath single-storey semi-circular Doric portico in side elevation, not centrally placed. Eaved roof. Small room panelled with the wooden blocks used for printing wallpapers. Subsequently owned by the Collins family, whose heiress married Major J. O. Aldworth. From 1916, the home of the Daly family.

Ardnargle, Limavady, co Derry (OGIL-BY/LGI1937Supp). A plain 2 storey 5 bay house of *ca* 1780, built by John Ogilby; given a porch, a 3 sided bow, window surrounds with console brackets and a modillion cornice *ca* 1854 by R. L. Ogilby. Victorian Classical plasterwork in hall and main reception rooms.

Ardo (also known as **Ardogena**), **Ard-more, co Waterford** (MCKENNA/LGI1912). A gingerbread Carcassonne on a bare cliff-top overlooking the Atlantic, consisting of a plain 2 storey house to which a tall battle-mented square tower and numerous round turrets, with pointed windows, hood mould-ings and quatrefoil openings, were added in the late-Georgian period; the turrets con-tinuing far beyond the house itself, joined by straight and curving castellated walls, to form a line of brittle fortifications. Fine staircase hall, its walls decorated with Classical reliefs in plasterwork. In the latter part of C18 and early C19, Ardo was the home of Jeremiah Coghlan, a gentleman of slender means whose wife, known as "Madam", maintained a recklessly grandi-ose and extravagant way of life here which she supported by helping the smugglers who frequented the coast. 2 of her 4 children were idiots; but she also had 2 beautiful daughters, one of whom she married off to "Cripplegate", 8th and last Earl of Barry-more (*see* BARRY/IFR), and the other to 9th Duc de Castries. The Coghlans—like the Barrymores—ended with a financial crash; but the Duc de Castries was rich and Ardo, though leased, remained in his family. It eventually passed to his grandson by his 1st marriage, the great Marshal Macmahon, victor of Magenta and President of France in·the early years of the Third Republic, who sold it 1874 to Sir Joseph McKenna of the National Bank, uncle of the politician Reginald McKenna. Ardo was abandoned *ca* 1918; it eventually became roofless and is now a crazy ruin.

Ardowen House, co Sligo. A plain Georgian house of 2 storeys over a base-ment. 4 bay front, with single-storey 3 sided bow at one side. Return.

Ardoyne House, Edenderry, co Antrim (ANDREWS/IFR). A house said to be basically late C17, but enlarged and remodelled in the late-Georgian period. 2 storey; 3 bay front, with deep end bow and simple Doric porch.

Ardowen House

Ardress House, Charlemont, co Armagh (ENSOR/LGI1894). A 2 storey 5 bay gable-ended house of *ca* 1664 with 2 slight projections at the back, enlarged and modernized *ca* 1770 by the Dublin architect, George Ensor—brother of the better-known architect, John Ensor—for his own use. Ensor added a wing at one end of the front, and to balance it he built a screen wall with dummy windows at the other end. These additions were designed to give the effect of a centre block 2 bays longer than what the front was originally, with 2 storey 1 bay wings having Wyatt windows in both storeys. To complete the effect, he raised the facade to conceal the old high-pitched roof; decorating the parapet with curved upstands and a central urn; the parapet of the wings curving downwards on either side to frame other urns. Ensor also added a pedimented Tuscan porch and he altered the garden front, flanking it with curved sweeps. Much of the interior of the house was allowed to keep its simple, intimate scale; the oak staircase dates from before Ensor's time. But he enlarged the drawing room, and decorated the walls and ceiling with Adamesque plasterwork and plaques of such elegance and quality that the work is generally assumed to have been carried out by the leading Irish artist in this style of plasterwork, Michael Stapleton. Ardress now belongs to the Northern Ireland National Trust and is open to the public.

Ardrum, Inniscarra, co Cork (COLTHURST, Bt/PB). A Georgian house with a long elevation. The original seat of the Colthurst family, who gave up living in the house in mid-C19, when they built the new Blarney Castle (*qv*); it is now demolished.

Ards, Sheephaven, co Donegal (WRAY/LGI1863; STEWART/LGI1912). The former seat of the Wray family. In the C18, the last William Wray of Ards was a celebrated figure, eccentric and autocratic but kind and generous; he lived at Ards in feudal state, building roads at his own expense across the mountains and always having 20 stalls ready in his stables for the horses of his guests, and 20 covers on his dinner table for their masters. As a result of his extravagance, the estate was sold 1781 to Alexander Stewart, brother of 1st Marquess of Londonderry. The house was rebuilt *ca* 1830 by Alexander Stewart towards the end of his life, to the design of John Hargrave, of Cork. The main front of 2 storeys, with a central feature consisting of a rather flattened Venetian window, set under a relieving arch below a curved pediment, and a single storey portico with a triangular pediment. 3 bays and an additional canted

Ardress House

Ardress House: Drawing Room

end bay on either side of the central feature. 3 storey range at back. Good plasterwork frieze in hall, with birds in high relief; also friezes in drawing room and dining room. Sold *ca* 1925; subsequently owned by Franciscans, who demolished it *ca* 1965.

Ardsallagh, Navan, co Meath (FRENCH/LGI1912). A Tudor-Revival house of 1844; with steeply-pointed gables and dormer-gables, oriels, mullions and tall chimneys.

Ardsallagh, Fethard, co Tipperary (FARQUHAR, Bt/PB). A gable-ended double bow-fronted C18 house of 2 storeys over a basement; the bows being 3 sided and having between them a Venetian window over a pedimented and fanlighted tripartite doorway. Broad flight of steps with railings up to hall door. Hall open to spacious staircase; drawing room and dining room with modern plasterwork friezes in late C18 style. Origi-

Ardsallagh, co Tipperary

nally the seat of the Frend family; bought after World War II by Mrs Reginald Farquhar who has made a notable garden here, with a series of delightful walled enclosures, one of which is laid out as an Italian garden with a pool; and also a wild garden planted with many rare trees and shrubs.

Ardtully

Ardtully, Kenmare, co Kerry (ORPEN/IFR). A Victorian Baronial house, with a high roof, stepped gables and dormers and a battlemented round tower and turret at one corner. Built by Sir Richard Orpen on the site of an earlier house which in turn had replaced an old MacCarthy stronghold. Burnt 1921.

The Argory

Argory (The), Charlemont, co Armagh (MACGEOUGH BOND/IFR). Built *ca* 1820 by Walter MacGeough (who subsequently assumed the surname of Bond), to the design of 2 architects named A. & J. Williamson, one or both of whom worked in the office of Francis Johnston. A house with imposing and restrained Classical elevations, very much in the Johnston manner, of 2 storeys, and faced with ashlar. Main block has 7 bay front, the centre bay breaking forward under a shallow pediment with acroteria; Wyatt window in centre above porch with Doric columns at corners. Unusual fenestration: the middle window in both storeys on either side of the centre being taller than those to the left and right of it. Front prolonged by wing of same height as main block, but set back from it; of 3 bays, ending with a wide three-sided bow which has a chimneystack in its centre. 3 bay end to main block; other front of main block also of 7 bays, with a porch; prolonged by service wing flush with main block. Dining room has plain cornice with mutules; unusual elliptical overdoors with shells and fruit in plasterwork. Very extensive office ranges and courtyards at one corner of house: building with a pediment on each side and a clock tower with a cupola; range with polygonal end pavilions; imposing archway. The interior is noted for a remarkable organ; and also houses the important modern art collection of the present owner.

Armagh Palace, co Armagh. The Palace of the (C of I) Archbishops of Armagh and Primates. A plain and dignified late C18 block, 9 bays long and 4 bays deep, originally of 2 storeys over a high rusticated basement.

Armagh Palace

Built 1770, to the design of Thomas Cooley, by Primate Richard Robinson, afterwards 1st Lord Rokeby, who added a 3rd storey 1786, his architect then being Francis Johnston. Later, a large enclosed porch was added, with pairs of Ionic columns set at an angle to the front. Flanking the entrance front of the Palace is the Primate's Chapel, a detached building in the form of an Ionic temple. The exterior, of 1781, is by Cooley; but the interior was carried out after Cooley's death 1784 by Francis Johnston, who succeeded him as architect to Primate Robinson. Johnston's interior, a modification of Cooley's design, is one of the most beautiful surviving C18 ecclesiastical interiors in Ireland; with a coffered barrel-vaulted ceiling, a delicate frieze, Corinthian pilasters, a gallery with a curved rear wall, and splendid panelling and pews. The Palace is surrounded by a well-wooded demesne, in which there is an obelisk, also by Johnston. The Church of Ireland is at present building a modern residence for the Primate on Cathedral Hill, so that the future of the Palace is uncertain.

Artramont House, Castlebridge, co Wexford (LE HUNTE/LGI1912; NEAVE, Bt/PB). A late C18 house, remodelled after being burnt 1923. 2 storey; entrance front with a pediment of which the peak is level with the coping of the parapet, and the base is well below the level of the main cornice. In the breakfront central feature below the pediment are 2 windows and a tripartite Venetian doorway; 2 bays on either side of the central feature.

Ashbourne, Glounthaune, co Cork (BEAMISH/IFR; HALLINAN/IFR). A plain 2 storey 5 bay late-Georgian house with additions in the late-Victorian or Edwardian half-timbered style. Interiors of the period: fancy timber studding in the walls, oak panelling, beamed and fretted ceilings. Garden with noted collection of trees and shrubs; straight yew walk, long flight of steps bordered by hedges. A seat of the Beamish family; bought after World War I by Major T. F. D. Hallinan, who sold it *ca* 1958. Now an hotel.

Ashbrook

Ashbrook, nr Derry, co Derry (BERESFORD-ASH/IFR). A 2 storey bow-fronted gable-ended C18 house, reputed to incorporate a house built by John Ash 1686. Unusual fenestration: 2 windows on either side of the central curved bow in the upper storey, but only 1 on each side below. All the windows in the front and the entrance doorway have rusticated surrounds. Both sides of the house are gabled and irregular.

Ashburn

Ashburn, Limerick, co Limerick. A 2 storey house of 1829 built onto a 3 storey C18 house. 3 bay front with central breakfront and semi-circular Ionic porch; roof parapet and corner pilasters. Bought 1870 by the Dunphy family; sold 1949, demolished *ca* 1960.

Ashfield, Rathfarnham, co Dublin (CUSACK-SMITH, Bt/PB; DENIS-TOTTENHAM, *sub* TOTTENHAM/IFR). A Georgian house of 2 storeys over a high basement. 3 bay front; solid roof parapet with urns; C19 porch. Blind lunette windows in side elevation. The seat of Sir William Cusack-Smith, 2nd Bt, Baron of the Court of Exchequer in Ireland 1801–36.

Ashfield Lodge, Cootehill, co Cavan (CLEMENTS/IFR). A 2 storey late-Georgian house with a wide curved bow in the centre of its front, and a bowed end elevation. 1 bay on either side of central bow; recessed panels between upper and lower storeys. Lower service wing at rear. Sold after the death of Lt-Col M. L. S. Clements 1952; subsequently demolished.

Ashford Castle, co Galway (BROWNE, ORANMORE AND BROWNE, B/PB; GUINNESS, Bt/PB). A vast and imposing Victorian-Baronial castle of rather harsh rough-hewn grey stone in a superb position at the head of Lough Corrib close to co Mayo village of Cong; built onto an earlier house consisting of a 2 storey 5 bay Georgian shooting-box enlarged and remodelled in French château style. The shooting-box and estate originally belonged to the Oranmore and Browne family; they were sold by the Encumbered Estates Court in 1855 and bought by Benjamin Lee Guinness, afterwards 1st Bt, head of Guinness's Brewery, who transformed the shooting box into the French château. From the 1870s onwards, his son, Arthur, 1st and last Lord Ardilaun, added the castle, which was designed by James Franklin Fuller and George Ashlin. He also built the tremendous castellated 6 arch bridge across the river, with outworks and an embattled gateway surmounted by a

Ashford Castle

Ashford Castle: Bridge and Outworks

gigantic "A" and a Baron's coronet, which is the main approach; from the far side of this bridge the castle looks most impressive. Its interior, however, is a disappointment, like the interiors of so many late-Victorian houses. The rooms are not particularly large, and some of them are rather low; everything is light oak, with timbered ceilings and panelling. The main hall was formed out of 2 or more rooms in the earlier house, and has a somewhat makeshift air; it is surrounded by an oak gallery with thin uprights and a staircase rises straight from one side of it. Another room has an immense carved oak mantel with caryatids and the Guinness motto. Magnificent gardens and grounds; large fountain, vista up the hillside with steps; castellated terrace by the lake. Sold *ca* 1930; now an hotel.

Ashgrove, co Cavan. A 2 storey 3 bay c18 house with a rusticated Venetian doorway below a Venetian window.

Ashgrove, Cobh, co Cork (BEAMISH/IFR). A plain 3 storey late Georgian house built for Councillor Franklin by Abraham Hargrave, overlooking the water between Great Island and the mainland. 3 bay entrance front with large central door. Other front has shallow curved bow at one side. Frieze of paired dolphins joining lyres in dining room. Now a ruin. Old keep by entrance gate.

Ash Hill Towers, Kilmallock, co Limerick (EVANS, *sub* CARBERY, B/PB; JOHNSON, *sub* HARRINGTON, E/PB). A c18 pedimented house, the back of which was rebuilt in Gothic 1833, probably to the design of James and George Richard Pain, with two slender round battlemented and machicolated towers. Rectangular windows

with wooden tracery. Good plasterwork in upstairs drawing room in the manner of Wyatt and by the same hand as the hall at Glin Castle (*qv*); saloon with domed ceiling. The towers have, in recent years, been removed. Originally a seat of the Evans family; passed in the later c19 to John Henry Weldon. Now the home of Major Stephen Johnson.

Ash Hill Towers

Ashley Park, Nenagh, co Tipperary (HEAD/LGI1958; ATKINSON/IFR). A 2 storey house of early c19 appearance, said to incorporate older building. Polygonal ends; external shutters; veranda.

Ashline, Ennis, co Clare (MAHON/LGI-1912). A 2 storey Georgian house with a curved bow in the centre of its front, incorporating the entrance doorway; and with 1 bay on either side. Windows grouped away from the corners, leaving wide expanses of blank wall at either side of the facade. Extension set back and lower wing.

Ash Park

Ash Park, Feeny, co Derry (STEVENSON/IFR). A 2 storey 5 bay house, built *ca* 1796 by James Stevenson, of Knockan, co Derry (*qv*), as a residence for his elder son, William. High pitched roof, partly gable-ended, partly hipped.

Ashton House, Castleknock, co Dublin. An imposing Victorian Italianate house, consisting of a 3 storey main block with single-storey wings. Both the main block and the wings have balustraded roof parapets; the main block has a central projection, with a small segmental pediment, and a pilastered and balustraded enclosed porch. Small triangular pediment on each wing.

Ashurst, Killiney, co Dublin (DOBBS/IFR). A Victorian house with gables, pointed windows and a pointed belfry; built 1861–1863 for W. C. Dobbs, MP, Judge of Landed Estates Court, to the design of Charles (afterwards Sir Charles) Lanyon and William Henry Lynn. In recent years the residence of Most Rev J. C. McQuaid, Catholic Archbishop of Dublin.

Ashline

Askeaton Castle

Askeaton Castle: C17 or C18 House in Bailey

Assolas: Front incorporating C17 facade

Askeaton Castle, Askeaton, co Limerick
(FITZGERALD, DESMOND, E/DEP). One of the
chief castles of the FitzGeralds, Earls of
Desmond, mostly C15 and extending round
2 courtyards on a small rocky island in the
River Deel. The buildings include a magnificent mid-C15 banqueting hall raised on a
basement of vaulted chambers. Also in the
castle bailey is the ruin of an enigmatic
house of rubble stone with red brick dressings, which old pictures show to have had a
very high roof and tall chimneys. It has a
curved bow at one side of each of its two
principal fronts, one of them with a
Venetian window. This could be the earliest
known example of a Venetian window on
the curve, not just in Ireland but anywhere,
if, as is possible, the house dates from late
C17. It may not, however, have been built
until *ca* 1740s, when it is said to have been
the headquarters of the Limerick Hell Fire
Club. In C19, it was used as a barracks.
Askeaton Castle is now a ruin maintained as
a National Monument.

Assolas, Kanturk, co Cork (WRIXON-
BECHER, Bt/PB). A truncated tower-house,
with a late C17 2 storey 3 bay facade surmounted by a pediment-gable incorporating
a chimneystack, to which a 2 storey bow-
ended range was added in C18, to provide a
new front at right angles to C17 facade. The
side of the house incorporating the latter

was made nearly symmetrical by the addition of a 2 storey wing with a curved bow,
balancing the curved end bow of C18 front
on the other side of the old tower. The
house was re-roofed with exceptionally
wide eaves, probably in the early C19. The
interior contains some C17 and C18 panelling. Acquired *ca* 1714 by Rev Francis
Gore; subsequently acquired by the Wrixon
family. Now owned by Mrs Bourke.

Assolas: C18 Front

Athavallie, Castlebar, co Mayo (LYNCH-
BLOSSE, Bt/PB). A long, low plain 2 storey
house; its main block being of 5 bays, with
an entrance door set in a broad stone arch;
the front being extended by a 4 bay range of
the same height, but set back. Now a
convent.

Athcarne Castle, Duleek, co Meath
(GERNON/LGI1912). An old tower house with
a 3 storey, 3 bay later wing which is plain
but for a battlemented porch and a rather
thin turret. Now a ruin.

Athclare Castle, Dunleer, co Louth. A
C16 tower-house with a hall wing attached.
Part Gothic, part Renaissance fireplace.

Athgoe Park, Hazelhatch, co Dublin
(SKERRETT/LGI1886; O'CARROLL/LGI1958;
KENNEDY-SKIPTON/IFR). A mid-C18 house of
2 storeys and 5 bays, with a steep pediment-
gable, a high sprocketed roof and a pedimented and fanlighted doorcase; standing
alongside the well-preserved medieval
tower-house of the Locke family, who also
built C18 house. A lower wing connects the
house to buildings behind the old tower.
After the death of Peter Warren Locke *ca*
1832, Athgoe passed to his two sisters, Mrs
Skerrett and Mrs O'Carroll, who were his
heirs-at-law. Some years later, Mrs O'Carroll's son, Redmond O'Carroll, was looking
through a bundle of old leases when a paper
fell out which he found was the Will of
Peter Warren Locke, leaving all his estates
and property to his illegitimate daughter.
Being a man of strict honour, Redmond
O'Carroll did not destroy the fatal document, as others might have done; but
promptly handed it over to the lady who
would benefit from it; even though this

meant that he and his family as well as his
Skerrett cousins would be destitute. Eventually, however, Athgoe passed to his
nephew, F.J.L. O'Carroll. In recent years
it was the home of the late H.K. Kennedy-
Skipton, FRSA.

Attyflin, Patrickswell, co Limerick
(WESTROPP/IFR; HEWSON/IFR). A 2 storey
early to mid-C18 house. 5 bay centre with

pediment; 2 storey 2 bay early C19 wings slightly lower than the centre block.

Auburn, Athlone, co Westmeath (BAIRD (*formerly* ADAMSON)/LGI1958). A 2 storey over basement and 5 bay house with a fan-lighted doorway; built or remodelled 1805 by John Hogan, whose father, a solicitor, had acquired the estate from the previous owners, a branch of the Naper family, who had mortgaged it to him to pay his vast costs in a lawsuit. The estate takes its name from Oliver Goldsmith's poem, *The Deserted Village*, which describes the surrounding countryside. Sold 1848 to William Henry Daniel; sold 1864 to G. A. G. Adamson.

Aughentaine Castle

Aughentaine Castle, Fivemiletown, co Tyrone (KNOX-BROWNE, *sub* BROWNE/IFR; HAMILTON STUBBER/IFR). A large Victorian mansion, built 1860 by T. R. Browne, consisting of a symmetrical 2 storey main block, and a lower 2 storey wing, with 2 very tall Italianate campaniles of equal height, one at each end, to give the building that air of near-symmetry so beloved of many Victorian architects. Open porch; 2-light and 3-light windows, some rectangular, others round-headed. Prominent roofs. Sold following the death of Mervyn Knox-Browne 1954, to Major J. H. Hamilton Stubber, who demolished it and built a modern Classical house to the design of Hon Claud Phillimore.

Augher Castle, co Tyrone (*see* SPUR ROYAL).

Aughrane Castle (also known as **Castle Kelly**), **Ballygar, co Galway** (O'KELLY/LGI1863; BAGOT/IFR). A castellated house of C19 appearance; little bartizans at corners, plain windows with hood mouldings, simple battlemented porch. Gabled range at one end and gabled tower behind.

Avondale, Rathdrum, co Wicklow (PARNELL-HAYES, *sub* CONGLETON, B/PB). A square house of 2 storeys over a basement, built 1779 for Samuel Hayes, a noted amateur architect who possibly designed it himself. 5 bay entrance front, the 3 centre bays breaking forward under a pediment; small Doric porch with paired columns, Coade stone panels with swags and medallions between lower and upper windows. Garden front with central bow; the basement, which in the entrance front is concealed, is visible on this side and its windows have Gibbsian surrounds. Magnificent and lofty 2 storey hall with C18 Gothic plasterwork and gallery along inner wall. Bow room with beautiful Bossi chimneypiece. Dining room with elaborate neo-Classical plasterwork on walls and ceiling; the wall

Avondale

decoration incorporating oval mirrors and painted medallions. Passed to William Parnell-Hayes, brother of the 1st Baron Congleton, and grandfather of Charles Stewart Parnell, the Irish nationalist leader, who was born here and lived here all his life with his mother and elder brother. Now owned by the Department of Lands, Forestry Division, which maintains the splendid demesne as a forest park and centre of forestry research. The house has in recent years been restored by the Board of Works.

Avonmore, Annamoe, co Wicklow. A 2 storey Georgian house with an unusually long front of 11 bays. Eaved roof; entrance door not central.

Ayesha Castle (formerly known as **Victoria Castle**), **Killiney, co Dublin** (WARREN/LGI1912; LLOYD *of Lossett*/LGI1958; AYLMER/IFR). A romantic C19 castle of ashlar with a round tower and various turrets by the side of Killiney Bay, built *ca* 1850 by Robert Warren, of Killiney Castle, who named it Victoria Castle, presumably in honour of the Queen's visit to Dublin for the Exhibition of 1853. It later became a residence of Rev Humphrey Lloyd, FRS, of Lossett, co Cavan, Provost of Trinity College, Dublin 1867–81, and remained in the Lloyd family until the present century. Gutted by fire towards the end of the Lloyd ownership; afterwards restored, and its name changed to Ayesha Castle. Bought by Col R. M. Aylmer 1947.

Ayesha Castle

B

Bagenalstown House, Bagenalstown, co Carlow. A 2 storey Georgian house with a front of 2 curved bows joined by a conservatory. The home of Mr John Hedges Becher (of the family of BECHER/IFR, but not actually included in the pedigree).

Bailieborough Castle, Bailieborough, co Cavan (YOUNG, Bt, *of Bailieborough*/PB; COCHRANE, Bt/PB). An irregular 2 storey Victorian house with a gabled and buttressed Gothic porch. The seat of C19 politician and proconsul, Sir John Young, 1st and last Lord Lisgar, Chief Secretary for Ireland, Lord High Commissioner of the Ionian Isles, Governor of New South Wales and Governor-General of Canada.

Ballaghtobin, Callan, co Kilkenny (KNOX/IFR; GABBETT/IFR). A Georgian house, built by a descendant of William Baker, who was granted the estate, which had originally belonged to the Tobin family, 1660; subsequently reduced in size and inherited towards the end of C19 by a branch of the Knox family, from whom it passed by inheritance to the present owner, Lt-Col R. E. Gabbett. In 1953, finding the house "ugly and awkward", Col Gabbett demolished the greater part of it, and built a 2 storey modern house in the Georgian style, incorporating what remained. The architect of the new house was Mr Donald A. Tyndall.

Ballea Castle, Carrigaline, co Cork (HODDER/IFR; DORMAN/IFR). An "L"-shaped C17 tower-house with a doorway guarded by an iron yett, given regularly-disposed sash windows in the Georgian period. Large drawing room on first floor. Small courtyard at one side of castle with old chapel, still roofed and intact. A seat of the Hodder family; bought in the present century by R. H. Dorman, sold after his death 1949. Bought late 1950s by Mr A. F. Clark, now of Ringabella House (*qv*), who remodelled the interior of the castle, making a new drawing room downstairs. Now the home of Mr David Jackson.

Ballibay House, Ballybay, co Monaghan (LESLIE/LGI1912). A fine Classical house of 1830 by John B. Keane, built for C.A. Leslie. Of 2 storeys, over a high basement; 3 bay entrance front, the centre bay being recessed, with a Wyatt window above a single-storey Doric portico. Adjoining front of 5 bays, the centre bay breaking forward under a pediment-gable and having a tripartite window in its lower storey. Apart from this window, all the windows in the

lower storey were set in arched recesses; also those in the basement, and the centre window in the upper storey of the side elevation. Eaved roof on bracket cornice. A 3 storey gable-ended range was added behind the house later in C19. Now demolished.

Ballinaboola House, co Wexford. A house with an eaved roof and a C19 single-storey 3 sided bow.

Ballinaboy, Clifden, co Galway (MORRIS/IFR). A late-Georgian house of 1 storey over a basement, which becomes a ground floor on the garden front where the ground falls away. 3 bay entrance front; fanlighted doorway. Recently enlarged by the addition of a wing at one side in the contemporary style, with "picture" windows, containing a large reception room on the upper floor.

Ballinacarriga

Ballinacarriga, Kilworth, co Cork (CORBAN-LUCAS, *sub* LUCAS/IFR). A 3 storey 5 bay C18 house, originally a seat of the Pyne family; bought *ca* the 1850s by Laurence Corban, who lived nearby at Maryville (*qv*), as a wedding present for his daughter when she married John Lucas; the son of the marriage, A. J. Corban-Lucas, refaced the house *ca* 1880 and added single-storey 2 bay wings, as well as an enclosed porch entered at the side and with a round-headed front-facing window glazed in Romanesque style. The porch was replaced by a simpler porch by A. J. L. Corban-Lucas 1936, when the centre of the house had to be reconstructed owing to a severe attack of dry-rot. 2 drawing rooms opening into each other with double doors to form a ballroom, one of the 2 rooms being in one of the wings. Both rooms have C19 plasterwork cornices; the room in the wing has a more elaborate one, and also a more ornate chimneypiece: Victorian, and of white marble.

Ballinaclough House, Nenagh, co Tipperary (BAYLY/IFR). A 2 storey gable-ended house with irregular fenestration; round-

Ballinaclough House

headed windows, with simple fanlights in all of them; fanlighted entrance doorway, which is not central to the front. Ogee headed windows in gable end.

Ballinacor

Ballinacor, Rathdrum, co Wicklow (KEMMIS/IFR; LOMER, *sub* ST ALBANS, D /PB). A 2 storey late C18 house, enlarged, refaced and reroofed in C19. 3 bay entrance front, Wyatt window in centre of upper storey, single-storey Ionic portico below. End elevation of 6 bays, 3 being in a shallow curved bow. Entablatures on console brackets over windows in both storeys. C19 gabled office wing and conservatory at right angles to side elevation, with Italianate campanile at junction of main block and wing. Clock with two faces in campanile, the same age as Big Ben, which keeps time for the whole countryside. Stone-flagged entrance hall with C19 plasterwork cornice. Large toplit 2 storey hall with oval lantern and oval gallery with ironwork balustrade. Magnificent demesne, with wooded hills crowned by high mountains. Mile-long oak walk; mile-long avenue from front gate to house, bordered by rhododendrons and firs. Deer park with red and Japanese deer; the River Avonbeg flows below the house with many cascades and gorges. On the death of Captain W. D. O. Kemmis 1965, Ballinacor was bequeathed to his maternal cousin, Major Richard Lomer.

Ballinafad

Ballinafad, Balla, co Mayo (BLAKE/IFR).
A rather conservative late-Georgian house
built 1827 by Maurice Blake and his wife,
Anne, daughter and heir of Marcus Lynch;
who were, incidentally, the maternal grand-
parents of George Moore, the writer. Of 2
storeys over a high, slightly rusticated basement; 5 bay entrance front, with wider
spacing between the centre bay and the
bays on either side of it, than between the
outer bays. Arched perron and double steps
and iron railings in front of the fanlighted
hall door, which is now obscured by a later
C19 enclosed porch with pretty diamond
glazing. Parapeted roof; chimneys grouped
into one exceptionally long stack (the
longest which Dr Craig knows of). Symmetrical 5 bay rear elevation with large
fanlighted staircase window in centre.
Square entrance hall with plasterwork
frieze. Staircase of wood with slender
turned balusters; short lengths of plaster-
vaulted corridor. Drawing room ceiling
with circular and rectangular mouldings;

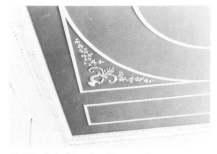

Ballinafad: Drawing Room ceiling

central acanthus rosette and pretty plasterwork in corners: birds, a tripod, a lyre,
shamrocks and cornucopiae. Dining room
with simple cornice and oval of plasterwork
in centre of ceiling; early C19 black marble
Ionic chimneypiece. Acquired from Lt-Col
Llewellyn Blake *ca* 1908 by African Mis-
sionary Brothers, who enlarged it sympathetically in the same style as a college.
The college has recently closed down; in
1976 the property was for sale.

Ballinakill House

Ballinahina, White's Cross, co Cork
(HALL/IFR). A Georgian house with a fanlighted doorway.

Ballinahy, co Tipperary (*see* ANNER
CASTLE).

Ballinakill House: Drawing Room

**Ballinakill House, Waterford, co Water-
ford** (POWER/IFR). A gable-ended late C17
or early C18 house of 2 storeys with a
dormered attic, incorporating an old tower-
house which is not visible from the outside.
5 bay front, made irregular *ca* 1770 by the
insertion of 2 much larger windows in the
upper storey at one end, lighting the 1st
floor drawing room which was formed at
that time. Porch with 2 Tuscan columns
and pediment. Lower 2 storey 1 bay wing.
Slightly curving C18 wooden staircase going
up to the top of the house, and lit by small
fanlighted windows. Spacious 1st floor
landing with shouldered doorcases. On one
side of the landing is a room in the old
tower, which has a recently-uncovered C17
stone fireplace, as well as a small C18
chimneypiece of black marble. On the other
side is the drawing room, which has a
magnificent plasterwork ceiling of *ca* 1770,
with foliage and husk ornament in compartments, and a cornice of flowers. The
room also has particularly fine C18 joinery:
a dado, a shouldered doorcase and shouldered and scrolled architraves round the
windows, which are on three sides, those at
one end commanding a spectacular view of
Waterford Harbour. Originally the seat of
the Dobbin family; sold 1788 to Nicholas
Power, whose son, Nicholas Mahon-Power,
ceased to occupy it when he acquired the
nearby Faithlegg House (*qv*) 1819. It was
subsequently acquired by another branch
of the Dobbins, from whom it was inherited
by Mrs Patricia Gossip. Mrs Gossip and
her son, Mr George Gossip, have, over the
past few years, been carrying out a thorough
and sympathetic restoration of the house.
The drawing room ceiling, part of which
had fallen, was restored by Mr William
Garner under the auspices of the Irish
Georgian Society 1970.

Ballinaminton, Clara, Offaly. A C18
house of 3 storeys over a basement. 5 bay
front; doorcase with baseless pediment on
console brackets, round-headed window
over. Wall carried up to be roof parapet. In
1814 the residence of George Marsh.

Ballinamona, Cashel, co Tipperary
(GILBEY, Bt/PB). A 2 storey late-Georgian
house. 3 bay front, fanlighted doorway
obscured by later 2 bay side-entered porch
with simple pilasters and corner-pilasters;
round-headed tripartite windows in lower
storey on either side of centre. 3 bay side.
Internal fanlight between hall and stairs.
The seat of the Murphy family; passed by
inheritance to Mrs Ralph Gilbey.

Ballinamona Park

**Ballinamona Park, nr Waterford, co
Waterford** (CAREW/IFR). A 2 storey basically
C18 centre block of 4 bays, with single-
storey 3 bay wings added 1866. Centre block
has an eaved roof carried on a bracket cornice; C19 entablatures over ground floor
windows; fanlighted doorway and elegant
late-Georgian portico with coupled Ionic
columns of wood. In its present form, the
house is a rebuilding following a fire 1894,
which gutted the centre block. Before the
fire, the centre block was of 3 storeys; presumably the "well built house" mentioned
by Charles Smith in his *History of Waterford*
1746 as the seat of Thomas Carew; a house
built on the site of a house or castle of 1488,
the foundations of which can be seen in the
present basement. Panelled hall; large
drawing room opening into a charming C19
conservatory which, like the portico, survived the fire. Dining room with carved oak
overmantel. The house still faces along the
"handsome canal" which existed in Smith's
time; but it is now more of a lake, having
been given a naturalistic appearance in C19.

Ballinamona Park

On a hill in the park there is a C16 brick
watch-tower, occupying the site of an older
Danish tower. Particularly handsome farm
buildings, including barns with massive
stone pillars carrying their roofs. Robert
Carew of Ballinamona, the son of Thomas

Carew who owned the estate when it was described by Smith, was known as "Boots" Carew from having once attended a Parliamentary debate in his boots. (He is not to be confused with "Tottenham in his Boots", who lived at Tottenham Green, co Wexford —*qv*).

Ballinamore House

Ballinamore House, Kiltimagh, co Mayo (ORMSBY/IFR). A mid to late C18 house of 2 storeys over a basement, with a simple 5 bay front of unusually satisfying proportions. Pedimented tripartite doorway, with broad flight of steps leading up to it. Sold 1938 to Order of St John of God, which gave it to the Western Care Association as an institution for mentally handicapped children 1974.

Ballina Park, Ashford, co Wicklow (TIGHE/IFR). A long, low, 2 storey house, originally built at the end of C17 by an ancestor of the present owner, but long used only as a secondary residence to the nearby Rossana (*qv*). It was re-roofed, remodelled and a wing added some time in C18 or early C19; so that the present fenestration of the 7 bay principal front, which has a projecting central bay with a Wyatt window in its upper storey, is late-Georgian. Low-ceilinged rooms; an attractive small, partly curving staircase with slender balusters of wood.

Ballinclea, Killiney, co Dublin (TALBOT, *sub* TALBOT DE MALAHIDE, B/PB). A 2 storey house of early to mid-C19 aspect. Entrance front with single-storey portico between 2 shallow 3 sided bows with Wyatt windows. Triangular and segmental pediments over windows; balustraded roof parapet. Now demolished.

Ballinderry, Ballinasloe, co Galway (COMYN/IFR). A plain mid to late C18 house, now derelict.

Ballinderry, Carbury, co Kildare. A 2 storey 3 bay mid-C18 house with a Venetian window above a pedimented doorway. In 1814, the residence of Thomas Tyrrell.

Ballindoon House (formerly **Kingsborough**), **Derry, co Sligo** (STAFFORD-KING-HARMAN, Bt/PB and *sub* KINGSTON, E/PB). An early C19 house with a dome, in the manner of John Nash. Now the home of Mrs Peter Baden-Powell.

Ballingarrane (formerly known as **Summerville**), **Clonmel, co Tipperary** (WATSON/IFR). A house of *ca* 1797, possibly an early work of Richard Morrison, who was living in Clonmel at that time; of 2 storeys over a basement in front and 3 storeys behind.

Ballingarrane

Front of 5 bays, doorcase with baseless pediment and Doric column; steps with elegant wrought-iron railings; good quoins. Small 2 storey 1 bay wings set back; gateway with tall piers and pineapple finials at side, leading to yard. Slightly curving stairs with slender wooden balusters at back of hall; drawing room with Adamesque frieze; dining room with black marble chimneypiece which probably came out of an earlier C18 house, as did another black marble chimneypiece in a bedroom. Very attractive garden laid out by present owners, Col Sidney Watson, the historical biographer, and Mrs Watson; with vistas of lawns, flowers and shrubs extending in several directions; garden gate made from the doorcase of a demolished house in Clonmel.

Ballingarry, co Limerick: The Turret (ODELL/LGI1958). A 3 storey house, 1 room deep, with a curvilinear gable at one end of its front; built 1683 by Major John Odell; said to have incorporated a turret surviving from an old house of the Knights Hospitallers, hence its name. Became a presbytery at the end of C19, when an enclosed porch was added on the front and a wing at the back.

Ballinkeele, nr Enniscorthy, co Wexford (MAHER/IFR). A Classical house of *ca* 1840 by Daniel Robertson. 2 storey, long office wing at one side. Massive porte cochère with monolithic Tuscan columns. Corinthian columns and pilasters of scagliola in hall. Stair rail curving round stone column at foot of stairs. Old keep in park near house.

Ballinlough Castle

Ballinlough Castle, Clonmellon, co Westmeath (NUGENT, Bt, *of Ballinlough*/PB). The Nugents of Ballinlough (who are really O'Reillys, having assumed the surname of Nugent to inherit a legacy 1812) are almost unique in being a Catholic Celtic-Irish family who still live in their ancient castle; for the other Celtic-Irish families who have remained Catholic and kept their ancestral homes have almost all abandoned their castles in favour of houses built at a

later period. At Ballinlough, the old castle was never abandoned but reconstructed in 1730s so that it assumed the appearance of a pleasant 2 storey 7 bay house of the period, with narrow windows, a breakfront centre and a segmental-pedimented doorcase; originally it had a high-pitched roof, but was re-roofed at a later date, probably *ca* 1780 when the breakfront was raised a storey to form a tower-like central attic, which was battlemented, like the rest of the roof-line, to make it in keeping with the higher 2 storey castellated range which was added at this period at right angles to the original front, by Hugh O'Reilly (afterwards 1st Bt), who eventually assumed the surname of Nugent. The new range, which has two slender round corner towers, is rather similar to one side of Malahide Castle, co Dublin (*qv*), the home of Hugh O'Reilly's brother-in-law, which was re-built about 10 years earlier; so that it seems likely that the work at Ballinlough and Malahide is by the same architect or builder; Dr Rowan suggests it might be the amateur architect, Thomas Wogan Browne, of Castle Browne (*qv*), who was himself connected to both families. The delicate Gothic plasterwork in the drawing room and dining room incorporates some neo-Classical elements; and the drawing room chimneypiece is identical to one known to be by Wyatt at Curraghmore, co Waterford (*qv*). The other notable interior is the hall, in the earlier part of the

Ballinlough Castle: Hall

castle and dating, in its present form, from *ca* 1750. It rises through 2 storeys and is spanned by a bridge-gallery, behind which is the staircase; a very unusual arrangement for its period, though one of which there is another example only a couple of miles away across the Meath border at Drewstown (*qv*). The decoration of the hall at Ballinlough is of a much higher quality than that of the Drewstown hall; there are panels of fruit and flowers in plasterwork on the walls, a cornice in the same style and a richly carved frieze of acanthus below the gallery balustrade; which, like that of the staircase, has slender wooden balusters.

Ballinrobe, co Mayo (KENNY/IFR). A 2 storey Georgian house at Ballinrobe, built *ca* 1740 by Courtney Kenny so that he could keep an eye on the family corn mill here; the former family seat, Roxburgh, being too far from the town to be convenient. 7 bay front, which must have been altered towards the end of C18 or at the beginning of C19, since it has a central Wyatt window above a late-Georgian fanlighted doorway with recessed Ionic columns. At one end of the house is an archway. The house now has a road running immediately in front of it; but before the road was made, it faced over a pleasure-ground by the River Robe. After the advent of the road, a tunnel was constructed under it to enable the family to reach their pleasure-ground without, as was said, being run over by donkey-carts. There are attractive grounds behind the house, including a formal garden and a beech walk. The home of Mr Courtney Kenny, the well-known concert pianist.

Ballinsperrig, co Cork (*see* ANNGROVE).

Ballintaggart, Colbinstown, co Kildare (BONHAM/IFR). A gabled late C19 house rather like a Scotch lodge, added 1893-94 to a plain early C19 house with a Wyatt window by Col John Bonham, whose architect is said to have been Richard Orpen, brother of Sir William Orpen, the painter. Of limestone random ashlar; high gable at one side, small dormer-gables near it; some window mullions of stone, others of wood; porch with pointed gable and finial.

Ballin Temple

Ballin Temple, Tullow, co Carlow (BUTLER, Bt, *of Cloughgrenan*/PB). A handsome 3 storey mid or late Georgian house with a 5 bay entrance front of which the central bay was given emphasis by a Venetian window and a pedimented Grecian Doric porte-cochère; the latter being presumably an early C19 addition. In the centre of the garden front was a colonnaded semi-circular bow. The house stood as a shell for many years after being burnt; but has now been demolished.

Ballintober, Ballinhassig, co Cork (MEADE, CLANWILLIAM, E/PB; MEADE/LG 1972). A house of 2 storeys with a dormered attic built during 2nd half of C17 by Lt-Col William Meade. 7 bay centre with gable-ended projecting wings; pediments over 1st floor windows; tall chimneys. Long 2 storey service range at side. Forecourt with railings and tall rusticated piers; formal garden with banked terraces and balustraded steps to a gateway, also with rusticated piers. In 1765 Sir John Meade, 4th Bt, married the heiress of the Hawkins Magill family of Gill Hall,

Ballintober

co Down (*qv*), becoming 1st Earl of Clanwilliam 1776. His interests were henceforth centred on his wife's estates, and he sold Ballintober and his other estates in co Cork 1787 to his cousin, Rev John Meade, whose nephew was the ancestor of the Meades who lived at Ballintober until the present century. The house was demolished in 1940s.

Ball's Grove, Drogheda, co Louth (BALL/IFR). A very good early C18 house of brick. 2 storeys over basement; solid roof parapet with shallow recessed panels. Fine triumphal arch at entrance to demesne, with armorial bearings in tympanum and wicket gate surmounted by oval recess. The seat of the Ball family.

Ballyanahan, Rockmills, co Cork. A small Georgian house. Handsome pedimented front with cut-stone dressings. The seat of a branch of the Barry family; in recent years of Dr T. St J. Barry, father of Rev N. P. Barry, OSB, Headmaster of Ampleforth College.

Ballyanne House, New Ross, co Wexford (TYNDALL/LGI1912). A house with fine late C18 interiors. Staircase with alternate wood and iron balusters; plasterwork panels on walls. Ballroom, afterwards dining room, with coved ceiling. Drawing room with transitional plasterwork in low relief. Library with Adamesque ceiling. In 1814 the residence of Gen Ambrose. Now totally demolished.

Ballyarnett, Derry, co Derry (MCCORKELL/LGI1958; and *sub* BROWNE/IFR). A late C19 house, built by D. B. McCorkell, incorporating an earlier house said to date back to the Siege of Derry.

Ballyarthur, Woodenbridge, co Wicklow (BAYLY, *sub* ANGLESEY, M/PB). A 2 storey 5 bay late C17 house, refronted in early C19 with battlements, a battlemented pediment and Wyatt windows. Interior panelling; late C17 painting in dining room. Late C18 drawing room.

Ballyarthur

Ballybricken, Ringaskiddy, co Cork (CONNER/IFR). A C18 house of 2 storeys over a basement on the southern side of Cork Harbour. 6 bay entrance front, with a mezzanine storey fitted in on either side of the centre, as at Kilshannig (*qv*). Pair of round-headed windows in centre above pedimented tripartite doorcase with fanlight, round-headed flanking windows, engaged columns and pilasters.

Ballybroony, co Mayo. A 2 storey 5 bay mid-C18 house of rough-cut stone, flanked by quadrants, one of them with niches. Gibbsian doorcase. C19 roof.

Ballyburly

Ballyburly, Edenderry, Offaly (WAKELY/LGI1912). A house of late C17 or early C18 aspect, probably built either by John Wakely who was MP for Kilbeggan in 1692 and died *ca* 1713, or by his son, Thomas. 11 bay front, 5 bay centre with very high pediment; doorcase with entablature and pilasters; high-pitched roof on bracket cornice. Burnt 1888; afterwards rebuilt to the design of James Franklin Fuller.

Ballycanvan House, Waterford, co Waterford (POWER/IFR; GALLWEY/IFR). A C18 house built onto an old castle. Doorway with broken pediment and engaged Doric columns, not centrally placed. The seat of the Bolton family, before they built the nearby Faithlegg House (*qv*); bought, together with Faithlegg, by the Power family 1819 and eventually inherited by Mrs H. W. D. Gallwey (*née* Power). Afterwards demolished; the doorway is now at Georgestown House (*qv*).

Ballycarron House, Golden, co Tipperary (BUTLER/IFR). A 2 storey 5 bay Georgian house. 1 bay pedimented breakfront; round-headed window above fanlighted doorway. Interior fanlight at back of hall. Handsome entrance gates, with pedimented and rusticated wickets; Gothic lodge facing.

Ballycastle, co Antrim: Manor House (BOYD/LGI1958). A mid-C18 house. Archway above which was set a statue of an

Indian river god, probably brought home by Major-Gen Hugh Boyd of the Bengal Army at the time of the Mutiny. Stable block with cutstone window surrounds. Now a Barnardo Home; little remains of the original house.

Ballyclough, Kilworth, co Cork (BURY-BARRY/LGI1958 and *sub* BURY/IFR). A 2 storey house with a mildly Gothic c19 front of 7 bays. Stepped gables, battlements, a pair of buttresses at either end; mullioned windows. Hall with impressive Tudor-Revival staircase. The greater part of the house has now been demolished.

Ballyclough House, Ballysheedy, co Limerick (FURNELL/IFR). A plain 2 storey 5 bay late c18 house with an eaved roof and a projecting porch. Sold 1973.

Ballyconnell House, co Cavan

Ballyconnell House, Ballyconnell, co Cavan (ENERY/LGI1863; ROE/LGI1912). A house built 1764 by G. Montgomery on the site of Ballyconnell Castle, which had been burnt. 2 storey; 5 bay front; 2 bay side; high-pitched roof. c19 bowed porch.

Ballyconnell House, Falcarragh, co Donegal (OLPHERT/LGI1912). A long, rambling, 2 storey house, with a few mid-c19 Tudor-Revival touches: low-pitched gables, hood mouldings over some of the windows, and single-storey mullioned rectangular bows.

Ballyconra House (during 1st Butler Rally)

Ballyconra House, Ballyragget, co Kilkenny (BUTLER, MOUNTGARRET, V/PB; CA-HILL/IFR). An early c18 gable-ended house with a high, parapeted roof; the seat of the Butlers, Viscounts Mountgarret, after they abandoned their earlier seat of Ballyragget Castle. 2 storey, with an attic lit by windows in the gable ends; 7 bay front, doorway with pilasters and entablature, above which is a stone panel with a coat-of-arms, brought from another old Butler castle in the neighbourhood. Low ceilinged rooms. Large hall, with a ceiling of somewhat bucolic rococo plasterwork; doorcases of good c18 joinery. Wooden staircase going up round inner hall, with additional flight to attic. Drawing room to left of hall had plasterwork ceiling which fell earlier this century and was re-

placed with a plain ceiling; more plasterwork in small study to the right of hall. Dining room behind study, divided in the middle by a thick arch pierced through the main wall of the house, the other half of the room being an addition. This room is said to be haunted by the ghost of Edmund, 12th Viscount Mountgarret and 1st and last Earl of Kilkenny, who died 1846 and was the last Mountgarret to live here; a benign spectre in a high collar and stove pipe hat, who has also been seen going up the stairs. After the death of the Earl of Kilkenny, the house was occupied by Michael Cahill, agent to the subsequent Viscount Mountgarret, by whose descendants it was afterwards acquired.

Ballycross, Bridgetown, co Wexford (ROWE/LGI1858). A 3 storey 5 bay Georgian house with a small portico.

Ballycullen, Askeaton, co Limerick (NAISH/LGI1875). A 3 storey c18 house with a tripartite fanlighted doorway. Plasterwork of mid-c18 type in hall ceiling; staircase of good joinery with gallery. Recently restored.

Ballycurrin Castle, co Mayo (LYNCH/VSA). A late-Georgian house built 1828 by Capt Peter Lynch, replacing an earlier house said to have been built in c17 by Maurice Lynch. Of 2 storeys over a basement, with cut-stone quoins and other facings. Fine situation overlooking Lough Corrib; ruined castle in grounds.

Ballycurry: Entrance Front

Ballycurry, Ashford, co Wicklow (TOT-TENHAM/IFR). A c18 house of the Boswell family, of 2 storeys and 7 bays with a pedimented breakfront centre, which passed to the Tottenhams with the marriage of Frances Boswell to Charles Tottenham, MP; who rebuilt the house *ca* 1808 to the design of Francis Johnston. Of 2 storeys; entrance front of 6 bays without pediment; single-storey Grecian Doric portico with fluted columns and triglyph frieze. At one end of the front there is now a projecting wing added in the Victorian period. Garden front with 1 bay on either side of shallow curved bow. Hall with screen of fluted

Ballycurry: Garden Front

Grecian Doric columns and frieze of triglyphs and ox-skulls. The bow-fronted drawing room, the dining room and the library, all have typical early c19 plasterwork friezes. Pedimented bookcases in library.

Ballydarton, nr Leighlinbridge, co Carlow (WATSON/IFR). An early to mid-c19 Gothic house, possibly by one of the Robertsons, of Kilkenny. Main square battlemented tower flanked by gables and polygonal turret. The home of Robert Watson, a famous Victorian MFH, who was so fond of hunting that he thought he would be reincarnated as a fox; at his funeral mourners cried "Gone away!"

Ballydivity, Ballymoney, co Antrim (STEWART MOORE/IFR). A 2 storey 3 bay house of *ca* 1760; door with square fanlight. Added to from *ca* 1810. Central staircase; drawing room extended 1911.

Ballydonelan Castle

Ballydonelan Castle, Loughrea, co Galway (DONELAN/LGI1912; MAHON/LGI-1912 and *sub* MAHON, Bt/PB). A long low and narrow 2 storey c17 house with an old castle at one end of it, the seat of the Donelans; enlarged and remodelled by a c18 Donelan who transformed the castle into a flanking wing higher than the c17 range and built a similar wing to balance it at the other end; the wings being treated as end-pavilions, with truncated pyramidal roofs and cupolas and Venetian windows. One of these Venetian windows lit a vast room running the full depth of the left-hand wing, with a bow at the back. The low c17 range in the middle was given sash windows; it was of 8 bays and had 2 doorways, one being the entrance and the other a dummy, to balance it; the centre of the front being taken up with the drawing room. Some time *post* 1787 the cupolas were removed and the wings were given less steep pyramidal roofs; and the centre range was given a 4 bay pedimented breakfront. Ballydonelan subsequently became the seat of a branch of the Mahon family. One wing was burnt some time *ante* 1913; the house is now in ruins.

Ballyduff, Thomastown, co Kilkenny (CONNELLAN/LGI1912; SOLLY-FLOOD/LGI 1912). A Georgian house with a fanlighted doorway joined by a wing to an old tower. Library with carved oak bookcases. Inherited by Marguerite, Mrs Solly-Flood (*née* Connellan); now the home of her son-in-law and daughter, Major & Mrs D. J. O. Thomas.

Ballydugan House, Portaferry, co Down (KEOWN-BOYD/LGI1886; BROWNLOW/IFR). A 3 storey, 5 bay Georgian house, with 2 storey bow-fronted wings.

Ballyedmond, Midleton, co Cork (COURTENAY, *sub* BELL/LGI1958; SMITH-BARRY/IFR). An imposing winged house of different periods, partly by the elder and the younger Abraham Hargrave. The main block late Georgian, 2 storey over basement, 6 bay, parapeted roof, 2 bay breakfront centre with die and Doric porch. The wings were of the same height as the main block, set at right angles to it and joined to it by lower links; they also resembled the main block in style, but were more early Victorian in character, having roofs carried on bracket cornices. In the entrance front, the wings ended with blank walls, each relieved with a shallow recess framed by concentric arches between 2 niches. Entrance hall with pilasters and floor of black and white marble pavement. Imposing staircase of wood, with barley-sugar uprights, in room to right of entrance hall. Large drawing room and dining room in garden front; drawing room latterly decorated in Louis Seize style, with panels of watered silk. Smaller rooms in wings, which contained additional living rooms rather than offices. Handsome stable range facing entrance front. Entrance gates with twin lodges. Passed by descent to R. H. Smith-Barry, 4th son of John Smith-Barry of Fota, co Cork (*qv*) and Eliza-Mary Courtenay; sold *ca* 1960 by Guy Smith-Barry. Subsequently demolished and the demesne devastated.

Ballyedmond, Killowen, co Down (DOUGLAS-NUGENT/IFR). A Victorian Tudor-Baronial house, with pointed gables, mullioned windows and a battlemented tower and conical-roofed turret. Now an hotel.

Ballyeigan, Birr, Offaly (MULLINS/LG 1875). A Classical house of *ca* 1830; 2 storeys over basement, 3 bay front; entrance door recessed beneath a Grecian propylaeum, with two Doric columns and acroteria. Eaved roof on bracket cornice.

Bally Ellis

Bally Ellis, nr Gorey, co Wexford (JERVIS-WHITE-JERVIS, Bt/PB1940). A double gable-ended 2 storey early C18 house. 5 bay front, doorway with blocking, small single-storey Doric portico with paired columns, presumably a later addition. Derelict by the end of C19.

Ballyfin, Mountrath, co Leix (WELLESLEY-POLE, *sub* WELLINGTON, D/PB; COOTE, Bt/PB). The grandest and most lavishly appointed early C19 Classical house in Ireland; built between 1821 and 1826 by Sir Charles Coote, 9th Bt; replacing a long, plain house of 1778 which had been the seat of William Wellesley-Pole, afterwards 1st Lord Maryborough and 3rd Earl of Mornington, a brother of the great Duke of Wellington. Coote, the Premier Bt of Ireland, who bought the estate from Wellesley-Pole *ca* 1812, seems originally to have employed an architect named Dominick Madden, who produced a design for a 2 storey house with a long library at one side running from front to back, and extending into a curved bow in the centre of the side elevation; a room very similar to the library at Emo Court (*qv*), a few miles away. When this end of the house —which also contained a top-lit rotunda, another feature doubtless inspired by Emo —had been built, Coote switched from Madden to Sir Richard Morrison, who, assisted by his son, William Vitruvius Morrison, completed the house according to a modified plan, but incorporating Madden's library wing which forms the side elevation of Morrison's house, just as it would have done of Madden's; it is of 1 bay on either side of the central curved bow, which is fronted by a colonnade of giant Ionic columns. The side elevation is now prolonged by a gracefully-curving glass and iron conservatory of *ca* 1850. The principal front is of 13 bays with a giant pedimented Ionic portico; the 2 end bays on either side being stepped back. The interior, almost entirely by the Morrisons, is of great magnificence and beautifully finished, with exciting spatial effects and a wealth of rich plasterwork, scagliola columns in Siena, porphyry, green and black; and inlaid parquetry floors; originally the rooms contained a fine collection of pictures and sculpture and furniture said to have been made for George IV as Prince of Wales. A rather restrained entrance hall, with a coffered ceiling and a floor of mosaic brought from Rome, leads into the great top-lit saloon in the centre of the house, which has a coved ceiling decorated with the most elaborate plasterwork and a screen of Corinthian columns at each end. The saloon is flanked by the rotunda, which is surrounded by Ionic columns and has a coffered dome, and the staircase hall, which has pairs of engaged and recessed columns round its upper storey; the balustrade of the stairs and gallery being of brass uprights. There is a splendid vista through the centre of the house, from the staircase hall to the library, which lies at right angles to this central axis, beyond the rotunda; it is divided by screens of Ionic columns. The drawing room has a characteristic Morrison ceiling and gilt Louis Quinze decoration on the walls dating from 1840s and by a London decorator. Classical entrance gates with piers similar to those at Killruddery, co Wicklow and Fota, co Cork (*qqv*); and a folly castle in the park. Ballyfin was sold by the Coote family 1920s and is now a college run by the Patrician Brothers.

Ballyfin

Ballyfin: Rotunda

Ballyfin: Saloon ceiling

Ballygally Castle, nr Larne, co Antrim.
A unique example of a C17 Plantation Castle surviving intact, inhabited and un-

Ballygally Castle

Ballygally Castle : Doorway

changed, apart from the insertion of sash windows. Built 1625 by James Shaw. With its high roof, its 2 pepperpot bartizans, and its 2 curvilinear dormer-gables, which do not quite match, it looks for all the world like a little C16 or early C17 tower-house in Scotland. In 1814, the residence of Rev Thomas Alexander. Now an hotel.

Ballygarth Castle, Julianstown, co Meath (PEPPER/LGI1912). A tall tower-house with a 2 storey 3 bay castellated wing added to it. The old tower has C18 or early C19 battlements and a tripartite Gothic doorway.

Ballygawley Park, Ballygawley, co Tyrone (STEWART, Bt, of *Athenree*/PB). An early C19 Classical house of 2 storeys, with a 2 storey portico supported by two giant Doric columns and a shallow dome; built between 1825 and 1833 by Sir Hugh Stewart, 2nd Bt, MP, to the design of John Hargrave, of Cork. Now derelict.

Ballygiblin

Ballygiblin, nr Mallow, co Cork (WRIXON-BECHER, Bt/PB). A house re-modelled in Tudor-Baronial style, with a turret and spire, ca 1836, by William Vitruvius Morrison. The house flanked on one side by a detached Gothic orangery, with buttresses and pinnacles. Now a ruin.

Ballyglan, Woodstown, co Waterford (PAUL, Bt, *of Paulville*/PB1959; PROFUMO/ LGI1952). A 2 storey late C18 house overlooking Waterford Harbour; built by Sir Joshua Paul, 1st Bt. 7 bay front; pedimented doorcase with sidelights below slightly wider central window. 3 sided bow on side elevation, which formerly had an iron veranda along it. The house was formerly noted for its library. Sold *ca* 1963 to Major Philip Profumo, brother of John Profumo, sometime Secretary of State for War; re-sold *ca* 1971.

Ballyglunin Park

Ballyglunin Park

Ballyglunin Park, Monivea, co Galway (BLAKE/IFR). A C18 house of 2 storeys and 3 bays, with large mid and late C19 additions at the back of it and to one side. The C18 house has a 1 bay pedimented breakfront, with a Diocletian window above a Venetian doorway, both having blocked surrounds. The doorway has been made into a window, the entrance being now at what was originally the side of the house; in a gable-end of the C19 addition; where there is a very elaborate Victorian stone porch with balustrading and bits of entablature. At the back of C19 range is a squat round tower with a conical roof. Oval room, formerly hall, in centre of C18 front; with cornice of mutules, rococo plasterwork including eagle over

doors and C19 stencilled decoration on flat of ceiling. Drawing room adjoining with frieze of plasterwork, shouldered doorcases and good chimneypiece of white marble and Siena, with large reclining *putto*. Victorian staircase. Outbuildings close to house with square pyramidal-roofed tower. Sold *ca* 1964 by Mr Acheson Blake; now owned by Opus Dei and used as a conference centre.

Ballyhaise House, Ballyhaise, co Cavan (HUMPHRYS/LGI1912). An important house by Richard Castle, built *ca* 1733 for Brockhill Newburgh. Of 2 storeys over a basement, and 7 bays; faced in brick, with ashlar dressings. Entrance front with pedimented central feature of 4 Ionic pilasters superimposed on a Doric entablature and 4 Doric pilasters. Garden front with central curved bow, which has round-headed windows and a doorway under a consoled pediment. The bow contains an oval saloon which Dr Craig considers may well be the earliest surviving oval room in the British Isles; it keeps its original plasterwork on its ceiling, which, surprisingly, is a brick vault; the ground floor as well as the basement being vaulted over, as in the King House at Boyle, co Roscommon (*qv*). The doors and chimneypiece in the saloon are all curved. Sold *ca* 1800 to William Humphrys, who extended the house by adding 2 storey wings of the same height as the original block and also of brick with stone facings; but with a neo-Classical flavour; the slightly projecting end bays on the entrance front being framed by broad corner strip-pilasters, supporting entablatures with dies. The windows in these bays are tripartite, with entablatures over them on console brackets. Sold by the Humphrys family in the present century; now an agricultural college.

Ballyheigue Castle, nr Tralee, co Kerry (CROSBIE/IFR). The original house of the Crosbies here was long, low and thatched, facing onto an enclosed bawn or courtyard, in a corner of which was a strong stone tower, part of an old castle of the De Cantillons. It was in this tower that, in 1730, Thomas Crosbie placed the chests of silver which he had rescued from the Danish East Indiaman *Golden Lyon* when that vessel was lured into Ballyheigue Bay by wreckers and wrecked; his exertions in

Ballyhaise House

Ballyheigue Castle

saving the treasure and the crew of the ship proved too much for him, and he died from exposure and fatigue. Some months later the castle was attacked by rapparees and the treasure carried off; it was alleged that the attack was organised by Thomas Crosbie's widow, who subsequently obtained the bulk of the treasure. A new house appears to have been built *ca* 1758, which Col James Crosbie turned into a romantic castle *ca* 1809. His architects were Richard and William Vitruvius Morrison, the design being actually produced by the latter, though he was only 15 at the time. Like other Gothic and Tudor-Revival houses by the Morrisons, it was intended to represent a building dating from two different periods; the entrance front, in the words of Neale, "exhibiting the rich and ornamental style of the early part of the reign of Henry VIII"; whereas the elevation towards the sea had "the character and appearance of the castellated mansions of King Henry VI". In fact, the seaward elevation betrays itself very much as a 2 storey Georgian house which has been battlemented and had round and square towers and other pseudo-medieval features added to it; while the adjoining entrance front is a not very inspired gabled affair. And whereas Neale's well-known view shows the castle dramatically situated at the edge of a sheer cliff above the sea, it stands less spectacularly at the top of a gently sloping lawn, quite some way from the water's edge. A castellated outbuilding is joined to the castle by a long wall. Pierse Crosbie, the son of Col James Crosbie, had trouble with his wife, who eloped to the Continent with a groom—having previously bestowed her favours on stable-lads—and was never heard of again. The castle was burnt 1921, and is now a ruin.

Ballyhemock (or **Ballyhimmock**), **co Cork** (*see* ANNES GROVE).

Ballyhossett

Ballyhossett, Downpatrick, co Down (ANDERSON/LGI1958). A 2 storey, 5 bay C18 house with a single bay wing set back. The main block has a porch with Ionic pilasters, and the wing has a miniature breakfront, with pediment.

Ballyin, Lismore, co Waterford (ANSON, *sub* LICHFIELD, E/PB). A miller's house to which the prosperous flour-miller P. Foley added a new front in early C19, of 3 bays with a 1 bay breakfront and pediment-gable. Round-headed windows. Bought in 1930s by Hon Claud Anson.

Ballykealey

Ballykealey, Tullow, co Carlow (LECKY/LGI1937Supp). A somewhat stylized Tudor-Revival house of stucco with stone facings, built *ca* 1830 for John James Lecky to the design of Thomas A. Cobden, of Carlow. Symmetrical front of 2 storeys and high attic, with 3 unusually steep gables ending in finials; recessed centre with 3-light round-headed window edged with stone-work in a rope pattern above a stone Gothic porch of three arches. Tall Tudor chimney-stacks at either end; slender battlemented pinnacles rising from corbels at the angles of the roof parapet. Battlemented single storey wing at one side, prolonged by battlemented screen wall with Gothic gateway. Irregular wing with steep gables and dormers at back. Sold *ca* 1953. Now a Novitiate of the Patrician Brothers.

Ballykilcavan

Ballykilcavan, Stradbally, co Leix (WALSH-KEMMIS/IFR). A 2 storey early or mid-C18 house; entrance front of 7 bays with an open-bed pediment and advanced end bays, rather similar to the main block of Landenstown, co Kildare (*qv*). Staircase hall with unusual and very bucolic plaster-work on ceiling: shells and wings, circular and octangular panels. Small, low library with alcove on one side of hall, dining room of similar size on the other. Large and lofty drawing room in a late C18 addition built out at the back of the house, and entered from the half-landing of the stairs; it has an early C19 frieze of foliage. The drawing room addition, which is of 2 storeys, makes the garden front unbalanced; according to family tradition, a dining room was to be built to balance it, but work was suspended owing to 1798 Rebellion. The public road from Athy to Stradbally is aligned on the entrance front of the house, giving the impression of a long, straight avenue; the

Ballykilcavan: Stable Yard

vista from the house being closed at the far end by a church of *ca* 1800, with a Gothic tower. Near the house is an impressive stable yard, with a pediment and facings of ashlar.

Ballykilty, co Limerick (*see* PLASSEY HOUSE).

Ballyknockane, Ballingarry, co Limerick. A villa built from 1794 onwards by Capt Michael Scanlan, with single-storey bows at the sides and one in the centre of the front, serving as a porch. In the latter is a delightful curving fanlighted doorway with engaged Ionic columns between the door and sidelights; the fanlight being unusual in incorporating an enchanting little group of Classical figures. Interior fanlight between hall and staircase. Now the home of Mrs Murray.

Ballyknockane Lodge

Ballyknockane Lodge, Ballypatrick, co Tipperary (BUTLER, ORMONDE, M/PB). A shooting-lodge of the Ormonde family at the foot of Slievenaman; Victorian, of stone, with gables, overhanging roofs and bargeboards. The home of 5th Marquess of Ormonde, towards the end of his life, after he had given up living at Kilkenny Castle (*qv*).

Ballylin, Ferbane, Offaly (KING/LGI1958). A 2 storey early C19 villa by Richard Morrison; with a 3 bay entrance front identical to those of two other Morrison villas in Offaly, Bellair and Cangort Park (*qqv*); dominated by a remarkable deep arched recess with a concave surround, beneath which the entrance door was set. Side elevation with 1 bay on either side of a central curved bow; the ground floor windows being recessed under blind arches. Single storey addition with pilasters at the side of the entrance front. Now demolished.

Ballyline House (formerly **White House**), **Callan, co Kilkenny** (BARTON/IFR). An early Georgian house with a return added 1798. Occupied 1729 by William Chandler.

Ballylough House, Bushmills, co Antrim (TRAILL/IFR). A C18 house originally belonging to Archibald Stewart of Ballintoy; bought by the Traill family 1789. 2 storey over basement; 3 bay front. The front was subsequently given Wyatt windows; battlemented segmental flanking walls with niches were built 1815; and a wing was added, also in early C19. At some other date, the Tuscan doorcase was moved from the centre of the front to the right-hand bay, thereby spoiling the symmetry. Plasterwork in hall which may be contemporary with the original building of the house; plasterwork festoons, flowers and foliage elsewhere, probably later.

Ballymack House, Cuffesgrange, co Kilkenny (BARTON/IFR). A small Georgian house with a regular front and a fanlighted doorway; projection in centre of rear elevation. Acquired *ca* 1851 by the Townsend family.

Ballymaclary House, Magilligan, co Derry. An unusual probably mid-C18 house of 1 storey and an attic lit by windows in the gable-ends; said to have been a summer residence of the Cather family. 5 bay front; breakfront centre, with handsome pedimented tripartite doorway, the entablature being supported by Ionic half-columns and pilasters. Good C18 staircase rising from hall.

Ballymacmoy

Ballymacmoy, Killavullen, co Cork (HENNESSY/IFR). A 2 storey late-Georgian house on a rock overhanging the River Blackwater. Entrance front of 3 bays and curved bow; Wyatt windows, subsequently re-glazed with central mullions; fanlighted doorway now obscured by plain porch. Adjoining 3 bay front also with re-glazed Wyatt windows, facing onto terrace over river. Simple battlemented arch at opposite end of house. Hall with elaborate early to mid-C19 plasterwork: reeded cornice with rosettes, central oval of acanthus. Partly curving stair with slender wooden balusters at inner end of hall beyond arch with rope ornament. Fine doorcases with Doric entablatures and rope ornament on architraves. Cornices of oakleaves in drawing room and ante room. Bow-ended ballroom with higher ceiling than the other principal rooms and simpler and presumably earlier C19 plasterwork: oval moulding in centre of ceiling, with flat fan pendentives at corners. Fluted pilasters on walls. Oak chimneypiece in the "Arts and Crafts" style, with overmantel incorporating needlework panel, carved in 1905 by Harriette, widow of J.W. Hennessy. There is a similar oak fireplace in the dining room, which has been entirely done over in Edwardian Tudor; with a

beamed ceiling, timber-studded walls and painted coats-of-arms. Sold 1932 by Mr C. J. Hennessy to his kinsman, the late Monsieur J.R. Hennessy, of La Billarderie, Cognac. Now tenanted by Mr Ian Sherriff (*see* COOTE, Bt/PB), who runs it as a guest house.

Ballymacool

Ballymacool, Letterkenny, co Donegal (BOYD/LGI1958). A house said to have been originally built *ca* 1770, but rebuilt in Tudor-Revival early to mid-C19. 2 storey with a gabled and dormer-gabled attic; symmetrical entrance front, with projecting porch-gable between 2 wider gables; rectangular mullioned windows with hood mouldings over them, corbelled oriel above entrance door. Side elevation with 2 dormer gables and a gable, and a single-storey 3 sided bow. Other side with narrow tower-like projection, surmounted by small gable and finial. Single-storey wing at back.

Ballymagarvey, Balrath, co Meath. A 2 storey 5 bay gable-ended mid-C18 house with a steep pediment. Battlemented tower, probably early C19. The seat of the Osborne family.

Ballymaloe

Ballymaloe, Cloyne, co Cork (BOYLE, CORK AND ORRERY, E/PB; CORKER, *sub* CORCOR/LGI1912). A castle built towards the end of C16 by the FitzGeralds of Imokilly, enlarged 1602 by Sir John FitzEdmund FitzGerald; confiscated by Cromwell; occupied for a period after the Restoration by William Penn, of Pennsylvania, when he was managing his father's estate at Shanagarry, nearby; subsequently occupied by 1st Earl of Orrery, presumably while he was repairing and improving his nearby seat of Castle Martyr (*qv*); acquired towards end of C17 by Lt-Col Edward Corker; sold by him *ante* his death 1734 to Hugh Lumley, who added some new buildings to the castle some time *ante* 1750. As a result of Lumley's additions, Ballymaloe is now predominantly early C18 in character; consisting of a plain 2 storey 6 bay range with an old tower built into one end of it, and a 3 storey gable-ended range at right angles to the 2 storey range, and joined to it by a return; forming a house on an "L"-plan. Some of the

windows have thick early C18 glazing-bars. A staircase with thin turned balusters rises from the inner end of the hall, which has a ceiling with simple Adamesque decoration. The large room to the right of the hall has simple Adamesque frieze. *Ca* 1800, Ballymaloe was the residence of the Penn Gaskell family, who were descended from William Penn. In 1814, it was the residence of William Abbot. In 1837, it was owned by a Mr Forster; in 1908, it was occupied by William Litchfield. Until *ca* 1947, it was the home of Mr & Mrs J. M. Simpson; since then, it has been the home of Mr & Mrs Ivan Allen. Mrs Allen—who, as Myrtle Allen, is a well-known writer on cookery—now runs the house as a guest house and restaurant.

Ballymanus, Stradbally, co Leix (DENNEHY/LGI1958). A long, low 2 storey house of C19 appearance, with a gabled projection at either end and a recessed 3 bay centre. The end projections have a Wyatt window in their lower storey and are joined by a glazed loggia. Now the headquarters of Vasa Mink (Ireland).

Ballymascanion, co Louth: The Cottage. A single-storey early C19 gentleman's "cottage", with wide eaves, a central bow and a portico. In 1837 the seat of Mrs Rogers.

Ballymascanlon House, Ballymascanlon, co Louth (MCNEILL, *sub* MCNEILE/LGI1972). A Tudor-Revival house built *ca* 1840 for James Wolfe McNeill; with gables, mullioned windows, hood-mouldings and a recessed doorway. Now an hotel.

Ballymena Castle

Ballymena Castle, Ballymena, co Antrim (ADAIR, Bt/PB). A large Scottish-Baronial castle of 1870s by William Henry Lynn. Of rough-hewn ashlar, with a tall tower in the Balmoral manner. Some of the rooms had stained glass windows commemorating various members of the Adair family. Now demolished.

Ballymore, Cobh, co Cork (HARE, *sub* LISTOWEL, E/PB; O'DONOVAN/IFR). A 2 storey house of *ca* 1860 in the late-Georgian manner. 6 bay entrance front with fanlighted doorway, not centrally placed; front prolonged by archway to yard. Adjoining front, overlooking Cork Harbour, with 3 sided bow. The seat of a branch of the Hare (Listowel) family; bought *post* World War II by Mr V.T. O'Donovan. Now the home of Mr & Mrs E. F. Heckett.

Ballymore, Camolin, co Wexford (DON-OVAN/LGI1912). An early to mid-C18 gable-ended house. Pedimented front of 5 bays; Diocletian window in pediment; windows in upper storey higher than those below. Other front, also of 5 bays, with pedimented and rusticated doorcase and roof dormers.

Ballymore Castle

Ballymore Castle, Laurencetown, co Galway (SEYMOUR, *sub* HALE/LGI1958). An old tower house with a 2 storey, wide-eaved, bow-fronted house of *ca* 1800 built against the front of it; curved fanlighted doorway in bow.

Ballymoyer House

Ballymoyer House, Belleek, co Armagh (HART-SYNNOT/IFR). A 3 storey C18 block, with a pedimented doorway and a shallow curved bow, to which a much taller 3 storey block was added; the latter either built or refaced in 1st half of C19. This taller block had a projection with a curved bow, the lower storey of which was adorned with engaged Ionic columns; and a balustraded roof parapet. Brig-Gen A. H. S. Hart-Synnot sold the demesne, demolished the house owing to damage suffered from requisitioning and gave the avenue and glen to the National Trust 1938.

Ballynacourty, Ballysteen, co Limerick (STACPOOLE/IFR). A small Georgian house cleverly enlarged by its present owners, Mr George Stacpoole, the antique dealer and his wife Michelina, the designer of fashion knitwear, by the addition of an arcaded gallery along the front and a single-storey wing containing a large reception room.

Ballynacourty, co Limerick

Ballynacourty, Tipperary, co Tipperary (MASSY-DAWSON, *sub* MASSY, B/PB). A plain 2 storey cut-stone house with a polygonal pyramidal-roofed tower. Now demolished.

Ballynacree House

Ballynacree House, Ballymoney, co Antrim (MOORE, Bt, *of Moore Lodge*/PB). An earlier house of 2 storeys and 5 bays, remodelled in Victorian Italianate style 1861 to the design of Fitzgibbon Louch; faced in red brick with sandstone dressings. Segmental pediments on console brackets over ground floor windows; single-storey Ionic portico, the window over it being set in a recess; eaved roof on bracket cornice. Hall with Tower of the Winds columns; double staircase with iron balusters; richly moulded circles of acanthus on ceilings of 2 principal reception rooms, with cornices to match.

Ballynaguarde

Ballynaguarde, Ballyneety, co Limerick (CROKER/IFR). A house of 2 storeys over a high basement built 1774. 5 bay front with 3 bay pedimented breakfront; wing with an Ionic porch. The seat of the Crokers, of whom the notorious "Boss" Croker of Tammany was the grandson of a younger son (*see* GLENCAIRN, co Dublin). The house fell into ruin earlier this century; according to the writer, Frank O'Connor, there was a proposal to take the fine statue of Hercules, which stood by the front of the house, to Limerick; "but a committee of inspection, having studied him carefully fore and aft, decided that he would never do for the confraternities".

Ballynahinch Castle, Connemara, co Galway (MARTIN/IFR; BERRIDGE/IFR). A long, many-windowed house built in late

C18 by Richard Martin, who owned so much of Connemara that he could boast to George IV that he had "an approach from his gatehouse to his hall of thirty miles length" and who earned the nickname of "Humanity Dick" through founding the RSPCA. When Maria Edgeworth came

Ballynahinch Castle

Ballynahinch Castle

here 1833 the house had a "battlemented front" and "four pepperbox-looking towers stuck on at each corner"; but it seemed to her merely "a whitewashed dilapidated mansion with nothing of a castle about it". The "pepperbox-looking towers" no longer exist; but both the entrance front and the 8 bay garden front, which overlooks a superb stretch of water, have battlements, stepped gables, curvilinear dormers and hood mouldings; as does the end elevation. The principal rooms are low for their size. Entrance hall with mid-C19 plasterwork in ceiling. Staircase hall beyond; partly curving stair with balustrade of plain slender uprights. Long drawing room in garden front; oval of C18 plasterwork foliage in ceiling, rather like the plasterwork at Castle ffrench (*qv*). Also reminiscent of Castle ffrench are the elegant mouldings, with concave corners, in the panelling of the door and window recesses. Maria Edgeworth thought the drawing room "tolerably well furnished"; while remarking on how "the want of window curtains and rattling of window shutters and the total lack of bookcases gave the whole an unfinished, unlivable appearance". The principal rooms still have their doors of "magnificently thick well-moulded mahogany" which Miss Edgeworth thought "gave an air at first sight of grandeur"; though she complained that "not one of them would shut or keep open a single instant". The drawing room now has a C19 chimneypiece of Connemara marble. The dining room has an unusually low fireplace, framed by a pair of Ionic half-columns. "Humanity Dick" Martin was renowned for his extravagant way of life, and in order to escape his creditors he retired to Boulogne, where he died. He left the family estates heavily mortgaged, with the result that his granddaughter and eventual heiress, Mary Laetitia Martin, known as "The Princess of Connemara", was utterly ruined after the Great Famine, when Ballynahinch and the rest of her property was sold up by the Encumbered Estates Court; she and her husband being obliged to emigrate to America, where she died in childbirth soon after her arrival. Ballynahinch was bought by Richard Berridge, whose son sold it 1925; after which it was acquired by the famous cricketer, "Ranji", otherwise Maharaja Ranjitsinhji, Jam Sahib of Nawanagar. It is now an hotel.

Ballynahown Court

Ballynahown Court, Athlone, co Westmeath (MALONE/LGI1912; ENNIS, Bt/PB-1884; O'DONOGHUE OF THE GLENS/IFR; CROFTS-GREENE, *sub* CROFTS/IFR). One of the very few red-brick houses in this part of Ireland, built 1746 by Edmond Malone, MP. 3 storeys over basement; 3 bay front; pedimented and fanlighted tripartite doorway, the pediment extending over the door and side-lights and carried on pilasters. Parapeted roof. Single-storey wing, from its appearance an early C19 addition, at one side. Sold *ca* 1830 to Andrew Ennis; inherited by the family of The O'Donoghue of The Glens, by whom it was sold *ca* 1965 to Mr Basil Crofts-Greene, who re-sold it *ca* 1976.

Ballynalacken Castle, Lisdoonvarna, co Clare (O'BRIEN/LGI1912). A single-storey house with a curved bow, close to an old keep on a rock. The seat of the O'Brien family of which Lord Chief Justice Peter O'Brien, Lord O'Brien of Kilfenora (known irreverently as "Pether the Packer") was a younger son.

Ballynaparka, Cappoquin, co Waterford (DAVIS-GOFF, Bt/PB; VILLIERS-STUART/IFR). A 2 storey double bow-fronted early C19 house with an eaved roof. The home of the parents of Miss Muriel Bowen, the writer and journalist; afterwards the home of Sir Ernest Davis-Goff, 3rd and present Bt; now of Mr & Mrs James Villiers-Stuart, who formerly lived at Dromana (*qv*), nearby.

Ballynastragh, Gorey, co Wexford (ESMONDE, Bt/PB). Originally a C17 house, built by James Esmonde; enlarged and modernized by Sir Thomas Esmonde, 8th Bt, probably soon after he succeeded 1767; so that it became a house of mid-C18 appearance, of 3 storeys over a basement. Handsome 7 bay front with 3 bay breakfront; niche with statue in centre, above entrance

Ballynastragh

door; parapeted roof; good quoins; statues at ends of area parapet. Various alterations were carried out by Sir Thomas Esmonde, 9th Bt, between 1803 and 1825; including, probably, the addition of the single-storey Doric portico on the entrance front. Later in C19, the house was embellished and slightly castellated; probably in 2 phases; the architect, at any rate of the 2nd phase, being George Ashlin. A slender 5 storey battlemented tower was added on one side, and a projection with round-headed windows on the other. The parapet of the roof, as well as that of the portico, was battlemented. The garden front was given 2 Victorian 3 sided bows, of a style very characteristic of Ashlin, with 3 tiers of pilasters. The house was burnt 1923 and replaced 1937 by a new house in the Georgian style to the design of Mr Dermot Gogarty (son of Oliver St John Gogarty, of Renvyle—*qv*), who worked under Lutyens; and a connexion of the Esmonde family. It is of brick, 2 storeys and 5 bays; with a high-pitched sprocketed roof and a veranda recessed under the upper storey.

Ballynatray, Glendine, co Waterford (HOLROYD-SMYTH/IFR; PONSONBY/IFR and *sub* BESSBOROUGH, E/PB). A house of 2 storeys over a basement and 11 bays, built 1795-97 by Grice Smyth, incorporating some of the walls of a much earlier house

Ballynastragh

which itself was built on the foundations of an old castle; refaced in stucco and its principal rooms re-decorated early in the C19 by Grice Smyth; some work having been done *ca* 1806 by Alexander Deane. Entrance front with 3 bay recessed centre between 4 bay projections joined by single-storey Ionic colonnade with a statue in a

Ballynatray

Ballynatray

Ballynatray: Hall

Ballynatray: Billiard Room frieze

niche at either end. Balustraded roof parapet with urns. Garden front, facing down the Blackwater estuary, with 3 bay pedimented breakfront and 4 bays on either side. 5 bay side elevations. Early C19 interior plaster-work. Frieze of bulls' heads—as distinct from the neo-Classical ox-skulls or bucrania, a demi-bull being the Smyth crest—in hall. Unusual frieze of cues and billiard balls in billiard room. Wide arched doorways be-tween most of the principal rooms. By means of these arches, the library runs right through the house, with windows facing both the river and the park. The house is gloriously situated at a point where the river does a loop. Woods sweep outwards and round on either side and continue up and downstream for as far as the eye can see. On the landward side of the house is a hill, with a deer park full of bracken. There is an extraordinary sense of peace, of remoteness from the world. A short distance from the house is a ruined medieval abbey on an island which was joined to the main-land by a causeway built 1806 by Grice Smyth, who put up a Classical urn within the abbey walls in honour of Raymond-le-Gros, Strongbow's companion, who is said to be buried here. Also within the abbey walls is a statue of its founder, St Molanfide, which Grice Smyth's widow erected 1820. The 2nd daughter of Grice Smyth was the beautiful Penelope Smyth, whose runaway marriage with the Prince of Capua, brother of King Ferdinand II of the Two Sicilies (*see* RFW), caused an international furore in 1836. On the death of Mr Horace Holroyd-Smyth 1969, Ballynatray passed to his cousins, the Ponsonby family, of Kilcooley Abbey, co Tipperary (*qv*).

Ballyneale House, Ballingarry, co Lim-erick. A house of early C19 appearance, with flanking wings with elliptical arches. Centre block of 3 storeys over a high base-ment; 5 bay front, 1 bay breakfront; high

Ballyneale House

eaved roof on bracket cornice. In 1914, the residence of Daniel Hederman.

Ballynegall

Ballynegall, Mullingar, co Westmeath (SMYTH/IFR). A house built 1808 by James Gibbons, using stone from the old castle here, which was called Castle Reynell after the former owners of the estate, the Reynell family. Main block of 2 storeys over a basement; entrance front of 6 bays with 2 bay breakfront centre; single-storey Ionic portico; single-storey 2 bay wings. Dentil cornice below roof parapet. Garden front with central curved bow, and a single Wyatt window on either side of it in both storeys. Hall with fluted Ionic columns and plaster-work frieze in fan pattern. Stairs in inner hall with brass uprights. Drawing room with C19 wallpaper in pink and gilt, sten-cilled to represent decorative panels and pilasters; statuary marble chimneypiece with caryatids. Dining room in bow of garden front with plasterwork ceiling in an ivy-leaf pattern. Left by James Gibbons 1846 to his nephew by marriage, J. W. M. Berry, who carried out various improve-ments to the house and collected books for the library; and who left Ballynegall to a cousin, T. J. Smyth 1855. Remained in the Smyth family until 1963, when it was sold.

Ballynoe, Tullow, co Carlow (BARRATT/LGI969). A small late-Georgian house of 2 storeys over a basement. 3 bay front and sides; glazed and curving porch; eaved roof. Extended by 2 bay Victorian addition of 2

Ballynoe, co Limerick

storeys with pediment; further extensions again. In recent years the home of Major & Mrs S. G. R. Elton-Barratt.

Ballynoe, Ballingarry, co Limerick (COX/LGI1899). A 3 storey 4 bay Georgian block, probably a *ca* 1770 rebuilding by Hugh Cox of an early C18 house, itself a rebuilding of a C17 house. C19 eaved roof and pillared porch. Curved staircase. Now derelict.

Ballynoe House, Rushbrooke, co Cork (MURPHY/IFR). A 2 storey C19 house in the late-Georgian manner.

Ballynure, Grange Con, co Wicklow (CARROLL/LGI863). A 2 storey stucco-faced early C19 house of 4 bays between pedi-mented ends. Horizontal panels over central upper windows.

Ballyowen

Ballyowen (formerly **New Park**), **Cashel, co Tipperary** (PENNEFATHER, *sub* FREESE-PENNEFATHER/LGI1958; MCCAN, *sub* POWER and O'CONNELL/IFR). A house of 3 storeys over a basement built *ca* 1750 by the Pennefather family. 6 bay front; 2 bay pedimented breakfront; Venetian doorway framed by frontispiece of 4 engaged Corin-thian columns and entablature with a Venetian window on either side. Prominent roof; lunette window in pediment. 2 bay side. Main staircase rising to top storey. Plaster ceiling in drawing room similar to one at Glin Castle (*qv*). Pedimented stable block at side of house. Sold after the Famine to the Davies family. Resold 1864 to the McCan family.

Ballyquin House, Ardmore, co Water-ford (MASSY, B/PB; CARLYON, *sub* KINAHAN/IFR). A Georgian house overlooking the sea; owned in recent years by Mrs Hugh Massy (*see* CREGG CASTLE and TEMPLENOE HOUSE, co Cork) who completely remodelled the interior so that the ground floor now con-sists only of a vast hall, containing the elegant and spacious wooden Georgian stair, and a vast reception room. The plaster has been stripped from the walls of both rooms to expose the bare stone and the ceilings removed to reveal the joists and underside of the floor-boards above, which have been stained brown. The effect is somewhat Spanish, or Latin American. Ballyquin is now the home of Mr & Mrs Peter Carlyon.

Ballyragget Grange, co Kilkenny (*see* GRANGE (THE), Ballyragget).

Ballysaggartmore, Lismore, co Water-ford (KEILY, *sub* USSHER/IFR; ANSON, *sub* LICHFIELD, E/PB). A late-Georgian house built round a courtyard, on the side of a

Ballysaggartmore

steep hill overlooking the River Blackwater, to which a new front was subsequently added. Neither the front nor the older range behind it had a passage, so that it was necessary to go through the front set of rooms or those at the back to get to the front door. A seat of the Keily family. Arthur Keily, who assumed the surname of Ussher 1843, built 2 remarkable Gothic follies in the demesne, to the design of his gardener, J. Smith; one of them a turreted gateway, the other a castellated bridge over a mountain stream. "Nothing can be more romantic than this castle in the woods", a local historian wrote enthusiastically of the latter soon after it was built. According to a story, these follies were intended to be the prelude to a castle which Mrs Keily *alias* Ussher persuaded her husband to build as a rival to his brother's castle of Strancally (*qv*); but which never materialized owing to the money running out. The house was bought at the beginning of the present century by Hon Claud Anson, who sold it 1930s. It was subsequently demolished. The follies remain, one of them being now occupied as a house.

Ballysallagh, Johnswell, co Kilkenny. An early C18 house of 2 storeys over a basement and 5 bays. 1 bay pedimented breakfront centre; doorway with Gothic-glazed fanlight and blocking; lunette window in pediment. High-pitched roof. The seat of the Doyle family.

Ballyscullion

Ballyscullion, Bellaghy, co Derry (HER-VEY, BRISTOL, M/PB; BRUCE, Bt, *of Downhill*/PB; MULHOLLAND, Bt/PB). One of 3 eccentric palaces of Frederick Hervey, 4th Earl of Bristol and Bishop of Derry, the other 2 being Downhill Castle (*qv*), also in co Derry, and Ickworth in Suffolk. Built near the shore of Lough Beg, the small lough at the north-west corner of Lough Neagh; begun 1787, the architect being Michael Shanahan, a Corkman who was the Earl-Bishop's architect, adviser and confidant. Like Ickworth, it was in the form of a central domed rotunda joined by curved sweeps to rectangular pavilions or wings; the Earl-Bishop having got the idea from

the circular house on Belle Isle in Lake Windermere. On the entrance side of the rotunda was a pedimented portico of four giant Corinthian columns. In the centre of the house was a double corkscrew staircase, like that at the Château of Chambord; a grand stair going round a smaller one for the servants, so constructed that people on one could not see those on the other. There was a large library of segmental shape, like some of the rooms at Ickworth. The Earl-Bishop lost interest in the house, which came to be known as Bishop's Folly and was still uncompleted at the time of his death 1803; though it was inhabited and partly furnished. Together with Downhill, it was left to the Earl-Bishop's kinsman, Rev Henry Hervey Aston Bruce, who was immediately afterwards created a Bt. Not wishing to have to maintain 2 great palaces in the same county, and preferring Downhill, the 1st Bt demolished Ballyscullion a few years after inheriting it. Part of the facade, including the portico, was re-erected as the front of St George's Church, Belfast; while some pink marble columns from the interior, as well as some chimneypieces, are now at Portglenone House, co Antrim (*qv*). Other chimneypieces are at Bellarena, co Derry (*qv*). Some of the stone was later used in the building of a new and more modest house at Ballyscullion, to the design of Charles (later Sir Charles) Lanyon, for Adm Sir Henry Bruce, 2nd son of 1st Bt. It was until lately the seat of Sir Henry Mulholland, 1st Bt, Speaker of the Northern Ireland Parliament.

Ballyseedy

Ballyseedy, Tralee, co Kerry (BLENNER-HASSETT/IFR; BLENNERHASSETT, Bt/PB). A large 3 storey block of *ca* 1760 with 2 curved bows on the entrance front and another bow at the side, given a battlemented parapet, hood mouldings and other mildly baronial touches late C19 by James Franklin Fuller. At one side of the front is a long and low castellated service wing, with round and square turrets, the other side of which has a sham wall, consisting of a long range of false windows. This Gothic work dates from 1816 and may well be by Sir Richard Morrison. Rather narrow bifurcating staircase rising behind a screen of Doric columns at one end of the hall. Bequeathed 1965 by Miss Hilda Blennerhassett to her kinsman Sir Adrian Blennerhassett, 7th Bt, who sold it 1967. Now an hotel.

Ballyshanduffe House (also known as **The Derries**), **Portarlington, co Leix** (ALLOWAY/LGI 1879). A C19 castellated house, originally built 1810 by W. J. Alloway on the site of an old house of the O'Dempseys;

remodelled and partly rebuilt *ca* mid-C19 by R. M. Alloway. 2 principal fronts, one of them low and nearly 200 feet in length, with battlements and pointed doors and windows; the other front higher and with a square tower. Old arch opposite hall door, surviving from the O'Dempsey house.

Ballyshannon House, Ballyshannon, co Donegal. A 3 storey castellated house with narrow turrets.

Ballytrent, Broadway, co Wexford (RED-MOND/IFR; HUGHES/IFR). A 2 storey Georgian house. 5 bay front, projecting ends, each with a Wyatt window in both storeys. Adamesque plasterwork. The home of John Redmond, MP, leader of the Irish Parliamentary Party.

Ballyvolane, co Cork (COPPINGER/LGI 1912). A handsome 3 storey gable-ended early Georgian house, fronted by a forecourt with imposing gate piers, in the northern outskirts of Cork city. The home of Marianne Coppinger, 1st wife of the Prince Regent's crony, the 11th ("Jockey") Duke of Norfolk (*see* PB). Recently demolished.

Ballyvolane, Castlelyons, co Cork (PYNE, *sub* PHIPPS/IFR; GREEN, *sub* BLAKE, Bt, *of Menlough*/PB). A Victorian Italianate house with a roof on a heavy cornice. Pillared hall. The seat of the Pyne family. Bought *ca* 1953 by late C. H. Green.

Ballyvonare, Buttevant, co Cork (HAR-OLD-BARRY/IFR). A 3 storey C18 block. 5 bay entrance front; fanlighted doorway with blocking and coat-of-arms.

Ballywalter Park, Newtownards, co Down (MULHOLLAND, DUNLEATH, B/PB). Ireland's finest C19 Italianate palazzo; in the words of Dr Rowan, "a building with a metropolitan air and all the architectural trappings of a London club". Built *ca* 1846 for Andrew Mulholland, Mayor of Belfast 1845 and chief owner of the great York Street Flax Spinning Mills, to the design of Charles (afterwards Sir Charles) Lanyon; incorporating an earlier house of *ca* 1810, formerly belonging to the Matthews family and known as Springvale; though the existence of this earlier structure is not now apparent, except in the basement. Main block of 3 storeys over basement, with single-storey overlapping wings; entrance front of 5 bays in main block plus 1 additional bay in each wing; the end bays of the main block in the 2 lower storeys and also the wings having tripartite windows; those in the wings being framed by pedimented Corinthian aedicules. Large single-storey porte-cochère with coupled Doric columns and end piers, surmounted by latticed balustrade; also latticed balustrade round area. Eaved roof on bracket cornice on main block; balustraded roof parapets on wings. On the garden front, the main block is of 6 bays and the wings end in shallow curved bows. Spacious and sumptuous interior. Entrance hall, panelled in mahogany. Vast and magnificent 2 storeyed central hall, 60 feet in length, with Doric columns below, supporting the gallery, and Corinthian columns and pilasters marbled porphyry

Ballywalter Park

Ballywalter Park: Hall

balustrade; surrounded, in the upper storey, by arcades lighting the bedroom corridors, and niches with sculpture. The other end, separated from the staircase by a screen of columns, is treated below as a saloon—its walls hung with scarlet brocade—and as a picture gallery above. Drawing room with screen of Corinthian columns at one end and elaborate coved and coffered ceiling. In 1863 Andrew Mulholland added a single-storey billiard room wing, prolonging the garden front; with, at right angles to it, a large and splendid conservatory, also designed by Lanyon, with Corinthian columns along its front and a glass dome. Andrew Mulholland's son, 1st Lord Dunleath, installed the ornate pedimented bookcases in the library, which, like the drawing room, has a coved ceiling. 2nd Lord Dunleath added a service wing *ca* 1902, to the design of W. J. Fennell, of Belfast; he later enlarged this wing, in order, as is said, to put up the visiting XI during his cricket week. After World War II, this wing was curtailed. The garden front of the house overlooks wide-spreading lawns with paths and statues, beyond which is a notable collection of ornamental trees and shrubs.

Ballyward Lodge

Ballyward Lodge, Ballyward, co Down
(HIGGINSON/IFR). A very attractive gentleman's "cottage" of *ca* 1800 in a beautiful situation overlooking a lake; originally owned by William Beers. 2 subsequent additions; sensitively restored and much improved by present owner, W/Cmdr J. S. Higginson. 2 storey, upper storey partly in attic with dormer-gables; projecting single-storey porch, the same height as the rest of the front, with large and very elegant fan-lighted doorway. Battlemented projection at end; the upstairs end windows, which are pointed, with Georgian Gothic astragals, were put in recently. Long low-ceilinged library, with columns brought from Downhill Castle (*qv*) on either side of alcove. Drawing room divided by arch, formed out of two rooms, with a simple marble chimneypiece at either end. Stairs with iron handrail leading up to large bedroom landing, with fanlighted window. Impressive formal garden south of house, with statues and urns, laid out by present owner.

Ballywhite House, Portaferry, co Down
(KER/IFR; BROWNLOW/IFR). A 2 storey, double gable-ended C18 house, enlarged and embellished in the Italianate manner *ca* 1870 for a Mr Warnock, solicitor, of Downpatrick. The entrance door in the side of a large pedimented projection built in the centre of the front, with coupled Corinthian pilasters in its upper storey. Entablatures over the ground floor windows of the front, segmental pediments over the windows in

above; lit by two richly ornamented glazed domes on pendentives springing from the cornice. At one end of the hall rises an imperial staircase of stone with an ironwork

Ballywhite House

the gable ends; and at one end, a single storey bow. The other end of the house is joined to a single-storey ballroom wing by a pleasant Victorian conservatory. Owned for a period by Capt Richard Ker, of Portavo (*qv*), who sold it to the Brownlow family 1916.

Ballywillwill House

Ballywillwill House, nr Castlewellan, co Down. A handsome 2 storey house built 1815–16 by Rev G. H. McD. Johnson. 5 bay front; Wyatt windows in outer bays and centre of upper storey. Unusually long single-storey portico, supported by 10 Doric columns, with urns and a large recumbent lion on its entablature; the centre 4 columns breaking forward. The centre bay in the upper storey is framed by Ionic pilasters; the 3 inner bays being framed by bands of rusticated quoins.

Balrath, Kells, co Meath. A late-Georgian stucco-faced house with a pediment and superimposed orders of columns along the front.

Balrath Burry

Balrath Burry, nr Kells, co Meath (NICHOLSON/IFR). Originally a 2 storey pedimented c18 house of 7 bays with a curved bow at either end of the front. Subsequently enlarged by the addition of 3 bays to the right of the front, and 7 bays with another pediment as well as 2 more bays to the left,

so that the front extended for a total of 19 bays, plus 2 bows. After suffering damage when used as a barracks 1939–42, the house was reduced in size 1942 to the original block, which at the same time was rebuilt in an American Colonial style. The front kept its pediment, but lost its bows, and a colonnaded veranda was built along the full length of the ground floor. A pillared loggia was made under the pediment, and a porte-cochère was added to the end of the house, which is the entrance front; the columns for this and the veranda having been brought from Rosmead (*qv*). The present arrangement of the interior, and the proportions of the rooms, dates from this rebuilding; the principal rooms being on either side of a large hall with a bifurcating staircase. Long Georgian stable range, with pediment.

Baltiboys

Baltiboys, Blessington, co Wicklow (SMITH, *sub* STANNUS/IFR). A 2 storey late-Georgian house; 5 bay front, the centre bay breaking forward under a small pediment and having a Wyatt window above the entrance doorway. Roof on bracket cornice. The front prolonged by a lower 2 storey 2 bay addition, and then by a long 2 storey wing of 6 bays ending with a greenhouse. A seat of the Smith family; subsequently the home of Mr Kenneth Besson.

Baltrasna, Oldcastle, co Meath (O' REILLY/LGI1912). A house with a gable-end which is possibly a fragment of an earlier c18 house, of 2 storeys with quoins and shouldered architraves round the windows.

Balyna

Balyna, Moyvalley, co Kildare (MORE O'FERRALL/IFR). The ancestral home of the O'More family, the land having been granted to them by Elizabeth I as a small compensation for their forfeited territories in Leix; a tree in the demesne is said to have grown from the stick of Col Rory O'More, the Irish leader in 1641, who plunged it into the ground when he paused here as a fugitive. A new house was built 1815, which was burnt 1878; this was replaced by the present house, built 1880s. It is slightly Italianate, with a Mansard roof carried on a bracket cornice; of 2 storeys

with a dormered attic. Entrance front with two 3 sided bows and a single-storey Ionic portico. 5 bay garden front with pediment, the windows on either side being larger than those in the centre. Imposing staircase with handrail of decorative ironwork; ceiling of staircase hall has modillion cornice. Chapel in garden. Sold *ca* 1960; subsequently owned by Bewley's Oriental Cafés Ltd.

Bancroft House, co Down. A 3 storey 5 bay Georgian house with a fanlighted doorway.

Bangor Castle

Bangor Castle, Bangor, co Down (WARD, *sub* BANGOR, V/PB; BINGHAM, CLANMORRIS, B/PB). An Elizabethan-Revival and Baronial mansion by William Burn, built 1847 for Robert Ward, a descendant of 1st Viscount Bangor. Mullioned windows; oriels crested with strapwork; rather steep gables with finials. At one end, a battlemented tower with a pyramidal-roofed clock turret. Partly curved bows, very characteristic of Burn. Inherited by Robert Ward's daughter and heiress, Matilda Catherine, wife of 5th Lord Clanmorris. Featured in *Peers and Plebs* by Madeleine Bingham. Now owned by the town of Bangor.

Bannow House

Bannow House, Bannow, co Wexford (BOYSE/LGI1912 and *sub* BRUEN/IFR). A large 2 storey late-Georgian house. Entrance front with 3 bays on either side of break-front centre with 2 bays in upper storey and entrance door flanked by 2 windows below, under single-storey Ionic portico with iron balcony. 6 bay side. Eaved roof on bracket cornice.

Bansha Castle, Bansha, co Tipperary (BUTLER/IFR). A 2 storey Victorian house with a round tower at one end, a square tower at the other and a gabled porch. Odd-shaped windows and a few blind loops; but no castellations or other pseudo-medieval features.

Bantry House (formerly **Seafield** and before that, **Blackrock**), Bantry, co Cork (SHELSWELL-WHITE/IFR). A mansion of which the nucleus is a square 3 storey 5 bay house of *ca* 1740, built by the Hutchinson family. A wing was added at one side later in c18; probably *ca* 1770, after the property had been acquired by Richard White. It is of the same height as the original block, but of 2 storeys only; with a curved bow at the front and back and a 6 bay elevation at the side. The house was greatly enlarged and remodelled in 1845 by Richard White, Viscount Berehaven and afterwards 2nd Earl of Bantry, whose father had been raised to the peerage as a reward for his efforts in organizing the local defences when the French fleet appeared off Bantry 1796. 2nd Earl of Bantry travelled extensively in Europe building up the art collection for which the house is famous; and in enlarging the house, which he probably did to his own design, his object seems to have been to give it the air of a palace of the Baroque period somewhere on the Continent; he also may have been influenced by English architecture of late c17 and early c18. The long 14 bay front which he added at the opposite side of the original block to the late c18 wing, consisting of a 6 bay centre of 2 storeys over a basement and 3 storey 4 bay bow-ended wings, is lined with giant Corinthian pilasters of red brick; the intervening spaces being of grey stucco with red brick window surrounds. The rest of the house was also adorned with pilasters and other facings of brick; and the whole building was given a rather delicate balustraded roof parapet, which follows the Baroque undulations of the facades: the bows being echoed by concave curves. The house is entered through a glazed Corinthian colonnade, built onto the original c18 front in c19; there is a similar colonnade on the original garden front. The hall is large but low-ceilinged and of irregular shape, having been formed by throwing together 2 rooms and the staircase hall of mid-c18 block; it has early c19 plasterwork and a floor of black and white pavement, incorporating some ancient Roman tiles from Pompeii. From one corner rises the original staircase of c18 joinery. The 2 large bow-ended drawing rooms which occupy the ground floor of the late c18 wing are hung with Gobelins tapestries; one of them with a particularly beautiful rose-coloured set said to have been made for Marie Antoinette. The dining room is of two different heights, being partly in the original block and partly in c19 addition; the 2 sections being separated by a screen of Corinthian columns of marble with gilded capitals. The walls are royal blue, which sets off the gilt ornament of the ceiling, and the riot of gilt foliage framing copies of the familiar Allan Ramsay portraits of George III and Queen Charlotte. From the half-landing of the stairs, a lobby leads to the great library, which runs the whole length of the centre of c19 front; it is divided by 2 screens of marble Corinthian columns and has a compartmented ceiling. The library formerly led into an immense glass conservatory, built onto the centre of c19 front, which has since been removed. Flanking the entrance front is an imposing stable range, with a pediment and cupola. The house is surrounded by Italian gardens with balustrades and statues and has a magnificent view over Bantry Bay to the mountains on the far

Bantry House

Bantry House: Hall

Bantry House: Drawing Room

Bantry House: Dining Room

Bantry House: Library

George Ingoldsby. Doorcase with broken segmental pediment. The ends of the house were altered subsequently. Interior plasterwork with foliage and ribbon decoration and painted medallion; plasterwork fan over doorway. Sold by H. I. L. Smythe (a cousin of Miss Pat Smythe, the equestrian and author) 1955. Now the offices of a German company.

Barbavilla

shore. The demesne is entered by a fine archway. Bantry House is now the home of Mrs Shelswell-White, great-niece of 4th and last Earl of Bantry, who opens the house regularly to the public; having started doing so more than 30 years ago, before any other country house in Eire was regularly open.

Barbavilla, Collinstown, co Westmeath (SMYTHE, *sub* SMYTH/IFR). A long low 2 storey 9 bay house with a pediment, built *ca* 1730 by William Smythe who named it after his wife, Barbara, daughter of Sir

Barberstown Castle, Straffan, co Kildare. A tower-house with a long plain 2 storey wing attached. In 1814, the residence of Jos Atkinson; in 1837, of Capt Robinson.

Bargy Castle

Bargy Castle, Tomhaggard, co Wexford
(HARVEY/IFR; DE BURGH/IFR). An old castle,
originally belonging to the Rossiter family,
added to at various periods and given
regular sash windows with segmental
pointed heads and Georgian Gothic astragals. Interior full of ups and downs, winding
stairs and secret chambers; some c16 or c17
panelling, with the initials of the Rossiters;
also some carved panelling which was probably brought from elsewhere. Some of the
rooms have massive beams. A large room
with pointed arches, now the dining room,
is said to have been originally a chapel. The
home of Bagenal Harvey, the United Irish
leader, who commanded the United Forces
in Wexford 1798; after the defeat of the
insurgents he was captured and hanged off
Wexford Bridge; Bargy and the rest of his
estates were confiscated under the Act of
Attainder, but restored 1810 to his brother,
John Harvey. Sold by the Harveys 1947 to
Mr Thomas H. Paget. Re-sold *ca* 1960 to
Gen Sir Eric de Burgh; now the home of
his son-in-law and daughter, Lt-Col & Mrs
C. J. Davison, who run it as an hotel during
the summer months. Col Davison has added
a new wing to the castle, with correct
battlements.

Barmeath Castle, Dunleer, co Louth
(BELLEW, B/PB). An old castle of the Pale,
enlarged and remodelled mid-c18 so that it
became a plain 3 storey 7 bay double gable-
ended house, which was further enlarged
and castellated 1839 by Sir Patrick Bellew,
7th Bt, afterwards 1st Lord Bellew, possibly to the design of John B. Keane. Two
round corner turrets were added on the
former entrance front, which became the
garden front, a new entrance being made
under a Romanesque arch guarded by a
portcullis in a square tower which was built
at one end of the side elevation. On the
other side of the castle, a long turreted
wing was added, enclosing a courtyard. The
castle kept its Georgian sash-windows,
though some of them lost their astragals
later in c19. Staircase of magnificent c18

Barmeath Castle

Barmeath Castle: Turreted Wing

joinery, with Corinthian balusters and a
handrail curling in a generous spiral at the
foot of the stairs, opening with arches into
the original entrance hall; pedimented doorcases on 1st floor landing, one of them with
a scroll pediment and engaged Corinthian
columns. Long upstairs drawing room with
Gothic fretted ceiling. Very handsome mid-
c18 library, also on 1st floor; bookcases
with Ionic pilasters, broken pediments and
curved astragals; ceiling of rococo plasterwork incorporating Masonic emblems. The
member of the family who made this room
used it for Lodge meetings. When Catholics
were no longer allowed to be Freemasons,
he told his former brethren that they could
continue holding their meetings here during
his lifetime, though he himself would
henceforth be unable to attend them.

Barnabrow, Cloyne, co Cork. A 3 storey
3 bay double gable-ended c18 house with
single-storey 2 bay c19 wings. Wyatt windows in 2 lower storeys of c18 block. In
1814, the residence of Timothy Lane; in

1837, of J. R. Wilkinson; in recent years. of
Lt-Cmdr & Mrs Whitehouse.

Barnane

Barnane, nr Templemore, co Tipperary
(CARDEN/IFR). Purchased by Jonathan Carden 1701, and from then onwards the seat
of the senior branch of the Cardens. A long,
irregular range of buildings, mostly 2
storeyed, dating from various periods in
c18 and c19, with c19 battlements, gables,
lancet windows and hood mouldings. At
one end, a massive keep-like tower. The
home of John Carden (known as "Wood-
cock", as he was so often shot at by his
tenants), who attempted to abduct Miss
Eleanor Arbuthnot 1854 and was consequently imprisoned. Sold by A. M.
Carden *ca* 1920; subsequently fell into ruin.

Barne

Barne, Clonmel, co Tipperary (THOM-
SON-MOORE/IFR). A large 3 storey house of
early c18 appearance with a front of 11
bays, the 2 end bays on either side projecting forwards. Central feature rather similar
to that of Furness, co Kildare, and Clermont, co Wicklow (*qqv*), consisting of a
frontispiece of paired engaged Doric
columns and entablature, surmounted by
an aedicule of 2 engaged Ionic columns and
a pediment framing the central first-floor
window. In c19, the house was given a
high-pitched roof in the French château
style, with dormers.

**Barons Court, Newtownstewart, co Tyr-
one** (HAMILTON, ABERCORN, D/PB). A large
and complex 2 storey Georgian house, of
which the nucleus is a block 7 bays long and
externally of *ca* 1780, when 8th Earl of
Abercorn employed as his architect George
Steuart; with a 3 bay pedimented breakfront, urns along the roof parapet and on
the pediment, and plain entablatures over
the ground-floor windows. In 1791–92, 1st
Marquess of Abercorn employed John
(afterwards Sir John) Soane to remodel the
house, which was further enlarged and
given a rich neo-Classical interior early in
c19 to the design of William Vitruvius
Morrison. Robert Woodgate also worked
here at some stage. The original block now

Barons Court: Garden Front

Barons Court: Porte-Cochère

Barons Court: Rotunda

Barons Court: Staircase Hall

Barons Court: Dining Room

Barons Court: Ceiling

Baronston: as it originally was

Baronston: with the centre block rebuilt

oculus in a coffered dome, supported by Ionic columns. The staircase hall has a ceiling of rectangular coffering with a rich acanthus frieze, supported by fluted half-columns; the stair itself has a balustrade of delicate ironwork. The library has a circular ceiling on pendatives; other rooms have plasterwork ceilings of varying designs and walls lined with Corinthian half-columns and pilasters. A modern "living space" has recently been created in the interior by the present Duke's son, Marquess of Hamilton.

Baronston, Ballinacargy, co Westmeath (MALONE, SUNDERLIN, B/DEP; MALONE/LGI-1912). A late C18 house consisting of a 3 storey centre block joined to 2 storey wings by curved sweeps; largely built by Richard Malone, 1st and last Lord Sunderlin, who is immortalized in Sir John Betjeman's poem, *Sir John Piers*:

And from the North, lest you, Malone,
should spy me
You, Sunderlin of Baronstown, the
peer,
I'll fill your eye with all the stone that's
by me
And live four-square protected in my
fear.

The centre block had a 7 bay front with a pedimented breakfront; *oeil de boeuf* window in pediment; 3 bay projecting porch. The wings were of 5 bays. After suffering 2 successive fires, the centre block was replaced 1903 by a large gabled Edwardian villa to the design of James Franklin Fuller; the original C18 curved sweeps and wings remaining on either side, to produce an effect of grotesque incongruity. Sold *ca* 1929; afterwards demolished.

Barraghcore House, Goresbridge, co Kilkenny (FLEMING/LGI1904). A 2 storey Georgian house with a Wyatt window above a pedimented and fanlighted porch. 2 bays on one side of the centre, triple windows on the other. Vast castellated mill with turrets and *machicoulis* at corner of demesne.

Barretstown Castle, Ballymore Eustace, co Kildare (BORROWES, Bt/PB1939). An old tower-house with a 2 storey slightly Ruskinian Gothic Victorian addition. The latter has rectangular, pointed and segmental-pointed plate glass windows, some of those in the upper storey rising into stepped dormer-gables. At one side of the front is a 4 storey tower with a stepped

forms the centre of a long garden front, having been prolonged on either side by 2 storey 4 bay wings, of the same height and in the same style, but set back, so that the original block stands out from the front by the depth of 4 bays. Originally, the entrance was on this side of the house; it was then moved to the present entrance front, where there is a pedimented porte-cochère of 4 giant Ionic columns with wreaths on the entablature, enabling the original entrance hall and the rooms on either side of it to be thrown together into a great gallery, which is divided by screens of fluted Corinthian columns; and has a ceiling of elaborate plasterwork. The rest of the interior is no less sumptuous. There is a rotunda lit by an gable. Owned in recent years by Miss Elizabeth Arden, the *parfumiére*; afterwards by Mr W. G. Weston, who has presented it to the Irish nation.

Barrettstown House, Newbridge, co Kildare (DE PENTHENY O'KELLY/LGI1958; MANSFIELD/IFR). A C19 house with gables and bargeboards, hood mouldings and a turret and spire. The home of Lt-Col H. L. Mansfield, and of his widow after his death 1948.

Barrowmount, co Kilkenny (BUTLER/IFR). A 2 storey early C18 house, with a 3 bay recessed centre and projecting end bays. Eaved roof; bold quoins.

Barrymore Lodge, Castlelyons, co Cork (BARRY/IFR; COLLIS, *sub* COOKE-COLLIS/IFR; PHILIPPI, *sub* MEADE/LGI1972). A double gable-ended house said to date back to C17 and to have been the dower house of Castle Lyons (*qv*). 5 bay front with camber-headed windows. C19 3 sided bow at one end. In recent years the home of Capt & Mrs E. A. Philippi.

Barry's Court, Carrigtwohill, co Cork (BARRY/IFR). A medieval castle, rebuilt 1585. Chapel; chimneypiece with inscription. One of the principal seats in C16 and C17 of the Barry family, Earls of Barrymore, whose descendants from early C19 onwards had their seat nearby on Fota Island (*qv*). Now a ruin.

Baymount

Baymount: Stable Yard

Baymount, Clontarf, co Dublin. A Georgian house of 3 storeys over a basement with a curved bow in the centre of one of its fronts, mildly castellated in early C19; with a battlemented parapet and 2 rather thin turrets on either side of the bow. Classical interior. Castellated stable yard. The residence of Dr Trail, Bishop of Down and Connor; later, *ca* 1837, the residence of J. Keily. Now owned by the Society of Jesus.

Beamond House, Duleek, co Meath. A 2 storey 5 bay late-Georgian house with an

eaved roof and a single-storey Doric portico. The home of R. A. Cornwall until his death *ca* 1956.

Beardiville

Beardiville: Entrance archway

Beardiville, Cloyfin, co Antrim (MAC-NAGHTEN, Bt/PB; LECKY/IFR). A mid-C18 house originally belonging to the Mac-naghten family; 2 storeys over basement, 5 bays. Centre bay on front breaks forward; porch with Tuscan columns added later. Roof on cornice. Staircase with fluted balusters. Drawing room in single-storey early C19 wing, with plasterwork of the period. Simple pedimented archway at entrance to demesne, flanked by single-storey lodges with partly blocked-up Diocletian windows. Passed to the Lecky family C19.

Bearforest

Bearforest, Mallow, co Cork (DE LA COUR/LGI1958; PURDON COOTE, *sub* COOTE, Bt/PB; MOORE, *sub* DIGBY, B/PB). A villa built in 1807–1808 for Robert Delacour to the design of Richard (afterwards Sir Richard) Morrison, who intended it to display "his taste and talents as a villa architect" and "his capacity for designing and executing a residence that should combine simplicity and elegance with a convenience and extent of accommodation suitable for the purposes of a large family, or of affluent fortune, while it retained the modest character becoming the habitation of an unostentatious private gentleman". Of 2 storeys; 3 bay front, semi-circular porch with engaged fluted Doric columns, between Wyatt windows under relieving arches; 4 bay side elevation

with semi-circular fanlighted conservatory; eaved roof on bracket cornice. Compact, but spacious plan: oval hall, extending into the porch, with columns flanking the doorcases, as at Castlegar and Isercleran (*qqv*); central top-lit staircase hall; large, well proportioned drawing room and dining room. All in all, the house lives up to Morrison's intentions; though surprisingly, in an age which set a high store on views and prospects, he made the southern side of the house, where there is an attractive view to the Nagles Mountains, the back; so that it was largely blinded by a service wing. The house subsequently passed to the Purdon Coote family; it was burnt *ca* 1920 and afterwards rebuilt, without the conservatory and with an extra storey on the porch, which now has the effect of central curved bow. The Morrison interior decoration, which was naturally lost in the fire, was not reinstated. Bearforest was sold by the Purdon Cootes a few years ago to Mr C. A. & Hon Mrs Moore who have solved the problem of the house's orientation by demolishing the original service wing and making a patio where it stood, and building a new service wing on the north side of the house. They have also re-floored the hall in marble.

Beaulieu

Beaulieu

Beaulieu, Drogheda, co Louth (PLUNKETT, LOUTH, B/PB; TICHBORNE, FERRARD, B/DEP; MONTGOMERY, *sub* WADDINGTON/IFR). The finest and best-preserved country house of 2nd half of C17 in Ireland; and one of 1st country houses to be built in Ireland without any fortification; though until C19 it was surrounded by a tall protective hedge, or palisade. Built 1660–67 by Sir William Tichborne, whose father, Sir Henry Tichborne, a prominent military commander in the Civil War, obtained the estate from the Plunkett family; traditionally by purchase rather than through confiscation. Of 2 storeys, with a dormered attic in the high, eaved roof, which is carried on a massive wooden modillion cornice; 7 bay entrance front, the 2 end bays on either side breaking forward; 6 bay side elevation. The facades are rendered, with dressings of warm red brick; on the entrance front there is a brick doorcase with a segmental pediment and Corinthian pilasters; on the side elevation, there are 2 triangular pedimented doorcases with Ionic pilasters. The 2 tall moulded chimneystacks are also of brick. The large 2 storey hall has its original C17 chimneypiece and overmantel, arched doorways and cornice; it was adorned with rich woodcarving early C18. The decoration of the drawing room and dining room is also almost entirely of late C17; the 2 rooms have bolection-moulded panelling and ceilings with central ovals surrounded by heavy garlands of plaster flowers and foliage; that in the drawing room being filled with a *trompe-l'oeil* perspective painting in the manner of Verrio. The staircase of elegant joinery with newels in the form of fluted Corinthian columns dates from *ca* 1720; and would, like the carvings in the hall, have been put in by the son of the builder of the house, Sir Henry Tichborne, 1st and last Lord Ferrard. Lord Ferrard lost both his sons—the elder was drowned when crossing to England 1709—and Beaulieu eventually passed to the descendants of his granddaughter, who married Rev Robert Montgomery. On the death of Richard Montgomery 1939, Beaulieu passed to his daughter, Mrs Nesbitt Waddington, whose husband was for many years manager of the Aga Khan's Irish stud farms.

Beau Parc

Beau Parc

Beau Parc, co Meath (LAMBART, Bt/PB). A 3 storey house of 1755, built for Gustavus Lambart, MP, and attributed to the amateur architect, Nathaniel Clements; joined to 2 storey wings with convex quadrants *ca* 1778 by Charles Lambart, MP, advised by another talented amateur, Rev Daniel Beaufort. The main block is faced in ashlar and has an entrance front of 5 bays, with the classic sequence of a Diocletian window above a Venetian window above a tripartite doorway; the latter pedimented and with Doric columns. Parapeted roof. The garden front, overlooking the River Boyne, is of 2 bays on either side of a curved central bow.

Bective House, Bective, co Meath (BOLTON/LGI863; WACHMAN, *sub* DALY/IFR). A plain 2 storey house of *ca* 1790. 7 bay

front, enclosed porch with fluted Doric columns; 5 bay side. Good staircase hall. The childhood home of Mr James Stern, the writer; sold to Mr William Bird 1922. Recently the home of Mr Norman Wachman, who sold it to the Tower Cement Mines Co.

Bedford House, Listowel, co Kerry (RAYMOND/LGI863; BATEMAN/LGII912). A 2 storey 7 bay C18 house with a cut-stone front. Camber-headed windows with triple keystones; cornice. In 1837, the residence of S.S. Raymond.

Beechmount

Beechmount, Rathkeale, co Limerick (LLOYD/IFR). A 3˙ storey 5 bay Georgian house with single-storey 3 bay C19 wings, one of them being a conservatory. Triple window in centre of 2 upper storeys, above C19 glazed porch; solid roof parapets.

Beechwood Park, Nenagh, co Tipperary (TOLER, *sub* NORBURY, E/PB; OSBORNE, Bt/PB; BLAKE/LGI972). A tall 3 storey early to mid-C18 house built onto the end of an earlier house; its front extended by single-storey wings. 7 bay front, with 2 additional bays on either side in the wings; 3 bay pedimented breakfront. Bold quoins; pedimented doorcase. Recently the home of Mr Philip Blake, the genealogist; now the property of the O'Brien Machinery Co, of Pennsylvania, USA.

Beechy Park (formerly **Bettyfield**), **Rathvilly, co Carlow.** A 3 storey 5 bay mid to late C18 house. Diocletian window in centre of top storey of entrance front, above win-

dow with entablature on console brackets, above later Doric porch. Bold string courses.

Belan, co Leix. A 2 storey 3 bay C18 house. Primitive Venetian windows with slightly pointed heads on either side of round-headed rusticated doorcase; Wyatt windows above.

Belan House, Ballitore, co Kildare (STRATFORD, ALDBOROUGH, E/DEP). One of the largest of C18 gable-ended houses, built 1743 for John Stratford, MP, afterwards 1st Earl of Aldborough, to the design of Richard Castle in collaboration with the amateur architect, Francis Bindon. Of 3 storeys; 11 bay front, the 3 centre bays and the 2 outer bays on each side breaking forward. Central Venetian window over tripartite doorway. Solid roof parapet with recessed panels and urns. According to a writer of 1825, the rooms were remarkable neither for their elegance, nor for their size. Fine stable block; domed Doric rotunda in park, also several follies. The house was still intact and furnished 1837, but was afterwards abandoned by the family, who fell on evil days before the extinction of the earldom 1875. It has long been a ruin. The rotunda temple and 2 obelisks survive in nearby fields.

Belcamp Hall, Balgriffin, co Dublin (NEWENHAM/IFR). A fine red brick house of *ca* 1786. Of 3 storeys over a basement; 7 bay breakfront entrance front with rusticated stone frontispiece; garden front with curved central bow and 2 bays on either side. Round-headed ground floor windows. Rather similar plan to Lucan, co Dublin and Mount Kennedy, co Wicklow (*qqv*); oval room extending into garden front bow. Good interior plasterwork. Tower in grounds erected in honour of George Washington 1778 by Sir Edward Newenham, MP, a member of the Patriot Party. Now a college.

Belcamp House (also known as **Belcamp Hutchinson**), **Balgriffin, co Dublin** (HYDE/IFR). A 2 storey double bow fronted

Belan House

Georgian house, the bows being close together. Porch with Ionic columns. Now the home of Count Karl Waldburg.

Belcamp Park, Balgriffin, co Dublin (JERVIS-WHITE-JERVIS, Bt/PB1940). A 2 storey 3 bay C18 house. Central breakfront; pedimented doorcase; massive stone cornice.

Belfast Castle

Belfast Castle: "Elizabethan" staircase (Mr & Mrs John Whyte of Loughbrickland—qv—in foreground)

Belfast Castle, co Antrim (CHICHESTER, DONEGALL, M/PB; ASHLEY-COOPER, SHAFTESBURY, E/PB). The original Belfast Castle was a tall, square semi-fortified house with many gables, built at the beginning of C17 by the Lord Deputy Sir Arthur Chichester, uncle of 1st Earl of Donegall. It stood surrounded by formal gardens and orchards going down to a branch of the River Lagan, and was the seat of the Donegalls until 1708 when it was destroyed by a fire "caused through the carelessness of a female servant"; 3 of 6 daughters of 3rd Earl perishing in the blaze. The castle was not rebuilt and its ruin was subsequently demolished; its site and that of its gardens is now occupied by Castle Place and the adjoining streets, in what is now the centre of the city. For much of C18, the Donegalls lived in England; later, they lived at Ormeau (qv), just outside Belfast to the south-east. 3rd Marquess of Donegall found Ormeau inconvenient; and so, towards the end of 1860s, he and his son-in-law and daughter, afterwards 8th Earl and Countess of Shaftesbury, built a large Scottish-Baronial castle at the opposite side of the city, in a fine position on the lower slopes of Cave Hill, overlooking the

Lough; it was named Belfast Castle, after Sir Arthur Chichester's vanished house. The architects of the new Belfast Castle were Sir Charles Lanyon and William Henry Lynn; stylistically, it would seem to be very much Lynn's work; but it may also perhaps have been influenced by a design by William Burn, having a plan almost exactly similar to those of several of Burn's

Scottish-Baronial castles. Tall square tower, of 6 storeys, in the manner of Balmoral. Projecting pillared porch in "Jacobethan" style, with strapwork on columns. On the garden front, a fantastic snaking Elizabethan staircase of stone leading down to the terrace from the *piano nobile* was added 1894. Entrance hall in base of tower; larger hall opening at one end into staircase well with a massive oak stair; arcaded first floor gallery. Reception rooms *en suite* with rather uninspired fretted ceilings. Now owned by the City of Belfast.

Belfort

Belfort, Charleville, co Cork (CLANCHY/LGI1958). A 2 storey Victorian house in the Georgian manner, with a pediment and a pillared porch. Demolished 1958.

Belgard Castle, Clondalkin, co Dublin (KENNEDY-SKIPTON/IFR; LAWRENCE, Bt, *of Lucknow*/PB; MAUDE, *sub* HAWARDEN, V/PB). A large 3 storey C18 block attached to a medieval tower with Georgian-Gothic windows and battlements. Drawing room ceiling of Adamesque plasterwork. Belgard was originally the seat of a branch of the Talbot family, from whom it passed by inheritance to a branch of the Dillon family at the end

Belgard Castle

Belgard Castle: Upstairs Hall

of C17. In 1788 it was leased to Francis Cruise, whose family still occupied it 1814. Later in C19 it was bought by Dr Evory Kennedy, President of Royal College of Physicians Ireland; it subsequently passed to his grandson, Sir Henry Lawrence, 2nd Bt (who was also the grandson of the great Sir Henry Lawrence, founder of British rule in the Punjab and defender of Lucknow), whose widow sold it in 1910 to A. F. Maude. Sold *ca* 1962 by Mr Hugh Maude.

Belgrove

Belgrove, Cobh, co Cork (GUMBLETON, *sub* MAXWELL-GUMBLETON/LG1952; BAGWELL/IFR; BUTLER, *sub* DUNBOYNE, B/PB). A Georgian house consisting of a 2 storey main block with a long curved wing, overlooking East Ferry, a heavily-wooded backwater of Cork Harbour. Impressive and graceful bifurcating staircase of wood. Fine garden, with C18 terrace. Originally the seat of the Harper family; owned in C19 by Rev George Gumbleton, who took his services in the pleasant little Victorian Gothic church by the water's edge on the opposite side of the Ferry to the house. His elder son, William, was a great gardener and an eccentric character who did not mince words: when shown a plant of which he did not think very much, he would exclaim "Pish!", "Tush!" or "Pooh!", depending on its degree of commonness.

When he died, in 1911, he left Belgrove to his cousins, the Bagwell family, who were descended in the female line from the Harpers. Since they already owned the nearby Eastgrove (*qv*), where they preferred to live, Belgrove was let to tenants during the succeeding years. Then, *ca* 1954, having stood empty for a long period, it was demolished. The property was subsequently bought by Mr James Butler, who has built a modern house here.

Bellaghy Castle, Bellaghy, co Derry (THOMPSON, *sub* CLARK/IFR). A C17 "Plantation castle" in a good state of repair. The home of Dr G. M. Thompson.

Bellair, Ballycumber, Offaly (HOMAN-MULOCK/LGI1912; WINGFIELD, POWERS-COURT, V/PB). A 2 storey early C19 villa by Richard Morrison, with a 3 bay entrance front identical to those of two other Morrison villas in Offaly, Ballylin and Cangort Park (*qqv*); dominated by a remarkable deep arched recess with a concave surround, beneath which the entrance door is set. Side elevation has curved bow. Single-storey pilastered addition. Passed to the writer, Mrs Claude Beddington, daughter of F. B. Homan-Mulock; then to Mrs Beddington's daughter, Sheila, Viscountess Powerscourt.

Bellamont Forest, Cootehill, co Cavan (COOTE, BELLAMONT, E/DEP; O'GOWAN/IFR). One of the most perfect examples in the British Isles of a Palladian villa; built *ca* 1730 for Thomas Coote, Lord Justice of the King's Bench in Ireland, to the design of his nephew, Sir Edward Lovett Pearce; inspired in particular by Palladio's Villa Rotonda at Vicenza and his Villa Pisani at Montagnana. Of red brick, with ashlar facings; 2 storeys over a rusticated basement, with a mezzanine fitted in at the sides. The upper storey treated as an attic, above the cornice. 5 bay front with pedimented Doric portico; side elevations with central Venetian windows, the centre light of each being blind; one of them having entablatures and recessed columns, the other more simply treated. The hall has a high coved ceiling with a modillion cornice and a moulding in the keyhole pattern; the walls are decorated with roundels containing busts, some of which are said to represent members of the Coote family. The saloon has a richly ornamented coffered ceiling and a pedimented doorcase. The dining room has a deeply coved coffered ceiling (described by Dr Craig as "eminently characteristic of Pearce"); and a screen of engaged fluted Ionic columns at one end. The bedrooms are arranged around a central upper hall, lit by an oval lantern enriched with plasterwork. The coved and coffered ceiling of the library dates from 1775, and was put in by Thomas Coote's grandson, Charles, who succeeded his cousin as 5th Lord Colooney 1766 and was made Earl of Bellamont of 2nd creation 1767. In honour of this, he changed the name of the house, which had formerly been Coote Hill, to Bellamont Forest. Lord Bellamont was a somewhat absurd figure, ultra-sophisticated and ardently Francophile—he insisted on making his maiden speech in the Irish House of Lords in

Bellamont Forest

Bellamont Forest: Hall

Bellamont Forest: Saloon ceiling

Bellarena

Bellarena: Library

French—pompous and an inveterate womanizer. He left several illegitimate sons, to one of whom he bequeathed Bellamont, his only legitimate son having pre-deceased him. In 1874 Bellamont was sold to the Dorman-Smith (now O'Gowan) family. The present owner's uncle was the politician, Sir Reginald Dorman-Smith, Governor of Burma at the time of the Japanese invasion.

Bellarena, Magilligan, co Derry (GAGE/IFR and LGI1972; HEYGATE, Bt/PB). A predominantly late-Georgian house which evolved in several different phases around what is probably a late C17 core. Marcus McCausland, son of the heiress of Bellarena, who assumed the name of Gage, added to the house 1797; his son, Conolly Gage, made the present library and contrived to fit in a 3rd storey at the back of the house 1822. In 1830s, Charles (afterwards Sir Charles) Lanyon was employed to redecorate the house, remodel the hall and add the present porch; it seems that Conolly Gage's wife, Henrietta, did not wish to be outdone by her sister, Marianne, who was the wife of her husband's cousin, Marcus McCausland, owner of the nearby Drenagh (*qv*) which was rebuilt in grand style to the design of Lanyon at this time. A final addition seems to have been made by Conolly and Henrietta Gage's daughter and heiress, Marianne, who married Sir Frederick Heygate, 2nd Bt, 1851. For all its complicated evolution, the house has an air of compactness. 2 storey 5 bay entrance front; faced, like the other elevations, in dark coursed basalt. Unusually wide Venetian window in centre of upper storey, rising into a baseless floating pediment. Below the Venetian window is Lanyon's porch, semi-circular and fronted by a pair of engaged Ionic columns on either side of the doorway. At one side of the entrance front is a wing, but set back. The rear of the main block is of 4 bays, all with Wyatt windows in both storeys; this is prolonged by the rear face of the wing, of the same height as the main block but with ordinary rectangular sashes. Along the top of the rear elevation is a row of squat Wyatt windows lighting Conolly Gage's 3rd storey; they are, in fact, half-dormers, breaking upwards through the cornice and into the roof. The hall, as remodelled by Lanyon, who obtained the space necessary for the desired grand effect by adding the porch, contains a double staircase with cast iron balusters, rising between 2 Corinthian columns painted to resemble marble. The drawing room has a ceiling of elaborate plasterwork, similar to the plasterwork at Drenagh. The most notable room in the house is the library of 1822, a large and lofty room with a coved ceiling, surrounded on 3 sides by a gallery with a balustrade of delicate ironwork. It is possible that this balustrading, and the slightly bowed window frames, came from Ballyscullion (*qv*), as did the library chimneypiece, as well as that in the smoking room. At the back of the house is a large cobbled office courtyard, with a central pond and fountain; the imposing stable block having a pediment and spire. Beyond is an unusually complete range of early C19 farm buildings. Bellarena was the home of Sir John Heygate, 4th Bt, novelist and journalist, who married, as his 1st wife, Hon Evelyn, daughter of 1st and last Lord Burghclere (*see* PB1921), who was also 1st wife of Evelyn Waugh (*see* LG1952).

Belleek Manor

Belleek Manor, Ballina, co Mayo (KNOX-GORE, *sub* KNOX/IFR). A large Tudor-Gothic house almost certainly by John B. Keane; built *ca* 1825 for Francis Knox-Gore, afterwards 1st Bt. Symmetrical front with 3 stepped gables flanked by slender polygonal battlemented turrets and pinnacles; oriels at sides, porch in centre with twin corbelled oriel above it. Lower wing with turret. Now an hotel.

Belle Isle, Lisbellaw, co Fermanagh (GORE, Bt/PB; PORTER, *sub* BAIRD/IFR). A house beautifully situated on an island in Upper Lough Erne; the seat of a distinguished C18 soldier, Sir Ralph Gore, 6th Bt, 1st and last Earl of Ross and Viscount Belleisle, who was C-in-C in Ireland 1788. Bought early in C19 by Rev J. G. Porter. The present house appears to incorporate a 2 storey C18 range with a 3 sided bow at one end, to which a range of 1820–30 was added at right angles, with a staircase hall, top-lit by an octangular lantern, in the re-entrant. The house was re-modelled *post* 1880 in the plain English Tudor manor-house style made popular by Norman Shaw and his disciples; producing a gabled entrance front with mullioned windows, a projecting porch and a tall, church-like battlemented tower at the corner of the 1820–30 range. The latter range, which is the garden front facing the lough, remains unaltered, apart from having Victorian plate-glass windows; at one end is the end bow of C18 range, with Georgian astragals. Inside the house, arches were opened up between the staircase hall and the rooms at either end of it, to make a much larger hall; the staircase hall was also widened at the expense of the rooms in 1820–30 range, the old wall being replaced by a massive oak beam. An oak staircase with barleysugar balusters replaced the original stairs; the walls were panelled in oak, or decorated with half-timbering. The octangular ceiling lantern, however, was left undisturbed. The drawing room, in 1820–1830 range, was redecorated, having been reduced in width, and given a chimneypiece of old oak carving, possibly of more than one period and nationality. The room extending into the bow of C18 range, which is now the drawing room, was given a stone Tudor fireplace; but it still keeps its original doors with shouldered C18 architraves. In 1907 the entrance front was prolonged by a wing in Tudor style containing a long and lofty gallery, with a timbered roof, an elaborate Tudor fireplace and overmantel and

a minstrels' gallery, the balustrade of which has slender turned uprights and would appear to be late C17 or early C18 woodwork brought from elsewhere. At this end of the entrance front stands a pedimented and gable-ended office wing which would appear to date from quite early in C18. After the death of N. H. A. Porter 1973, Belle Isle was inherited by his niece, Miss Lavinia Baird.

Belle Isle, Lorrha, co Tipperary (YELVERTON, AVONMORE, V/PB1910). A C18 house of 2 storeys with an attic. Pedimented front and ends, each pediment having a lunette window. The seat of a branch of the Yelverton family; passed through marriage to the O'Keefe family, and then back to another branch of the Yelvertons through the marriage of Cecilia O'Keefe to 3rd Viscount Avonmore.

Belleview, co Cavan. A C18 house consisting of a 2 storey centre block, joined by screen walls to flanking wings. Centre block of 3 bays; tripartite doorway with pediment on console brackets; keystones over ground floor windows.

Belleville Park, Cappoquin, co Waterford (POER/LG1863; KEANE, Bt/PB). A plain 2 storey 7 bay Georgian house with a wing at the back.

Bellevue, co Galway (*see* LISREAGHAN).

Bellevue, co Leitrim. A 2 storey 3 bay early C19 house with a simple fanlighted doorway.

Bellevue, co Wicklow

Bellevue, Delgany, co Wicklow (LA TOUCHE/IFR). A house built 1754 by the wealthy Dublin banker, David La Touche, at a cost of £30,000. 2 storey; pedimented entrance front of 9 bays, the 2 outer bays on each side projecting forward. Dentil cornice under parapet and round pediment; urns on parapet. 4 bay side, without cornice; irregular rear elevation. Later in C18, some of the principal rooms, which were described (1793) as being of "the most brilliant hue", were given ceilings of neo-Classical plasterwork, in the manner of Michael Stapleton. At about the same time, or soon afterwards, a small single-storey Doric portico was added on the entrance front. Also a chapel was built near the house, to the design of Richard Morrison, who did other work here. As well as building the house, David La Touche laid out a landscape garden, which he and his son, Peter, adorned with numerous ornaments and follies; including a Gothic "dining room" and a Turkish tent, by the elder and younger Francis Sandys or

Bellevue, co Wicklow: Conservatory

Bellevue, co Wicklow: House and Conservatory

Sands. Peter La Touche also constructed the remarkable glass conservatory or "glazed passage" which snaked across the lawn for more than 500 feet, joining the house to a formidable succession of greenhouses. It was completed by 1793, when a visitor wrote of it: "You walk under glass in a wandering path for six or seven hundred feet". Some years after the death of a subsequent Peter La Touche, in 1904, Bellevue was sold by his sisters and co-heiresses. The house was afterwards allowed to fall into disrepair. Parts of it were still standing 1945; but it was finally demolished in 1950s.

Bellevue House, Slieverue, co Kilkenny (POWER/IFR). A 3 storey Georgian house with a top storey almost as high as those below, creating an unusual effect. 8 bay front; entrance doorway with recessed columns fitted in between 2 narrower windows, under an unusual C19 2 storey canted portico, almost like an Indian veranda, with 4 widely spaced polygonal columns of no recognizable order in each storey, the upper storey forming a covered balcony with a wrought-iron balustrade; the upper entablature being adorned with St Hubert's Stag, the crest of the Power family. Prominent moulded string courses; parapeted roof. Entirely plain 4 bay side elevation. Owned in early C19 by the politician, Richard Lawlor Shiel, MP, from whom it was bought by Patrick Power, MP. Sold 1940 by A.R. Power; afterwards dismantled, the ruin standing for some years until it collapsed.

Belline, Piltown, co Kilkenny (PONSONBY, BESSBOROUGH, E/PB; MURRAY SMITH, *sub* BURNHAM, B/PB). A tall late C18 house of 3 storeys over a basement with a 3 sided bow in the centre of its entrance front; flanked by 2 most unusual detached 3 storey circular pavilions with conical roofs. The house has a fine Classical doorcase in the entrance front bow, with many steps leading up to it; and good stone facings. Octagon hall; drawing room and dining room each with a small room, like an alcove, opening off it. Rustic lodge with portico of tree-

Belline

trunks. The house was built by Peter Walsh; but was bought *ca* 1800 by 3rd Earl of Bessborough, whose seat, Bessborough (*qv*), was nearby. From then until 1934, the house was occupied by successive agents of the Bessborough estate; one of whom, 2nd half of C19, was F. W. Walshe (*see* IFR), whose family was different from that of the builder of the house. The house is believed to have been lent to William Lamb (afterwards Viscount Melbourne, the Prime Minister) and his wife, the notorious Lady Caroline (daughter of 3rd Earl of Bessborough) 1812, when he brought her to Ireland in the hope that it would make her forget Byron. After being sold by the Bessboroughs, Belline was for some years the home of Major & Mrs G.W. Murray Smith, who built a 2 storey addition along the back of the house containing a back hall and a new kitchen. The parapet of this addition, as well as the terrace wall round the sweep, is now adorned with splendid C18 stone urns, which were formerly on the roof parapet of Bessborough. Belline is now the home of Mr Donal O'Neill-Flanagan, the architect, and Mrs O'Neill-Flanagan.

Bellinter

Bellinter : Hall

Bellinter, Navan, co Meath (PRESTON/ IFR). A Palladian house of rubble with ashlar facings by Richard Castle, one of the last country houses designed by him; built *ca* 1750 for John Preston, MP. 5 bay centre

block of 2 storeys over basement, joined to 2 storey 5 bay wings by straight arcades; the elevation being prolonged, beyond the wings, by curved quadrant walls as at Powerscourt (*qv*), with gateways and piers with urns. The main block has a central feature of a modified Venetian window, in which the central opening is a niche formerly sheltering a statue; and the side-lights are as wide as the other windows of the facade, and framed by Ionic pilasters. Below is a fanlighted tripartite doorway with a broad broken pediment extending over the door and the side-lights which, again, are of the full width. The flight of steps up to the hall door is unusually wide and long, with plain iron railings which are continued on either side in front of the area. The windows of the centre block have entablatures over them; those in the lower storey, and in the lower storey of the wings, have rusticated surrounds; the entrance doorway being also rusticated. Good interior plasterwork; panels of trophies on the walls of the hall, which has a tremendous stone chimneypiece with a Bacchantic mask. The secondary staircase is spiral, and of wood. In the time of the builder's grandson, another John Preston, who became 1st and last Lord Tara of 2nd creation 1800, 2 drawing rooms in the garden front were made to open into each other with large folding doors. Other alterations were carried out at this period, in which Lady Tara seems to have been the prime mover; the most notable being the Gothic-glazing of the two arcades joining the house to the wings, so as to convert them into orangeries. Bellinter later passed by inheritance to the Briscoe family. It is now a convent of Our Lady of Sion.

Bellwood

Bellwood, Templemore, co Tipperary. A 2 storey C19 house with low-pitched gables and fancy bargeboards. Wide windows with astragals.

Belmont, Banbridge, co Down. A 2 storey 3 bay ashlar-faced Georgian house with a single-storey Ionic portico.

Beltrim Castle

Beltrim Castle, Gortin, co Tyrone (COLE-HAMILTON, *sub* ENNISKILLEN, E/PB; BLAKIS-TON-HOUSTON/IFR). A plain square Georgian house with a long wing.

Belvedere

Belvedere, Mullingar, co Westmeath (ROCHFORT, *sub* BELVEDERE, E/DEP; ROCH-FORT/LGI1912; MARLAY/LGI1912; HOWARD-BURY, *sub* SUFFOLK AND BERKSHIRE, E/PB; and BURY/IFR). An exquisite villa of *ca* 1740 by Richard Castle on the shores of Lough Ennell; built for Robert Rochfort, Lord

Bellfield, afterwards 1st Earl of Belvedere, whose seat was Gaulston (*qv*), *ca* 5 miles away. Of 2 storeys over a basement, with a long front and curved end bows—it may well be the earliest bow-ended house in Ireland—but little more than 1 room deep. The front has a 3 bay recessed centre between projecting end bays, each of which

originally had a Venetian window below a
Diocletian window. Rusticated doorcase
and rusticated window surrounds on either
side of it; high roof parapet. The house
contains only a few rooms, but they are of
fine proportions and those on the ground
floor have rococo plasterwork ceilings of the
greatest delicacy and gaiety, with cherubs
and other figures emerging from clouds; by
the same artist as the ceilings formerly at
Mespil House, Dublin, one of which is now
at Áras an Uachtaráin (*qv*). The staircase,
wood and partly curving, is in a projection
at the back of the house. Soon after the
house was finished, Lord Bellfield's beautiful wife confessed to him that she had
committed adultery with his brother; where-
upon he incarcerated her at Gaulston, where
she remained, forbidden to see anyone but
servants, until his death nearly 30 years
later; while he lived a bachelor life of great
elegance and luxury at Belvedere. Another
of his brothers lived close to Belvedere at
Rochfort (afterwards Tudenham Park—*qv*);
having quarrelled with him, too, Lord Belvedere—as he had now become—built the
largest Gothic sham ruin in Ireland to blot
out the view of his brother's house; it is
popularly known as the "Jealous Wall". In
c19, the Diocletian windows in the front of
the house were replaced with rectangular
triple windows; and the slope from the front
of the house down to the lough was elaborately terraced. Belvedere passed by inheritance to the Marlay family and then to
late Lt-Col. C. K. Howard-Bury, leader of
the 1921 Mount Everest Expedition; who
bequeathed it to Mr Rex Beaumont.

Belvoir, Sixmilebridge, co Clare (WIL-
SON LYNCH/LGI1958). An early c19 "gingerbread Gothic" house; later porch, ogee
doorcase and pinnacles. Simple Gothic
chapel joined to house by screen; according
to an inscription on a stone, it was "erected
in return for the devoted attention of a wife
during an illness in 1862–63". The house is
now a ruin but the chapel is still roofed and
in use.

Belvoir Park, co Down

Belvoir Park, Newtownbreda, co Down
(HILL-TREVOR, *sub* TREVOR, B/PB; DE YAR-
BURGH-BATESON, DERAMORE, B/PB; WILSON/
LGI1912). A large 3 storey mid-c18 house,
refaced *ca* 1820. Top storey treated as an
attic, above the cornice. 7 bay front, 3 bay
breakfront centre with 4 giant Doric pilasters supporting pediment in attic storey,
flanked by two oculi. Curved bow on side
elevation. Impressive staircase hall; stairs
with wrought-iron balustrade; gallery on
console brackets. Renovations carried out
by William J. Barre *ca* 1865. Leased towards
end of c19 by W. H. Wilson, whose family
continued to lease the house after his death.
Demolished 1950s to make room for a
housing estate.

Belvoir Park, co Down

Belvoir Park, co Down: Hall

Benburb, co Tyrone: Manor House
(BRUCE/LGI1912). A large late-Victorian
house with gables, high-pitched roofs and
rectangular plate glass windows, built 1887
to the design of William Henry Lynn. Of
red brick, with bands of stone to give structural polychromy. Now a Servite Priory.
Nearby, on a cliff above the River Blackwater, is an early c17 fort, built by Sir
Richard Wingfield.

Manor House, Benburb

Benekerry, nr Carlow, co Carlow
(NEWTON, *sub* BAGENAL/IFR; BAGENAL/IFR).
A house of 7 bays and 2 storeys, with an
attic lit by dormers in the roof, dating originally from end of c17 or early c18. In the
late-Georgian period, a single-storey neo-
Classical addition was built along the whole
length of the entrance front; consisting of
an enclosed 3 bay porch in the centre, with
a short open colonnade of Doric columns on
either side. One room has an apsed end with

Benekerry

a screen of two Grecian Ionic columns. In
1832, Philip Newton, son of Col Philip
Newton of Benekerry, assumed the name of
Bagenal in accordance with the wishes of
his mother and his grandfather, Col Beau-
champ Bagenal, of Dunleckney, co Carlow
(*qv*). At about this time, 1st cricket ground
in co Carlow was here.

Bennett's Court, Cobh, co Cork (BENNETT/
LGI1886). A 2 storey early to mid-c19 house
with a 3 sided central bow on its principal
front and Wyatt windows. Entrance door at
end of house; courtyard behind. Impressive
gate lodge with portico. Now owned by a
religious order.

Benown (also known as **Harmony Hall**),
Athlone, co Westmeath (CAULFEILD, *sub*
CHARLEMONT, V/PB; HARRIS-TEMPLE, *sub*
HARRIS, B/PB). A late c18 house of 2 storeys
over a basement built by a member of the
Caulfeild family. 5 bay front; central Wyatt
window; doorway with graceful segmental
fanlight extending over door and sidelights
and Tuscan columns going up as far as
the fanlight glazing and thus supporting
nothing. Sold to the Chaigneau family;
passed in later c19 to Capt Hon Arthur
Harris, afterwards Harris-Temple, who married the widow of Capt Arthur Chaigneau.
Owned by the Fox family from the beginning of the present century until 1971;
afterwards the home of Mr Wilson. Let,
during 1880s, to Dr Gleeson, founder of the
Athlone Woollen Mills.

Benvarden

Benvarden, Dervock, co Antrim (MAC-
NAGHTEN, Bt/PB; MONTGOMERY/IFR). Originally the seat of the Macnaghtens, including John Macnaghten who shot Mary Anne
Knox, of Prehen (*qv*) 1760 while trying to
abduct her, and was consequently hanged;
at the first attempt to execute him, the rope
broke, and the crowd urged him to escape;
but he said "I couldn't go about the country as 'Half-Hanged Macnaghten'" and
mounted the scaffold again; the rope did
not break a 2nd time. A 2 storey c18 house
with a central curved bow in each of its two

fronts, 1 containing the entrance hall. Sold 1798 to Hugh Montgomery, afterwards co-founder of Montgomery's Bank (which became the Northern Bank), who had returned from Virginia, USA; and who enlarged Benvarden *ca* 1805, by adding 2 wings with 3 sided bows, of the same height as C18 block, but with higher ground floor ceilings; containing a dining room and a drawing room or ballroom. At the same time, or perhaps later, a service wing with a curved bow was added at one end, prolonging the facade still further. In mid-C19, an Italianate porch with flanking corridors was added on the entrance front, and another service wing was built. Also in C19, the astragals were removed from the windows. Elegant semi-circular cantilevered stair and oval light well in hall; some good plaster-work. Rhomboidal stable courtyard, with a pedimented archway crowned by a wooden lantern.

Berkeley Forest, New Ross, co Wexford (DEANE/LGI1912; TYNDALL/LGI1952Supp). A 2 storey 5 bay Georgian house, with a pillared porch and a Venetian window in the centre of the upper storey. Eaved roof. Adamesque plasterwork. Originally belonged to the Berkeley family, from whom it passed by inheritance to the Deane family, and thence to the Tyndall family.

Bermingham House, Tuam, co Galway (LOUTH, E/DEP; CUSACK-SMITH, Bt/PB). A plain, square 2 storey C18 house. 3 bay entrance front with round-headed doorway, the windows being set very far apart; 5 bay side. Late C18 interior plasterwork; shouldered doorcases; pedimented door between entrance hall and staircase hall; staircase of wood with slender turned balusters. Originally the seat of the Bermingham family, Lords Athenry; 22nd Lord Athenry was made Earl of Louth 1759; he features in an unfortunate episode in Dorothea Herbert's *Retrospections* (see ARDFRY). When he died, the Earldom of Louth became extinct and the Barony of Athenry dormant. In C19, Bermingham became the seat of the Dennises and was the home of John Dennis, founder of the Galway Hounds (afterwards known as the "Blazers") and one of the most famous hunting men of his day. His great-great-grand-niece, Lady Cusack-Smith, the present owner of Bermingham, is herself a legendary horsewoman and MFH.

Bert, Athy, co Kildare (DE BURGH/IFR). A gable-ended house of 1725–30, enlarged early in C19 by the addition of 2 storey Classical overlapping wings, of the same height as the centre block; which is of 3 storeys over a basement with two 7 bay fronts. On one front, the top storey is treated as an attic above the cornice and has blank windows. On this front, the wings are of 3 bays with, on the ground floor, a Wyatt window between two niches. On the other front, the wings project further and are joined by a Doric colonnade. Plasterwork ceiling in drawing room; screen of columns in dining room. In recent years, the home of the Misses Geoghegan.

Besborough, Blackrock, co Cork (PIKE/LGI1958). A 3 storey house of mid to late C18 appearance, rendered with cut-stone facings. 7 bay front; pedimented breakfront with Diocletian window above Venetian window on console brackets above a pedimented doorcase which seems to have been substituted for the original doorcase in the Victorian period. Blind elliptical oculus in pediment; keystones over all the windows; well-moulded cornice; string course over ground floor. C19 single-storey wing fronted by an elaborate glass and iron conservatory with a curved roof and ending in a 2 bay bow-ended pavilion framed by quoins; with a die and two camber-headed recesses in which the windows are set. In 1814 the residence of J. Spence. For most of C19 and during the earlier years of the present century, the seat of the Pike family. Now a convent.

Bessborough

Bessborough, Piltown, co Kilkenny (PONSONBY, BESSBOROUGH, E/PB). A large house by Francis Bindon, consisting of a centre block of 2 storeys over a basement joined to 2 storey wings by curved sweeps. Built 1744 for Brabazon Ponsonby, 1st Earl of Bessborough, replacing an earlier house; the "Bess" in whose honour the estate received its name—which was singled out by Swift in his scornful attack on the custom of naming houses and estates after peoples' wives—having been the wife of a C17 Ponsonby. Entrance front of 9 bays; 3 bay pedimented breakfront with niche above pedimented Doric doorway; balustraded roof parapet with urns; rusticated basement; perron and double stairway with ironwork railings in front of entrance door. Ingeniously contrived Gibbsian doorways in the curved sweeps, their pediments being above the cornice; niches on either side of them. 6 bay garden front with 4 bay breakfront; Venetian windows in upper storey above round-headed windows. Later wing at side. Hall with screen of Ionic columns of Kilkenny marble, their shafts being monolithic. Saloon with ceiling of rococo plasterwork and chimneypiece with female herms copied from William Kent. The entrance front, never a very inspired composition, was not improved by the removal of the perron and the substitution of a porch at basement level early in the present century, so as to enable the hall to be used as a sitting room; the architect of this work being Sir Thomas M. Deane. The house was burnt 1923. It was afterwards rebuilt to the design of H. S. Goodhart-Rendel; but in the end the family never went back to live in it, and it stood empty until it was sold 1944. It now belongs to a religious order, and has been added to and altered; the urns have been removed from the parapet and are now at Belline (*qv*).

Bessmount, co Monaghan. A High Victorian Ruskinian Gothic house with a fantastic carved porch.

Bettyfield, co Carlow (*see* BEECHY PARK).

Bingfield, Crossdoney, co Cavan (STORY/IFR). A 3 storey 3 bay mid-C18 house, built *ca* 1745 by Ven Joseph Story, Archdeacon of Kilmore. Venetian window over pedimented tripartite doorway. 2 storey wing.

Bingham Castle

Bingham Castle, Belmullet, co Mayo (BINGHAM/LGI1912; and *sub* CLANMORRIS, B/PB). A symmetrical castle of early C19 appearance consisting of 2 large 3 storey towers with machicolated galleries joined by a 2 storey 3 bay centre. Turreted central feature and porch; tracery windows. Screen wall at one side of front which appears to have been originally a single-storey wing. Bingham Castle is now in ruins.

Birchfield, co Clare. An early C19 castellated house of 2 storeys. Symmetrical front; slender round turrets at sides; battlemented parapet; porch. Now a ruin. The embattled stable and outbuildings survive. Built by Cornelius O'Brien, MP, who was responsible for O'Brien's lookout tower on the Cliffs of Moher nearby. A monument surmounted by an urn to his memory, with a lengthy inscription stands on the road to the north of the house.

Birr Castle, Offaly (PARSONS, ROSS, E/PB). A castle of different periods, incorporating a gatehouse and 2 round flanking towers built or rebuilt between 1620 and 1627 by Sir Laurence Parsons in the precincts of an O'Carroll castle which he had been granted. The castle was burnt 1643 and besieged 1690; during the course of C17, the gatehouse was transformed into a dwelling-house, being joined to the two flanking towers, which were originally free-standing, by canted wings; so that it assumed its present shape of a long, narrow building with embracing arms on its principal front, which faces the demesne; its back being turned to the town of Birr and its end rising above the River Camcor. Not much seems to have been done to it during C18, apart from the decoration of some of the rooms and the laying out of the great lawn in front of it, after the old O'Carroll keep and the early C17 office ranges, which formerly stood here, had been swept away *ca* 1778. From *ca* 1801 onwards, Sir Laurence Parsons (afterwards 2nd Earl of Rosse), enlarged and remodelled the castle in Gothic, as well as building an impressive Gothic entrance to the demesne. His work on the castle was conservative; being largely limited to facing it in ashlar and giving a unity to its facade which before was doubtless lacking; it kept its original high-pitched

Birr Castle

Birr Castle: Staircase

roof containing an attic and two C17 towers at either end of the front were not dwarfed by any new towers or turrets; the only new dominant feature being a 2 storey porch in the centre of the front, with a giant pointed arch over the entrance door. At the end of the castle above the river, 2nd Earl built a single-storey addition on an undercroft, containing a large saloon. He appears to have been largely his own architect in these additions and alterations, helped by a professional named John Johnston (no relation of Francis Johnston). In 1832, after a fire had destroyed the original roof, 2nd Earl added a third storey, with battlements. The entrance hall of the castle is long and narrow, being the room over the arch of the original gatehouse; the arch itself being now at basement level. The staircase is of yew and dates from between 1660 and 1681, when Thomas Dinely referred to it as "the fairest staircase in Ireland". It rises through 3 storeys and has bold turned balusters and a gracefully curving handrail; the ceiling above it being of plaster Gothic vaulting and dating from the reconstruction after 1832 fire. The staircase is not the castle's

Birr Castle: Saloon

Birr Castle: Dining Room

only surviving C17 interior feature; there is also a frieze of early C17 plasterwork in one of the round towers. There is C18 plaster-work in the Yellow Drawing Room—which was formed by throwing together three small rooms *ca* 1908—and also in the study; the library, adjoining, used to have an elaborately coffered C18 ceiling, but this was destroyed by fire 1919. These rooms all

keep their C18 chimneypiece. The large saloon in 2nd Earl's addition has a lofty and elegant plaster Gothic vault on slender columns. The dining room, at the other end of the castle, which is hung with scarlet Victorian flock-paper, has a somewhat later C19 Gothic ceiling of curving tracery. The garden, extending far into the demesne from the front of the castle, is world-famous and open to the public. One of its features is the Gothic observatory built in early 1840s by the astronomer 3rd Earl which contains the tube of his telescope—until 1917 the largest reflecting telescope in the world.

Bishopscourt

Bishopscourt, Straffan, co Kildare (PONSONBY, *sub* BESSBOROUGH, E/PB; PONSONBY, V/DEP; SCOTT, CLONMELL, E/PB1935; KENNEDY, Bt/PB1970; MCGILLYCUDDY OF THE REEKS/IFR). A large Classical house built *ca* 1780–90 for Rt Hon John Ponsonby, Speaker of the Irish House of Commons, in the manner of James Gandon and most probably an early work by Richard Morrison; completed by Speaker Ponsonby's son, 1st Lord Ponsonby of Imokilly. 4 bay entrance front with pedimented portico of 4 giant Ionic columns; the outer bays have pedimented ground floor windows and circular plaques instead of windows in the upper storey. Roof parapet on dentil cornice. Side elevation with recessed centre and 3 bay projection at either side, joined by veranda of slender columns with ironwork balcony. Curved bow on other side of house. Imperial staircase. Sold 1838 to 3rd Earl of Clonmell. Re-sold in the present century to E. R. Kennedy, who bred the famous racehorse *The Tetrarch*. Inherited by Mr Kennedy's daughter, Mrs Dermot McGillycuddy.

Black Castle, Navan, co Meath (FITZHERBERT/IFR). Originally a single-storey late C18 gentleman's "cottage", with a thatched roof and 2 curved bows on the entrance front; to the back of which a 2 storey slate-roofed wing was added, probably *ca* 1791 and with the advice of that talented amateur architect, Rev Daniel Beaufort. This "cottage" was replaced, some time *post* 1826, by a plain 2 storey early C19 house. Principal front of 6 bays with 2 bay breakfront centre. Single-storey Doric portico at side; 3 sided bow at other end.

Blackhall, Clane, co Kildare (WOLFE/IFR). A 2 storey C18 house with a 7 bay front, the 3 centre bays being recessed. Flat roof, with a fantastic cupola sprouting from it. The seat of Theobald Wolfe, after whom was named Theobald Wolfe Tone, the patriot, whose family were freehold tenants on the Blackhall estate.

Black Hall, Termonfeckin, co Louth. A 2 storey 3 bay house which, from its appearance, would be *ca* 1800 and of the school of Francis Johnston. Windows set in arched recesses. Folly tower on hill behind. The seat of the Pentland family.

Blackrock, Bantry, co Cork (*see* BANTRY HOUSE).

Blanchville, Gowran, co Kilkenny (KEARNEY/USA). A house built by Lt-Gen Sir James Kearney, KCH 1830.

Blandsfort

Blandsfort, Abbeyleix, co Leix (BLAND/IFR). An early C18 house of 3 storeys over a basement and 5 bays, built 1715 on the ruins of an O'More fortress. Parapeted roof; later porch; Georgian Gothic staircase window in rear elevation. Large hall, probably formed out of original hall and a room to one side of it; corner fireplace and C18 panelling, decorated with one or two Corinthian pilasters. Staircase hall at back; stairs of noble joinery, with carved decoration on stringings. 2 small parlours at front and back, with corner fireplaces; what must have been a similar room, on the other side of the house, has been enlarged by a presumably C19 addition to form a larger dining room, with a modillion cornice. Conservatory of *ca* 1850. Stables of 1792 by Patrick Farrell. Garden wall shaped like a C18 sham ruin.

Blarney Castle, Blarney, co Cork (MACCARTHY, CLANCARTY, E/DEP; JEFFERYES, *sub* COLTHURST, Bt/PB; COLTHURST, Bt/PB). An exceptionally large keep with an angletower, built 1446 by the McCarthys of Muskerry, and world-famous for having the Blarney Stone built into its battlements. Having been forfeited by Donogh MacCarthy, 4th Earl of Clancarty, who fought for James II in the Williamite War, it was acquired by the St John Jefferyes family. In the mid to late C18, James St John Jefferyes built a 4 storey Georgian-Gothic house onto the old keep; with a central bow and a turret and cupola; pointed windows and curvilinear pinnacled battlements. The Jefferyes family also laid out a landscape garden known as the Rock Close, with great stones arranged to look as though they had been put there in prehistoric times. The C18 house was burnt early in C19 and not rebuilt; its ruin now forms a picturesque adjunct to the keep. In 1874 a new house was built, on a different site further into the demesne and overlooking the lake. It is in the Scottish Baronial style, of rough-hewn ashlar; of 2 storeys over a high basement with a gabled attic. Round corner-turret and bartizans with conical roofs; stepped gables and dormer-gables; rectangular plate-glass

Blarney Castle: old castle and C18 house

windows. Porch with 2 Ionic columns on entrance front, the window above being framed by Corinthian pilasters, an entablature and strapwork. 2 storey curved bow with strapwork cresting on garden front. Entrance hall with timbered ceiling and flight of stone steps leading up to the level of the principal rooms. Top-lit inner hall with Jacobean-style oak staircase; first floor landing with arches and Corinthian pilasters. Large and small drawing rooms *en suite*, with friezes of Adam-Revival plasterwork. Adam-Revival frieze also in dining room. Passed through marriage to the Colthurst family.

Blarney Castle: 1874 house

Blayney Castle

Blayney Castle (also known as **Hope Castle**), **Castleblayney, co Monaghan** (BLAYNEY, B/DEP; HOPE/LG1937; PELHAM-CLINTON-HOPE, NEWCASTLE, D/PB). A 3 storey 5 bay Georgian block, built near the site of a C17 "Plantation Castle"; refaced

and embellished during the Victorian period. Entablatures over windows; scrolled cresting on roof parapet; segmental pediment with arms on garden front. Entrance front with central curved bow, to which a projecting porch, and a canopy of orna-

Blayney Castle

mental cast iron work and glass, was added. Top storey treated as attic, above cornice. Lower service wing, and single-storey 4 bay C19 addition with roof on bracket cornice prolonging garden front. Centre 1st floor window of garden treated as a niche, sheltering a statue. Sold 1853 by 12th and last Lord Blayney to Henry Hope, of Deepdene, Surrey, son of Thomas Hope, the great exponent of neo-Classicism and a member of the Scottish-Dutch banking family, famous for its ownership of the Hope Diamond. Passed by descent to Lord Henry Francis Hope Pelham-Clinton-Hope, afterwards 8th Duke of Newcastle. Now a convent.

Blessingbourne

Blessingbourne

Blessingbourne: Hall

Blessingbourne, Fivemiletown, co Tyrone (MONTGOMERY/IFR). There was originally no house at Blessingbourne, an estate which came to the Montgomerys through marriage early in the C18; the family seat being Derrygonnelly Castle in co Fermanagh, which was burnt later in C18 and not rebuilt. The family lived for some years at Castle Hume (*qv*), which they rented; then, at the beginning of C19, a romantic thatched cottage was built by the side of the lough at Blessingbourne by Hugh Montgomery (known as "Colonel Eclipse") as a bachelor retreat for himself after he had been crossed in love. His bachelorhood ended 1821, when he married a Spanish girl; but during the next 50 years the family lived mainly abroad, so that his cottage was all they needed for their occasional visits to co Tyrone. The present Victorian Elizabethan house was built by his grandson, Hugh de Fellenberg Montgomery, between 1870 and 1874, to the design of F. Pepys Cockerell. Pepys Cockerell, son of the better-known C. R. Cockerell, was an artist as much as an architect; his patron and his patron's wife were also people of taste; so that Blessingbourne is an unusually attractive and successful example of its style and period. The grey stone elevations are not overloaded with ornament; such as there is has restraint: caps on the chimneys, small finials on the gables, curved and scrolled pediments over some of the mullioned windows. The interior of the house is comfortable, with great character. The hall has a staircase incorporated in a screen of tapering wooden piers. Through glazed arches one looks across an inner hall to the lough and mountains. The principal rooms have

Blessingbourne: Dining Room

chimneypieces of carved stone in a Tudor design, flanked by niches for logs; some of them being decorated with William de Morgan tiles. The dining room still keeps its original William Morris wallpaper of blue and green grapes and foliage; while there is another original Morris paper in the library. The present owner, Capt P. S. Montgomery, former President of the Northern Ireland Arts Council, has recently stylishly redecorated much of the interior, which houses his collection of modern Irish art.

Blessington

Blessington, co Wicklow (BOYLE, BLESINTON, V/DEP; BLESINTON, E, *sub* STEWART, Bt, *of Ramelton*/PB; HILL, DOWNSHIRE, M/PB). One of the largest late C17 Irish country houses, built by Michael Boyle, Archbishop of Armagh and the last ecclesiastical Lord Chancellor of Ireland, who was granted the manor of Blessington 1669 by Charles II and laid out the town. The house was of 2 storeys with a dormered attic in its high-pitched roof; of brick, and built on an "H"-plan. Principal front with 5 bay centre recessed between two 3 bay projecting wings joined by a single-storey balustraded colonnade. Roof on bracket cornice; single-storey wing at one side. The house stood at the end of an avenue in a fine demesne with a deer park. Primate Boyle's son was made Viscount Blesinton in his father's lifetime; but the peerage became extinct in 1732 and the Blessington estate passed to the 2nd and last Viscount's sister, Anne, wife of 2nd Viscount Mountjoy, whose son was made Earl of Blesinton. This 1st Earl of Blesinton was also the last, and after his death, the Blessington estate passed to the Earl of Hillsborough, afterwards 1st Marquess of Downshire, whose great-grandmother was a daughter of Primate Boyle. The house was burnt by the insurgents 1798. The early C19 Earl of Blessington, husband of the celebrated Lady Blessington, was descended in the female line from a brother of 2nd Viscount Mountjoy, and therefore had no hereditary connexion with the Blessington estate.

Bloomfield

Bloomfield, Claremorris, co Mayo (RUTTLEDGE/IFR). A 3 storey Georgian block, enlarged, altered and refaced *ca* 1769 and later. 5 bay front, doorway with shallow fanlight over door and sidelights below 2 central Wyatt windows; 5 bay side. Interior redecorated 1833. Stairs lit by immense 2 storey round-headed window. Good ceiling decoration and chimneypieces. Sold 1924, subsequently demolished.

Bloomfield, co Westmeath (CAULFEILD, *sub* CHARLEMONT, V/PB). A house built 1828 to the design of H. A. Baker; with a curved bow, a single-storey portico and a courtyard at the back.

Bloomsbury, Kells, co Meath (BARNEWALL, TRIMLESTOWN, B/PB). A 2 storey 5 bay early C19 house with a Doric porch.

Boakefield, Ballitore, co Kildare. A 2 storey 5 bay mid-C18 house with a high-pitched roof and a rusticated doorway; the front being prolonged by lower wings which though they appear to be contemporary and balance each other in size, are asymmetrical as regards fenestration. The seat of the Boake family.

Bogay, Newtowncunningham, co Donegal. A square 2 storey house of the 1730s, with a dormered attic in its slightly sprocketed roof. 5 bay front, pedimented surround to central window in lower storey; tall stacks at sides. In 1814 the residence of Rev Thomas Pemberton.

Bolton Castle, Moone, co Kildare. A double gable-ended house of early C18 appearance with a battlemented tower attached. In recent years the home of the eminent gynaecologist, Senator Prof R. P. Farnan. Now a Cistercian monastery.

Bonnettstown Hall

Bonnettstown Hall, Kilkenny, co Kilkenny (BLUNDEN, Bt/PB; KNOX/IFR; MARESCAUX DE SABRUIT/IFR). One of the most perfect medium-sized early C18 country houses in Ireland; built 1737 for Samuel Mathews, Mayor of Kilkenny, whose name and the date are inscribed on quoins at either side of the entrance front. Of 2 storeys over a high basement. 6 bay entrance front, with tripartite round-headed rusticated doorcase; blank tympanum over door instead of fanlight. Windows in lower storey have rusticated surrounds; those above, shouldered surrounds on consoles; basement windows camber-headed with keystones. Quoins; broad flight of steps with ironwork railings up to hall door. High, sprocketed roof.

Bonnettstown Hall

Garden front also of 6 bays but plain; with 2 large windows in the centre and below them a door with an enchanting miniature Baroque perron in front of it, complete with double iron-railed curving steps. Large hall, from the back of which rises a staircase of noble joinery, with Corinthian newels and acanthus carving on the ends of the treads. Black marble chimneypiece in hall contemporary with building of house; ceiling over staircase decorated with geometrical plaster panels. Large lobby above hall open to head of stairs with rococo plasterwork. Drawing room and dining room with plain cornices; chimneypiece in drawing room contemporary with house; that in dining room, of Kilkenny marble with scroll pediment, probably earlier, having been brought from Kilcreene House (*qv*). Drawing room hung with cream and gold wallpaper of slightly Chinese design, originally made for Allerton Park, Yorks. Study with original C18 fielded panelling, and another chimneypiece from Kilcreene.

Boom Hall, Derry, co Derry (ALEXANDER/IFR; and CALEDON, E/PB; MATURIN-BAIRD/LG1952; COOKE/IFR). The original Boom Hall belonged to Robert Alexander, elder brother of the wealthy "Nabob" James Alexander, 1st Earl of Caledon. The house was so named because of being near where the boom of Derry was placed during the Siege. James Alexander built a new house here *ca* 1772, to the design of Michael Priestley, soon after returning from India, and before buying the estate of Caledon, co Tyrone (*qv*), which was to become his principal seat and from which he was to take his title. Of cut stone; 2 storeys over a basement. 7 bay entrance front with 3 bay breakfront centre; projecting porch added later. Garden front with 3 sided bow; side elevation of 5 bays. Window surrounds with blocking, even in basement; blocked quoins. Moderately high roof, on cornice. Large cubical central hall. Sold 1840 to Daniel Baird, through whose daughter it passed to the Maturin-Bairds. Afterwards the seat of the Cooke family.

Borris House, Borris, co Carlow (KAVANAGH/IFR). A plain 3 storey late C18 block, incorporating part of an old castle; badly damaged 1798 and restored *ca* 1820 by Richard and William Vitruvius Morrison, who gave it a Tudor exterior and a rich and largely Classical interior. The exterior, which remained symmetrical, was given a roofline of Tudor battlements and finials, hood mouldings, some of them ogee shaped, over the windows, a portico with pointed arches and four square corner turrets,

Borris House

Borris House: Hall

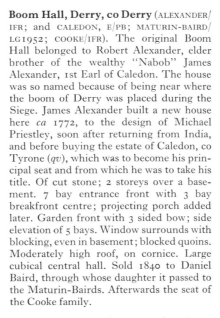
Borris House: Dining Room

crowned with cupolas, rather similar to those at Glenarm Castle, co Antrim (*qv*) and Kilcoleman Abbey, co Kerry (*qv*). A castellated office wing was also added, which has now been partly demolished, joining the house to a chapel. The entrance hall, though square, has a circular ceiling of rich plasterwork, treated as a rotunda with segmental pointed arches and scagliola columns; eagles in high relief in the spandrels of the arches and festoons above. Dining room with Ionic columns of scagliola screening the sideboard recess. Upstairs library with ceiling of alternate barrel and rib vaults, above a frieze of wreaths that is a hall-mark of the Morrisons. Chapel with ribbed ceiling. 20 years before 1798 Rebellion, the house featured in the saga of Eleanor Butler and Sarah Ponsonby, those two friends who later became celebrated as the "Ladies of Llangollen". Eleanor was kept here in disgrace after she and Sarah had tried to run away together, it being the home of her

Borris House: Library

Borris House: Chapel

sister, who was the wife of Thomas Kavanagh. One night she managed to escape and went to join Sarah, who lived with her cousins at Woodstock, co Kilkenny (*qv*). In C19, Borris was the home of the remarkable Arthur MacMorrough Kavanagh, who was born without arms or legs, but led an active and adventurous life, rode, shot and travelled in remote parts of Asia and elsewhere, as well as becoming an MP and a Privy Councillor. On one of his visits to Abbey Leix (*qv*), he remarked to Lady De Vesci: "It's an extraordinary thing—I haven't been here for five years but the stationmaster recognized me."

Borrismore House (formerly **Marymount**), **Urlingford, co Kilkenny** (NEVILLE/IFR). A Georgian house built by Garrett Nevill about the time of his marriage 1765 to Mary Hodson, after whom he named it Marymount.

Bowen's Court (with Mark Bence-Jones)

Bowen's Court, Kildorrery, co Cork (BOWEN/IFR). A classic example of the tall and square C18 Irish house. Built by Henry Bowen and completed by 1776, the work having allegedly taken 10 years; replacing an earlier house built by the Nash family, who from 1697 leased the estate which had been granted to the Cromwellian Col Henry Bowen—according to the family tradition, he was offered as much Irish land as his pet hawk could fly over, and it flew so far that people believed he had made a pact with the Devil. The house is attributed to Isaac Rothery; and indeed, the silvery-grey cutstone elevations, for all their simplicity, had a beauty of proportion that would suggest an accomplished hand. Of 3 storeys over a basement; 7 bay entrance front, slight 3 bay breakfront emphasized by quoins; simple pedimented doorcase; plain but well-moulded window surrounds; moderately high roof with parapet. Both sides of the house were intended to be of 6 bays, but only the west side was completed; work ceased before the north-east corner had been built, for the inevitable reason that the money ran out. In 2nd half of C19, Robert Bowen filled in this corner of the house with a lower service wing. Inside the house, the rooms were few, but of noble proportions; the hall, drawing room, dining room and library had friezes of C18 plasterwork. The hall had shouldered doorcases with segmental pediments and a chimneypiece of Kilkenny marble with a scroll pediment. At the back of the hall was the staircase hall lit by a Venetian window framed by Corinthian pilasters and an entablature; the stairs themselves were of fine oak joinery. Above the hall was a large upper hall known as the Lobby; and on the top floor there was a still larger room running right through the centre of the house with windows at either end. This, known as the Long Room, had its counterpart in the gallery at Mount Ievers (*qv*), and in the long galleries of Elizabethan and Jacobean houses in England; but was an unusual feature in a C18 Irish house. It was intended as a ballroom, but the floor would not stand dancing; and like the house itself, it was never finished; its coved ceiling was left plain, except for two rather primitive ovals of plaster decoration. It has to be reached by the upper flight of the back stairs, which came up, rather surprisingly, through its floor; since the extra flight of grand stairs that should have led up to it was to have been in the missing corner of the house. Bowen's Court was the home of Elizabeth Bowen (Mrs Alan Cameron), the novelist, who modelled the house in *The Last September* on it, and writes poetically in *Bowen's Court* of the house, which, "with its rows of dark windows set in the light facade against dark trees has the startling, meaning and abstract clearness of a house in a print, a house in which something important occurred once, and seems, from all evidence, to be occurring still". Owing to the rising costs of upkeep, Miss Bowen was obliged to sell Bowen's Court 1959; it was demolished by its subsequent owner *ca* 1961.

Boyle, co Roscommon (*see* KING HOUSE).

Boyne House, co Meath (*see* STACKALLAN HOUSE).

Boytonrath, Cashel, co Tipperary (BUTLER/IFR). An early C18 house consisting of a 2 storey centre and single-storey wings. The centre has 5 windows in its upper storey, the 2 outer ones on either side being close together; but only 1 window on either side of the doorway in the lower storey. The wings are 1 bay. High-pitched roofs.

Bracklyn Castle

Bracklyn Castle, Killucan, co Westmeath (FETHERSTONHAUGH/IFR). A C18 house consisting of a 2 storey 5 bay centre block with single-storey 1 bay wings. Wall carried up to form roof parapet. Early C19 pillared porch. Rustic stone arch at entrance to demesne.

Brade House

Brade House: Plasterwork

Brade House, Leap, co Cork (JERVOIS/IFR). A 3 storey, 5 bay C18 house with a fanlighted doorway. C18 plasterwork frieze in hall, incorporating the arms of the Jervois family. After the death of Samuel Jervois the younger 1794, it went to his illegitimate sons, who are reputed to have squandered the entire property; which had passed out of the family by *ca* 1850.

Braganstown, Castlebellingham, co Louth (GARSTIN/LGI1912). A showy C19 Gothic house.

Braganza, Carlow, co Carlow. By Thomas A. Cobden, of Carlow; built *ca* 1818 for D. S. Hill. 2 storey, with a wide eaved roof carried on brackets and a shallow curved bow at either side of both the front and the rear elevations. Small single storey Tuscan portico with pediment between the two bows of the front, which have a Wyatt window in each storey, the lower one being set under a relieving arch. Another Wyatt window in the centre, above the portico. Bold string course between the storeys, con-

Braganza

tinuing round the side of the house. Hall with flat circular ceiling over pendentives. Fine large drawing room, running the full depth of the house, with a bow at each end and an unusually broad frieze of plaster-work. Curving staircase in room on opposite side of hall to drawing room. A few years after it was built, the house became the residence of the Catholic Bishops of Kildare and Leighlin; which it continued to be until recently.

Braganza: Drawing Room

battlemented turret set at an obtuse angle to the facade. Sold *ca* 1960; now an hotel.

Brianstown, Cloondara, co Longford (ACHMUTY/LG1850–53). A cut-stone house of 2 storeys over a basement, with a dormered attic in a high-pitched roof; built 1731 for Samuel Achmuty, whose arms are incorporated in the modified Venetian doorway, above which there used to be a niche between 2 windows. Gibbsian window surrounds. After a fire in the present century, the house was reconstructed without the upper storey.

Bridestown

Bridestown, Glenville, co Cork. A 2 storey late-Georgian house with a forecourt flanked by earlier office ranges of cut-stone, at the front of which are two polygonal towers, joined by wrought-iron railings and entrance gates. According to tradition, the towers were built by Jonathan Morgan, a

Cork wine merchant, to please his French wife, whom he met on a visit to Bordeaux; for in France, even as late as C18, a tower on either side of the entrance to a house denoted the owner's nobility. The towers at Bridestown are certainly rather French in flavour; they have round-headed windows and niches below elliptical *oeils-de-boeuf*, now blocked up; and they formerly had pyramidal roofs, though one of them is now roofless. From a date-stone, it would seem that one of the forecourt ranges was not built until towards the end of C18; while the present house is later still, the original house having been burnt. In fact, the present house turns its back on the forecourt, having an entrance front with a fanlighted doorway on the other side. There is pleasant early C19 decoration in its drawing room and dining room. In the grounds, to the right of the forecourt, is a slender folly tower. Bridestown was sold by the Morgans during 2nd half of C19; they are said to have been ruined by the gambling of Lady Louisa Morgan (*née* Moore—*see* PERCEVAL-MAX-WELL/IFR), who was known as "Unlimited Loo". It afterwards passed to the Lindsay family.

Bridestream House, Knocknatulla, co Meath. A mid-C18 house consisting of a 2 storey pedimented centre block with small, square wings or pavilions. The fenestration of the centre block has been much altered and a large porch added; but it is possible to attribute the house to the amateur architect, Nathaniel Clements, from the similarity of the wings to the wings of other houses by Clements or attributed to him. In 1814, the residence of John Coates.

Brightfieldstown

Brightfieldstown: Plasterwork

Brightfieldstown, Minane Bridge, co Cork (ROBERTS, Bt, *of Glassenbury and Brightfieldstown*/PB). A long, 2 storey house one room deep with a return at the back, above Roberts Cove on the coast between Cork Harbour and Kinsale. From its appearance, early or mid-C18, but altered in late C18, or at the beginning of C19. 3 bays on either side of a baseless gable pediment in which there is a lunette window. Below the pediment, 3 windows, those on the out-

Breaghwy

Breaghwy, Castlebar, co Mayo (BROWNE/IFR). A large Victorian Baronial mansion of rough-hewn grey stone with red sandstone round the windows; unusually long for its height. Entrance front with single-storey battlemented porch. Garden front with stepped gables, polygonal corner turret with battlements and pointed roof, and another

Brightfieldstown: Staircase

side being narrower than that in the middle. Below again, two narrow windows, which are lower than the others, on either side of an exceptionally wide and somewhat urban doorway, with an elegant leaded fanlight and sidelights. Good ironwork railings on either side of front door steps. The present doorway was clearly put in during the later years of C18, or at the beginning of C19; probably at the same time as 3 principal rooms—a spacious hall and a large drawing room and dining room on either side of it—were given their friezes and cornices of delicate plasterwork. In the middle of the flat of the hall ceiling there is also an oval of delicate but more primitive plasterwork in very low relief. The staircase, behind the hall and in the return, lit by a Venetian window at right angles to the front of the house, is of wood with slender uprights and would seem to be contemporary with the doorway and the plasterwork in the main rooms. The Roberts family ceased to live in the house *ca* mid-C19; it subsequently became the home of the MacDonald family, by whom it was sold 1958. It is now derelict.

Brittas, Clonaslee, co Leix (DUNNE/ LGI 1912). A castellated house of sandstone with limestone dressings built 1869 by Major-Gen Rt Hon Francis Plunkett Dunne, MP, to the design of John McCurdy.

Brittas, co Meath

Brittas, co Meath

Brittas, Nobber, co Meath (BLIGH, *sub* BARRINGTON/IFR). A house of several periods. The long garden front consists of a

plain C18 centre, of 1 bay on either side of a curved bow, prolonged to the right by a 4 bay wing of similar style and height, added soon *post* 1800 to the design of Francis Johnston; and with, on the left, an earlier wing which is lower and now has mullioned windows. The entrance front is C19 Tudor Revival, of cut stone, with mullioned windows and a doorway with latticed side-lights recessed under an arch below the central gable. Small entrance hall. Room in central bow with simple C19 cornice. Frieze with garlands in dining room. Ballroom in Johnston wing, with elaborate early C19 plasterwork frieze and straight entablatures over 4 doorcases.

Brittas Castle, co Tipperary

Brittas Castle, Thurles, co Tipperary (LANGLEY/IFR; KNOX/IFR). The earlier castle here was burnt *ca* 1820, when occupied by Henry Grace Langley. His nephew, Major Henry Langley, began building what, if it had been completed, would have been the first "archaeological" C19 castle in Ireland; more closely based on medieval originals than any earlier Irish Medieval-Revival castle, and surrounded by a moat. It was designed by the versatile William Vitruvius Morrison; but in 1834, when only the great gate-tower had been built, Major Langley was killed by a falling stone and the work was abandoned. The gate-tower is of massive stonework, the gateway being set beneath a tall arch and flanked by polygonal turrets. It rises stark from the surrounding meadow, fronted by part of the moat which still holds water. Behind it is the very modest single-storey C19 house with which subsequent owners of Brittas have made do. The estate was sold 1853 to a branch of the Knox family.

Brockley Park

Brockley Park, Stradbally, co Leix (JOCELYN, RODEN, E/PB; YOUNG/LGI1912). A house built 1768 for 2nd Viscount Jocelyn, afterwards 1st Earl of Roden, Auditor-General of Ireland, to the design of Davis Duckart. Of 3 storeys over basement; 7 bay entrance front with breakfront centre; garden front of 4 bays with a projection at one side ending in a three-sided bow. 2 storey wing. Good interior plasterwork. By 1825, the Rodens had ceased to live at Brockley, which afterwards became the seat of the Young family; it was demolished 1944.

Brooklands

Brooklands, Belfast (OWDEN, *sub* GREER/ IFR). A 2 storey Georgian house with a 3 bay front, prolonged at one end by a 2 bay single-storey wing, and a 5 bay side. Pilastered porch; single-storey partly-bowed projection on side elevation. Eaved roof on bracket cornice. The seat of the Owden family.

Brook Lodge, Glanmire, co Cork. A 2 storey Georgian house with a front of 1 bay on either side of a curved central bow. Curved end bow. In the present century, the seat of the Berry family.

Brook Lodge, Halfway House, co Waterford (BOLTON *of Mount Bolton*/ LGI1912). A Georgian house originally belonging to the Penrose family, acquired in C19 by the Bolton family, who rebuilt it in an Italianate style with a roof on a bracket cornice.

Browne's Hill

Browne's Hill, Carlow, co Carlow (BROWNE-CLAYTON/IFR). A distinguished mid-C18 house of 3 storeys over a basement, faced in very regular granite ashlar; built 1763 for Robert Browne, to the design of an architect named Peters. 6 bay entrance front, with 2 bay pedimented breakfront. Partly enclosed pedimented Doric porch, with coupled columns at sides. Shouldered window surrounds. Solid roof parapet; balustraded area parapet. Curved entrance

Browne's Hill: Staircase

hall with mutule cornice and frieze of swags, and pedimented Doric doorcase, shaped to the curve, with fluted half-columns. Staircase hall decorated with plasterwork foliage; wooden stairs with turned balusters and carved ends to treads. Drawing room with ceiling of rococo plasterwork incorporating birds in high relief, in the manner of Robert West. Octagon bedroom. Some alterations carried out 1842, probably to the design of Thomas Alfred Cobden. Magnificent triumphal arch at entrance to demesne, with pediment, pilasters, volutes and rusticated wicket-gates, surmounted by lions; now removed to Lyons, co Kildare (*qv*). Browne's Hill was sold by Lt-Col W. P. Browne-Clayton 1951.

Brownhall, Ballintra, co Donegal (HAMILTON/LGI1937Supp). A 3 storey late-Georgian block by Robert Woodgate. 4 bay front with later single-storey portico; 3 bay side; 2 storey wing set back. Quoins. Hall with triglyph frieze. Heavy mid-C19 cornice in drawing room; late cornice in dining room.

Brownlow House

Brownlow House, Lurgan, co Armagh (BROWNLOW, LURGAN, B/PB). A large Elizabethan-Revival house by William Playfair, of Edinburgh, built from 1836 onwards for Charles Brownlow, 1st Lord Lurgan, whose son, 2nd Baron, owned the famous greyhound *Master McGrath*, and whose brother-in-law, Maxwell Close, built Drumbanagher

(*qv*), also to the design of Playfair. Of honey-coloured stone, with a romantic silhouette; many gables with tall finials; many tall chimneypots; oriels crowned with strapwork and a tower with a lantern and dome. The walls of 3 principal reception rooms are decorated with panels painted to resemble verd-antique; while the ceilings are grained to represent various woods. The grand staircase has brushwork decoration in the ceiling panels, and the windows are filled with heraldic stained glass. Sold 1903 to the Orange Order, its present owners, by whom it is used for occasional functions. Its grounds have become a public park.

Brownsbarn, Thomastown, co Kilkenny (MARSH/LGI1958; SHORE, TEIGNMOUTH, B/PB). A High Victorian Ruskinian-Gothic house by Sir Thomas Newenham Deane, of grey stone with bands of red sandstone giving a polychromic effect. On a high basement, which was the basement of an earlier house; so that as Victorian houses go, it has an unusually compact and straightforward plan, and its rooms have comfortable Regency proportions. Large square hall, with staircase at one side; large and small drawing room en suite. Doors and staircase of pitch pine, stained pleasantly dark; elaborately moulded marble chimneypieces, with flanking columns of different coloured marbles; reminiscent of the altars in Irish Catholic churches of later C19. Passed to the Teignmouths through the marriage of Anna Adelaide Caroline Marsh to 6th Lord Teignmouth.

Brownswood, Enniscorthy, co Wexford. An elegantly proportioned early C19 house of 2 storeys and 5 bays; the centre bay breaking forward. Pillared porch; eaved roof. Rising from the centre of the roof, a tower with a gracefully pointed roof, in the manner of Gola or Ancketill's Grove (*qqv*).

Bruree House, Bruree, co Limerick (SHELTON/LGI1958; VERNON, *sub* WESTMINSTER, D/PB). A 2 storey Victorian house with gables and pointed and shoulder-headed windows. Prominent roofs with simple cresting. In recent years the home of Major Stephen & Lady Ursula Vernon.

Bullock Castle, Dalkey, co Dublin. A medieval castle with 2 square Irish-battlemented towers and a plain 3 storey 3 bay later wing. In 1910 the residence of S. A. Quan-Smith.

Buncrana Castle

Buncrana Castle, Buncrana, co Donegal (RICHARDSON/LGI1912). A very distinguished early C18 house, built 1716 by George Vaughan, close to the shore of Lough Swilly. 2 storeys over basement; 7 bay centre block with 2 storey 1 bay overlapping wings.

Doorway with scroll pediment. Panelled interior. Axial approach by a 6-arched bridge over the river, near which stands an old tower-house of the O'Dohertys, Lords of Inishowen; and through a curving forecourt. Originally, the house was surrounded by elaborate gardens and terraces. By *ca* 1840, Buncrana belonged to a Mrs Todd; it later became a seat of Alexander Airth Richardson, son of Jonathan Richardson, MP, of Lambeg, and his wife, Margaret Airth. It is now falling into decay.

Bunowen Castle, Clifden, co Galway (BLAKE, Bt, *of Menlough*/PB1970). A dramatic but somewhat insubstantial C19 castle on the shores of Bunowen Bay, at the south-western tip of Connemara.

Bunratty Castle

Bunratty Castle, co Clare (O'BRIEN, INCHIQUIN, B/PB; and THOMOND, E/DEP; STUDDERT/IFR; RUSSELL/IFR; VEREKER, GORT, V/PB). One of the finest C15 castles in Ireland, standing by the side of a small tidal creek of the Shannon estuary; built *ca* 1425, perhaps by one of the McNamaras; then held by the O'Briens, who became Earls of Thomond, until 6th Earl surrendered it to the Cromwellian forces during the Civil War. A tall, oblong building, it has a square tower at each corner; these are linked, on the north and south sides, by a broad arch just below the topmost storey. The entrance door leads into a large vaulted hall, or guard chamber, above which is the Great Hall, the banqueting hall and audience chamber of the Earls of Thomond, with its lofty timbered roof. Whereas the body of the castle is only of 3 storeys—there being another vaulted chamber below the guard chamber—the towers contain many storeys of small rooms, reached up newel stairs and by passages in the thickness of the walls. One of these rooms, opening off the Great Hall, is the chapel, which still has its original plasterwork ceiling of *ca* 1619, richly adorned with a pattern of vines and grapes. There are also fragments of early C17 plasterwork in some of the window recesses. After the departure of the O'Briens, a C17 brick house was built between the two northern towers; Thomas Studdert, who bought Bunratty early in C18, took up residence here 1720. Later, the Studderts built themselves "a spacious and handsome modern residence in the demesne" and the castle became a constabulary barracks, falling into disrepair so that, towards the end of C19, the ceiling of the Great Hall collapsed. Bunratty was eventually inherited by Lt-Cmdr R. H. Russell, whose mother was a

Studdert, and sold by him to 7th Viscount Gort 1956. With the help of Mr Percy Le Clerc and Mr John Hunt, Lord Gort carried out a most sympathetic restoration of the castle, which included removing c17 house, re-roofing the Great Hall in oak and adding battlements to the towers. The restored castle contains Lord Gort's splendid collection of medieval and c16 furniture, tapestries and works of art, and is open to the public; "medieval banquets" being held here as a tourist attraction. Since the death of Lord Gort, Bunratty and its contents have been held in trust for the Nation.

Burgage, Leighlinbridge, co Carlow (VIGORS/IFR). A plain 2 storey 3 bay c18 house. Tripartite doorway with blocking.

Burnchurch House, Bennettsbridge, co Kilkenny (BUTLER, *sub* DUNBOYNE, B/PB; DE MONTMORENCY/IFR). A 2 storey 3 bay late-Georgian house built for Rev Richard Butler, Vicar of Burnchurch. Large drawing room. Remained in the Butler family until 3rd quarter of c19, being occupied by succeeding vicars; then sold to the Mosse family, millers, of Bennettsbridge. Bought by Capt J.P. de Montmorency, formerly of Castle Morres (*qv*), 1949.

Burnham House

Burnham House

Burnham House, Dingle, co Kerry (EVELEIGH DE MOLEYNS, *sub* VENTRY, B/PB). From its appearance, a 3 storey 7 bay Georgian block enlarged by the addition of 2 storey wings, refaced and embellished in the mid to late c19. Entrance front with central feature of engaged Doric columns supporting sections of entablature and a steep pediment above a balustraded and pedimented Doric porte-cochère; tympana of pediments decorated with acanthus carving. Eaved roof on centre and wings; that of the centre being on a modillion cornice. Garden front with 2 storey rectangular projections in the centre and 3 sided bows at the ends of the wings. Now an institution.

Burntcourt Castle, Clogheen, co Tipperary (CHEARNLEY/LGI1912). One of the largest and also probably the last of the gabled semi-fortified early c17 houses; consisting of a centre block of 2 storeys over a high basement with a gabled attic, and 4 gabled corner towers; the whole building

Burntcourt Castle

having no less than 26 gables. Regularly-disposed mullioned windows; tall chimneys; projecting corbels of stone to support timber defensive galleries. Built from 1640 onwards by Sir Richard Everard, afterwards a member of the Supreme Council of the Confederation of Kilkenny, who was hanged by Ireton, Cromwell's son-in-law, 1651. In the previous year, when the Cromwellian troops approached his still unfinished house, Lady Everard set it on fire in order to prevent it falling into their hands. It has remained a ruin ever since. In early c18, Anthony Chearnley, the painter, built a 2 storey 5 bay gable-ended house with a dormered attic in front of the ruin in the bawn, and laid out a formal garden outside the bawn wall. The remnants of this house are now used as farm buildings.

Burrenwood, Castlewellan, co Down (HAWKINS-MAGILL, *sub* HAWKINS/IFR; MEADE, *sub* CLANWILLIAM, E/PB). A single-storey early c19 cottage ornée, originally thatched and rather similar to Derrymore, co Armagh (*qv*); built *ca* 1820 by Gen Hon Robert Meade, and having, as one of 2 wings which extend back from it on either side of a narrow open-ended court, an earlier cottage built by his mother, Theodosia Hawkins-Magill, Countess of Clanwilliam, from whom he inherited the property. Lady Clanwilliam's cottage is said to have been built for her in six weeks, as a stopping place on the road south from her home, Gill Hall (*qv*), when there was an epidemic at Rathfriland, where she normally stayed. The front of the 1820 cottage has a doorway surmounted by a small dormer-gable, between 2 Wyatt windows. The roof has wide eaves supported by logs to form a rustic veranda or colonnade.

Burton Hall, co Carlow

Burton Hall, Carlow, co Carlow (MAINWARING-BURTON/IFR). An important early c18 house, begun 1712. Of 3 storeys on a high plinth; 9 bays; 3 bay breakfront centre. Rusticated entrance doorway up many steps; pointed window above it, round-headed window above that again. Bold

quoins; solid roof parapet with recessed panels. A bow window was added to the garden front 1840–44; and at some period, the top storey was removed. Sold 1927 by W.F. Burton; demolished 1930.

Burton Park (formerly **Burton House**), **Churchtown, co Cork** (PERCEVAL, EGMONT, E/PB; RYAN-PURCELL/IFR). Originally a fine cut-stone house built in several stages between *ca* 1665 and 1686 for Sir John Perceval, 1st Bt, and his two sons, Sir Philip, 2nd Bt and Sir John, 3rd Bt; designed by Capt William Kenn, his son, Benjamin, and Thomas Smith. Of 2 storeys over a basement, with a dormered attic; 7 bay front, with unusually tall windows. The roof was surmounted by a row of tall chimneys and a lantern with a copper ball on top of it. The house stood within a series of walled enclosures, with turrets at the outer corners. Like his brother, the 3rd Bt died young, 1686, leaving several infant sons, one of whom eventually became 1st Earl of Egmont. In 1690 the house was burnt by James II's troops as they retreated south after the Battle of the Boyne. A new 2 storey house was built by an Earl of Egmont in the late-Georgian period; it was subsequently acquired by the Purcell family, who refaced it in Victorian cement and gave it a high roof with curvilinear dormer-gables. Hall with staircase rising round it; stairs of wood, with thin balusters. Pedimented Georgian doorcases put in later. Large drawing room with ceiling of delicate late-Georgian plasterwork; walls decorated in the Louis Seize style. Victorian dining room. Castellated entrance gateway, from which a straight avenue of trees leads up to the house.

Burtown House

Burtown House, Athy, co Kildare (FENNELL/LGI1958). An early to mid-c18 house joined by screen walls to small wings, of which only the facade of one remains, and part of the facade of the other; remodelled internally later in c18; re-roofed and the facade of the entrance front remodelled in early c19. The entrance front, of 2 storeys and 3 bays, now has the appearance of an early c19 villa; with the centre bay breaking forward and the fanlighted entrance door recessed in an arch; the upstairs windows have been made taller by adding false sections to them. The roof is eaved, on a bracket cornice. The screen walls, however, have blocked-up round-headed c18 doorways with rustications, and in the remaining wing facade there is a blocked-up Diocletian window. The garden front has a central 3 sided bow, with irregular fenestration on either side of it; like the entrance front it is 2 storey, but there is a mezzanine fitted in at the sides. The hall has a doorway with an internal fanlight at its inner end; the ceiling is of Wyatt-style plasterwork; there are oval wall medallions surrounded by wreaths and busts in 4 corners. The dining room and study keep their plain early or mid-C18 cornices and doors with shouldered architraves; the dining room has an alcove with a rather Baroque curve. Behind the hall is a corridor with a frieze of mutules and foliage; leading to the elegant wooden staircase, which is not central, and to the drawing room, which has a curved end, in the garden front bow, a Wyatt-style plasterwork frieze, and an alcove decorated rather more exuberantly with vases and foliage. There is more plasterwork on the staircase and in some upstairs rooms. Burtown was originally built by a member of the Houghton family; it subsequently belonged to the Wakefield family, from whom it passed by inheritance to the Fennells.

Butlerstown Castle

Busherstown

Busherstown, Moneygall, Offaly (MINCHIN/IFR). A partly castellated 2 storey house built on the site of an old castle originally called Bouchardstown, after the original owner, Bouchard de Marisco. Granted in C17 to Charles Minchin; an early C18 house being built on the site of the old castle by Humphrey Minchin, MP, and improved by his son, another Humphrey. The house was partly burnt 1764, having been set on fire by robbers; it was subsequently rebuilt and given a slightly castellated facade, rather similar to the nearby Mount Heaton (*qv*). Round tower at one end; 3 bay centre, with Georgian sash windows; bow-ended square tower with segmental pointed windows at other end of front. Battlemented and machicolated parapet. The side of the house is not castellated,

but quite plain; of 3 bays, the centre bay breaking forward. Lower service wing with gable at other end of house. Painted ceiling decoration in reception rooms. Early C19 round tower on the summit of a wooded hill behind the house. Sold 1973.

Bushfield, co Kerry (*see* KILCOLEMAN ABBEY).

Bushy Park, Terenure, co Dublin (SHAW, Bt/PB). A plain 3 storey Georgian house with large C19 ground floor windows and external shutters. Belonged, *ca* 1800, to Abraham Wilkinson; later became the seat of his son-in-law, Sir Robert Shaw, 1st Bt, MP and Lord Mayor of Dublin (a 1st cousin of George Bernard Shaw's grandfather) who had previously lived nearby at Terenure (*qv*).

Butlerstown Castle, Tomhaggard, co Wexford (BOXWELL/IFR). A square 2 storey late-Georgian house with a Victorian roof. 3 bay front, projecting centre with gable and Victorian bargeboard and Georgian Gothic window above fanlighted doorway. Courtyard at one end of house, enclosed by

office ranges and wall, and with a well-preserved old tower-house at one corner. Small chapel-like building, with belfry and Gothic tracery window, projecting from one side of tower-house, prolonged by battlemented wall.

Buttevant Castle, Buttevant, co Cork (ANDERSON, Bt, *of Fermoy*/PB1861; LLOYD/LGI1912). One of the old fortifications of the town of Buttevant, made into a castellated house early in C19 by the enterprising Army contractor, John Anderson, who laid out the town of Fermoy. A tall and narrow building, with a round tower at one side and a curved end at the other. Gothic windows. Subsequently owned by the Lloyd family.

Byblox, Doneraile, co Cork (MORROGH-BERNARD/IFR; PREECE, *sub* FARQUHAR, Bt/PB). A 3 storey bow-ended house which appears to have been built *ca* 1793 by Robert Fennell Crone. 6 bay front; doorway with wide segmental fanlight extending over door and sidelights. Elegant curving staircase in one of the end bows. In recent years the home of Mr & Mrs J.R. Preece; and then of Mr & Mrs Terence Millin. Now demolished.

C

Cabinteely House (formerly **Clare Hill**), **Cabinteely, co Dublin** (NUGENT, E/DEP; BYRNE/LGI1863; ORMSBY-HAMILTON, *sub* ORMSBY/IFR). A C18 house built round 3 sides of a square; with well-proportioned rooms and good decoration. Built by that genial Irishman on the C18 English political scene, Robert, 1st and last Earl Nugent, on an estate which belonged to his brother-in-law, George Byrne, and afterwards to his nephew and political protegé, Michael Byrne, MP. The house was originally known as Clare Hill, Lord Nugent's 2nd title being Viscount Clare; but it became known as Cabinteely House after being bequeathed by Lord Nugent to the Byrnes, who made it their seat in preference to the original Cabinteely House; which, having been let for a period to John Dwyer—who, confusingly, was secretary to Lord Chancellor Fitzgibbon, 1st Earl of Clare—was demolished at end of C18 and a new house, known as Marlfield and afterwards a seat of the Jessop family (*see* LGI1912), built on the site. The new Cabinteely House (formerly Clare Hill), afterwards passed to the Ormsby-Hamilton family. In recent years, it was the home of Mr Joseph McGrath, founder of the Irish Sweep and a well-known figure on the Turf.

Cabra Castle, Kingscourt, co Cavan (PRATT, *sub* DE MONTMORENCY/IFR; SHEPPARD/LGI1958). The original Cabra, seat of the Pratts, was on the opposite side of the road to where the C19 castle of that name, the family seat in more recent years, now stands. It was an early C18 villa with a pediment extending over the whole front, in the full Palladian tradition; so that the Knight of Glin considers it to have been almost certainly by Sir Edward Lovett Pearce. The pediment was adorned with statues and had a lunette window in its tympanum. The C18 villa was later added to and engulfed; then, *ca* 1830, Col Joseph Pratt bought the adjoining property, Cormey Castle, which had formerly belonged to a Mr Foster, and enlarged the house here to make a new seat for his family, re-naming it Cabra Castle. The original house became known as Old Cabra and was used as a ballroom, until its destruction by fire 1950s. Col Pratt's new Cabra Castle, completed by 1837, probably incorporates the old Cormey Castle, which was also C19 Gothic. It is a stucco-faced castle of what appears to be vast extent, for its outbuildings are joined to it and also castellated; but somewhat insubstantial; its battlements, towers and turrets being a little thin. Though its windows are all either rectangular or pointed—

Cabra Castle

Cabra Castle: Entrance Door

Cabra Castle: Study

Cabra Castle: Staircase

Cabra Castle: Drawing Room

and now mostly plate-glass—it seems, from a contemporary description, that its architect's intention was to produce a "castellated mansion in the Norman style of architecture"; and indeed, the square tower with corner turrets at one end of the rambling edifice is a miniature stucco version of a Norman *donjon* like the keep of Rochester Castle. The entrance door, deeply recessed under a pointed arch, is in this tower; it leads into a low-ceilinged hall from which a bifurcating staircase with a metalwork balustrade ascends to the first floor, which is in effect the *piano nobile*. The staircase hall is surrounded by a gallery at second floor level, partly carried on iron brackets, and has a ceiling of rather thin fretting. At the head of the stairs is a charming Victorian drawing room, with an original gilt wall-paper. The other rooms are undistinguished, apart from a small study with elegantly-glazed bookcases set in ogee-arched recesses; while some of the corridors have attractive pointed arches. Cabra Castle was inherited by Mr M. C. ff. Sheppard, who sold it *ca* 1966. It is now an hotel.

Cabra (or **Cabragh**) **House, co Dublin** (SEGRAVE/LG1972). A 3 storey house of early C18 appearance. Front with 3 bay centre and 2 bays breaking forward on either side. Doorcase with entablature on console brackets; wall carried up to be parapet; single-storey gabled addition at side with round-headed windows; low buildings at back.

Caherelly Grange, Herbertstown, co Limerick (FURNELL/IFR). An old castle, not lived in since mid-C19.

Cahir, co Tipperary (BUTLER, GLENGALL, E/DEP; CHARTERIS, *sub* WEMYSS, E/PB). Cahir Castle, seat of the Butlers, Barons Caher and afterwards Earls of Glengall, is the largest and best preserved C15 and C16 castle in Ireland; it stands on an island in the River Suir by the town of Cahir and has a magnificent park stretching away southwards from it. Within its curtain wall are several courtyards, a massive keep and a great hall, which was re-roofed in C19. Unlike most medieval castles, Cahir never really became a ruin; but the family ceased to live in it during C18 and built a house of 3 storeys and 5 bays with a central Venetian window (now Cahir House Hotel) facing the main square of the town and backing onto the Castle park. Either the 10th Baron Caher and 1st Earl of Glengall—whose father was a very distant kinsman of the 8th Baron, and whose mother, according to Dorothea Herbert, had been a beggar in the

Cahir: Swiss Cottage (2 views)

Cahir Park

Cahir Castle

streets of Cahir—or his son, the 2nd Earl, who succeeded 1819, built a delightful cottage ornée known as Swiss Cottage in a romantic situation at the southern end of the park, traditionally for a mistress; it has thatched roofs and elaborate rustic verandas and was probably designed by John Nash. Its principal room has a Dufour wallpaper, *Rives du Bosphore*. 2nd Earl, whose name figures in a list of candidates for Court appointments whom the Prince Consort turned down because they were "Dandies and Roués of London and the Turf", usually lived in Swiss Cottage when he was at Cahir; at any rate during his bachelor days. After his marriage to the daughter of a rich government contractor, he seems to have contemplated building a new house; but nothing had been done by the time of his death 1858, when the earldom became extinct and the estate went to his daughter, Lady Margaret Charteris. It was she who built the house known as Cahir Park, or Cahir Lodge, across the river from the Castle, which served as the family seat from now on. Begun in 1861, to the design of Lanyon, Lynn & Lanyon, it was worthy neither of its architects nor of its glorious setting; being a singularly dull and dour essay in watered-down Baronial, with steep gables, pointed plate-glass windows and a turret with a pyramidal roof. Its interior was no less uninspired, with meanly-proportioned rooms which in later years were to a certain extent redeemed by some handsome French furniture. In the present century, Lt-Col R. B. Charteris added a large billiard room-cum-library with a ceiling of neo-Caroline plasterwork. The house was gutted by fire soon after the estate had been sold following Col Charteris's death, at the age of 94, 1961.

Cahircalla

Cahircalla, Ennis, co Clare (STACPOOLE/IFR; CROWE/LG11958). A 2 storey house of C19 appearance; front of 5 bays, with 1 bay pedimented breakfront; projecting porch, entablatures on console brackets over ground floor windows. Roof on bracket cornice. Lower wing at back. Occupied by Richard Stacpoole 1820s; afterwards became the seat of Wainwright Crowe.

Cahircon (also known as **Cahiracon**), **Killadysert, co Clare** (KELLY, *sub* ROCHE-KELLY/IFR; VANDELEUR/IFR). A late-Georgian block of 3 storeys over a basement with 2 storey mid-C19 wings and other additions, facing across the Shannon estuary. Main block of 5 bays, with Ionic porch; wings with 3 sided bows. Prominent roofs. At one end, a single-storey addition with a lantern; at the other, a large conservatory. "U"-shaped stables of 1820; gate lodge with

Cahircon

Doric portico. The seat of the Scott family; afterwards of the Kelly and Vandeleur families. Now owned by a religious order.

Cahirduggan, Midleton, co Cork (O'CAL-LAGHAN/LGI1958). A 2 storey house of late-Georgian appearance. 5 bay front, with fanlighted doorway; 5 bay side. Eaved roof.

Cahir-Guillamore

Cahir-Guillamore, Kilmallock, co Limerick (O'GRADY, GUILLAMORE, V/PB1953). A 2 storey late C17 house. High roof with dormers; projecting end bays. Now totally derelict.

Cahirmoyle

Cahirmoyle, Ardagh, co Limerick (O'BRIEN, *sub* INCHIQUIN, B/PB). A 2 storey Victorian house of rough-hewn ashlar in the Celtic-Romanesque style, built 1871 for Edward O'Brien, son of the Young Ireland leader William Smith O'Brien, to the design of J. J. McCarthy. The facades are decorated with a carved string course, the roof is carried on a cornice like a miniature cor-belled arcade, and there is much structural polychromy; courses of pink stone inter-spersed with the general grey; grey and white voussoirs in the round window arches, which are supported on columns with pink marble shafts. There are similar arches, supported by pairs of pink marble columns, on 3 sides of the large balustraded porte-cochère. At one end of the entrance front is a 3 storey pyramidal-roofed tower. The ad-joining garden front has a 3 sided bow and a single-storey 2 bay rectangular balustraded projection. 2 storey hall surrounded by ar-cades with polished marble columns; capi-

Cahirmoyle: Porte-Cochère

tals of columns with carvings of human figures, animals and foliage. Chimneypieces in reception rooms of stone inlaid with different coloured Irish marbles. The house now belongs to a religious order and has been sympathetically enlarged in the same style; as well as being restored after a recent fire.

Cahirnane, Killarney, co Kerry (HER-BERT/IFR). A plain gabled Victorian house with plate-glass windows, some of them mullioned; built 1877 by Henry Herbert. Now an hotel.

Cahore House, Cahore Point, co Wexford (GEORGE/LGI1958). An early to mid-C19 Tudor-Gothic house, with gables and a tall battlemented tower.

Cairndhu, Larne, co Antrim (STEWART-CLARK, Bt/PB). A 2 storey, many-gabled Victorian house, given a Chinese flavour by the design of the ornate open-work barge-boards, and of the elaborate wooden veranda and balcony running along most of its front.

Cairndhu

Caledon, co Tyrone (BOYLE, CORK AND ORRERY, E/PB; ALEXANDER, CALEDON, E/PB). A seat of 5th Earl of Orrery (a friend of Dean Swift), who described the house here (1738) as "old, low, and though full of rooms, not very large". Sold by 7th Earl to James Alexander, a wealthy East Indian "Nabob", who subsequently became 1st Earl of Caledon; and who replaced Lord Orrery's house with a house built on a different site, to the design of Thomas Cooley 1779. 2 storey; 7 bay entrance front with pedimented breakfront centre; garden front with 1 bay on either side of a broad central curved bow, the downstairs window in each of these bays being of the so-called Wyatt type, set under a relieving arch; 5 bay side. The plan has a strong resemblance to that of Mount Kennedy (*qv*); a large hall with a screen of yellow scagliola Doric columns at its inner end, a Doric frieze and plasterwork in the Wyatt manner on the walls and ceiling, opens into an oval drawing room extending into the garden front bow. On one side of the drawing room is the dining room; on the other, a boudoir with a slightly vaulted ceiling of delicate plaster-work in "Harlequin" style, coloured in chocolate, scarlet, apple green and tortoise-shell, incorporating a circular painted me-dallion; the walls of the room being hung with an apple-green Chinese or "India" paper which was probably brought back from the East by "Nabob" Alexander him-self. In 1812, 2nd Earl enlarged and em-bellished the house to the design of John Nash. 2 single-storey domed wings or pa-vilions were added, flanking the entrance front and projecting forwards from it; joined by a colonnade of coupled Ionic columns, to form a long veranda or *stoep* such as Lord Caledon had probably grown

Caledon

used to sitting under when he was Governor of the Cape of Good Hope. One of the two wings contains a large and splendid library, with a coffered dome and Corinthian columns of porphyry scagliola. Nash also re-decorated the oval drawing room, making it one of the most perfect Regency interiors in Ireland; with friezes of gilt Classical figures and mouldings in cut paper work; elaborately shaped drapery pelmets and mirrors supported by swan-necked consoles. In 1835, towards the end of his life, 2nd Earl carried out further additions to the house, when his architect may have been Joseph Pennethorne, who continued Nash's practice after his death 1834. A 3rd storey was added to the central block, the pediment being replaced at the higher level; and the entrance was moved round to one end of the house, where a single storey extension containing a domed octagonal hall, fronted by a hexastyle Ionic porte-cochère, was built; the original hall becoming the saloon. In the park is c18 Bone House, its pillars and arches faced with ox bones; the only surviving relic of 5th Earl of Ossory's rococo garden. Towards the end of c19, the park was inhabited by wapiti and black bears, brought back by 4th Earl of Caledon who had hunted and ranched in the Wild West. His 3rd son was Field Marshal Earl Alexander of Tunis, whose boyhood was spent here.

Camass House

Camass House, Bruff, co Limerick (BEVAN/IFR). A plain 2 storey house of 5 bays with a porch. External shutters. Small battlemented tower near entrance gate.

Camla Vale, Monaghan, co Monaghan (WESTENRA, ROSSMORE, B/PB). A late-Georgian house of 1 storey over a high basement, with wide three-sided and curved bows and a pillared porch. Parapeted roof; windows set under relieving arches. At one side, a long wing, of 2 storeys, but lower than the main block and with no roof parapet. Large hall; large bow-fronted drawing room. The estate, which adjoins that of Rossmore Park (*qv*), originally belonged to a branch of the Montgomery family. It was bought early in c19 by Lt-Col Henry Westenra, who left it to his nephew, 3rd Lord Rossmore. *Post World War II*, 6th Lord Rossmore came to

live here, having abandoned Rossmore Park; and the pictures and furniture brought from Rossmore gave an air of great splendour to the large and lofty Regency rooms. From the drawing room ceiling hung a pair of particularly beautiful crystal chandeliers; the library was fitted with handsome bookcases which came from the library at Rossmore. Camla Vala was sold *ca* 1962 and has since been demolished.

Camlin

Camlin, co Donegal (TREDENNICK/LGI-1912). A Tudor-Gothic house of *ca* 1840, by John B. Keane, rather similar to Keane's building at Castle Irvine, co Fermanagh (*qv*). 2 storey; main block symmetrical, having 2 bays on either side of a central gable with a corbelled oriel over a castellated porch; 1 bay deep. Battlemented parapet and tall and slender octagonal corner turrets. Wing at back incorporating part of earlier house. Gothic gateway.

Camolin Park, Camolin, co Wexford (ANNESLEY, VALENTIA, V/PB; CAULFEILD, *sub* CHARLEMONT, V/PB). A square block of superior quality, dating from the first half of c18. Good doorcase with segmental pediment. The seat of the Annesleys, Earls of Mountnorris and Viscounts Valentia; sold by them 1858. A ruin for many years; demolished altogether *ca* 1974.

Camphire, Cappoquin, co Waterford (USSHER/IFR; DOBBS/IFR). A 2 storey 5 bay early c19 house in an attractive situation by the Blackwater estuary. Porch; roof on cornice; irregular side.

Cangort

Cangort, Shinrone, Offaly (ATKINSON/IFR). The seat of the Atkinson family 1600–1957. Original castle besieged and destroyed by the Cromwellian forces and the family fled. They returned at the Restoration and built a house on the right of the castle, which was subsequently altered from time to time; 2 very small rooms from the castle surviving at the back of the present house. The front of the house was rebuilt in early-Victorian Tudor-Gothic, being finished 1850; with steep pointed gables and plain mullioned windows.

Caledon

Caledon: Boudoir ceiling

Caledon: Oval Drawing Room

Cangort Park

Cangort Park, Shinrone, Offaly (TRENCH, *sub* ASHTOWN, B/PB). An elegant 2 storey villa, built for William Trench, brother of 1st Lord Ashtown, and completed by 1807. Conclusively attributed to Richard Morrison by Mr McParland, who describes it as "full of spatial surprises, introduced by the extraordinary funnelled entrance". The latter is a deep arched recess, beneath which the entrance door is set; it has a wide, concave surround and is the dominant feature of the 3 bay entrance front; a front identical to those of two other Morrison villas in Offaly, Ballylin and Bellair (*qqv*). The interior is ingeniously planned, with domed lobbies and rooms that are bowed or covered with trellis-work barrel vaults. The plasterwork is by James Talbot, who was associated with Morrison on other houses.

Capard

Capard, Rosenallis, co Leix (PIGOTT/ LGI1912). A 2 storey early C19 house with a 5 bay front; the centre bay pedimented and projecting boldly, with a window in a rectangular recess above a Doric portico. The Pigott family tree is painted on a wall in one of the rooms. Straight canal in garden.

Cappagh House, Cappagh, co Waterford (USSHER/IFR; CHAVASSE/IFR). A 2 storey Victorian house built 1875 by R. J. Ussher to the design of the engineer who constructed the railway from Cork to Rosslare; replacing an earlier house, which was subsequently used as outbuildings. Camber-headed windows cutting through string-courses; 3 sided bow on principal front; roundheaded staircase window with Romanesque tracery; highish roof. Sold 1944 by Mr Arland Ussher, the writer, to Col Kendal Chavasse.

Cappamurra, Dundrum, co Tipperary. A 2 storey house with round-headed windows in its upper storey and windows of unusual shape below. A seat of the Grene family.

Cappoquin House

Cappoquin House, Cappoquin, co Waterford (KEANE, Bt/PB). A square 2 storey house of 1779 with a handsome 7 bay ashlar front facing over the town of Cappoquin to the River Blackwater: 3 bay breakfront centre with round-headed windows; quoins; balustraded roof parapet with urns. The house was burnt 1923, but afterwards rebuilt and the fine late C18 interiors reproduced exactly as they were; the architect of the rebuilding being Richard Orpen, brother of Sir William Orpen, the painter. When the house was rebuilt, the front facing the Blackwater, which was formerly the entrance front, became the garden front; and what was formerly the back of the house became the entrance front; it is of 6 bays with a frontispiece of engaged columns and faces onto an attractive courtyard, entered

through an arch. The present entrance hall has a stone flagged floor and a frieze of plasterwork in late C18 manner. Beyond is an impressive top-lit staircase hall with a coffered dome. Beyond again is the former hall, now the drawing room, which has a screen of Ionic columns and an Adamesque ceiling.

Carbury Castle, co Kildare (*see* CASTLE CARBERY).

Careysville, Fermoy, co Cork (CAREY/ LGI1863; MONTGOMERY *of Killee*/LGI1912; CAVENDISH, DEVONSHIRE, D/PB). A C18 house of 2 storeys over a high basement and 5 bays, above the River Blackwater. Subtly spaced windows. The seat of the Carey family; passed by inheritance to the Montgomery family, from whom it was bought by the Duke of Devonshire, whose Irish seat, Lismore Castle (*qv*), is a few miles further down the river.

Cargins Park, Roscommon, co Roscommon (DROUGHT/LGI1912). A 2 storey 3 bay Victorian house with a porch.

Carker House, Doneraile, co Cork (EVANS/LGI1912). A 2 storey C18 house. 6 bay front; 2 bay breakfront, with small pediment-gable; tripartite round-headed doorcase. Now derelict.

Carnagh, New Ross, co Wexford (LAMBERT/LGI1912; LAMBERT/LGI1958). A Georgian house with a fanlighted doorway; pillars between hall and staircase; Adamesque plasterwork.

Carnalway Glebe, Kilcullen, co Kildare (GUINNESS/IFR). An unusually attractive and spacious early to mid-C19 glebe house in the Gothic taste, its entrance front flanked by a Gothic outbuilding which looks like a chapel or orangery. Hall with trefoil-headed panels; three reception rooms *en suite*, with simple Gothic decoration. Lately the home of Mrs M. S. Booth (*née* Guinness), now married to Mr Thomas Long.

Carnelly

Carnelly, Ennis, co Clare. A 3 storey mid-C18 house of pink brick, built for George Stamer almost certainly to the design of his brother-in-law, Francis Bindon. 5 bay front; Venetian doorway, windows with keystones, those in the top storey touching the frieze of the cornice. The front is prolonged by a 2 storey 3 bay wing, with rusticated window surrounds. Elaborately decorated drawing room; ceiling of foliage in low relief; modillion cornice; frames, festoons and pedimented mirrors on walls. At one end of the room is an unusual feature of 2 pairs of fluted Corinthian columns supporting an entablature with Corinthian pilasters behind them and a round-headed frame containing a mirror; it might have been imagined that the room was once a Catholic chapel and that the altar was here; but this cannot have been the case, for the Stamers were Protestants descended from a Cromwellian soldier who is said to have brought a curse on the family through taking part in the burning of a convent.

Carnew Castle

Carnew Castle, Carnew, co Wicklow (FITZWILLIAM, E/PB; SPICER/LG1952). An old castle which was in ruins by the end of C18—according to the popular account, it was battered by Cromwell's troops from a rock above the village—and which was re-roofed and modernized *ca* 1817 by 4th Earl Fitzwilliam, whose Irish seat, Coolattin (*qv*), is nearby. As restored, it is of 3 storeys with regularly disposed Georgian sash windows; there is a round tower at one side of the front, and a porch with a Georgian-Gothic door. The parapet is battlemented in a simple manner. The entrance from the village street is through a Gothic gateway with an ogee arch. Having been restored, the castle was used as the Rectory. *Post World War II*, it became the home of Capt S. R. F. Spicer.

Carramore, Ballina, co Mayo (JACKSON/LGI1912). A 2 storey early C19 house. 3 bay entrance front; fanlighted doorway with sidelights; windows on either side set in arched recesses. 4 bay side elevation. Eaved roof on bracket cornice. Originally the seat of the Vaughan family; passed to the Jackson family through marriage early in C19. Now ruinous.

Carrick-on-Suir, co Tipperary: The Castle (BUTLER, ORMONDE, M/PB). A house built *ca* 1568 by "Black Thomas", 10th Earl of Ormonde, similar to many English Tudor manor houses but unique in Ireland in having survived intact and in being unfortified; though it had the protection of the 2 towered C15 castle in front of which it was

built; the house, which is horseshoe-shaped, forming three sides of a small inner court, and the castle the fourth. The house is of 2 storeys with a gabled attic; the towers of the castle rise behind it. The gables are steep, and have finials; there are more finials on little piers at the corners of the building. There are full-sized mullioned windows on the ground floor as well as on the floor above, the lights having the slightly curved

The Castle, Carrick-on-Suir

heads which were fashionable in late C16. There is a rectangular porch-oriel in the centre of the front, and an oriel of similar form at one end of the left-hand side elevation. The finest room in the house is a long gallery on the first floor, which has 2 elaborately carved stone chimneypieces—one of which was removed to Kilkenny Castle (*qv*) 1909, but has since been returned—and a ceiling and frieze of Elizabethan plaster-

work. The decoration includes busts of Elizabeth I, who was a cousin of "Black Thomas" Ormonde through her mother, Anne Boleyn, and used to call him her "Black Husband"; she is said to have promised to honour Carrick with a visit. The old castle served as part of the house and not merely as a defensive adjunct to it; containing, among other rooms, a chapel with carved stone angels. Carrick was the favourite house of 12th Earl, afterwards the Great Duke of Ormonde, in his younger days; but afterwards the family deserted it, while continuing to own it down to the present century. In 1780s, when Dorothea Herbert and her family were living near Carrick, it was let to an elderly couple named Galwey. By the beginning of this century it was in a state of romantic decay, untouched by C19 "improvements", its grey walls covered in ivy and lichen; empty and silent but for the "chatter of the jackdaws" and "the rustling of the tall water-weeds that part the castle from the Suir". Had it been in England, someone would have fallen in love with it and restored it sympathetically as a house to live in; but in Ireland, during the earlier years of this century, no such "rescuer" was forthcoming; so that it fell increasingly into disrepair until it was taken over by the Office of Public Works, which is gradually restoring it as a national monument. Much of its magic has been lost through having its demesne developed as a housing-estate.

Carrick Barron, Stradbally, co Waterford (BARRON/IFR; OSBORNE, Bt/PB; OSBORNE/LG1863). A 2 storey 5 bay C18 house with a 1 bay pedimented breakfront having a round-headed window above a fanlighted doorway. A seat of the Barron family; subsequently belonged to the Osbornes of Newtown Anner, co Tipperary (*qv*) and known for a time as "Lady Osborne's Summer House".

Carrickblacker, Portadown, co Armagh
(BLACKER/IFR). A house dated 1692, but
much embellished in C19. 3 storey 5 bay
front with curvilinear "Dutch" gable in the
centre; balustraded parapet to roof and urns
on skyline; balustrade above entrance door.
Now demolished.

Carrickmore House (formerly **Carrick-**
more Hall), **Carrickmore, co Tyrone**
(STEWART, Bt, *of Athenree*/PB; ALEXANDER/
IFR; SCOTT/IFR). Plain 2 storey house of *ca*
1840, of sandstone ashlar, square in plan,
with two small wings at rere. 3 bay front,
with projecting porch. Roof on plain cornice. Bold string course. Leased to H. G. S.
Alexander. Used as Rectory from *ca* 1923 to
ca 1970. Bought by Mr R. T. M. Scott 1972.

Carrigacunna Castle, Killavullen, co
Cork (FOOTT/LGI1912; HUMPHREYS/LGI-
1958). A 2 storey early C19 house alongside
an old tower-house above the River Blackwater. 3 bay front with Wyatt windows; 2
storey extension, set a little back, also with
Wyatt windows; Victorian enclosed porch
with round-headed windows and round-
headed entrance door at side. Fine avenue.

The Cottage, Carrigaholt

Carrigaholt, co Clare: The Cottage
(BURTON, *sub* CONYNGHAM, M/PB). A C19
house of random ashlar consisting of a 2
storey centre with pointed windows, flanked
by single-storey gabled wings; overlooking
the mouth of the Shannon, close to the ruins
of an old castle of the MacMahons which
was captured by the O'Briens of Thomond
and afterwards passed to the Burton family.
Now rebuilt; but the old C18 pink brick
garden walls still survive.

Carrigglas Manor, nr Longford, co
Longford (NEWCOMEN, V/DEP; LEFROY/IFR).
Originally a manor of the (C of I) Bishops
of Ardagh; left to Trinity College, Dublin
in C17, and leased by Trinity in C18 to the
Newcomen family. Magnificent stables
were built here *ca* 1790, to the design of
James Gandon, extending round two courtyards, with pedimented and rusticated archways; as well as an entrance gateway to the
park, also by Gandon. After the failure of
the Newcomens' bank—which caused the
suicide of one member of the family—
Carrigglas was leased to Chief Justice
Lefroy, who later bought the freehold of
the estate, and who rebuilt the house in
Tudor-Gothic to the design of Daniel
Robertson, of Kilkenny, 1837/40. Symmetrical entrance front, with central gable
and oriel over porch, flanked by two slender
polygonal battlemented turrets. Gables and
oriels with Gothic tracery on side elevation;
orangery on garden front. Lower service
wing. Square entrance hall opening into

Carrigglas Manor

staircase hall lit by stained glass window;
stairs with cast iron handrail. Drawing
room, library and dining room *en suite* along
garden front. Drawing room ceiling with
plaster Gothic ribs and cornice of foliage,
coloured pale blue and gold. Gothic panels
to doors. Library with Gothic bookcases of
oak. Dining room with Tudor-style ceiling,
and cornice of foliage.

Carriglea, Dungarvan, co Waterford
(ODELL/LGI1863). An early C19 Tudor-
Revival house of a pleasant pink coloured
stone, built for John Odell *ante* 1837, possibly to the design of Daniel Robertson, of
Kilkenny. Symmetrical front; central feature in the form of a scaled-down gate-
tower, with slender turrets; gables; mullioned windows. Cantilevered staircase with
brass balusters. Now the Bon Sauveur
Convent.

Carrigmore, Ballineen, co Cork (CON-
NER/IFR; LYSAGHT/IFR; GRAHAM-TOLER, NOR-
BURY, E/PB; PURCELL/IFR). A 2 storey house
in the late-Georgian manner, built 1842 by
James Lysaght on the site of an earlier
house, known as Connerville, which had
formerly belonged to the Conner family and
which he purchased from them. Sold to 3rd
Earl of Norbury who sold it *ca* 1860 to
James Holmes. Sold 1876 to James Purcell;
subsequently bought back by the Conners,
who sold it to James Henry Morton 1905.
Now the home of Mrs R. Langran.

Carrigmore, Montenotte, Cork, co Cork
(MURPHY/IFR). A very handsome C19 Classical house, faced in a Roman cement which
closely resembles stone. Of 2 storeys over a
basement. 6 bay front with pediment, giant
corner-pilasters and semi-circular single-
storey portico. Modillion cornice; shouldered window surrounds; pedimented
doorcase. Bow at end and projecting wing
at rear. The residence of a branch of the
Murphy family; afterwards of late J. Craig
McKechnie. Now ruinous.

Carrignavar, co Cork (MACCARTIE/LGI
1912). A late C19 castellated house incorporating some fragments of an old castle.
Battlemented bow at one end; high-pitched
roof with dormers. Curved wooden staircase. The house stands in a fine position

Carrigglas Manor: Stables

above a small river; there was formerly an artificial cascade on the opposite side of the valley. The seat of the senior surviving branch of the once Sovereign House of M'Carty. Bought in the present century by Mr John Sheedy, who sold it *ca* 1950 to the Sacred Heart Fathers.

Carrig Park, Mallow, co Cork (FRANKS/ IFR). A 2 storey bow-ended Georgian house.

Carrigrenane, Little Island, co Cork (BURY/IFR; SULLIVAN/IFR). A pleasant square late-Georgian house of 2 storeys over a basement on a promontory jutting out into Lough Mahon. Perron in front of entrance doorway with double steps and simple railings, now partly obscured by porch. Compact but spacious interior; 2 drawing rooms *en suite*. Castellated tower by water's edge. A seat of the Bury family. Occupied in 1st half of C19 by John M. Ashlin, father of the architect, George Ashlin, who was born here 1837. In recent years the home of the late Judge D. B. & Mrs Sullivan.

Carrigrohane Castle, Carrigrohane, co Cork (WALLIS/IFR; HOARE, Bt, *of Annabella*/ PB). A C19 castellated house incorporating part of an old castle of the Barrett family on a crag above the River Lee. The estate was subsequently owned by the Wallis family, from whom it passed by marriage to the Hoares in late C18; the castle was a ruin for many years before it was built into the present house; which has a front of 3 storeys with a central gable flanked by dormers behind the battlements; and large mullioned windows with round-headed lights. Carrigrohane Castle features in a recent book of highly evocative reminiscences, *The Road to Glenanore*, by M. Jesse Hoare.

Carrowdore Castle, Donaghadee, co Down (DE LA CHEROIS-CROMMELIN, *sub* STONE/IFR). A Georgian Gothic castle built 1818 by Nicholas de la Cherois-Crommelin. 3 storey; 4 bay front with 4 slender poly-

Carrowdore Castle: Stable Yard tower

Carrowdore Castle

gonal turrets; Gothic portico. Round tower at one end. Very graceful Gothic plasterwork fretting on hall ceiling. Subsequently the home of May de la Cherois-Crommelin, traveller and author of *The White Lady* and other books.

Carrowgarry, Beltra, co Sligo (CRICHTON/ IFR). A Victorian house built *ca* 1880 by A. J. Crichton.

Carrowmore (also known as **Fairfield House**), **Aughrim, co Galway** (WADE, *sub* HYDE/IFR). A plain 3 storey 5 bay Georgian house. Tripartite doorway, Victorian triple windows on ground floor.

Carrowmore House, Carrowmore-Lacken, co Mayo (PALMER/LG1875; MC-CORMICK, *sub* KNOX/IFR). A 2 storey 3 bay house of *ca* 1830 with a fanlighted doorway, incorporating a C18 house. Now the home of Mr & Mrs Nial McCormick.

Carrowroe Park, Roscommon, co Roscommon (GOFF/LGI1912). An early C19 Classical house faced in limestone; of 2 storeys, with a pediment and central Wyatt window above a Doric portico; the front being prolonged on one side by a wing with a pair of pediments and columns, and on the other by a wing with only 1 pediment. Garden front with colonnade and 2 arched loggias.

Carstown

Carstown, Drogheda, co Louth (PLUN-KETT, *sub* LOUTH, B/PB). An early C17 house dated 1612, consisting of 1 storey over a high basement with an attic of 5 gables. Subsequently given sash windows. Still intact.

Carton, Maynooth, co Kildare (TALBOT DE MALAHIDE, B/PB; FITZGERALD, LEINSTER, D/PB; NALL-CAIN, *sub* BROCKET, B/PB). The lands of Carton always belonged to the FitzGeralds, Earls of Kildare, whose chief castle was nearby, at Maynooth; in C17, however, they were leased to a junior branch of the Talbots of Malahide, who built the original house here. After the attainder of Richard Talbot, Duke of Tyrconnell, James II's Lord Deputy of Ireland, Carton was forfeited to the Crown and sold 1703 to Major-Gen Richard Ingoldsby, Master-General of the Ordnance and a Lord Justice of Ireland; who added a 2 storey 9 bay pedimented front to the old house, with wings joined to the main block by curved sweeps, in the Palladian manner. In 1739 Thomas Ingoldsby sold the reversion of the lease back to 19th Earl of Kildare, who decided to make Carton his principal seat and employed Richard Castle to enlarge and improve the house. Castle's rebuilding obliterated all trace of the earlier house, except for a cornice on what is now the entrance front and the unusually thick interior walls. He added a storey, and lengthened the house by adding a projecting bay at either end; he also refaced it. He gave the entrance front a pediment, like its predecessor; but the general effect of the 3 storey 11 bay front, which has a Venetian window in the middle storey of each of its end bays, is one of massive plainness. As before, the house was joined to flanking office wings; but instead of simple curved sweeps, there were now curved colonnades. The work was completed after the death of 19th Earl for his son, 20th Earl, who later became 1st Duke of Leinster and was the husband of the beautiful Emily, Duchess of Leinster and the father of Lord Edward FitzGerald, the United Irish leader. 3rd Duke, Lord Edward's nephew, employed Sir Richard Morrison to enlarge and remodel the house *ca* 1815, having sold Leinster House in Dublin. Morrison replaced the curved colonnades with straight connecting links containing additional rooms behind colonnades of coupled Doric columns, so as to form a longer *enfilade* along what was now the garden front; for he moved the entrance to the other front, which is also of 11 bays with projecting end bays, but has no pedi-

Carton: Garden Front (former Entrance Front)

Carton: present Entrance Front

ment. The former music room on this side of the house became the hall; it is unassuming for the hall of so important a house, with plain Doric columns at each end. On one side is a staircase hall by Morrison, again very unassuming; indeed, with the exception of the great dining room, Morrison's interiors at Carton lack his customary neo-Classical opulence. Beyond the staircase, on the ground floor, is the Chinese bedroom, where Queen Victoria slept when she stayed here; it remains as it was when decorated 1759, with Chinese paper and a Chinese Chippendale giltwood overmantel. The other surviving mid-C18 interior is the saloon, originally the dining room, in the garden front, dating from 1739 and one of the most beautiful rooms in Ireland. It rises through 2 storeys and has a deeply coved ceiling of Baroque plasterwork by the Francini brothers representing "the Courtship of the Gods"; the plasterwork, like the decoration on the walls, being picked out in gilt. At one end of the room is an organ installed 1857, its elaborate Baroque case designed by Lord Gerald FitzGerald, a son of the 3rd Duke. The door at this end of the saloon leads, by way of an anteroom, to Morrison's great dining room, which has a screen of Corinthian columns at each end and a barrel-vaulted ceiling covered in interlocking circles of oak leaves and vine leaves. The demesne of Carton is a great C18 landscape park, largely created by 1st Duke and Emily Duchess; "Capability" Brown was consulted, but professed himself too busy to come to Ireland. By means of a series of dams, a stream has been widened into a lake and a broad serpentine river; there is a bridge by Thomas Ivory, built 1763, an ornamental dairy of *ca* 1770 and a shell house. Various improvements were carried

Carton: Saloon ceiling

out to the gardens towards the end of the C19 by Hermione, wife of 5th Duke, who was as famous a beauty in her day as Emily Duchess was in hers; she was also the last Duchess of Leinster to reign at Carton, for her eldest son, 6th Duke, died young and unmarried; and her youngest son, 7th Duke, was unable to live here having, as a young man, signed away his expectations to the "50 Shilling Tailor" Sir Henry Mallaby-Deeley, in return for ready money and an annuity. As a result of this unhappy transaction, Carton had eventually to be sold. It was bought 1949 by 2nd Lord Brocket, and afterwards became the home of his younger son, Hon David Nall-Cain, who opened it to the public. It was sold once again in 1977.

Carton: Dining Room

Cashel House, Cashel, Connemara, co Galway (BROWNE-CLAYTON/IFR). A Victorian house built 1870; rebuilt 1951–52 by Lt-Col W. P. Browne-Clayton. Outstanding garden.

Cashel Palace

Cashel Palace, Cashel, co Tipperary. The Palace of the (C of I) Archbishops of Cashel; built 1730–32 by the scholarly and cultivated Archbishop Theophilus Bolton to the design of Sir Edward Lovett Pearce. Of 2 storeys over a basement, with a dormered attic in the high-pitched roof. The dignified Palladian entrance front, of rose-coloured brick with stone facings, stands back from the main street of the town, framed by the trees of the forecourt; it is of 7 bays, with a 3 bay central breakfront. In the lower storey, the 2 end windows on either side are replaced by a single Venetian window with a rusticated surround. The other lower storey windows also have rusticated surrounds, and there is a pedimented doorcase with banded Ionic columns; the

upper storey windows have plain entablatures. The lower storey windows are firmly set on a string course above the plinth; the bases of those above being likewise tied together. The quoins only go up as far as the top of the lower storey. The 7 bay garden front, which is wholly of stone, is quite plain except for a repetition of the string courses and curtailed quoins; the ground floor windows now cut through the string course on which they were meant to rest, having been lengthened at the beginning of C19. Large panelled hall, with a screen of fluted Corinthian columns and pilasters, a pair of black marble bolection chimneypieces facing each other on either side, arched doorcases adorned with scrolls and a modillion cornice. Splendid carved wood staircase in staircase hall at side; twisted and fluted balusters, Corinthian newels, ends of treads decorated with scrolls, acanthus frieze in entablature below landing. The head of the staircase is open to the panelled bedroom corridor, which has a curved ceiling. The 3 main reception rooms in the garden front, facing towards the Rock of Cashel, which rises like a stupendous "eyecatcher" above the trees at the bottom of the lawn, were redecorated in a simple manner at the beginning of the C19 by Archbishop Charles Agar, afterwards Archbishop of Dublin and 1st Earl of Normanton; the Palace having suffered damage 1798. A long room at one side of the forecourt formerly housed Archbishop Bolton's magnificent library, which he partly inherited from the great Archbishop William King of Dublin and bequeathed to Cashel; the books have since been removed to a building near the Cathedral. From 1839,

when the See of Cashel was amalgamated with that of Waterford, until the end of 1950s, the Palace was partly occupied by the Dean. The Church of Ireland then decided to sell it; for a time, its future was uncertain; but through the good offices of the Irish Georgian Society a purchaser was found who restored it without altering its character and opened it as an hotel.

Castle Archdale

Castle Archdale, Irvinestown, co Fermanagh (ARCHDALE/IFR). A noble house of 1773 on the shores of Lough Erne, built by Col Mervyn Archdale to replace a "Plantation castle" originally built by John Archdale 1615. 3 storeys over basement; 6 bay entrance front with 2 bay breakfront centre; tripartite doorway with Ionic pilasters, entablature and pediment, the latter breaking forwards on 2 Ionic columns to form a porch, which appears to have been a subsequent alteration. 3 bay side elevation, the bottom storey having Venetian windows with Gothic astragals in its outer bays. Bold, rusticated quoins; solid roof parapet. Derelict since 1959 and now ruinous.

Castlebar House

Castlebar House, Castlebar, co Mayo (BINGHAM, LUCAN, E/PB). The original seat at Castlebar of the Bingham family, afterwards Earls of Lucan, was a castle which had been "burnt many years" when Rev Daniel Beaufort came here 1787. All that remained of it then was "two great round towers", one of which had rooms added to it on either side of a long corridor by the Lord Lucan of the time, who was 1st Earl; Dr Beaufort described them as "tolerably good and convenient, furnished with some pictures of which a few have merit"; though he regarded the furnishing as "far from elegant" and was clearly not impressed with the "large heavy chimneypiece of black marble" in one of the rooms. This adequate if somewhat makeshift dwelling was destroyed in the Rebellion of 1798 and replaced with a house that had even less pretensions to being a nobleman's seat: a plain 2 storey 5 bay late-Georgian house with the entrance at one end. It had, however, a large drawing room and was redeemed by its romantic situation high above the river and by its "verdant, handsome, old-fashioned park studded with large trees" which afforded "a pleasant promenade to the inhabitants of the town". A traveller of 1852 who came here to visit 3rd Earl of Lucan, of Balaclava fame, was impressed by his up-to-date methods of farming; he even had a steam-engine in his yard. The 5th Earl, grandfather of the vanished 7th Earl, sold Castlebar House *post* World War I. It became a convent, but was subsequently burnt.

Castle Bellingham

Castle Bellingham, co Louth (BELLING-HAM, Bt/PB). The original castle here, called Gernonstown, which was acquired by Henry Bellingham mid-C17, was burnt by King James's soldiers before the Battle of the Boyne, when its then owner, Colonel Thomas Bellingham, was fighting for King William. Col Bellingham built a new house 1690/1700 and named it Castle Bellingham; it had a high-pitched roof and is said to have resembled Beaulieu, in the same county (*qv*); Mrs Delany, described it (1745) as "one of the prettiest places I have seen in Ireland". The house was remodelled in later C18, when a 3rd storey was added, and again in early C19, when it was given a battlemented parapet, some turrets and a few other mildly medieval touches. The final result was not so much a castle as a castellated house, with plain Georgian sash windows. The 9 bay entrance front, which is prolonged by a battlemented office wing, appears to be only of two storeys owing to the higher ground on this side; the entrance, through a Gothic porch not centrally placed, is, in fact, on the first floor, where the principal rooms are situated. The opposite front, which also just misses being symmetrical—with 3 bays on one side of a shallow, curving bow and 2 bays and a turret on the other—is of 3 storeys; so is the end of the house, which also has a curved bow. Simple, pleasant rooms; a small staircase in a narrow hall at right angles to the entrance. Garden with terraces overlooking the River Glyde, formerly adorned with statues brought from Dubber Castle, the seat of another branch of the Bellinghams; vista to shrine of the Virgin Mary, erected by Sir Henry Bellingham, a convert to Catholicism during the later years of the Oxford Movement. Straight avenue aligned on the entrance front of the house, terminated at the opposite end by a castellated gatehouse facing the village green. Having been sold by the Bellinghams *ca* 1956, Castle Bellingham is now a hotel.

Castle Bernard, Bandon, co Cork (BERNARD, BANDON, E/PB). The old castle of the O'Mahonys, formerly known as Castle Mahon, was acquired by the Bernards early

Castle Bernard, co Cork: Skating Party, Christmas 1880

Castle Bernard, co Cork: Entrance Front

Castle Bernard, co Cork: Garden Front

in C17 and its name was eventually changed to Castle Bernard. During 1st half of C18, 2 new fronts were added to the castle, by Francis Bernard, Solicitor-General of Ireland, Prime Serjeant and Judge of the Court of Common Pleas, and by his son, Francis Bernard, MP. They were of brick, with Corinthian pilasters and other enrichments of Portland stone, and were surrounded by formal gardens with statues, fountains, cascades and *jets d'eau*. In 1798 Francis Bernard, 1st Viscount Bandon and afterwards 1st Earl of Bandon, pulled down the two early C18 fronts and began building a new house alongside the old castle, to which it was joined by a corridor. It was of 2 storeys, with a 9 bay entrance front overlooking the Bandon River and a garden front of 3 bays on either side of a deep curved central bow. Prominent roof with parapet and dentil cornice; bold quoins. In the early C19—probably in 1815—1st Earl of Bandon gave the house a Gothic coating that was literally skin-deep; a facade of battlements and two slender turrets on the entrance front, which continued round the side for part of the way and then stopped; the garden front being left as it was, except for the insertion of Gothic tracery in its windows, similar to that in the windows of the entrance front

and side; and the addition of hood mouldings. The old castle, an adjoining range and the connecting corridor also had C19 battlements. The interior of the house was spacious, with a straightforward plan. A square entrance hall with Ionic pilasters and columns opened into a wide central corridor running the whole length of the main block with a curving staircase at one end. On the opposite side of this corridor to the hall was a large oval room, extending into the garden front bow. Castle Bernard was burnt *ca* 1921; it is now a ruin smothered in climbing roses that forms an object in the garden of the modern house nearby, which was built in 1960s by 5th and present Earl of Bandon.

Castle Bernard (subsequently known as **Kinnitty Castle**), **Kinnitty, Offaly** (BERNARD/LGI1912; DE LA POER BERESFORD, DECIES, B/PB). A Tudor-Revival castle of 1833 by James and George Richard Pain.

Castle Bernard, Offaly

Impressive entrance front with gables, oriels and tracery windows and an octagonal corner tower with battlements and crockets; all in smooth ashlar. Subsequently the home of 6th Lord Decies, by whom it was sold *ca* 1950. Now a forestry centre.

Castleblayney, co Monaghan (*see* BLAYNEY CASTLE).

Castle Blunden, Kilkenny, co Kilkenny (BLUNDEN, Bt/PB). A highly romantic mid-C18 house with water on both sides of it so that it seems to float; the water being two lakes probably formed out of the moat of the earlier house or castle here. It was built either for John Blunden, MP, or for his son, Sir John Blunden, 1st Bt. Of 3 storeys over a vaulted basement; 6 bay front, central niche with statue below square armorial panel and above single-storey pedimented Doric portico. Quoins; rusticated surrounds to all the windows and the niche. Slightly sprocketed roof. The back of the house consists of 2 gables with a projection between them containing the principal and secondary staircases. The decoration of the interior is late c18 and was probably carried out by the 2nd Bt after his marriage to a bride who, according to Dorothea Herbert, brought him "a clear £8,000 a year". Hall with frieze of rams' heads. Drawing room with ceiling of Adamesque plasterwork. Before 2nd Bt married, he and his sisters kept the house constantly filled with young people; in the evenings, there were boating parties on one of the lakes, when, according to Dorothea, the girls would step from the windows into the pleasure boat "whilst six or seven fiddles serenaded us on the water". The young men of the party would also serenade the girls at night outside their bedroom, and sometimes "burst in", catching them "*en chemise*". A wing has recently been added to the house, designed by Mr Jeremy Williams, containing an additional sitting room.

Castleboro: Entrance Front

Castleboro: Garden Front

Castle Blunden

Castle Blunden: Drawing Room ceiling

Castleboro, nr Enniscorthy, co Wexford (CAREW, B/PB). A very large and imposing Classical house by Daniel Robertson, of Kilkenny; built *ca* 1840 for 1st Lord Carew. Its style was unusually archaic for the period in which it was built; for not only did it follow the Palladian plan of a central block flanked by wings and pavilions; but the 3 storey main block, in which the top storey was treated as an attic, above a boldly-projecting cornice, had an affinity with certain English mansions of early c18; notably Wynde's Buckingham House. But for the inevitable c19 lushness, one might have believed the garden front to date from 100 years earlier than it actually did; it had a central 3 sided bow with engaged Corinthian

columns at the angles supporting the entablature, 2 bays on either side of the centre and a pair of Corinthian pilasters at each end. The 7 bay entrance front was more obviously of its period, having a rather deep 2 storey Corinthian portico, with a straight entablature which was, in fact, the main entablature of the house carried outwards.

Castleboro: Hall

As in the garden front, there were pairs of Corinthian pilasters at either end of the facade, the outer one in each case being a corner-pilaster. The wings and pavilions, which were 2 storey, had more of a neo-Classical flavour in the entrance front; particularly the front walls of the pavilions, which had no windows, but a deep blind central recess with Ionic columns, flanked by niches. The garden front of the wings was plainer, with a central feature of four engaged Ionic columns in the end pavilions. Impressive 2 storey hall with gallery. 2 drawing rooms *en suite*, decorative panels of wallpaper framed with mouldings on walls; one of the 2 rooms having a screen of Corinthian columns. 2 storey library with metalwork gallery. Burnt 1923; now a ruin; some of the cut-stone having at various times been removed, to Monksgrange (*qv*) and elsewhere.

Castle Browne, Clane, co Kildare (WOGAN-BROWNE/LGI1912). A 3 storey house rebuilt as a symmetrical Gothic Revival castle 1788 by Thomas Wogan Browne, who acted as his own architect; with round corner towers and Irish battlements. Round

Castle Caldwell

Castle Cooke

room with Adamesque plasterwork on domed ceiling. Castle Browne was sold 1814 by Gen Michael Browne to the Society of Jesus, and became the nucleus of the famous Jesuit public school, Clongowes Wood College.

Castle Caldwell, Belleek, co Fermanagh (CALDWELL, Bt/PB1858; BLOOMFIELD/LGI1912). A C18 house of 2 storeys over a basement, on the shores of Lough Erne, with a delightful Georgian "pasteboard Gothic" facade. Pointed and quatrefoil windows, 2 little projecting turrets, and a battlemented pediment-gable at either end, surmounted by a pointed arch, like a belfry; the main block being linked by diminutive battlemented curved sweeps to a pair of tower-pavilions. An octagon temple in the grounds near the water. Passed to the Bloomfields through the marriage of Frances, daughter and co-heiress of Sir John Caldwell, 6th Bt, of Castle Caldwell, to John Bloomfield 1817. The house was ruinous by the end of C19.

Castle Carbery

Castle Carbery, Carbury, co Kildare (COLLEY, *sub* WELLINGTON, D/PB; and HARBERTON, V/PB). A fortified Jacobean manor-house, with tall chimneys, former seat of the Colleys, ancestors of the Dukes of Wellington; built on the site of a medieval castle of the de Berminghams. Still inhabited by the Colleys *ca* 1750, but became a ruin soon afterwards.

Castlecaulfeild, co Tyrone (CAULFIELD, CHARLEMONT, V/PB). A "U"-shaped Plantation castle originally of 3 storeys, with mullioned windows and massive chimney stacks; built 1612 by Sir Toby Caulfeild, burnt during the Rising of 1641, sub-

sequently rebuilt but abandoned by 1700 and now a ruin. Also in the village of Castlecaulfeild is Castlecaulfeild House, formerly the dower-house of the Caulfeild (Charlemont) family; 2 storey, 7 bay, lowbuilt and plain; of late C18 or early C19 appearance, though it may be basically C17.

Castlecomer House

Castlecomer House

Castlecomer House, Castlecomer, co Kilkenny (WANDESFORD, E/DEP; BUTLER, *sub* ORMONDE, M/PB; PRIOR-WANDESFORD/LGI1958). A very large C18 and C19 house, consisting of a square 2 storey main block with fronts of 5 bays, and a slightly lower 3 storey wing of great length, recessed for its 1st 6 bays and then stepped forward. Battlemented parapet on main block and wing; rectangular Georgian sash-windows, mostly with astragals; pointed Georgian-Gothic windows on ground floor of entrance front of main block; hood mouldings over windows of main block. John Johnston, who worked at Birr Castle (*qv*), was also employed here. Enclosed Gothic porch. Largely demolished in recent years.

Castle Cooke, Kilworth, co Cork (COOKECOLLIS/IFR). The old castle of Dungallane was acquired by Thomas Cooke, a Cork Quaker merchant, in 2nd half of C17, and subsequently renamed Castle Cooke. A house was built near the old castle, and

added to at various periods, so that it ended as an irregular structure consisting of several gable-ended ranges, with C19 eaved roofs; and a 2 storey projecting gabled porch. At beginning of C20, a wing resembling a keep, rather higher than the rest of the house and with a flat roof, was added by Col William Cooke-Collis. Burnt 1921.

Castlecoole, Enniskillen, co Fermanagh (LOWRY-CORRY, BELMORE, E/PB). The most palatial late C18 house in Ireland, built 1790–98 by 1st Earl Belmore to the design of James Wyatt, who adapted earlier designs by Richard Johnston, and also showed himself to be much influenced by Stuart and Revett's *Antiquities of Athens*, so that the house is an unusually perfect example of late C18 Hellenism, massive and restrained; yet keeping certain Palladian features such as Venetian windows and a balustraded roof parapet; and following the traditional Palladian plan of a centre block and wings. The centre block of 2 storeys and 9 bays, with a pedimented portico of 4 giant Ionic columns on the entrance front, and a curved central bow lined with giant fluted Ionic columns on the garden front; the wings single storey and consisting, on the entrance front, of deep colonnades of fluted Doric columns ending in small Doric pavilions, and on the garden front of 5 bay links and end pavilions with Venetian windows. The ends of the wings have central features of 4 fluted Doric columns and are as perfectly finished as the major elevations; all being of beautifully cut masonry in a pale silvery Portland stone which was brought here at great expense, being shipped to Ballyshannon, taken overland to Lough Erne, shipped to Enniskillen and taken the last 2 miles in bullock carts. It was no less expensive getting English plasterers to come here under the supervision of Joseph Rose; and it seems that the austerity of the interior plasterwork was to some degree for reasons of economy; though in fact it is entirely suited to the Grecian purity of the house. The single-storey hall is of great depth and dramatic simplicity, its only adornments being a Doric frieze, a pair of small Doric chimneypieces by Westmacott facing each other on either side and a screen of Doric columns in porphyry scagliola at the lower end. The splendour is reserved for the oval saloon in the middle of the garden front, which is lined with grey scagliola Corinthian pilasters and has a frieze of swags and delicate ornament on the flat of the ceiling; it is flanked by the drawing room and the dining room, forming a magnificent enfilade. The library, which has its original delicately moulded bookcases, is on one side of the hall, separated from the drawing room by the staircase hall, which contains a double stone staircase of great length, leading up

Castlecoole

Castlecoole: Hall

Castlecoole: Saloon

the present house was completed, the earlier house, which was small, built 1709 and with a rather heavy pediment, was burnt to the ground. The earlier family pictures and furniture were probably lost in this fire; which would explain why the house contains comparatively few portraits, making for large stretches of unrelieved wall, again very much in keeping with the Grecian simplicity. As a contrast, however, there is the sumptuous gilt Regency furniture in the saloon, introduced by 2nd Earl; and the bed, festooned with flame silk, in the state bedroom, said to have been decorated for George IV, who, however, never slept here. The garden front of the house overlooks a lake on which there is the oldest non-migratory flock of greylag geese in the British Isles; it is said that if ever they go, the Belmores will also go. There are some wonderful trees in the park, and fine stables by Sir Richard Morrison. Castlecoole has been maintained by the Northern Ireland National Trust since 1951 and is open to the public.

Castle Cor, Kanturk, co Cork

Castle Cor, Kanturk, co Cork (DEANE FREEMAN, *sub* DEANE/LGI1912; BARRY/LGI-1958; MURRAY, *sub* WRIXON-BECHER, Bt/PB). A late C17 or early C18 house consisting of a 2 storey 7 bay block with 2 storey 1 bay pyramidal-roofed corner towers. 3 bay pedimented breakfront; doorcase with scroll pediment. High-pitched roof with dormered attic. Built by the Freemans, on the site of an old castle. Enlarged at the beginning of the C19 by Edward Deane Freeman by the addition of a higher 2 storey wing at one end, running from the front of the house to the back, extending both the entrance and garden fronts by 1 bay, and with a 4 bay side elevation. The intention was to have a balancing wing at the other end of the house, but this was never built. At some period, a 3 storey curved bow was built into the garden front. In the space between the main block, the new wing and the 2 corner towers at this side, an impressive top-lit staircase hall was formed; with a graceful wooden staircase. This hall, and the large and lofty drawing room and dining room in the new wing, provided a pleasant contrast to the smaller and lower rooms in the main block. Sold *post* 1840 by a subsequent Edward Deane Freeman to Richard Barry. Adelaide (*née* Wrixon-Becher), widow of W. N. Barry, who lived at Castle Cor until her death at a very great age 1959, was for many years the oldest member of the Duhallow Hunt; a legendary figure and a fearless rider to hounds when she was well up in her 80s. Castle Cor was inherited by her nephew, Mr Hope Murray, who sold it *ca* 1960; it was subsequently demolished.

to a landing with a screen of yellow and brown scagliola Doric columns. The 1st floor lobby, lit by glass domes, rises into an attic storey which is not visible from the outside of the house; and is surrounded by a gallery with a colonnade probably inspired by the interiors of the Parthenon and the Temple of Poseidon at Paestum. In 1797, just before

Castlecor, co Longford

Castlecor, co Longford: Octagon Room

Castlecor, Ballymahon, co Longford
(HARMAN, *sub* KING-HARMAN/LG1937Supp;
PARSONS, ROSSE, E/PB1970). A mid to late
C18 house, built by Very Rev Cutts Harman,
Dean of Waterford, probably as a hunting
lodge for Newcastle (*qv*); with a plan that
seems to have been inspired by Stupingi,
the hunting palace of the Dukes of Savoy
near Turin, consisting of a central octagon
with four short 2 storey wings projecting
from four of its faces. The octagon contains
a single lofty vaulted chamber with a central
pillar the base of which is adorned with
marbled Corinthian columns at its four
corners, a Corinthian entablature and segmental pediments on console brackets; and
has a fireplace in each of its 4 faces. To
complete the Italian Baroque effect, the
room has a marble floor; so that it was
described (1825) as "this great central region
of cold and damps". To make the house
more habitable, a conventional 2 storey
front was built onto it early in C19, either by
Peyton Johnston, who rented the house
after it had been inherited by the Earl of
Rosse, or by Thomas Hussey, the subsequent tenant who bought the property
ante 1825. This front joins 2 of the wings,
so that its ends and theirs form obtuse
angles. In the space between it and the
octagon is a top-lit stair. Early in the present
century, a wider front of 2 storeys and 3
bays in C18 manner, with a tripartite pedimented doorway, was built onto the front of
early C19 front. Castlecor subsequently
passed to a branch of the Bonds, and was

eventually inherited by Mrs C. J. Clerk (*née*
Bond). It is now the Ladies of Mary
Convent.

Castle Crine, Sixmilebridge, co Clare
(BUTLER/IFR; MASSY, CLARINA, B/PB1949;
BUTLER-HENDERSON, *sub* FARINGDON, B/PB).
A mildly castellated late-Georgian house,
consisting of a 2 storey block with 2 curved
bows side by side at one end, one of them
with pointed Gothic windows, and a 3 storey
tower. Small battlements; corbelled turret
on tower. Inherited by Sophia Mary, Lady
Clarina, then by her daughter, Hon Mrs
E. B. Butler-Henderson, who sold it *ca* 1950.
Now demolished.

Castle Daly

Castle Daly, Loughrea, co Galway
(DALY/IFR). A 3 storey C18 house with a
pedimented centre recessed between two 2
storey wings, one of them incorporating an
old tower-house. The fenestration of the
centre is somewhat reminiscent of Raford
(*qv*), another Daly house in the same county,
with a large semi-circular window above the
tripartite fanlighted entrance doorway and
two small windows above that again. In
C19, the ends of the wings were raised and
finished off with battlements, so as to look
like towers; the pediment was also given a
battlemented outline. A long, low countrified stable range flanking the house, with
primitive rusticated doorways of cut stone.
Castle Daly is now demolished, and only
the front wall remains standing, like a folly
or a piece of stage scenery.

Castle Dillon: mid-C18 house

Castle Dillon: C19 house

Castle Dillon, Armagh, co Armagh
(MOLYNEUX, Bt, *of Castle Dillon*/PB1940). A
large and austere mansion of 1845 by
William Murray; built for Sir George

Castle Dillon: Stables

Molyneux, 6th Bt, to replace a rather low
and plain mid-C18 winged house, which had
itself replaced the 2nd of 2 earlier houses
again. 2 storey 9 bay centre block with
single-storey 3 bay wings; the entrance
front, and the garden front facing the lake,
being similar and without any ornament at
all, except for a simple pillared porch on the
entrance front. A straightforward and conservative plan; a large hall with a screen of
columns dividing it from a wide central
corridor running the full length of the house,
and having a curved stair at one end; a
saloon flanked by dining room and drawing
room in the garden front. A library and
morning room on either side of the hall;
additional living-rooms in 1 wing, offices in
the other, which in fact consists of 2 shallow
ranges with a yard between them. Fine
pedimented C18 stables by Thomas Cooley.
Fine entrance gates of 1760, described as
"the most costly park gates perhaps at that
time in the three kingdoms", erected by Sir
Capel Molyneux, 3rd Bt, MP, who also
built an obelisk near the park to commemorate the winning of independence by the
Irish Parliament 1782. Castle Dillon was
sold *ca* 1926. It is now a hospital.

Castle Dobbs, Carrickfergus, co Antrim
(DOBBS/IFR). An early C18 house in the
manner of Sir Edward Lovett Pearce, built
1730 by Arthur Dobbs, Surveyor-General
of Ireland, Governor of N Carolina, agri-
culturalist and organizer of expeditions to
discover the NW passage from Hudson's
Bay to the Pacific. 2 storey over high basement; 7 bay front with 3 bay pedimented
breakfront centre. Entablature over lower
storey; high solid parapet to roof. Later
wings of 1 storey over basement, with
bracket cornices, extending front by 3 bays
on either side; windows of lower storey of
main block given entablatures on console
brackets in C19.

Castle Dodard, Lismore, co Waterford.
A small castle with pointed roofs in the
manner of a French château, spectacularly
situated in the Knockmealdown Mountains
among vast banks of *rhododendron ponticum*.
Now the home of Col & Mrs Stephenson,
who have added an extra storey but have replaced the pointed roofs as they were before.

Castle Durrow, Durrow, co Leix
(FLOWER, ASHBROOK, V/PB). An early C18
house of an attractive pinkish stone, with a
high-pitched roof and tall stacks; built
1716–18 by Col William Flower, MP, afterwards 1st Lord Castle Durrow, who employed a builder named Benjamin Crawley
or Crowley. Of 2 storeys—originally with a

Castle Durrow: Entrance Front

Castle ffrench

Castle Durrow: Garden Front

dormered attic in the roof—and 9 bays; the front being divided into 3 groups of 3 bays by giant Doric pilasters, originally crowned with urns. Doorcase of Doric pilasters and entablature with urns; now erected on the front of a C19 enclosed porch. Alternate triangular and segmental pediments over ground floor windows. Originally the house was flanked by single-storey outbuildings with mullion-and-transom windows; but these have since been replaced by other outbuildings; while the front has been extended by the addition of 2 projecting bays at one side. The interior was originally panelled, the hall and dining room in oak; but the panelling now survives only in two rooms. Subsequent generations of the family, who from 1751 held the title of Viscount Ashbrook, adorned the house with C18 plasterwork and C19 stained glass; as well as building the impressive castellated entrance gate in the square of the little town of Durrow. Castle Durrow was sold by 9th Viscount Ashbrook 1922 and is now a convent school. In recent years, the attic dormers have been removed.

Castle ffrench: Hall

Castle ffrench, Ahascragh, co Galway (FFRENCH, B/PB). An elegant ashlar-faced house of 3 storeys over a basement, built 1779 by Sir Charles ffrench, Mayor of Galway; replacing a late C17 house on a different site which itself replaced a castle built by the ffrench family soon after they bought the estate in late C16. 5 bay entrance front with 3 bay breakfront, the outer bays being very wide. Fanlighted and pilastered doorcase; solid roof parapet with urns. 3 bay side; 4 bay rear elevation with twin round-headed windows in the centre, lighting the main and secondary staircases. Interior plasterwork of a style characteristic to

co Galway, with delicate naturalistic foliage and flower swags. Foliage and trophies on ceiling of hall; Irish harps and other emblems in drawing room frieze; flowers, foliage and birds in sideboard alcove of dining room. Doors and shutters of handsome joinery, with octagonal and lozenge-shaped panels. Slightly curving staircase behind hall with balustrade of plain slender wooden uprights. Early in C19, 2nd Lord ffrench lost a great deal of money owing to the carelessness of the manager of the family bank; the family fortunes suffered a further blow with the Famine, when 3rd Lord ffrench refused to collect any rents from his tenants; so that in 1848 Castle ffrench had to be sold. It was, however, bought back by the parents of the present Lord ffrench 1919.

Castlefield, co Kilkenny. A 3 storey bow-fronted Georgian house, the bow having a trefoil window and battlements. Pillared porch.

Castle Forbes, Newtownforbes, co Longford (FORBES, GRANARD, E/PB). A C19 castle of random ashlar, built *ca* 1830 partly to the design of John Hargrave, of Cork; replacing an earlier house destroyed by fire. Of 2 storeys over a high basement, with 2 adjoining fronts, dominated by a tall, round corner tower. Entrance front with door in square tower, prolonged by low service wing and gateway to yard in French style, with high roof and conical-roofed turret and bartizan, added *ca* 1870 to the design of J. J. McCarthy. Adjoining front with 4 bay block prolonged by lower gabled wing. Heavy battlements and machicolations; lancet windows separated by stone mullions and some Early English tracery windows. Corbelled stone balconies with pierced balustrades. The interior of the castle was done up in great splendour following the marriage of 8th Earl of Granard to Beatrice, daughter of Ogden Mills, of Staatsburg, Dutchess County, USA, 1909.

Castle Ellen

Castle Ellen, Athenry, co Galway (LAMBERT/IFR). A 2 storey 5 bay early to mid-C19 house with a balustraded Ionic porch and entablatures over the ground floor windows.

Castle ffogarty, Thurles, co Tipperary (RYAN-LENIGAN/LGI1912; RYAN/IFR). A rather insubstantial C19 castle; burnt 1922 and now a ruin except for 1 tower which has been rebuilt. The seat of the ffogarty family, from whom it passed by inheritance successively to the Lenigan, Ryan-Lenigan and Ryan families.

Castle Forbes

Castle Freke

Castlegar

Castle Forward, Newtowncunningham, co Donegal (FORWARD-HOWARD, WICKLOW, E/PB). A long, low 2 storey Georgian house of 9 bays; the windows of 4 outer bays on either side being grouped in pairs. Shallow pilastered porch, with a window on either side of the door. Originally the seat of the Forward family, whose heiress was the wife of 1st Viscount Wicklow and was herself created Countess of Wicklow 1793.

Castle Freke, Rosscarbery, co Cork (EVANS-FREKE, CARBERY, B/PB). The original Castle Freke was an old castle formerly belonging to the Barrys, which was bought by the Frekes in C17; Capt Arthur Freke defended it for several months during the Williamite War, but it was afterwards captured by the forces of King James and partly burnt. It continued to serve as the family seat until late 1780s, when Sir John Evans-Freke, 2nd Bt, after coming of age, found it so neglected and dilapidated that he abandoned it and built a new house on a more convenient site, with splendid views over Rosscarbery Bay; a plain rectangular block of 2 storeys over a high vaulted basement; one of its fronts being of 9 bays, with a 3 bay breakfront; the other of 8 bays, with a 6 bay breakfront. The house had a fine hall and staircase and several large reception rooms, including a drawing room "in the gallery style". When the offices came to be built, which not until *ca* 1820, it occurred to Sir John (by this time 6th Lord Carbery) that "the whole might be thrown into the character of a Castle"; and so he commissioned Sir Richard Morrison to carry out a transformation. Morrison added a castellated office court with 1 or 2 slender round and polygonal towers and a gateway complete with portcullis; he also built a tall polygonal tower at one end of the principal front of the house, and a square tower at the other, incorporating a new entrance. The roof parapet of the house was crenellated in a mild way, and adorned with corner-bartizans; but below that the facades remained unmistakably Classical, with handsome and prominent quoins. The house was gutted by fire 1910 and rebuilt with steel window-frames, reinforced concrete between the floors and a largely Edwardian-Jacobean interior: panelling, ceilings of heavy plasterwork and elaborately carved oak chimneypieces, a large and ornate oak staircase. The hall was divided into 3 sections by arcading of a somewhat Romanesque flavour. The work was finished by 1913, when a ball was given here for the coming-of-age of 10th Lord Carbery, who sold Castle Freke *post* World War I. The house was dismantled 1952 and is now a ruin.

Castlegar, Ahascragh, co Galway (MAHON, Bt/PB). The grandest of Sir Richard Morrison's villas, built from 1803 onwards for Ross Mahon, afterwards 1st Bt; replacing an earlier house. Square, compact plan; front of 2 storeys, back of 3; but with a 2 storey side elevation. Shallow curved bow in centre of front, with die and pedimented Ionic porch; 1 bay on either side, with pedimented triple windows in lower storey. 4 bay side elevation, the duality being resolved by a central pediment on 2 broad superimposed pilasters or framing bands. Rich interior, characteristic of Morrison, with good spatial effects. Elliptical hall or saloon leading into central top-lit staircase hall leading into domed back hall with Doric columns and entablature. The elliptical hall or saloon has pairs of recessed fluted Tower of the Winds columns and a domed ceiling with swags of foliage. The staircase hall, though not particularly large, has an air of great height. The staircase, which has a simple metal balustrade,

Castlegar: Staircase Hall

rises to a magnificent domed landing, with yellow Siena scagliola columns of the Composite order at either end. The dome is carried on fan pendentives; the tympana and soffits below the dome are decorated with swags and other plasterwork. The 5th Bt, who succeeded 1893, added a service wing and built a new porch at the back of the house; so that the Doric back hall became the entrance hall. In 1898 he commissioned Arrowsmith of London to transform the dining room into a classic interior of its period; with a fretted ceiling, a massive carved oak chimneypiece and a wallpaper of scarlet and pink stripes below a frieze of female figures and yellow and green foliage by Sibthorpe. In 1904 the drawing room was done up, also by Arrowsmith; the Morrison plasterwork in the ceiling was retained; but the room was given a frieze, chimneypiece, overmantel and doorcases in the Adam-Revival style; and a pink striped "Adam" wallpaper now faded to a beautiful colour.

Castlegarde, Pallasgreen, co Limerick (O'GRADY, GUILLAMORE, V/PB1953). A c16 tower-house, modernized *ca* 1820 and a lower castellated wing added to it by Waller O'Grady, son of the eminent lawyer Standish O'Grady, afterwards 1st Viscount Guillamore; probably to the design of

Castlegarde

James and George Richard Pain. At the same time, the old castle bawn was restored and given battlements and a castellated gateway, incorporating c18 primitive garden statuary. Drawing room with c19 Gothic panelling in dark oak and slightly vaulted ceiling. Passed on death of 9th Viscount Guillamore 1955 to his cousin Mr H.E. O'G. Thompson.

Castle Gore, Ballina, co Mayo (BOURKE/ LGI1899; GORE, ARRAN, E/PB; CUFF, TYRAW-LEY, B/DEP). Deel Castle, a c16 tower-house of the Bourkes close to the northern end of Lough Conn, passed, after Col Thomas Bourke had fought on the side of King James in the Williamite War, to the Gore family, afterwards Earls of Arran, who re-

Castle Gore: old castle

Castle Gore: Entrance doorway

Castle Gore: fragment of plasterwork frieze in Hall

named it Castle Gore. The tower-house had a large c18 wing with a handsome rusticated doorway added to it; possibly incorporating a c17 range. The front was flanked by a wall and a low office range which probably included parts of the old bawn. In the later c18, the estate somehow became alienated to 1st Earl of Arran's sister's son, James Cuff, MP (afterwards 1st and last Lord Tyrawley), who built a new house a short distance from the old castle *ca* 1790; a typical late c18 block of 3 storeys over a basement. 3 bay entrance front; tripartite doorway with engaged Tuscan columns and pediment extending over door and sidelights. Plain 5 bay garden front. Hall with frieze of delicate late-Georgian plasterwork. Long and narrow staircase hall at back of main hall, lit by very tall round-headed window; also with plasterwork frieze. Drawing room with niches on either side of fireplace. Low service wing; office court with stone arcade for coaches; barrel-vaulted underground service tunnel, passing beneath the formal garden. Many-arched bridge over the Deel River. The house was severely damaged and the original staircase destroyed during the Rebellion of 1798. Lord Tyrawley left Castle Gore to his illegitimate son, Col James Cuff, who scandalized the County by keeping a French mistress here. After his death, the estate reverted to the Earls of Arran. The house was burnt 1922 and not rebuilt; in recent

Castle Gore: illuminated address to 6th Earl of Arran and his Countess on their marriage

years the local authority tried to dynamite the ruin, regarding it as unsafe; but it proved to be so well built that only one corner was blown off. The old castle, which was still intact earlier this century, is now also a ruin.

Castle Grace, Clogheen, co Tipperary (GRUBB/IFR). A Georgian house, reconstructed *ca* 1825.

Castle Grove, Letterkenny, co Donegal (CAMPBELL-GROVE/IFR). A 2 storey Georgian house, repaired and modernized by Thomas Brooke (*né* Grove) *ca* 1825. Tripartite pedimented doorcase, with Doric columns and pilasters. Attractive early C19 conservatory of glass and wood flanking entrance front.

Castle Hacket, Belclare, co Galway (KIRWAN, *sub* PALEY/IFR; BERNARD, *sub* BANDON, E/PB; PALEY/LG1969). An early C18 centre block of 3 storeys over a basement, with 2 storey wings added later in C18, and a late C19 wing at the back. Burnt 1923; rebuilt 1928–29, without one of C18 wings and the top storey of the centre block. The seat of the Kirwans; inherited by Mrs P. B. Bernard (*née* Kirwan) 1875. Passed from Lt-Gen Sir Denis Bernard to his nephew Mr Percy Paley 1956. Notable genealogical library.

Castle Harrison

Castle Harrison, Charleville, co Cork (HARRISON/IFR). A 3 storey double gable-ended early C18 house, incorporating part of an old castle. 5 bay front; doorway with pilasters and entablature. Low-ceilinged hall with wooden stairs; low-ceilinged dining room and parlour with dark panelling on ground floor. Large drawing room with yellow wallpaper entered from half-landing of stairs. Fielded panelling in bedroom. Sold 1956 and subsequently demolished.

Castlehaven House, Castletownshend, co Cork (BECHER/IFR). A house built 1826 as a Rectory. Main block of 2 storeys and 4 bays, extended by a slightly lower range also of 2 storeys and 4 bays. Porch with fanlighted doorway at end of main block. Many improvements carried out by Brig F. R. Becher, who bought the house *ca* 1947 and sold it 1972.

Castle Hewson, Askeaton, co Limerick (HEWSON/IFR). A 2 storey early to mid-C18 house, with an old tower-house at one end of it. The C18 block has an entrance front with a central 3 sided bow in which there is a pedimented doorway; 2 bays on either side of it. The end of the house away from the old tower is of 3 storeys, owing to the ground falling away; with a single wide Georgian-glazed window in each storey. A lower Victorian wing ending in a gable extends at the back.

Castle Howard

Castle Howard, Avoca, co Wicklow (HOWARD-BROOKE, *sub* BROOKEBOROUGH, V/PB). A romantic early C19 castle rising from a wooded hill-top above the Meeting of the Waters built 1811 for Lt-Col Robert Howard to the design of Sir Richard Morrison, who set out to produce a building combining two different archaic styles, as his son did at Ballyheigue Castle, co Kerry (*qv*). In this case, the combination was meant to be that of a castle and an abbey, "to which the situation is peculiarly appropriate". The "castle" part consists of a 3 storey tower with two round turrets; the "abbey" of a 2 storey wing ending in a gable with pinnacles and a Perpendicular window. At right angles to the back of this monastic-military range runs a long, low 2 storey battlemented wing, in which the entrance is situated. The interior has a splendid brass banistered spiral stairway

Castle Hume, co Fermanagh (*see* ELY LODGE).

Castle Hyde

Castle Hyde, Fermoy, co Cork (HYDE (*now* SEALY)/IFR; WRIXON-BECHER, Bt/PB). A house built *ca* 1801 for John Hyde to the design of the elder Abraham Hargrave, of Cork; consisting of a centre block of 3 storeys over a basement and 7 bays joined by straight corridors to bow-fronted pavilions; both the corridors and the pavilions being of 1 storey over a basement. The centre block has a 3 bay breakfront; the entrance door and the 2 flanking windows are round-headed, as is the central 1st floor window; all the basement windows are semi-circular, and all the windows in the front have keystones. The corridors are of 3 bays, divided by Ionic pilasters; and there are 3 round-headed windows in the bows of the pavilions, which are curved. Large hall with screen of fluted Corinthian columns; frieze of transitional plasterwork; plaster

panelling on walls. The drawing room, on one side of the hall, has a rather similar frieze. Long and wide corridors—more like galleries—lead from the hall to oval rooms in the pavilions, which are very much of their period in containing additional reception rooms rather than offices. The latter would almost invariably have been the case had the house been a few years earlier; though in some other respects it seems old-fashioned for its date, and might possibly be a rebuilding of an earlier house. But if the wings are very much of 1801, so is the splendid oval cantilevered staircase of stone with its elegant wrought-iron balustrade, which rises to the top of the house in a domed staircase hall behind the main hall. Surprisingly, one has to climb to the top of this beautiful staircase to reach the garden, for the house stands beside the River Black-water with its back up against a cliff. From the top of the stairs one crosses the chasm between the house and the cliff by a bridge; then, after climbing a few more steps cut in the rock one goes through a door and finds oneself at the end of a broad vista between colossal beech hedges, looking towards a church tower. There is an old ruined castle of the Condons rising from the cliff immediately above the house. Handsome entrance gates, with trefoil-arched wickets surmounted by sphinxes and flanked by tall piers with Doric friezes. The seat of the Hydes, of which Douglas Hyde, founder of the Gaelic League and 1st President of Ireland, was a cadet. Sold in mid-C19 during the lifetime of John Hyde, son of the builder of the house, by order of the Encumbered Estates Court. Subsequently the seat of William Wrixon-Becher, a great yachtsman (who sailed his cutter across the Atlantic and back 1856), and a great hunting man who hunted for 60 years with almost every pack in Ireland. Now the home of Mr & Mrs Henry Laughlin, who bought Castle Hyde between the wars.

Castle Ievers, Croom, co Limerick (IEVERS/IFR). A 2 storey 4 bay early C19 house with a single-storey Doric portico.

Castle Irvine (also known as **Necarne Castle**), **Irvinestown, co Fermanagh** (IRVINE/LG11912). A 4 storey castle, probably C17, with round turrets and later battlements, to the front of which a 2 storey

Castle Irvine

Tudor-Gothic range by John B. Keane, rather similar to Camlin, co Donegal (*qv*), was added 1831; so that the old castle rises above the centre of the newer facade. The Tudor-Gothic building has a Classical interior; there are Corinthian columns of scagliola in the hall, which opens to form one long room with the rooms on either side.

Castle Kelly, co Galway (*see* AUGHRANE CASTLE).

Castle Kevin, co Cork

Castle Kevin, Mallow, co Cork (REEVES/LGI1912). A C19 castle built *ca* the 1830s by E. Badham Thornhill to the design of an architect named Flood. 3 storey 3 bay battlemented front flanked by semi-circular 4 storey towers with battlements and machicolations; turreted porch; single-storey wing at side with battlements and pointed tracery windows. Hall lit by armorial stained-glass window in central lantern tower. Passed to the Reeves family mid-C19.

Castle Kevin, Annamoe, co Wicklow. A 2 storey house with two adjoining fronts, one of 3 bays with a round-headed doorway and a wide-eaved roof; the other of 5 bays with battlements and a pillared and pedimented porch. Battlemented screen wall and lower wing. The seat of the Frizell family.

Castle Lackin

Castle Lackin, nr Ballycastle, co Mayo (PALMER, Bt, *of Castle Lackin*/PB1910; KNOX/LGI1912). A plain, 2 storey late Georgian house, with a wide curved bow at one end of its garden front; simple entablatures over ground floor windows. A vast complex of outbuildings at the rear of the house, partly surrounded by a high battle-

Castle Lackin: Entrance to yard

mented wall with castellated gate piers. "Eyecatcher" folly on hill opposite. The house and outbuildings are now in ruins, and some of the walls have collapsed.

Castle Leslie

Castle Leslie: side elevation and Cloister

Castle Leslie: Hall

Castle Leslie (also known as **Glaslough House**), **Glaslough, co Monaghan** (LESLIE, Bt, *of Glaslough*/PB; LESLIE-KING/IFR). A grey stone Victorian pile by Sir Charles Lanyon and William Henry Lynn, built *ca* 1870 for John Leslie, MP (afterwards 1st Bt), incorporating part of an earlier house. The somewhat dour exterior of gables, 3 sided bows and rectangular plate-glass windows is very much redeemed by the glorious

lake-side setting. Also by the delightful Italian Renaissance cloister (said to have been copied from Michelangelo's cloister at Santa Maria degli Angeli in Rome) joining the main block to a single-storey wing containing the library and billiard-room, and by the rich Italian Renaissance flavour of the interior, where one can detect the hand of Lanyon—and also that John Leslie, who had travelled much in Italy—rather than that of Lynn, who is very much in evidence in the exterior of the house. The great hall has a shallow barrel-vaulted ceiling with a dentil cornice, Ionic columns of grey marble and walls painted a warm brown. The ceilings of the drawing room and dining room have modillion cornices and friezes of swags; the drawing room has a blue and white Della Robbia chimneypiece. Behind the cloister runs a long top-lit gallery divided by many arches, with frescoes of rather pre-Raphaelite angels and other figures on their piers and in their spandrels; these were painted by 1st Bt, a talented artist who had the distinction, when a subaltern in the Life Guards, of winning the Grand Military Steeplechase and painting a picture which was hung in the Royal Academy in the same year. 1st Bt also painted frescoes of himself and members of his family on the walls of the gallery, which are framed to look like hanging family portraits. 2nd Bt

Castle Leslie: Gallery

married Leonie, one of the 3 beautiful daughters of Leonard Jerome, of New York, and a sister of Lady Randolph Churchill; during the years when she was châtelaine, Castle Leslie was much frequented by Edwardian fashionable society. The young Winston Churchill paid visits here to his uncle and aunt; except when he was temporarily banished by his uncle on account of his espousal of Home Rule. Later this century, Castle Leslie was the home of Sir Shane Leslie, the writer. Sir John Leslie, the present Bt, made it over to his sister, Mrs Bill Leslie-King (Anita Leslie, the writer), who in turn has passed it jointly to her younger brother, Mr Desmond Leslie, and to her son, Mr Tarka Leslie-King.

Castle Lough, co Tipperary (PARKER/ LGI1894). A 2 storey 5 bay Georgian house with a high roof.

Castle Lyons, Fermoy, co Cork (BARRY/ IFR; ANDERSON, Bt, *of Fermoy*/PB1861). A c16 fortified mansion, built on the foundations of the castle of the O'Lehans, from whom the place took its name; principal seat of the Earls of Barrymore. Built round a central courtyard, with, on one side, the great hall, hung with weapons; on another, the kitchen, to which water came by an aqueduct. On 1 of 2 remaining sides of the courtyard was a 2 storey gallery 90 feet long; but this was not yet finished 1750. One front of the house overlooked gardens with a large canal; the demesne included a deer park. The house was burnt 1771, through the carelessness of a workman, and never rebuilt. The then Earl of Barrymore died at an early age 2 years after the fire; his eldest son, 7th and penultimate Earl, was the notorious rake "Hellgate", who squandered the family fortunes and sold Castle Lyons and his other co Cork estates to the enterprising Army contractor John Anderson, of Buttevant Castle (*qv*). The ruin of Castle Lyons now forms a prominent object in the surrounding countryside, with its numerous tall chimneys.

Castle Mac Garrett

Castle Mac Garrett

Castle Mac Garrett, Claremorris, co Mayo (BROWNE, *sub* ORANMORE AND BROWNE, B/PB). The original house here, a castle of the Prendergasts, passed to the Brownes with the marriage of Geoffrey Browne and Mary Prendergast in late c16. A subsequent Geoffrey Browne built a new house here 1694 which was burnt in 1811, and replaced by an unpretentious early c19 Tudor-Gothic house, built by Dominick Browne, 1st Lord Oranmore and Browne. At the beginning of the present century, 3rd Lord Oranmore and Browne built extensive additions in an Edwardian baronial style faced in cement; so that the house became

Castlemartin

large and rambling, extending round a three-sided court; with an elaborate pillared, pedimented and partly balustraded porch in the central range. Typical Edwardian hall, with wooden staircase and gallery, the walls of which are decorated with swags of plasterwork in late c17 manner. Large drawing room and dining room with very good reproduction Adam ceilings, by Dublin craftsmen. Library with beamed timbered ceiling and inglenook fireplace. Now a home for the elderly.

Castlemartin, co Kildare (SHAEN CARTER/ IFR; BLACKER, *sub* BLACKER-DOUGLASS/LGI-1912; POLLOK/LGI1958; RUTHVEN, GOWRIE, E/PB). An early c18 "U"-shaped house, built *ca* 1720 by a Dublin banker named Harrison, using materials from the old Eustace castle here. Of 2 storeys over a basement; dormered attic in roof; 9 bay breakfront front and side elevations. Doorcase in entrance front of exceptional beauty, with a scrolled pediment on console brackets, and a bolection moulding. Triangular pediment over central window in side elevation. Hall with large plaster panels, pilasters and some carvings in wood. Sold 1730 to Capt Henry Boyle Carter. Used by Lt-Gen Sir Ralph Dundas as his headquarters during 1798 Rebellion. Sold to T. S. Blacker 1854. At some period the house was re-roofed, and lost its dormers; and the interior was much altered in the 1st half of c19, having suffered damage 1798. The house faces along a straight lime avenue at the end of which are magnificent c18 wrought iron gates. On the death of Mrs Blacker (*née* Pollok), widow of Lt-Col Frederick Blacker, of Castlemartin, 1967, Castlemartin was inherited by Mrs Blacker's great-nephew, 2nd and present Earl of Gowrie, the politician, who sings of the house in his poem, *Easter 1969*, published

Castle Martyr: old castle

in *A Postcard from Don Giovanni*:

Behind me, also rooted raptured to a corner
    of earth and Ireland, the eighteenth-century
    house
Grey face, dummy windows alternating
    with true
were in the northern dawn succinct at 6 a.m.

Lord Gowrie sold Castlemartin, which is now the home of Mr A. J. F. O'Reilly, the well-known Rugby football player and businessman.

Castle Martyr: Entrance Front

Castle Martyr, co Cork (BOYLE, CORK AND ORRERY, E/PB; BOYLE, SHANNON, E/PB; ARNOTT, Bt/PB). Originally an old castle of the FitzGeralds, Seneschals of Imokilly, to which an early c17 domestic range was added by Richard Boyle, the "Great" Earl of Cork, who bought it from Sir Walter Raleigh, to whom it had been granted, along with other confiscated Geraldine estates. Having been damaged during the Civil Wars, it was repaired and made "English like" by Lord Cork's 3rd son, 1st Earl of Orrery, to whom it had passed; only to suffer worse damage in the Williamite War, after which it was left as a ruin, and a new house built alongside it early in c18 by Henry Boyle, who became Speaker of the Irish House of Commons and eventually 1st Earl of Shannon. The house was greatly enlarged by 2nd Earl between 1764/71, and further remodelled in late-Georgian period. While giving it an abnormally long facade, the subsequent additions did not take away from the house's early c18 character, being on the same scale and in the same style as the original building. Entrance front of 2 storeys and 17 bays, consisting of a 5 bay recessed centre with a giant pedimented portico between projecting wings, the forward-facing 1 bay ends of which are prolonged by a further 5 bays on either side. The ends of the projecting wings on either side of the centre are framed by rusticated pilasters, and formerly had Venetian windows in their lower storey, which have now been made into ordinary triple windows; there is also a rusticated pilaster at either

Castle Martyr: Garden Front

end of the facade. The front is unusual in having 3 entrance doorways, of similar size, 1 under the portico and 1 in the centre of the 5 outer bays on either side; originally these doorways had plain architraves, but these were replaced by rusticated doorcases early this century. High-pitched, slightly sprocketed roofs. Irregular garden front; range of 3 bays on either side of a curved central bow, then a 4 bay range set slightly back with a balustraded colonnade of coupled Doric columns along its lower storey, then a range set further back again, of the same height as the rest of the facade but of 1 storey only, with 3 tall windows. Long, narrow and low-ceilinged hall with bifurcating wooden staircase at one end; late-Georgian frieze. A wide pilastered corridor runs from the staircase end of the hall, opening into a series of reception rooms along the garden front; they are of modest size, low-ceilinged and simply decorated. In contrast to them is the magnificent double cube saloon or ballroom at the opposite end of the hall, which rises the full height of the house and is lit by the 3 tall windows in the single-storey part of the garden front. It has a coved ceiling with splendid rococo plasterwork in the manner of Robert West—birds, swags, flowers, foliage and cornucopiae in high relief—and a doorcase with fluted Ionic columns and a broken pediment. This room was one of 2nd Earl's additions; it was finished by 1771, when it was seen by Arthur Young, who considered it to be the best room he had seen in Ireland. It certainly rates among the dozen or so finest Irish country house interiors; or anyhow would have done when it had its chimneypiece and its original pictures and furnishings. The entrance front

Castle Martyr: Saloon

of the house overlooks a sheet of water which is part of the remarkable artificial river made *ante* 1750 by 1st Earl; it winds its way between wooded banks through the demesne and round the neighbouring town of Castlemartyr; broad and deep enough to be navigable by what was described in C18 as "an handsome boat". The entrance gates from the town are flanked by tall battlemented walls shaped to look like Gothic towers; from the side they reveal themselves to be no more than stage scenery. Castle Martyr was sold early in the present century to the Arnott family; it was subsequently re-sold and is now a Carmelite College.

Castle Mary, Cloyne, co Cork (LONG-FIELD/IFR). A house on which the C18 architect, Davis Duckart, worked; being recorded as having designed a "difficult" roof for it. The house was subsequently rebuilt as a C19 castle, dominated by a square battlemented tower and with mullioned windows; it was burnt *ca* 1920 and is now an ivy-covered ruin, the family having made a new house in the nearby stable quadrangle.

Castle Mattress (also known as **Castle Matrix), Rathkeale, co Limerick** (SOUTH-WELL, V/PB). A tall C15 keep of the Desmond FitzGeralds on the bank of the River Deel; modernized 1837 by the Southwell family and a 2 storey castellated wing built onto it, extending right to the water's edge. The keep has corner bartizans and Irish battlements. Unoccupied for more than 30 years from 1931; recently restored.

Castlemore, Tullow, co Carlow (EUS-TACE-DUCKETT/IFR). A 2 storey house of late-Georgian appearance, with two long adjoining fronts, both having battlements and hood mouldings over the windows. Plain enclosed porch, not centrally placed. Quoins.

Castle Morres

Castle Morres, Kilmaganny, co Kilkenny (DE MONTMORENCY, Bt/PB; DE MONT-MORENCY/IFR). A magnificent mid-C18 house by Francis Bindon. Of 2 storeys over a basement. 9 bay front with a bay on either side of the 3 bay centre breaking forward and given additional emphasis by being framed by quoins and having a rusticated ground floor. Balustraded roof parapet and area; impressive balustraded perron and double stairway leading up to pedimented doorway with Ionic columns. Single-storey wings. Elaborate plasterwork in hall; military trophy under scroll pediment with eagle above scroll-pedimented black marble chimneypiece; cartouche of helmet and musical instruments on wall opposite; frieze of foliage below unusual modillion cornice. Sold *post* World War I; partially demolished *ca* 1930, though much remains to be seen.

Castle Morres

Castle Morres: plasterwork and chimneypiece in Hall; and the same view today

Castle Oliver (also known as **Clonodfoy), Kilfinane, co Limerick** (OLIVER/IFR; TRENCH, *sub* ASHTOWN, B/PB). A large C19 castle of red sandstone in an Irish version of Scottish Baronial; built *ca* 1850 by the Misses Mary & Elizabeth Oliver-Gascoigne (afterwards Mrs F. C. Trench and Lady Ashtown), in order to give employment after the Famine; replacing an earlier house which was the birthplace of Marie Gilbert (better known as the adventuress, Lola Montez, the love of Ludwig I of Bavaria—see RFW). The Misses Oliver-Gascoigne had

Castle Oliver

Castle Pollard

hall, with an elegantly cantilevered brass-railed stair leading up to a spacious bedroom lobby lit by a coloured glass dome. Now an institution.

Castlerea, co Mayo

Castlerea, Killala, co Mayo (KNOX/IFR). 2 storey late C18 or early C19 front, with 4 bays between two curved bows. 3 storey 5 bay range at right angles, possibly earlier, ending in battlemented tower. Front flanked by high battlemented screen wall, with an imposing belfry and cupola rising above it. In C18, the home of "Diamond" Knox; in C19, the home of L.E. Knox, MP, who founded the *Irish Times* 1859. Sold 1936, demolished 1937.

Castlerea House, co Roscommon

an estate in Yorks as well as their co Limerick estate; and they employed a York architect, G. Fowler Jones, to design Castle Oliver. It has a massive tower like a keep, and many stepped gables and corbelled oriels; also a tall battlemented turret that formerly had a pointed roof. On the entrance front is a gabled porch-tower, carried on battered piers and segmental-pointed arches to form a porte-cochère. A terrace with a pierced "Jacobethan" parapet adorned with heraldic beasts runs along the two principal fronts. At the back of the castle is a long service range, enclosing a court. Large oak staircase. The framework of the high-pitched roofs is of iron, which would have made the castle very much in advance of its time. On the hill above the castle is a Gothic "eyecatcher", dating from the days of the earlier house and known as Oliver's Folly. Castle Oliver passed to Hon William Trench, step-grandson of Elizabeth (*née* Oliver-Gascoigne), Lady Ashtown, one of 2 sisters who built the present castle.

Castle Park, Limerick, co Limerick (DELMEGE/IFR). A 2 storey 5 bay mid-C18 house, regarded by the Knight of Glin as possibly by Francis Bindon. Floating pediment with lunette window supported—in a characteristically Bindon manner—on the keystone of the Venetian window below it; which is itself above a tripartite pedimented doorcase with banded piers. At one end of the house is a 3 sided bow and a single-storey wing; at the other, a screen wall joins it to the stump of an old tower-house, which is treated as a pavilion. The roof of the house is concealed by a high parapet like a blind attic which is higher than the pediment; and which was finished off with Irish battlements early in C19, at the same time as the wing, the screen wall and the old tower were similarly crenellated. Sold 1969.

Castle Pollard (formerly **Kinturk**), **co Westmeath** (POLLARD-URQUHART/LGI-1958). A 3 storey 5 bay Georgian block enlarged and remodelled 1821 for W.D. Pollard by C.R. Cockerell, who added a single-storey Greek Ionic portico, two short single-storey wings with blind walls and niches on the entrance front, and a wing on the garden front. Eaved roof; balustraded area. Cockerell also formed a new staircase

Castle Otway

Castle Otway, Templederry, co Tipperary (OTWAY-RUTHVEN/IFR; VERNEY-CAVE, BRAYE, B/PB). A handsome 2 storey mid-C18 house with a vast and largely C19 tower-house at its back. The tower-house incorporated part of the original Clohonan or Cloghanane Castle which was granted to John Otway 1665 and later renamed Castle Otway. The C18 house, which Dr Craig considers to have been designed by the same architect or builder as Lissenhall, co Tipperary (*qv*), another house of the Otways, had a 7 bay front with a pedimented breakfront centre, and a pedimented doorcase; and a 4 bay side elevation. The roof was high-pitched, but the expanded tower-house rose above it. Burnt 1922.

Castle Saunderson

Castlerea House, Castlerea, co Roscommon (SANDFORD, MOUNT SANDFORD, B/ DEP; WILLS-SANDFORD/LGI1958). A large C18 block of 3 storeys over a basement, with C19 wings of 2 storeys over a basement. The main block of 7 bays are plain except for string courses; C19 eaved roof on bracket cornice. The wings of 2 bays, with balustraded parapets. The 3 bay side of the left-hand wing served as the entrance front; it had a central pedimented breakfront with 2 windows above a wide Victorian glass door at the head of a flight of steps. From the right-hand wing ran a 1 storey-over-basement service range. The house is now demolished; the demesne is maintained as a public park by the town of Castlerea.

Castlerichard, co Waterford (*see* GLEN-CAIRN ABBEY).

Castle Ring, Dundalk, co Louth (BOLTON/ LGI1912). A 2 storey 5 bay gable-ended C18 house with a simple round-headed doorway.

Castle Saffron, co Cork (*see* CREAGH CASTLE).

Castle Saunderson, Belturbet, co Cavan (SAUNDERSON/IFR). A large castellated mansion combining both baronial and Tudor-Revival elements, built *ca* 1840; from its close stylistic resemblance to Crom Castle (*qv*), about 5 miles away in co Fermanagh, it can be attributed to Edward Blore. Entrance front symmetrical, with a battlemented parapet, square end turrets and a tall central gatehouse tower which is unusual in having the entrance door in its side rather than in its front. The adjoining garden front is more irregular, with a recessed centre between 2 projecting wings of unequal size and fenestration, each having a Tudor gable; the 2 wings being joined at ground floor level by a rather fragile Gothic arcade. To the left of this front, a lower "L"-shaped wing with a battlemented parapet and various turrets, ending in a long Gothic conservatory. Castle Saunderson has stood empty for many years and is now semi-derelict.

Castle Shane, co Monaghan

Castle Shane, nr Monaghan, co Monaghan (LUCAS, *sub* LUCAS-SCUDAMORE/LG-1972). A house built 1836, replacing an earlier house which may have incorporated a castle built 1591. The 1836 house consisted of a 4 storey tower with corner bartizans copied from the O'Neill tower at Ardgonnel, co Armagh, and a 3 storey block of rubble faced with cement in what was intended to be Elizabethan or Jacobean style. Entrance front of 3 bays between 2 3 sided bows and 1 bay on either side of them; curvilinear battlement-gables along

roofline; 2 storey slightly-projecting porch with corbelled oriel over doorway. Windows with cross mullions; hood mouldings over them in 2 lower storeys; bold string-courses. Not quite regular 4 bay side elevation. Large square tower with square corner bartizans rising from behind the house. Tall, Tudor-style chimneys. Burnt 1920.

Castlesize, Sallins, co Kildare (GRAHAM/ LGI1958). A 2 storey late C18 house of 7 bays, the 2 outer bays on either side projecting slightly. Original doorcase hidden by later enclosed porch with corner pilasters and door at side. In 1814, the residence of George Chace.

Castle Talbot

Castle Talbot, Blackwater, co Wexford (TALBOT, *sub* O'REILLY/IFR). A 3 storey 5 bay Georgian block with curved sweeps. Would appear to be basically early or mid-C18; but the fenestration looks late-Georgian; perhaps also 3rd storey is a later addition, since the house looks too high in proportion to the sweeps. Good quoins and pedimented and fanlighted doorcase, with rusticated piers. In each of the sweeps there is a door with a shouldered architrave between 2 niches; doors and niches having fluted keystones. Ball finials on the coping of the sweeps. Good C18 gate piers with ball finials; slender battlemented tower in grounds.

Castle Taylor, Ardrahan, co Galway (SHAWE-TAYLOR/IFR). A massive tower-house with C18 tracery windows, to which a 3 storey house was added in early C19. The early C19 house was plain except for a stepped battlement and a pair of gables with blind tracery at one side of its front; it had a curved bow at one end. The home of John Shawe-Taylor, a prominent figure in the Irish Revival at the beginning of this century. Sold 1930s or 1940s by his son, Michael Shawe-Taylor; subsequently demolished.

Castle Tenison, co Roscommon (*see* KILRONAN CASTLE).

Castletown, Carlow, co Carlow (FAULK-NER/LGI1958). A small early C19 Tudor-Gothic house by William Robertson, of Kilkenny, incorporating a truncated tower-house. Of 1 storey and an attic with gables and dormer-gables apart from the central battlemented tower, which is 3 storey. At the foot of the tower is a porch flanked by small turrets, and there is a polygonal turret at one end of the front. Mullioned windows.

Castletown, Celbridge, co Kildare (CONOLLY/LGI1912; CONOLLY, *sub* LONG-FORD, E/PB; CONOLLY-CAREW, CAREW, B/PB; GUINNESS, *sub* MOYNE, B/PB). The largest of

the great Irish Palladian houses; also the earliest, having been begun 1722 by William Conolly, Speaker of the Irish House of Commons, who, from modest beginnings, had risen to being the richest man in the Ireland of his day. Designed by the Italian architect, Alessandro Galilei, and also in part by Sir Edward Lovett Pearce, who supervised the work in its later stages. The centre block, of 3 storeys over a basement, has 2 more or less identical 13 bay fronts reminiscent of the facade of an Italian Renaissance town palazzo; with no pediment or central feature and no ornamentation except for a doorcase, entablatures over the ground floor windows, alternate segmental and triangular pediments over the windows of the storey above and a balustraded roof parapet. Despite the many windows and the lack of a central feature, there is no sense of monotony or heaviness; the effect being one of great beauty and serenity. The centre block is joined by curved Ionic colonnades to 2 storey 7 bay wings; the wings and colonnades having been designed by Pearce, who also designed the impressive 2 storey entrance hall, which has a gallery supported by Ionic columns. Apart from the hall, the long gallery upstairs and some rooms with simple wainscot, the interior of Castletown was still unfinished at the time of Speaker Conolly's death, and remained so until after his great-nephew, the popular Irish patriot Tom Conolly, married Lady Louisa Lennox (daughter of 2nd Duke of Richmond and sister of Emily, Duchess of Leinster) 1758. In the following year, Tom Conolly and Lady Louisa employed the Francini to decorate the walls of the staircase hall with rococo stuccowork; and in 1760 the grand staircase itself—of cantilevered stone, with a noble balustrade of brass columns—was installed; the work being carried out by Simon Vierpyl, a protegé of Sir William Chambers. The principal reception rooms, which form an enfilade along the garden front and were mostly decorated at this time, are believed to be by Chambers himself; they have ceilings of geometrical plasterwork, very characteristic of him. Also in this style is the dining room, to the left of the entrance hall. It was here that, according to the story, Tom Conolly found himself giving supper to the Devil, whom he had met out hunting and invited back, believing him then to be merely a dark stranger; but had realized the truth when his guest's boots were removed, revealing him to have unusually hairy feet. He therefore sent for the priest, who threw his breviary at the unwelcome guest, which missed him and cracked a mirror. This, however, was enough to scare the Devil, who vanished through the hearthstone. Whatever the truth of this story, the hearthstone in the dining room is shattered, and one of the mirrors is cracked. The doing-up of the house was largely supervised by Lady Louisa, and 2 of the rooms bear her especial stamp: the print room, which she and her sister, Lady Sarah Napier (*see* OAKLY PARK, co Kildare) made *ca* 1775; and the splendid long gallery on the first floor, which she had decorated with wall paintings in the Pompeian manner by Thomas Riley 1776. The gallery, and the other rooms on the garden front, face along a 2 mile vista to the Conolly Folly, an obelisk raised on arches which was built by Speaker

Castletown, co Kildare

Castletown, co Kildare

Castletown, co Kildare: Dining Room

Castletown, co Kildare: Hall (previously and now)

Castletown, co Kildare: Print Room

whose mother was a Conolly of the Pakenham line. He sold it 1965; the estate was bought for development and for 2 years the house stood empty and deteriorating. Then, in 1967, Hon Desmond Guinness courageously bought the house with 120 acres as the headquarters of the Irish Georgian Society, and in order to save it for posterity. Since then the house has been restored and it now contains an appropriate collection of furniture, pictures and objects, which has either been bought for the house, presented to it by benefactors or loaned. The house is open to the public.

Castletown (sometimes known as **Castletown Cox** to distinguish it from the more celebrated Castletown in co Kildare—*qv*), **Piltown, co Kilkenny** (COX, *sub* VILLIERS-STUART/LGI1912; WYNDHAM-QUIN, DUNRAVEN, E/PB; BLACQUE/LGI1958, and *sub* WATERFORD, M/PB). One of the most beautiful houses in Ireland, the masterpiece of Davis Duckart (Daviso de Arcort), the architect-engineer of Franco-Italian descent who came here in mid-C18, having been in the Sardinian service. Built 1767–71 for Michael Cox, Archbishop of Cashel, whose father, Sir Richard Cox, Lord Chancellor of Ireland, had obtained a lease of the estate from the Duke of Ormonde. Centre block of 3 storeys over a basement and 7 bays, flanked, in the Palladian manner, by stable and kitchen wings, which prolong 2 fronts of the house and then run outwards at right angles to form a partially enclosed forecourt. The centre block has a more or less similar facade on each of its two fronts, which is a variant of William Wynde's Buckingham House in London: a centrepiece of 4 fluted

Conolly's widow 1740, probably to the design of Richard Castle. The ground on which it stands did not then belong to the Conollys, but to their neighbour, the Earl of Kildare, whose seat, Carton (*qv*) is nearby; the Folly continued to be part of the Carton estate until 1968, when it was bought by an American benefactress and presented to Castletown. At the end of another vista, the Speaker's widow built a remarkable corkscrew-shaped structure for storing grain, known as the Wonderful Barn. One of the entrances to the demesne has a Gothic lodge, from a design published by Batty Langley 1741. The principal entrance gates are from a design by Chambers. Castletown was inherited by Tom Conolly's greatnephew, Edward Michael Pakenham, who took the name of Conolly. It eventually passed to 6th and present Lord Carew,

Corinthian pilasters rising through the two lower storeys, and a Corinthian entablature running all round the building below the top storey, which is treated as an attic. The roof parapet is balustraded. The house is built of dressed sandstone and unpolished Kilkenny marble; the main block being of very finely cut stone, contrasting with the rougher stonework of the wings, which have ashlar dressings. The wings on either side of the garden front are arcaded, and terminate in pavilions with octagonal domes and cupolas. Magnificent rococo plasterwork in the principal rooms by the Waterford stuccodore, Patrick Osborne; the hall, staircase hall and dining room having decorative plaster panels on their walls, as well as plasterwork ceilings. The hall has a screen of monolithic fluted Corinthian columns of the same unpolished Kilkenny marble as that used in the exterior of the house; and a chimneypiece with terms. Castletown passed by inheritance to a branch of the Villiers-Stuart family; it was sold 1909 to Col W. H. Wyndham-Quin, who laid out an elaborate knot-garden at one side of the house and introduced various

Castletown, co Kilkenny

Castletown, co Kilkenny: Hall

Castletown, co Kilkenny: Drawing Room ceiling

Castletown, co Kilkenny: Dining Room

the Eastwoods. James Eastwood, *ca* 1837, planned to make a residence for himself out of the old castle, which then served as offices for late C18 house; but nothing seems to have been done in this respect. Passed by inheritance to the Bigger family. Folly tower built by Patrick Byrne 1780.

Castletown Castle, co Louth

Castletown, co Kilkenny: Arcade, Pavilion and Knot-Garden

pieces of statuary. *Ca* 1928, having succeeded as 5th Earl of Dunraven 1926, he sold it to Major-Gen E.R. Blacque (son-in-law of Adm Lord Beresford), whose son, Mr Charles Blacque, re-sold it 1976. Its future is uncertain. The delightful little Georgian church with a steeple, at the corner of the park, is at present being restored as an ecumenical chapel, as funds permit.

Castletown Castle, Dundalk, co Louth (BELLEW, B/PB; HAMILTON-RUSSELL, BOYNE, V/PB; EASTWOOD/LGI1863). An impressive and well-preserved C15–C16 castle of the Bellew family, with crow-step or Irish battlemented corner-towers, adjoining which a plain 2 storey 3 bay house with a fanlighted doorway was built in late C18. Having passed from the Bellews to the family of Viscount Boyne, it was acquired subsequently by

Castletown Conyers, Ballyagran, co Limerick (CONYERS/IFR). A 2 storey gable-ended early C18 house, to which a single-storey bow-fronted wing was subsequently added on one side, and a 2 storey stable block on the other. The front of the main house was originally of 5 bays, with a break-front centre; but at a later date the 2 right-hand windows were replaced in each storey by a single Wyatt window. Central window flanked by 2 narrow windows above simple tripartite doorway. Bold quoins; simple shouldered window surrounds with key-stones. The bow-fronted wing, which has since been demolished, contained a large room. Facing the front of the house is a charming pool with a statue of Neptune rising from it, aligned on the hall door.

Castletown Manor, Enniskillen, co Fermanagh (BRANDON/IFR). A Victorian house built 1869, with a wing at the back which was built *ca* 1750 to accommodate the caretaker of Monea Castle after it was burnt.

Castletown Manor, Pallaskenry, co Limerick (WALLER/IFR). A large Georgian block, built by John Waller. Good frieze in dining room. Now demolished.

Castle Townshend, co Cork (TOWNSHEND/IFR). A castellated house, consisting of 2 battlemented towers joined by a range with dormer gables. Panelled hall. The tower of the parish church rises picturesquely from among the trees immediately above the house, which stands by the shore of Castle Haven.

Castle Upton, Templepatrick, co Antrim (UPTON, TEMPLETOWN, V/PB; KINAHAN/IFR). Basically a Plantation castle, built at end of C16 and beginning of C17 by Sir Robert and Sir Humphrey Norton, who named it Castle Norton. Sold 1625 to Capt Henry Upton and the name changed to Castle Upton. From 1783 onwards, Clotworthy Upton, 1st Lord Templetown, and his son, afterwards 1st Viscount, employed Robert Adam to modernize the interior and give the exterior a "castle air". Adam raised and machicolated the two round towers of the original castle, and gave them high conical roofs; he also added a wing with a 3rd machicolated round tower. The whole effect was very impressive, rather like one of Adam's castles in Scotland. Adam was also commissioned to design a chaste little Classical mausoleum in the nearby churchyard, and a magnificent castellated stable range; both of which were completed 1789. The stables are the most important surviving range of office buildings in Adam's castle style; they have tall battlemented gateways and corner octagons. In 1837 Edward Blore was employed by 2nd Viscount to remodel the castle; he put in mullioned windows and did away with most of Adam's interiors; raising and panelling the hall, and redecorating the principal rooms in a restrained Elizabethan style, with fretted ceilings. Castle Upton was sold by the Templetowns early this century; the subsequent owner re-roofed the main building, so that Adam's romantic skyline was lost. During the years that followed, the wing added by Adam was allowed to fall into ruin. In 1963, the castle was bought by Sir Robin Kinahan; he and Lady Kinahan have since restored the castle most sympath-

Castle Townshend

Castle Upton: as it is now; and Adam's Stables

etically. Their most spectacular achievement was the rebuilding of the ruined Adam wing, which now contains an elegant ballroom, with a Doric frieze copied from a surviving fragment of Adam's plasterwork in the adjoining round tower; and an Italian marble chimneypiece that was formerly at Downhill Castle (*qv*).

Castleview, Conna, co Cork *see* (GLYNNATORE).

Castleward, Strangford, co Down (WARD, BANGOR, V/PB). A grand mid-C18 house of 3 storeys over a basement and 7 bays; built 1760/73 by Bernard Ward (afterwards 1st Viscount Bangor), and his wife, Lady Anne, daughter of 1st Earl of Darnley, to replace an earlier house. Probably by an English architect; and faced in Bath stone, brought over from Bristol in Mr Ward's own ships. It seems that the Wards could not agree on the style of their new house; he wanted it to be Classical; but she was of what Mrs Delany called "whimsical" taste and favoured the fashionable new Strawberry Hill Gothic. The result was a compromise. The entrance front was made Classical, with central feature of a pediment and 4 engaged Ionic columns rising through the two upper storeys, the bottom storey being rusticated

and treated as a basement. The garden front, facing over Strangford Lough, was made Gothic; with a battlemented parapet, pinnacles in the centre, and pointed windows in all its 3 storeys and 7 bays—lancet in the central breakfront, ogee on either side. All the windows have delightful Strawberry Hill Gothic astragals. This front of Castleward, and Moore Abbey, co Kildare (*qv*), are the only two surviving examples of mid-C18 Gothic in major Irish country houses which are not old castles remodelled. The interior of Castleward is remarkable in that the rooms on the Classical side of the house are Classical and those on the Gothic side Gothic; thus the hall—now the music room—has a Doric frieze and a screen of Doric columns; whereas the saloon has a ceiling of fretting and quatrefoils, pointed doors and a Gothic chimneypiece. The dining room, with its grained plaster panelling, is Classical and the sitting room is Gothic with spectacular plaster fan vaulting. Mr Ward, however, managed to be one up on his wife in that the staircase, which is in the middle of the house, is Classical; lit by a Venetian window in one of the end bows. If we believe Lady Anne, this was not the only time when he got his own way at her expense; for, having left him, as it turned out, for good, she wrote accusing him of

Castle Upton: as it was

Castleward: Classical Front

Castleward: Gothic Front

Castleward: Saloon

bullying her. In C19, a porch was added to one of the end bows of the house, making a new entrance under the staircase; so that the hall became the music room. In the grounds there is a 4 storey tower-house, built at the end of C16 by Nicholas Ward; also a temple modelled on Palladio's Redentore, dating from *ante* 1755; it stands on a hill, overlooking an early C18 artificial lake, or canal. On the death of 6th Viscount 1950, Castleward was handed over in part payment of death duties to the Northern Ireland Government, who gave it, with an

endowment, to the National Trust. The house and garden are now open to the public, and the Trust has set up various projects in different parts of the estate.

Castlewellan, co Down (ANNESLEY, E/PB; ANNESLEY, *sub* SOWERBY/LG1972). Although the Annesley family bought the Castlewellan estate 1741, they did not build themselves a mansion here until more than a century later; living either in the Grange, a pleasant group of C18 farm and stable buildings round 3 courtyards; or at Castlewellan Cottage, a single-storey Georgian house with projecting wings and a Venetian doorway. In 1856 the young 4th Earl Annesley began building a castle, to the design of William Burn, which was completed 1858. It is a large and somewhat austere granite pile; of 3 storeys plus an attic of dormer-gables, and with a massive 4 storey tower at one side; at the opposite side there is a rather slender round tower and turret. Plain rectangular windows. The demesne is of great beauty, and contains a famous arboretum. Inherited by Mr Gerald Sowerby (nephew of 6th Earl), who assumed the name of Annesley; sold by him to the Northern Ireland Government *ca* 1965. The demesne is now a forest park.

Castle Widenham, Castletownroche, co Cork (ROCHE OF FERMOY, V/DEP; BRASIER-CREAGH/IFR; SMYTH/IFR; COTTER, Bt/PB). The old castle of the Viscounts Roche of Fermoy, on a rock high above the Awbeg River; consisting of a tall keep and a baily enclosed by a curtain wall with bastions and other fortifications. During the Civil War, the castle was heroically defended against the Cromwellian forces by the Lady Roche of the time; but she was eventually obliged to surrender. The estate was confiscated and granted to the Widenham family; Lord Roche failed to recover it after the Restoration and was reduced to dire poverty. Later in C17, or early C18, a house of 2 storeys and an attic was built onto the keep, incorporating some of the walls of the old castle; it stood within the bailey, the wall of which was still intact 1790s. *Ca* 1820s, Henry Mitchell Smyth, whose wife, Priscilla (*née* Brasier-Creagh), was the eventual heiress of the Widenhams, castellated the house and extended it at the opposite end to the old keep; giving it a skyline of battlements and machicolations and a turreted porch on its entrance front. Probably at the same

Castlewellan

Castle Widenham: as it was in the 1790s

Castle Widenham: Spiral Staircase

Castle Widenham: Entrance Front

Castle Widenham: corner of Drawing Room

Castle Widenham: Garden Front

Castle Widenham: Dining Room

time, the bailey wall was largely demolished; though parts of it still survive, together with some of the outworks and a detached building which is thought to have been a chapel. A terrace was built along the garden front later in C19 by H. J. Smyth. The rooms of the house have plain cornices and charming Georgian-Gothic shutters in the deep window recesses; the drawing room has segmental-pointed doorways with rope ornament. The principal staircase has slender turned balusters; there is also a delightful little spiral staircase of wood, rather similar to that at Dunsany Castle (*qv*), which goes up to the attic storey, whence a door leads into an upper room of the keep.

From *ca* 1963 to 1976, Castle Widenham was the home of Sir Delaval Cotter, 6th and present Bt—whose old family seat, Rockforest (*qv*) was nearby—and Lady Cotter. Sir Delaval & Lady Cotter carried out an admirable restoration of the castle, which was in poor condition when they bought it; the rooms, as redecorated by them, were greatly improved and gained much from their fine furniture and the Cotter family portraits. They also made a garden in the outworks of the castle and opened up the views down to the river, which had become completely overgrown. Unfortunately, in 1976, circumstances obliged them to sell Castle Widenham and move to England.

Castle Wilder (also known as **Cloghdoo**), **Abbeyshrule, co Longford** (O'REILLY/ IFR). A 3 storey gable-ended house.

Castlewillington, Nenagh, co Tipperary (WILLINGTON/LGI1958). A tower-house with a 3 storey 3 bay gable-ended Georgian wing. Low top storey, more like an attic; pedimented doorcase with rusticated piers.

Castle Wray, Letterkenny, co Donegal
(WRAY/LGI1863; MANSFIELD/LGI1912). A 2 storey Georgian house.

Cavangarden, Ballyshannon, co Donegal (ATKINSON/LGI1958). A 2 storey gable-ended house built 1781 by John Atkinson. Entrance front of 1 bay on either side of a central bow, to which an enclosed pillared porch was later added. Attic lit by windows in gable-ends; gable-ends truncated, making the roof partly hipped.

Cecil Manor

Celbridge Abbey

Celbridge Abbey

H

Cecil Manor, Augher, co Tyrone (GERVAIS/LGI1912). A rather severe 3 storey early C19 block, probably by William Farrell, with windows set wide apart in the solid expanses of wall. Entrance front with Classical porch, prolonged by a wing of the same height. Slightly overhanging roof with bracket cornice; chimneystacks grouped together in a long line. Now demolished.

Celbridge Abbey, Celbridge, co Kildare (MARLAY/LGI1912; GRATTAN/LGI1863 and IFR; LANGDALE, *sub* MOWBRAY, SEGRAVE AND STOURTON, B/PB; DEASE, *sub* BLAND/IFR). The house of Esther Vanhomrigh, Swift's "Vanessa"; a rustic seat by the River Liffey is said to have been favoured by Swift as a place to retire with his love. Dr Richard Marlay, Bishop of Waterford, uncle of the statesman, orator and patriot, Henry Grattan, rebuilt the house in Georgian-Gothic towards end of C18; it is of 2 storeys over a basement and has a front of 6 bays, the 2 centre bays breaking forward and rising above the parapet on either side to form a central battlemented attic; the parapet on either side being battlemented also, with small pinnacles at the corners. The windows on either side of the centre are pointed, and have the most enchanting Georgian-Gothic astragals, in the form of delicate Gothic tracery. Attractive Georgian-Gothic entrance gates. Occupied *ca* 1837 by J. Ashworth, owner of the woollen manufactory in Celbridge. Passed to Henry Grattan, MP, son of the great Henry Grattan; then to his daughter and co-heiress, Henrietta, wife of C. J. Langdale. Afterwards the seat of a branch of the Dease family.

Celbridge Lodge

Celbridge Lodge (formerly **Kildrought Parsonage**), **Celbridge, co Kildare** (MCDOWELL (*formerly* PLATT)/LGI1969). A house of *ca* 1830. 2 storeys over basement, 3 bay front, with single-storey portico of coupled fluted Doric columns. Eaved roof on bracket cornice. Hall with modillion cornice and bifurcating staircase rising at its inner end. Drawing room and dining room ceilings with good C19 plasterwork cornices and ovals of foliage in centre. Used for many years as a Glebe House. Now the home of Mr Henry McDowell, the genealogist and writer, and Mrs McDowell.

Chaffpool, Ballymote, co Sligo (ARMSTRONG, *sub* KEMMIS/IFR). A simple gabled house.

Chanter Hill, Enniskillen, co Fermanagh. A 2 storey house built 1780 as a Glebe for Rev Thomas Smyth, DD. Front of 1 bay between 2 3 sided bows. Solid roof parapet.

Charlemont Fort, co Armagh (*see* ROXBOROUGH CASTLE, co Tyrone).

Charlesfort, Kells, co Meath (TISDALL/IFR). A 2 storey house of *ca* 1800, with a lower wing. Hall with Corinthian columns. Drawing room in early C18 style, with panelling. Library with simple frieze. Interior rearranged by Rev Daniel Beaufort. Sold *ca* 1971.

Charlestown, Clogher, co Roscommon (KING, Bt, *of Charlestown*/PB). A 2 storey late-Georgian house. Entrance front of 3 bays, centre bay recessed with enclosed Ionic porch. Garden front of 3 bays, with Wyatt windows throughout. Parapeted roof; entablatures over windows; lower wing.

Charlestown House, Clara, Offaly (GOODBODY/IFR). A 2 storey near-symmetrical Victorian Italianate house with curved

Charlestown House, Offaly

bows, entablatures on console brackets over the windows and a fancy pierced roof balustrade, standing near one of the family mills by a mill-race lined with yews and other trees, giving it the appearance of a garden canal.

Charleville, co Cork (BOYLE, CORK AND ORRERY, E/PB). A fine house built 1661 to his own design by 1st Earl of Orrery, who at the same time developed the nearby town which he named Charleville after Charles II. The house stood on one side of a fortified enclosure; it had extensive gardens and a park. It was burnt 1690 during the Williamite War by the troops of Duke of Berwick and not rebuilt.

Charleville, Castlebar, co Mayo (FITZGERALD/IFR). A square C18 house, now in ruins.

Charleville, co Wicklow

Charleville, Enniskerry, co Wicklow (MONCK, V/PB). A house built 1797 for 1st Viscount Monck to the design of Whitmore Davis; replacing an earlier house destroyed by fire 1792. Of 2 storeys, faced in ashlar; with a Palladian facade clearly inspired by that of Lucan House, co Dublin (*qv*), with the same central feature of a pediment raised on a 3 bay attic and carried on 4 engaged Ionic columns standing on the lower storey which, below them, is treated as a basement and rusticated; the front, however, is of 9 bays to Lucan's 7. It would seem that the house was not finished until the time of 2nd Viscount, who became 1st (and last) Earl of Rathdowne; probably the Rebellion of 1798 put a stop to the original building work. On the side of the house there are large Wyatt windows which would appear to date from the early C19; while the decoration of the interior is also early C19, with ceilings of rich Grecian Revival plasterwork probably designed by Sir Richard Morrison. Large entrance hall with screen of fluted Ionic columns and floor of inlaid parquet; impressive staircase with balustrade of brass uprights in hall behind. Sitting room with barrel vaulted ceiling; plasterwork in coffering. Immense walled garden; conservatory in the form of a Doric temple facing down long yew walk; yew tunnel. The Moncks gave up living at Charleville after the death of 5th Viscount's widow 1929. In 1941 it

was bought by Mr Donald Davies, who subsequently established one of the factories making his world-famous shirt dresses in the stable-yard at the back of the house.

Charleville Forest

Charleville Forest: corbelled arch over entrance door

Charleville Forest: Hall

Charleville Forest: Gallery

Charleville Forest, Tullamore, Offaly (BURY/IFR). The finest and most spectacular early C19 castle in Ireland, Francis Johnston's Gothic masterpiece, just as Townley Hall, co Louth (*qv*), is his Classical masterpiece. Built 1800–12 for Charles William Bury, 1st Earl of Charleville, replacing a C17 house on a different site known as Redwood. A high square battlemented block, with, at one corner, a heavily machicolated octagon tower, and at the other, a slender round tower rising to a height of 125 feet, which has been compared to a castellated lighthouse. From the centre of the block rises a tower-like lantern. The entrance door, and the window over it, are beneath a massive corbelled arch. The entire building is cut-stone, of beautiful quality. To the right of the entrance front, and giving picturesque variety to the composition, is a long, low range of battlemented offices, including a tower with pinnacles and a gateway. The garden front is flanked by square turrets. The interior is as dramatic and well-finished as the exterior. In the hall, with its plaster groined ceiling carried on graceful shafts, a straight flight of stairs rises between galleries to *piano nobile* level, where a great double door, carved in florid Decorated style, leads into a vast saloon or gallery running the whole length of the garden front. This is one of the most splendid Gothic Revival interiors in Ireland; it has a ceiling of plaster fan vaulting with a row of gigantic pendants down the middle; 2 lavishly carved fireplaces of grained wood, Gothic decoration in the frames of the windows opposite and Gothic bookcases and side-tables to match. The drawing room and dining room, on either side of the hall, are also of noble proportions; the dining room has a coffered ceiling and a fireplace which is a copy of the west door of Magdalen College chapel, Oxford. Staircase of Gothic joinery leading to the upper storeys, with Gothic mouldings on walls. Small octagonal library in octagon tower; charming little boudoir in round tower, with plaster vault surmounted by an eight-pointed star. Very heavily oak-wooded demesne, with grotto and serpentine walks; castellated entrance gateway. With the death of 5th Earl of Charleville 1875, the title became extinct; Charleville Forest passed to a sister of 4th Earl, then to her son, and then to the grandson of another of 4th Earl's sisters. After standing empty for many years, the castle has been let to Mr M. G. McMullen, who has restored it.

Charleville Forest: Boudoir in Round Tower

Charleville Park (also known as **Sanders Park**), **Charleville, co Cork** (SANDERS/IFR; AYLMER/IFR). A 3 storey, 6 bay late C18 house, built by Christopher Sanders; given an eaved roof on a bracket cornice with a small pediment, a single-storey 3 sided porch-bow, and pediments on console brackets over the second and fifth first-floor windows, in the C19. Bought 1948 by J.W. Aylmer, formerly of Courtown, co Kildare (*qv*), who sold it 1952. Now divided into flats.

Chief Secretary's Lodge, Dublin (*see* UNITED STATES EMBASSY).

Church Hill

Church Hill, Maghera, co Down (KIRK-PATRICK/IFR). An early to mid-C18 2 storey gable-ended house of 5 bays; extended towards the end of C18 to form a new drawing room, the addition being of the same height as the original front, and also gable-ended; but single-storey, with a 3 sided bow in its front and end walls. At the same time, presumably, the entrance door was moved to the left-hand bay of the original front, being given a delicately-glazed fanlight and sidelights; in the Victorian period, a graceful open wooden porch was added, with a curving roof on turned supports. In 1930s, the end bow of the drawing room was raised a storey and a balancing gable-ended wing with a 2 storey 3 sided bow was built alongside the drawing room extension, containing a new dining room. At the same time, the hall was enlarged by taking in the former dining room; and a new semi-circular staircase was constructed.

Church Hill, Chapeltown, co Kerry (DENNY, Bt, *of Castle Moyle*/PB). A C18 house with a central breakfront and a curved bow at the back.

Cill-Alaithe

Churchtown House, Churchtown, co Kerry (MAGILL/IFR). A 3 storey 5 bay C18 house. Doorcase with entablature on console brackets flanked by narrow windows. Fine gate piers with pineapples.

Clandeboye

Clandeboye

Clandeboye: Railway arch

Cill-Alaithe, Killala, co Mayo. A 2 storey mansion of *ca* 1900 with a small pediment in the centre of its entrance front, above a balustraded portico of pink marble columns with Romanesque capitals. Pedimented projection in side elevation.

Clandeboye, nr Bangor, co Down (HAMILTON-TEMPLE-BLACKWOOD, DUFFERIN AND AVA, M/PB). A comfortable and unpretentious 2 storey late-Georgian house of *ca* 1820, which evolved from a plain C18 block in at least 2 stages; the architects concerned being R. A. Woodgate and Sir Richard Morrison. 7 bay entrance front, the 5 inner bays breaking forward boldly, with a 3 bay pedimented breakfront in the centre. Ground floor windows round-headed, with a fanlighted tripartite window at either end. Single-storey Doric portico. Adjoining garden front with 3 bays on either side of a broad curved bow; an additional bay subsequently added at the end of this front. Office ranges on the other two sides of the house, but at a lower level, owing to the fact that the ground falls away steeply here; so that the house is a complete square, with a small inner court, which is bisected at the lower level by the single-storey former kitchen. Originally, the door under the portico led into an entrance hall, to the right of which was the imposing room known as the Gallery; consisting of a room in the entrance front opening with an arch into the staircase hall. Imperial staircase with balustrade of simple ironwork. To the right of the Gallery, the 3 main reception rooms, in the garden front; a central bow-fronted saloon, with a typically 1820 ceiling of simple rectangular coffering; on one side of it the drawing room, on the other, the dining room, with a screen of columns at one end, dividing the main part of the room from the additional bay. 5th Lord Dufferin, afterwards 1st Marquess of Dufferin and Ava, the Victorian statesman, diplomat, Governor-General of Canada and Viceroy of India, was a romantic with a passion for building. He had dreams of rebuilding Clandeboye in a style more to his taste, and obtained plans from various architects; notably from William Henry Lynn, whose scheme, in the words of Lord Dufferin's nephew, Sir Harold Nicolson, "suggested, at one and the same time, François Premier and the Prince Consort". Any sort of radical transformation of the house was, however, beyond Lord Dufferin's means; so he contented himself with various alterations, in which he was helped originally by a factotum named Henry, and later by Lynn. He made a library by knocking the original entrance hall into the adjoining study; a most successful room, imposing yet comfortable, full of light and mellow with the graining of the bookcases, which are of a simple Classical design, inscribed in gilt with the names of Greek gods and goddesses. He made a new entrance to the house at the lower level, in one of the office ranges; turning the former scullery and kitchen into an outer and inner hall. His new front door was in the middle of a blank wall, the penalty for moving the entrance round to this side; Lynn proposed enlivening this wall with battlements and turrets, but it remained blank until the present Marquess added a porte-cochère. The two halls formed out of the old scullery and kitchen were, at various periods in Lord Dufferin's lifetime, given fretted plaster ceilings and other touches such as a "quaint Elizabethan" doorway of pitch-pine; but they derived their main character from being filled with Lord Dufferin's collection

Clandeboye: Helen's Tower

of curios from all over the world; the "many lovable objects" which Sir Harold Nicolson remembered from his childhood visits here; ranging from a Red Indian fertility idol—"on the whole, a friendly beast"—to a huge and menacing grizzly bear and its more benign but equally large neighbour, a mummy case. From the inner hall, a flight of stairs leads up to the Gallery and the main rooms of the house. Lord Dufferin also put in 2 windows instead of the original 1 to the right of the portico in the former entrance front, to give more light to the Gallery; and to the right again he added a 3 sided single-storey bow to enlarge the drawing room. As well as carrying out alterations to the house, Lord Dufferin transformed the surrounding fields into a vast and idyllic park landscape, with a great lake; and he built 1 or 2 follies; notably the baronial private entrance to the nearby railway station, which has an arch under the line, crowned by a vigorously carved coat-of-arms with supporters and flanked by turrets; and the more famous Helen's Tower, a tower with pepper-pot bartizans rising from a hill at the southern end of the demesne, completed 1862 to a design by William Burn. It was built in honour of his mother, Helen, Lady Dufferin, one of three beautiful and lively sisters who were the granddaughters of Richard Brinsley Sheridan; in a room near the top of the tower, lined with delicate Gothic woodwork, the walls are adorned with poems on bronze tablets expressing the love between mother and son; including a poem written specially for Lord Dufferin by Tennyson:

Helen's Tower here I stand
Dominant over sea and land
Son's love built me, and I hold
Mother's love in lettered gold.

Clanwilliam House, co Antrim (*see* DANESFORT).

Clara House, Clara, Offaly (GOODBODY/ IFR). A compact Georgian block 3 bays long and 3 bays wide, of 3 storeys over a base-

ment. Rusticated ground floor; porch with columns and corner piers. In 1837 the seat of Edward Cox; afterwards passed to the Goodbody family.

Clare Hill, co Dublin (*see* CABINTEELY HOUSE).

Claremont, Claremorris, co Mayo (BROWNE, *sub* ORANMORE AND BROWNE, B/PB; and SLIGO, M/PB; BLACKER, *sub* BLACKER-DOUGLASS/LGI1912). A C18 Palladian house of grey stone, built by Col Dominick Browne. Afterwards acquired by Rt Hon Denis Browne, brother of 1st Marquess of Sligo. The house was noted for its banshee, which unlike other visitants of this kind, was a portent of good. A seat of the Blacker family early in this century.

Clare Park

Clare Park, Ballycastle, co Antrim (MC-GILDOWNY/LGI1958; SMYTHE-WOOD/IFR). A long, irregular, partly castellated house, the nucleus of which is a 3 bay gable-ended house of late C17. 2 storey and not quite regular wings were added in C18, one of them being prolonged soon afterwards by a stable range. Finally, some time *post* 1880, the original block was given 2 bows and a battlemented parapet; overhanging oriel windows were added to the wings; and a slender 3 storey square battlemented tower with string-courses, rather like the tower of a church, was built at the junction of the right-hand wing and the stable range.

Clarisford

Clarisford, Killaloe, co Clare. The Palace of the (C of I) Bishops of Killaloe, a late C18 block of 3 storeys over a basement in a demesne by the River Shannon outside the town; built 1774–78 by Bishop Robert Fowler (*see* IFR). 5 bay front; triple window with unusually narrow sidelights in centre, above tripartite Doric doorcase with pedimented porch on 2 columns; steps with curving iron railings up to hall door. C19 eaved roof on bracket cornice. 3 bay side.

Clashenure House, Ovens, co Cork (ALLEN/IFR). A 2 storey 5 bay Georgian house, renovated 1819 and again 1960.

Classiebawn Castle

Classiebawn Castle, Mullaghmore, co Sligo (PALMERSTON, V/DEP; ASHLEY, *sub* SHAFTESBURY, E/PB; MOUNTBATTEN OF BURMA, E/PB). A Victorian-Baronial castle spectacularly situated on a bare headland jutting out into the Atlantic; built, towards the end of his life, by the statesman, Lord Palmerston; who is said to have sat on the grass and watched the new castle go up on a visit to his co Sligo estate. Designed by Rawson Carroll; of yellowish brown sandstone, consisting of a plain, gabled range and a central tower and conical-roofed turret. Carved coats-of-arms on entrance front. The principal rooms are raised on a very high basement. Bequeathed by Palmerston to his wife's grandson, Rt Hon Evelyn Ashley, MP, grandfather of the late Countess Mountbatten of Burma. Now the Irish seat of Earl Mountbatten of Burma.

Cleggan Lodge, Ballymena, co Antrim (O'NEILL, RATHCAVAN, B/PB). Originally a hunting lodge, owned at various times by the O'Neills and the O'Haras. 2 storey; front with two bows, linked by a wooden first-floor balcony. Dormer-gables; roof formerly thatched and windows formerly latticed. Octagonal drawing room and dining room; imposing double staircase. Modern additions at back. The home of Lord Rathcavan, formerly Rt Hon Sir Hugh O'Neill, MP; 1st Speaker of the Northern Ireland Parliament, and one-time "Father" of the House of Commons at Westminster.

Clermont, co Wicklow (LEESON, *sub* MILLTOWN, E/PB). A 3 storey house of 1730, built for the Yarner family, thought to be by Francis Bindon and with an identical front to that of the centre block of Furness, co Kildare (*qv*), except that it is of brick, whereas Furness is of stone, and its roof parapet is balustraded, whereas that of Furness is solid. Of 3 bays, with a lunette window above a central window framed with a pedimented aedicule on console brackets, above a frontispiece of coupled Doric columns framing the entrance door. 4 bay rear elevation. Richly ornamented plasterwork ceilings, in the manner of Pearce; good chimneypieces. In 1814, the residence of Hon William Leeson.

Clifden Castle, Clifden, co Galway (D'ARCY/LGI1894 and IFR). A castle built by John D'Arcy who settled here 1815 and developed the town of Clifden from scratch. 2 storey; porch tower with slender round turrets; round tower to one side and rectangular tower behind. Gothic windows and doorway. Visited by Thackeray, who described it somewhat inaccurately as "a fine château". Fine pleasure grounds; lawns sloping down to Clifden Bay; grotto with stream running through it; shell-house or "marine temple".

Clifden Castle

Cliff

Cliff, Ballyshannon, co Donegal

Cliff, Ballyshannon, co Donegal (CON-OLLY/LGI1912). A rather austere late-Georgian house of 2 storeys over a basement, in a fine position above the River Erne; built of random ashlar. Curved central bow with 2 bays on either side of it; Wyatt windows in lower storey on either side of bow; eaved roof on bracket cornice.

Cliffs (The), Baily, co Dublin (BELLINGHAM, Bt/PB). A C19 house added to at various times in the present century, and full of Edwardian charm. Large drawing room, like those living-room-halls which were so popular with the Edwardians; boudoir with modern plasterwork; partly octagonal dining room with balcony overlooking the sea.

Clifton, Montenotte, Cork, co Cork (MURPHY/IFR). A 2 storey 5 bay early C19 house, with a single-storey 2 bay wing balanced by a conservatory, behind which is a chapel, with a lantern. The main block has a fanlighted doorway, an eaved roof and rectangular panels above 1st floor windows. The home of Nicholas Murphy and of his son, John Nicholas, who was created Count Murphy, of the Papal States. Now a convent.

Clinshogh, co Dublin (*see* WOODLANDS).

Clobemon Hall, Ferns, co Wexford (DE RINZY/LGI1843/9; DUNDAS/LGI1912; MURPHY, Bt, *of Wyckham*/PB1963; GRENFELL, B/PB). A 2 storey "L"-shaped house of *ca* 1820, by Thomas A. Cobden, of Carlow. 5 bay entrance front with single-storey Grecian Doric portico. Adjoining front is 3 bay, centre bay projecting and with a framing band on either side. Wide eaved roof. Hall with coffered barrel vaulted ceiling. Now the home of Cmdr H. F. P. Grenfell.

Cloghdoo, co Longford (*see* CASTLE WILDER).

Clogher House, Ballyglass, co Mayo (LYNCH/LGI1863; FITZGERALD-KENNEY/LGI-

Clogher House, co Mayo

1912). A 3 storey house of *ca* 1790 built by the Lynch family. 6 bay front, 2 bay breakfront; tripartite pedimented and fanlighted doorcase. Rooms with ceilings of Adamesque plasterwork, including curved room. Passed by inheritance from the Lynch family to the FitzGerald-Kenney family.

Clogher Palace (subsequently known as **Clogher Park**), **Clogher, co Tyrone** (PORTER/LGI1912 and *sub* BAIRD/IFR). The former Palace of the (C of I) Bishops of Clogher; a restrained cut-stone Classical mansion of 1819–23, begun by Lord John Beresford, afterwards Archbishop of Armagh, while Bishop of Clogher (*see* WATERFORD, M/PB); continued by the next Bishop, the ill-fated Hon Percy Jocelyn (*see* RODEN, E/PB), who was unfrocked for sodomy 1822 and ended his days as a domestic servant; completed by Bishop Jocelyn's successor, Lord Robert Tottenham (*see* ELY, M/PB). Centre block of 3 storeys over a high basement, with lower wings. The entrance front, standing back from the street of the town beside the Cathedral, has an enclosed portico of fluted columns. The garden front, overlooking the large demesne, is of 6 bays in the centre block, which has a high arcaded basement. After being given up by the See, it became the seat of T. S. Porter and was known as Clogher Park. It is now a convent.

Cloghroe House, Blarney, co Cork (MAHONY/IFR). A Georgian house built on the site of an old castle.

Clogrenane, Carlow, co Carlow (BUTLER, Bt, *of Cloughgrenan*/PB; ROCHFORT/LGI1912). A late-Georgian house with a pediment and a wide central window, built by the Rochfort family near the ruin of an old castle of the Butlers. The house, which itself is now a ruin, was approached through one of the gateways of the castle.

Clohamon House, nr Ferns, co Wexford (SWEETMAN/IFR; HUDSON-KINAHAN, *sub* KIN-

Clohamon House

AHAN/IFR; LEVINGE, Bt/PB). A 2 storey Georgian house; curved bow in centre of front with entrance door, and 2 bays on either side of it.

Clonageera House, Durrow, co Leix. A square 2 storey 3 bay late-Georgian house with a single-storey Doric portico and an eaved roof. Larger rooms than the exterior would suggest.

Clonalis: old house

Clonalis, Castlerea, co Roscommon (O'CONOR DON/IFR). The seat of The O'Conor Don, senior descendant of the last High Kings of Ireland. Originally a double gable-ended early C18 house of 2 storeys over a basement and 5 bays, the windows of the front being grouped together away from the corners; with wings of 1 storey over a basement and 3 bays. Roof of main block on heavy timber modillion cornice; 4 large chimneystacks in the gable ends. In the late-Georgian period, the facade was adorned with a framing-band at either end, each with a niche in the upper and lower storey; a Gothic-glazed porch was also added, with corner-piers and similar niches. In its low-lying position close to the River Suck, the house came to be regarded by the family as unhealthy; so between 1878 and 1880 Rt Hon Charles Owen O'Conor Don, MP, built a new house on a different site to the design of F. Pepys Cockerell. The old house was abandoned but remained intact until 1961, when it was wrecked by a storm. The new house is of 2 storeys over a basement with an attic in the roof and is in a style that comes half way between Victorian Italianate and the "Queen Anne" which Norman Shaw made so popular in England

Clonalis: Entrance Front

during 1870s and 1880s. Unlike Shaw's "Queen Anne" houses, however, it is faced not in brick but in cement. The entrance front is more or less symmetrical and the adjoining garden front is entirely so; the entrance front has 3 bays on either side of a central tower with a low pyramidal roof. The entrance door is in the base of this tower, in a slightly Baroque balustraded

Clonalis: Garden Front

Clonalis: Rt Hon Denis Charles O'Conor, O'Conor Don, with his niece, butler, gamekeeper, gardener and other dependants in his 2 motor-cars, ca 1912

porch; on either side are Doric pilasters with Ionic pilasters in the storey above. Some of the windows have scroll-pediments over them and are set in round-headed recesses. The garden front has a centre which breaks forward and projecting ends; the centre being crowned with a pedimented dormer-gable and a balustraded balcony on very heavy console brackets; the side projections being also surmounted with balustrades and smaller dormer-gables. In the centre is a doorcase with a scroll pediment. The high-pitched roof is carried on a cornice of elaborately moulded brackets; the chimneystacks are tall and wide; some of them are decorated with mouldings and recessed panels; others are pierced with arches. Large hall with Ionic columns of pink Mallow marble; modillion cornice; marble bolection chimneypiece; stairs with oak handrail and pitch-pine balusters behind arcade; broad arched corridor leading from one side of hall to principal reception rooms. Charming Victorian drawing room. Library with mahogany bookcases and marble chimneypiece flanked by niches for turf; Pepys Cockerell incorporated similar niches in the stone Tudor-Revival chimneypieces which he designed for Blessingbourne, co Tyrone (*qv*). Clonalis contains portraits, objects, manuscripts and documents of great historic interest; it is now open to the public.

Clonard, nr Wexford, co Wexford. A Georgian house of 2 storeys over a basement. 3 bay weather-slated front; handsome fanlighted doorcase with blocking and keystone; diamond shaped astragals in fanlight. Broad flight of steps to entrance door.

Clonattin House, Gorey, co Wexford (BLAND/IFR). An early house, partly burnt 1798 and rebuilt c19. Bought 1963 by Major Edward Whitley, son of Mrs A.M. Whitley (*née* Bland).

Clonbrock

Clonbrock, Ahascragh, co Galway (DILLON, CLONBROCK, B/PB1926; DILLON-MAHON, *sub* MAHON, Bt/PB). A house of 3 storeys over a basement built between 1780 and 1788 by Robert Dillon, afterwards 1st Lord Clonbrock, to the design of William Leeson; replacing the old castle of this branch of the Dillons which remained intact until 1807 when it was burnt owing to a bonfire lit to celebrate the birth of 2nd Baron's son and heir. 7 bay entrance front with 3 bay pedimented breakfront; doorway with blocked engaged Tuscan columns and entablature. A single-storey Doric portico by John Hampton was added *ca* 1824; while in 1855 3rd Baron added a single-storey 2 bay bow-ended wing to the right of the entrance front, which is balanced by a single-storey wing on the left hand side, though the two do not match. Good interior plasterwork of the 1780s, in the manner of Michael Stapleton. Classical medallions and husk ornament on the walls of the hall, at the inner end of which stood a splendid organ in a mahogany case surmounted by a baron's coronet. Medallions and husk ornament also on the walls of the staircase hall, which has an oval ceiling of particularly graceful plasterwork on fan pendentives; coloured salmon pink, brown, pale grey and white. Stone staircase with balustrade of brass uprights. Large drawing room with coved ceiling and modillion cornice in 1855 wing opening with double doors into a smaller drawing room in the main block, to form what is in effect one long room; which, a few years ago, still had a delightful early-Victorian character; with a grey watered silk wallpaper and curtains of cream and faded pink as a background to the glitter of 2 crystal chandeliers and of the many gilt frames of the pictures and of the mirror over the fine statuary marble chimneypiece. When the room was being fitted up, 3rd Baron's son, who at the time was a young diplomat in Vienna, wrote home to give instructions on how the floor was to be laid, so that it might be suitable for dancing the latest waltzes. After the death of 5th and last Baron 1926, Clonbrock passed to his sister, Hon Ethel Dillon; it was subsequently made over to her nephew, Mr Luke Dillon-Mahon, who sold it 1976.

Cloncarneel, co Meath (*see* CLOWN).

Cloncorick Castle, Carrigallen, co Leitrim (SIMPSON/LG1875). A 2 storey early to mid-c19 Tudor-Gothic house with buttresses and stepped gables.

Cloncoskraine, Dungarvan, co Waterford (NUGENT, Bt, *of Cloncoskoran*/PB1929; WYNTER BEE/LG11958). A 2 storey mid-c19 house probably incorporating an earlier house. Entrance front with 1 bay on either side of a central 3 sided bow, from which

projects a single-storey porch. Garden front of 5 bays, with a pediment on console brackets over the central first-floor window and an entablature over the central window below. Parapeted roof. Lower 2 storey service wing at side. Drawing room with handsome Victorian gilt pelmets. The seat of the Nugents, formerly Nugent Humble; sold *ca* 1959 by Mrs A.R. Wynter Bee (*née* Nugent).

Clonbrock: Hall

Clonbrock: ceiling of Staircase Hall

Clonbrock: large and small Drawing Rooms

Clonearl, Philipstown, Offaly (MAGAN/IFR). An early c19 house built for W. H. Magan to the design of William Farrell. Demolished.

Clonebraney, Crossakeel, co Meath (WADE/IFR). An early c19 house, of which only 2 ruinous wings remain. Handsome stable yard with pedimented archway.

Clonfert Palace, Eyrecourt, co Galway (TRENCH/LG11958; and *sub* CLANCARTY, E/PB; MOSLEY, Bt/PB). The Palace of the (C

Clonfert Palace

of I) Bishops of Clonfert, deep in the country by the little medieval cathedral with its splendid Irish-Romanesque doorway. A long low and narrow house of 2 storeys with an attic of dormer-gables; basically mid-C17, dating from when the original Palace was rebuilt by Bishop Dawson; but partly rebuilt late C18. Venetian windows set in arched openings. The Palace has C17 oak beams and joists and possibly its original C17 roof. Yew avenue. When the Diocese was amalgamated with those of Killaloe and Kilfenora 1833, the Palace was bought by J.E. Trench. In 1952 it became the Irish home of Sir Oswald Mosley, Bt; but it was badly damaged by fire 1954. It is now derelict.

Clongowes Wood, co Kildare (*see* CASTLE BROWNE).

and a shallow projecting porch. 3 sided bow at end. Long 2 storey wing at back of house.

Clonlost, Killucan, co Westmeath (NUGENT, *sub* WESTMEATH, E/PB and LG1863; PALMER/LGI1912). A tall Georgian block with a central pedimented attic. Now a ruin.

Clonmannon, Rathnew, co Wicklow (TRUELL/LGI1912). A late C18 house with a frontispiece rather similar to that of Mount Kennedy (*qv*). Among its outbuildings is a remarkable little building of brick, with a pediment and pilasters on a rusticated lower storey; it is rather in the manner of Inigo Jones and would appear to date from late C17 or early C18 and to have been part of an earlier house.

Clonmeen, Banteer, co Cork (GREHAN/ LGI1958). A late-Victorian house of rough-hewn red sandstone ashlar with half-timbered gables; built 1893 by Stephen Grehan; replacing a Georgian house nearby, which was kept in repair as a secondary residence. Near-symmetrical front with central gable above mullioned window above balustraded porch; single-storey 3 sided mullioned bow on either side; lower service wing ending in another gable. Impressive top-lit staircase hall; pitch-pine staircase and gallery. Sold *ca* 1975.

Clonshavoy, co Limerick (POWELL/LG-1863). A single-storey early C19 house in the "cottage" style, with gables.

Clonshire House, Adare, co Limerick (GREENALL, DARESBURY, B/PB). A late-Georgian house of 1 storey over a basement. Fanlighted doorway; shallow curved bow at either side of facade.

Clonskeagh Castle, co Dublin (THOMPSON/LGI1912). A symmetrical castellated house of 2 storeys with 3 storey 1 bay corner towers. Entrance front of 3 bays between 2 towers, with a single-storey Doric portico.

Clonmeen

Clontarf Castle, Clontarf, co Dublin (VERNON/LGI1912). A Tudor-Revival house of 1836 by William Vitruvius Morrison, attached to a tall old tower on the site of a medieval commandery of the Knights Templar and afterwards of the Knights Hospitaller of St John of Jerusalem. The house had an interior of sombre richness, with heavily moulded ceilings painted in dull colours, brown or black panelling from floor to ceiling, and stained glass, heraldic or historical, in every window. Lofty hall with timbered roof and galleries, and a double screen of arches separating it from a bifurcating staircase, on the landing of which was a handsome stained glass window containing portraits of Henry VII and Elizabeth of York. A wonderful effect was produced by the light from the stained glass windows playing on the gilt of the mouldings. Drawing room hung with gold brocade. The home of E.V. Vernon, maternal grandfather of Cyril Connolly, the author and critic. Now an hotel.

Clonhugh

Clonhugh, Multyfarnham, co Westmeath (GREVILLE, B/PB; HOPE-JOHNSTONE, *sub* LINLITHGOW, M/PB; HARVEY-KELLY/IFR). A 2 storey Victorian house consisting of 2 ranges at right angles to each other, and forming one corner of a large office courtyard. Rebuilt *ca* 1858 by Fulke Greville-Nugent, afterwards 1st Lord Greville. Eaved roof; symmetrical entrance front with gable-pediment and three-light centre window, above porch with Ionic columns. Sold 1917 to E. W. Hope-Johnstone; sold 1927 to the Harvey-Kelly family.

Clonleigh, Ballindrait, co Donegal (KNOX, *sub* RANFURLY, E/PB). A 2 storey 3 bay Georgian house with Wyatt windows

Clonmore House

Clonmore House, Piltown, co Kilkenny (MORRIS/IFR). A low 2 storey Georgian house, with a slightly irregular 5 bay front.

Clonodfoy, co Limerick (*see* CASTLE OLIVER).

Clonteadmore

Clonteadmore, Coachford, co Cork (GILLMAN/IFR). A square 2 storey house of *ca* 1830. 3 bay front, 4 bay side, eaved roof.

Clontra, Shankill, co Dublin. A delightful Ruskinian Gothic villa, almost certainly by Sir Thomas Newenham Deane and possibly designed by his brilliant young partner, Benjamin Woodward, shortly *ante* his death 1861. Built 1860-62 for James Lawson, a

Clontra

Clontra

lawyer. Of 2 storeys, or, more precisely, a basement and an attic; the principal rooms being in the attic, which is in fact a *piano-nobile*, rising into a very high roof, and lit by trefoil-headed windows in the gables; Dr Girouard sees this arrangement as that of the familiar single-storey-over-basement late-Georgian Dublin villa translated into High-Victorian Gothic. Of stone, with a certain amount of brick polychromy. Main entrance under wooden trellised veranda. Long conservatory with twisted Gothic columns of cast iron. High rooms, with sloping beamed ceilings under the roofs; the walls of the principal rooms frescoed by John Hungerford Pollen 1862, with pre-Raphaelite scenes of a knight and his lady, and *The Seven Ages of Woman*. Pollen also painted the spaces between the beams with birds, flowers and foliage, with backgrounds of blue and terra-cotta. Sold by the Lawsons early this century; subsequently the home of Judge Quinn.

Clonyn Castle

Clonyn Castle, Delvin, co Westmeath (NUGENT, WESTMEATH, E/PB; GREVILLE, B/PB). A square symmetrical 2 storey C19 castle of cut limestone, with four tall round corner towers. Large 2 storey hall with gallery and massive arcading. The seat of the Nugents, Earls of Westmeath, whose original castle here was burnt as Cromwell's Army approached. On the death of 8th Earl and 1st and last Marquess of Westmeath 1871, Clonyn passed to his only surviving child, Rosa, wife of 1st Lord Greville. A late C17 house, reconstituted in C18 Gothic style, also still remains not far away in the park.

Cloonacauneen Castle, Claregalway, co Galway. An old tower-house with a 2 storey 3 bay castellated wing attached.

Cloonamahon, Collooney, co Sligo (MEREDITH/LG1875; TWEEDY/LGI1912). A High-Victorian Tudor-Gothic house of polychrome brick, with gables, dormer-gables and a turret and spire. 2 storey hall with large staircase and stained glass window. Built from 1856 onwards by Capt T.J. Meredith to the design of an architect named Montgomery. The place was said to have a curse on it, to which Yeats alludes in *The Ballad of Father O'Hart*. Certainly the Victorian house was not very fortunate; Capt Meredith died before it was finished. The walls failed to keep out the damp and so were plastered over, except on the front. For much of the time that it was a private residence, it was let; then, early in the present century, after it had passed through marriage to the Tweedy family, it was sold and became a convent. It is now owned by the Passionist Fathers.

Clooncahir, Mohill, co Leitrim. A plain 2 storey 4 bay house of *ca* 1820. In 1837 the residence of Rev A. Crofton.

Cloonyquin, Elphin, co Roscommon (FRENCH/IFR). A plain 2 storey 3 bay Georgian house, originally a shooting-lodge but occupied permanently by the Frenches after their original house, about a mile away, was burnt; subsequently enlarged at various dates, notably by the addition of a single-storey lean-to with a porch at one end of it, and a 2 storey wing. The boyhood home of Percy French, entertainer, writer of immortal Irish songs and watercolourist. Sold *ca* 1955 by Mr H. A. St G. French; afterwards demolished.

Cloverhill, Belturbet, co Cavan (SANDERSON/LGI1912; PURDON/IFR). Built 1799–1804 for James Sanderson to the design of Francis Johnston. 3 storey, the top storey being concealed in the front, which is of 3 bays, the centre bay breaking forward and having a single-storey pedimented Ionic portico. Ground floor windows of front set under relieving arches. Wide curved bow at one side, with Wyatt windows. Bow-ended drawing room. Passed by inheritance to the Purdons; sold by Major J. N. Purdon *ca* 1958.

Clown (now known as **Cloncarneel**), **Trim, co Meath.** An older house enlarged and remodelled 1801 for Walter Dowdall to the design of Francis Johnston. 2 storeys, 5 bays; 1 bay breakfront centre with recessed fanlighted doorway under ironwork balcony. Adamesque plasterwork over sideboard recess in dining room.

Colamber (*see* COOLAMBER).

Colebrooke, Brookeborough, co Fermanagh (BROOKE, BROOKEBOROUGH, V/PB). An austere Classical house of 1825 by William Farrell; built for Sir Henry Brooke, 1st Bt of 2nd creation. 2 storey 9 bay front, with a pedimented portico of 4 giant Ionic columns; 3 storey irregular side; eaved roof. Of cut-stone, with a sprinkling of red sandstone ashlars which gives the elevation a

Colebrooke

pleasant reddish tinge. Large entrance hall; double staircase in back hall. Drawing room with original white and gold damask wallpaper. Sitting room with C19 arabesques. Large dining room, which Lord Craigavon, 1st Prime Minister of Northern Ireland, christened "Golgotha" on account of the numerous deer skulls covering the walls. The home of Sir Basil Brooke, 5th Bt and 1st Viscount Brookeborough, Prime Minister of Northern Ireland 1943–63; he and the late Lady Brookeborough made an attractive sunken formal garden at one end of the house. Since the death of Lord Brookeborough, Colebrooke has stood empty; a sale having been held of the contents 1974. The present Viscount continues to live at Ashbrooke, a smaller house on the estate.

The Manor House, Coleraine

Coleraine, co Derry: The Manor House (*formerly* **Jackson Hall**). A house of 2 storeys over a basement with a dormered attic, and 6 bays, originally built 1680; but enlarged and remodelled 1770s by R. Jackson, who gave it an unusual roof parapet of curving open-work, in the Chinese taste; with what look like miniature open porches, surmounted by ball finials, in front of all the dormers. At the same time, the windows were given octagonal glazing. The house was originally faced in brick, but was cement rendered 1920s; the windows have mostly been re-glazed and the parapet balustrading has gone. It is now the County Council offices.

Colganstown, Newcastle, co Dublin. A small but very distinguished Palladian house, built 1760s for the Yates or Yeates family, who also owned Moone Abbey, co Kildare (*qv*); attributed to the amateur architect, Nathaniel Clements. The house is unusual in that the centre block, of 2 storeys over a basement, stands forward from its 2 storey 3 bay flanking wings or pavilions, to which it is linked by curved sweeps starting from its back, rather than its front, corners. The elevation is further prolonged by gated walls joining the pavilions to the gable-ends of farm buildings, which run back to form the sides of yards on either side of the back of the house, partly enclosed by curved walls echoing the sweeps. Thus the house and farm buildings are all part of the one

Colganstown

composition, in the true Palladian manner. The entrance front of the house is of 3 bays, and similar to that of Newberry Hall, co Kildare (*qv*), except that it has no pediment; there is a breakfront centre with a Diocletian window above a tripartite fanlighted and pedimented doorway; the glazing of the fanlight being delightfully original. The back of the house is of 1 bay on either side of a curved central bow, into which the staircase extends. The interior contains some excellent rococo plasterwork in the manner of Robert West; there is a Chinese dragon over the staircase window and many birds in high relief; some of which have unfortunately had their heads shot off at one time or other as an after-dinner sport. Now the home of Mr & Mrs Felim Meade.

Collierstown House, Collierstown, co Meath (HALLINAN/IFR). A late C18 house, built *ca* 1775.

Collon, co Louth (*see* ORIEL TEMPLE).

Combermere, Glounthaune, co Cork. An early C19 "gentleman's cottage", mostly of 1 storey, with a small castellated wing. Large reception rooms. Attractive garden, with fine collection of magnolias, on hillside overlooking Lough Mahon and the upper reaches of Cork Harbour. The home of the Harrington family.

Convamore, Ballyhooly, co Cork (HARE, LISTOWEL, E/PB; HIRSCH, *sub* INCHCAPE, E/PB). A large, plain, 2 storey early C19 house, partly by James Pain, standing above one of the most beautiful reaches of the River Blackwater. The entrance front has a single-storey Doric portico; the front facing the river is punctuated with Doric pilasters. The block which contained the principal rooms is faced with Victorian stucco and had plate glass windows; the long office range keeps its late Georgian character and had windows with astragals. Burnt 1921, now a ruin almost totally submerged in undergrowth and ivy. Down river from the house, close to the entrance to the demesne, is the old Roche castle of Ballyhooly, the upper rooms of which were restored in Baronial style *ca* 1860 and used by 3rd Earl and Countess of Listowel for entertaining. The walls of the castle are still stained with tar from a beacon that was lit when Edward VII paid a visit as Prince of Wales. The castle now belongs to Major J. H. Hirsch, whose father built a gabled fishing lodge adjoining it.

Conway, Dunmurry, co Antrim (BARBOUR, Bt/PB1949). A 2 storey Victorian house with a symmetrical front of two shallow curved bows and a central projection; on either side of which runs a pillared and balustraded veranda, joining at one end to a single-storey wing, and at the other to a pilastered conservatory. Roof on bracket cornice from the centre of which rises a vaguely Italianate tower. Now an hotel.

Convamore

Cookstown House, co Meath (*see* CORBALTON HALL).

Coolamber, Street, co Westmeath (O'REILLY/LGI1958; SAXONY/RFW). A 2 storey late-Georgian house with an eaved roof. 5 bay front, pillared porch. Bought after the end of World War II by Prince Ernest of Saxony.

Convamore: as a ruin

Convamore: old castle of Ballyhooly and new fishing lodge

Coolamber Manor, Lisryan, co Longford (STANLEY, *sub* TYNDALL/LGI1952Supp; WINGFIELD, *sub* POWERSCOURT, V/PB). A house of *ca* 1820, by John Hargrave, of Cork; built for Major Blackall. 2 storey; eaved roof; angle piers; front with bowed projection in centre and porch with slender pillars on one side. Attractive curved rooms. Subsequently the home of the Stanleys and eventually of Brig A. D. R. Wingfield and Mrs Wingfield (*née* Stanley). Sold *ca* 1960; now a rehabilitation centre.

Coolavin

Coolavin, Monasteraden, co Sligo (MACDERMOT, PRINCE OF COOLAVIN/IFR). A late-Victorian house built 1897–98 by Rt Hon Hugh MacDermot, The MacDermot, Prince of Coolavin, to the design of James Franklin Fuller. Of cut stone, with red sandstone dressings; rather in the style of an early C17 hall in the North of England.

Steep porch-gable, decorated with balls on pedestals; dormer-gables on either side. Mullioned and sash windows, the latter, rather surprisingly for their period, with Georgian astragals. End gables, also with pedestals and balls.

Coolbawn

Coolbawn: as a ruin

Coolbawn, nr Enniscorthy, co Wexford (BRUEN/IFR). An impressive Tudor-Revival pile faced in granite ashlar, built *ca* 1830s for Francis Bruen to the design of the younger Frederick Darley. Symmetrical front; alternate triangular and curvilinear gables; many finials; massive central porch tower, with mullioned window and carved tracery over doorway. Screen walls with curvilinear battlements prolonging the facade on either side, one of them with windows lighting a range behind it. Monolithic stone mullions in windows; grand staircase of stone in hall to right of entrance. Extensive office court, with gables and finials, at right hand side of house. Burnt *ca* 1914, now a ruin.

Coolcarrigan

Coolcarrigan, Naas, co Kildare (WILSON/IFR; WILSON-WRIGHT/IFR). A 2 storey C19 house, with 3 bay elevations, the windows being well spaced out; parapet along entrance front, bracket cornice under roof at sides; projecting porch. The main block is flanked by two 2 storey blocks at the back, which do not quite balance each other; these are joined to the back of the main block by lower ranges, enclosing a courtyard which is prolonged beyond them by walls, and enclosed at the opposite end to the house by an outbuilding. The home of Sir Almroth Wright, the eminent pathologist, originator of the system of Anti-

Coole, Millstreet, co Cork

Typhoid Inoculation and author, who married the daughter and heiress of Robert Wilson, of Coolcarrigan.

Coolderry House, Carrickmacross, co Monaghan (BROWNLOW/IFR). A 2 storey late C18 house of 5 bays between 2 semi-circular bows. Tripartite doorway with baseless pediment and fanlight. Blocked surrounds to windows. Parapeted roof; the parapet over 2 bows being mildly battlemented. Sold 1920 by Col G. J. Brownlow; afterwards demolished.

Coole, Millstreet, co Cork. A long and low 2 storey Georgian house with a plain 7 bay front. In 1837 the residence of H. O'Donnell.

Coole Abbey, Fermoy, co Cork (PEARD/ LG1863; ROSE, Bt, *of Rayners*/PB). A house built *ca* 1765 by Henry Peard; attributed, on stylistic grounds, to Davis Duckart. Of 2 storeys over a basement; handsome ashlar facade of 1 bay on either side of a 3 bay breakfront with superimposed Doric and Ionic pilasters; the pilasters in the upper storey and those on either side below being heavily rusticated. Round-headed central window over doorway with semi-circular fanlight set in rectangular surround; bold quoins; shouldered window surrounds, some with keystones; broad steps up to hall door, platform with iron railings. C19 eaved roof. Curved quadrant walls link the back of the house to stables with arches of plain cut stone blocks, forming a handsome courtyard. Large hall with staircase of solid C18 joinery.

Coole Park, Gort, co Galway (GREGORY/ IFR). A 3 storey block of *ca* 1770, built by Robert Gregory, a wealthy East Indian "Nabob". Entrance front with Diocletian window above Venetian window above doorway, which was later obscured by a plain square enclosed porch. Early-Victorian bows added on garden front. Impressive 3 sided stable block with tall dovecot. Romantic and heavily wooded demesne with river and lake. The home of Augusta, Lady Gregory, poet, author and playwright, co-founder of the Abbey Theatre and patron of the arts; in whose time Coole was much frequented by Yeats and other leading figures of the Irish literary and artistic revival;

the place often features in Yeats's poems. In 1927 the estate was sold to the Department of Lands, Lady Gregory being allowed to live there during her lifetime. In 1941, nine years after Lady Gregory's death, the house was demolished; a fate which Yeats had foretold:

> Here, traveller, scholar, poet, take your
> stand
> When all those rooms and passages are
> gone,
> When nettles wave upon a shapeless
> mound
> And saplings root among the broken
> stone . . .

Cooleville, Clogheen, co Tipperary (GRUBB/IFR; SACKVILLE-WEST, SACKVILLE, B/ PB). A pleasant early C19 house of 2 storeys over a basement and 3 bays, with a pillared porch and a 2 storey service wing; built by one of the Grubb family who owned the mill, the ruin of which stands beside the avenue and now, hung with creepers, forms a feature of the garden. From 1956 until his death 1965, the home of Edward Sackville-West, 5th Lord Sackville, the author and music critic, who decorated the house in a delightful Victorian manner as a background to his notable collection of modern pictures. The drawing room was hung with a maroon-coloured flowered paper; the library with a paper of Prussian blue, which set off the orange pine bookcases and the warm colours of a Graham Sutherland landscape over the fireplace. The library opens into a Gothic conservatory which Lord Sackville added *ca* 1963, to the design of Mr Donal O'Neill-Flanagan.

Coolhull Castle, co Wexford. An old castle with a tower at one end and a lower building at the other. Irish battlements.

Coolkelure

Coolkelure, Dunmanway, co Cork
(SHULDHAM/LGI1912; EVANS-FREKE, CAR-
BERY, B/PB; BERNARD, BANDON, E/PB; CAP-
RON/LGI1965). A late-Victorian house of
stone, with gables of timber open-work in
the Swiss manner and a pyramidal-roofed
tower. The estate originally belonged to the
Shuldham family and passed by inheritance
to Georgiana (*née* Evans-Freke), wife of 4th
Earl of Bandon; subsequently to late Mr
Dennis Capron.

Coollattin (also known as **Malton**), **Shil-
lelagh, co Wicklow** (FITZWILLIAM, E/PB).
A 2 storey house built 1801–1804 for 4th
Earl Fitzwilliam—who became Lord-
Lieutenant of Ireland 1795 but was recalled
after 3 months on account of his sympathy
for Catholic Emancipation—replacing a
house which he built 1796, and which was
burnt 1798. It was designed by the veteran
English architect, John Carr of York, with
whom Lord Fitzwilliam, as a great Yorks
magnate, would have had contacts; and as
would thus be expected, its design is con-

Coollattin: Hall and Staircase

Coollattin

servative; the entrance front of 5 bays, with
a 3 bay breakfront and a wide pediment;
the side elevations each with a central curved
bow. The entrance door is under a simple
pillared porch. In the absence of the octo-
genarian Carr, the work of building was
supervised by Thomas Hobson, a mason
from Yorks. Later in C19, the house was
enlarged, the new addition being at the
back and having a lower ground floor, since
the ground falls away steeply on this side.
The later additions include a monumental
hall and a dining room. The rooms in the
earlier part of the house, which include a
bow-ended room with apses, were altered
and redecorated later C19. Good stable yard
with wide pediment on centre block. Sold
1977 to Mr Brendan Cadogan and Mr
Patrick Tattan.

Coolmain Castle, Kilbrittain, co Cork
(STAWELL/LGI1912; RUSKELL/LGI1958). A 2
storey 7 bay gable-ended C18 house with a
pediment-gable on the shore of Courtmac-
sherry Bay; enlarged C19 by the addition of
a castellated wing with dormer-gables and
surrounded by battlemented curtain walls
and outworks.

Coolmore, Carrigaline, co Cork (NEW-
ENHAM/IFR). A large late C18 block of 3

Coolmore

storeys over a basement, built 1788 by
W. W. Newenham to replace a house built
ca 1701 built by Thomas Newenham. 6 bay
entrance front; 2 bay breakfront; doorcase
with engaged Tuscan columns and baseless
pediment. 6 bay garden front overlooking
the Owenboy estuary. The house is faced in
stucco over weather-slating, with stone
dressings. Very large hall with late C18 or
early C19 organ; 2 wooden staircases in
separate halls on either side. Drawing room
and dining room in garden front, both with
friezes of late C18 plasterwork. The drawing
room has a C19 wallpaper with delightful
stencilled decoration in tempera in beautiful
faded reds and greens, and painted medallions of Classical figures on a blue ground.
Sitting rooms on either side of the hall with
rather Soanian curved ceilings. In recent

years, the dining room was reduced in size
in order to make a new kitchen; but the
frieze was reproduced on the new partition
wall and the chimneypiece moved so as to
be central to the room as altered. The
entrance gates are flanked by 8 lodges in the
"Cottage Gothic" style, arranged in the
form of an open court; they were built in
1815 by W. H. Newenham to the design of
an English architect, the elder Thomas
Cundy.

Coolmore, Thomastown, co Kilkenny
(CONNELLAN/LGI1912). A 2 storey 5 bay
late-Georgian house with a single-storey
wing. Single-storey Doric portico with die;
entablatures over ground-floor windows;
roof on cornice supported by unusually
heavy brackets.

Coolnamuck, Carrickbeg, co Waterford
(SANDERS/IFR). A 3 storey C18 block with a
lower wing at one side. 3 bay entrance front
with tripartite pedimented doorcase. Deep
curved bow in adjoining front, with domed
roof. Fine ballroom extending into bow.
Straight lime avenue. C18 Gothic tower by
River Suir. Formerly the seat of a branch of
the Wall family. It is said that one of the
families who owned it in the past lived
very extravagantly; and when, as a result,
they went bankrupt, they committed mass-
suicide by driving their coach over the cliff
at Tramore. In the present century, the
main block became derelict; a house was
made in the wing, which in recent years was
the home of Mr C. C. Sanders. The house
has now been demolished.

Cooper Hill, co Limerick

Cooper Hill, Clarina, co Limerick
(COOPER/LGI1912 and LGI1863). A house built
1741 of 2 storeys at the front and 3 at the
back. 6 bay front; 2 bay pedimented breakfront; doorcase with segmental pediment
flanked by 2 small windows; quoins.

Coopershill, co Sligo

Coopershill, Riverstown, co Sligo (COO-
PER, *sub* O'HARA/IFR). A 3 storey house

attributed by the Knight of Glin to Francis Bindon. Started *ca* 1755, for A. B. Cooper, who is said to have provided a tub of gold guineas to cover the cost of the building before engaging in the undertaking; but according to the story, the last guinea had been spent before the walls showed above the surface of the ground. As a result, the house was not finished until 1774; Cooper had to sell property in order to raise funds to continue, and the stone took 8 years to quarry. It is certainly a house of high quality, built of local ashlar, with 2 similar fronts; entrance front with 2 bays on either side of a rusticated Venetian door, with a rusticated Venetian window above it and a three-light window in the centre of the top storey. All the other windows in the front have rusticated surrounds. Good bold cornice, now rather in the shadow of a C19 eaved roof.

Coote Hill, co Cavan (*see* BELLAMONT FOREST).

Coppinger's Court, Rosscarbery, co Cork. An impressive early to mid-C17 semi-fortified house built by Sir Walter Coppinger; with gables, machicolations and mullioned windows. Now a ruin.

Corballymore

Corbally, Taghadoe, co Kildare. A small early C18 gable-ended house of 2 storeys over a basement. Attractive 5 bay front with floating pediment and round-headed door-way with blocking. In 1814, the residence of William Geraghty.

Corballymore (formerly **Summerville**), **Dunmore East, co Waterford** (FORTESCUE, E/PB; GALLWEY/IFR). A Victorian Baronial house overlooking the Back Strand of Tramore Bay, built by Hon Dudley Fortescue. Of dark random ashlar with bands of lighter-coloured stone; gables, dormer-gables, high-pitched and half-conical roofs. Bought early in the present century by Mr & Mrs H. J. Gallwey; restored after a fire 1935. Now a hotel.

Corbalton Hall (formerly **Cookstown House**), **Tara, co Meath** (CORBALLY/LG1863; CORBALLY-STOURTON, *sub* MOWBRAY, SEGRAVE AND STOURTON, B/PB1970). A 3 storey C18 house with a front of originally 7 bays and flanked by curved screen walls; to which a 2 storey villa by Francis Johnston was added 1801–1807 for Elias Corbally; the older building and the new being joined at an acute angle. The front of Johnston's addition became the new entrance front: 3 bays, 1 bay breakfront centre; Wyatt window above single-storey Ionic portico; ground floor windows set in rather Soanian

Corbalton Hall

arched recesses. Johnston also changed the fenestration of the front of the old house to 3 bays; and replaced the original staircase with a spiral secondary stair lit by a large polygonal cupola. His new block contained a large drawing room and dining room on either side of a hall with a curved staircase extending into a bowed projection at the back. Along the front of the old house is an elegant glass conservatory with a curving roof; from its appearance, it would have been added fairly early in C19. Adjoining the house on this side is a handsome pedimented stable range, with a cupola clock. Inherited through his mother by Col Hon Edward Stourton, who assumed the additional surname of Corbally; and who sold Corbalton 1951.

Cor Castle, Innishannon, co Cork

Cor Castle, Innishannon, co Cork (CORCOR/LG11912). A small, early Gothic Revival castle, its doorway being a Gothicized Venetian window in the Batty Langley manner.

Corduff, Ballinamore, co Leitrim. A 2 storey 5 bay house probably of late C18. 3 storey centre bow. In 1814, the residence of George Percy; in 1914, of Frederick James Penrose.

Corick

Corick, Clogher, co Tyrone (STORY/IFR). A house originally built at the end of C17, as a double gable-ended block of 2 storeys over a basement and 5 bays; extended in early C19 by the addition of a 2 storey 2 bay wing; and largely rebuilt "with comfortable mid-Victorian informality" 1863, to the design of Charles (afterwards Sir Charles) Lanyon and William Henry Lynn.

Cork, co Cork: Bishop's Palace. The Palace of the (C of I) Bishops of Cork; a compact 3 storey block with a fanlighted doorway, built between 1772 and 1789 by Bishop Mann on the site of the earlier palace, a rambling building said to have dated from C16 and shown in an illustration on a French map of 1650 to have had a tower and cupola. Handsome entrance gates.

Corkagh House, Clondalkin, co Dublin (FINLAY/LG11912; COLLEY, *sub* HARBERTON, V/PB). A 3 storey 8 bay late C18 house with a parapeted roof, built by Col John Finlay, MP. Inherited by Edith, daughter of H. T. Finlay, who married G.P.A. Colley 1909. Sold *ca* 1960.

Corkbeg

Corkbeg, Whitegate, co Cork (PENROSE-FITZGERALD, *sub* UNIACKE/IFR). A square 2 storey early to mid-C19 house on an island just inside the entrance to Cork Harbour joined to the mainland by a causeway; built to replace an earlier house nearer the water's edge. 3 bay entrance front; large enclosed porch with door at side between recessed Grecian Ionic columns. Adjoining 3 bay front with single-storey curved central bow flanked by large triple windows. Very impressive central top-lit staircase hall; stone staircase with brass balusters. Sold *ca* 1945

Corkbeg: Drawing Room

by Capt R. F. U. Penrose-FitzGerald; an hotel for some years, and then completely demolished to make way for an oil refinery.

Cornacassa, Monaghan, co Monaghan (HAMILTON/LGI1912). A restrained and dignified early C19 Classical house of the school of Francis Johnston. 2 storey over basement; ashlar-faced. 3 bay entrance front, 1 bay breakfront centre, single-storey Doric portico. Lower 2 storey service wing. Balustraded area parapet, added in late C19 or at beginning of C20. 5 bay side elevation. Plain roof parapet. Drawing room with screen of fluted columns at one end and arched recesses filled with looking-glass. Now demolished.

Cornacassa

Cornahir, Tyrrellspass, co Westmeath (VIGNOLES/LGI1879). A 2 storey double bow-fronted Georgian house.

Corradoo, Ballinafad, co Sligo (PHIBBS/LGI1912). A house built 1768 by William Phibbs, of Hollybrook (*qv*), for use as a school. Renovated as a house for himself 1866-67 by Owen Phibbs, son of William Phibbs, of Seafield; continued to serve as a dower house for the Phibbses of Seafield (afterwards known as Lisheen—*qv*) until sold by Geoffrey Phibbs 1939 to Major Fraser.

Corries, Bagenalstown, co Carlow (RUD-KIN/LGI1937Supp; WYNNE/IFR; BAYLISS, *sub* LOFTUS/IFR). A late C17 or early C18 house, built by the centenarian Henry Rudkin. Very thick walls, small rooms with beams encased in plaster. Sold *ca* 1830 to the Wynne family. A wing containing a drawing room was added at one end *ca* 1880, projecting forwards from the front; also a projecting porch; the two projections being joined by a single-storey corridor along the ground floor of the front. Inside, this addition provides a delightful feature, a long narrow room like a gallery, running from the porch to the drawing room. Re-sold 1943 to Capt H. T. Bayliss, who in turn sold it *ca* 1958 to Mr & Mrs Henry A. Rudkin, of Pepperidge Farm, USA; Mr Rudkin be-

ing a descendant of the original owners of Corries. Mrs Rudkin invented a special bread, originally for her son, who was ill at the time and allergic to most foods; it was so good that she marketed it as Pepperidge Farm Bread.

Corville, Roscrea, co Tipperary (O' BYRNE/LGI1912). A C18 house with a break-front centre. Rusticated doorcase with entablature on console brackets. Decorated ceilings.

Costello Lodge, Costello, co Galway (ISMAY/LGI1952; HERDMAN/IFR). A fishing lodge in Connemara, owned earlier this century by J. Bruce Ismay, head of the White Star Line at the time of the sinking of the *Titanic* and one of the survivors from that ill-fated ship. Burnt 1922 and rebuilt 1925; a 2 storey house with gables, dormer-gables and a pantiled roof.

Courtown, Kilcock, co Kildare (AYLMER/IFR; DRUMMOND, *sub* PERTH, E/PB; O'BRIEN, Bt/PB) A plain 2 storey house of *ca* 1815, built by John Aylmer to replace the earlier house here, which was burnt and looted 1798 during the ownership of his father, Michael Aylmer, who had been unable to rebuild it, not having received sufficient compensation from the State. 5 bay front, with strip-pilasters. Much enlarged *ca* 1900 by J.A. Aylmer, who added a wing at right angles to the original block to form a new entrance front, with a 3 sided bow and an open porch, at one side of a pedimented projection; containing, among other rooms, a hall with a massive oak staircase. Fine beech avenue, half a mile long. Sold 1947 by J. W. Aylmer to George Drummond; now the home of Mr & Mrs John O'Brien.

Courtown House, Gorey, co Wexford (STOPFORD, COURTOWN, E/PB). A C18 house, overlooking the sea at Courtown Harbour, much altered and enlarged C19 after being sacked during 1798 Rebellion. The front of the house consisted of a "U"-shaped block of 2 storeys and a dormered attic in the high-pitched, château-style roof; the dormers being pedimented. 5 bay centre and 1 bay in the end of each of the projecting wings; the space between the latter being filled, at ground floor level, by a large open porch, fronted by a porte-cochère carried on 4 piers. The side of the house was of 3

bays, interrupted by a massive chimney-stack, beyond which was a 3 storey 3 sided bow. The side elevation was further prolonged by a 2 storey block with an ordinary eaved roof on a plain cornice; of 3 bays in its upper storey, and with a single large 3 light window, fronted by pilasters and an entablature, below. Large hall with double staircase. Sold *post* World War II; subsequently demolished.

Craigavad, co Down (MULHOLLAND, DUN-LEATH, B/PB). A restrained Classical house on the shores of Belfast Lough, built *ca* 1852 for John Mulholland, afterwards 1st Lord Dunleath, to the design of the Belfast architect, Thomas Turner. Top-lit central hall with a circular gallery and a glazed dome. Now a golf club.

Craigavon, Strandtown, co Down (CRAIG, CRAIGAVON, V/PB). A 2 storey Victorian house with a front of 2 bays on either side of a central bow. Round-headed windows in lower storey, camber-headed windows above. Pavilion with pedimented portico at back of house, joined to main block by orangery. The home of James Craig, 1st Viscount Craigavon, 1st Prime Minister of Northern Ireland. Given to the nation.

Craigdunn Castle

Craigdunn Castle, Dunminning, co Antrim (MCNEILL-MOSS/IFR). A Victorian Scottish-Baronial castle of basalt, built by Edmund McNeill. 2 storey and gabled attic; massive 5 storey tower with pepperpot bartizans. Drawing room with Classical plasterwork ceiling.

Cranagh Castle, Templemore, co Tipperary (LLOYD/IFR). A 3 storey house of 1768 built on to a medieval round tower. 5 bay front with central Venetian window

Courtown House, co Wexford

Crawfordsburn

over round-headed doorway with blocking and sidelights. Curved bow at one end, possibly intended to balance the old round tower, which can be seen in juxtaposition with it at the side of the house. Eaved roof, presumably C19.

Cranaghan House, Ballyconnell, co Cavan. A house with an Ionic portico rising through the full height of its front.

Crawfordsburn, Bangor, co Down (SHAR-MAN-CRAWFORD/LGI1912). Originally a 2 storey 5 bay gable-ended C18 house overlooking Belfast Lough. Triple window above fanlighted doorway. Return. Enlarged in C19 gabled style. Now a hospital and much altered.

Creagh, Skibbereen, co Cork

Creagh, Skibbereen, co Cork (BECHER/ IFR; WRIXON-BECHER, Bt/PB; HAROLD-BARRY/IFR). A pleasant Regency house of 2 storeys over a basement, built *ca* 1820. Entrance front with a single deep semicircular bow and 1 bay; fanlighted doorway beneath trellised porch; a second bow is said to have been intended, but never built. Side elevation of 3 bays and a 3 sided bow. Eaved roof. Curving staircase, with slender wooden balusters; drawing room extending into the semi-circular bow, dining room in the three-sided bow. Delightful gardens laid out by the present owner, Mr P. J. Harold-Barry, extending to the shore of the estuary and along the banks of a mill-race and millpond, with the ruined mill providing a folly-like "object".

Creagh, Ballinrobe, co Mayo (KNOX/ LGI1912). A house built 1875 for Capt C. H. C. Knox to the design of S. U. Roberts.

Creagh Castle, Doneraile, co Cork

Creagh Castle, Doneraile, co Cork (BRASIER-CREAGH/IFR; BLACK/LGI1958). A house of 2 storeys over a basement and 5 bays built 1816 by Capt W. J. Brasier-Creagh on the site of an earlier house known as Castle Saffron which was destroyed by fire in 2nd half of C18; and which in 1750 was the seat of John Love and said to have rooms with plasterwork by the Francini brothers. The 1816 house, which from its appearance could be earlier—and probably incorporates the burnt front of Castle Saffron—is faced in ashlar and has a handsome doorcase with engaged Ionic columns and a fanlight below the entablature; and a perron with double steps and an iron railing. There are corner-pilasters, scroll keystones over some of the windows, and a well-moulded cornice. The front was extended by 2 bays at one side early in the present century to provide a larger drawing room; the extension is in exactly the same syle as the original block, complete with scroll keystones and corner pilasters; but it has a dormered attic on its side elevation and no basement windows. On the other side of the front stands a well-preserved tower-house. Spectacular Gothic entrance gates, built 1827 by G.W. Brasier-Creagh; consisting of a central arch flanked by two smaller ones, all liberally adorned with pinnacles, finials and battlements. Sold 1977.

Crebilly, Ballymena, co Antrim (O'HARA/ LGI1863). A 2 storey C19 Italianate house which from its appearance could be an early work of Sir Charles Lanyon. 7 bay front, the end bays breaking forward; rectangular, round-headed and camber-headed windows. Porch in the form of a 3 arched loggia, with Tuscan columns, surmounted by pierced parapet with armorial bearings in centre. Rock-faced rustication on side piers of porch, round inner lower-storey windows and elsewhere. Entablatures on console brackets over outer lower-storey windows. Roof on bracket cornice. Astragals in windows.

Creevaghmore, Ballymahon, co Longford. A 2 storey gable-ended mid-C18 house, with 2 lower wings extending back towards the farmyard, which is immediately behind the house. 7 bay pedimented front; doorway with blocking and a large keystone, the stones on either side of it defined with an architrave-moulding. Open-well staircase of wood in entrance hall.

Cregg Castle, Fermoy, co Cork (HYDE/ IFR; MASSY, B/PB). A house of mid-C18 appearance, of 3 storeys over a basement; the top storey being treated as an attic, above the cornice. 6 bay front; 2 bay breakfront; round-headed doorway flanked by narrow windows. 2 storey 3 bay wing at one side, and set back; with a truncated pyramidal roof. Staircase of fine C18 joinery at back of hall. The house stands above the River Blackwater; in the grounds is a more or less intact tower-house of the Condons. Cregg Castle was, until lately, the home of Mr & Mrs Hugh Massy, who made an elaborate Italian garden at the back of the house.

Cregg Castle, co Galway

Cregg Castle, Corrandulla, co Galway (KIRWAN/LGI1912; BLAKE/LGI886). A tower-house built 1648 by a member of the Kirwan family, and said to have been the last fortified dwelling to be built west of the Shannon; given sash-windows and otherwise altered in Georgian times, and enlarged with a wing on either side: that to the right being as high as the original building, and with a gable; that to the left being lower, and battlemented. In C18 it was the home of the great chemist and natural philosopher, Richard Kirwan, whose laboratory, now roofless, still stands in the garden. It was acquired *ca* 1780 by James Blake. The hall, entered through a rusticated round-headed doorway with a perron and double steps, has a black marble chimneypiece with the Blake coat-of-arms. The dining room has a plasterwork ceiling. Sold 1947 by Mrs Christopher Kerins (*née* Blake), to Mr & Mrs Alexander Johnston. Re-sold 1972 to Mr Martin Murray, owner of the Salthill Hotel, near Galway.

Crevenagh House, Omagh, co Tyrone (AUCHINLECK, *sub* DARLING/IFR). A 2 storey house built *ca* 1820 by D. E. Auchinleck, great-uncle of Field Marshal Sir Claude Auchinleck. 3 bay entrance front with Wyatt windows in both storeys and projecting porch. 3 bay side with central Wyatt window in both storeys. A slightly lower 2 storey range was subsequently added by D. E. Auchinleck's son, Major Thomas Auchinleck, behind the original block and parallel with it; its end, which has a single-storey bow, forming a continuation of the side elevation, to which it is joined by a short single-storey link. The principal rooms in the main block have good plaster-work ceilings, and the hall has a mosaic floor depicting the Seven Ages of Man. There are doors made of mahogany from the family plantations in Demerara.

Crobeg, Doneraile, co Cork (STAWELL/LGI1912). A plain 2 storey Georgian house with an enclosed porch.

Crocknacrieve, Enniskillen, co Fermanagh (RICHARDSON/IFR; ARCHDALE/IFR; LOANE/IFR). A Georgian house, built by Capt John Johnston, whose widow married H. M. Richardson, of Rossfad; who, when he inherited the latter estate, and part of Rich Hill (*qv*), handed Crocknacrieve over to his cousin, Nicholas Archdale, who added a wing, said to have been built with stone from the old Folliott castle at Ballinamallard. Sir Edward Archdale sold the property 1901; in 1921 it was bought by S. C. Loane, whose wife (*née* Barton) was the grand-daughter of H.M. Richardson.

Crom Castle

Crom Castle, Newtown Butler, co Fermanagh (CRICHTON, ERNE, E/PB). A large castellated mansion combining baronial and Tudor-Revival elements, by the side of one of the many inlets of Upper Lough Erne; built 1829 to the design of Edward Blore. The entrance front has a gabled projection with a corbelled oriel at each end, but they are not entirely similar; while the tall, battlemented entrance tower, which incorporates a porte-cochère, is not central but to one side, against the left hand gable. The adjoining garden front is symmetrical, dominated by a very tall central tower with slender octagonal turrets, inspired by various Tudor gatehouse towers in England, but without a doorway. On either side of it is a gable and oriel. In the park are the ruins of the earlier Crom Castle, a Plantation castle of 1611, destroyed by fire 1764.

Cromore, Portstewart, co Derry (MONTAGU, *sub* MANCHESTER, D/PB). A mid-C18 house of 2 storeys with a dormered attic and 4 bays, enlarged and remodelled 1834 by John Cromie, who added a 2 storey wing on

Cromore

either side, of the same height as the centre; with a single large many-paned window in each storey. The front was further prolonged by the addition of a single-storey pavilion, in the form of a Doric temple, at one end; this was, in fact, the entrance porch, joined to the main block by a short corridor. Later, a balancing pavilion was built at the other end of the house; it was glazed as a conservatory. Impressive hall of 1834 with Ionic screen behind which rises a staircase with elegant cast-iron balusters. Passed to the Montagus through the marriage of Ellen, daughter and heiress of John Cromie, to Lord Robert Montagu, MP (2nd son of 6th Duke of Manchester), a prominent Victorian public figure and Catholic convert who reverted to Protestantism as a protest against Mr Gladstone's Irish policy. Cromore is now a residence for post-graduate university students.

Cromwellsfort, co Wexford (CORNOCK/LGI1912). A C18 house of 3 storeys over basement. 5 bay front; Venetian window in centre, with triple window above and tripartite doorway below. High basement; balustraded roof parapet; prominent quoins. The name of the house comes from the Irish *cromwelk*, "the sloping wood".

Croney Byrne, Rathdrum, co Wicklow (BYRNE/IFR). A 2 storey 3 bay late-Georgian house with an eaved roof. Porch with plain pillars. Gothic gate lodge. The home of Rt Rev Herbert Byrne, OSB, titular Abbot of Westminster and former Abbot of Ampleforth.

Cronroe, Ashford, co Wicklow (CASEMENT/IFR). A Victorian house with bargeboards, eaved roofs and a tower.

Crossdrum, Oldcastle, co Meath (HARMAN/LGI1958). A house attributed by Dr Watkin to C. R. Cockerell, probably built 1825 for J. L. Naper, of Loughcrew (*qv*), to be occupied by a tenant. 2 storey, 3 bays, fanlighted doorway with elegant sidelights. Shallow window surrounds with blocking.

Crossdrum, Oldcastle, co Meath (ROTHERAM/LGI1958). A late C18 house of 2 storeys over a basement; 5 bay front with tripartite rounded doorcase; parapeted roof.

Crosshaven House, Crosshaven, co Cork (HAYES/IFR). A 3 storey house built 1769 by William Hayes, with 2 identical fronts of crisp grey ashlar which, as Mr A. H. Gomme has pointed out, almost certainly derive from Isaac Ware's design for Clifton Hill House, Bristol, in his *Complete Body of Architecture*. Each front is of 5 bays with a 3 bay pedimented breakfront; the ground floor is treated as a basement and rusticated. Fanlighted doorcase with engaged Ionic columns on entrance front. The house is flanked by free-standing wings or pavilions which originally accommodated the male and female servants; they are of 2 storeys and have handsome pedimented elevations on the garden front with Diocletian windows above Venetian doorways and with oculi in the pediments. On the entrance front the wings have rudimentary pediment-gables and arched openings into which coaches or carts could be driven. The house has a cantilevered staircase, and there is plasterwork in some of the principal rooms.

Croney Byrne

Crossdrum (HARMAN)

Crosshaven House: Entrance Front

Crosshaven House: Garden Front

The garden front of the house, rising above the demesne wall, dominates the village square by the little harbour of Crosshaven in a manner reminiscent of some Continental schloss or château. Crosshaven House was sold by Col Pierse Hayes 1973 to Mr Graham Flint, of Florida, USA; it was subsequently re-sold and is now a community centre.

Crossogue House, Ballycahill, co Tipperary (MOLLOY, *sub* DE LA POER/IFR). An early-Victorian house with a high basement. The home of Mr & Mrs Anthony Molloy.

Crotto

Crotto, Kilflynn, co Kerry (PONSONBY, *sub* BESSBOROUGH, E/PB). A house built 1669 by a branch of the Ponsonbys descended from Henry Ponsonby, younger brother of Sir John Ponsonby from whom the Earls of Bessborough and the other Irish Ponsonbys descend. Of 2 storeys; entrance front consisting of 5 bays recessed between projecting wings with 1 bay forward-facing ends. Steep pediment-gable with lunette window over 3 centre bays; rusticated window surrounds. In 1705 Rose Ponsonby, the heiress of Crotto, married John Carrique; their descendants bore the additional surname of Ponsonby. Some alterations were carried out *ca* 1819 by a member of the Carrique Ponsonby family to the design of Sir Richard Morrison, who gave the wings "Elizabethan" gables with coats-of-arms and tall chimneys; he also added a curvi-

linear-gabled porch. In other respects, the exterior of the house kept its original character. The estate was sold by the Carrique Ponsonbys 1842. A few years later, the new owner leased the house to Lt-Col H. H. Kitchener, whose son, the future Field Marshal Earl Kitchener of Khartoum (*see* PB), spent his boyhood here. Now demolished.

Crowhill, Annaghmore, co Armagh (ATKINSON/LGI1958). A 2 storey late-Georgian house; 5 bay front with 1 bay pedimented breakfront. Lunette attic window in tympanum of pediment; doorway with very wide elliptical fanlight extending over the door and sidelights; the voussoirs of the fanlight arch being very prominent. Some late-Georgian plasterwork in interior. The estate originally belonged to the Hopes and passed to the Atkinsons through the marriage of Sarah Hope to Joseph Atkinson 1791. Sold 1951/52 to Northern Ireland Ministry of Agriculture.

Cuba Court

Cuba Court, Banagher, Offaly. Described by Dr Craig as "perhaps the most splendidly masculine house in the whole country"; an early C18 house of noble proportions and bold, self-confident detail; of 2 storeys over a basement, with 2 adjoining pedimented breakfront elevations, one of 5 bays and the other of 7. The longer of 2 fronts had a Venetian window above a pedimented door-

case flanked by two windows; the shorter had a doorcase with a pediment on tapering pilasters copied from Sir John Vanbrugh's door at King's Weston, Glos, which in turn derived from Michelangelo. Roof on massive cornice with tall stacks. The house is said to have been built for a family named Fraser; it seems likely that Sir Edward Lovett Pearce had at least a hand in its design. By end of C18 it belonged to a branch of the Daly family; early in C19 it became a school, one of the masters of which was the uncle of Rev A. B. Nicholls, who brought his bride, Charlotte Bronte, to stay here on their honeymoon 1854. The house was unroofed *ca* 1946; and in recent years, much of the ruin has been demolished.

Cuffesborough, Durrow, co Leix (PRIOR-PALMER/LGI1958). A 3 storey house of 1770 which from both its elevation and plan would appear to have been built about 30 years earlier. Front of 2 bays on either side of a centre consisting of a rusticated pedimented and fanlighted doorcase flanked by 2 small windows below a window flanked by 2 niches, below a window flanked by 2 blank windows. Good string courses and quoins. Shouldered doors with triple keystones set into arched recesses in hall. Staircase at back of hall rising to top of house.

Cullamore, Carney, co Sligo (GORE-BOOTH, Bt/PB). A house built by Sir Robert Gore-Booth, 4th Bt, MP, some time *ante* 1833, as a dower house for Lissadell (*qv*); to the design of Francis Goodwin, of London. Described as an "Italian villa", but rather more Grecian in character. 2 storey; 3 bay centre slightly recessed between pedimented projecting end bays, surrounded by framing bands and with channelling in their lower storey. Porch with square piers and ironwork balconies on either side.

Cuba Court: as it is today

Cullane, Sixmilebridge, co Clare (STUD-DERT/IFR). A Georgian house with a bow window, overlooking the lake. Had a good scrolled overmantel in one room. Now a ruin. A gazebo on hill nearby.

Culmore House, Ballykelly, co Derry. A good quality late-Georgian house of brilliant red brick, built 1805. 2 storey over high basement; 5 bay front, central window flanked by 2 narrow windows above, fanlighted doorway flanked by 2 niches below. Circular staircase.

Cultra, Craigavad, co Down (KENNEDY/LGI1958). Originally, a large, plain house with a central bow and a battlemented parapet. Towards the end of the C19, or in the opening years of the C20, Robert (afterwards Sir Robert) Kennedy, a diplomat who eventually became Minister to Uruguay, replaced the house with a long 2 storey mansion built of rubble with ashlar facings, which he named Cultra Manor. Front with projecting pedimented ends, joined by balustraded Ionic colonnade; the right-hand section of it breaking forwards, as a porch. Balustraded roof parapet. Long 2 storey service wing, joined to main block by lower link.

Cultra, co Down: Bishop's Palace. A gabled Victorian house with a battlemented tower at one corner.

Curragh, Lisnaskea, co Fermanagh (CHARTRES/IFR). A 2 storey 3 bay house with quoins, said to have been originally built *ca* 1690–1700. 2 storey 5 bay wing of rubble with limestone dressings. The windows are said to have been altered *ca* 1820–30 by Capt William Chartres; and the house was re-roofed at the beginning of C20. Outer and inner halls paved in stone; C18 doorcases and alcoves; staircase with finely-turned balusters. Sold 1900.

Curragh Chase

Curragh Chase, Adare, co Limerick (DE VERE, and *sub* HUNT/LGI1912; DE VERE, *sub* INCHIQUIN, B/PB). A large house of 2 storeys over a basement with two adjoining fronts. The shorter of 2 is C18, by a Limerick architect, with 2 bays on either side of a central 3 sided bow; lower storey windows with shouldered architraves and simple entablatures; upper storey windows with shouldered architraves on console brackets. The longer front is early C19, probably added 1829 by Sir Aubrey de Vere, 2nd Bt (author of *Julian the Apostate* and *The Duke of Mercia*), to the design of an English architect, Amon Henry Wilds; of 11 bays, the 3 end bays on either side breaking forward; it is plain, except for prominent quoins, and has a curved bow at one end. A terrace with a broad flight of steps leading

up to it runs along the whole length of this front, concealing the basement. Large library. The house is in what Mr James Lees-Milne describes as "one of the most remote and romantic settings conceivable"; above a reed-fringed lake with woods stretching away to distant hills. The landscape was largely created by Sir Aubrey de Vere, 2nd Bt; with whom, in the words of his son, the C19 Catholic poet Aubrey de Vere, "landscape gardening was one mode of taking out the poetry which was so deeply seated within him". Aubrey de Vere was born here and though only a younger son, lived here for most of his long life; dying here at the age of 87 in the same small room which he had occupied as a child. His friend, Tennyson, often came to visit him here; and while here wrote *Clara Lady Vere de Vere*. Curragh Chase passed to a great-nephew of Aubrey de Vere, R. S. V. O'Brien, of the Inchiquin family, who assumed the surname of de Vere. The house was gutted by fire 1941; the ruin and its surroundings are now kept in good order by the Department of Lands, which maintains the demesne as a forest park.

Curraghmore, co Mayo

Curraghmore, Ballinrobe, co Mayo. From its appearance, a 2 storey 3 bay ashlar-faced house of *ca* 1830, of which the centre bay has been altered and embellished in the High Victorian period: framed by buttresses, with 2 small round-headed windows inserted into the space of what was formerly a central Wyatt window, and a tripartite doorway of no easily definable style in which the door and sidelights are separated by polygonal piers. At one side of the house is a narrow, tower-like projection topped by a little pediment-gable. The seat of the Martyn family.

Curraghmore, Portlaw, co Waterford (DE LA POER BERESFORD, WATERFORD, M/PB).

A medieval tower, remodelled C18 and refaced in Classical style C19, with a large 3 storey house 7 bays wide and 7 bays deep behind it. The tower survives from the old castle of the Le Poers or Powers; the house was in existence 1654, but was rebuilt 1700 and subsequently enlarged and remodelled; it extends round 3 sides of a small inner court, which is closed on 4th side by the tower. The 1700 rebuilding was carried out by James Power, 3rd and last Earl of Tyrone of 1st creation, whose daughter and heiress, Lady Catherine Power, married Sir Marcus Beresford, afterwards 1st Earl of Tyrone of the 2nd creation; a marriage which the ghost of the bride's uncle had predicted to the bridegroom's mother (*see* GILL HALL). The 1st Beresford Earl of Tyrone remodelled the interior of the old tower and probably had work done on the house as well. His son, 2nd Earl, afterwards 1st Marquess of Waterford, had the principal rooms of the house—which in the earlier C18 were decorated with wall and ceiling paintings by the Dutch artist, Johann van der Hagen—redecorated to the design of James Wyatt 1780s; and at the same time he probably built the present staircase hall in the inner court and carried out other structural alterations. The tower and the house were both refaced mid-C19. The house has a pediment in the centre of its principal front, which is the garden front; and, like the tower, a balustraded roof parapet. The tower has 3 tiers of pilasters framing the main entrance doorway and the triple windows in the two storeys above it; and is surmounted by St Hubert's Stag, the family crest of the Le Poers. It stands at the head of a vast forecourt, a feature which seems to belong more to France, or elsewhere on the Continent, than to the British Isles; having no counterpart in Ireland, and only 1 or 2 in Britain, notably the forecourt at Seaton Delaval, Northumberland, a house to which the Beresfords became connected by marriage; though not until half-a-century after the building of the Curraghmore forecourt, which dates from the time of the 1st Beresford Earl of Tyrone, probably from 1750–1760. It is by the Waterford architect, John Roberts, and is a magnificent piece of architecture; the long stable ranges on either side being dominated by tremendous pedimented archways with blocked columns and pilasters. There are rusticated arches and window surrounds, pedimented niches with statues, doorways with entablatures; all in

Curraghmore, co Waterford

Curraghmore, co Waterford: Courtyard

beautifully crisp stonework. The ends of the two ranges facing the front are pedimented and joined by a long railing with a gate in the centre. The entrance hall, in the old tower, has a barrel vaulted ceiling covered with plasterwork rosettes in circular compartments which dates from *ca* 1750; this being one of the rooms redecorated by the 1st Beresford Earl of Tyrone, the other being the room above, now the billiard room, which has a wonderful coved ceiling probably by the brothers Paul & Philip Francini, decorated with foliage, flowers, busts and ribbons in rectangular and curvilinear compartments. The chimneypiece, which has an overmantel with a broken pediment and *putti*, is probably by John Houghton, Richard Castle's carver. At the inner end of the room is a recess in the thickness of the old castle wall with a screen of fluted Corinthian columns. There is a similar recess in the hall below, in which a straight flight of stairs leads up to the level of the principal rooms in the house. These lie on three sides of the great staircase hall, which has Wyatt decoration and a stair with a light and simple balustrade rising in a sweeping curve. Of the other Wyatt interiors, the finest are the dining room and the Blue Drawing Room, two of the most beautiful late C18 rooms in Ireland. The dining room has delicate plasterwork on the ceiling and walls, the former incorporating roundels attributed to Antonio Zucchi or his wife, Angelica Kauffman; the latter, *grisaille* panels by Peter de Gree. The Blue Drawing Room has a ceiling incorporating roundels by de Gree and semi-circular panels attributed to Zucchi. In the garden is a shell-house built *ca* 1750 and containing a statue by the younger John van Nost of

Curraghmore, co Waterford: ceiling of Blue Drawing Room

Catherine, Countess of Tyrone, who put up the shells with her own hands. The demesne of Curraghmore is unsurpassed in Ireland in its size, its romantic scenery and its splendid woods, which are part of a primeval forest. The River Clodagh flows through it and is spanned, a little way from the house, by a many-arched medieval bridge, built, according to tradition, for King John. On a hill at the north-east of the demesne is a copy of an ancient Irish round tower erected by 1st Marquess of Waterford in memory of his 12 year old eldest son who was killed when jumping his horse over the forecourt railing. Later Beresfords were renowned for their dashing horsemanship; 3rd Marquess was one of the most famous MFHs of his time; while the sporting exploits of 3 brothers of 5th Marquess, Lord Charles Beresford ("Charlie B"), the Admiral, Lord William Beresford, who won the VC in the Zulu War and Lord Marcus Beresford, who managed the racing stables of Edward VII and George V, are legendary.

Curraglass, co Cork (WALLIS/IFR; GUMBLETON, *sub* MAXWELL-GUMBLETON/LG1952). A 3 storey Georgian house. Square fish-pond surrounded by walks overshadowed by elms. A seat of the Wallis family; afterwards of H. C. Gumbleton, brother of R. W. Gumbleton, who built the nearby Glynnatore (*qv*). The house stood for many years as a ruin, a pleasant landmark on the road from Conna to Tallow, which turned 4

Currarevagh

right-angled corners in order to avoid it. Recently, however, the road was straightened and it was swept away.

Currarevagh, Oughterard, co Galway. A plain 2 storey slightly rambling C19 house in a magnificent situation overlooking Lough Corrib. Attractive staircase with turned wooden balusters rising round large staircase hall. The seat of the Hodgson family, who now run it as a guest house.

Curravordy, co Cork (*see* MOUNT PLEASANT).

Cuskinny, Cobh, co Cork (FRENCH/LG 1937Supp). A 2 storey house of C19 appearance, with an entrance door in the side of a gabled projection at one end; and a long, plain side elevation. Eaved roof. The seat of the French family, from whom the present owner, Mrs J. G. Ronan, is maternally descended.

D

Daisy Hill, co Derry (*see* ROE PARK).

Dalgan Park, Kilmaine, co Mayo (MAIT-LAND-KIRWAN/LGI1937; KIRWAN/LGI1912). A 2 storey early C19 Classical house of cut limestone. 9 bay front, the 3 centre bays being framed by Ionic pilasters; medallion and plaque over entrance door. Parapeted roof. Bow at end. Impressive hall with Corinthian columns, lit by dome. In 1914 the home of A.J.J. Algie. Now owned by a religious order.

Dalyston

Dalyston, Loughrea, co Galway (DALY/IFR; O'FARRELL/LGI1912). A good 3 storey late C18 house, built for Rt Hon Denis Daly, MP. 3 bay entrance front, of cut stone; tripartite doorcase with pilasters and pediment extending over door and sidelights; plain window surrounds. Deep and elaborately moulded roof cornice. Plain 5 bay side elevation. Small room off hall with decorated ceiling. Became the seat of the O'Farrell family *ante* mid-C19. Now a ruin.

Damer House

Damer House, Roscrea, co Tipperary (DAMER, *sub* PORTARLINGTON, E/PB). A very distinguished early C18 house, built within the walls of the old Butler castle in the town of Roscrea by Joseph Damer (father of 1st Earl of Dorchester and maternal grandfather of 1st Earl of Portarlington), who

Damer House: Staircase

bought the castle 1715. Of 3 storeys and 9 bays, it has a scroll pedimented doorway and a magnificent carved staircase, rather similar to the staircase at Cashel Palace (*qv*). Like the King House at Boyle (*qv*), it was used as a barracks for most of C19, then as a school, after which it housed the County Library and Engineering Offices. By 1973 it was in poor repair and threatened with demolition; but it has been saved by the Irish Georgian Society, which has leased it and is restoring it gradually, as funds permit.

Danesfort

Danesfort (formerly **Clanwilliam House**), **Belfast, co Antrim** (BARBOUR, Bt/PB1949; DUFFIN, *sub* GARDNER/IFR). One of the finest High-Victorian mansions in Ire-

land, built 1864 for Samuel Barbour to the design of William J. Barre. Described by Mr Brett as "a sort of a French-Italian-English château"; dominated by a tall and very ornate tower with a mansard roof resting on an arcade of what Mr Brett calls "square cabbagey columns", which constitutes a porte-cochère. Inherited by Margaret, daughter of Samuel Barbour, wife of Charles Duffin. Now used as headquarters by the Electricity Board.

Dangan Castle, Trim, co Meath (WEL-LESLEY, WELLINGTON, D/PB; BURROWES/IFR). The seat of the Wesley family, inherited by Richard Colley who assumed the name of Wesley (which later became Wellesley) and was created Lord Mornington; his son, 1st Earl of Mornington, was the father of the great Duke of Wellington; who, according to tradition, was born here. The house appears to have been early to mid-C18, of 2 storeys and with a solid roof parapet; it was described (1739) as having "a noble piazza of seven curious turned arches in front of it". Near the house was a stable block with a central turret and pedimented ends. The grounds were said (1739) to boast of at least 25 obelisks, a Rape of Proserpine "weighing 3 tons" and a fort with cannon which fired salutes on family birthdays down by the lake; where 3 vessels—a 20 ton man of war, a yacht and a packet boat—rode at anchor. By end of C18, there was also a column, which is now at Furness, co Kildare (*qv*) and wrought-iron gates, now at St Patrick's College, Maynooth. The Duke of Wellington's eldest brother, Richard, 2nd Earl of Mornington, who was made Marquess Wellesley while Governor-General of India, sold Dangan *ca* 1793 to Col Thomas Burrowes, MP, an East Indian "Nabob" who improved the house by adding wings to it, containing a library and a chapel with a painted window, after Raphael, of St Paul preaching to the Athenians. The estate remained in the Burrowes family until sold by Col Burrowes's great-grandson; but by 1803 the house had been let to Roger O'Connor, a United Irishman like his brother, Arthur, who had been made an honorary General by Napoleon; he was said to have taken the house in order to be able to entertain Napoleon there. By 1807 the place was dilapidated, trees were cut down and the gardens overgrown. A few years later, the house was in ruins. Despite his oft-quoted remark about being born in a stable not making one a horse, the great Duke of Wellington had sufficient feeling for Dangan to contemplate buying back the estate; but nothing came of the plan.

Daramona House, Street, co Westmeath (WILSON/IFR). A house with a pillared porch on its 3 bay front, a single-storey addition and a domed observatory.

Dardistown Castle

Dardistown Castle, Julianstown, co Meath. A medieval castle with 2 wings, one probably added C17, the other C18. The seat of the Osborne family.

Dargan Villa, co Dublin (*see* MOUNT ANVILLE).

Dartrey

Dartrey (formerly **Dawson Grove**), **Rockcorry, co Monaghan** (DAWSON, DARTREY, E/PB1933). A large Elizabethan-Revival mansion by William Burn, built 1846 to replace a house of *ca* 1770. This earlier house, described 1778 by Rev Daniel Beaufort as "a new brick building, neat and well

contrived but rather heavy both in its external appearance and inside decorations", was of 3 storeys over a basement; the entrance front was of 7 bays with a 3 bay pedimented breakfront, the garden front of 1 bay on either side of a central 3 sided bow. On one side, the house was joined to a low pedimented pavilion by a single-storey link; the corresponding pavilion at the other side does not appear to have been built, or was demolished at some stage. The house had a high-pitched roof and a solid roof parapet adorned with urns; on either side of the bow in the garden front there was a Venetian window under a relieving arch. The hall had a recess at its inner end, behind a screen of columns; the saloon extended into the bow of the garden front, which was curved on the inside. The staircase was in a separate hall at one side. The Elizabethan-Revival mansion which took the place of this house, built by Richard Dawson, 3rd Lord Cremorne and afterwards 1st Earl of Dartrey, had long and somewhat monotonous elevations of curvilinear gables, mullioned windows and oriels, with, every now and then, a square turret and cupola. There was an army of Tudor chimneys, a generous application of strapwork and a 2 tier terrace along the garden front with many yards of latticed balustrading. The quoins were partly curved, a mannerism very characteristic of Burn. The house overlooked Lough Dromore, where, on a wooded island, Thomas Dawson, 1st Lord Dartrey and afterwards Viscount Cremorne, built a domed mausoleum *ca* 1770 in memory of his 1st wife, Lady Anne, to the design of James Wyatt; containing a dramatic life-sized sculptural group, including an angel with outstretched wings, by Joseph Wilton. The Elizabethan-Revival mansion, after standing empty for some years, was demolished *ca* 1950; the mausoleum, which had become roofless, so that the monument was suffering from the weather as well as from vandalism, was repaired by the Irish Georgian Society 1961.

Darver Castle, Dundalk, co Louth (BOOTH/LGI1958). An old tower-house, with a 2 storey gabled porch and late C18 doorcase; to which a plain 2 storey Georgian wing with Wyatt windows has been added. The castle is approached through a medieval gatehouse; and part of the bawn still stands.

Davidstown House, Castledermot, co Kildare (ARCHBOLD/LGI1894; GALLWEY/IFR). A plain 3 storey Georgian block, with a 5 bay front and sides of 5 and 4 bays; extended at the back by 2 storey wings, to form a small 3 sided court. The entrance front has a magnificent doorway with a delicately-

Davidstown House

Davidstown House: Doorway

leaded fanlight and side-lights, engaged Ionic columns and a baseless pediment extending over all. Late C18 and C19 interior plasterwork. Passed by inheritance from the Archbold family to Mr G. P. Gallwey.

Dawson Grove, co Monaghan (*see* DARTREY).

Dean's Hill, Armagh, co Armagh (ARMSTRONG/IFR). Formerly the Deanery. A Georgian house built 1772–74 by Very Rev Hugh Hamilton, Dean (C of I) of Armagh, subsequently Bishop of Clonfert and Bishop of Ossory; altered 1887 under the supervision of J. H. Fullerton; a wing added 1896 to the design of H. C. Parkinson.

Debsborough

Debsborough, Nenagh, co Tipperary (BAYLY/IFR). Original house demolished during War of 1939–45. New house built in its place 1955, in the manner of a 2 storey 3 bay Georgian house, with slightly lower 2 storey 1 bay wings set slightly back; but with modern windows.

Deel Castle, co Mayo (*see* CASTLE GORE).

Deeps (The), Crossabeg, co Wexford (REDMOND/IFR). A single-storey house of *ca* 1800, with a colonnaded veranda along most of its front, which gives it the air of a

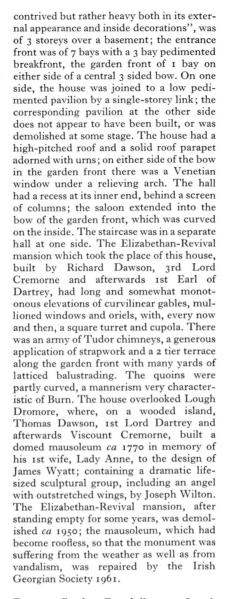

bungalow in India. The colonnade is not quite central, having 1 bay on one side of it, and 1 bay and a somewhat narrower bay on the other. The bays on either side of the colonnade are adorned with pilasters, which, like the columns, support an entablature with a modillion cornice. Somewhat incongruously, the windows on either side of the colonnade have Gothic tracery; though this adds to the exotic flavour of the house. The home of John Redmond, MP, great-uncle of the more famous John Redmond who led the Irish Party.

Delaford, Rathfarnham, co Dublin (OTTLEY/LG1952). A 3 storey house, originally an inn, onto which an elegant single-storey bow-ended front was built *ca* 1800 by Alderman Bermingham. The front is of 5 bays, the two bays on either side breaking forwards; the slightly recessed centre being emphasised by two urns on the parapet. In the centre is a very wide fanlighted tripartite doorway, the segmental fanlight extending over the door and the sidelights, which have curving astragals. Large bow-ended rooms on either side of the hall. Subsequently a seat of the Ottley family.

Delamont, Killyleagh, co Down (GORDON (*now* GORDON-PUGH)/IFR). A mildly Tudor-Revival early to mid-c19 house, rather like a simplified version of one of Richard Vitruvius Morrison's Tudor houses. Of 2 storeys, plus an attic with dormer-gables. Front with central polygonal bow, raised above the skyline to give the effect of a tower, flanked by 2 narrow oriels topped by dormer-gables. Irregular gabled side elevation, considerably longer than front. Slender polygonal turret with cupola at back of house. Altered 1968, to the design of Mr Arthur Jury.

Delville, Glasnevin, co Dublin. A 2 storey early c18 house with a 5 bay front; pedimented porch with engaged Ionic columns, 3 sided end bow; lower 2 storey wing extending back; solid roof parapet; rusticated window surrounds. Staircase with wrought-iron balustrade under barrel vaulted ceiling. In c18, the seat of Dr Patrick Delany, Dean of Down, whose wife was the famous Mrs Delany, the letter-writer and autobiographer. Together, they landscaped the grounds in the manner made fashionable in England by Pope, who was one of Dr Delany's close friends; so that Delville, though on a small scale, was Ireland's 1st naturalistic garden. It had a grotto, and an Ionic temple, which Mrs Delany painted with a fresco of St Paul, and a medallion bust of Mrs Johnson, "Stella", who in the past used to come here with Swift. In 1837, Delville was the residence of S. Gordon. Towards end of c19, it was the residence of Sir Patrick Keenan, whose niece, Daisy, Countess of Fingall, a prominent figure in the Irish Revival as well as in Edwardian fashionable society, had her wedding reception here. The temple was demolished 1940s, and the house some time *post* 1951.

Delvin Lodge, Gormanston, co Meath (JAMESON/IFR). A plain 3 storey house with gables and dormer-gables. Now a convent.

Derk

Derk, Pallasgreen, co Limerick (CONSIDINE/IFR). A 2 storey house of *ca* 1770 with an eaved roof; 5 bay front; pedimented and fanlighted Ionic doorcase; pedimented centre window above. The boyhood home of Father Daniel Considine, SJ, author of *Words of Encouragement* and of other popular spiritual works. Sold 1971.

Derrabard, Omagh, co Tyrone (VESEY/LG11912). A 2 storey Georgian house of rough stone blocks with ashlar facings; front of 1 bay on either side of shallow curved centre bow; window surrounds with blocking, flush with the rough stone. Solid roof parapet; bold quoins and string course. 3 bay end elevation with Ionic porch. The house was derelict and falling into ruin by 1970.

Derreen

Derreen, Lauragh, co Kerry (PETTY-FITZMAURICE, LANSDOWNE, M/PB; BIGHAM, *sub* MERSEY, V/PB). A house splendidly situated at the head of Kilmakilloge Harbour on the southern side of the estuary of the Kenmare River; enlarged between 1863 and 1866 by 4th Marquess of Lansdowne, who built a new wing; further enlarged *post* 1870 by 5th Marquess, who was subsequently Viceroy of India and British Foreign Secretary. The house was burnt 1922 and rebuilt by 5th Marquess in a similar style 1924; it underwent a further reconstruction, having been attacked by dry-rot, 1925–26. As enlarged and rebuilt, the house is pleasant, comfortable and unassuming; of 2 storeys over a basement, with white rendered walls, dormer-gables and 2 simple half-timbered gables at one end of its principal front. Derreen is famous for its garden, which extends over the greater part of the peninsula on which the house is built. It was originally planted by 5th Marquess; but the collection of trees and shrubs has been constantly added to by his successors. In the moist and mild climate, tender and exotic species flourish; while the older trees have grown to an incredible height and girth. The garden is particularly noted for its rhododendrons and tree ferns. As a foil to the luxuriant plantings, there are great natural outcrops of rock. After World War II, Derreen passed to Lady Nairne (now Viscountess Mersey), sister of 7th Marquess, who was killed in action 1944. It is now the property of her son, Hon David Bigham; the garden is open to the public.

Derries (The), co Leix (*see* BALLYSHANDUFFE HOUSE).

Derry, co Cork

Derry, Rosscarbery, co Cork (TOWNSHEND/IFR; SULLIVAN/IFR). A house of late-Georgian appearance, consisting of a 2 storey 4 bay centre block joined by single-storey 1 bay links set a little back to 2 storey 2 bay wings. The entrance door was at one end of the centre block, in the angle between the centre block and the link. The wing at the other side was prolonged by a lower range with a late-Victorian or Edwardian half-timbered gable. A seat of the Townshends; inherited by Charlotte Frances Payne-Townshend, wife of George Bernard Shaw, the dramatist, who sold it. Early in the present century, Derry was the home of A. M. Sullivan, KC, the last Irish Serjeant-at-Law. It was burnt *ca* 1922.

Bishop's Palace, Derry

Derry, co Derry: Bishop's Palace. The Palace of the (C of I) Bishops of Derry, adjoining the Cathedral. A square Georgian block of 3 storeys over a high basement; built originally *ca* 1761 by Bishop Barnard; said to have been largely rebuilt by the Earl-Bishop, Frederick Hervey, Earl of Bristol, later c18; damaged while occupied as a barrack 1802 and subsequently repaired by Bishop Knox. c19 eaved roof on cornice.

Derrycarne, Dromod, co Leitrim (ORMSBY-GORE, HARLECH, B/PB). A house on a promontory in the River Shannon between Lough Boderg and Lough Bofin, consisting of a 2 storey 3 bay bow-ended late-Georgian front with Wyatt windows and an enclosed Doric porch; and a 2 storey 4 bay castellated wing extending back at right angles. Now derelict.

Derrylahan Park

Derrymore House

Derryquin Castle

Derrylahan Park, Riverstown, co Tipperary (HEAD/LGI1958). A High Victorian house with steep gables and roofs, plate glass windows and decorative iron cresting on the ridges. Built 1862 at a cost of £15,000, to the design of Sir Thomas Newenham Deane. Burnt 1921.

Derrymore House, Bessbrook, co Armagh (CORRY/LGI1886). A single-storey thatched cottage ornée of Palladian form, consisting of a bow-fronted centre block and 2 flanking wings, joined to the main block by diminutive canted links. The central bow of the main block is 3 sided, and glazed down to the ground, with mullions and astragals; it is flanked by 2 quatrefoil windows, under hood mouldings. There is also a mullioned window in each wing. Built *ante* 1787 by Isaac Corry, MP for Newry and last Chancellor of the Irish Exchequer. The Act of Union is said to have been drafted in the fine drawing room here. Now owned by the Northern Ireland National Trust and open to the public.

Derryquin Castle

Derrynane

Derrynane, Waterville, co Kerry (O'CONNELL/IFR). The best surviving example of the "Big House" of a Gaelic Catholic family in c18; the home of Eileen O'Connell, author of the *Dirge of Art O'Leary* (1773); of Daniel, Count O'Connell of the French Army; and, of course, of Daniel O'Connell, "The Liberator", leader of the struggle for Catholic Emancipation. The house, which is believed to have been 1st slate-roofed house in this remote and mountainous part of the country, originally consisted of 2 unpretentious ranges at right angles to each other, probably built at various times between *ca* 1700 and 1745 and somewhat altered in later years; one range being of 2 storeys and the other mainly of 2 storeys and a dormered attic, which, in 2nd half of c18, became a 3rd storey. Between 1745 and 1825 a wing was built at what was then the back of the house, the side towards Derrynane Bay; and in 1825 the great Daniel O'Connell extended this wing in the same unpretentious style with rather narrow sash

windows; so that what had previously been the back of the house became the front, with reception rooms facing the sea. O'Connell also built a square 2 storey block with Irish battlements at right angles to his main addition, forming an attractive 3 sided entrance court, the other 2 sides being 1745 –1825 wing and one of the original ranges. The battlemented block is weather-slated, as indeed all O'Connell's additions were originally; he also weather-slated some of the older parts of the house. Finally, in 1844, O'Connell built a new chapel in thanksgiving for his release from prison. It flanks the entrance court on the side furthest from the sea and is Gothic, based on the chapel in the ruined medieval monastery on Abbey Island nearby; it was designed by O'Connell's 3rd son, John O'Connell, MP. The interior of the house is simple, and the ceilings are fairly low. The two principal reception rooms are the drawing room and dining room which are one above the other in 1825 wing; they have plain cornices; the dining room has a Victorian oak chimneypiece, the drawing room an early c19 Doric chimneypiece of white marble. The benches and communion rail in the chapel are of charmingly rustic Gothic openwork. The house is now owned by the Commissioners of Public Works, who demolished one of the original ranges in 1965. The rest of the structure has been restored and is now open to the public, the principal rooms containing O'Connell family portraits and objects related to Daniel O'Connell's life and career.

Derryquin Castle, Sneem, co Kerry (BLAND/IFR). A Victorian castle of rough-hewn stone by James Franklin Fuller, built for the Blands. Main block of 3 storeys over a basement, with a 4 storey tower in the form of an elongated octagon running through its centre; entrance door at one end, flanked by 2 storey partly curving wing. Straight wing running at right angles to the other end of the main block. Rectangular, pointed and camber-headed windows; battlements and simple machicolations. Sold by J. F. Bland to Lt-Col C. W. Warden, who lived at Derryquin until it was burnt 1922.

Derryvolgie

Derryvolgie, Lisburn, co Antrim (EWART, Bt/PB). A square 2 storey house of *ca* 1840 with an eaved roof and an iron veranda, built onto a cottage said to date from the early c18 or late c17. Enlarged 1898 by S. W. Ewart, who added a wing with a 3

Derryvolgie: Hall

Desart Court: Entrance Front

Desart Court: Garden Front

Desart Court: Hall

Desart Court: Staircase

sided bow surmounted by a half-timbered gable. The interior appears to have been altered at about the same time: a large hall formed by making an arch between the staircase hall, which contains a curving staircase, and the adjoining room; both rooms being given fretted ceilings; while the drawing room was given a frieze of Georgian style plasterwork and an Adam Revival chimneypiece set under an inglenook arch. Sold 1972 by Sir Ivan Ewart, 6th and present Bt, to the Ministry of Defence.

Derryvoulin House

Derryvoulin House, Woodford, co Galway. A 2 storey 3 bay late C18 house. 1 bay breakfront; fanlighted doorway, surround with blocking. Ground floor windows wider than those above. Single-storey projection at side.

Desart Court, Callan, co Kilkenny (CUFFE, DESART, E/PB1934; MILBORNE-SWINNERTON-PILKINGTON, Bt/PB). A Palladian house consisting of a centre block of 2 storeys over a basement joined to 2 storey wings by curved sweeps; built *ca* 1733 for John Cuffe, 1st Lord Desart, almost certainly to the design of Sir Edward Lovett Pearce. Centre block with 7 bay front; central feature of 4 superimposed engaged Doric and Ionic columns and Doric entablature. Rusticated niche over rusticated doorway; ground floor windows also rusticated. Balustraded roof parapet; perron with double steps. Rusticated basement. Engaged Doric columns on curved sweeps. In the garden front of the centre block the entire lower storey was rusticated and the central feature consisted only of 4 engaged Ionic columns in the upper storey. There was also a balustraded parapet on this side and a large perron. Hall with wood dado, plasterwork panels, pedimented doorcases and ceiling of elaborate rococo plasterwork. In separate halls at each end of the house were 2 grand staircases with magnificent carved scroll balustrades; leading up to a bedroom corridor lit by a lantern. The drawing room, in the centre of the garden front, had a ceiling of rococo plasterwork similar to that in the hall. The house was burnt 1923; it was afterwards rebuilt by Lady Kathleen Milborne-Swinnerton-Pilkington, daughter of 4th Earl of Desart; the architect of the rebuilding being Richard Orpen. Some years later, however, it was sold and then demolished.

Doe Castle, Creeslough, co Donegal. The medieval castle of MacSweeney Na Doe, a rather grim keep with outworks surrounded by sea and rocks. After being de-

Desart Court: Ceiling

serted, it was restored in C18 and C19 by the Hart family and again occupied; a lean-to range with sash windows was built against one side of it, the outworks were battle-

Doe Castle

mented; a sash window was pierced in the keep itself, surmounted by a hood moulding in the shape of a Georgian-Gothic ogee arch. In the upper part of the keep, where there were few windows, a room was made which was lit by a lantern in the roof.

Dolanstown, Knocknatulla, co Meath (JONES *late of Headfort*/LGI1937Supp). An early C18 house of 2 storeys and 7 bays, with a central breakfront, a Venetian window and a tall, pedimented doorcase. Brackets under eaves on one side rather similar to those at Eyrecourt Castle, co Galway (*qv*). In 1814, the residence of Cunningham Jones, (who was probably a son of Walter Jones, of Lavagh, co Leitrim, and his wife Charlotte (*née* Cunningham)).

Dollardstown, Slane, co Meath (MERE-DYTH, Bt, *of Greenhills*/PB1909; SOMERVILLE, ATHLUMNEY, B/PB1929). A house grandly remodelled in red brick *ca* 1730 for Arthur Meredyth, probably by Richard Castle. 3 storey over a high basement and with a parapet-attic of blind windows above the cornice. 7 bay front, 3 bay breakfront centre, with Castle's favourite sequence of a blind oculus above a niche above the entrance doorway, which is pedimented and pillared. 2 bay side elevation, with Venetian windows in both principal storeys, triple windows above and triple blind windows in the attic and also in the basement; which, instead of being of brick faced with stone, is of stone faced with brick. The principal front is flanked by 2 tall pedimented pavilions. Passed by inheritance to the Somerville (Athlumney) family; occupied by a farmer as early as 1837. Now a ruin.

Dolly's Grove, Dunboyne, co Meath. A 2 storey late-Georgian house; 3 bay front, with ground floor windows set in arched recesses; 4 bay side. Oval staircase. In 1814, the residence of James Hamilton.

Donacomper, Celbridge, co Kildare (KIRKPATRICK/LGI1958). A house enlarged and very successfully remodelled in Tudor-Revival by William Kirkpatrick *ca* 1835. Simple elevations with partly-stepped gables, mullioned windows and hood-mouldings; polygonal lantern and cupola.

Lofty hall with timbered ceiling. Drawing room running the full depth of the house with good plasterwork ceiling. Library of great beauty: ribbed timber ceiling, oak bookcases with carving and Gothic tracery, original C19 wallpaper in brown and gold. Staircase newels carved to resemble swans; cut-down oil portraits and coats-of-arms arranged round cupola over gallery of staircase. Formal garden with attractive vista from garden front of house. The home of late Sir Ivone Kirkpatrick, the diplomatist, sometime head of the British Foreign Office. After his death, it was sold to Mr J. Bruce Bredin, who resold it to Mr Brendan McGonnell 1977.

Donadea Castle, co Kildare (AYLMER, Bt/PB). A medieval and C17 castle, with a bowed centre of *ca* 1800 by Richard Morrison. Medieval doorways and fireplaces in some rooms; Doric entablatures in others on the first floor. Castellated gateway. Bequeathed by Miss C. M. Aylmer 1935 to the Church of Ireland, by which it was subsequently sold. The castle is now a ruin.

Donaghadee, co Down: Manor House (DE LA CHEROIS, *sub* STONE/IFR). A plain 2 storey Georgian house with its entrance front behind railings on the High Street of the town; 6 bay entrance front with pillared porch; 3 sided bow in side elevation.

Donahies (The), co Dublin. A 2 storey 3 bay Georgian house with 3 sided end bows and a pillared porch. Adamesque interior plasterwork. The seat of the Casey family. Now demolished.

Donamon Castle, Roscommon, co Roscommon (CAULFEILD, *sub* CHARLEMONT, V/PB). A C15 castle with a tall arch between its towers, like that at Bunratty Castle (*qv*), given regular sash windows and Georgian-Gothic battlements towards end of C18 and further altered and enlarged mid-C19. Staircase gallery with plaster fan vaulting. Now owned by the Divine Word Missionaries.

Donard House, Dunlavin, co Wicklow (HEIGHINGTON/LGI1912). A 2 storey 5 bay house with a fanlighted doorway; built 1813–14 for William Heighington, to the design of William Vierpyl, presumably a son or relative of Sir William Chambers's protégé, the stonemason Simon Vierpyl,

Manor House, Donaghadee

Donacomper

Donard House, co Wicklow

who worked on the staircase at Castletown, co Kildare (*qv*). Donard is now the home of Mr Brian Hussey.

Donard Lodge

Donegal Castle

Donard Lodge, Newcastle, co Down (ANNESLEY, E/PB). A distinguished 2 storey Classical house of granite ashlar, built in 2 stages 1830s by 3rd Earl Annesley as a marine residence. The architect at first was John Lynn, who later acted merely as contractor, carrying out plans by Thomas Duff, of Newry, and his partner, Thomas Jackson, of Belfast. Entrance front with central projecting bay (in fact a 2 storey porch) and a boldly projecting 3 sided bow at either side; the centre being joined on each side to the projecting ends by a short Doric colonnade; one of these colonnades serving as the en-

trance portico, the door being in one side of the central projection. Garden front with curved and three-sided bows and round-headed ground floor windows. Elegant semi-circular conservatory by John Lynn at one end of the house. Donard Lodge is now demolished.

Donegal Castle, co Donegal (BROOKE, BROOKEBOROUGH, V/PB). A massive square keep, built 1505 by Red Hugh II O'Donnell, to which a fortified gabled manor house was added *ca* 1623 by Sir Basil Brooke; who remodelled the keep in the same style as his new range, with gables and mullioned windows. The great hall on the first floor of the keep contains a vast and elaborately carved Jacobean chimneypiece. Donegal Castle has long been a ruin.

Doneraile Court, Doneraile, co Cork (ST LEGER, DONERAILE, V/PB). Sir William St Leger, Lord President of Munster in the reign of Charles I, bought the lands of Doneraile from the son of Edmund Spenser, the poet; and established himself in a castle close to the village on the north side of the Awbeg river—the "Gentle Mulla", of which Spenser sang. Having been burnt by the Confederates 1645, the castle was rebuilt

Doneraile Court: Entrance Front

Doneraile Court: Garden Front

later in C17 and a great formal garden laid out on 2 sides of it. Then, not so very long afterwards, the castle was abandoned in favour of a new house across the river, which was probably built by Arthur St Leger, who became 1st Viscount Doneraile of the earlier creation 1703. A new 3 storey 7 bay cut-stone front was built onto the house *ca* 1730 to the design of Isaac Rothery; it has a 3 bay breakfront, blocked quoins, crisply-moulded window surrounds with scroll keystones in 2 upper storeys and a doorcase with Ionic columns and a scroll pediment; now incorporated in an early C19 balustraded porch. Later in C18, curved end bows were added; later again, possibly when the house was being reconstructed after a fire 1805, the side elevation was extended by a bow-fronted addition, so that it became a garden front of 3 bays between 2 bows, the newer of the 2 being slightly larger than the older. On the other side of the house, a wing containing a new dining room was added 1869 by 4th Viscount Doneraile of the later creation. The C19 porch, which is 3 bays wide, is in fact an extension to the hall, divided from it by a screen of Ionic columns. At the back of the hall is an oval late-Georgian staircase hall in which a staircase with slender wooden balusters rises gracefully to the top of the house beneath a ceiling of Adamesque plasterwork. To the right of the staircase hall is one of the rooms of the original house, with a corner fireplace and fielded panelling; it was possibly in here that, *ca* 1713, Elizabeth St Leger was initiated as one of the only 3 women Freemasons in history, after she had been caught spying on a Lodge meeting held by her father. Behind this room was the vast and splendid dining room of 1869, which formerly had an immense mahogany sideboard in a mirrored alcove confronting a full-length portrait of 4th Viscount with his favourite hunter. He was one of the great Victorian hunting men; ironically, he died of rabies through being bitten by a pet fox. The 3 drawing rooms on the other side of the house are early C19 in character and probably date from the reconstruction after the fire; they have simple but elegant friezes, overdoors with volutes and windows going right down to the floor. The end drawing

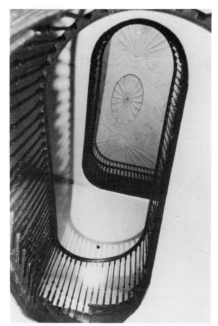

Doneraile Court: Staircase Hall

Doneraile Court: Panelled Room

Doneraile Court: Dining Room

room formerly opened into a slightly Gothic conservatory which is now ruinous; it is charmingly evoked by Sir Harold Nicolson, who remembered sitting in it on a hot, wet afternoon in his youth: "inhaling the smell of the tube roses, listening to the rattle of the rain upon the glass roof, listening to the gentler tinkling of the fountain as it splashed

Doneraile Court: Pink Drawing Room

among the ferns". The long connexion of the St Legers with Doneraile ended when Mary, Viscountess Doneraile died 1975. The garden, which boasts of a Lime Walk and a long "fishpond" or canal surviving from the original c18 layout, is now maintained by the Department of Lands; as is the park, in which there is still a herd of red deer. The house, after standing empty for several years and becoming almost derelict, is in the process of being restored by the Irish Georgian Society, with a view to finding someone who would be willing to take it on. The 1869 dining room wing, which had fallen into disrepair worse than the rest of the house, has been demolished.

Donore, Multyfarnham, co Westmeath (NUGENT, Bt, *of Donore*/PB). A plain 3 storey Georgian block. Now demolished.

Donore House, Prosperous, co Kildare. A 2 storey late c18 house of brick, with wings extending back to form a "U"-plan. Pedimented Ionic doorcase in central 3 sided bow with 3 bays on either side, the end bays projecting slightly. Now a ruin.

Doolistown, Trim, co Meath (THE FOX/ IFR). A 2 storey 3 bay Georgian house with a good doorcase. For 6 years the home of T. H. White, author of *The Once and Future King* (filmed as *Camelot*), etc, and his beloved dog "Brownie".

The Doon

Doon (The), Togher, Offaly (ENRAGHT-MOONY/IFR). A square 2 storey house built 1798 by R. J. Enraght-Moony, incorporating a late c17 or early c18 house which had been the dower house when the family lived in the old castle nearby. 3 bay front with single-storey portico; 3 bay side.

Doonass, Clonlara, co Clare (MASSY, Bt/ PB1870; MASSY-WESTROPP, *sub* WESTROPP/ IFR). A 2 storey house of *ca* 1820 in the late-Georgian villa style. Entrance front with slightly recessed centre; 1 bay on either side, the windows being set in 2 storey blind arches. Fanlighted doorway under 2 windows in centre; Wyatt windows on either

side in lower storey. Eaved roof; curved bow at side. The back wing of the house has been demolished. A notable folly tower dating from *ca* 1760 stands down by the river. It has a detached turret for a spiral staircase. A hell-fire club is said to have met there.

Doory Hall, Ballymahon, co Longford (JESSOP/LGI1912). A house of *ca* 1820, by John Hargrave, of Cork. 2 storey, 5 bay, centre bay projecting. Pediment; wide entrance door under porch with fluted Doric columns; wide window over. Curved bow at end. Now a ruin.

Downhill Castle

Downhill Castle: as rebuilt after fire of 1851

Downhill Castle, nr Coleraine, co Derry (HERVEY, BRISTOL, M/PB; BRUCE, Bt, *of Downhill*/PB). One of 3 eccentric palaces of Frederick Hervey, 4th Earl of Bristol and Bishop of Derry, the other two being Ballyscullion (*qv*), also in co Derry, and Ickworth, Suffolk. Built on a bare cliff-top above the Atlantic; begun in early 1770s and continued in various stages until *ca* 1785; the architect being Michael Shanahan, a Corkman who was the Earl-Bishop's architect, adviser and confidant; and who may have made use of a design by the Milanese architect, Placido Columbani. Of 2 storeys over a high basement; principal front of 3 bays between 2 wide 3 sided bows, with 2 much longer wings running back towards the sea, prolonged by office ranges. The long elevations of the wings were relieved by pairs of curved bows, and ended with domes. From 1784 onwards, the front and the wings were given facades of granite ashlar, with giant fluted Corinthian pilasters on a rusticated basement. The interior of the house was filled with the pictures, statuary and other works of art which the Earl-Bishop collected on his travels in Italy and elsewhere. The principal staircase was of stone, with a balustrade of gilded ironwork; it curved round the inside of a bow, under a dome painted with *The Dividing of the Light from the Darkness*; the walls being painted with "rustic scenery". The 2 largest rooms were the library and the great 2 storey picture gallery, which had a ceiling painted with *Aurora*; at one end of the room were pairs of Corinthian columns, supporting an entablature above which were the arms of bishopric and earldom in plasterwork. One of the small 1st floor rooms had a gilt arabesque ceiling. A short distance from the house, on the very edge of the cliff, the Earl-Bishop built a domed rotunda, surrounded by Corinthian columns, and named it the Mussenden Temple to commemorate his friendship with his kinswoman, Mrs Mussenden; it contained a library and a lower room which the Earl-Bishop, always tolerant in matters of religion, allowed the local Catholics to use for Mass. When he died, the Earl-Bishop left Downhill and Ballyscullion to Mrs Mussenden's brother, Rev H. H. A. Bruce, who was immediately afterwards created a Bt. The 1st Bt gave added drama to the exterior of the house by building crenellated walls and bastions of basalt on the seaward side of the office ranges; he also further embellished the interior by bringing here all the works of art from Ballyscullion, which he demolished. Downhill suffered a disastrous fire 1851, in which many works of art were lost; most of the centre and the wing containing the gallery being gutted. The house was rebuilt between 1870 and 1874, to the design of John Lanyon; with plate glass windows, which gave the long elevations a great bleakness; and without the domes. The interior was fitted up with much Victorian woodwork and cast-iron, including a formidable heating system; the great gallery being re-roofed with pitch pine match-boarding. A little of the original plasterwork survived, however, and also some of the Earl-Bishop's fine chimneypieces. After standing empty for many years, the house was demolished 1950; it is now a crumbling ruin, though the Mussenden Temple, the entrance gates and other monuments in the demesne are maintained by the National Trust. One of the chimneypieces is now at Castle Upton (*qv*); and a pair of columns from one of the rooms here is now at Ballyward Lodge, co Down (*qv*).

Dowth Hall

Dowth Hall, nr Slane, co Meath (NETTERVILLE, V/DEP; GRADWELL/LGI1958).

A small and extremely elegant mid-c18 house, built for 6th Viscount Netterville; with a 2 storey front, but with an extra storey fitted in as a mezzanine at the back. The front, of ashlar, is 5 bay; the lower storey is rusticated; the windows in the upper storey are higher than those below, and have alternate triangular and segmental pediments over them. Urns on roofline; pedimented doorway with Doric columns and frieze. Splendid interior plasterwork, possibly by Robert West, who may in fact have been the architect. Doric frieze in hall. Beautiful rococo decoration on walls and ceiling of drawing room. Dining room ceiling with birds and clouds. Library with simple rococo ceiling and

Dowth Hall: Drawing Room

swags on walls. A little way from the house is a famous prehistoric burial mound, one of several in the neighbourhood; 6th Viscount Netterville, who was a somewhat eccentric character, used to sit on top of it and "attend" Mass by training a telescope on a distant chapel. Dowth Hall was acquired mid-c19 by the Gradwell family, who sold it *ca* 1951. It subsequently became the home of Mr Clifford Cameron.

Drenagh

Drenagh: Central Hall

Drenagh (formerly Fruit Hill), Limavady, co Derry (MCCAUSLAND/IFR).

The earliest major country house by Charles (afterwards Sir Charles) Lanyon, built *ca* 1837 for Marcus McCausland, replacing an early c18 house on a different site. Of significance in the history of c19 Irish domestic architecture in that it is a competent late-Georgian design by an architect whose buildings of the following decade are definitely Victorian. 2 storey; of an attractive pinkish sandstone ashlar. 5 bay entrance front with the centre bay recessed and a single-storey Ionic portico in which the outer columns are coupled. Adjoining front of 6 bays with 2 bay pedimented breakfront; the duality of the elevation being emphasized rather than resolved by the presence of 3 giant pilasters, supporting the pediment. Rear elevation of 1 bay between two 3 sided bows, with fanlighted tripartite garden door. Lower service wing at side. Balustraded parapet round roof and on portico. Single-storey top-lit central hall with screens of fluted Corinthian columns; graceful double staircase with elegant cast-iron balusters rising from behind one of these screens. Rich plasterwork ceilings in hall, over staircase and in drawing room; simpler ceilings in morning room and dining room. At the head of the stairs, a bedroom corridor with a ceiling of plaster vaulting and shallow domes goes round the central court or well, the lower part of which is roofed over to form the hall. Very large and extensive outbuildings. Vista through gap in trees opposite entrance front of house to idyllic landscape far below, the ground falling steeply on this side; straight flight of steps on the axis of this vista leading down to bastion terrace with urns. Chinese garden with circular "moon gate", laid out by Lady Margaret McCausland 1960s. Gate lodge by Lanyon with pedimented Ionic portico.

Drewstown, Athboy, co Meath (MCVEAGH/LGI1958).

An imposing 3 storey cutstone house of *ca* 1745, attributed to Francis Bindon; built for Barry Barry. 7 bay entrance front with 3 bay central breakfront; round-headed window framed by pilasters and segmental entablatures in the centre of each of 2 upper storeys; ground floor windows with rusticated surrounds, shouldered architraves round windows in upper storeys. Later enclosed porch with fanlight and Ionic columns and pilasters. Curved bow in one side elevation, but not in the other. 2 storey hall with the staircase rising behind a bridge-gallery; a rare feature in Irish country houses of this date, though there is another example of it only a couple of miles away across the Westmeath border at Ballinlough Castle (*qv*). As at Ballinlough, both the stair and gallery have slender wooden balusters; and there is c18 panelling on the walls. The doorcases, both upstairs and down, have heavy triangular or segmental pediments; and the ceiling is decorated with somewhat bucolic plasterwork. Drewstown was bought 1780s by Major Joseph M'Veagh, who married Margery, daughter of Governor Alexander Wynch of Madras, a wealthy East Indian "Nabob". It remained in the M'Veagh or McVeagh family until 1950.

Drimina House, Sneem, co Kerry
(BLAND/IFR; LEYCESTER/LG1952). A gabled
Victorian house on the shores of Sneem
Harbour. Noted sub-tropical garden.

Dripsey Castle, Dripsey, co Cork (BOW-
EN-COLTHURST/IFR). A 3 storey Georgian
house with a pedimented breakfront centre.
Old castle nearby.

Drishane, Castletownshend, co Cork
(SOMERVILLE/IFR). A 2 storey 6 bay weather-
slated house with a fanlighted doorway built
ca 1790 by Thomas Somerville. A new
entrance doorway was subsequently made
in the 2 bay end of the house, which is
prolonged by a lower 2 storey wing. The
principal rooms have doors of mahogany,
one of the commodities which Thomas
Somerville, a successful merchant, imported
into Ireland from the West Indies. Drishane
was the home of Edith Somerville, celebrated for her great writing partnership
with her cousin, Violet Martin ("Martin
Ross"), of Ross, co Galway (*qv*).

Drishane Castle: Drawing Room

Drishane Castle

Drishane Castle, Millstreet, co Cork
(WALLIS/IFR). A 3 storey C18 house built
alongside the keep of a C15 castle of the
MacCarthys by the Wallises, castellated and
extended between 1845 and 1860. Battlemented parapet; entrance front with square
corner-towers and central porch tower—
with a presumably later battlemented porte-
cochère built onto its front—prolonged by a
single-storey range joining it to a 2 storey
wing or pavilion with Irish-battlemented
corner towers. Adjoining front with 3 sided
bow and mullioned windows, prolonged by
a slightly lower wing ending in a square
tower, joined by high battlemented walls to
the old keep, which stands on a mound at
this corner of the house. 2 storey hall with
gallery; Georgian doorcases with entablatures. 2 drawing rooms opening into each
other with an arch. The old keep was completely restored some time *post* 1879 by
Lady Beaumont, mother of Major H. A. B.
Wallis, the last member of the family to live
at Drishane, which was sold 1908 by order
of the Court of Chancery. It was re-sold a
year later to the Sisters of the Infant Jesus,
who opened a boarding school and domestic
economy school here.

**Dromahair Castle, Dromahair, co Lei-
trim** (VILLERS, Bt/EDB and *sub* JERSEY, E/PB).
A large "strong-house" built 1626 by Sir
William Villiers, 1st Bt, whose half-brother,
James I's and Charles I's favourite, the
Duke of Buckingham, was granted an ex-

Drishane Castle: Hall

tensive tract of land here. It had blank,
forward-facing gables and many massive
chimney-stacks. Now a ruin.

Dromana, Cappoquin, co Waterford
(VILLIERS-STUART/IFR; and *sub* BUTE, M/PB).
A house rising sheer from a ledge of rock
high above one of the loveliest stretches of
the Blackwater estuary, incorporating parts
of the old castle of the FitzGeralds, Lords
of the Decies, whose heiress married Gen
Edward Villiers late C17. The castle, which
probably surrounded a courtyard, was badly
damaged during mid-C17 wars; later in
C17 and early C18, 2 adjoining sides of it
were rebuilt as 2 storey gable-ended ranges,
which are plain except for a handsome
Gibbsian doorway in the range at right
angles to the river. The old castle walls
can be seen at the base of the range on the
river side; at one end there is even a medi-

eval window, lighting what is now a cellar.
These two ranges were intended to serve as
a temporary house "till a more commodious
one could be built". The more commodious
house, which was begun 1780s, by George
Mason-Villiers, 2nd Earl Grandison of 2nd
creation, took the form of a very large 2
storey rectangular block; its shorter side,
which had a wide curved bow, being a continuation of the range along the river; its
longer side forming a new 9 bay entrance
front with a 3 bay breakfront. The back of
the new block formed 3rd side of a courtyard
with 2 older ranges; a low office range
forming 4th side. The Gibbsian doorway
was hidden from sight in the courtyard. The
new block was very much done over *ca*
1840s by Henry Villiers-Stuart, 1st and last
Lord Stuart de Decies (whose mother was
2nd Earl Grandison's only child and heiress); one suspects that owing to Lord
Grandison's fondness for gambling, it was
still unfinished when he died 1800; while
his daughter and son-in-law would have
been prevented from doing much to it by
their untimely deaths only a few years after
his. Lord Stuart de Decies faced the entrance front in cement, with triangular and
Baroque-curved pediments over the ground
floor windows and entablatures over the
windows above; there was a larger Baroque
pediment over the fanlighted entrance door,
containing his arms and coronet. Inside the
house, he made a very impressive hall, with
an imperial staircase behind a screen of
fluted columns; and he gave the principal
reception rooms cornices of early-Victorian
plasterwork. The drawing room or ballroom
and the library, both of vast size and height,
lay on either side of the hall, forming a
spacious enfilade. The drawing room or
ballroom was a magnificent room extending
into the great curved bow above the river,
which was reflected by a similar curve in the
inner wall; it had a pair of late-Georgian
chimneypieces and an original early-Victorian wallpaper in white and gold. Though
redecorated by Lord Stuart de Decies, it
had been completed in its final form by
1806, when it was seen and admired by Rev
Daniel Beaufort. Downstream of the house

Dromana

Dromana: Hall

Dromana: front of Georgian block

Dromana: C17 or early C18 range

Dromana: Gibbsian Doorway

Dromana: Hindu-Gothic Gateway

Dromaneen Castle, Banteer, co Cork
(O'CALLAGHAN/IFR). A gabled early C17
semi-fortified house on a rock above the
River Blackwater; now a ruin. Entrance
court with Jacobean doorway.

Dromaneen Castle

Dromin House, Dunleer, co Louth.
Georgian house of 2 storeys over basement;
5 bay front with later porch; parapeted roof.

Dromkeen, co Cavan (SAUNDERSON/IFR;
LUCAS-CLEMENTS/IFR). A 2 storey early C19
house; front of 2 bays on either side of a
central 3 sided bow, crowned with battlement-gables and finials. Plain entablatures
over ground floor windows. Now a convent
and much altered.

**Dromkeen House, Pallasgreen, co Lim-
erick** (HUSSEY DE BURGH/IFR). A gable-
ended Georgian house of 2 storeys over a
basement and 5 bays. Simple doorcase.

**Dromoland Castle, Newmarket-on-
Fergus, co Clare** (O'BRIEN, INCHIQUIN, B/
PB). Originally a large early C18 house with
a pediment and a high-pitched roof; built
for Sir Edward O'Brien, 2nd Bt; possibly
inspired by Thomas Burgh, MP, Engineer
and Surveyor-General for Ireland. Elaborate formal garden. This house was demolished *ca* 1826 by Sir Edward O'Brien, 4th
Bt (whose son succeeded his kinsman as
13th Lord Inchiquin and senior descendant
of the O'Brien High Kings) and a wide-
spreading and dramatic castle by James and
George Richard Pain was built in its place.
The castle is dominated by a tall round
corner tower and a square tower, both of

is a C18 terrace garden with what was described (1746) as "a neat bastion" by the
waterside. At the northern end of the demesne is a delightful Hindu-Gothic gateway, the only example in Ireland of the
Brighton Pavilion taste; with a dome, slender minarets and pointed windows; it is
approached by a bridge over the Finisk
river, a tributary of the Blackwater. According to the story, it was first built 1826 as a
temporary structure to welcome Henry
Villiers-Stuart (the future Lord Stuart de
Decies) and his bride when they returned
from their honeymoon; and they were so
charmed by it that they had it copied in
more permanent materials. In 1957 Mr
James Villiers-Stuart sold most of the estate
to the Department of Lands. The house and
some of the grounds were bought by his
cousin, Mr FitzGerald Villiers-Stuart; he
and Mrs Villiers-Stuart remodelled the two

Dromana: Drawing Room or Ballroom

older ranges to form a self-contained house
with pleasant rooms of comfortable size,
and eventually demolished the later block.
Its disappearance, though naturally regret-
table, has opened up the courtyard, enabling
it to be transformed into a delightful forecourt; the Gibbsian doorway has come into
its own once again as the front door. The
splendid woodlands of the demesne are
being well cared for by the Forestry Service;
the Hindu-Gothic gateway, which spans
what is now a public road, is also being well
maintained, having been restored 1967–68
by the Irish Georgian Society after it had
fallen into disrepair.

Dromoland Castle

Dromoland Castle: Long Gallery

them heavily battlemented and machicolated; there are lesser towers and a turreted porch. The windows in the 2 principal fronts are rectangular, with Gothic tracery. The interior plan is rather similar to that of Mitchelstown Castle, co Cork (*qv*), also by the Pains; a square entrance hall opens into a long single-storey inner hall like a gallery, with the staircase at its far end and the principal reception rooms on one side of it. But whereas the Mitchelstown rooms had elaborate plaster Gothic vaulting, those at Dromoland have plain flat ceilings with simple Gothic or Tudor-Revival cornices. The dining room has a dado of Gothic panelling. The drawing room was formerly known as the Keightley Room, since it contained many of the magnificent C17 portraits which came to the O'Brien family through the marriage of Lucius O'Brien, MP, to Catherine Keightley, whose maternal grandfather was Edward Hyde, the great Earl of Clarendon. The other Keightley portraits hung in the long gallery, which runs from the head of the staircase, above the inner hall. Part of C18 garden layout survives, including a gazebo and a Doric rotunda. In the walled garden is a C17 gateway brought from Lemeneagh Castle (*qv*), which was the principal seat of this branch of the O'Briens until they abandoned it in favour of Dromoland. The Young Ireland leader, William Smith O'Brien, a brother of 13th Lord Inchiquin, was born at Dromoland in C18 house. Dromoland Castle is now an hotel, having been sold 1962 by 16th Lord Inchiquin, who built himself a modern house in the grounds to the design of Mr Donal O'Neill Flanagan; it is in a pleasantly simple Georgian style.

Dromore, co Down: Bishop's Palace. A fine 3 storey late C18 block, built 1781 by Hon William Beresford, Bishop (C of I) of Dromore, afterwards Bishop of Ossory, Archbishop of Tuam and 1st Lord Decies (*see* PB). "Improved" by Beresford's successor, Thomas Percy, the antiquary and poet, who laid out plantations, gardens and a glen, adorned with painted obelisks. In Bishop Percy's time, the Palace was frequented by a circle of poets and painters, notably the poet Thomas Stott and the painter Thomas Robinson, a pupil of Romney. Sold 1842, when the diocese of Dromore was merged with Down and Connor; used for some years in late C19 as a school, and after that empty; now ruinous.

Dromoland Castle

Dromoland Castle: Dining Room

Dromoland Castle: Keightley Room

Dromore Castle, Kenmare, co Kerry (MAHONY/IFR; HOOD, V/PB; WALLER/IFR). An early C19 castle by Sir Thomas Deane, built *ca* 1831–38 for Rev Denis Mahony; replacing a long low 2 storey house on a different site built on one side of a courtyard with the stables on the other, which still survives; and which itself replaced an old castle of the O'Mahonys, on a different site again. The present castle is of 2 storeys over a basement and is faced in a golden-brown Roman cement imitating ashlar, with grey limestone dressings. The entrance front, which is dominated by a machicolated round tower and turret, at one side of a central heavily machicolated porch-tower, has a certain grimness; the windows are few and narrow. The garden front, facing down wooded

slopes of sub-tropical luxuriance to the Kenmare River, is more graceful and friendly; there are fewer machicolations and the windows are wider; in the centre is a Perpendicular window of great height. At either end of the garden front is a three-sided bow, with corner-bartizans. Apart from the staircase window, the windows are rectangular, and combine wooden Gothic tracery with Georgian glazing; some of them incorporating rather unusual half-Gothic fanlights. Inside the castle, a vast hall, like a long gallery, runs almost the full length of the front; it has a timbered ceiling and oak-grained doors with panels of Gothic tracery. In the centre, opposite the front door, an arch opens onto an imperial staircase of oak with Gothic balusters, lit by the great Perpendicular window. The reception rooms have Gothic doors and heavily ornamented cornices. There are original braided curtains dating from 1830s and massive gilt pelmets of Gothic design. The dining room is hung with a Victorian wallpaper of faded red with gold fleurs-de-lys and Tudor roses. The large drawing room has a Victorian chimneypiece of white marble, elaborately carved with foliage. In the smaller circular drawing room there are curved doors. On the death of Harold Mahony 1905, Dromore passed to his sister, Nora Eveleen, wife of Lt-Col Edward Hood. It passed to Mrs Hood's cousin, Mr H. B. Waller, 1951.

Dromore Castle, Pallaskenry, co Limerick (PERY, LIMERICK, E/PB). The most archaeologically correct C19 Irish castle, rising from a wooded ridge above a lough; built 1867–70 for 3rd Earl of Limerick to the design of the English architect and "aesthete", Edward William Godwin, who measured and studied the construction of at least a dozen old Irish castles before producing his plans. The grouping, the strength of detail, the solidity of the light grey stonework all make it a building of exceptional quality. A tall main block, with a massive keep at one end balanced by a reproduction of an ancient Irish round tower at the other, has a lower hall range attached to it at right angles, as at Askeaton Castle; forming two sides of a courtyard

Dromore Castle, co Kerry: Entrance Front

Dromore Castle, co Kerry: Garden Front

entrance to the banqueting hall, which had a high timber barrel roof and a large stone fireplace with a sloping hood carried on corbels; on the other was the entrance to the main block, from which a straight flight of stone stairs under a very unusual stepped barrel vault led up to 1st floor corridor, off which opened the dining room and 2 drawing rooms. The larger drawing room, in the keep, had pointed arches in the thickness of its walls, some of which were supported by marble columns. All 3 rooms had timbered ceilings with painted decoration in which Celtic motifs were mixed with Japanese; Godwin being one of the chief protagonists of the Japanese taste. As if cut through the solid stone, the staircase continued up to

Dromore Castle, co Limerick: view in Courtyard

which is enclosed on the other 2 sides by battlemented walls with corner towers and a narrow gateway. The walls of the castle are as much as 6 feet thick, with a batter; the details, which are beautifully wrought, are copied exactly from Irish originals; if not of C13 and C14, as Godwin believed, at any rate of C15 and C16; there are Irish battlements, bold chimneys, bartizans and

machicoulis on stout corbelling, trefoil windows and angle loops. All the main rooms were made to face into the courtyard, and on the ground floor there is hardly a single outside window; though this was not just archaeological but, as the *Building News* explained at the time, "so that in the event of the country being disturbed, the inmates of Dromore Castle might not only feel secure themselves but be able to give real shelter to others"; this being the year of the Fenian rising, when at least one other Irish country house, Humewood, co Wicklow (*qv*)—also by an English architect—was designed with a view to defence. A vaulted gateway, over which was a chapel, led into the courtyard; on one side of it was the

Dromore Castle, co Limerick: Banqueting Hall

Dromore Castle, co Limerick: Architect's Perspective

Dromore Castle, co Limerick: Aerial View

Dromore Castle, co Limerick: Silhouette

Dromore Castle, co Limerick: Vault over Entrance Steps

Dromore Castle, co Limerick: Drawing Room

Dromore Castle, co Limerick: Ceiling

Dromore Castle, co Limerick: Bedroom Corridor

the bedroom floor, where the corridor was particularly attractive, with a long row of deep window recesses and a timber barrel roof. The walls of the main rooms were to have been painted by the historical painter, Henry Stacy Marks, who actually started work; but the scheme had to be dropped owing to the damp—something which also caused Godwin trouble at his other Irish country house, Glenbeigh Towers, co Kerry (*qv*). Dromore was sold by the Limerick family between the 2 World Wars to the McMahon family, who occupied it until *ca* 1950. An attempt was then made to find a buyer for it; and when this proved unsuccessful, the castle was dismantled. The ruin remains; as solid as any of the old ruined castles of the Irish countryside, but larger and more spectacular than most of them.

Dromore (Old), co Cork (*see* OLD DROMORE).

Drumadarragh House

Drumadarragh House, Kilbride, co Antrim (DIXON, GLENTORAN, B/PB). A 2 storey 3 bay C18 house with a fanlighted doorway, to which 2 wings were added, probably 1827; they are of 2 bays each, similar in style and proportion to the centre; but each has a pediment gable with an *oeil-de-boeuf* window. The rear of the house is similar, except for a wing in the same style as the rest of the house, added 1903.

Drumalis

Drumalis, Larne, co Antrim (SMILEY, Bt/PB). A rambling 2 storey late-Victorian or Edwardian mansion, dominated by a 4 storey central tower and turret. Eaved roof; camber-headed windows; pillared porch; solid parapet on tower and turret. The seat of Sir Hugh Houston Smiley, 1st Bt, whose 2nd son married the sister of the late Ernest Simpson, former husband of the Duchess of Windsor (*see* GRF).

Drumbanagher

Drumbanagher, Poyntzpass, co Armagh (CLOSE/LG1937Supp). A very large Italianate house by William Playfair of Edinburgh, built *ca* 1837 for Maxwell Close, brother-in-law of 1st Lord Lurgan who built Brownlow House (*qv*), also to the design of Playfair. 2 storey centre block with higher 3 storey wings set at right angles to it, and projecting beyond it both in the entrance and garden fronts; the space between the wings in the entrance front being filled by a vast arched porte-cochère. Roofs of wings eaved and carried on bracket cornices; roof of centre block with balustraded parapet. Plain pilasters framing downstairs windows in ends of wings. Now demolished.

Drumboe Castle, Stranorlar, co Donegal (HAYES, Bt/PB1912). A Georgian house consisting of a 3 storey centre with a 3 sided central bow and pillared porch, and bow-ended wings. A Wyatt window on either side of the centre bow.

Drumcairn, Stewartstown, co Tyrone (CAULFEILD, CHARLEMONT, V/PB). A late-Georgian house with a magnificent view across Lough Neagh to the Mourne Mountains. 2 storey; 3 bay front with wide windows; single-storey Doric portico with coupled columns; eaved roof.

Drumcar

Drumcar, Dunleer, co Louth (MCCLINTOCK/IFR; and RATHDONNELL, B/PB). A square block of 1778, 3 storeys over a basement with a 5 bay front, embellished C19 and extended by the addition of 2 large single-storey Italianate wings prolonging 2 adjoining fronts, one of them ending in a handsome archway. Doorcase with 4 engaged Ionic columns and pediment over middle 2; mid to late C19 Doric portico; segmental pediments over ground floor windows. Doorcase with Tuscan pilasters in hall. Ballroom in one of the wings. Now owned by St John of God Brothers.

Drumcarban, Crossdoney, co Cavan. A late C18 house of 3 storeys and 3 bays; doorcase with very delicate fanlight; flues grouped in one long stack.

Drumcashel, Castlebellingham, co Louth (MACAN/LGI1912). A C19 Tudor-Revival house with hood-mouldings.

Drumcondra House

Drumcondra House, Drumcondra, co Dublin (COGHILL, Bt/PB). A very important 3 storey early C18 house, with 2 adjoining fronts. The grander of the two, which has a boldly projecting central feature of giant Corinthian pilasters supporting a balustraded Corinthian entablature and is richly adorned with niches, aedicules, and triangular and segmental pediments over the windows and 2 doorways, of unknown authorship; the simpler, which is plain but for a 2 storey pedimented frontispiece with a pilastered Venetian window in its upper storey, by Sir Edward Lovett Pearce; his earliest recorded private house work, which he carried out 1727 for Marmaduke Coghill, MP, Chancellor of the Exchequer and Judge of the Prerogative Court. The interior, which has c18 panelling and good contemporary chimneypieces, has been altered at various times; but some of it is by Pearce. On the lawn is a temple with a pediment and Corinthian pilasters, probably by Alessandro Galilei, the Italian architect who designed the main block of Castletown, co Kildare (*qv*). Drumcondra House has long been All Hallows College.

Drumcree House, Collinstown, co Westmeath (SMYTH/IFR). A distinguished early to mid-c18 house of ashlar; 2 storeys over a basement. Pedimented breakfront centre, oculus in pediment; doorcase with segmental pediment, Doric pilasters and frieze; Venetian window with Ionic columns and pilasters above, flanked by niches. Now derelict.

Drumhierney, co Leitrim. A 2 storey 6 bay house with a 2 bay pedimented breakfront and a conservatory with fluted Ionic pilasters. Now derelict.

Drumlargan, co Meath (BOMFORD/IFR). A 2 storey double gable-ended house, probably early c18 but with c19 windows and a c19 2 storey gabled projecting porch. Owned by the Bomford family until *ca* 1850.

Drummilly, Loughgall, co Armagh (COPE/LG1937Supp). A plain, vaguely Georgian house with a remarkable 2 storey elliptical structure of glass and art-nouveau ironwork projecting from its centre and constituting the entrance. Elliptical windows in the upper storey of this addition.

Drumnasole

Drumnasole, Garronpoint, co Antrim (TURNLY/IFR). An early c19 house, in what was described (1845) as "a most romantic and sheltered site at the base of the perpendicular hills". Begun some time *ante* 1819 and not completed until *ca* 1840; built for Francis Turnly, who had been in the East India Company and spent much of his early life in China. Of basalt from the hill behind; 2 storey over basement; entrance front has

K

breakfront centre with window flanked by 2 narrower windows above and fanlighted doorway under shallow porch of 4 engaged Doric columns below; 1 bay on either side. Side of house is 5 bay. Long hall with plasterwork ceiling; stair-well lit by dome.

Drumreaske House, Monaghan, co Monaghan (KANE/LG11912). A 2 storey c19 Tudor-Revival house of the "cottage" type, with gables and decorated bargeboards.

Drumsill, co Armagh (MACGEOUGH BOND/IFR). Owned by the MacGeough family from the c17. A house of *ca* 1788, remodelled by Francis Johnston, *ca* 1806. Sold 1916. An hotel 1957–72, when it was blown up.

Duarrigle Castle

Duarrigle Castle, Millstreet, co Cork. A castellated house of early c19 appearance, consisting of a 3 storey block and a 2 storey block with a round turret at their junction. Simple battlements; regularly disposed mullioned windows with ogival-headed lights; entrance doorway with ogival fanlight at the head of a flight of steps with wrought-iron railings. Hood mouldings. The seat of the Justice family; more recently of the O'Connors, maternal forebears of Mr Norman St John-Stevas, MP (whose mother, Mrs Stephen S. Stevas, was formerly Miss Kitty St John O'Connor, of Duarrigle Castle). Now a ruin.

Duckett's Grove

Duckett's Grove

Duckett's Grove, nr Carlow, co Carlow (EUSTACE-DUCKETT/IFR). A square house of 2 and 3 storeys, transformed into a spectacu-

Duckett's Grove: Gateway

iar castellated Gothic fantasy by Thomas A. Cobden, of Carlow, for J. D. Duckett 1830. Numerous towers and turrets, round, square and octagonal; notably a heavily machicolated round tower with a tall octagonal turret growing out of it. The walls enlivened with oriels and many canopied niches sheltering statues; more statues and busts in niches along the battlemented wall joining the house to a massively feudal yard gateway; yet more statues manning the battlements of one of the towers, and disposed around the house on pedestals. At the entrance to the demesne is one of the most stupendous castellated gateways in Ireland: with a formidable array of battlemented and machicolated towers and 2 great archways giving onto two different drives; the principal archway having a portcullis, and being surmounted by an immense armorial achievement, which was originally coloured. The house was burnt 1933 and is now a ruin.

Duckspool

Duckspool, Dungarvan, co Waterford (GALWEY/IFR). A tall 3 storey 5 bay house of late-Georgian appearance. Fanlighted doorway; eaved roof. The seat of J. M. Galwey, MP, whose son, Edward, lost his estates and money as a result of the Great Famine. Now owned by Augustinian Fathers.

Duleek House, Duleek, co Meath (O'BRIEN, INCHIQUIN, B/PB). A 3 storey pedimented cut-stone house of *ca* 1750, attributed to Richard Castle or his school; built for Thomas Trotter, MP. 3 bay front; central breakfront with triple window above Venetian window above pedimented tripartite doorway. Balustraded roof parapet. Owned, in early part of c19, by 2nd Marquess of Thomond.

Dunany House, Togher, co Louth (BELL-INGHAM, Bt/PB; ENGLAND/LG1969). A "U"-shaped house with a courtyard, partly early c18, but much altered late c18 and made to look Gothic in early c19. Bolection chimneypiece in hall.

Dunboden Park, Mullingar, co Westmeath (COOPER/IFR). A house of early to mid-c19 appearance, of 2 storeys over a basement and square in plan; with 5 bay front and side elevations. Porch with engaged columns; entablatures over windows.

Dunboy Castle

Dunboy Castle

Dunboy Castle: arches spanning Hall

Dunboy Castle, Castletownberehaven, co Cork (PUXLEY/LG1972). A castellated house of 1838 and earlier facing up Berehaven, to which H. L. Puxley, owner of the Berehaven Copper Mines, added a vast new building of razor-sharp ashlar 1880s: a solid, vigorous, 3 dimensional composition in which Ruskinian Gothic arches and windows were combined with "Old English" oriels. While the overall effect was High Victorian, it was not wholly uninfluenced by subsequent trends in English domestic architecture, having certain similarities to Norman Shaw's Cragside, Northumberland. There were no battlements, but a skyline of steep and pointed roofs and tall chimneys. A high-roofed tower rose from the middle of the entrance front, and another from a corner of the front facing the water, which had an arcaded basement beneath it; at one side of the latter tower was a tremendous buttress, combined with a chimneystack. The chief feature of the interior was the series of transverse diaphragm arches spanning the hall. Burnt 1921; now a spectacular ruin.

Dunboyne Castle, Dunboyne, co Meath (BUTLER, DUNBOYNE, B/PB; SADLEIR, *sub*

Dunboyne Castle

TRENCH/IFR; MANGAN, *sub* TINDAL-CARILL-WORSLEY/LG1972; WACHMAN, *sub* DALY/IFR). The c18 house which replaced the old castle here as the seat of the Dunboynes. From its appearance, dating from 2 different periods, the front being later; probably inspired by Sir William Chambers's Charlemont House in Dublin and added either by Pierce Butler, 10th Lord Dunboyne, who succeeded 1768, or by his son, 11th Baron, who died 1785. Of 3 storeys and 7 bays, the ground floor being rusticated and treated as a basement and the 1st floor as a *piano nobile* with pediments over the windows. Tripartite pedimented and fanlighted entrance doorway; urns on roof parapet. Single-storey 4 bay rusticated wing. Good interior rococo plasterwork. 11th Lord Dunboyne was succeeded as 12th Baron by his 70-year-old uncle, Rt Rev and Hon John Butler, Catholic Bishop of Cork, who caused a sensation two years later by turning Protestant and marrying, in what proved to be the vain hope of producing an heir. During the remaining years of his life, 12th Lord Dunboyne lived at Dunboyne Castle. He was reconciled to the Catholic Church before his death 1800, and—against the advice of the Catholic Archbishop of Dublin—made a Will leaving his co Meath property to Maynooth College. The Will was disputed by his sister, Hon Mrs O'Brien-Butler; in the end half the property went to Maynooth —which used it towards founding the Dunboyne Establishment for higher ecclesiastical studies—and the other half, including Dunboyne Castle, to the O'Brien-Butler family; the Dunboyne peerage having gone to a distant kinsman. Later in c19, Dunboyne Castle passed to Mary (*née* O'Brien-Butler), wife of Nicholas Sadleir. Later again, it passed to the Mangan family; and for a period it was leased by the Morragh-Ryan family. In recent years, it was the home of Mr Norman Wachman; it is now the Good Shepherd Convent.

Dunbrody Park, Arthurstown, co Wexford (CHICHESTER, TEMPLEMORE, B/PB; and DONEGALL, M/PB). A pleasant, comfortable, unassuming house of *ca* 1860 which from its appearance might be a c20 house of vaguely "Queen Anne" flavour. 2 storey; 5 bay centre, with middle bay breaking forward and three-sided single-storey central bow; 2 bay projecting ends. Moderately high roof on bracket cornice; windows with cambered heads and astragals. Wyatt windows in side elevation.

Dundalk House, Dundalk, co Louth (HAMILTON, CLANBRASSILL, E/DEP; JOCELYN, RODEN, E/PB; CARROLL/IFR). A Georgian Gothic house of 2 storeys, with pointed windows and a 3 sided bow; originally a seat of the Earls of Roden, who inherited the estate from the Earls of Clanbrassill of 2nd creation; acquired c19 by the Carrolls, owners of the tobacco firm of P. J. Carroll & Co., whose factory was nearby. Demolished *ca* 1900 owing to its site being unhealthy, and replaced by red brick gabled house of the period, which was given to P. J. Carroll & Co. for use as offices 1936. The demesne of Dundalk House was one of 1st in Ireland to be landscaped, following the fashion started in England by Pope and William Kent. By 1752, 1st Earl of Clanbrassill of 2nd creation (then Viscount Limerick) had made "an artificial serpentine river" here; he had also erected "a Chinese bridge" and "a thatch'd open house supported by bodies of fir trees".

Dundanion, Blackrock, co Cork. A 2 storey 5 bay early c19 villa which was the home of the Cork architect, Sir Thomas Deane, who supervised its building, though it was designed by the Morrisons. Single-storey Ionic portico; eaved roof. More recently the home of the McNamaras; sold *ca* 1950 after the death of Lt-Gen Sir Arthur McNamara.

Dunderave

Dunderave: Central Hall

Dunderave, Bushmills, co Antrim (MAC-NAGHTEN, Bt/PB). A very fine Italianate palazzo by Charles (afterwards Sir Charles) Lanyon; built 1847 for Sir Edmund Workman-Macnaghten, 2nd Bt, to replace a castellated house which his father, Sir Francis Macnaghten, had built only 10 years earlier. Sir Edmund, like his father, had spent much of his life in India, where he had made a great deal of money; it is possible that Calcutta—then in its heyday as the "City of Palaces"—gave him a preference for Classical houses, high ceilings and pillars. Both outside and in, Dunderave has all the dignity and spacious splendour of a London club; and indeed, it seems that Lanyon's design for the house was directly influenced by Charles Barry's Reform Club, which was completed 1840. The house is of 2 storeys and square in plan, with a lower service wing at one side; the three fronts are all different, and boldly ornamented in a crisp, pinkish sandstone. Some of the windows are surrounded by Corinthian aedicules, surmounted by latticed balustrading of a design very characteristic of Lanyon; others have pediments or entablatures on console brackets. The roof is carried on a deep bracket cornice. The entrance porch is an Italianate loggia with Corinthian pilasters and engaged columns; while in the adjoining front there is a central feature of a single-storey curved bow, also adorned with engaged Corinthian columns. The porch leads into a narrow entrance hall with a barrel ceiling and Classical reliefs on the walls, very like the passage leading into the *cortile* of a palazzo. The *cortile* is there; but as at the Reform Club, it is in the form of a vast and magnificent central hall, of immense height, surrounded by a broad gallery at first floor level, with Corinthian columns carrying a lantern storey. The gallery is carried on an arcaded lower storey with Doric pilasters and frieze. To add to the sense of richness, the walls and columns are painted to represent Siena, porphyry and other marbles; and there is no staircase to take away from the sense of space; the main stair being relegated to a small well at the back. Of the reception rooms arranged round the hall, the grandest is the ballroom, with an elaborate plasterwork ceiling of geometrical design. The other rooms have ceilings with modillion cornices; and there are handsome doorways with entablatures on consoles.

Dundermot

Dundermot: Drawing Room

Dundermot, Ballintober, co Roscommon (O'CONOR DON/IFR; KELLY/LGI1958). A 3 storey C18 double gable-ended house of 3 bays, with 2 storey 2 bay wings almost as high as the centre. Regency ironwork porch; ironwork balconies in front of ground floor windows of wings. Tall and massive chimneystacks on gable ends of centre block. The seat of a branch of the O'Conor Don family; afterwards of the Blake Kelly family.

Dundrum, co Tipperary (MAUDE, HAWARDEN, V/PB). A C18 Palladian house consisting of a centre block of 2 storeys over a high basement joined by short links to flanking wings or pavilions, very much in the style of

Dundrum

Sir Edward Lovett Pearce; the seat of the Maude family, Viscounts Hawarden. Entrance front of 7 bays, with 3 bay pedimented breakfront; links and wings of 1 bay each. Central round-headed window with keystone above pedimented doorcase; similar windows on either side of door and in wings. Graceful perron in front of door with partly curving double stairs and iron railings. Oculi and camber-headed windows in basement; prominent quoins on centre block and wings. Large hall with compartmented ceiling. Impressive double-pedimented stable block at right angles to entrance front. An extra storey, treated as an attic above a continuous cornice, was added to the centre block *ca* 1890 by 4th Viscount Hawarden, who was 1st (and last) Earl de Montalt. This did away with the pediment and spoilt the proportions of the house; making the centre block massive and ungainly, so that it dwarfs the wings. After being sold by the Maudes, the house was for many years a convent; but it is now in private occupation once again.

Dundullerick, Lisgoold, co Cork (CREAGH-BARRY, *sub* BARRY/IFR). A Georgian house consisting of a 2 storey 3 bay centre with single-storey 2 bay wings.

Duneske, Cahir, co Tipperary (SMITH/IFR). A 3 storey asymmetrical Victorian house with a high roof and some gables; built *ca* 1870 for R.W. Smith to the design of Sir Thomas Drew. Plate glass windows, bows in various places. Porch with sinuous, rather art-nouveau style decoration in stucco. An impressive straight flight of stairs between walls leads up to 1st floor, where the principal reception rooms are situated; there are 2 drawing rooms with friezes of simple Victorian plasterwork; one of them has a characteristically late-Victorian alcove in a projecting bow, set at an odd angle.

Dungar, Coolderry, Offaly. A 2 storey C19 house with a front and side elevation of 3 bays, the centre bay of the front being recessed, and that of the side breaking forwards. Porch with arches and rusticated piers; single-storey curved bow in centre of side elevation; prominent quoins; entablatures over ground floor windows; eaved roof on bracket cornice. The home of Mr Harry Read, who in 1911–12 had the unique distinction of playing for Ireland at cricket, tennis and Rugby football. Some years ago, Mr & Mrs Read moved to a new house which they had built for themselves near an old castle in the grounds, and which is named The Old Castle House.

Dungiven Castle, Dungiven, co Derry. A C19 castle with a long 2 storey battle-mented front, having a central polygon tower with a pointed Gothic doorway and a pointed window over, and a round tower at each end. 5 bays on either side of the centre.

Dunguaire Castle, Kinvara, co Galway (MARTYN/LGI1912; GOGARTY/IFR; RUSSELL, AMPTHILL, B/PB). An old tower-house with a bawn and a smaller tower, on a creek of Galway Bay; which was for long roofless, though in other respects well maintained by the Martyn family, of Tulira (*qv*), who owned it C18 and C19; and which was bought in the present century by Oliver St John Gogarty, the surgeon, writer and wit, to save it from a threat of demolition. More recently, it was bought by the late Christabel, Lady Ampthill (the central figure in the celebrated "Russell baby" case), and restored by her as her home; her architect being Mr Donal O'Neill Flanagan, who carried out a most successful and sympathetic restoration. The only addition to the castle was an unobtrusive 2 storey wing joining the main tower to the smaller one. The main tower has 2 large vaulted rooms, one above the other, in its 2 lower storeys, which keep their original fireplaces; these were made into the dining room and drawing room. "Medieval" banquets and entertainments are now held here.

Duninga, Goresbridge, co Kilkenny (BOOKEY, *sub* RIALL/LGI1958). A house with a 3 storey centre and 2 storey projecting wings, joined by a Doric colonnade. The seat of the Bookey family.

Dunkathel

Dunkathel: Staircase

Dunkathel (also known as **Dunkettle**), **Glanmire, co Cork** (TONSON, *sub* TONSON-RYE/IFR and RIVERSDALE, B/DEP; TRANT/LGI1958; MORRIS/LGI879; GUBBINS/LGI937-Supp; RUSSELL/IFR). A house in the Palladian manner, consisting of a 2 storey 9 bay centre block joined by screen walls with rusticated niches to office wings extending back; the front ends of the wings being treated as 2 storey 2 bay pavilions with oculi in their upper storey. The front of the centre block has quoins at its sides and framing a 3 bay breakfront; a solid roof parapet and a fanlighted doorcase with an entablature and engaged Tuscan columns. Built *post* 1780 by Abraham Morris, a wealthy Cork merchant who became an MP after a celebrated electoral case which ended in the unseating of his successful opponent, Lord Kingsborough; the architect of the house is not known, but the Knight of Glin has suggested that it might be by an associate of Davis Duckart, who designed the nearby Lota (*qv*); since the design clearly owes much to Duckart's influence. The wings form 2 sides of a courtyard at the back of the house, being joined by a range containing a room with a frieze of C18 plasterwork, which is possibly a remnant of the previous house, built by Dominick Trant, MP—who had a fine collection of pictures here—itself the successor to an earlier house on a different site built by Richard Tonson, MP. The present house has an impressive bifurcating staircase of stone with graceful iron balustrades behind a wide arch at the back of the hall, which is adorned with fluted Corinthian pilasters of wood. The hall keeps its early C19 decoration, the walls marbled to represent Siena, the ceiling painted as a blue sky with clouds. The other main rooms have simple friezes. The house stands in a fine situation overlooking the Lee estuary just below the mouth of the Glanmire River. Sold *ca* 1870 by Jonas Morris to the Wise Gubbins family, from whom it was inherited by the Russell family.

Dunleckney Manor

Dunleckney Manor, Bagenalstown, co Carlow (NEWTON, *sub* BAGENAL/IFR; VESEY *sub* DE VESCI, V/PB). A C19 Tudor-Gothic house by Daniel Robertson, of Kilkenny. Built *ca* 1850 for Walter Newton, who inherited the estate from his mother, the heiress of the Bagenal family of Dunleckney. Faced in smooth limestone ashlar; steep gables and overhanging oriels; a slender polygonal corner turret decorated with panels of miniature tracery in the manner of English Perpendicular architecture; similar ornament on the bow of the garden front. Interior has plaster fan vaulting. Elaborately carved staircase of wood. Inherited by S.P.C. Vesey, whose maternal grandfather was P.J. Newton; sold by his widow 1942. Subsequently owned by Mr Thomas Donnelly; re-sold *ca* 1958.

Dunluce Castle, co Antrim (MCDONNELL, ANTRIM, E/PB). The ancestral stronghold of the McDonnells, Earls of Antrim, dramatically situated at the end of a rocky promontory jutting out into the sea off the north Antrim coast. The castle, which was built at various periods from C14 to C17, eventually consisted of several round towers and a gatehouse with rather Scottish bartizans, joined by a curtain wall; with domestic buildings inside this enclosure. The latter included a

Dunluce Castle

mid-C16 loggia with sandstone columns, and a 2 storey Elizabethan or Jacobean house, with 3 large oriels. These 2 buildings were in 1st of 2 courtyards into which the castle enclosure was divided; the other and lower yard containing offices and servants' quarters. There were also buildings on the mainland, erected early C17. In 1639, part of the curtain wall of the castle collapsed into the sea, together with some of the servants' quarters and a number of servants. After the Civil Wars, the castle was abandoned by the family in favour of Glenarm Castle (*qv*); it is now a romantic ruin.

Dunmanway, co Cork: The Manor House (COX, *sub* VILLIERS-STUART/LGI1912; LUCAS/IFR). A 2 storey 3 bay house of 1819, with Wyatt windows and an enclosed porch.

Dunmore, Carrigans, co Donegal (MC-CLINTOCK/IFR). A gable-ended mid-C18 house which Dr Craig considers may be by Michael Priestley. 2 storey, with an attic lit by windows in the gable-ends; 5 bay front, with central Venetian window above tripartite doorway, later obscured by a porch. Lower 2 storey wing added later. Staircase extending into central projection at back of house.

Dunmore, Durrow, co Leix (STAPLES, Bt/PB; and MACGEOUGH BOND/IFR). An early-Georgian house of brick, plastered over, consisting of a 3 storey 5 bay gable-ended centre block with 2 storey projecting wings. Centre block with pediment and high-pitched roof. The seat of a branch of the family of the Staples Bts. Now a ruin.

Dunmore House, co Galway

Dunmore House, Dunmore, co Galway (SHEE, Bt/PB1869; DERING, Bt/PB). A late C18 house of 3 storeys over a basement, incorporating an earlier house. 3 bay bow-ended entrance front, with 1 bay central breakfront. Wide fanlighted doorway.

Dunmore House (also known as **Dunmore Palace**), **Kilkenny, co Kilkenny** (BUTLER, ORMONDE, M/PB). A C17 red brick house on a palatial scale built *post* Restoration by Duchess of Ormonde, wife of the Great Duke. Its chief interior feature was a staircase of carved wood, "so large that twenty men might walk abreast". The Duchess also laid out elaborate gardens here. When the Duke was showing some people his improvements at Kilkenny Castle, one of them said: "Your Grace has done much here"; to which he replied, pointing in the direction of his wife's house, "Yes, and there the Duchess has Dunmore; and if she does any more, I shall be undone". The house was neglected and eventually demolished during C18.

Dunnstown, co Kildare. A 2 storey pedimented C18 house flanked by 2 free-standing wings with small pediments. The pediment of the main block was made into a bargeboarded gable C19.

Dunore House

Dunore House, Aldergrove, co Antrim. The only full-blown country house example in Ireland of the Egyptian taste; and a rather late example, having been built *post* 1857. Of smooth rusticated granite; the doorcase being composed of 4 terms with Pharaohs' heads, originally surrounded by hieroglyphics; the pediment being topped with an obelisk.

Dunsandle

Dunsandle, Athenry, co Galway (DALY/IFR). A large plain mid to late C18 Palladian house, until recently the finest C18 house in co Galway; very tentatively attributed by the Knight of Glin to Davis Duckart. Built for Rt Hon Denis Daly, MP. Centre block of 3 storeys over a basement with 5 bay entrance and garden fronts, each having a 3 bay pedimented breakfront; joined by long straight screen walls with pedimented doorways and niches to low and wide-spreading 2 storey wings extending round courtyards open at the ends. Elaborate plasterwork in saloon: wall panels with garlands identical to those in Duckart's most important country house, Castletown, co Kilkenny (*qv*). Coved rococo ceiling in morning room. Adamesque ceiling in drawing room. Staircases with carved balusters at either side of hall. Sold *ca* 1954 by Major Bowes Daly; subsequently demolished.

Dunsany Castle: Library

Dunsany Castle

Dunsany Castle, Dunsany, co Meath (PLUNKETT, DUNSANY, B/PB). A castle founded *ca* 1200 by Hugh de Lacy; and which, in 1403, passed by marriage, along with the neighbouring castle of Killeen (*qv*), to Sir Christopher Plunkett; who left Killeen to his eldest son, ancestor of the Earls of Fingall, and Dunsany to his 2nd son, 1st Baron of Dunsany. The castle eventually consisted of two tall blocks, each with a pair of square corner-towers, joined by a hall range so as to enclose a shallow 3 sided court. 13th Lord Dunsany restored and modernized the old castle 1780s, filling in the old court between the projecting tower-blocks to form a spacious staircase hall, putting in pointed Georgian-Gothic windows and decorating the principal rooms in the fashionable style of the period. 14th Lord Dunsany carried out various additions and alterations to the castle *ca* 1840, which can safely be attributed to James Shiel, who was working at the nearby Killeen Castle at that time. Shiel replaced the Georgian-Gothic windows on the entrance front and at the end of the castle with tracery and mullioned windows; but he was much more sparing with his medievalism here than he was at Killeen; so that the old grey castle with its square towers keeps all the character and atmosphere of a house that has grown through the ages, rather than looking merely like a castle of C19. The small and rather low entrance hall is one of the interiors of 1780s; it has a semi-vault and Gothic pilasters, with delicate plasterwork on the flat of the ceiling. Beyond is the wonderfully spacious and lofty 1780s staircase hall, in which a staircase with slender wooden balusters makes a graceful and partly curving ascent through 3 storeys, by way of a gallery at first floor level off which opens the drawing room, in what was originally the upper part of the hall range; another delightful interior of 1780s, with a ceiling of delicate

plasterwork by Michael Stapleton. A door at one end of the drawing room leads to a charming little late C18 spiral staircase of wood; there is a rather similar staircase at Castle Widenham, co Cork (*qv*), as though late-Georgian craftsmen, when working in medieval castles, tried to produce their own version of the medieval newel stair. At the other end of the drawing room is the library, which runs through the full depth of the old tower-block on this side, with a window at each end. This is one of the rooms decorated by Shiel, with Gothic bookcases and a plain ribbed ceiling surrounded by corbelled half-vaults; the mellow oak graining of the woodwork and the dark red brocade damask on the walls make it a room of extraordinary beauty. Some of the graining incorporates Gothic tracery painted in *trompe l'oeil*. At the back of the castle is a large panelled Edwardian billiard room by George Jack, in a single-storey wing added 1910 by 18th Lord Dunsany, who as well as being a highly imaginative poet and prose writer and a figure in the Irish Revival of the beginning of this century, was a traveller, soldier and sportsman. His uncle, Sir Horace Plunkett, the great Irish agricultural reformer, lived much at Dunsany during late C19. Close to the castle is a large ruined C15 church. There are Gothic gateways at 3 of the entrances to the demesne; one in the form of a sham ruin.

Dunsland, Glanmire, co Cork (PIKE/LGI1958). A late-Victorian house with an eaved roof, half-timbered gables and pediments and entablatures on console brackets over the ground floor windows. Burnt *ca* 1920.

Dunsoghly Castle

Dunsoghly Castle, Finglas, co Dublin (DUNNE/LGI1912). A C15 castle built by Thomas Plunkett, Chief Justice of the King's Bench; consisting of a tall 3 storey tower with tapering corner-turrets rising above the parapet of the centre block. At one side of the tower is a detached chapel, built 1573 by Sir John Plunkett, Chief Justice of the Queen's Bench, and his 3rd wife, Genet Sarsfield. The lowest storey of the tower is vaulted; those above had timber floors. The castle still keeps its original roof, with massive oak timbers. Passed to the Dunnes through the marriage of Margaret, daughter and co-heiress of Nicholas Plunkett, to Francis Dunne.

Durrow, co Leix (*see* CASTLE DURROW).

Durrow Abbey, Tullamore, Offaly (GRAHAM-TOLER, NORBURY, E/PB; SLAZENGER, *sub* POWERSCOURT, V/PB). Originally a plain 3 storey 7 bay C18 house with a pillared porch; replaced *ca* 1837 by a Tudor-Gothic house built for 2nd Earl of Norbury, who was murdered here 1839. The house now consists of 2 2 storey ranges at right angles to each other, one of them standing on slightly lower ground, with a small battlemented tower at their junction. The higher range has a central projecting porch-gable, with a corbelled oriel over the entrance door; and a slightly stepped gable at each end. There are tall, Tudor-style chimneys and a few pinnacles. The house was rebuilt in the same style 1924. Nearby is the site of an ancient abbey, with a fine C10 High Cross. Durrow passed to the descendants of a younger son of 2nd Earl; it was sold *ca* 1950 and was afterwards the home of Mr & Mrs Ralph Slazenger; it is now the home of Mr & Mrs Michael Williams.

Dysart

Dysart

Dysart, Delvin, co Westmeath (OGLE/IFR). A house of 2 storeys over a basement, which is concealed at the front but visible at the sides and back; built 1757 to the design of George Pentland for Nicholas Ogle, whose 2nd wife was Elizabeth Lambart, of Beau Parc, co Meath (*qv*), a house built 1755 and which, although on a much grander scale, may have influenced Dysart; since both houses have the same sequence of tripartite pedimented doorway, Venetian window and Diocletian window as their central feature. Since Dysart has only 2 storeys to Beau Parc's 3, the Diocletian window is accommodated in a pediment. The centre of the Venetian window is a niche, as at Bellinter, co Meath (*qv*). 1 bay on either side of the centre, which breaks forward. Large curved end bows; pediment-gable in rear elevation.

E

Eastgrove, Cobh, co Cork (BAGWELL/IFR; JENKINSON, Bt/PB). An early C19 house in the "Cottage Gothic" style overlooking East Ferry, a heavily-wooded backwater of Cork Harbour; built by Dorcas (*née* Bagwell), wife of Benjamin Bousfield, on land which had belonged to her mother's family, the Harpers of Belgrove (*qv*). Shallow gables with bargeboards; trellised iron veranda on front overlooking Ferry. A polygonal tower, with an eaved roof, was subsequently added at one end of the house and known as the Wellington Tower. It contains a large and impressive dining room with curved walls. There is also a large and handsome drawing room. At one side of the house is a range of castellated outbuildings, with a slender tower like a folly; there is another tower in the woods. After Mrs Bousfield's death, Eastgrove was inherited by the Bagwells. It was sold *ca* 1958 by Major W.E.G. Bagwell to Mr Robin Jenkinson, who re-sold it to Mr Dermot Griffith.

Ecclesville, Fintona, co Tyrone (ECCLES, sub MCCLINTOCK/LGI1912; LECKY-BROWNE-LECKY, *sub* BROWNE/IFR). A plain late-Georgian house. The home of Raymond Saville Charles De Montmorency ("Tibby") Lecky-Browne-Lecky, actor-musician and noted female impersonator. Now a home for the elderly.

Echlinville (afterwards **Rubane House**), **Kircubbin, co Down** (ECHLIN/LGI1912). An early to mid-C18 house, largely rebuilt 1850; but the library, a 4 bay pavilion with Ionic pilasters and Gothic astragals in its windows, survives from the earlier house; inside is a vaulted ceiling with 2 floating domes. In the grounds there is a small Classical bridge and a pebble house with pinnacles. Subsequently the seat of a branch of the Cleland family, its name being changed to Rubane House.

Edenfel, Omagh, co Tyrone (BUCHANAN, *sub* HAMMOND-SMITH/IFR). A Victorian house with gables and bargeboards. The home of the Buchanan family, of which James Buchanan, 15th President of the United States, was a cadet (*see* PFUSA).

Eden Hall, Ballyragget, co Kilkenny (BRENAN/IFR). The former seat of a branch of the Purcell family, rebuilt in a very mildly Gothic style early C19 by Gerald Brenan, having been ruinous. 2 storey; 5 bay front with 1 bay central breakfront. Hood mouldings over windows; fanlighted doorway beneath delicate Gothic portico of timber.

Edenmore, Stranorlar, co Donegal (COCHRANE/IFR). A 2 storey gable-ended late C18 house. Front with 3 sided central bow and 1 bay on either side of it. The house is flanked by detached office wings running back, one much longer than the other; the front ends of these wings have 3 sided bows, matching the bow in the centre of the house; they are linked to the house by walls, forming one long elevation. Sold 1954.

Eden Vale

Eden Vale, Ennis, co Clare (STACPOOLE/IFR). A C18 house, enlarged and embellished during 2nd half of C19 by Richard Stacpoole. Irregular entrance front with 3 bays on one side of a tower-like central feature, and 4 bays on the other. Porch with pilasters and pierced parapet. At the end of the house are 2 Venetian windows, one on top of the other. Sold *ca* 1930; now an old peoples' home.

Edermine

Edermine

Edermine, Enniscorthy, co Wexford (POWER, *sub* O'REILLY/IFR). A 2 storey Italianate villa by John B. Keane, built *ca* 1839 for the Powers, owners of the firm of John Power & Son, Distillers, of Dublin. Eaved roof on bracket cornice; 3 bay front, with pillared porch, and triangular pediments over downstairs windows. 5 bay side

elevation, with a central Venetian window recessed in a giant blind arch. Grecian interior; fluted Doric columns in hall, paired Ionic columns and pilasters on staircase landing. A Gothic chapel was subsequently built at one side of the house to the design of A.W. Pugin, a family friend; it was originally free-standing, but was afterwards joined to the house by an addition at the back which includes a small Italianate campanile. At right angles to the chapel, a magnificent early Victorian iron conservatory, gracefully curving in the Crystal Palace manner, was built; probably by the Malcolmson Works in Waterford, or the Hammersmith Iron Works in Dublin; it is joined to the corner of the chapel by a cast iron veranda.

Edgeworthstown House

Edgeworthstown House, Edgeworthstown, co Longford (EDGEWORTH/LGI1912; MONTAGU, *sub* MANCHESTER, D/PB). An early C18 house built by Richard Edgeworth, MP, with small windows, low, wainscoted rooms and heavy cornices; much enlarged and modernized after 1770 by Richard Lovell Edgeworth, the inventor, writer on education and improving landlord, father of Maria Edgeworth, the novelist. Of 2 storeys over a basement, with two adjoining fronts; prominent roof and dentil cornice. Entrance front of 3 bays between 2 triple windows in the upper storey, with doorway in a pillared recess between 2 shallow single-storey curved bows below; in the Victorian period, the right-hand triple window was replaced by 2 windows and the right-hand bow by a rectangular single-storey projection. Adjoining front with 3 bay breakfront rising above the roofline as a pedimented attic, and 2 bays on either side; on the ground floor, Richard Lovell Edgeworth enlarged the rooms by throwing them into single-storey 3 bay rectangular projections, linked in the centre by an arcaded loggia; in the Victorian period one of the projections was replaced by a glass lean-to conservatory, and the loggia was removed. Curved top-lit staircase in centre of house. In Richard Lovell Edgeworth's time, the house was full of labour-saving devices: sideboards on wheels, pegs for footwear in the hall, leather straps to prevent doors banging, a water pump which automatically dispensed ½d to beggars for each half-hour that they worked it. Inherited 1926 by Mrs C. F. Montagu (*née* Sanderson), whose mother was an Edgeworth; sold by her to Mr Bernard Noonan, who bequeathed it to an order of nuns, by whom it is used as a nursing home; the exterior of the house having been much altered, and the interior gutted and rebuilt.

Edgeworthstown Rectory

Edgeworthstown Rectory, Edgeworthstown, co Longford (EDGEWORTH/LGI1958). A 3 storey 3 bay gable-ended early C18 house. The birthplace of Henry Essex Edgeworth, better known as Abbé Edgeworth de Fermont, who attended Louis XVI on the scaffold.

Edmondsbury (formerly **Newtown**), **co Leix** (BUTLER (*now* BUTLER-SLOSS)/IFR). A house probably built by Edmond Butler soon *post* 1734. Good chimneypiece in hall. Sold 1910.

Edmondstown, co Roscommon. A High Victorian house of stone with brick polychromy; pointed windows; pyramidal-roofed turret.

Eglantine, Hillsborough, co Down (MULHOLLAND, *sub* DUNLEATH, B/PB). A C19 house with a remarkable double-ramped staircase.

Manor House, Eglinton

Eglinton, co Derry: Manor House (DAVIDSON/IFR). A 2 storey late-Georgian house with an eaved roof and a fanlighted doorway, built by the London Company of Grocers, who owned and developed the village of Eglinton. Bought by James Davidson *ca* 1840, and subsequently enlarged by the addition of a battlemented wing, with a small battlemented turret at the junction of the wing and the original house. The wing and turret have large vermiculated quoins; and the original house has similar quoins.

Eglish Castle, Birr, Offaly. A 2 storey house with a pediment. In 1837 the residence of Capt English.

Elm Hill

Elm Hill, Ardagh, co Limerick (STUDDERT/IFR). A weather-slated C18 house of 2 storeys over a high basement. 6 bay front; pedimented doorway with sidelights. Archway of curving Baroque shape, the main arch being surmounted by a round-headed opening, at side of house, leading to yard.

Elm Park, Farran, co Cork (ASHE, *sub* WOODLEY/IFR). A 2 storey 5 bay early C19 house, the 2 left-hand bays of the front projecting forwards, with a glazed pilastered porch in the angle thus formed. The other end of the house is slightly curved. Eaved roof. Early in the present century the residence of C.W. Ashe.

Elm Park, co Limerick

Elm Park, Clarina, co Limerick (MASSY, CLARINA, B/PB1949). An irregular early C19 cut-stone castellated house, mostly of 2 storeys over a basement; with round and square towers. Rectangular windows, some of them with Georgian astragals. Now demolished, except for the gate arch.

The Elms

Elms (The), Portarlington, co Leix (STANNUS/IFR). A Georgian house consisting of a gable-ended centre of 3 storeys over a basement, with lower asymmetrical wings. The centre with a 3 bay front and a large fanlighted staircase window not centrally placed in its rear elevation. The home of Lt-Col T. R. A. Stannus, father of Dame Ninette de Valois, the ballerina and choreographer.

Ely Lodge (on the same estate as **Castle Hume**), **nr Enniskillen, co Fermanagh**

Ely Lodge

(HUME, Bt/EDB; LOFTUS, ELY, M/PB; GROSVENOR, WESTMINSTER, D/PB). Richard Castle built his 1st Irish Palladian house here for Sir Gustavus Hume, Bt, MP 1729; it was named Castle Hume. Fine stable-court, with rusticated openings, some of them surmounted by oculi, and an interior of vaults supported by Doric columns, as at Strokestown (*qv*). The estate subsequently passed to the Ely family through the marriage of the Hume heiress to Nicholas Loftus, afterwards 1st Earl of Ely. In 1830s, a new house was built a couple of miles away, on a promontory in Lough Erne, by 2nd Marquess of Ely, and named Ely Lodge; to provide stone for it, the main block of Castle Hume was demolished, so that only the stable-court remains. Ely Lodge, which was to the design of William Farrell, consisted of a 2 storey 5 bay gable-ended block with Doric pilasters along its whole front and a Doric porch, the gable-ends being treated as pediments; at one end was a single-storey wing set back, with corner-pilasters and a curved pilastered bow in its side elevation. In 1870, Ely Lodge was blown up as part of 21st birthday celebrations of the 4th Marquess, who intended to build a new house; it is also said that he blew the house up in order to avoid having Queen Victoria to stay. In the event, the new house was never built; doubtless for the reason that the young Lord Ely spent too much money on rebuilding his other seat, Loftus Hall, co Wexford (*qv*). The former stables of Ely Lodge have since been extended to form a house, which is the Irish seat of the Duke of Westminster; it contains a number of interior features of the now demolished Eaton Hall, Cheshire.

Emell Castle, Moneygall, Offaly (STONEY/IFR). A large C16 tower-house of the O'Carrolls, with a gable-ended C18 house of 2 storeys over a basement and 5 bays built onto the front of it. Fanlighted doorway. The C18 addition was almost certainly built by Capt Robert Johnstone, who bought the property 1782 and left it at his death 1803 to his nephew, Thomas Stoney. Some work was carried out on both the tower and the house during C19, without altering the original character of either. Sold 1959 by Mr A.R.J. Stoney.

Emo Court (also known as **Emo Park**), **Portarlington, co Leix** (DAWSON-DAMER, PORTARLINGTON, E/PB; CHOLMELEY-HARRISON/IFR). The only country house by James Gandon in the monumental style of the Dublin Custom House and his other public buildings; begun *ca* 1790 for John Dawson, 1st Earl of Portarlington, a man of architectural interests who had been instrumental in bringing Gandon to Ireland; replacing an earlier house on a different site known as

Emo Court: Entrance Front

Emo Court: Garden Front

Emo Court: Rotunda

Mid-Victorian Emo: Lord Portarlington riding and Lady Portarlington in her carriage

Mid-Victorian Emo: Ante-Room (now Library)

Mid-Victorian Emo: Lady Portarlington in her Boudoir

Mid-Victorian Emo: Library (now Saloon)

Emo Court: Saloon (formerly Library)

Dawson's Court; the name Emo being an Italianised version of the original Irish name of the estate, Imoe. Described by Mr McParland as "Gandon's anti-Wyatt manifesto, rising in defiance of Wyatt's greatest Irish house, Castlecoole" (*qv*). Of 2 storeys over a basement, the sides of the house being surmounted by attics so as to form end towers or pavilions on each of the two principal fronts. The entrance front has a 7 bay centre with a giant pedimented Ionic portico; the end pavilions being of a single storey, with a pedimented window in an arched recess, beneath a blind attic with a panel containing a Coade stone relief of *putti*; on one side representing the Arts, on the other, a pastoral scene. The roof parapet in the centre, on either side of the portico, is balustraded. The side elevation, which is of 3 storeys including the attic, is of 1 bay on either side of a central curved bow. The house was not completed when 1st Earl died on campaign during 1798 rebellion; 2nd Earl, who was very short of money, did not do any more to it until 1834–36, when he employed the fashionable English architect, Lewis Vulliamy; who completed the garden front, giving it its portico of 4 giant Ionic columns with a straight balustraded entablature, and also worked on the interior; being assisted by Dublin architects named Williamson. It was not until *ca* 1860, in the time of 3rd Earl—after the house had come near to being sold up by the Encumbered Estates Court—that the great rotunda, its copper dome rising from behind the garden front portico and also prominent on the entrance front, was completed; the architect this time being William Caldbeck, of Dublin, who completed the other unfinished parts of the house and added a detached bachelor wing, joined to the main block by a curving corridor. Photographs taken only a few years after the house was completed show the rooms already thick with mid-Victorian clutter; while a few years later again, some of them were lined with wholly incongruous oak panelling; which was still there when the house was sold 1930 to the Society of Jesus, for use as a seminary. So it can in truth be said that Emo never really came into its own until *post* 1969, when it was bought from the Society of Jesus by its present owner, Mr C. D. Cholmeley-Harrison, who has restored and redecorated the house most sympathetically and has furnished it with great taste and splendour; his advisers in the work of restoration being the firm of Sir Albert Richardson & Partners. The single-storey apse-ended entrance hall has recently been most successfully painted in *trompe l'oeil* to represent the plaster decoration which Gandon intended for the room but which was never carried out. The entrance hall opens into the rotunda, a room of great magnificence, lit by a lantern in its high, coffered dome and surrounded by Corinthian pilasters in Siena with gilded capitals; its floor of richly inlaid parquetry. On one side of the rotunda is the dining room, with a ceiling of particularly handsome 1830s plasterwork by Vulliamy; on the other side is the library, formerly the ante-room, where the ceiling is covered with bold and sinuous C19 rococo decoration in dull gold and there is a stupendous white marble chimneypiece of the same period carved with *putti* and vines. Beyond the present library is the former library, now the saloon, which has the proportions of a long gallery, running from the front of the house to the back; divided by 2 screens of green marble Ionic columns with gilt capitals, and extending into a wide curved bow in the middle of one of its long sides. The present owner has also set to work restoring the garden and park, and is planting many new trees. He has carried out improvements to the lake and has brought the long Wellingtonia avenue, planted by 3rd Earl as the grand approach to the house, into use once again. In late C19, when there was the idea of acquiring an Irish residence for the Prince of Wales, afterwards Edward VII, Emo was one of the houses considered.

Emsworth, Malahide, co Dublin. The only one of James Gandon's villas to survive intact; built *ca* 1790 for J. Woodmason, a Dublin wholesale stationer. A pediment extends over the whole length of the 2 storey 3 bay centre, which is flanked by single-storey 1 bay overlapping wings. Fanlighted doorway under porch of engaged Doric columns and entablature; ground floor windows of centre, and windows of wings, set in arched recesses. Chimney-urns on wings. Now the home of Mr & Mrs John McGuire.

Enniscoe

Enniscoe, Crossmolina, co Mayo (JACKSON/LGI1912; PRATT, *sub* DE MONTMORENCY/IFR; NICHOLSON/IFR). A 2 storey house of *ca* 1790, built onto the front of an earlier 3 storey C18 house. 5 bay entrance front; central window flanked by sidelights above pedimented tripartite doorway with Doric columns and pilasters. 5 bay side elevation. Elegant late-Georgian interior plasterwork, which probably dates from *post* 1798 Rebellion, in which the house was damaged. Large entrance hall with frieze of foliage and Adamesque decoration in centre of ceiling. Oval staircase hall and staircase

Enniscoe: Landing at head of Stairs

behind entrance hall; stairs with balustrade of plain slender uprights; frieze of urns and foliage; glazed dome surrounded by foliage and oval medallions of Classical figures. Behind the staircase hall is a lobby with a delicate interior fanlight, opening onto the staircase of the earlier house; of good C18 joinery. Drawing room and dining room with friezes of sphinxes and foliage; drawing room hung with wallpaper of a faded salmon pink; the frieze being in pale blue and white. Library in older part of house, but extended; simple early C19 cornice of reeding and acanthus. Originally the seat of the Jacksons; passed to the Pratts through the marriage of Madeline Jackson to Mervyn Pratt, of Cabra Castle, co Cavan (*qv*), 1834. Inherited by Prof J.A. Nicholson from his cousin, Major Mervyn Pratt, 1950.

Enniscorthy Castle

Enniscorthy Castle, co Wexford (WALLOP, PORTSMOUTH, E/IFR). A C13 four-towered keep, like the ruined castles at Carlow and Ferns, restored at various dates

and rising above the surrounding roof-tops of the town of Enniscorthy like a little French *chateau-fort*, with its neat row of *tourelles*. Once the home of Edmund Spenser, the poet. Now a museum.

Enniskillen Castle, co Fermanagh (COLE, ENNISKILLEN, E/PB). A large and impressive fortress at one side of the island in the River Erne on which the town of Enniskillen is built; with walls enclosing a ward or courtyard, an inner keep and a tall and frowning water gate with two conical-roofed bartizans. Until C18 the castle stood on a small island of its own, separated from the rest of the island by a ditch of water crossed by a draw-bridge. The castle was originally built C15, by the Maguires; it was granted 1607 to Captain William (afterwards Sir William) Cole, who rebuilt the keep as a house for himself, and renovated all the fortifications; the water gate probably dates from his time. The Coles continued to live on and off at the castle until 1739; afterwards, they established themselves permanently at Florence Court (*qv*). The castle then became barracks, and the keep was rebuilt once again. The buildings remain in good repair.

Ennismore, Cork, co Cork (LEYCESTER/LGI1952). An early C19 single-storey "villa in the cottage style" with wrought-iron verandas; facing down the Lee estuary. Long and wide hall, running through the middle of the house; large and lofty reception rooms, which formerly contained a notable collection of pictures. Sold *ca* 1952; now owned by a religious order.

Ennistymon House

Ennistymon House, Ennistymon, co Clare (MACNAMARA/IFR). A 2 storey 7 bay gable-ended C18 house with a 2 bay return prolonged by a single-storey C19 wing ending in a gable. 1 bay pedimented breakfront with fanlighted tripartite doorway; lunette window in pediment. Some interior plasterwork, including a frieze incorporating an arm embowed brandishing a sword—the O'Brien crest—in the hall. Conservatory with art-nouveau metalwork; garden with flights of steps going down to river. The home of Francis Macnamara, a well-known bohemian character who was the father-in-law of Dylan Thomas and who married, as his 2nd wife, the sister of Augustus John's Dorelia; he and John are the *Two Flamboyant Fathers* in the book of that name by his daughter, Nicolette Shephard.

Erindale, Carlow, co Carlow (VIGORS/LGI1912; ALEXANDER/IFR). A remarkable 2 storey red-brick house of *ca* 1800, with a Gothic flavour and an ingenious plan made up of curved bows; so that one of the two bows on the entrance front serves as one of the end-bows of the adjoining elevation, which itself has a single centre bow. The windows in the entrance front are pointed; 1st floor centre window, and also 2 centre ground-floor windows of the bows, being Venetian windows made Gothic. There is a very large semi-circular fanlight extending over the door and side-lights, with elaborate fancy glazing which Dr Craig considers to be original. Wide eaved roof.

Errew Grange, Crossmolina, co Mayo (KNOX/IFR). A large plain Victorian Gothic house on a peninsula jutting out into Lough Conn; rather similar to Mount Falcon (*qv*), and, like it, probably by James Franklin Fuller; built *ca* 1870s. Became an hotel and gutted by fire 1930s; recently half rebuilt, also as an hotel.

Esker House, Lucan, co Dublin. A 2 storey Georgian house with a 5 bay centre and a 2 sided bow at either side; the bows being of the same height as the centre, but with their upper storey windows close to the cornice so as to make the ground floor rooms higher. Small porch. In recent years the home of Miss J. E. Bellaney.

Everton House, Crockaun, co Leix. A 2 storey C18 house with a front consisting of 2 deep curved bows separated by 1 bay with a fanlighted doorway; with an additional bay to the left of the left-hand bow and a curved end-bow. Later 2 storey wing prolonging the front to the right of the right-hand bow. In 1814, the residence of Rev Dr Thomas.

Evington House, Carlow, co Carlow. A 2 storey 3 bay late-Georgian house with an eaved roof. Doorway with large fanlight extending over door and sidelights.

Eyrecourt Castle, Eyrecourt, co Galway (EYRE/IFR). One of the only 2 important mid-C17 Irish country houses to survive intact into the present century, the other being Beaulieu, co Louth (*qv*). Built 1660s; of brick faced with rendered rubble. Of 2 storeys, with a dormered attic in the high, wide-eaved sprocketed roof; 7 bay entrance front, with 3 bay pedimented breakfront centre; 6 bay side. Massive wooden modillion cornice. Splendid if somewhat bucolic doorcase of wood, with Corinthian pilasters,

Eyrecourt Castle: Meet of East Galway Hunt ante *1914*

Eyrecourt Castle

an over-wide entablature, carved scrolls, a mask and an elliptical light over the door surrounded by a frame of foliage. Windows with C18 Gothic glazing. Richly decorated interior. Hall divided by screen of arches and primitive wooden Corinthian columns from vast and magnificent carved oak staircase with two lower ramps and a single central return leading up to a landing with elaborately moulded panelling and a plasterwork ceiling. The stairs and gallery have cut-through scroll balustrades, exuberantly carved with acanthus, and crowned with numerous carved flower-filled urns. This is the only surviving Irish example of a type of staircase found in many C17 English houses; the only other one which existed in Ireland this century, at Desart Court, co

Eyrecourt Castle: Staircase

Kilkenny (*qv*), having been burnt. Alas, the Eyrecourt staircase is no longer in Ireland, but in store at Detroit Institute of Arts, having been removed there after the house was left to decay from 1920 onwards; since when it has fallen into total ruin.

F

Factory Hill, Glanmire, co Cork (HOARE, Bt, *of Annabella*/PB; DRING/IFR). A small Georgian house in the Palladian manner, consisting of a centre block joined to tiny pavilions by curved sweeps; and with the farmyard at the back. A seat of the Hoare family; bought *ca* 1954 by Mr John Dring, who sold it some years later.

Fahagh Court, Beaufort, co Kerry (MORROGH-BERNARD/IFR). An irregular 2 storey house with a shallow battlemented bow and a rusticated doorcase of sandstone on its front, and a gable at the back. Now an hotel.

Fairfield House, co Galway (*see* CARROW-MORE).

Fairy Hill, Mallow, co Cork (SARSFIELD/LGI1958). A late-Georgian house of 1 storey over a basement. Irregular facade with bow and Wyatt window.

Fairy Hill, Borrisokane, co Tipperary. A 2 storey 3 bay C18 house with a pediment and a fanlighted doorway with sidelights and blocking. In 1837 the seat of W.H. Cox.

Faithlegg House

At Faithlegg House

Faithlegg House, Waterford, co Waterford (POWER/IFR; GALLWEY/IFR). A 3 storey 7 bay block with a 3 bay pedimented breakfront, built 1783 by Cornelius Bolton, MP, whose arms, elaborately displayed, appear in the pediment; bought 1819 by the Powers who *ca* 1870 added 2 storey 2 bay wings with single-storey bow-fronted wings beyond them. At the same time the house was entirely refaced, with segmental hoods over the ground floor windows; a portico or porch with slightly rusticated square piers was added, as well as an orangery prolonging one of the single-storey wings. Good C19 neo-Classical ceilings in the principal rooms of the main block, and some C18 friezes upstairs. Sold 1936 by Mrs H. W. D. Gallwey (*née* Power); now a college for boys run by the De La Salle Brothers.

Falmore Hall, Dundalk, co Louth (BIGGER, *sub* HAMILTON/IFR; WINDHAM-DAWSON, *sub* DARTREY, E/PB1933). A 2 storey Georgian house of 5 bays, with an eaved roof and a bow on one front. The seat of the Bigger family; more recently, of Mr Richard Windham, son of Lady Edith Windham-Dawson.

Fanningstown Castle

Fanningstown Castle, Croom, co Limerick (JACKSON/LG1863). A C19 castle by P. Nagle of Cork, consisting of a 2 storey battlemented range with a square tower at one end, and a smaller tower at the other; standing in a corner of the bawn of an old medieval castle.

Farmleigh

Farmleigh, Castleknock, co Dublin (TRENCH, *sub* ASHTOWN, B/PB; GUINNESS, IVEAGH, E/PB). A 3 storey Victorian-Georgian mansion of Portland stone, built 1881 for Edward Guinness, afterwards 1st Earl of Iveagh; incorporating an earlier house, which belonged, in 1st half of C19, to Charles Trench. Entrance front with pedimented breakfront between 2 3 sided bows and with deep single-storey balustraded porte-cochère; the facade being prolonged by a 3 storey wing with a 3rd bow, added *ca* 1900. Balustraded roof parapet; triangular and segmental pediments over ground floor windows. Garden front with 3 sided bow at one end. Hall with rather Byzantine Corinthian columns and staircase with balustrade of elaborate gilded metalwork. Oak-panelled dining room in late C17 style, with carving in the manner of Grinling Gibbons. Drawing room in 2 sections, one with a curved and rather Soanian ceiling with delicate plasterwork. Adam-Revival ballroom in *ca* 1900 wing. Magnificent 2 storey library with oak panelling and bookcases rising from the floor to the wooden coffered ceiling; and with a gallery of light gilded metalwork. Victorian billiard room hung with the original faded red printed linen, similar to that in one of the bedrooms, where it is most effective with the grained woodwork. Panelled study in Austrian style. In 1975, the present Earl of Iveagh lent Farmleigh for an important meeting of the EEC Foreign Ministers.

Farney Castle, Thurles, co Tipperary (HEATON-ARMSTRONG/IFR). An old tower with a later 2 storey battlemented wing on a high basement, and an octagon turret at the opposite end. Battlemented terrace in front of entrance door, with steps leading up to it. Rectangular tracery windows under hood mouldings.

Farnham, Cavan, co Cavan (MAXWELL, FARNHAM, B/PB). The estate here was granted by James I to the Waldrons; Henry Waldron, later in C17, followed the popular custom of naming it after his wife; but instead of giving it a name incorporating her Christian name, he gave it her maiden name, which was Farnham. A few years later the estate was sold to Robert Maxwell, Bishop of Kilmore, whose cathedral was nearby. The Bishop's son, John Maxwell, built a new house here *ca* 1700, which was improved *ca* 1780 by Barry Maxwell, 3rd Lord Farnham and 1st Earl of Farnham of 2nd creation, who added a library designed by James Wyatt. From 1802 onwards, 2nd Earl employed Francis Johnston to rebuild the house. Johnston produced a house consisting of 2 somewhat conservative 3 storey ranges at right angles to one another; one of them, which incorporated part of the earlier

Farnham

Farnham: Staircase

house, including Wyatt's library, having a front of 8 bays, with a die over a 2 bay breakfront, and a single-storey Doric portico; the other having a front of 9 bays with a 3 bay pedimented breakfront; prolonged by 1 bay in the end of the adjoining range. The interior was spacious but restrained, the principal rooms having simple ovolo or dentil cornices. Elliptical staircase hall, with simple geometrical design in the ceiling; stone stair with elegant metal balustrade. In 1839, 7th Lord Farnham (a distinguished scholar and genealogist who, with his wife, was burnt to death 1868 when the Irish mail train caught fire at Abergele, North Wales) enlarged the house by building new offices in the re-entrant between the two ranges. Also probably at this time the main rooms were changed around; the library becoming the dining room, and losing any Wyatt decoration it may have had; Wyatt's bookcases being moved to the former drawing room. *Ca* 1960, the present Lord Farnham, finding the house to be badly infested with dry-rot, demolished the range where the entrance had formerly been situated, as well as the additions of 1839; and remodelled the surviving Johnston range to form a house in itself; being assisted in the work by Mr Philip Cullivan. The pedimented front is still the garden front, as it was formerly; the back of the range being now the entrance front, with the portico re-erected at one end of it; so that the entrance is directly into the staircase hall. The surviving range contains Johnston's dining room, which has been the drawing room since C19 rearrangement; as well as the boudoir and the former study, now the dining room. One of Wyatt's bookcases is

now in the alcove of the former staircase window. The demesne of Farnham has long been famous for its beauty; a landscape of woods, distant mountain views and lakes, which are part of the great network of loughs and islands stretching southwards from Upper Lough Erne.

Farragh

Farragh

Farragh (also known as **Farraghroe**), **Longford, co Longford** (BOND/LGI1958). A somewhat composite house, originally a shooting-box but greatly enlarged by Willoughby Bond between 1811 and 1833, his architect being John Hargrave, of Cork. Subsequent additions were made in the Victorian period. Entrance front of 3 storeys and 5 bays, with Wyatt windows in centre above pillared porch. Side elevation of 2 storeys and 3 bays framed by giant plain pilasters; round-headed windows in arched recesses in upper storey of outer bays; 2 windows in middle above a single-storey Victorian bowed and balustraded projection. Other elevation of 3 storeys and 4 bays with a pediment extending over its whole length. Large 2 storey central hall with gallery and bifurcating staircase, top-lit through skylight with stained glass incorporating the family motto, "*Deus providebit*", which had been set by mistake the wrong way round, so that from below the letters read back to front; people said that this had been done intentionally, so that the

Almighty, looking down from above, would be able to read the motto and thus be reminded of His obligations. Farragh was sold *ca* 1960 by Mr B. W. Bond; it was subsequently demolished.

Farran, Coachford, co Cork (CLARKE/IFR). A somewhat rambling stucco-faced Victorian Italianate house of 2 storeys over a basement; consisting of a 3 bay front with a projecting porch, 1 bay wings with triple windows set back and another 1 bay wing further back again with a 3 sided end bow. Modillion cornice extending round all the elevations; pediments on console brackets over the principal windows.

Faughart, Dundalk, co Louth (MAC NEALE/LGI1912; and *sub* MCNEILE/LGI1972). A 2 storey gable-ended house of *ca* 1770. 5 bay front, pedimented Doric doorcase.

Favour Royal, Aughnacloy, co Tyrone (MOUTRAY/LGI1912). A somewhat austere Tudor-Gothic house of 1825, said to be by an architect named William Warren; built for John Corry Moutray to replace a house of 1670 destroyed by fire 1823. 2 storey with attic of rather low-pitched gables in front; 3 storey at the back. The front of the house has large rectangular windows with elaborate Gothic tracery and hood mouldings over them. Now owned by the Forestry Commission.

Fellows Hall, Killylea, co Armagh (MAXWELL, *sub* FARNHAM, B/PB; ARMSTRONG/ IFR; STRONGE, Bt/PB; MCCLINTOCK/IFR). A Victorian Italianate rebuilding of a house of 1762, itself a rebuilding of a C17 house burnt 1752. 2 storeys over basement; 5 bay front, round-headed windows with keystones in upper storey, rectangular windows with entablatures on console brackets above them in lower storey. Tripartite doorway with triple window above it. Roof on bracket cornice. Passed through marriage from the Maxwell family to the Armstrong and Stronge families, and then to the McClintock family.

Fellsfort, co Cork (*see* MITCHELLSFORT).

Fenagh House, Bagenalstown, co Carlow (PACK-BERESFORD/IFR). A plain and austere C19 house of stone. Irregular in plan, and extensive; but with a symmetrical entrance front of 3 bays, the centre bay being recessed with a pillared porch.

Fenaghy House, Galgorm, co Antrim. A 2 storey, 5 bay gable-ended C18 house, refaced as a stucco Italianate villa in mid-C19. Entablatures on console brackets over ground floor windows; 2 storey projecting porch with a Corinthian column on either side of the entrance doorway; pierced roof balustrade. Conservatory at end of house, of pretty ironwork. Good interior plasterwork.

Fennypark, co Kilkenny. A Georgian house consisting of a 2 storey 3 bay centre with Wyatt windows and a pedimented pillared porch, joined to 1 storey 1 bay pedimented wings by links with iron verandas. The home of Major Keating.

Fermoy House, Fermoy, co Cork (ANDERSON, Bt, *of Fermoy*/PB1861; COOKE-COLLIS/IFR). A house of *ca* 1790, consisting of a centre block and wings. The seat of John Anderson, the enterprising Army contractor who laid out the town of Fermoy. Later a seat of the Cooke-Collis family. Now demolished.

Ferns Palace, Ferns, co Wexford. The Palace of the (C of I) Bishops of Ferns and Leighlin until 1836, when 2 Dioceses were joined to that of Ossory. Begun 1785 by Bishop Walter Cope (*see* LG1937Supp), who died 1787; finished by his successor Bishop William Preston. A large square stone house; late-Georgian staircase in side hall rising to the top storey. The Palace was plundered and severely damaged during 1798 Rebellion. In 1834, Bishop Thomas Elrington carried out various additions to the design of Thomas Alfred Cobden; they presumably included the porch, with its 4 Doric pilasters.

Ferrans, co Meath (BOMFORD/IFR). A 2 storey 5 bay late-Georgian house with an eaved roof. Sold *ca* 1970; burnt 1972, subsequently rebuilt for institutional use.

Ferry Quarter, Strangford, co Down (COOKE/IFR). A large stucco early-Victorian house, overlooking the entrance to Strangford Lough.

ffranckfort Castle, Dunkerrin, Offaly (ROLLESTON/IFR). A Georgian castellated house, with a battlemented parapet, pointed windows and a turret, incorporating part of a medieval castle and surrounded by the original fosse and a fortified wall of predominantly late C18 or early C19 appearance, with twin Gothic gateways opening into a forecourt in front of the house. Originally the seat of the ffrancks; passed to the Rollestons through the marriage of the adopted daughter of Capt James ffranck to Francis Rolleston 1740. Now demolished, except for some of the walls and moat.

Fields of Odin, co Dublin (*see* HERMITAGE).

Finnebrogue

Finnebrogue, Downpatrick, co Down (PERCEVAL-MAXWELL/IFR). A fine late C17 house, built on an "H"-plan: a central range with wings projecting at the front and back. Of 2 storeys over a basement, with an attic storey in the side and rear elevations. Entrance front of 5 bays, with 2 additional bays in the end of each wing. The upper storey of the central range is treated as a *piano nobile*, with higher windows than those below. The house was altered and brought up-to-date at end of C18 by Dorothea, Mrs Waring-Maxwell, sister and heiress of

Finnebrogue

Edward Maxwell, of Finnebrogue, having stood empty for some 25 years. The original high-pitched roof was replaced by a roof that was lower, though still high by late C18 standards; late-Georgian sash windows were inserted, and some of 1st floor rooms were given high coffered ceilings similar to those of the Down Hunt Rooms in Downpatrick, which date from the same period. Some of the internal partition walls are of turf (peat), as in certain other Irish houses.

Finnstown

Finnstown, Lucan, co Dublin (NASH/IFR). A Victorian house of 2 storeys over a basement. Symmetrical pedimented front; single-storey portico with clusters of columns. Windows with cambered heads and keystones.

Florence Court: Staircase

Finvoy Lodge, Ballymoney, co Antrim. 2 storey gable-ended Georgian house; 3 bay front; later projecting porch; 3 bay return.

Fisherwick Lodge, Ballyclare, co Antrim (CHICHESTER, DONEGALL, M/PB). A hunting lodge of the Marquesses of Donegall; rebuilt *ca* 1805 as a hollow square with two single-storey fronts of 9 bays each. Tall windows, reaching almost to the ground; pedimented wooden doorcase, with fluted columns.

Fishmoyne, nr Templemore, co Tipperary (CARDEN/IFR). The seat of the junior branch of the Cardens; a 3 storey C19 block, built to replace an earlier house destroyed by fire. Pedimented entrance door in 3 sided bow in middle of front, 2 bays on either side. Entablatures over ground floor and first floor windows; eaved roof. Octagonal hall. Sold by Major R. H. L. Carden 1955.

Flesk Castle, co Kerry (*see* GLENFLESK CASTLE).

Flood Hall, Thomastown, co Kilkenny (SOLLY-FLOOD/LGI1912; HANFORD-FLOOD/LGI1912). A 2 storey Georgian house with C19 Gothic embellishments. Front with pediment flanked by small crockets; single-storey three-sided bow below. Hood mouldings. Irregular C19 end. The home of Henry Flood, the great C18 statesman and Irish patriot. Demolished 1950.

Florence Court, Enniskillen, co Fermanagh (COLE, ENNISKILLEN, E/PB). A tall, early to mid-C18 block of 3 storeys over a basement and 7 bays, its front heavily enriched with rustications, balustrades, pedimented niches and other features; joined by long arcades with rusticated pilasters to pedimented and pilastered single-storey pavilions. The centre block was probably built by John Cole, MP, afterwards 1st Lord Mountflorence, whose mother was the Florence after whom the house is named; the name was probably originally given to a shooting-box built here in the days when the family lived at Enniskillen Castle (*qv*). The arcades and pavilions seem to date from *ca* 1770, and would have been added by William Cole, 1st Earl of Enniskillen; they were possibly designed by Davis Duckart. They blend perfectly with the centre block, and the whole long, golden-grey front has a dream-like Baroque beauty that is all the greater for being somewhat bucolic. The centre block has a 3 bay breakfront with a central pedimented niche between 2 win-

Florence Court

Florence Court: Dining Room

dows in the top storey, a Venetian window between 2 niches in the storey below, and a pedimented tripartite doorway on the ground floor. The rear elevation has a central 3 sided bow with rusticated window surrounds; but there is nothing like the lavish ornament here that there is on the front. Curved sweeps join the back of the house to outbuildings. The interior contains some wonderfully vigorous rococo plasterwork, in the manner of Robert West and apparently dating from 1755. In the hall, which is divided from the staircase by an arch, the decoration is architectural, reflecting the outside, with banded pilasters and a Doric frieze. Through the arch and up the staircase of splendid joinery with its handrail of tulip wood, the plasterwork becomes more rococo: great panels of foliage on the walls, and a cornice of pendants and acanthus. From the half landing one gets a view downwards to the hall and upwards through 2 arches at the top of the stairs to the Venetian Room, lit by the great Venetian window, which has what is probably the finest ceiling in the house; with a swirl of foliage and eagles and other birds of prey in high relief. The drawing room, to the right of the foot of the staircase, has a cornice of acanthus foliage, masks of "Tragedy" and "Comedy", baskets of fruit and birds. The ceiling of the dining room, on the other side of the staircase hall, is more elaborate, with foliage and birds and a central panel of cherubs puffing from clouds. There was formerly a delightful ceiling in the nursery on the top floor, with drums, rocking horses and other toys incorporated in the ornament. The park, which is dramatically overshadowed by the sombre mountains of Benknocklan and Cuilcagh, contains the original Irish or Florence Court yew. The 5th Earl and his son, the late Viscount Cole, gave Florence Court to the Northern Ireland National Trust 1953. 2 years later, the centre of the house was severely damaged by fire; fortunately the staircase and much of the plasterwork was saved, and most of what was lost was restored under the direction of the late Sir Albert Richardson. No photographic record existed of the nursery ceiling, which was among those destroyed; so this was not reinstated. Florence Court is open to the public.

Forenaghts, Naas, co Kildare (WOLFE/IFR). A 3 storey early or mid-C18 house, probably originally of 5 bays but subsequently extended to form a 3 storey front of 7 bays, with an addition of *ca* 1831 which is of 2 storeys on the entrance front and a single high storey on the garden front. Also in the C19 the house was given an eaved roof on a bracket cornice and a single-storey Doric portico; and it was refaced in stucco. The garden front is of 6 bays, with a 2 bay projection at one end; C19 wing on this side has a curved bow. Low-ceilinged rooms in the main block; hall with slightly curving staircase at back, enlarged early C20 by taking in the adjoining room to the left, which in turn has been opened, with arches on either side of its fireplace, into the library beyond, which has bookcases incorporated in its panelling. Beautiful early C19 drawing room in the garden front of the wing, with a curved bow and a high coved ceiling decorated with elaborate C19 plasterwork. This room was probably made—and the wing added—by Rev Richard Wolfe, for his fashionable wife, who was Lady Charlotte Hely-Hutchinson, sister of 2nd Earl of Donoughmore.

Fort Etna, Patrickswell, co Limerick (PEACOCKE/LGI1912; REILLY, *sub* SIMONDS-GOODING and PEART/LGI1958). A 2 storey 5 bay C18 house with a Venetian window and a pedimented and shouldered doorcase. 5 bay side. Gable-ended farm buildings treated as wings. The seat of the Peacocke family; afterwards of the Reilly family.

Fortfergus (also known as **Mountfergus**), **Killadysert, co Clare** (ROSS-LEWIN/LGI1912; STACPOOLE/IFR). A long, irregular house of vaguely Georgian appearance, incorporating, or on the site of, a house built by Capt George Ross 1688. Passed by descent to Ross-Lewins; transferred by W. G. Ross-Lewin to his uncle, John Stacpoole, 1800. Sold under Encumbered Estates Act 1855 to Major William Hawkins Ball. Burnt 1922.

Fortfield, Terenure, co Dublin (YELVERTON, AVONMORE, V/PB1910). A 3 storey house built *ca* 1785 for Chief Baron Yelverton, afterwards 1st Viscount Avonmore. 7 bay front; central Venetian window above single-storey portico and with 3 oculi in the centre of the top storey. Very wide staircase.

Fort Frederic, Virginia, co Cavan (SANKEY/LGI1912). A 2 storey mid-C18 house with a central 3 sided bow and 2 bays on either side of it. Georgian Gothic doorcase. Single-storey wings, one of them with 2 bows in its end wall.

Fortgranite, Baltinglass, co Wicklow (DENNIS/IFR). A house of *ca* 1730 built by George Pendred, of Saunders Grove (*qv*)—whose son assumed the name of Saunders—which came to T. S. Dennis through his marriage to Katherine Saunders 1810; he remodelled it 1810–15, so that it is now

Fortgranite

predominantly late-Georgian in character. 2 storey; entrance front with recessed centre and single storey Doric portico; adjoining front is 5 bay with 2 single-storey 3 sided bows. Parapeted roof. The house was modernized 1870–71 by M. C. Dennis. The grounds contain a notable arboretum, planted *ca* 1820.

Fortland, Easkey, co Sligo (BRINKLEY/LGI1912). A Georgian house. Tripartite doorway with rusticated piers and pediment extending over door and sidelights.

Fort Robert

Fort Robert, Ballineen, co Cork (CONNER/IFR). A late C18 weather-slated house of 2 storeys over a high basement, built by R. L. Conner 1788. 8 bay front, with wide fanlighted doorway. 3 bay side. Empty and decayed by 1854; ruinous by end of C19.

Fort Stewart, Ramelton, co Donegal (STEWART, Bt, *of Ramelton*/PB). A 3 storey double gable-ended C18 house. 7 bay entrance front, with single-storey, 2 bay wings. C19 pilastered porch with door at side. Entrance hall with 4 engaged Tuscan columns and shallow rib-vaulting rising from them. Early C19 decoration in reception rooms.

Fort William, Doneraile, co Cork (*see* KILMACOOM).

Fort William, Tivoli, co Cork (BAKER/IFR). A late-Georgian house consisting of a 2 storey 5 bay centre block with single-storey bow-ended wings. Now part of the Silver Springs Hotel.

Fortwilliam, Ballinasloe, co Galway (D'ARCY/IFR). A small Georgian house with Victorian additions.

Fort William, Lismore, co Waterford (GUMBLETON, *sub* MAXWELL-GUMBLETON/LGI1952; GROSVENOR, WESTMINSTER, D/PB). A 2 storey house of sandstone ashlar with a few slight Tudor-Revival touches, built 1836 for J. B. Gumbleton to the design of

Fota Island: Entrance Front

Fota Island: Garden Front

James & George Richard Pain. 3 bay front with 3 small gables and a slender turret-pinnacle at either side; doorway recessed in segmental-pointed arch. Georgian-glazed rectangular sash windows with hood mouldings. Tudor chimneys. Other front of 7 bays; plain 3 bay side elevation. Large hall; drawing room with walls decorated in Louis XV style. From *ca* 1946 until his death 1953, the Irish home of 2nd Duke of Westminster. Afterwards the home of Mr & Mrs Henry Drummond-Wolff; then of Mr & Mrs Murray Mitchell.

Fosterstown, Trim, co Meath (CHAMBERS/LG1937Supp). A 2 storey 3 bay gable-ended late C18 house. The residence of the great Duke of Wellington when (as Hon Arthur Wellesley), he was Member for Trim in the Irish Parliament.

Fota Island, Carrigtwohill, co Cork (SMITH-BARRY (*now* VILLIERS)/IFR). After Barry's Court (*qv*) had been abandoned by the Barrymores, a hunting box was built on the nearby Fota Island, in Cork Harbour, by Hon John Smith-Barry, a younger son of 4th Earl of Barrymore, to whom Fota and some of the other Barrymore estates were given 1714. This house, of 3 storeys and 7 bays, was greatly enlarged *ca* 1820 by John Smith-Barry to the design of Sir Richard Morrison, so that it became a wide-spreading Regency mansion of stucco with stone dressings. The original house, given a single-storey Doric portico with fluted columns and acroteria beneath a pedimented Wyatt window, remained the centre of the composition; flanked by 2 storey projecting wings with pedimented ends on the entrance front and curved bows on the garden front. A long 2 storey service range was added at one side. In 1856, a billiard room wing, in the same style as the Morrison wings but of 1 storey only, was added on the entrance front, projecting from the end of the service range. The space between this and the main building was filled in *ca* 1900 by Arthur Smith-Barry, 1st (and last) Lord Barrymore of a new creation, with a single-storey range containing a long gallery. The exterior simplicity of Fota is a foil to the splendours within; for the interior has that richness which Sir Richard Morrison and his son, William Vitruvius, were so well able to create. The hall, which runs the entire length of the front of the original house, is divided by screens of paired Ionic columns in yellow scagliola. A doorway opposite the entrance door leads into the staircase hall, which is of modest size, being

Fota Island: Hall

Fota Island: Staircase

Fota Island: Drawing Room

Fota Island: Dining Room

Fota Island: Library

the staircase hall of the original house; but it has been greatly enriched with plasterwork. The ceiling is domed, with wreaths on the pendentives and eagles in the lunettes; there is a frieze of wreaths and at the head of the stairs 2 fluted Tower of Winds columns frame an enchanting vista to a 2nd and smaller staircase, leading up to the top storey. There are elaborate plasterwork ceilings in the library and dining room, which are in the Morrison wings, at either end of the hall; the dining room has a screen of grey marble Corinthian columns. The ceiling of the drawing room, which extends into one of the bows on the garden front, has a surround of foliage, birds and trophies in high relief, similar to that in the library, and late C19 stencilled decoration and panels of pictorial paper in the centre. The Edwardian long gallery has a ribbed ceiling with a modillion cornice and an ingle-nook fireplace flanked by mahogany Ionic columns; the walls are lined with mahogany bookcases, which formerly contained books of Irish interest. Until recently, the house contained a magnificent collection of pictures. In mid-C19, J. H. Smith-Barry laid out formal gardens behind the house, with lawns and hedges, wrought-iron gates and

rusticated piers, a temple and an orangery. He also began to plant the arboretum, which has since become world-famous. The planting was continued for more than a century after his death by his son, Lord Barrymore, and by Lord Barrymore's son-in-law and daughter, Major & Hon Mrs Bell; in the mild climate of Fota many rare and tender species flourish. The demesne of Fota extends over the entire island, which is skirted by the road and railway from Cork to Cobh; there are impressive Classical entrance gates by Morrison similar to those at Ballyfin, co Leix and Kilruddery, co Wicklow (*qqv*). On the point of the island is an early C19 castelated turret, by John Hargrave, of Cork. Fota was sold 1975 to University College, Cork.

Fota Island: Turret

Fountainstown House, Crosshaven, co Cork (HODDER/IFR). A 3 storey double gable-ended early C18 house built by Samuel Hodder.

Fox Hall, Letterkenny, co Donegal (CHAMBERS/LG1863). A stucco-faced house of mid-C19 appearance, but in a straight-forward late-Georgian manner, with large rectangular windows and astragals. Of 2 storeys over a basement. Projecting porch, with 2 ball finials, not centrally placed; roof on plain cornice.

Foyle Park House

Foyle Park House, Eglinton, co Derry (DAVIDSON/IFR). A plain 2 storey irregular late-Georgian house, built *ca* 1820 and opened 1827 as the North West of Ireland Society's Literary & Agricultural Seminary and School of Classics. Came to the David-son family by marriage later in C19; sold 1920 by James Davidson to Mr H. White-side, who sold it back to Lt-Col K. B. L. Davidson, of The Manor House, Eglinton (*qv*), 1968.

Frankville House, Athboy, co Meath. A 2 storey house of late-Georgian appearance. 3 bay front, with Wyatt windows and an enclosed porch with a die. 4 bay side, with 2 Wyatt windows in the lower storey, not related to the windows above. The seat of the Welsh family.

Frascati, Blackrock, co Dublin (FITZ-GERALD, LEINSTER, D/PB). The seaside house of the Leinsters in C18, where Emily, Duchess of Leinster, lived during her widowhood and where her son, the United Irish leader, Lord Edward FitzGerald, spent much of his youth. A long, plain 2 storey C18 house, with a pedimented door-way between 2 3 sided bows. Drawing room with ceiling by Thomas Riley, who decor-

Fox Hall

ated the gallery at Castletown, co Kildare (*qv*) for Emily Duchess's sister, Lady Louisa Conolly. Now derelict.

Frankville House

French Park, co Roscommon (DE FREYNE, B/PB). An early Palladian winged house of red brick; probably built 1729 by John French to the design of Richard Castle. 3 storey 7 bay centre block, 3 bay pedimented breakfront with lunette window in pediment; late-Georgian pillared porch. 2 storey wings 5 bays long and 4 deep joined to main block by curved sweeps as high as they are themselves; the curved sweeps having 3 windows in their upper storey and a door flanked by 2 windows below. 2 storey panelled hall; stairs with slender turned balusters ascending round it to gallery; panelling with bolection mouldings; walnut graining. Dining room originally hung with embossed leather which was later replaced with wallpaper; C19 plasterwork cornice and rosette and circle in centre of ceiling. Draw-

ing room on 1st floor above dining room, with a Bossi chimneypiece at one end and a late C18 Ionic chimneypiece at the other; good compartmented plasterwork ceiling executed for Arthur French, 4th Lord De Freyne, late C19. Fine C18 wrought-iron entrance gates. Now a roofless ruin, having been sold by 7th and present Lord De Freyne 1953 and afterwards demolished.

French Park: Hall

French Park: Dining Room

French Park

Fruit Hill, co Derry (*see* DRENAGH).

Frybrook, Boyle, co Roscommon (FRY/IFR). A 3 storey 5 bay mid-C18 house. Oculus in centre of top storey, above Venetian window, above tripartite doorcase with large pediment extending over door and flanking windows.

French Park: Hall and Staircase

French Park: Drawing Room

Frybrook

Furness, Naas, co Kildare (NEVILL, *sub* NEVILLE/IFR; DERING, Bt/PB; BEAUMAN/LG1886; SYNNOTT/IFR). A house built originally *ca* 1740 for Richard Nevill, and attributed by the Knight of Glin to Francis Bindon; consisting of a 3 storey centre block joined by single-storey links to 2 storey projecting wings of the same height as the links; the elevation being further prolonged by quadrants joining the wings to office ranges; so that it extends to a total length of 400 feet. The centre block has a 3 bay ashlar-faced entrance front, with a lunette window above a window framed by an aedicule on console brackets consisting of 2 engaged Ionic columns and a pediment; above a frontispiece of coupled Doric columns and a Doric entablature framing the entrance doorway. There is an almost identical elevation at Clermont, co Wicklow (*qv*). The garden front of the centre block is of 5 bays, with blocking round the ground floor windows. From *ca* 1780 onwards, Richard Nevill, MP, great-nephew of the builder of the house, carried out various additions and alterations; chief of which was the raising of the left-hand link, so that it became a 2 storey wing with a curved bow on the garden front. The whole of the centre block, on the entrance front, is taken up with a hall, consisting of 2 sections opening into each other with an arch; they were originally separate, but the Doric frieze is probably contemporary with the building of the house, as is the handsome staircase of Spanish chestnut, which rises on one side of the arch; though there are indications that it has been remodelled On the frieze of

Furness: Entrance Front

Furness: Garden Front

the staircase and gallery is a Vitruvian scroll decoration. The drawing room has a ceiling, probably by Michael Stapleton, of delicate late C18 plasterwork with a medallion of Minerva attended by a kneeling hero. The dining room, in the wing, is a large simple room with a curved bow. Richard Nevill, MP, also landscaped the grounds. At his death 1822, Furness passed to his daughter and heiress, the wife of Edward Dering. Later it was sold to the Beauman family. In 1897, by which time it had become very dilapidated, it was bought by N. J. Synnott, who carried out a thorough—and for those days, remarkably sympathetic—restoration. The vista from the entrance front of the house is now terminated by a column formerly at Dangan, co Meath (*qv*), the boyhood home of the great Duke of Wellington. It was brought here and erected 1962, as a 21st birthday present to Mr David Synnott from his father.

L

G

Galgorm Castle (formerly **Mount Colville**), **Ballymena, co Antrim** (MOORE, *sub* PERCEVAL-MAXWELL/IFR; HUGHES-YOUNG, ST HELENS, B/PB; CHICHESTER, *sub* O'NEILL, B/PB). A 3 storey C17 house, in a fortified enclosure or bawn, built *ca* 1645 by Rev Dr Alexander Colville. When Mrs Delany visited Galgorm 1758, the rooms still had their original oak panelling, which has since disappeared; though there is still an early oak stair with turned balusters and large round heads on the newels. Passed by inheritance to the Earls Mount Cashell; 3rd Earl altered and modernized the castle *ca* 1830, and more work was done subsequently. These alterations gave the castle regular fenestration, with sash windows in brick surrounds; as well as a roofline of curved battlements, with a curvilinear "Dutch" gable as the central feature of the 5 bay entrance front; similar gables being added on the side elevations. The gable surmounting the entrance front was repeated on a projecting porch, which was given a Renaissance doorcase by Sir Charles Lanyon, who also designed the doorcases inside the castle and the dining room fireplace. Sold 1851, through the Encumbered Estates Court, to Dr William Young; passed eventually to Mrs Arthur Chichester, daughter of Rt Hon W. R. Young.

Gallen Priory, Ferbane, Offaly (ARMSTRONG, Bt/PB). A 2 storey 7 bay C18 house with simple pinnacles, a central gable, a corbelled oriel and other C19 Gothic touches; standing near the site of an old monastery. Now a convent; new buildings have been added to the house as well as a large modern open porch.

Galtee Castle, Clogheen, co Tipperary. A Victorian-Baronial castle with a conical-roofed turret. Built by Abel Buckley, MP, of Ryecroft Hall, near Manchester. Demolished *ca* 1940.

Galgorm Castle

Gallen Priory

Galtrim House, Summerhill, co Meath (DAWSON, *sub* DARTREY, E/PB1933; THE FOX/IFR; EUSTACE/IFR; CONYNGHAM, M/PB). The finest of Francis Johnston's smaller houses, built *ca* 1802 as a glebe house for Very Rev Thomas Vesey Dawson. 2 storey centre block of 4 bays on entrance front, with single-storey 1 bay wings prolonged by

small quadrant-walls. Breakfront centre with 2 windows above and a door flanked by two windows below; the door and flanking windows being framed by engaged fluted Doric columns and an entablature. Ground floor windows in outer bays of centre block, and in wings, set in wide arched recesses. Roof parapet with central die. Garden front with curved central bow and 1 bay on either side of it; Wyatt windows in lower storey of outer bays. An interior of great subtlety, many of the rooms having curved ends and apsidal recesses. In the words of Dr Craig: "The decoration, in which much elegant play is made with almost imperceptibly recessed planes . . . is of the coolest kind imaginable". A new glebe house was built 1815, and Galtrim House became the seat of The Fox. In recent years it was owned by Mr J. F. F. Eustace, who sold it to Eileen, Countess of Mount Charles 1969.

Gambonstown, co Tipperary (*see* LAKEFIELD).

Garadice, Ballinamore, co Leitrim. A 2 storey late C17 or early C18 "U"-shaped house, consisting of a 3 bay centre, with short gable-ended wings projecting forwards. Hall with heavy cornice. The seat of the Percy family. One wing has been demolished.

Garbally Court: Amateur Theatrical Company (1865) including Ladies Anne & Sarah Le Poer Trench, Hon Frederick Le Poer Trench and Miss Gertrude Le Poer Trench

Garbally Court

Gardenmorris

Gardenmorris: O'Shee coat-of-arms in Conservatory

Garbally Court, Ballinasloe, co Galway
(LE POER TRENCH, CLANCARTY, E/PB). A large
and somewhat austere 2 storey house of
1819 by the English architect, Thomas
Cundy, built to replace an earlier house
burnt 1798. Square in plan, built round
what was originally a central courtyard;
similar many-windowed elevations on all
four sides, which look rather long for their
height. 11 bay entrance front with single-
storey Doric porte-cochère; alternate triangular and segmental pediments over
ground floor windows. Adjoining front of
11 bays, unrelieved except for pediments
over the ground floor windows as in the
entrance front. Single storey curved bow in
centre of rear elevation; while the remaining
front, which faces the offices, has advanced
end bays. Hall with Ionic pilasters and
niches, with arch leading into a great picture
gallery which was built in the central courtyard *ca* 1855; it has a barrel ceiling with
skylights and columns at one end. The
other principal rooms have a certain amount
of plasterwork and attractive overdoors.
There is a curious fluted obelisk in the
garden. Now owned by a religious order.

Gardenmorris, Kill, co Waterford
(O'SHEE/IFR). Originally a C17 house of red
brick; enlarged, refaced in stucco and
re-built in the style of a French château
mid-C19. Of 2 storeys, with a high roof, dor-
mergables, camber-headed Georgian-glazed
windows, an octagonal turret and spire, and
a balcony or two; the whole effect being
pleasantly modest and conveying the atmosphere of France with greater success than
many of the more elaborate houses in the
château style manage to do. The side of the
house adjoining the stables, where there is a
C17 cypher set into one wall, has something
of the air of a *basse-cour*; while the picture is
completed by the surroundings; the principal front does not rise from a typical rolling
Irish or British park, but faces over lawns
and a formal garden to a lake, covered in
summer with yellow water-lilies; beyond
which are thick woods. The house was
burnt 1923 but afterwards rebuilt as it was,

except that a 3rd storey at one end was
omitted. The bathroom fittings for the rebuilt house were obtained in France, so that
the visitor to Gardenmorris, when he goes
to have his bath, might well wonder if he
has not been magically wafted from co
Waterford to Normandy; for the taps are
labelled *Chaud* and *Froid*.

Garretstown House

**Garretstown House, Dunshaughlin, co
Meath** (JAMESON/IFR). A single-storey modern house in the Classical style, built for
Mr & Mrs Julian Jameson to the design of
Mr Austin Dunphy of O'Neill Flanagan &
Partners; completed 1976. Entrance front
with projecting wings and central pediment;
garden front with 2 balustraded curved
bows and pedimented Ionic doorcase

Garretstown House

Garretstown House: Dining Room

Garron Tower

Garvagh House

Garvagh House: White Drawing Room

Drawing room with screen of Corinthian columns; octagonal dining room in the Chinese taste, with tent-like ceiling; library with recessed bookcases in Regency style.

Garrettstown, Ballinspittle, co Cork (CUTHBERT-KEARNEY/LG1863; FRANKS/IFR). Some time *ante* mid-C18, the Kearney family—who, like other families along the south-west coast of Ireland, are reputed to have become rich through smuggling—began building themselves a grand house with 2 wings facing each other across a forecourt in the Palladian manner; levelling a site for it out of the solid rock above the sea at great expense. The two wings, of an attractive golden stone, their handsome pedimented facades, each with a rusticated doorway, facing each other across the forecourt, were completed. But whether the house itself was actually built is uncertain; though Charles Smith (writing 1750) implies that it was. If it existed, it cannot have survived for very long; for one of the wings subsequently became the house, being enlarged for this purpose by having its front, at right angles to the facade, more than doubled in length; and from the style of this enlargement, it would appear to have been carried out before end of C18. The other wing kept to its original size and served as a stable. The 2 wings continued to serve their respective purposes of house and stable until the property was sold; there were no subsequent alterations to take away from their early C18 character; while close to them in the garden and grounds there were handsome stone gate piers with pineapple finials and wrought iron gates, an orangery and a wrought iron *claire voie*, which were clearly all part of the original—or projected—grand layout. Towards end of C19, Garrettstown was inherited by the Franks family, who sold it *ca* 1950. It is now ruinous.

Garron Tower, Garronpoint, co Antrim (VANE-TEMPEST-STEWART, LONDONDERRY, M/PB). A romantic but austere cliff-top castle of black basalt, built between 1848 and 1850 by the redoubtable Frances, Marchioness

of Londonderry, who was the daughter and heiress of the very wealthy Durham coal-owning landowner, Sir Henry Vane Tempest, and whose mother was Countess of Antrim in her own right; Mr Brett believes that she intended Garron "to rival (if not upstage) Glenarm Castle" (*qv*), the Antrim family seat a few miles to the south. Her architect has been proved by Mr Brett to have been Lewis Vulliamy, of London; it seems that she wanted her castle to be something on the lines of Burg Rheinstein, a castle of the Archbishops of Trier on the Rhine which was restored 1820s by Prince Frederick of Prussia; but in fact Vulliamy only copied a few details from Rheinstein, and followed it in having a dominant tower; which is at one end of the long building, polygonal with a square turret. At the other end of the front a short wing projects forwards, ending in a rectangular tower and turret. Apart from the rather plain machicolations and crenellations, the walls have hardly any ornament. Lady Londonderry enlarged her newly-built castle by adding a hall 1852. The principal front is flanked by a terrace with a battery of cannon. Became an hotel 1898; largely gutted by fire between the wars; sympathetically restored *post* 1950 to the design of Mr P. Gregory, for use as a school.

Garry Castle, Banagher, Offaly (ARMSTRONG/LG11912). A medieval castle with a bawn and gate tower and a simple white C18 house set in the bawn wall.

Garrycloyne, Blarney, co Cork (TRAVERS/IFR; TOWNSHEND/IFR; MAHONY/IFR). A square 2 storey 4 bay late-Georgian house with an attic in the roof.

Garryhinch, Portarlington, Offaly (WARBURTON/LG11958). A house of early to mid-C18 appearance, of 3 storeys, with a 3 bay centre recessed between 2 projecting 1 bay wings. Pointed doorway; 2 storey 3 bay range at one side and set back. Burnt *ca* 1914.

Garvagh House, Garvagh, co Derry (CANNING, GARVAGH, B/PB). A house said to have been first built in early C17, and enlarged twice since that time; eventually of late-Georgian appearance, with a front of 3 bays between 2 3 sided bows and an eaved roof on a bracket cornice. Long enfilade of reception rooms, one with a modillion cornice and a Georgian bow; another with a broken pediment of C19 appearance over its doorcase. The seat of the Cannings; George Canning, father of the Prime Minister and grandfather of the Viceroy of India, Earl Canning, was the eldest son of Stratford Canning, of Garvagh; but was disinherited on account of his marriage to a penniless Irish beauty, so that the estate went to his brother, the father of 1st Lord Garvagh. The son of another brother of the disinherited George Canning was Sir Stratford Canning, 1st Viscount Stratford de Redcliffe, the great Ambassador.

Garvey House, Aughnacloy, co Tyrone (MONTGOMERY-MOORE/LGI1912). A massive 3 storey late-Georgian block by Francis Johnston, built for Nathaniel Montgomery, MP, who assumed his mother's maiden name of Moore, having inherited Garvey from her family. 7 bay front, with break-front centre; 6 bay side. Symmetrical plan with twin stairs at sides of hall. Now a ruin.

Gaulston

Gaulston (also known as **Gaulston Park**), **Rochfortbridge, co Westmeath** (ROCH-FORT, BELVEDERE, E/DEP; and ROCHFORT/ LGI1912; BROWNE, KILMAINE, B/PB). A late C18 house consisting of a 3 storey 7 bay centre block joined to 2 storey wings by single-storey links; built by 2nd Earl of Belvedere, replacing the earlier house where his mother had been incarcerated by his father for nearly 30 years (*see* BELVEDERE). The entrance front had a central Gothic-glazed Venetian window below a window flanked by 2 medallions of lion masks, and above an enclosed porch with a fanlighted doorway and coupled Doric columns which appears to have been added later, after the house had become a seat of the Kilmaines; for there were 2 Kilmaine eagles on its parapet. Bold quoins, window surrounds and string courses; solid roof parapet. Adamesque decoration on friezes and over-doors in principal rooms. Staircase with ironwork balustrade and spacious first floor landing. Library in one of the wings. Sold 1784 by 2nd Earl of Belvedere to Sir John Browne, 7th Bt, MP, afterwards 1st Lord Kilmaine. Sold 1918 by 5th Lord Kilmaine; burnt 1920.

Gaulstown, co Meath. A small early C19 villa; 2 storey, 5 bay, central Wyatt window above simple porch; eaved roof. In recent years, the home of Hon Mrs Knight.

Gaybrook, Mullingar, co Westmeath (SMYTH/IFR). A late C18 block of 3 storeys over a basement, built 1790 by Ralph Smyth; replacing a gabled C17 house on an estate that originally belonged to the Gaye family, of which John Gay, author of *The Beggar's Opera*, is reputed to have been a member. Curved bow in centre of garden

front, with 1 bay on either side of it; Wyatt windows in these outer bays on ground floor. 5 bay side. Single-storey C19 wing. Curving staircase. Sold *ca* 1960.

Geashill

Geashill: as a ruin

Geashill, Offaly (FITZGERALD, LEINSTER, D/ PB; DIGBY, B/PB). A house built alongside an ancient castle of the O'Dempseys, and afterwards of the Kildare FitzGeralds, who were also Barons of Offaly, which passed to the Digbys through the marriage of Sir Robert Digby to the heiress of 11th Earl of Kildare; a lady who, in her widowhood, stood siege in castle for several months 1641–42. The house was of 7 bays, with a recessed 3 bay centre, a high plain roof parapet and a lower wing at one side. It was burnt 1922. Geashill had the name for being badly haunted; the manifestations being as-sociated with an ancient cauldron which was formerly preserved here.

Georgestown House, Kilmacthomas, co Waterford (BARRON/IFR; DE LA POER BERESFORD, *sub* WATERFORD, M/PB1970). A Georgian house of 2 storeys over a basement and 3 bays, with a lower wing. Segmental pediments over the windows of the lower storey; simple dentil cornice under roof. The side of the house is weather-slated. A seat of the Barron family; more recently the home of the late Lord William Beresford, who gave the house its present very hand-some doorway, with engaged Doric columns and a broken pediment, which came from Ballycanvan House, near Waterford (*qv*). Georgestown is now the home of Lord William's sister, Lady Patricia Miller.

Gibbings Grove

Gibbings Grove, Charleville, co Cork (GIBBINGS/LGI1912). A simple 2 storey 3 bay Georgian house with a fanlighted doorway. Gate lodge with pediment, blind lunette and niches.

Gibbstown, Navan, co Meath (GERRARD/ LGI1937Supp). A Victorian Italianate house with a rusticated ground floor; prolonged by a single-storey domed wing, ending in a campanile tower.

Gill Hall

Gill Hall: house and old bridge over River Lagan

Gill Hall: Staircase

Gill Hall, Dromore, co Down (HAWKINS-MAGILL, *sub* HAWKINS/IFR; MEADE, CLAN-WILLIAM, E/PB). A 3 storey 7 bay house built between 1670 and 1680 by John Magill. Enlarged and improved *ca* 1731 by Robert Hawkins-Magill, MP, probably to the de-sign of Richard Castle; a 3 storey wing, fronted with a shallow curved bow, being added on either side of the front. Each bow has a modified form of Venetian window—with the side windows set further from the window in the centre than is customary—in its middle storey; with similarly spaced triple windows above and below. The windows in the bows are heavily rusticated, and there are rustications round the centre windows of the original block to give unity to the facade. The entrance doorway is particularly magnificent; the door opening is under a segmental arch, with carved stone dolphins in the spandrels, and is rusticated on either side; all this being framed by Doric columns and a Doric entablature surmounted by a segmental pediment. Until recently, the original block retained its c17 carved wood panelling and its fine staircase with barley-sugar banisters and carved swags of foliage. At one end of the house is an old stone bridge with pointed arches spanning the River Lagan. Gill Hall is the scene of the celebrated "Beresford Ghost Story". One night in 1693, when Nichola, Lady Beresford, was staying here, her schooldays' friend, John Power, Earl of Tyrone, with whom she had made a pact that whoever died first should appear to the other to prove that there was an after-life, appeared by her bedside and told her that he was dead, and that there was indeed an after-life. To convince her that he was a genuine apparition and not just a figment of her dreams, he made various prophecies, all of which came true; notably that she would have a son who would marry his niece, the heiress of Curraghmore (*qv*) and that she would die on her 47th birthday. He also touched her wrist, which made the flesh and sinews shrink, so that for the rest of her life she wore a black ribbon to hide the place. Lord Tyrone was far from being the only ghostly visitant to Gill Hall, which shared with Leap Castle, Offaly (*qv*), the dubious title of being the most haunted house in Ireland. When 5th Earl of Clanwilliam (whose forebear had married the Hawkins-Magill heiress 1765) brought his bride to Gill Hall 1909, she found the ghosts more than she could bear; and so the house was abandoned by the family in favour of Montalto (*qv*), which 5th Earl bought *ca* 1910. From then onwards, Gill Hall stood empty and deserted. In 1966, when the house was in an advanced state of decay, the Irish Georgian Society carried out some timely repairs, without which it would very soon have been past saving; in the hope that, having thus been made watertight, it would stand a chance of being properly restored at a later date. This hope, alas, was not to be realized; for a few years after the Georgian Society's admirable "rescue operation", the house fell a victim to fire.

Glananea, Killucan, co Westmeath (SMYTH/IFR). A late c18 house of 2 storeys over a basement by Samuel Woolley, who designed the triumphal arch at the entrance to the demesne which was so grand that the Smyth of the day came to be known as "Smyth with the gates"; growing tired of this, he disposed of the arch to a neighbour of his, at Rosmead (*qv*), only to be known as "Smyth without the gates". The house at Glananea has a 6 bay entrance front, with a 2 bay breakfront centre and a pedimented and fanlighted tripartite doorway. Garden front of 7 bays, with 3 bay breakfront, the 3 central ground floor windows being roundheaded and treated as an arcade. Good interior plasterwork in the manner of James Wyatt. Hall with frieze of swags and shallow

Glananea

arcading. Large staircase hall with ceiling of radial pattern; stairs with slender metal balusters. Inlaid mahogany doors in drawing room. Sold *ca* 1960.

Glandalane, Fermoy, co Cork (HALLINAN/IFR). A late-Victorian or Edwardian house with a high gabled roof and an ogival-roofed turret.

Glanduff Castle, Broadford, co Limerick (IEVERS/IFR). A simple castellated house with a tower at one corner.

Glanleam

Glanleam, Valentia Island, co Kerry (FITZGERALD, Bt, KNIGHT OF KERRY/PB; SPRING RICE, MONTEAGLE OF BRANDON, B/PB; UNIACKE/IFR). A large plain irregular house on Valentia Island, with extensive subtropical gardens.

Glanmire House, Glanmire, co Cork (MORROGH BERNARD/IFR; RUSSELL/LGI1958; SULLIVAN, *sub* MAUNSELL/IFR). A 3 storey 7 bay Georgian house with projecting end bays joined by a graceful Regency iron veranda. Fanlighted entrance doorway at side of house, not central. The walls of the house are of stucco on weather-slating. A seat of the Morrogh Bernard family and afterwards of the Russell family; more recently of Brig-Gen E. L. Sullivan, father of Anne, Duchess of Westminster (*see* PB), the owner of *Arkle*.

Glanmore, Charleville, co Cork (RUSSELL/LGI1958). A 2 storey 5 bay early c19

house with an eaved roof and a porch with the entrance door in its side.

Glanmore Castle, Ashford, co Wicklow (SYNGE/IFR). A castle of symmetrical design by Francis Johnston, built *ca* 1804 for Francis Synge, MP, great-grandfather of the poet and playwright J. M. Synge, whose uncle's home it was. Of 2 storeys over a basement, with round corner towers; 3 storey 3 sided battlemented projection in the centre of one front, 3 storey central feature with bartizans in the front adjoining. Simple Classical interior; curved staircase. Sold 1943 by Mrs Anthony Farrington (*née* Synge); afterwards dismantled and then partly rebuilt by new owner. In recent years the home of Herr Kurt Oehlert.

Glannanore, co Cork (*see* GLENANORE).

Glasdrumman House, Annalong, co Down (GREER/IFR; LOWRY/IFR). A picturesque house built during 2nd quarter of c19; 2 storey, the upper storey being an attic with high pointed dormer-gables. Wyatt windows in lower storey, ordinary rectangular windows with Georgian astragals above. Simple projecting porch with door at side. Wing to right of front. Low-ceilinged rooms. Inherited by late Cmdr R. G. Lowry on death of his aunt Miss E. M. Greer 1951.

Glaslough House, co Monaghan (*see* CASTLE LESLIE).

Glasnevin House, Glasnevin, co Dublin (LINDSAY, *sub* CRAWFORD, E/PB). A plain 2 storey C19 house with a single-storey high-roofed wing at right angles.

Glasshouse, Shinrone, Offaly (SMITH/ IFR; ROLLESTON-SPUNNER, *sub* ROLLESTON/ IFR). A house built on the site of an ancient glass factory. Originally the seat of the Smith family; in 1837, the seat of Thomas Spunner, from whom it passed by inheritance to the Rolleston-Spunners. Now demolished.

Glenade, Manorhamilton, co Leitrim (TOTTENHAM/IFR). A single-storey late-Georgian house with a Doric porch and colonnade along the front. Wreathes on frieze; fanlighted doorway.

Glenanna (also known as **Glenanna Cottage**), **Ardmore, co Waterford** (BARRON/ IFR). A simple long and low house. Gothic folly, with two round towers, battlements and pointed windows, nearby. Described 1837 as "the marine residence of H. Winston Barron, Esq".

Glenanore (also known as **Glannanore**), **Castletownroche, co Cork** (PURCELL/IFR; HOARE, Bt, *of Annabella*/PB). A 5 bay Georgian house with a central Wyatt window above a fanlighted doorway. Service wing ending in a building like a Gothic folly. The house features in a recent book of highly evocative reminiscences, *The Road to Glenanore*, by M. Jesse Hoare.

Glenarde

Glenarde, co Galway (PERSSE/IFR). A 2 storey C19 house with irregular fenestration and a single-storey 3 sided bow.

Glenarm Castle, Larne, co Antrim (MCDONNELL, ANTRIM, E/PB). Originally a castle built 1603 by Sir Randal MacDonnell, afterwards 1st Earl of Antrim, as a hunting-lodge or secondary residence; became the

Glasdrumman House (with Mrs R. G. Lowry and late Cmdr Lowry)

Glenarm Castle

Glenarm Castle: in C18

Glenarm Castle: Dining Room

Glenarm Castle: Hall

Glenarm Castle: Bridge and Barbican

principal seat of the family after Dunluce Castle (*qv*) was abandoned. Rebuilt *ca* 1750 as a 3 storey double gable-ended block, joined by curving colonnades to 2 storey pavilions with high roofs and cupolas. The main block had a pedimented breakfront with 3 windows in the top storey, a Venetian window below and a tripartite doorway below again; flanked on either side by a Venetian window in each of the two lower storeys and a triple window above. The pavilions were of 3 bays. *Ca* 1825, the heiress of the McDonnells, Anne, Countess of Antrim in her own right, and her 2nd husband, who had assumed the surname of McDonnell, commissioned William Vitruvius Morrison to throw a Tudor cloak over Glenarm. He did very much the same as he had done at Borris, co Carlow (*qv*) and Kilcoleman Abbey, co Kerry (*qv*); adding 4 slender corner turrets to C18 block, crowned with cupolas and gilded vanes; he also gave the house a Tudor-Revival facade with stepped gables, finials, pointed and mullioned windows and heraldic achievements, as well as a suitably Tudor porch. The other fronts were also given pointed windows and the colonnades and pavilions were swept away, a 2 storey Tudor-Revival service wing being added in their stead. The interior of the castle remained Classical; the hall being divided by an arcade with fluted Corinthian columns; the dining room having a cornice of plasterwork in the keyhole pattern. In 1929 the castle was more or less gutted by fire; in the subsequent rebuilding, to the designs of Imrie & Angell, of London, the pointed and mullioned windows were replaced with rectangular Georgian sashes. Apart from the octagon bedroom, which keeps its original plasterwork ceiling with doves, the interior now dates from the post-fire rebuilding; some of the rooms have ceilings painted by the present Countess of

Glenart Castle

Antrim. The service wing was reconstructed after another fire 1967, the architect being Mr Donald Insall. In 1825, at the same time as the castle was made Tudor, the entrance to the demesne from the town of Glenarm was transformed into one of the most romantic pieces of C19 medievalism in Ireland; probably also by Morrison. A tall, embattled gate-tower, known as the Barbican, stands at far end of the bridge across the river; flanked by battlemented walls rising from the river bed.

Glenart Castle, Arklow, co Wicklow (PROBY, Bt/PB). Originally a hunting lodge, known as "the Cottage at Poulnahoney"; enlarged in the castellated style at the beginning of the C19 by John Proby, 1st Earl of Carysfort, and known for a period as Kilcarra Castle, before acquiring its subsequent name of Glenart Castle. Enlarged again 1869 to the design of John McCurdy. A rather plain building, mostly 2 storey, but partly 3 and dominated by a square battlemented tower. Large rectangular windows with hood mouldings; 3 sided bows and a battlemented parapet. Partly faced with a rather unusual random ashlar. Half the house was burnt *ca* 1920; but the surviving half continued to be occupied by the family as an occasional residence until it was sold during World War II to a religious order, which has since rebuilt the house in an institutional style.

Glenavon, co Tyrone. A C19 Italianate house with a campanile tower.

Glenavon House, Fermoy, co Cork. A 2 storey late-Georgian house with a front of 2 bays between 2 1 bay pedimented projections; each having a giant blind arch breaking through the base-mouldings of the pediments. Single-storey Ionic portico with die. Lower wing at side.

Glen Barrahane, Castletownshend, co Cork (COGHILL, Bt/PB). An irregular 2 storey C19 house with gabled projections and a 3 sided bow. Interior panelling.

Glenbeigh Towers, Glenbeigh, co Kerry (WINN, HEADLEY, B/PB). A grim Victorian-Medieval fortress built 1867–71 for Hon Rowland Winn to the design of the English architect and "aesthete", Edward William Godwin, who designed Dromore Castle, co Limerick (*qv*). Like Dromore, Glenbeigh was of very solid stonework and near to being archaeologically correct. It consisted of a massive square keep of 3 storeys and a gabled attic, raised on a battered platform or plinth so that the windows of the bottom storey were high above the ground; with a walled entrance court or bawn on one side of it, entered through a gateway defended by a corner bastion. The keep had a polygonal turret with a pointed roof on one of its faces. The windows were suitably narrow, either lancet or trefoil-headed; the walls were unrelieved by ornament except for bold string-courses; the complete absence of battlements, machicolations and other pseudo-medieval features served to make the building more formidable. The original design included a tower 100 feet high; but this was never built. Godwin's work at Glenbeigh harmed his reputation—which had already suffered through his elopement with the actress, Ellen Terry—for it ended with Winn threatening to sue him because the walls leaked and the cost was too high; causing him in later years to advise young architects: "When offered a commission in Ireland, refuse it". Glenbeigh was the home of Rowland Winn's son, 5th Lord Headley, who became a Muslim, made the pilgrimage to Mecca and was President of the British Muslim Society. It was burnt 1922; only a corner of the ruin now stands, looking even more convincingly medieval than the building did when it was intact.

Glenbevan, Croom, co Limerick (BEVAN/IFR; BROOKE, Bt, *of Summerton*/PB). A 2 storey early C19 house in the late-Georgian manner. C19 plasterwork in hall. Garden with terraces overlooking the River Maigue.

Glenbrook, Magherafelt, co Derry (CASSIDI/IFR). A slightly Gothic late-Georgian house; entrance in 3 sided battlemented bow between 2 gables with finials and small overhanging oriels.

Glenburn, Glanmire, co Cork (GALLWEY/IFR; DRING/IFR). An early C19 house in the "Cottage Gothic" style. Gothic plasterwork in hall. In C19, the seat of T. H. Gallwey; in the present century, of Col R. C. D'E. Spottiswoode; and later of Lt-Cmdr R. H. Dring.

Glencairn, Sandyford, co Dublin (CROKER/IFR). A house formerly belonging to Judge Murphy, bought 1904 by Richard Welstead Croker, the notorious "Boss" of Tammany Hall, on his return to his native Ireland, and extensively remodelled by him, so that it became a mixture of Baronial and

Glenbeigh Towers: remaining corner of ruin

Glenbeigh Towers

American Colonial; with a veranda of granite columns running round it and an Irish-battlemented tower. Here he had his famous stud, where his horses included *Orby*, winner of both the English and the Irish Derbys 1907. Glencairn is now the British Embassy.

Glenbrook

Glencairn Abbey (formerly **Castlerichard**), **Lismore, co Waterford** (GUMBLETON, *sub* MAXWELL-GUMBLETON/LGI1952; BUSHE/LGI1912). An early C19 Gothic house of 1 storey with a gabled attic begun *ca* 1814 by R. E. Gumbleton, completed by his brother-in-law H.A. Bushe, to whom he bequeathed it at his death 1819. The principal front is symmetrical with 2 projecting gable-ended wings, joined by a single-storey range inspired by a late-medieval cloister, with buttresses and crockets, battlements and large Perpendicular windows. At the inner corner of each of the wings is a large pinnacle with an ogee finial; there is a Perpendicular window in each of the gables above a single-storey 3 sided battlemented bow with rectangular tracery windows. Irregular side elevation with battlemented entrance porch. Became a convent of Cistercian nuns *ca* 1930; badly damaged by fire 1973.

Glencara

Glencara, Mullingar, co Westmeath (KELLY, *sub* HARVEY-KELLY/IFR; BELLINGHAM, Bt/PB). A 2 storey house of 1824, with a strong family likeness to some of Sir Richard Morrison's "villas", notably Issercleran, co Galway (*qv*). 3 bay front with 3 sided end bows; single-storey Doric portico; downstairs windows set in shallow arched recesses. Roof parapet on corbel brackets. Similar side elevations, with bow and 2 Wyatt windows in each storey. Imposing staircase lit by dome, with typical plasterwork of the period. Modillion cornices in some of the reception rooms; those extending into the bows having curved rather than 3 sided ends. Sold *ca* 1938 to Lt-Col A.S. Bellingham, who made part of one of the downstairs rooms into a small library with panelling and bookcases brought from Mrs Bellingham's home in Scotland, Rosemount, Ayrshire.

Glencairn Abbey

Glencarrig, Glenealy, co Wicklow (DROUGHT/LGI1912). A 2 storey 4 bay Georgian house with single-storey Victorian wings.

Glenconnor House (formerly known as **Larchgrove**), **Clonmel, co Tipperary** (WATSON/IFR; CLEEVE/IFR). A 2 storey 3 bay late-Georgian house, built *ca* 1797 as a dower house for Summerville, now Ballingarrane (*qv*); to which 2 storey wings, ending in slightly projecting ranges with shallow gables, were added *ca* 1884. Yard at rear. Eaved roof on main block; partly glazed single-storey portico added in 1904. Single storey battlemented projection in one wing. Owned earlier this century by Col George A. Elliot, who sold it 1938 to Mr H.J. Cleeve.

Glencormac, Kilmacanogue, co Wicklow (JAMESON/IFR). A red brick High Victorian house.

Glencullen House

Glencullen House, co Dublin (FITZ-SIMON/LGI1958). A 2 storey double gable-ended house said to date back to late C17, to which a new single-storey front was added *ca* 1800. This late-Georgian front is of 3 bays, with a pedimented Doric portico and an eaved roof.

Glendalough House, Annamoe, co Wicklow (BARTON/IFR; CHILDERS/IFR). A C19 Tudor-Gothic mansion, possibly by John B. Keane, incorporating a long, low 2 storey earlier house, the front of which can be seen at right angles to the present front, with later buildings on either side of it; it has Wyatt windows, a fanlighted doorway and an eaved roof on a bracket cornice. The interior of this earlier house also keeps its distinct character; particularly the hall, which has a staircase of thick but graceful joinery running round 3 sides of it, and the small dining room, which has a circle of simple plasterwork in its ceiling. T. J. Barton, who bought the estate from the Hugo family, built the main Tudor-Gothic range 1838. The front, symmetrical but for an overhanging oriel to the left, has dormer-gables and a battlemented 3 sided central bow; a Gothic porte-cochère, with finials, was added at a later date. One side of this range ends with the old house; the other, which incorporates another earlier building, is long, irregular and gabled. A range in a

Glendalough House

different style of Gothic was added *ca* 1880 to accommodate the children of Prof R. C. Childers, who came to live here with their uncle after the death of their father; it joins the old house to the long Gothic stable range, which was built 1838 and originally freestanding. The entrance under the porte-cochère leads into a hall with a stone Gothic fireplace and a flight of steps up to the level of the principal rooms. Beyond is an impressive staircase hall, lit by an elegant oval lantern; the stairs are of wood, with carved oak newels but with balusters of cast-iron foliage. Originally the stairs were in an adjoining hall and this main hall merely had a gallery; but they were moved here *ca* 1875 and the original staircase hall divided to form another room with a bedroom over. Drawing room with plain coved ceiling and white marble chimneypiece of exotic character—possibly Russian—with acanthus and fluted columns. Dining room with coved ceiling and wooden cornice and elaborate carved oak chimneypiece and overmantel; carved oak sideboards to match. The stable range, which has a clock and belfry at its far end, is prolonged by a fanlighted building like a conservatory. Formal garden with yew trees in the angle between the stables and the old house; enclosed garden beyond, with Gothic garden-house. Glendalough House stands in a magnificent setting of park, river, woodland and mountain. The children of Prof R. C. Childers who came to live here *ca* 1880 included Erskine Childers, author of *The Riddle of the Sands* and fighter for Irish independence. His cousin, Mr Robert Barton, of Glendalough, who died in 1976 at the age of 95, was also a prominent figure in the independence movement, the last surviving signatory of the Anglo-Irish Treaty of 1921. Glendalough is now the home of Mr & Mrs R. A. Childers. Mr Childers is the brother of the late President Erskine Childers, to whom Glendalough was also very much home.

Glendaragh, Killead, co Antrim (MC-CLINTOCK/IFR). A long, low single-storey house; large windows with wooden mullions.

Glenflesk Castle

Glenflesk Castle (also known as **Flesk Castle**), **Killarney, co Kerry** (CRONIN-COLTSMANN/IFR; MCGILLYCUDDY OF THE REEKS/IFR). An extensive and romantic early C19 castle of yellowish stone, on a wooded hill above the River Flesk. Built *ca* 1820s by John Coltsmann, who, after visiting Killarney and "becoming enamoured of its beauties", bought land and settled here. He is said to have acted to a certain extent as his own architect; but the quality of the building would suggest that he also employed a talented professional; perhaps Sir Thomas Deane, who designed Dromore Castle, near

Kenmare (*qv*). Round tower and octagon tower with turret; square tower with bartizans. Rectangular windows with Gothic tracery. 2 storey galleried hall with groined ceiling. Spiral staircase in round tower. Octagonal saloon in octagon tower, one of 5 reception rooms *en suite*. Sold early in present century to John McGillycuddy (known as "Jackgillycuddy"), a younger brother of Richard, The McGillycuddy of the Reeks. Re-sold and dismantled *ante* World War II; now a ruin.

Glengarriff Castle

Glengarriff Castle, Glengarriff, co Cork (SHELSWELL-WHITE/IFR). A mildly castellated house overlooking Glengarriff Harbour; consisting of a long 2 storey range with shallow curved bows and ogee-headed windows, at one end of which is a square tower; and at the other, a much taller battlemented round tower. The latter joins the main block to a battlemented wing set at an obtuse angle to its end. Now an hotel.

Glengarriff Lodge

Glengarriff Lodge, Glengarriff, co Cork (SHELSWELL-WHITE/IFR). A large 2 storey late-Georgian cottage orné built by 1st Earl of Bantry, romantically situated on an island in the river high up the glen of Glengarriff. Thatched roof with undulating eaves; 2 storey rustic veranda; gable with fancy bargeboard and Gothic tracery window of innumerable lights.

Glenlo Abbey, nr Galway, co Galway (PALMER, *sub* DE STACPOOLE/IFR). A long plain 2 storey house built onto a slender

tower with pointed openings near its top. The seat of the Palmer family.

Glenmaroon, Chapelizod, co Dublin (GUINNESS, *sub* IVEAGH, E/PB). A house in the Edwardian Tudor Manor House style, built for Hon Ernest Guinness. Now a childrens' home.

Glenmervyn, Glanmire, co Cork (HALL/IFR). A long 2 storey C19 house with gables and bargeboards, hood-mouldings over the windows, a single-storey and a 2 storey 3 sided bow and an iron veranda. Castellated entrance gate.

Glenmona

Glenmona, Cushendun, co Antrim (MCNEILL-MOSS/IFR). A house in the modern Georgian style built by the politician and author, Ronald McNeill, 1st (and last) Lord Cushendun, in 1923, to replace an earlier house which had been burnt. His architect was Mr Clough (now Sir Clough) Williams-Ellis, who also designed a square and a terrace of houses for him in the nearby village of Cushendun. 2 storeys in front, 3 storeys at the rear. Principal front with 2 3 sided bows joined by an arcade on Tuscan columns. High roof with solid parapet; external shutters to windows.

Glenmore, Crossmolina, co Mayo (ORME/LGI1912; FETHERSTONHAUGH/IFR;

Glenstal Castle

Glenveagh Castle

HURT/LG1965; SOAMES, *sub* EBURY, B/PB). A 2 storey 3 bay late-Georgian house; entrance doorway set in arch, round-headed windows on either side. Office wing at back. The home of Mr J. Douglas Latta *ca* 1958; now the home of Mr & Mrs Martin Soames.

Glenstal Castle, Moroe, co Limerick (BARRINGTON, Bt/PB). A massive Norman-Revival castle by William Bardwell, of London; begun 1837, but not completed until *ca* 1880. The main building consists of a square 3 storey keep joined to a broad round tower by a lower range; the entrance front is approached through a gatehouse copied from the gatehouse at Rockingham Castle, Northants. The stonework is of excellent quality and there is a wealth of carving; the entrance door is flanked by figures of Edward I and Eleanor of Castille; the look-out tower is manned by a stone soldier. Groined entrance hall; staircase of dark oak carved with animals, foliage and Celtic motifs, hemmed in by Romanesque columns; drawing room with mirror in Norman frame. Octagonal library in the base of the round tower, lit by small windows in very deep recesses; vaulted ceiling painted blue with gold stars; central pier panelled in looking-glass with fireplace. Elaborately carved stone Celtic-Romanesque doorway copied from Killaloe Cathedral between two of the reception rooms. Glen with fine trees and shrubs; river and lake, many-arched bridge. Now a Benedictine Abbey and a well-known boys' public school.

Glenveagh Castle, Churchhill, co Donegal (ADAIR/LG1863). A Victorian Baronial castle of rough-hewn granite at the end of a wooded promontory jutting out into Lough Veagh, surrounded by the bare and desolate hills of a deer-forest, so large as to seem like a world apart. Built 1870 by J. G. Adair, of Bellegrove, co Leix, whose wife was a rich American heiress; designed by his cousin, J. T. Trench. The castle consists of a frowning keep with Irish battlements, flanked by a lower round tower and other buildings; the effect being one of feudal strength. The

Glenstal Castle: Staircase Hall

Glenstal Castle: Central Pier in Library

entrance is by way of a walled courtyard. Glenveagh has always had an American connexion; after the death of Mrs Adair, it was bought by the distinguished American archaeologist, Prof Kingsley Porter; then, in 1938, it was bought by its present owner, Mr Henry McIlhenny, of Philadelphia. Mr McIlhenny, whose hospitality is legendary, has decorated and furnished the interior of the castle in a way that combines the best of the Victorian age with Georgian elegance and modern luxury; and which contrasts splendidly with the rugged medievalism of the exterior and the wildness of the surrounding glen. He has also made what is now one of the great gardens of the British Isles. There are terraces with busts and statues; there is a formal pool by the side of the lough, an Italian garden, a walled garden containing a Gothic orangery designed by M Philippe Jullian; while the hillside above the castle is planted with a wonderful variety of rare and exotic trees and shrubs.

Glenville, nr Cushendall, co Antrim. A late-Georgian house built by the Macaulay family, consisting of a tall and narrow main block of 3 storeys and 3 bays, with long single-storey battlemented wings linking it to 2 storey octagonal turrets. The windows in the wings and turrets are pointed. Recently, the facade of the central block was spoilt by the insertion of a modern door and wide modern casement windows in its 2 lower storeys. Owned in 1920s by James Finneghan.

Glenville, Waterford, co Waterford (DAVIS-GOFF, Bt/PB). A mid-C19 house in a mildly Italianate style. Sold *ca* 1957, afterwards damaged by fire and eventually demolished.

Glenville Park (known for a period as **The Manor** and at an earlier period again as **Mount Pleasant**), **Glenville, co Cork** (HUDSON-KINAHAN, *sub* KINAHAN/IFR; BENCE-JONES/IFR). Originally a 2 storey 5 bay C18 house, of rendered rubble with blocked window surrounds of cut stone; it was fronted by a semi-circular forecourt or enclosure, with a gate at either side. The seat of a branch of the Coppinger or Copinger, family (*see* LG11912), the estate having originally belonged to the O'Keefes. Bought between 1776 and 1788 by Dr Edward Hudson, who built a new house a short distance from the old one, and at right angles to it; consisting of a 3 storey 3 bay gable-ended centre, with a fanlighted doorway, and 2 storey 1 bay gable-ended wings. This house was the home of Dr Edward Hudson's son, William Elliott Hudson, composer, collector of ancient Irish music and Irish patriot, who composed the music of *The Memory of the Dead* (better known as *Who Fears to Speak of '98*). The estate eventually passed to William Elliott Hudson's nephew, Sir Edward Hudson-Kinahan, 1st Bt, who enlarged and remodelled the house to the design of Sandham Symes 1887. A new 2 storey front was built onto the house, making it twice as deep; other additions were built at the back, and the original part of the house was reconstructed with 2 storeys instead of the original 3, so as to make the rooms as high as those in the new additions. The new front is in the Victorian-Georgian style, faced in grey cement and of considerable length; it has a small pedimented breakfront with a pair of round-headed windows above a balustraded and fanlighted porch. On either side of the centre is a 3 sided bow between 2 bays; the facade being prolonged at one end by an additional bay, beyond which is a 3 storey 1 bay wing set back. Entablatures on console brackets above ground floor windows; shouldered window surrounds in upper storey; parapeted roof. At the back of the house is a bow-fronted pavilion-like wing, containing a single large room, joined to the main building by a corridor. Long hall running the full depth of the house, with staircase at its inner end, behind an arch with plasterwork mouldings; modillion cornice. Doorcases with segmental pediments in the hall and principal reception rooms, which have Victorian plasterwork cornices of flowers and foliage; the drawing room has an original c19 wallpaper in faded lemon and grey. Spacious landing or upper hall at head of stairs. Walled garden with old beech hedges and walls of faded pink brick; the back of the Coppinger house being at one side of it. Glen garden containing a notable collection of rhododendrons and other shrubs and trees; long flight of steps down hillside to formal pool. Bought 1949 from the trustees of Sir Robert Hudson-Kinahan, 3rd Bt, by Col Philip Bence-Jones, who carried out various alterations to the house and threw 3 small rooms together to make a chapel, which has stained glass windows by Mr Stanley Tomlin and Mr Patrick Pollen, and a stone altar by the late Seamus Murphy, above which is a statue of the Madonna which survived the fire at Annemount (*qv*).

Glenwilliam Castle, Ballingarry, co Limerick (MASSY/IFR; ATKINSON, *sub* RAWSON/IFR). A 2 storey house built 1797 by Rev William Massy, with a curved bow in the centre of the entrance and garden fronts. In the entrance front bow, which has 1 bay on either side of it, is a round-headed rusticated doorway. Glenwilliam is one of the many Irish country houses reputed to have been lost at cards; at any rate, it changed hands in c19, the new owner being Edward Atkinson (father of Lord Atkinson, an eminent lawyer) who built a castellated tower

Glenville Park, co Cork: C18 house

Glenville Park, co Cork

Glenville Park, co Cork

Glenville Park, co Cork: Landing at head of Stairs

at one side of the house, to the design of James & George Richard Pain.

Glin Castle, Glin, co Limerick (FITZGERALD, KNIGHT OF GLIN/IFR). A romantic white castellated house overlooking the estuary of the Shannon from among the trees of its demesne. Built *ca* 1780–89 by Col John FitzGerald, 24th Knight of Glin, as a plain 3 storey double bow-fronted house with a long service wing possibly incorporating the earlier house, which itself replaced a thatched house, burnt 1740, to which the Knights of Glin moved c17 when they abandoned their ancestral castle, of

which only the stump now remains, outside the present demesne. The 24th Knight never completed the 3rd floor of the house owing to his impending bankruptcy 1801. In the proceedings, which included a private Act of Parliament, it states that the house and offices cost "£8,000 and upwards". Given simple battlements and a couple of turrets on the service wing *ca* 1820–36 by the 25th Knight—nicknamed "The Knight of the Women" by the local people—so that from being known as Glin House, it became Glin Castle. The bows on the entrance front are curved; between them are 2 bays, with a pedimented and fanlighted cut-stone

Gloster

Glin Castle

Glinsk Castle

Gloster, Brosna, Offaly (LLOYD/IFR). A C17 house enlarged and grandly remodelled early C18 for Trevor Lloyd, a 1st cousin of the architect, Sir Edward Lovett Pearce; whose influence can certainly be seen both in the exterior and the interior of the house as it is now; yet, as Dr Craig has pointed out, it seems a little too provincial to be actually by Pearce himself. The unusually long and imposing 2 storey 13 bay garden front consists of a 9 bay C17 centre, with early C18 2 storey 2 bay wings. The centre has a 3 bay breakfront with a doorcase of Ionic pilasters and a Baroque up-curving entablature; the bays on either side of it are framed by a superimposed order of fluted Ionic and Doric pilasters. The wings have windows surrounded by pedimented aedicules in their lower storey, with niches above. There is a balustraded roof parapet along the whole front, that of the centre being higher than that of the wings. Much of the centre of the front is taken up by a magnificent 2 storey hall or saloon, with boldly architectural plasterwork on its walls. At 1st floor level, this lofty chamber is surrounded by niches with busts and an arcaded gallery, opening into an upper hall decorated in the same style, with a Doric entablature and a coffered barrel-vaulted ceiling. At the end of a vista in the park is an arch flanked by obelisks which is regarded as being without doubt by Pearce. Gloster was sold *ca* 1958 and is now a convent.

Glyde Court

Glyde Court, Tallanstown, co Louth (FOSTER, Bt, *sub* MASSEREENE AND FERRARD, V/PB). A late C18 house with a long elevation, remodelled in Jacobean style C19. Thackeray, in his *Irish Sketchbook* of 1843, speaks of a mansion "of the Tudor order" being built here at that time; but the work does not seem to have been completed until 1868. The long elevation has curvilinear gables and 2 curved bows; the entrance is in the end of the building, where there is a shorter front with 2 gabled projections joined by an arcaded cloister. The seat of Sir Augustus Foster, 4th and last Bt, who features with his wife and children in a large and highly romantic Edwardian family portrait by Sir William Orpen, now in the National Gallery, Dublin.

doorcase flanked by 2 windows on the ground floor; the windows in this front—and in the 6 bay side elevation—have mullions and transoms with Georgian-glazed lights in the Pain/Morrison manner. The garden front has 2 3 sided bows, with, between them, a round-headed window above a Venetian window lighting the stairs above a doorcase with a shouldered architrave and entablature. The windows on this side are ordinary Georgian sashes. Splendid hall, divided by screen of fluted Corinthian columns; with a ceiling of elaborate plasterwork in which Adamesque neo-Classical motifs are combined with flowers and foliage, Irish harps and other pleasantly naive decoration in high relief similar to that at a number of houses in the West of Ireland; notably Castle ffrench, co Galway and Ash Hill Towers, co Limerick (*qqv*). It incorporates the impaled escutcheon of the 25th Knight and his wife (*née* Fraunceis Gwyn, of Forde Abbey, Devon), who married 1789. The hall ceiling keeps its original colouring, with terracotta Classical plaques on an apple-green background. Staircase hall behind the main hall, with similar plasterwork, though with less relief, on its ceiling and elaborate cornucopias in the spandrels of the elliptical relieving arch above the Venetian window. The stairs, which are of wood, with slender balusters,

are almost unique in Ireland in having 2 lower ramps with a single flying run of steps from the half-landing to 1st floor landing, perhaps echoing those at Adam's Mellerstain, Berwickshire. The drawing room has a frieze and ceiling of simple but more conventional Adamesque plasterwork. The library has a frieze and ceiling of plasterwork rather similar to that in the hall and staircase hall; at one side of the room is an unusual inset mahogany bookcase, with a broken pediment surmounted by a bust of Milton and brass grilles in oval openings, one of which artfully conceals the door. The 25th Knight, who castellated the house, also built 3 delightful castellated entrances to the demesne, with "pasteboard" battlements (one of which the 29th and present Knight, the distinguished architectural historian, has made into a shop and eating house); as well as a hermitage and a Gothic folly.

Glinsk Castle, Ballymoe, co Galway (BURKE, Bt, *of Glinsk*/PB1908). A 3 storey C17 fortified house, rather similar to Monkstown Castle, co Cork (*qv*); with gables, corner machicolations, tall chimneys and a recessed centre. Built *ca* 1630–40 by Sir Ulick Burke, 1st Bt. Gutted by fire at an early date and a ruin ever since, now maintained by the Commissioners of Public Works.

Glynch House

Glynch House, Newbliss, co Monaghan (MAYNE/LGI1875; ADAMS/IFR). An early C19 Classical villa, of 2 storeys over a basement. 3 bay front, central Wyatt window above pedimented Grecian porch with 2 Doric columns. The window on either side of the porch set in an arched recess, with an unusual elongated sill running from one side of the recess to the other. Wide eaved roof on bracket cornice.

Glynn

Glynn, co Antrim (JOHNSTON, *sub* BROOM/IFR). A 3 storey Victorian house, with dormer gables and 2 storey 3 sided bows.

Glynnatore (also known as **Castleview**), **Conna, co Cork** (GUMBLETON, *sub* MAXWELL-GUMBLETON/LGI1952). A house built 1791 by R. W. Gumbleton, facing across the River Bride to the ruins of the old Desmond castle of Mogeely.

Glyntown, Glanmire, co Cork (M'CALL/LGI1863; DRING/IFR). A late-Georgian villa romantically situated on a wooded hill above the Glanmire River; built by Samuel M'Call. Owned in the present century by Lt-Cmdr R. H. Dring. Demolished between the Wars.

Glynwood, Athlone, co Westmeath (DAMES-LONGWORTH/LGI1912). A 2 storey C19 Italianate mansion. Curved bow at end of one front; balustraded roof parapet; pediments over windows. Lower 2 storey range at one side and single-storey wing, containing a large room, projecting outwards at right angles. Burnt *ca* 1920.

Glynwood

Gola, Scotstown, co Monaghan (WRIGHT (*now* WOOD-WRIGHT)/LGI1879; and WILSON-WRIGHT/IFR). A remarkable early C18 house of 2 storeys and 5 bays, with a high, gable-ended roof and a central attic tower. The tower, which was square, with a pyramidal roof surmounted by a lantern, had a Venetian window; Dr Craig considers that it may have derived from the central lantern or gazebo at Sir Edward Lovett Pearce's Woodlands, co Dublin (*qv*). Below the tower there was a floating broken pediment, with an elliptical window in the tympanum. The windows of the front all had triple keystones; those in the lower storey being segment-headed. There were rusticated quoins on the tower as well as on the body of the house; and a rusticated Venetian doorway. Single-storey 1 bay wings with Venetian windows were added at a somewhat later date. Gola, which was burnt 1920; can be regarded as the prototype of a small group of Irish Georgian and *post* Georgian country houses with central towers; the most notable of which is Ancketill's Grove (*qv*), also in co Monaghan.

Golden Grove, Brosna, Offaly (LLOYD-VAUGHAN/LGI1912 and *sub* LLOYD/IFR). A 3 storey 5 bay C18 house with a Venetian window in the centre of its front. Lower wing.

Gormanston Castle, Gormanston, co Meath (PRESTON, GORMANSTON, V/PB). The old Manor at Gormanston was low and gabled, with a "long blue parlour" stretching the whole length of the ground floor on one side. Adjoining it was a chapel, where Mass was said all through the Penal times. At the beginning of C19, 12th Viscount Gormanston rebuilt the house as a 3 storey Gothic Revival castle, of the early, symmetrical type; with Georgian sash windows, round corner towers and a tall gatehouse tower with 2 slender turrets as the central feature of its principal front. Great Hall rising through 2 storeys with plaster vaulted ceiling, marble pavement and oak panelling put in sometime later in C19. Simple stairs with plain, slender uprights. Dining room with classical doorcases, cornice of simple classical plasterwork and handsome chimneypiece of statuary marble, its entablature supported by caryatids. Library with cornice of simple classical plasterwork and Ionic chimneypiece. The old chapel, which survived the rebuilding, stands at one corner of the garden front. Its doorway, of C16 or early C17 type, has the date 1687 in an armorial panel above it, joined to the lintel by a stone carved with a C17 "Jansenist" crucifix, in which the arms of Christ are only partially extended. 12th Viscount intended the castle to be much larger; but he ceased all building work when his wife died 1820: "This day the light of my life has gone out", he wrote in his diary on the day of her death. Gormanston is famous for the foxes which collect at the castle when the head of the family is dying or has recently died; there being a fox in the family crest. In 1860, at the time of 12th Viscount's death, there was a meet of the local hunt in the neighbourhood; but a villager said: "Don't they know all the foxes have gone to see the old Lord die?" The same thing happened when 14th Viscount died 1907; Lord Fingall was out with his hounds and never found; and an old countryman told him: "My lord, you may go home. Every fox in Meath is at Gormanston". One of the sons of 14th Viscount, while keeping vigil at midnight in the chapel by his father's coffin, heard scratching, and snufflings, at the door; opening it, he found several foxes which tried to get past him into the building. In 1946, when the castle was for sale, Evelyn Waugh, who was then thinking of settling in Ireland, decided to bid for it; he described it in his *Diaries* as "a fine, solid, grim, square, half-finished block with tower and turrets". Then, on hearing that Butlins were starting a holiday camp in the neighbourhood, he changed his mind. The castle was eventually bought by the Franciscans, for use as a school.

Gola

Gormanston Castle

Gormanston Castle: Great Hall

Gormanston Castle: Dining Room

Gortigrenane, Minane Bridge, co Cork (DAUNT/IFR; STOUGHTON/LGI1912). A late C18 house of 3 storeys over a high basement, faced with stucco over weather slating. Front with 2 bays on either side of a central window flanked by 2 narrow windows; tripartite fanlighted doorway with pediment and columns; curved astragals in sidelights. The house is joined by screen walls with blind arches to office ranges running back, the front-facing gable-ends of which have blind arches below square recesses. Projecting bow at rear containing stairs. Small entrance hall; Doric frieze with rams' heads; simple Adamesque decoration in flat of ceil-

Gormanston Castle: caryatid chimneypiece

Gormanston Castle: Library

Gormanston Castle: Doorway of Chapel

ing; door set in apsidal arch leading to staircase hall behind. Staircase hall with ceiling of delicate Adamesque plasterwork; elegant curving stairs of wood with slender balusters and carved scroll ends to treads; vaulted ceiling with wreath ornament under gallery; doorcases with husk ornament set in arches. Dining room with cornice and frieze of plasterwork. Vaulted ceiling with Adamesque decoration over back stairs. Stone doorways and rusticated arches in yard; small chapel; stone dated 1817 and Royal Arms. A seat of the Daunt family; passed through marriage to the Stoughton family early C19; sold *ca* 1880. Inhabited until *ca* 1960; now derelict.

Gortnamona (formerly **Mount Pleasant**), **Tullamore, Offaly** (O'CONNOR-MORRIS/ LGI1912). A 2 storey late C18 house built by M. N. O'Connor. Front of 2 bays on either side of a central breakfront with 2 windows above a pedimented doorway flanked by 2 windows. High parapeted roof. 2 bay end elevation. Burnt 1922.

Gortner Abbey

Gortner Abbey, Crossmolina, co Mayo (ORMSBY/IFR). A gable-ended C18 house by the side of Lough Conn; of 2 storeys over a basement with a dormered attic. 5 bay front; tripartite doorway with blocking; long and broad flight of steps up to hall door. After being sold by the family, the house became the Lough Conn Hotel; it is now a convent. Large wings have been added on either side of it.

Gosford Castle, Markethill, co Armagh (ACHESON, GOSFORD, E/PB). The 1st Norman-Revival castle in the British Isles, a massive, widespread granite pile by the English architect, Thomas Hopper, who later designed the great Norman-Revival castle in North Wales, Penrhyn. Built 1819–20 for Archibald Acheson, 2nd Earl of Gosford, afterwards Governor of Canada, replacing a Georgian house burnt *ca* 1805; largely paid for by his wife, the daughter and heiress of Robert Sparrow, of Worlingham Hall, Suffolk; so that it is possible that the choice of so strange a style as Norman was hers; she was a life-long friend of Lady Byron so may have absorbed some of Byron's exotic and somewhat sinister brand of romanticism; and coming from Suffolk, she would have been familiar with Orford, Castle Hedingham and other East Anglian Norman keeps. These, as much as Rochester, where Hopper was brought up, could have inspired the great square keep at Gosford; a frowning *donjon* which dominates the rest of the castle; looming above the entrance front, tying together the rather shapeless mass of towers and buildings; for this front was added to by a later architect who lacked Hopper's skill. Flanked by the embattled gateway to an office court and with bastions on either side of the hall door, the entrance front has an air of extreme grimness; a real ogre's castle. The garden front, however, has a strange beauty; the stone seems paler, Norman becomes more like Southern Romanesque. The grouping is masterly; the walls are at different angles to each other, so that there is a great sense of movement. A round tower on this side is almost as great an element in the composition as the keep; and there is a square tower at the end of the long wing containing the private rooms of the family, which rises step by step to meet it. There are Norman mouldings round the window arches, Romanesque columns and arcading; heavy machicolation. The garden door has a portcullis. Although Norman was really unsuited to C19 living, the interior does not suffer from the heaviness one finds at Penrhyn. The entrance halls are, indeed, rather gloomy; and a dark, vaulted passage gives the impression of going into the very heart of the castle. It leads, however, to the

Gosford Castle

Gosford Castle

Gosford Castle: Dining Room

Gosford Castle: Library

Inner Hall, which is light and colourful, like the state rooms beyond; with a vaulted ceiling picked out in gold and walls painted green to represent drapery. The angles make the plan difficult to follow; the rooms seem to fit together like a Chinese puzzle. Between the larger rooms are 3 little anterooms, one hexagonal, with arched bookshelves; one with an apse. Across them there are delightful vistas to rooms which seem to lie in all directions. The dining room has white plaster Norman decoration and slender columns of pink Armagh marble. The Norman bookcases in the library are carved with a riot of mouldings, columns, flowers and beasts' heads; in the space between them is a fantastic pattern of intertwined wooden tendrils on a background of scarlet. In the round tower is the immense circular drawing room, which formerly contained French ormolu furniture. The carving in some of the rooms is by John Smyth, Master of the Dublin Society's Modelling School, who, like his father, Edward, was a talented sculptor. 2nd Earl and his Countess were eventually estranged, so that she spent the later years of her life at Worlingham in Suffolk, where she died; her husband sent a party of servants to convey her coffin to co Armagh for burial; but, being in a convivial mood, they lost it on the journey. It was, however, subsequently found in a church in the English Midlands, the clergyman having treated it with great respect on account of the coronet with

which it was adorned. 4th Earl was a friend of Edward VII and maintained a rather too lavish way of life; so that in 1921, a year before his death, the contents of the castle had to be sold; he had already sold the library some 30 years earlier to pay a racing debt. The estate remained in the family until *post* World War II, when most of it was bought by the Northern Ireland Forestry Commission. At one time the castle was used to house a circus: the roar of lions coming from the office court must have heightened its strangeness. During World War II, it was in military occupation; among the officers stationed here was Mr Anthony Powell, who may have had Gosford in mind when he wrote of "Castlemallock", as the place where the narrator "knew despair", in *The Valley of Bones*. In recent years, it was used to store public records; for which purpose it was admirably suited, being remarkably dry, in spite of having stood empty for long. The future of the castle is uncertain.

Government House, co Down (*see* HILLSBOROUGH CASTLE).

Gowran Castle, Gowran, co Kilkenny (AGAR-ROBARTES, CLIFDEN, V/PB; WHITE, ANNALY, B/PB). Originally an old castle with several towers, onto which a 2 storey 9 bay pedimented front was built 1713 by James Agar, grandfather of 1st Viscount Clifden. This was demolished 1816 by 2nd Viscount, being by then in bad repair; and replaced by a compact Classical house built during the course of the next 3 years, to the design of William Robertson, of Kilkenny. Of 2 storeys over a basement; 7 bay entrance front with 3 bay pedimented breakfront; rectangular niche in centre above Doric frontispiece. Garden front with rather awkward central feature of thin Composite halfcolumns, paired at the sides, under a pediment; with a central rectangular niche in both storeys to resolve a duality. 3 bay end. The house was originally free-standing; but a lower 2 storey wing was subsequently added at one side of it, which has since been demolished. Inherited by the daughter of 3rd Viscount Clifden, who married 3rd Lord Annaly; sold by 4th Lord Annaly *ca* 1955.

Gowran Grange, Naas, co Kildare (DE ROBECK/IFR). A mid-C19, gabled Tudor-Revival house of grey stone by John McCurdy; built partly 1857 and partly 1872 for John Fock, 4th Baron de Robeck. Heavily carved oak chimneypiece in hall.

Grace Dieu, Clogheen, co Waterford (ANDERSON/IFR). Originally a 2 storey villa of *ca* 1840 with an eaved roof, an entrance front of 3 bays with an Ionic porch and a garden front of 4 bays. The garden front is still visible; but the entrance front has been obscured by extensive late C19 additions, which have transformed the house into an irregular Italianate mansion with a front composed of 2 2 storey blocks, that to the right being set further forward than that to the left. From the latter projects a balustraded and pilastered porch; from the former, a single-storey curved bow, also balustraded. Joining the porch to the right-hand block is a single-storey glazed extension to

Gowran Castle: Entrance Front

Gowran Castle: Garden Front

Graiguenoe Park

the hall. A pedimented orangery prolongs the front to the right. Eaved roofs. Large and rambling hall with arches and an impressive wooden staircase with joinery of C18 style. Dining room and library in the garden front of the original house, with friezes and ceiling rosettes of mid-C19 plasterwork in high relief. In the newer wing there is a large and attractive drawing room with a frieze of Adam Revival plasterwork; the rest of the decorations being in the same style.

Gracefield, Ballylinan, co Leix (GRACE, *sub* BOWEN/LGI1912; WHITE/LGI1912; ROSS-DE MOLEYNS, *sub* VENTRY, B/PB). An early C19 villa in the cottage-orné style, built *ca* 1817 for Mrs Morgan Kavanagh (*née* Grace); based on a design by John Nash, which was considerably modified and cut down by William Robertson, of Kilkenny, who carried out the building. Of 2 storeys; entrance front of 3 bays, the centre bay projecting and rising to form a pediment-gable. Garden front with 3 sided bow at one side. 2 bay end elevation with curved corners. Lower service wing and small Gothic conservatory. Sash windows with hood mouldings; mullioned window under pediment-gable in entrance front. Veranda of elaborate ironwork extending round three sides of the house; ironwork porch, with cresting and urns. Roof on bracket cornice. Small curving staircase with slender wooden balusters. Bow-ended dining room. The house is in a Reptonian setting of steeply undulating parkland. In recent years, the home of Hon Francis Ross-De Moleyns; then of Mr & Mrs J. P. Carrigan; now, of Mr & Mrs Christopher Hughes.

Grace Hall, Moira, co Down (BLACKER-DOUGLASS/LGI1912). A 3 storey double gable-ended C18 house with a front of two curved bows and 1 bay in between. Wyatt windows throughout; later porch.

Gracehill House, Dervock, co Antrim. A late C18 house, enlarged and re-orientated at the beginning of C19. 2 storey 5 bay front, with pedimented breakfront not quite central. Round-headed window in upper storey of breakfront, doorway with shallow elliptical fanlight below. In 1814, the residence of James Stewart.

Graiguenoe Park, Holycross, co Tipperary (CLARKE/IFR). A house in the late-Georgian style, of 2 storeys over a basement which was concealed at the front, built 1833–35 for Charles Clarke, one of the sons of the remarkable Marshal Clarke who appeared in Tipperary as a penniless clergyman *ca* 1780 and died a wealthy landowner 1833. Eaved roof; entrance front of 6 bays in upper storey, and 2 bays on either side of an Ionic portico below. 4 bay side. The entrance front was extended 1903 by the addition of a wing of 1 storey over a basement, containing "the big room", the most generally used sitting room in later years. Burnt 1923; the ruins stood until 1960s, when they were levelled.

Gracefield

Grallagh Castle, Thurles, co Tipperary (BUTLER/IFR; MANSERGH/IFR). An old tower-house, wide for its height. Battered lower storey; pointed entrance doorway at ground level; 2-light lancet windows higher up. Curved *machicoulis* at corners of skyline.

Grange, Dungannon, co Tyrone (GREEVES/IFR). A 2 storey house, said to be basically late C17, but partly rebuilt 1835 by William Greeves. Porch and fanlighted doorway.

The Grange, Ballyragget, co Kilkenny

Grange (The), Rathfarnham, co Dublin (*see* MARLAY).

The Grange, Ballyragget, co Kilkenny: Fanlight

The Grange, Ballyragget, co Kilkenny: Husk ornament and painted Medallion

Grange (The), Ballyragget, co Kilkenny (LANNIGAN, STANNARD and DOWDALL, *sub* BANCROFT/IFR). An old farmhouse to which Georgian reception rooms were added, producing a house of 2 storeys and 9 bays, with a 3 bay breakfront centre higher than the bays on either side. Fanlighted doorway; high-pitched roof. Room with Adamesque plasterwork incorporating oval painted medallions.

M

The Grange, co Limerick

Grange (The), co Limerick (O'GRADY, *sub* CROKER/LGI1912). A 3 storey 6 bay C18 house refaced C19. 2 bay central breakfront with pedimented doorcase flanked by 2 windows. Entablatures on console brackets over ground floor windows. 3 bay end. Late C18 plasterwork of similar style to that at Glin Castle (*qv*). Elaborate stables round a court on axis behind house. Now a ruin.

Grange Con, nr Baltinglass, co Wicklow (O'MAHONY, *sub* MAHONY/IFR). A house rebuilt after being burnt *ca* 1920; in a rambling half-timbered style, with many gables, an archway under one range and a pillared loggia. Sold in recent years by Mrs Richard Kennett Page (*née* O'Mahony).

Granite Hall

Granite Hall, Dun Laoghaire, co Dublin (MORE O'FERRALL/IFR). A solidly built 2 storey Regency house of stone, with a front of 3 bays between 2 curved bows, each with a single Wyatt window in both storeys. Central Wyatt window above fanlighted doorway, which was recessed under an arch supported by Doric columns. Bold string course. Now demolished.

Granston Manor, Abbeyleix, co Leix (FITZPATRICK, UPPER OSSORY, E/DEP; and CASTLETOWN, B/PB1937; SMYTH/LGI1912 and *sub* GALWAY, V/PB). A large rambling house, partly late-Georgian and partly later; of 2 storeys with an attic in the roof. The entrance front, of 5 bays with a Wyatt window above a balustraded portico, is, in fact, the end of the house, which is much deeper than it is wide and has various lower wings of 1 and 2 storeys. Roof on bracket cornice. Long garden front with single-storey balustraded projections. The interior was much done over in the late-Victorian and Edwardian period, largely by Bernard FitzPatrick, 2nd and last Lord Castletown, a celebrated character who was a strong Irish nationalist and believed in fairies; whose father was the illegitimate son and heir of the last Earl of Upper Ossory. The hall was thrown into the adjoining room and panelled in oak, and made into one of those sitting-room-halls so beloved of the Edwardians, with an oak

staircase of Tudor design. There was a very large drawing room made out of two rooms, divided by columns. After the death of Lord Castletown 1937, Granston passed to his nephew, Lt-Col G. H. J. S. Smyth, who assumed the surname of FitzPatrick. It was bought in 1947 by the late Mr Kenneth Harper, whose son, Mr Peter Harper, sold it *ca* 1961. It afterwards became the home of Mr & Mrs Harold Duncan-Collie, but was almost completely gutted by fire 1977.

Grantstown Hall, Dundrum, co Tipperary (MASSY/IFR). A 2 storey Victorian house with gables and fancy bargeboards. Pretty Gothic gates with graceful battlemented arches over wickets.

Gravesend, Castledawson, co Derry (CLARK/IFR). A 2 storey 3 bay Georgian house with single-storey 1 bay wings. Pilastered porch; semi-circular Ionic colonnade at end of wing.

The Manor House, Greencastle

Greencastle, co Donegal: The Manor House (MCCLELLAN, *sub* CROSBIE/IFR). A C18 gable-ended house of 2 storeys over a basement, close to the water's edge at the entrance of Lough Foyle. Front of 2 bays on either side of a shallow curved bow. 2 storey return with Victorian porch. The seat of the McClellan family.

Greenhills, Roscrea, co Tipperary (MINCHIN/IFR). A C18 house of 3 storeys over a basement with a pedimented and fanlighted doorway. In 1914 the residence of Major R. W. Cradock. Now a ruin.

Greenmount, Patrickswell, co Limerick (STANHOPE, HARRINGTON, E/PB). A house of *ca* 1830, seat of the Green family; owned *post* World War II by Major P. Dennis. The property was subsequently acquired by 11th and present Earl of Harrington, who demolished the house and built a large modern house *ca* 1968 in its place, to the design of Mr Donal O'Neill Flanagan. The new house is externally quite plain, with modern steel-framed windows; but its rooms are of a size and loftiness rarely, if ever, found in houses of the present time; they include a 2 storey hall 40 feet square and a drawing room and library each 46 feet long by 30 feet wide by 15 feet high.

Greenwood Park, Ballina, co Mayo (KNOX/IFR; ARMITAGE/LG1969). A compact 2 storey 3 bay late-Georgian house built by Major John Knox; more or less the twin of the nearby Netley Park (*qv*), which was built by his brother. Sold to Mr E. H.

Armitage; re-sold by him, and demolished *ca* 1961; now a ruin.

Grenane House, Tipperary, co Tipperary (MANSERGH/IFR). A 2 storey 3 bay late-Georgian house with a long 2 storey service wing. Enclosed porch with round-headed windows; a Wyatt window on either side of it.

Grene Park, Dundrum, co Tipperary. A 2 storey 5 bay late-Georgian house with an eaved roof. Doorway with shallow segmental fanlight over door and sidelights set in arched recess. A seat of the Grene family.

Grey Abbey (known for a period as Rosemount), nr Newtownards, co Down (MONTGOMERY/IFR). A handsome mid-C18 3 storey block, built 1762 by William Montgomery on the site of 2nd of two previous houses, both of which were destroyed by fire; with 2 storey wings ending in curved bows. The house is now entered by a canted porch with engaged Doric columns in front of one of the wings, which is balanced by a similar canted projection at the opposite end of the facade. The garden front of the main block has a central 3 sided bow, with ogee-headed Georgian Gothic windows in its bottom storey; the octagonal drawing room lit by these windows being decorated in Georgian Gothic. This unusual appearance of Gothic in the garden front of an otherwise Classical C18 house would suggest the influence of Castleward (*qv*), at the opposite corner of Strangford Lough; it seems likely that the Gothic work dates from *post* 1782, when William Montgomery's son, Rev Hugh Montgomery, married a daughter of 1st Viscount Bangor, whose home was Castleward. The main block, as well as the wings, has balustraded roof parapets, which would appear to be C19. There is also a single-storey C19 wing to the left of the garden front. On the hill opposite the house, there is a charming late C18 Gothic "eye-catcher"; the entrance to the demesne is also Georgian Gothic.

Grove, Fethard, co Tipperary (BARTON/IFR; PONSONBY/IFR). To the centre of a plain Georgian house with lower wings William Barton *ca* 1820–30 added a much larger 2 storey block in the restrained villa style of the period, almost identical to Kilrush House, co Kilkenny (*qv*); its 5 bay side forming a symmetrical composition with the 2 earlier wings; the other front of the old house, which has a pediment and faces the yard, remaining unchanged. The 2 principal fronts of the new block were made at right angles to those of the old house; doubtless in order that the living rooms should enjoy the exceptionally beautiful view down the valley. 3 bay entrance front, the 2 outer windows in the lower storey being set in arched recesses. A single-storey Ionic portico was added to this front *ca* 1836, designed by William Tinsley, of Clonmel, who may well have been responsible for the whole of the new block. Eaved roof. Compact and satisfying plan, the main rooms lying on 3 sides of a long central top-lit staircase hall with a vaulted ceiling carried on columns and a circular well-gallery. Above this gallery is

Grey Abbey, co Down: Entrance Front

Grey Abbey, co Down: Garden Front

Grey Abbey, co Down: Drawing Room

Grey Abbey, co Down: ceiling of octagonal Gothic room

Gunsborough, Lisselton, co Kerry (GUN/ LGI1912; MAHONY/IFR). A 2 storey late-Georgian house with an eaved roof. 3 bay front with 1 bay breakfront. Side elevation of 1 bay, with Wyatt window in lower storey, and 3 bays set a little back.

Gunsborough

Gurrane, Fermoy, co Cork (BLACKLEY/ IFR). A Victorian house built *ca* 1850 for the Deanes, to the design of Alexander Deane, on the site of an old castle. Inherited by Mrs T. R. Blackley (*née* Deane).

Gurteen Le Poer, Kilsheelan, co Waterford (DE LA POER/IFR). A large Tudor-Baronial house of 1866 by Samuel Roberts, built for Edmond, 1st Count de la Poer and *de jure* 18th Lord le Poer and Coroghmore, to replace an earlier house which itself replaced an earlier house again. In his design, Roberts was probably influenced by William Burn; for Gurteen is very much a scaled-down version of one of Burn's great Tudor-Baronial mansions in Britain. There is the same arrangement of a massive main block with a lower service wing to one side; the same grouping of gables and 3 sided bows in the garden front with a great tower in the entrance front; almost the only difference being that the tower and subsidiary turrets have Irish battlements instead of the Scottish "pepper-pot" bartizans characteristic of Burn. The tower gives a particularly im-

a delightful little rotunda of columns and pilasters with a dome decorated with plasterwork glazed at the top. Dining room with alcoves at each end. 2 drawing rooms *en suite*. Library with Classical reliefs. After the death of C. R. Barton 1955, Grove was inherited by his cousins, the Ponsonby family of Kilcooley Abbey (*qv*).

Gunnock's, Clonee, co Meath (WARD/ IFR). A house which was originally thatched, and said to date in part from C17; onto which a late-Georgian front of 2 storeys and 3 bays with a fanlighted doorway was built 1806 by Laurence Ward. Wing at side set back. Modern glass porch. Now owned by Mr J. L. Ward.

Gunnock's

Gurteen Le Poer

Gurteen Le Poer: Hall

Gurteen Le Poer: Dining Room

posing air to the entrance front, which faces across a forecourt of castellated walls and flanking turrets to the River Suir and Slievenaman. The garden front is more Tudor and less Baronial, with curvilinear gables and large mullioned windows; it overlooks a formal garden of box hedges, topiary and clipped bay trees. Both fronts and the side elevation are of grey random ashlar with good detailing. The interior of Gurteen is spacious and satisfying. In the centre of the house is a galleried top-lit great hall, divided by a screen of Gothic arches behind which is the staircase. There are similar arches in 1st floor gallery, which, like the staircase, has a balustrade of wrought iron. The library—which is lined with bookcases and has walls the colour of faded calf bindings—the drawing room and the ballroom open into each other along the garden front. The dining room, on the other side of the hall, must be one of the most perfect Victorian Baronial interiors in Ireland. The walls are of faded red, above a dado of warm brown oak panelling, elaborately ribbed and moulded, which was supplied by Graham of Clonmel who made the immense carved oak sideboard, dated 1864. The chimneypiece, also of carved oak, is the *pièce de résistance*; with its heraldic angels holding shields of the family arms, and its head of St Hubert's Stag—the family crest —complete with antlers and crucifix, mounted on top of the mantelshelf like a trophy.

H

Hall Craig, Enniskillen, co Fermanagh
(WEIR/LGI1958). A 3 storey 3 bay gable-ended house built 1721 by Robert Weir in front of the old castle where his family had lived since settling here in the previous century and which they had named Hall Craig after Craigie Hall, the ancestral home of the Weirs in Linlithgowshire. Handsome scroll-pedimented doorcase flanked by sidelights; ground floor windows wider than those above. Sold at the end of C19 to William T. Scott.

Halston House, Moyvore, co Westmeath (ARMYTAGE, Bt/PB). An elegant house of *ca* 1820, square in plan, of 2 storeys over a basement. 3 bay entrance front with pillared porch; 3 bay garden front, the centre bay consisting of a Venetian window lighting the stairs, with a Diocletian window below it. 4 bay side. Eaved roof; prominent quoins. Long and spacious hall with scagliola columns, staircase at end; attractive view of garden through the Diocletian window, which is below the turn of the stairs.

Hamwood, Dunboyne, co Meath (HAMILTON/IFR). A small Palladian house of 1764. The centre block, which is joined to elegant little wings by curved sweeps, has a duality in its rear elevation.

Harbourstown, Fourknocks, co Meath (CADDELL, *sub* STANLEY-CARY/LGI1958). A handsome 2 storey late-Georgian house. 7 bay entrance front, with breakfront centre and single-storey Ionic portico. Side elevation of 5 bays, the end bays breaking forward and with Wyatt windows. Octagonal gazebo with balustraded roof parapet and—formerly—finials, on artificial mound in grounds; built mid-C18 by Richard Caddell (afterwards Farrell). The house has been demolished, but the gazebo still stands.

Hardymount, Tullow, co Carlow (EUSTACE-DUCKETT/IFR; MAUDE, *sub* HAWARDEN/PB). A 2 storey bow-ended Georgian house with giant pilasters at each end of the entrance front. The present owner, Mr H. A. C. Maude, has removed some of the chimneypieces from Belgard (*qv*) to this house.

Hare Island (The), Athlone, co Westmeath (HANDCOCK, *sub* CASTLEMAINE, B/PB). An engagingly hybrid single-storey early C19 "cottage" on an island in Lough Ree, giving the impression of having been concocted out of the "left-overs" from several different houses of various styles and periods: a C18 Classical doorcase with a

The Hare Island

pediment on console brackets, Georgian Gothic windows, a mullioned bow-window with leaded lights and a Regency veranda with slender iron columns under the eaves of the roof. Built by 1st Lord Castlemaine, whose seat, Moydrum Castle (*qv*), was a few miles away, and who was fond of "aquatic excursions".

Harley Park, Ballingarry, co Tipperary (POË/IFR). A 2 storey 5 bay C18 house with a fanlighted doorway and outbuildings in the form of flanking wings.

Harmony Hall, co Westmeath (*see* BENOWN).

Harristown House

Harristown House, Brannockstown, co Kildare (LA TOUCHE/IFR; BEAUMONT, *sub* ALLENDALE, V and BEAUMONT OF WHITLEY, B/PB). An ashlar-faced late-Georgian house designed by Whitmore Davis, originally of 3 storeys over a basement but rebuilt with only 2 storeys after a fire *ca* 1900; the architect of the rebuilding being James Franklin Fuller. 9 bay entrance front, 3 bay pedimented breakfront centre with 3 windows grouped together under a wide relieving arch containing a coat-of-arms and swags; single-storey Ionic portico, the outside columns being coupled. 5 bay side, with triple windows in centre; that in the upper storey being set under a relieving arch containing a medallion and swags. Curved bows

at rear. Bought 1946 by Major M. W. Beaumont (father of Rev Lord Beaumont of Whitley), who put up C18 Chinese wallpapers in 2 rooms and brought "The House of Confucius" from Wotton—originally from Stowe, Bucks—for the garden.

Harrybrook, Tanderagee, co Armagh (HARDEN/LGI1958). A 2 storey house of early to mid-C19 aspect. Long low front with Wyatt windows, small central pediment-gable and pillared porch. Irregular side.

Hatley Manor: Entrance Front

Hatley Manor: Garden Front

Hatley Manor, Carrick-on-Shannon, co Leitrim (ST GEORGE/LGI1863; WHYTE/LG1937Supp). A miniature Castleward (*qv*) of *ca* 1830, with one front Italianate and the other Gothic. The former is the entrance front, and faces across a forecourt to the main street of Carrick-on-Shannon; the Gothic front, which has a large central tracery window lighting the stairs, overlooks the demesne, which goes down to the river. Hall with modillion cornice and screen of columns; staircase at inner end. Originally the seat of a branch of the St Georges, and named after their ancestral home in England, Hatley St George, near Cambridge. The last St George who lived here is buried in an ornate Victorian-Classical mausoleum in the grounds; after his death Hatley Manor passed by inheritance to Petronella Hallberg (*née* Riksdagsman), wife of C. C. B. Whyte. It is now the home of Mr & Mrs Shane Flynn.

Hatley Manor: Mausoleum

Hazlewood, co Sligo: Entrance Front

Hazlewood, co Sligo: Garden Front

Hayes, Navan, co Meath (LAMBART, Bt/ PB; LEGGE-BOURKE, *sub* DARTMOUTH, E/PB). A house of *ca* 1770, of rough-cut stone, 2 storeys over basement, with 2 storey later wings which are almost the same height as the main block but have their windows at a lower level in each storey. The entrance front of the main block is of 7 bays, with a pedimented breakfront centre in which there is a single Wyatt window. The garden front of the main block has 3 bays on either side of a central 3 sided bow. Sold by Sir Henry Legge-Bourke, MP *ca* 1963.

Hazlewood, co Cork

Hazlewood, Mallow, co Cork (LYSAGHT/ IFR). A 2 storey Georgian house consisting of 2 ranges at right angles to one another; both of them with eaved roofs. Entrance front of 3 bays with a fanlighted doorway and an additional bay in the projecting end of the adjoining range; adjoining garden front of 5 bays, the end bays being framed by vertical framing bands. A home of the writer and poet, S.R. Lysaght.

Hazlewood, Sligo, co Sligo (WYNNE/IFR). A large Palladian house on a peninsula in Lough Gill, built 1731 for Owen Wynne to the design of Richard Castle. Centre block of 3 storeys over a basement and 3 bays joined by curved sweeps to 2 storey wings 3 bays long and 3 bays deep. The entrance front of the centre block has a window flanked by two roundels which formerly sheltered busts above a Venetian window with niches instead of sidelights and a tympanum of arms instead of glazing in its head above a pedimented and rusticated tripartite doorway. Rusticated surrounds to ground floor windows. The garden front has a central Venetian window also with a tympanum of arms in its head, above a rusticated Venetian doorway; the ground floor windows are here also rusticated, as they are in the 3 bay side elevation. At the other side of the garden front is a 2 storey 3 bay C19 wing. Hall with Doric half-columns, pilasters and frieze; niches with swags of drapery in their surrounds. Room with modillion cornice, vaulted ceiling and circle of foliage; doorcase framed by fluted Ionic pilasters. Now the Irish headquarters of the Italian fibre manufacturing firm, SNIA.

Headborough

Headborough, Tallow, co Waterford (SMYTH/IFR; PERCEVAL-MAXWELL/IFR). A house of different periods, partly dating from C17 but largely remodelled *ca* 1830. Long and low stucco-faced front of 5 bays between 2 bay projections, with pedimented and fanlighted porch, formerly joined to the projections by lean-to conservatories, now removed. Small single-storey wooden bows at either side. Lower 2 storey wing. Large low-ceilinged hall, hung with a coloured early C19 French pictorial paper, *The Dream of Happiness*, by Desfossé & Karth; staircase facing, open to hall. The hall and the reception rooms on either side of it form a long enfilade. The house stands on a hillside high above the confluence of the Bride and Blackwater estuaries; behind it is an attractive courtyard, cut out of the rock and surrounded by stone outbuildings. Entrance gates with exceptionally tall piers and railings. Inherited by the Perceval-Maxwell family; sold *ca* 1963; now the home of Mr & Mrs P.A. Cornell.

Headfort, Kells, co Meath (TAYLOUR, HEADFORT, M/PB). A large and severely plain mid-C18 house of 3 storeys and 11 bays, with long single-storey wings; described by George Hardinge (1792) as "more like a college or an infirmary"; its 2 almost identical fronts, of silvery-grey Ardbraccan stone, being unrelieved except by simple pedimented doorcases. Built between 1760 and 1770 by Sir Thomas Taylour, 1st Lord Headfort and afterwards 1st Earl of Bective, to a design by George Semple which was probably modified by someone else before the work was completed; the delay in building being explained by the fact that Lord Bective at one stage contemplated scrapping what had gone up already and beginning afresh to a more sophisticated design by Sir William Chambers. His adherence to the original scheme—which in the end was made plainer than ever—was probably due to shortage of money; he had decided to have a costly interior by Robert Adam, so had to economize on the exterior of the house. Adam's designs for the principal rooms (exhibited at RIBA Gallery 1973) were carried out from 1771 until *post* 1775; they are his only country house work in Ireland to survive in its entirety, much of his work at Castle Upton (*qv*) having been lost. The single-storey entrance hall has a boldly decorated ceiling and a stone chimneypiece. The saloon, in the centre of the garden front, has a ceiling coloured in pink, blue-green, pale chocolate and gold, the plasterwork incorporating painted medallions in the manner of Angelica Kauffmann. The square drawing room adjoining the saloon on one side was given a simpler ceiling, which set off the superb pinky-fawn Chinese landscape papers on 3 inner walls. On the other side of the saloon is the great "Eating Parlour" or ballroom, a double cube rising through two storeys; one of the grandest country house interiors in Ireland; with decoration by Adam on the coved ceiling and on the walls. In the centre of the ceiling, and in the 2 overmantels, are roundels painted with Classical subjects. The noble mahogany staircase, with balusters in the form of Tuscan columns, ascends as far as the top storey in a staircase hall which is much simpler than Adam intended it to be. The garden front overlooks an elaborate topiary layout; beyond, and on various islands in the River Blackwater, which flows through the park, is a magnificent collection of ornamental trees and shrubs, mostly planted in the early years of this century by 4th Marquess, who married the beautiful Miss Rose Boote. *Post* World War II, 5th Marquess made a self-contained house in one of the wings, with elegant doorcases in its hall; and he leased the greater part of the centre block and the other wing to a boys' preparatory school, keeping the state rooms for entertaining.

Headfort

Headfort: Hall

Heathfield

Headfort: Chinese Drawing Room

Headfort: "Eating Parlour" or Ballroom

Heath House, Ballybrittas, co Leix (O'REILLY/IFR; BLAKE, Bt, *of Menlough*/PB). A long, low 2 storey Georgian house, plain but for a pedimented doorcase. Sold by the Blake family *ca* 1961.

Heathburn Hall, Riverstick, co Cork (SHAW, Bt/PB). A square early C19 house of 2 storeys over a basement and 4 bays, with a lower 2 storey Victorian castellated wing joining it to a tall battlemented and machicolated round tower. Bought 1882 by Lt-Col F. G. Shaw, who was descended from a branch of the family of Shaw, Bt, of Bushy Park (*qv*); considerably embellished by him.

Heathfield, Ballycastle, co Mayo (BOURKE/LGI1904). A 2 storey 5 bay gable-ended early C18 house with a large pediment, now almost entirely obscured by a 2 storey C19 battlemented projection of cut-stone, which has the entrance door in its side. Return. Walled garden at back of house. The house keeps its original roof of heavy Mayo slates; but it is in a state of disrepair.

Herbertstown House, Dunboyne, co Meath. A house built 1916 by Capt Whitworth in an ornate Edwardian style. 2 storey, rather low for its length, with a high-pitched roof on a bracket cornice; at the side of the house, the roof is of the mansard type and accommodates a dormered attic. Central pediment-gable with broken entablature, through which rises the segmental pediment of the central window. Sash windows with Georgian glazing, those below having keystones; those above, external shutters. Long and deep projecting porch fronted by another broken pediment, with a carved swag in its tympanum, supported by a pair of engaged Doric columns; Ionic pilasters at the sides of the porch, the intervening space being filled with mullioned and partly leaded windows. There are also mullions and leaded lights in the curved bow on the side elevation. Elaborately carved oak staircase in late C17 style with urns on the newels. Drawing room with modillion cornice and oval with fan decoration on flat of ceiling. Subsequently the home of Mr J. P. McAuley.

Hermitage, Glanmire, co Cork (BROWNE/LGI1965). A single-storey late-Georgian house with 3 sided bows.

Hermitage (formerly called **Fields of Odin**), **Rathfarnham, co Dublin** (HUDSON, *sub* KINAHAN/IFR). A C18 house of 3 storeys and 3 bays, the top storey being treated as an attic, above the cornice; with a 2 storey early C19 portico of 4 Doric columns carrying an entablature and die. 2 storey wing at one side. Romantic grounds, with numerous small follies. According to tradition, the patriot, Robert Emmet, courted Sarah Curran here; the place then belonged to Dr Edward Hudson, father of William Elliott Hudson, composer, collector of ancient Irish music and Irish patriot (*see*

GLENVILLE PARK). In 1910 Padraig Pearse, who was to be the leader of the 1916 Rising, moved his famous school, St Enda's, here. The house and grounds were bequeathed to the Irish nation by Pearse's sister, Miss Margaret Pearse, 1970.

Hermitage, Castleconnell, co Limerick (MASSY, B/PB). An imposing 2 storey house built in 1800 for a banker named Bruce; afterwards a seat of the Lords Massy. 5 bay entrance front; pediment supported by paired giant Corinthian pilasters framing centre bay. Balustraded roof parapet; Coade stone enrichments. 5 bay garden front, the end bay on either side being framed by quoins. Small but richly decorated circular hall with niches for statues. Now demolished.

Heywood, Ballinakill, co Leix (TRENCH/LGI1863; DOMVILE/IFR; POË/IFR). A house consisting of a 3 storey 4 bay late C18 centre, with mansard-roofed Victorian wings of the same height but in a totally different style.

Herbertstown House

Herbertstown House

Herbertstown House: Staircase

Herbertstown House: Drawing Room

Heywood

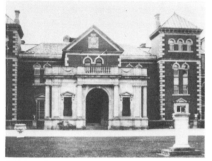
Heywood

Heywood: Dining Room

Heywood: House and Garden

Hillbrook

Hill Mount

Heywood: 3 views of Lutyens Garden

The c18 centre was built 1773 by M. F. Trench, who is said to have been the only man who ever called his house after his mother-in-law: Heywood having been that lady's maiden name. Trench was a talented amateur architect and is said to have designed the house himself; but he seems to have had some assistance from James Gan-don. The dining room was one of the most accomplished interiors of the Adam period in Ireland; with delicate plasterwork on the ceiling and in panels on the walls. As well as building the house, Trench laid out the grounds with 3 artificial lakes and Gothic follies made out of stonework from the nearby Aghaboe Abbey. Early in c20, an elaborate formal garden was laid out, to the design of Sir Edwin Lutyens. Passed by inheritance to the Domvile family, and subsequently to the Poë family. The Empress Elisabeth of Austria was entertained here when she came to Ireland to hunt 1879 and 1880; later, after she had been assassinated, the family put up a window to her memory in the local Protestant church. Heywood now belongs to a religious order, and the grounds are well maintained; but the house has been demolished.

Highfort, Liscarroll, co Cork (PURCELL, *sub* RYAN-PURCELL/IFR). A square late-Georgian house of 2 storeys over a basement. 3 bay front with fanlighted doorway; 4 bay side. The home of Sir John Purcell, who was knighted 1811 for the gallant defence he made when attacked by a gang of robbers. At the beginning of the present century, the home of D. S. Wigmore.

Hillbrook, Carnew, co Wicklow. A fine early c18 house of 2 storeys with a dormered attic and 5 bays. Shouldered doorcase with keystone, flanked by two narrow windows; high, sprocketed roof; tall chimneystack at each end. The house was altered in late c19

and the roof spoilt. The seat of the Symes family, of which Sandham Symes, the late c19 architect, was a member.

Hillburn House, Taghmon, co Wexford (BOYD/IFR). Late-Georgian; 2 storey, 3 bay. Round-headed doorway with blind recess over door; stone surround and keystone. c19 glazed porch with corner pilasters added in front of doorway, so that only the blind lunette now shows. Highish roof, with single central chimney stack.

Hill Mount, Dunminning, co Antrim. A 3 storey 5 bay gable-ended c18 house, believed to have been built by the Hill who founded the nearby Hill Mount bleach works, with 2 later single-storey bow-fronted wings. The main block has a central Wyatt window in its 2 upper storeys, above a fanlighted doorway. Handsome marble chimneypiece with caryatids in drawing room.

Hillsborough Castle (afterwards **Government House**), **Hillsborough, co Down** (HILL, DOWNSHIRE, M/PB; DIXON, GLENTORAN, B/PB). A large, rambling, 2 storey late-Georgian mansion of a warm, golden-orange ashlar; its elevations rather long for their height. It appears to incorporate a much smaller house of *ca* 1760; but was mostly built later in c18, to the design of R. F. Brettingham, by Wills Hill, 1st Marquess of Downshire, a prominent member of Lord North's Cabinet at the time of the American War. The work was not completed until 1797, 4 years after 1st Marquess's death. In 1830s and 1840s, the house was enlarged and remodelled, to the design of Thomas Duff, of Newry, and William Sands. The pedimented portico of 4 giant Ionic columns in the middle of the long 17 bay garden front—originally the entrance front—which is the principal exterior feature, dates from this period; as does the present appearance of the pedimented front adjoining to the left, with its asymmetrical projecting ends; as well as the treatment of the elevations of the 2 ranges at right angles

Hillsborough Castle

Hillsborough Fort

to each other which form 2 sides of the entrance forecourt; one of them having a rather shallow single-storey portico of four pairs of coupled Ionic columns. The forecourt, with its magnificent mid-C18 wrought-iron gates and railings, brought here 1936 from Rich Hill, co Armagh (*qv*), is on one side of the main square of the charming little town of Hillsborough, which is reminiscent of the *Schlossplatz* in a small German capital. Although the house backs onto a sizeable demesne, with a lake, the park is on the opposite side of the town. Its chief feature is Hillsborough Fort, a star-shaped fort built by Col Arthur Hill *ca* 1650. The gatehouse of the fort was rebuilt most delightfully in the Gothic taste *ca* 1758, perhaps to the design of Sanderson Miller himself. Hillsborough Castle became the official residence of the Governor of Northern Ireland 1925, and consequently became known as Government House; from then, until 1973, when the post of Governor was abolished, it was occupied by successive GOVERNORS (all PB); namely, 3rd Duke of Abercorn, 4th Earl Granville, 2nd Lord Wakehurst, Lord Erskine of Rerrick, and Lord Grey of Naunton; during this period, the house was frequently visited by members of the British Royal Family. In 1934 the house was seriously damaged by fire, and in the subsequent rebuilding the principal rooms were done up in a more palatial style, with elaborate plasterwork. The future of the house is now uncertain.

Hilltown, Collierstown, co Meath (BOY-LAN/IFR). A well-proportioned house of 2 storeys and 7 bays, built by Nicholas Boylan and completed 1810. 3 bay breakfront centre with single-storey Ionic portico; parapeted roof. The demesne has gates opening directly onto the picturesque little racecourse of Bellewstown, where a meeting is held once a year.

Hilton Park

Hilton Park (formerly **Maddenton**), **Clones, co Monaghan** (MADDEN/IFR). A large late-Georgian house of 2 storeys over a basement, 11 bay entrance front with the 5 centre bays breaking forward; rebuilt after a fire 1804. In 1872 the basement was excavated so that it became in effect a ground floor, as at Montalto, co Down (*qv*) and the house was refaced with Dungannon stone; with a pierced roof parapet and pediments over the windows of the principal storey. At the same time, a handsome Ionic porte-cochère was added, with coupled columns in the centre; and the principal reception rooms were given decorative ceilings.

Hoddersfield, Crosshaven, co Cork (MOORE-HODDER, *sub* HODDER/IFR). A house of 3 storeys over a basement built in either the last decade of C18 or the opening years of C19 for W. H. Moore-Hodder to the design of the elder Abraham Hargrave. 5 bay front with 3 bay breakfront, of stucco over weather-slating; stone cornice. Fan-lighted doorway with 4 engaged Ionic columns. Fine hall; doors flanked by Ionic pilasters; overdoor panels of transitional plasterwork, with foliage and cornucopiae; neo-Classical plasterwork on flat of ceiling. Oval-ended cantilevered stone staircase in side hall. Reception rooms opening into each other, so that it was possible to walk right round the house. Sold *ca* 1920 by W.H.J. Moore-Hodder. Occupied until a few years ago, then abandoned; now a ruin.

Holestone, Doagh, co Antrim (OWENS/LGI1912). An austere 2 storey Classical house of sandstone, built 1830. 5 bay bow-ended front; side of 6 bays, plus the bow. Parapeted roof; projecting porch with simple pilasters.

Holloden (formerly **Malcolmville**), **Bagenalstown, co Carlow** (VIGORS/IFR; O' GRADY/IFR). A mid-C18 house of 2 storeys over a basement, built for a Mr Mulhallen. Entrance front with 2 bays on either side of a pedimented breakfront, the pediment being baseless. Round-headed central window above fanlighted door, each flanked by narrow sidelights. The house is joined on one side by a curved sweep to an octagon pavilion. Hall with engaged columns and plaster panels on walls. Subsequently the seat of a branch of the Vigors family; passed to Miss Faith O'Grady, whose mother was a Vigors.

Hollybrook, co Cork

Hollybrook, co Cork

Hollybrook, Skibbereen, co Cork (BECHER/IFR; MORGAN, *sub* BAGNELL/IFR; O' DONOVAN/IFR). Originally a 2 storey C18 house with a front of 2 bays on either side of a pedimented breakfront centre, in which there was a central niche with flanking windows above a pedimented and pilastered porch. A seat of the Becher family. Passed to the Morgans; in 1903–1904 Lt-Col A. H. & Mrs Morgan built a new house on a different site, to the design of R. S. Balfour; the earlier house being demolished. The new house is in the style made popular in England during the late-Victorian and Edwardian periods by architects such as Norman Shaw and Philip Webb; it is of 2 storeys, with an attic in the high-pitched, gabled roof; the walls being rendered, and the gable-ends covered in red tile cladding; the roof itself being of red tiles. Near-symmetrical entrance front with segmental baseless pediment and modified Venetian window in recessed centre between gabled projections; Diocletian windows with keystones in the gable-ends, casements with astragals below. Near-symmetrical garden front with gabled projections joined by balustraded veranda with coupled Tuscan columns. Side elevation with central gable. Long service wing with simple casements; battlemented octagon tower at junction of service wing and main block. Large 2 storey galleried hall entered under the half-landing of a bifurcating staircase of oak with barley-

Hollybrook, co Cork: marquetry in Drawing Room

sugar balusters. Gallery carried on wide arches lined with oak panelling, above which are polygonal oak columns with Ionic capitals supporting the ceiling. Ionic columns framing Venetian window on half-landing. Woodcarving in the Grinling Gibbons style and neo-Caroline plasterwork. Similar plasterwork on ceiling and fireplace wall of dining room. Drawing room with 2 fireplaces on either side of a central stack; the chimneypieces, panelling and ceiling being all of elaborate marquetry in light and dark woods, incorporating arabesques, heraldic motifs and texts in Hebrew, Greek and English. The marquetry was made by Miss Jane Morgan for a house on Staten Island, New York, and brought over by Col Morgan, who was her nephew, when the new Hollybrook was being built. Circular study in octagon tower with oak panelling and bookcases and carved frieze. Fine stables dating from the time of the earlier house with stone arches and blocking; walled garden also from earlier house. Gardens with exotic trees and shrubs laid out in the present century. Inherited 1950 by Mrs A. H. Morgan's niece, Cornelia (*née* Bagnell), Madam O'Donovan.

Hollybrook House, Randalstown, co Antrim (CAMPBELL-GROVE/IFR). A 2 storey 5 bay house built *ante* 1777. Round-headed dormer windows.

Hollybrook House, Boyle, co Sligo (FFOLLIOTT/LGI1912; PHIBBS/LGI1912). A 3 storey 5 bay house of *ca* 1756 in a beautiful situation by the shore of Lough Arrow; given a single-storey Doric portico and an eaved roof on a bracket cornice in C19. The estate was granted to the Ffolliotts *ca* 1659; in mid-C18 it passed to an heiress, Mary Ffolliott, wife of John Harloe who demolished the original castle and built the present house. In 1775 Hollybrook passed by inheritance to William Phibbs, after whose death it was sold back to another branch of the Ffolliotts; the purchaser being John Ffolliott, whose mother was Barbara Allen, of the song. Sold *ca* 1945 to Major D.R. Sherriff, who re-sold it 1960.

Hollymount House, co Mayo

Hollymount House, Hollymount, co Mayo (VESEY, *sub* DE VESCI, V/PB; LINDSEY-FITZPATRICK/LGI1912). A C18 house on an estate which originally belonged to the Vesey family, and passed through marriage to the Lindseys. Front of 2 storeys over a basement and 7 bays; asymmetrical 3 storey 5 bay rear elevation. The front was refaced in a strongly "architectural" manner early in C19; with boldly-modelled giant pilasters of no recognizable order along the whole facade, a 3 bay pedimented breakfront, a high roof parapet and a shallow porch. Lunette window in pediment. Magnificent C18 gates, with rusticated piers and vases carved with figures and acanthus. Towards the end of C19, Hollymount passed to Mary Lindsey, wife of Heremon Fitzpatrick—who assumed the additional surname of Lindsey—brother of "Patsy", Mrs Cornwallis-West, one of the reigning beauties of Edwardian fashionable society. It is now a ruin; the gates have been removed and re-erected at Kinsale, co Cork.

Holly Park, Rathfarnham, co Dublin (FOOT/LGI1912 and LGI1952). A handsome late C18 house with fine Adamesque plasterwork in the reception rooms; built *ca* 1780 by Lundy Foot, a tobacco manufacturer. Now the nucleus of St Columba's College, the well-known public school.

Holly Park, Craughwell, co Galway (WHITE/IFR). A 2 storey 3 bay early C19 house with wide windows and an eaved roof. Originally the seat of a branch of the Blake family; passed to the White family through marriage.

Holly Park, Kilcornan, co Limerick (DE VERE, *sub* HUNT/LGI1912). A delightful Georgian-Gothic house built on the base of the keep of a castle of the Knights of Glin with pointed, Gothic-glazed windows; consisting of a 2 storey 5 bay centre and single-storey wings, one of which ends in a battlemented octagon. Originally the seat of the

Hollybrook House, co Sligo

Taylor family; subsequently owned by the de Vere family, of Curragh Chase (*qv*). Now the home of Mr John Philip Cohane, the writer; admirably restored by him after a fire some years ago.

Holybrooke House, Bray, co Wicklow (HODSON, Bt/PB). A Tudor-Revival house of 1835 by William Vitruvius Morrison, incorporating an earlier house. Oak-panelled galeried hall, with stained glass windows. The estate came to the Hodson family by inheritance from the Adairs, the most celebrated member of which was Robin Adair, the popular C18 doctor, hero of the song. Damaged by fire *ca* 1969; afterwards sold.

Holyhill, Strabane, co Tyrone (SINCLAIR/LGI1912). A plain 3 storey Georgian house; 5 bay front, projection with shallow curved bow in side elevation.

Hope Castle, co Monaghan (*see* BLAYNEY CASTLE).

Horetown House, Taghmon, co Wexford (DAVIS-GOFF, Bt/PB). A 3 storey Georgian house. Front with 2 bays on either side of a recessed centre. Triple windows in centre and pillared portico joining the 2 projections.

Horn Head

Horn Head, Dunfanaghy, co Donegal (STEWART/LGI1958). A plain C18 2 storey gable-ended house of 5 bays; with a central Wyatt window and a door with sidelights under a primitive pediment. Rambling outbuildings attached to house, with several archways. Sold 1934. The house was eventually almost buried under Atlantic storm-blown sands.

Hortland House, Kilcock, co Kildare (HORT, Bt/PB). A house by Richard Castle, built 1748 for Rt Rev Josiah Hort, Archbishop of Tuam. 2 storey, 5 bay; Venetian window with Doric pilasters above tripartite doorway with fanlight and baseless pediment. Wall carried up to form high roof parapet. Broad steps up to hall door. Owned 1913 by A. B. Warren. Now demolished.

Howth Castle, co Dublin (GAISFORD-ST LAWRENCE/IFR). A rambling and romantic castle on the Hill of Howth, which forms the northern side of Dublin Bay; the home of the St Lawrences for 800 years. Basically a massive medieval keep, with corner towers crenellated in the Irish crow-step fashion, to which additions have been made through the centuries. The keep is joined by a hall range to a tower with similar turrets which probably dates from early C16; in front of

Howth Castle: Entrance Court

Howth Castle

this tower stands a C15 gatehouse tower, joined to it by a battlemented wall which forms one side of the entrance court, the other side being an early C19 castellated range added by 3rd Earl of Howth. The hall range, in the centre, now has Georgian sash windows and in front of it runs a handsome balustraded terrace with a broad flight of steps leading up to the entrance door, which has a pedimented and rusticated Doric doorcase. These Classical features date from 1738, when the castle was enlarged and modernized by William St Lawrence, 14th Lord Howth, who frequently entertained his friend, Dean Swift, here; the Dean described Lady Howth as a "blue-eyed nymph". On the other side of the hall range, a long 2 storey wing containing the drawing room extends at right angles to it, ending in another tower similar to the keep, with Irish battlemented corner turrets. This last tower was added 1910 for Cmdr Julian Gaisford-St Lawrence, who inherited Howth from his maternal uncle, 4th and last Earl of Howth, and assumed the additional surname of St Lawrence; it was designed by Sir Edwin Lutyens, who also added a corridor with corbelled oriels at the back of the drawing room wing and a loggia at the junction of the wing with the hall range; as well as carrying out some alterations to the interior. The hall has C18 doorcases with shouldered architraves, an early C19 Gothic frieze and a medieval stone fireplace with a surround by Lutyens. The dining room, which Lutyens restored to its original size after it had been partitioned off into several smaller rooms, has a modillion cornice and panelling of C18 style with fluted Corinthian pilasters. The drawing room has a heavily moulded mid-C18 ceiling, probably copied from William Kent's *Works of Inigo Jones*;

Howth Castle: Dining Room

Howth Castle, Library

the walls are divided into panels with arched mouldings, a treatment which is repeated in one of the bedrooms. The library, by Lutyens, in his tower, has bookcases and panelling of oak and a ceiling of elm boarding. Lutyens also made a simple and dignified Catholic chapel in early C19 range on one side of the entrance court; it has a barrel-vaulted ceiling and an apse behind the altar. Howth Castle is celebrated for the custom, continued down to the present day, of laying an extra place at meals for the descendant of the chieftain who, several centuries ago, kidnapped the infant heir of the Lord

Howth Castle: Chapel

Humewood

Howth Castle: in the Gardens

Howth of the time in retaliation for being refused admittance to the castle because the family was at dinner, only returning him after the family had promised that the gates of the castle should always be kept open at mealtimes and an extra place always be set at the table in case the kidnapper's descendants should wish to avail themselves of it. Famous gardens; formal garden laid out *ca* 1720, with gigantic beech hedges; early c18 canal; magnificent plantings of rhododendrons.

Humewood, Kiltegan, co Wicklow (HUME (*now* DICK)/LGI1912; HUME-WEYGAND/LGI1958). A severe and imposing Victorian-Gothic pile of irregular-coursed granite, rightly described by Prof Girouard as "one of the most remarkable of Victorian country houses". Built 1867–70 for Rt Hon W. W. F. Dick (formerly Hume), MP, to the design of William White, a brilliant but

Humewood

Humewood: Staircase Hall

cranky many-sided genius who ended his days trying to prove that Shakespeare was Bacon. White undertook to design a house that would cost no more than £15,000; and even though his estimate was exceeded by £10,000—which resulted in an architectural *cause célèbre*—the fact that he was bound by a low maximum price meant that he had to cut down on detail and rely for effect on

line and mass alone; a treatment also dictated by the uncompromising nature of the granite, a material which he was particularly skilled in handling. With stepped gables, battered buttresses and chimneystacks, advancing and receding walls and pyramidal roofs, White built up a composition of pyramids and triangles; in Prof Girouard's words, "rising and falling but gradually mounting upwards to combine in one irregular pyramidal mass that culminates in the corner turret of the great central tower". This tower, together with the gables and spires and a tall round tower which is heavily battlemented, the tower by another architect added later, gives the house a dramatic silhouette in keeping with the mountain scenery around it. The windows are mostly plain and rectangular. The principal rooms are on a *piano nobile* above a high basement, which was intended to keep the house dry and also as a security measure; for the house was designed in the year of the Fenian Rising and like Dromore Castle, co Limerick (*qv*), by another rather eccentric English architect, Edward Godwin, was intended to be defensible; the vaulted porte-cochère has a room over it with spy-holes. The entrance under the porte-cochère leads into the bottom of a great staircase hall lit by stained glass windows; from which stone stairs ascend to a vaulted and arcaded landing with immensely thick columns of black Irish marble. The reception rooms open off this landing, and off the vaulted corridor which is its continuation; while the stairs—now of wood—continue upwards from the landing to the top of the house, where there are galleries under the vaulted ceiling. The reception rooms have ceilings of massive beams and White's highly individual woodwork. The drawing room opens through angular arches into one of the turrets. There is a large 2 storey banqueting hall. The stables, also by White and in the same style as the house, are a no less skilful composition. Humewood is now the home of Mme Hume-Weygand, daughter and heir of William Hume Hume and daughter-in-law of the celebrated General Maxime Weygand.

Huntington Castle, Clonegal, co Carlow
(ESMONDE, Bt/PB; DURDIN-ROBERTSON/IFR).
A castellated house of many periods, its
nucleus being a tower house built 1625 by
Laurence, 1st (and last) Lord Esmonde;
which, having been given sash windows at a
later date, forms the front facing down the
avenue. It was made more domestic by Sir
Laurence Esmonde, 2nd Bt, *ca* 1680, and a
wing was added *ca* 1720. Further additions
were carried out *ca* 1860 by Alexander
Durdin, whose uncle had married, as his 2
successive wives, 2 daughters and co-heiresses of Sir John Esmonde, 5th Bt; and
again *ca* 1895 by Alexander Durdin's
daughter, Helen, who married Herbert
Robertson. The later additions appear
mostly at the back of the house, facing the
yard, where there are irregular 2 storey
ranges with C19 battlements, a curved bow
and a battlemented gable, with the earlier
building rising above them. Upstairs drawing room with C18 panelling and a C19
Elizabethan style ceiling. Dining room with
oak panelling of C18 or late C17 style.
Another drawing room is hung with tapestry. A number of panelled bedrooms;
many narrow passages and small flights of
stairs, lined with wainscot or half-timbered
studding. Overmantel plasterwork in one
room, probably C17. Impressive vaulted
cellars; chapel at top of house made by
Helen Robertson (*née* Durdin). Various
alterations were carried out by Helen

Huntington Castle

Robertson's son, Manning Durdin-Robertson, who was himself a qualified architect.
Manning Durdin-Robertson married Nora,
author of *Crowned Harp*, daughter of Lt-
Gen Sir Lawrence Parsons; their children
include the artist and writer Miss Olivia
Robertson.

Hyde Park, Killucan, co Westmeath
(D'ARCY/IFR). A house of 2 storeys over a
basement, with a 5 bay front and a fanlighted
doorway with sidelights; built 1775 by
James D'Arcy.

Hyde Park, co Wexford (*see* TARA HOUSE).

I

Ileclash, Fermoy, co Cork (BENSON/LG1965; MOSLEY, Bt/PB; CORETH, *sub* ELWES/LG1965). A 2 storey late-Georgian house overlooking the River Blackwater. 5 bay entrance front with castellated porch; adjoining front with bow. Long hall divided from staircase by screen of columns; three reception rooms *en suite*. During 1950s and 1960s, Ileclash was owned successively by Mr P. G. R. Benson, Sir Oswald Mosley, 6th and present Bt, and Count Maurice Coreth.

Inane, Roscrea, co Tipperary. A simple 2 storey early to mid-C19 Tudor-Revival house with a front consisting of 2 gables joined by an arcade with an upper storey over it. Rectangular 2 light windows under hood mouldings. Impressive Georgian stables with pedimented archways facing the house across a forecourt, in the centre of which is a large and elaborate Neptune fountain. The seat of the Jackson family.

Inch, co Donegal. A 2 storey 7 bay Georgian house with a breakfront centre and a pedimented doorway.

Inch, Thurles, co Tipperary (RYAN/IFR). A C18 block of 3 storeys over a basement; said to incorporate parts of an earlier house. 6 bay front, 2 bay breakfront with Venetian doorway. Ground floor windows enlarged C19 and some of them glazed with diamond astragals. Low wing to one side containing chapel. Hall open to impressive bifurcating

oak staircase with slender turned balusters; probably early C19. Drawing room *en suite* with octagonal boudoir, both rooms having ceilings of particularly unusual C19 plasterwork and C19 wallpaper in white and gold.

Inch House, co Dublin

Inch House, Balbriggan, co Dublin (TAAFFE/IFR). A 2 storey 5 bay gable-ended C18 house with single-storey 1 bay wings; the front being prolonged by a higher single-storey wing at one side. Porch with fan-lighted doorway. Round-headed windows in wings.

Inchera, Little Island, co Cork (OLIVER/IFR; MURPHY/IFR). A 2 storey early C19 house with a lower 2 storey service wing; and a large single-storey Victorian addition,

Inch, co Tipperary

containing a top-lit billiard room, projecting at right angles to the garden front, which faced up the Lee estuary towards Cork city. Circular hall. A seat of the Oliver family; in the present century, of C. E. Murphy, after whose death, 1950, it was sold. A few years later, it was burnt.

Inchmore, Clara, Offaly (GOODBODY/IFR). A 2 storey Victorian house with gables, a pillared porch, a high, tower-like block and entablatures over some of the windows.

Innis Beg, Skibbereen, co Cork (MAC-CARTHY-MORROGH/IFR). A 2 storey Victorian house with a square pyramidal-roofed projection at one corner of its front and a somewhat different square projection at the other end. Roof on bracket cornice.

Innishannon, co Cork (FREWEN/LG1965). A square 2 storey Georgian house with 2 3 sided bows on its front and a castellated range at the back, said to have incorporated an earlier house. The Irish home of Moreton Frewen, MP, a celebrated figure in the late-Victorian and Edwardian period; whose brilliant but impracticable projects earned him the nickname of "Mortal Ruin". Winston Churchill, who was his wife's nephew, frequently stayed here with him when young. The house was burnt 1921.

Innisrath, Lisnaskea, co Fermanagh (BUTLER, *sub* LANESBOROUGH, E/PB). A gabled Victorian-Tudor house on an island in Upper Lough Erne, built *ca* 1860 by Hon Henry Cavendish Butler, half-brother of 5th Earl of Lanesborough.

Island (The), co Waterford (PURCELL-FITZGERALD/IFR). An old castle on an island in the estuary of the River Suir downstream of Waterford which always belonged to this branch of the FitzGeralds—of which the most famous member in recent times was Edward FitzGerald, the translator of Omar Khayyám—but which did not become the massive battlemented cut-stone pile it is now until *ca* 1900, when it was remodelled, modernized and had large wings added to it by Edward FitzGerald's great-nephew, Gerald Purcell-FitzGerald, to the design of Romayne Walker. The wings are almost as high as the centre, and, like it, have Irish battlements; the centre being flanked by 2 small turrets. The walls are more or less devoid of ornament; there are many stone-mullioned windows and a mullioned conservatory at one side of the building. The interior is Baronial and lavish Edwardian-Elizabethan; there is a great hall with walls

Inchmore

The Island, co Waterford

Island House, Castleconnell, co Limerick (DE BURGHO, Bt/PB1873). A single-storey house with a portico.

Islanmore, Croom, co Limerick (KELLY/IFR; MORLEY/LGI1958). A square 2 storey C19 house with a 5 bay front and side and an eaved roof. 1 bay breakfront; pedimented doorway; simple entablatures over ground floor windows. Staircase with wrought-iron balustrade; doorcases in staircase hall with entablatures and pilasters. Italo-Romanesque arcade at head of stairs, with coupled columns. Dining room with screen of Corinthian columns. Sold *ca* 1957 by Mr Derrick Morley.

Isercleran

Isercleran (also known as **St Clerans**), **Craughwell, co Galway** (BURKE COLE/IFR). A plain 2 storey late C18 house—built by the Burkes 1784 when they abandoned their ancestral castle nearby—onto the front of which a 2 storey bow-ended block by Sir Richard Morrison in his villa style was added 1811 by J. H. Burke. The new 5 bay front is, as Mr McParland points out, "a highly successful derivative of Gandon's Military Infirmary in Dublin"; with a 3 bay breakfront and a grouping of 3 arched recesses; a giant one rising the full height of the elevation in the centre, and 2 smaller ones on either side over the 2 neighbouring ground floor windows. A bold string course serves as the springing of the central arch, the lower part of which is filled with a single-storey portico. Entrance hall with domed ceiling on pendentives; paired columns in recesses. One of the sons of J. H. Burke, the builder of the new block, was Robert O'Hara Burke, who perished when leading the ill-fated Burke-Wills Expedition across Australia 1861. Isercleran was inherited 1914 by R. O'H. Burke's niece, who was the mother of the practical joker, Horace de Vere Cole and of Mrs Neville Chamberlain. It was sold 1954 and subsequently became the home of Mr John Huston, the film director and well-known follower of the Galway Blazers, who re-sold it *ca* 1971. The old castle remains in the Burke Cole family.

of Portland stone, Gothic arches and a stone fireplace carved with an impressive heraldic achievement; there is a very large dining room panelled in oak with an Elizabethan-style plasterwork ceiling, and other rooms in the same manner. After being let for some years, The Island was sold *ca* 1960 by Princess Ferdinando d'Ardia Caracciolo (*née* Purcell-FitzGerald).

Island (The), Kilmuckridge, co Wexford (BOLTON, *sub* HUGHES/IFR). An early or mid-C18 3 storey 5 bay block, with 2 storey wings that do not balance each other; that to the right being 3 bay, that to the left 1 bay, with a Victorian window in its lower storey. High solid parapets to roofs of main block and right hand wing. Fanlighted doorway now obscured by projecting porch with Doric pilasters. Low-ceilinged rooms. Dining room, running from front to back, with late-Georgian cornice. More elaborate Victorian plasterwork in ground floor room in left-hand wing. The Island has given its name to the well-known hunt, which was founded by William Bolton (*d* 1853) who kept a pack of hounds here and hunted the country at his own expense. After the death of the last William Bolton 1958, The Island was inherited by his nieces, the Misses Eva, Violet & Mary Hughes, who sold it 1962.

Island House, co Cork (*see* LITTLE ISLAND HOUSE).

J

Jackson Hall, Coleraine (*see* COLERAINE: THE MANOR HOUSE).

Jamesbrook, Ballinacurra, co Cork (GOOLD-ADAMS/LGI1958; BAGWELL/IFR). A bow-fronted Georgian house.

Jamestown, Drumsna, co Leitrim (O'BEIRNE/LGI1912). A hybrid house with a mixture of Georgian and Victorian features; probably a C18 house re-roofed and re-modelled C19. Gables with elaborate barge-boards; lunette windows above mullioned windows; 2 storey 3 bay end with pillared porch.

Jamestown, co Leix. A hybrid house with Diocletian windows under Victorian gables and fancy bargeboards. Pillared porch at end.

Jenkinstown

Jenkinstown, Ballyragget, co Kilkenny (BRYAN/LGI1904; BELLEW, B/PB). An early C19 house in "pasteboard Gothic", following the traditional Palladian plan of a centre block joined to wings by single-storey links; built for Major George Bryan to the design of William Robertson, of Kilkenny. 2 storey centre block; 2 storey projecting porch crowned with a battlemented gable and pinnacles; 2 storey end towers with quatrefoil windows. Links with pinnacles and triple ogee-headed windows, joining the centre block to the gable-ends of the wings, which ran back; one wing having a battlemented clock-tower, crowned with a little crocketed cupola. According to a description of 1829, the entrance hall was "a noble apartment, finished in the most florid style of Gothic architecture"; the great saloon and libraries were "chaste designs, cleverly executed"; while the corridor, containing a collection of ancestral portraits, led to "a theatre of elegant construction and sufficient magnitude" where amateur theatricals were performed "before a fashionable and a happy assemblage". Later in C19, one of the wings was rebuilt in a more substantial type of Gothic, with corbelled bartizans;

Jenkinstown

Jenkinstown

and either with a view to rebuilding it, or as the result of a fire, the centre block was demolished apart from one of its walls. In the event, the centre block was not rebuilt; instead, the 2 wings were joined by a somewhat makeshift single-storey corridor; and in the early years of the present century, the then owner, Major Hon George Bryan, afterwards 4th Lord Bellew, lived happily in one wing, his servants and kitchen being accommodated in the other. One day, the surviving wall of the centre block collapsed onto the corridor and Lord Bellew was cut off from his servants. He took it philosophically, and told his friends, with the characteristic humour of his generation, "I'm changing the name of the place from Jenkinstown to Ballyshambles".

Jigginstown House

Jigginstown House, Naas, co Kildare

(WENTWORTH, STRAFFORD, E/DEP; FITZ-WILLIAM, E/PB). The palace which Thomas Wentworth, afterwards Earl of Strafford, built *ca* 1636 when Lord-Deputy of Ireland, for his own use and also perhaps with a view to its being occupied by Charles I; though it was never a Royal Palace, but Strafford's own property, and remained the property of his descendants. It is said to have been designed by John Allen, who came to Ireland from Holland, was "factor" for the Dutch and "being skilful in architecture was esteemed and consulted by the most eminent of the nobility in their buildings". It appears to have consisted of one principal storey, of red brick, on a high, stone-faced basement; and with a high-pitched roof containing a dormered attic; it had a frontage of no less than 380 feet, consisting of a long central block flanked by 2 projecting pavilions or towers. Part of the basement was vaulted, of very fine brickwork, with panelled and moulded brick columns; there were brick fireplaces and massive brick chimneystacks. According to tradition, there was an elaborate formal lay-out with terraces and fishponds. Also according to tradition, the building was never completed; but this is not wholly true; Wentworth told Archbishop Laud 1637 that he had "in a manner finished it" at a cost of £6,000, and he seems to have been frequently in residence here, for many of his letters are written from "The Naas". It was here that the great Ormonde signed the "Cessation" with the Confederates 1643; after the Restoration, he removed some of the marble doorcases and chimneypieces to Kilkenny Castle, or Dunmore House (*qqv*). In C18, the building was allowed to fall into ruin; now all that remains are some of the walls and the vaulted basement. The ruins have recently been cleared of the ivy which for so long smothered them.

Johnsbrook, Kells, co Meath (DASHWOOD-TANDY, *sub* DF BURGH/IFR). A C18 house of 2 storeys, with a front of 1 bay on either side of a pedimented breakfront. Diocletian window in pediment, above window flanked by 2 narrower windows, above doorway with fanlight and baseless pediment flanked by 2 narrow windows. Good window surrounds with keystones. The seat of the Dashwood-Tandy family.

Johnstown, Enfield, co Meath. A 3 storey 5 bay early C18 house linked by blank walls to wings with Venetian windows. Parapeted roof; pedimented doorcase. The seat of the Rorke family.

Johnstown, co Tipperary

Johnstown (formerly **Peterfield**), **Puckaun, co Tipperary** (HOLMES/LGI1912). A 3 storey late C18 block with a similar elevation to the nearby Prior Park (*qv*), of 5 bays, the 3 central windows in each storey being grouped closely together, probably designed by William Leeson. Pedimented and fanlighted doorcase with 2 engaged Tuscan columns; keystones over windows. 6 bay side. Neo-Classical interior plasterwork. Built by Peter Holmes, MP; in 1837, the residence of J. S. Prendergast. Now a ruin.

Johnstown Castle, nr Wexford, co Wexford (ESMONDE, Bt/PB; GROGAN-MORGAN/ LGI1863; FORBES, GRANARD, E/PB; FITZ-GERALD, *sub* LEINSTER, D/PB). An old tower house of the Esmondes, engulfed in an impressively turreted, battlemented and machicolated castle of gleaming silver-grey ashlar built *ca* 1840 for H. K. Grogan-Morgan, MP, to the design of Daniel Robertson, of Kilkenny. Entrance front dominated by a single frowning tower, with a porte-cochère projecting at the end of an entrance corridor

and a Gothic conservatory at one end. Garden front with 2 round turrets, 3 sided central bow and tracery windows. Lower wing with polygonal tower. The castle stands in a lush setting of lawns and exotic trees and shrubs, overlooking a lake which has a Gothic tower rising from its waters and a terrace lined with statues on its far side. Impressive castellated entrance archways facing each other on either side of the road. After the death of H. K. Grogan-Morgan, Johnstown passed to his widow, who married as her 2nd husband, Rt Hon Sir Thomas Esmonde, 9th Bt, a descendant of the original owners of the old tower house. The estate afterwards went to H. K. Grogan-Morgan's daughter, Jane, Countess of Granard, and eventually to Lady Granard's daughter, Lady Maurice FitzGerald. It is now an agricultural institute, and the grounds are maintained as a show place. The old tower house was the home of Cornelius Grogan, who was unjustly executed for treason after 1798 Rebellion.

Johnstown House, Carlow, co Carlow

(CONNELLAN/LGI1912; and *sub* FAIRLIE-CUNINGHAME, Bt/PB). A 2 storey gable-ended house of early C18 appearance, built on the foundations of a medieval monastery and with C19 Tudor-Gothic embellishments. Entrance front not quite symmetrical; stepped gable and little turrets in centre, some battlements and buttresses with finials at the ends of the facade. Tall Tudor-style chimneys. In 1814, the residence of John Campion; now, of Lady (Phyllida) Couchman, daughter of C. L. Connellan, and of her son, Mr John Couchman.

Johnstown Kennedy, Rathcoole, co Dublin (KENNEDY, Bt/PB). A plain 3 storey Georgian house with a 3 bay front and a 5 bay, irregularly fenestrated, side. Later enclosed porch. Acanthus plasterwork on drawing room ceiling. Sold recently by Sir Derrick Kennedy, 6th and present Bt.

Johnstown Castle, co Wexford

K

Kanturk Castle

Kanturk Castle, Kanturk, co Cork. A very large 3 storey semi-fortified Jacobean house, built *ca* 1609 by MacDonagh Mac-Carthy, Lord of Duhallow; consisting of a rectangular centre block with 2 regular 3 bay fronts, one having a Jacobean doorway with pilasters, a frieze and a cornice, and 4 boldly-projecting corner-towers. It seems likely that these were intended to terminate in gables above corbelled galleries; but the house was never completed; MacCarthy, on hearing that his English settler neighbours were making complaints to the Privy Council that he was building a fortress, had the building stopped in a fit of rage; and ordered the glass tiles which had been made for covering the roof—so as to provide the equivalent of a sky-light—to be broken up.

Keale

Keale, Millstreet, co Cork (LEADER/IFR). An early C19 house of 2 storeys over a basement. 3 bay front; centre bay projecting boldly, framed by plain corner-pilasters with fanlighted doorway and twin-light window above, presumably a later C19 alteration. Plain corner-pilasters at sides of facade. Eaved roof.

Kenmare House, Killarney, co Kerry (BROWNE, *sub* GROSVENOR/IFR). The Brownes of Killarney, afterwards Earls of Kenmare,

Ross Castle, Killarney

Kenmare House: early C18 house

originally lived in Ross Castle on a promentory in Lough Leane. A wing was added to the old castle 1688 by Sir Valentine Browne, who became 1st Viscount Kenmare in the Jacobite Peerage a year later; but after the Battle of the Boyne, the castle, and the rest of his estates, were forfeited on account of his fidelity to James II. His grandson, 3rd Viscount, recovered the estates, but could not get possession of Ross Castle, which had been taken over as a military barracks; so *ca* 1726 he built a new house a little way to the north of the castle, closer to the town of Killarney. It was a rather old-fashioned house for its period: of 2 storeys with a dormered attic in its high-pitched roof, and with a front of 13 bays; the 3 outer bays on either side breaking forward. 3rd Viscount was his own architect, and the building work was done by tradesmen employed permanently on the estate; most of the materials came from near at hand, the hall being paved with marble from a quarry at Ross, the ceilings made of "laths from the mountains". The neighbouring gentry gave Lord Kenmare 16,000 slates "*gratis*". 4th Viscount, who had Charles James Fox to stay here—when Fox performed the rather surprising feat of swimming across one of the lakes—built a service wing onto the

house between 1775 and 1778; later a ball-room was added, which contained a painting of Handel being crowned by Orpheus. In C19, the original block was given plate-glass windows and an enclosed porch. Then, 1872, 4th Earl of Kenmare and his Countess decided to build a new house on a hilltop to the north-west, which commanded a spectacular view of the lakes and the surrounding mountains; a site which is said to have been chosen by Queen Victoria during one of her visits to Killarney. The old house was consequently demolished and a vast red-brick Victorian Tudor mansion was built on the chosen site, to the design of the English architect, George Devey; though the work seems to have been carried out by William Henry Lynn. It had many gables, some of them triangular, others curvilinear and pedimented; and many oriels, rectangular, 3 sided and semi-circular. It was decidedly Anglo-Saxon in flavour; though the spire of the domestic chapel, which was mounted on a dome, had Northern European ancestry. The interior of the house was panelled, or hung with boldly-patterned Spanish leather, and adorned with a profusion of rather small, carved wooden columns, reminiscent of an old-fashioned luxury liner. For 40 years Killarney House—as it was known—was one of the wonders of Ireland, and its splendours were legendary; then, 1913, it was gutted by fire. It was not rebuilt; instead, a house was made out of the stables of C18 house, entered by way of a pedimented porch in the courtyard; a house very characteristic of its period, with large, light, simply-decorated rooms. It was here that Valentine, Viscount Castlerosse—afterwards 6th Earl of Kenmare—the gossip columnist and *bon viveur*, entertained his friends in 1920s and 1930s. At the west end of the park, he laid out a golf course, regarded as one of the most beautiful in the world. In 1957 Mrs Beatrice Grosvenor, who had inherited the estate from her uncle, 7th and last Earl, sold this house together with part of the estate to a group of Americans; it is now the home of Mr John McShain, who purchased the interest of the other members of the group 1959, and is known as Killarney House, having previously been known as Kenmare House. The latter name was subsequently applied to the house which Mrs Grosvenor built for herself on the part of the estate which she retained; and afterwards to her present house, which she has also built. Both houses were designed by her cousin, Mr Francis Pollen, and are in a very pleasant Classical style. The first is on the site of the Victorian mansion, which having stood as a ruin, in a

Kenmare (Killarney) House: Victorian mansion

Kenmare (Killarney) House: Hall of Victorian mansion

The post 1913 Kenmare House (now known as Killarney House)

Kenure Park

Kenmare (Killarney) House: corridor in Victorian mansion

The post 1956 Kenmare House

The post 1974 Kenmare House

wilderness of shrubs and overgrown box hedges that had once been a formal garden, was cleared away *ca* 1956 to make room for it. The second house, to which Mrs Grosvenor moved *ca* 1974, is further from the town, towards the western end of the demense. It consists of a square 2 storey 3 bay block flanked by screen walls and single-storey wings; the main block has elevations adorned with fluted strip-pilasters; there is a pedimented doorcase beneath a recessed oculus in the centre of each of the 2 principal fronts.

Kenure Park, Rush, co Dublin (PALMER, Bt, *of Castle Lackin*/PB1911; FENWICK-PALMER, *sub* FENWICK/LG1965). A large mid-C18 3 storey house, grandly refaced 1842 to the design of George Papworth; mostly in stucco, with Corinthian corner pilasters reminiscent of those of Nash's London facades; but with a giant pedimented hexa-style Corinthian portico of stone, deep enough to serve as a porte-cochère. The entrance front is of 2 bays on either side of this great portico; the adjoining garden front is of 3 bays on either side of a curved central bow, with a semi-circular colonnade in front of its lower storey. The top storey is treated as an attic, above a modillion cornice; the roof parapet is balustraded. The entrance hall, with its engaged Doric columns and walls covered in yellow scagliola, dates from the Papworth remodelling, as does the vast central staircase hall, which is top-lit through windows of armorial stained glass in the cove of the ceiling. The staircase hall is also decorated in yellow scagliola, with Doric columns below and grey marbled Ionic pilasters above; there is an imperial staircase with an elaborate and ornate metal scrolled balustrade. Some of the reception rooms are on the ground floor, others on the floor above; the drawing room, and the room above it, which extend into the bow of the garden front, have ceilings of magnificent mid-C18 rococo plasterwork in the manner of Robert West. The rooms on the first floor include a long gallery. The dining room, next to the drawing room, has a cornice of Victorian plasterwork. The small library, next to the entrance hall, has (or had) mahogany bookcases. Sold *ca* 1964 by Col R. G. Fenwick-Palmer; now derelict.

Kerdiffstown, Naas, co Kildare (AYL-MER/IFR). A 3 storey C18 house of stone, with rusticated brick surrounds to the windows; originally belonging to the Hendricks. 3 sided bow in centre of front, containing entrance door; 2 bays on either side of this. The ends of the house are 3 bay; one side has round-headed, fanlighted windows on the ground floor, recessed in blind arches filled in with brick. Passed to a branch of the Aylmers with the marriage of Charlotte Hendrick to Michael Aylmer 1853. Sold by Col R. M. Aylmer 1938; subsequently a convent, when a chapel was built to one side of the front and an incongruous modern porch added to the central bow; now owned by Cement-Roadstone Ltd.

Kilballyowen, Bruff, co Limerick (o' GRADY/IFR). A 2 storey house of late-Georgian appearance, but with an old castle built into it. 5 bay front, with fanlighted doorway, prolonged by a 2 bay projecting wing at one end. Solid roof parapet. 3 bay side elevation with Wyatt windows under relieving arches in the 2 outer bays of the lower storey. Long garden front with 3 bay breakfront. Recently demolished and a new house built.

Kilbolane Castle, Charleville, co Cork (BOWEN/IFR; BRUCE/LGI1958). A house built 1695 or soon afterwards by John Bowen, whose family had hitherto lived in a lean-to within the walls of the old Desmond castle here, which had been granted to his maternal grandfather, the Cromwellian Capt John Nicholls. Of 2 storeys over a basement; 5 bay front. The house was refaced in the later Georgian period with a 1 bay breakfront, a central Wyatt window and a fanlighted doorway; and the windows were given thin astragals. At the back, however, the old square panes and thick glazing bars survived. Staircase at back of hall, separated from it by a doorway with an interior fanlight. 4 parlours on the ground floor, one with a corner fireplace; plasterwork of strong design in the two at the front. There was a lengthy dispute between the Bowen and Evans families as to the ownership of part of the Kilbolane estate, with litigation that lasted from 1759 to 1764. Then Henry Bowen built Bowen's Court (*qv*) on the original Bowen estate near Kildorrery, with the result that Henry Bowen's son, another Henry, sold Kilbolane 1795 to the Bruce family, of Miltown Castle, co Cork (*qv*). At the beginning of the present century, it was owned by David O'Leary Hannigan.

Kilboy, Nenagh, co Tipperary (PRITTIE, DUNALLEY, B/PB). A mid to late C18 house built for Henry Prittie, MP, afterwards 1st Lord Dunalley, to the design of William Leeson. Of 3 storeys over a basement; 5 bay entrance front with central feature of pediment and 4 giant engaged Doric columns; Doric entablature running the full length of the front, supported at the sides by coupled giant Doric pilasters; top storey treated as

Kilboy

Kilboy: Hall

an attic above the cornice. Ground floor windows with rusticated surrounds and alternate triangular and segmental pediments; rusticated basement; broad flight of steps up to entrance door. Side elevation almost plain, with no entablature or cornice; of 5 bays, with central Venetian window; keystones over windows and some simple blocking in the window surrounds. Large square hall, with heavy frieze of rather unusual plasterwork, combining *putti* and foliage with husk ornament and neo-Classical motifs; niche with entablature on console brackets; marble chimneypiece with swags of drapery, plasterwork panel over. Bifurcating staircase in back hall. The house was burnt 1922 and afterwards rebuilt without the top storey. The principal rooms, as rebuilt, had oak panelling in early C18 style; the bifurcating staircase was replaced by simple oak stairs. *Ca* 1955 the house was demolished and a single-storey house in a vaguely Georgian style was built on the original basement.

Kilbrack, Doneraile, co Cork (STAWELL/LGI1912). A square 2 storey late-Georgian house. Attractive wooden staircase. A seat of the Stawell family; in *ca* 1910, the residence of Capt W. H. Nichols; in more recent years, of Major & Mrs N. S. Regnart.

Kilbrittain Castle, Kilbrittain, co Cork (STAWELL/LGI1912). A C16 tower-house of the MacCarthys, protected by a turreted bawn, incorporated in a C18 house built *ante*

Kilbrittain Castle

1750 by Jonas Stawell, which was rebuilt as a castle in mid-C19. Of 2 storeys over a high basement, and faced in random ashlar; with a battlemented parapet, corner-bartizans and a square tower at one end. Mullioned windows, more or less regularly disposed; pointed entrance doorway opening onto a perron with long twin flights of steps. The castle stands on top of a hill, with wide views over the surrounding country and down a valley to the sea. The entrance front faces over a bawn, on one side of which there was formerly a less heavily castellated C18 range with a Venetian window. The castle was burnt in early 1920s and stood for nearly half-a-century as a spectacular ruin; parts of it, including the range with the Venetian window, being demolished. Then, from *ca* 1968 onwards, the surviving main building of the castle was restored by Mr Russell Winn.

Kilbyrne

Kilbyrne, Doneraile, co Cork (GROVE-WHITE/IFR). A 2 storey 3 bay late-Georgian house with a single-storey Doric portico, with a Victorian wing at one side. The home of Col James Grove-White, the antiquary and historian of North Cork. Sold *ca* 1956; now demolished.

Kilcarra Castle, co Wicklow (*see* GLENART CASTLE).

Kilcarty, Kilmessan, co Meath. A delightful "hobby farm" of *ca* 1770–80, built for Dr George Cleghorn, Prof of Anatomy, to the design of Thomas Ivory. The 2 storey 5 bay gable-ended dwelling house and the farm buildings are all part of the one composition, in the true Palladian manner. The front of the house, which has a round-headed doorway with blocking, is prolonged by single-storey 2 bay wings; linking it to gable-ends of the farm buildings, which are treated as pediments, with oculi; they stand a little back, rising above curved sweeps. The 2 farm buildings extend back, forming 2 sides of a large courtyard behind the house, which is balanced on 4th side by a centrally-placed barn. In the words of Dr Craig, "the total effect is one of bland serenity". In 1814, the residence of Ross Fox; now, of Mr Peter Harper.

Kilcascan Castle

Kilcascan Castle, Ballineen, co Cork (DAUNT/IFR). A 2 storey early C19 castellated house. Symmetrical entrance front with projecting bays joined by battlemented cloister; rectangular tracery windows. Battlemented bow and square turret.

Kilclooney, co Galway (*see* QUARRY-MOUNT).

Kilcoleman, co Cork: 1911

Kilcoleman, co Cork: 1921

Kilcoleman, Bandon, co Cork (LONG-FIELD/IFR). A 3 storey house of mid-C18 appearance, with camber-headed windows. 5 bay entrance front; C19 enclosed porch with paired corner-pilasters, Wyatt window at front and round-headed entrance doorway at side. 3 bay side elevation with later single-storey 3 sided bow. Burnt 1921.

Kilcoleman Abbey (formerly **Bushfield**), **Milltown, co Kerry** (GODFREY, Bt/PB). A plain 3 storey Georgian block, built *ca* 1800 by Sir William Godfrey, 1st Bt, MP; altered 1819 by Sir John Godfrey, 2nd Bt, to the design of William Vitruvius Morrison, who threw one of his thinner Tudor-Revival cloaks over the house and gave it 4 slender corner-turrets with cupolas, similar to those at Glenarm Castle, co Antrim and Borris, co Carlow (*qqv*). A 2 storey service wing

Kilcoleman Abbey, co Kerry: in its heyday; and as it was 1976

with curvilinear gables was also added. Inside the house, Morrison formed a 2 storey galleried hall, opening with arches onto the staircase. The house was lived in by the Godfreys until *ca* 1960; after which it was abandoned, and has now fallen completely into ruin; most of it having been demolished.

Kilcolgan Castle

Kilcolgan Castle, Clarinbridge, co Galway (ST GEORGE, *sub* FRENCH/IFR; BLYTH, B/PB; FFRENCH, B/PB). A small early C19 castle, built *ca* 1801 by Christopher St George, the builder of the nearby Tyrone House (*qv*), who retired here with a "*chère amie*" having handed over Tyrone to his son. It consists of 3 storey square tower with battlements and crockets and a single-storey battlemented and buttressed range. The windows appear to have been subsequently altered. The castle served as a dower house for Tyrone, and was occupied by Miss Matilda St George after Tyrone was abandoned by the family 1905; it was sold after her death 1925. Subsequent owners included Mr Martin Niland, TD; Mr Arthur Penberthy; Lord Blyth; and Mrs T.A.C. Agnew (sister of 7th and present Lord ffrench); it is now owned by Mr John Maitland.

Kilconner, Bagenalstown, co Carlow (WATSON/IFR). A house of C17 origin, enlarged and altered in C19 Gothic 1872, to the design of L. Buck.

Kilcooley Abbey, Thurles, co Tipperary (PONSONBY/IFR and *sub* BESSBOROUGH, E/PB). A large winged house built *ca* 1790 by Sir

Kilcooley Abbey

William Barker, 4th and last Bt, whose family had previously lived in the old abbey here, which was made into a house in C17. Centre block with 7 bay entrance front; broad flight of steps guarded by heraldic beasts up to hall door; flanking wings continued by screen walls. In the garden front, which faces the old abbey, the centre block is of 5 bays, with a breakfront centre of 4 giant Ionic pilasters supporting a plain entablature; the wings on this side are pedimented, and of 2 bays, joined to the centre block by lower links. Impressive balustraded perron with double flights of steps up to central door; roof parapet with urns. The house was partly destroyed by fire *ca* 1840; during the rebuilding, the family once again occupied the old abbey. Either then, or later in C19, two 3 sided bows were added on the entrance front, and smaller bows on the garden front, where balustraded loggias were built between the centre block and the wings. A glass porch was also at some date added on this side. The interior largely dates from after the fire. Vast 2 storey galleried hall, partly top-lit by a glazed dome; with low panelling. Stone staircase with wrought-iron balustrade, probably contemporary with the building of the house, in staircase hall to one side. Panelled dining room. Library with Victorian bookcases of carved oak. After the death of Sir William Barker, the builder of the house, Kilcooley passed to his nephew, Chambré Brabazon Ponsonby, the half-brother of Sarah Ponsonby, one of the two "Ladies of Llangollen".

Kilcor Castle, Castlelyons, co Cork (PHIPPS/IFR). A C19 castellated house with Wyatt windows.

Kilcornan

Kilcornan, Clarinbridge, co Galway (REDINGTON/LGI1899; WILSON-LYNCH/LGI-1958). A large C19 Tudor-Gothic pile begun by Sir Thomas Redington 1837; with gables and oriels, a pinnacled porch-tower and a much-pinnacled chapel. Long gallery with fretted ceiling. Passed by inheritance to the Wilson-Lynch family. Now an institution.

Kilcornan: Long Gallery

Kilcosgriff, Shanagolden, co Limerick (LANGFORD/IFR). A simple 2 storey 3 bay house, with a single-storey rectangular projection on either side of the entrance door. Prominent roof.

Kilcreene House

Kilcreene House, Kilkenny, co Kilkenny (EVANS, Bt/EDB; DE MONTMORENCY, Bt/PB; SMITHWICK/IFR). A very important late C17 house. Of 2 storeys over a basement; "U"-shaped, the 2 wings projecting on either side of the entrance front and each having 2 bays in its end. High, sprocketed roof on bracket cornice. Brick chimney stacks with recessed panels. Front prolonged by screen walls with niches and large rusticated arches. Good quoins. Later pilastered porch. 6 bay garden front, the 2 outer bays on either side breaking forward. Single storey entrance hall, with stairs in separate room at side of hall. Very fine chimneypieces, notably one of grey Kilkenny marble with a scroll pediment. The house was demolished in fairly recent years; some of the chimneypieces are now at Bonnettstown Hall (*qv*) and one is at Kilcreene Lodge (*qv*).

Kilcreene Lodge

Kilcreene Lodge, Kilkenny, co Kilkenny (SMITHWICK/IFR). A pleasant 2 storey stucco-faced Victorian house, built *ca* 1860 by J.W. Smithwick, incorporating an older, smaller house. 4 bay front with triangular pediments on console brackets over ground floor windows, and gabled wing at one end. Roof of main block on bracket cornice.

Irregular adjoining garden front, with single-storey curved and balustraded bow; decorative ironwork cresting on ridge of roof. Ornate overdoors in the hall and drawing room, the latter being a large and handsome room in Louis Quinze style. Good late C17 or early C18 chimneypiece brought from Kilcreene House (*qv*) in billiard room. Attractive garden with lake spanned by bridge.

Kilcrenagh, Carrigrohane, co Cork (PIKE/LGI1958). A house of late Georgian appearance, consisting of a centre of 3 storeys over a basement and 3 bays with 2 storey 3 bay wings set a little back. Round-headed entrance doorway in centre flanked by 2 storey bows. Burnt *ca* 1920.

Kildangan: Entrance Front

Kildangan: Garden Front

Kildangan, Monasterevin, co Kildare (MORE O'FERRALL/IFR). The old castle here, which had square corner towers, originally belonged to a branch of the FitzGeralds, Earls of Kildare. It was sold *ca* 1705 to the brothers Edward & Edmund Reilly, of co Cavan, prosperous merchants in Dublin, of which city Edmund was an Alderman. Passed to the More O'Ferralls with the marriage of Edmund's descendant, Susan O'Reilly, to C. E. More O'Ferrall 1849. In 1784, the old castle was abandoned by the family in favour of a single-storey thatched house, which was burnt 1880. 2 years later, D. M. J. More O'Ferrall had the old castle dynamited, presumably to provide stone for the large new house which he built between then and 1886, to the design of W. J. Hopkins, of Worcester. The house is in a restrained Victorian Jacobean style, with long, asymmetrical elevations on both the entrance and garden fronts; of 2 storeys, with a gabled and dormered attic in the high-pitched roof. Curvilinear gables; windows mostly rectangular sashes, originally with plate glass; except for a large mullioned window in the garden front, lighting the stairs. Many improvements to the house were carried out by Mr Roderic More O'Ferrall during the years following the end of the Second World War. The exterior, which had formerly been faced in red brick,

Kildangan: Drawing Room

was made much more attractive by being rendered in grey cement; and at the same time astragals were put into the windows. The sitting room was hung with a grey and white early C19 French pictorial wallpaper; and the large drawing room, which at times in the past had been divided into 2 separate rooms, was charmingly redecorated in Georgian Gothic; the orange colour of the walls being set off by the white of the slender Gothic piers and other Gothic ornament. Mr More O'Ferrall has also laid out a garden with a notable collection of trees and shrubs.

Kilderry, co Donegal (HART/LG1937 Supp). A rambling 2 storey house.

Kildevin, Street, co Westmeath (TYNDALL/LG1952Supp). A 2 storey late-Georgian house built 1833 by Robert Sproule, possibly a member of the family of architects of that name. 2 storey; 1 bay on either side of a deep central bow, which is balustraded and rises a storey above the rest of the front and continues as a balustraded attic through the depth of the house to form a similar bow at the back, facing the farmyard. Entrance door in bow, with pilasters and entablature. Bracket cornice. Subsequently the home of Mr & Mrs H. S. Tyndall.

Kildrought Parsonage, co Kildare (*see* CELBRIDGE LODGE).

Kilfane, Thomastown, co Kilkenny (BUSHE/LGI1912; POWER, Bt, *of Kilfane*/PB). A house of late-Georgian appearance consisting of a 3 storey 5 bay centre block with 3 bay wings which are single-storey at the front and 2 storey at the back. On the front of the centre block there is a 1 bay breakfront and a single-storey portico of fluted Doric columns. Fine straight lime avenue; ruined medieval church with fortified rectory at edge of park. The church contains a large and celebrated C14 effigy of a knight, known as "Long Cantwell". Originally the seat of a branch of the Bushe family, of which the great Charles Kendal Bushe came of another branch, established at the neighbouring house, Kilmurry (*qv*). Passed to the Powers through the marriage of Harriett Bushe to Sir John Power, 1st Bt, founder of the Kilkenny Hunt and brother of the talented amateur actor, Richard Power, who ran the Kilkenny Theatre in its great days in early C19. Sold *ca* 1967; now the home of Mr & Mrs T. H. Clarke.

Kilfera, Kilkenny, co Kilkenny (STOP-FORD, *sub* COURTOWN, E/PB). A long low house in early C19 cottage ornée style, built onto an old tower and with a Regency ironwork veranda at one end. The drawing room has a large Gothic doorway opening onto this veranda, which frames a Reptonian landscape of sweeping lawn, river and woods. The seat of the Hunt family; now the home of Mr Montagu & Mrs Stopford (*née* Hunt).

Kilfinnan Castle, Glandore, co Cork (HUSSEY DE BURGH/IFR). A castellated house overlooking Glandore Harbour. In recent years, the home of Mrs McCarthy Essaye.

Kilfrush, Knocklong, co Limerick (GUB-BINS/LG1937Supp). A plain 2 storey early C19 house. 7 bay entrance front with porch; 5 bay side. Attractive pillared gate lodge.

Kilkea Castle

Kilkea Castle, Mageny, co Kildare (FITZGERALD, LEINSTER, D/PB). A medieval castle of the FitzGeralds, Earls of Kildare, particularly associated with C16 11th Earl of Kildare, the famous "Wizard Earl". After Carton (*qv*) became the family seat in C18, it was leased to a succession of tenants; one of them being the Dublin silk-merchant, Thomas Reynolds, a friend of Lord Edward FitzGerald through whom he became a United Irishman, only to turn informer when he realized the full aims of the movement. His role as informer did not prevent the unhappy Reynolds from having the castle, which he had only recently done up in fine style, sacked by the military; who tore up the floor-boards and tore down the panelling on the pretext of searching for arms. Subsequent tenants caused yet more damage and there was a serious fire 1849; after which the 3rd Duke of Leinster resumed possession of the castle and restored and enlarged it as a dower-house for his family. The work was sympathetically done, so that the tall, grey castle keeps its air of medieval strength with its bartizans and its massively battered stone walls; though its battlements and its rather too regularly placed trefoil-headed windows are obviously C19. At one side of the castle a long, low, gabled office range was added, in a restrained Tudor-Revival style. The interior is entirely of 1849; for the lofty top storey, where the principal rooms were originally situated, was divided to provide a storey extra. The ceilings are mostly beamed, with corbels bearing the Leinster saltire. In 1880s, the beautiful Hermione, Duchess of Leinster (then Marchioness of Kildare), lived here with her amiable but not very inspiring husband; finding the life not much

to her taste, she composed the couplet: "Kilkea Castle and Lord Kildare / Are more than any woman can bear". After the sale of Carton 1949, Kilkea became the seat of the 8th and present Duke of Leinster (then Marquess of Kildare); but it was sold *ca* 1960 and is now an hotel.

Kilkenny, co Kilkenny: Bishop's Palace. A Georgian house built on the foundations of the medieval palace probably by Charles Este, who was (C of I) Bishop of Ossory from 1736 to 1745. Plain facade with Gibbsian doorcase. Panelled staircase hall; staircase of handsome joinery with Corinthian newels; doorcase with Corinthian pilasters. In 1760 Bishop Pococke built a Doric colonnade joining the Palace to St Canice's Cathedral, which incorporated a delightful single-storey pedimented and bow-ended Robing Room. The colonnade was subsequently demolished, but the Robing Room remains as a feature of the Palace garden. The Palace was well restored *ca* 1963 by the then Bishop, Dr H. R. McAdoo.

Kilkenny, co Kilkenny: Deanery (C of I). A mid-C18 house with a rusticated doorway. Large and small drawing rooms opening into each other.

Kilkenny Castle: as remodelled after Restoration by great Duke of Ormonde

with 4 round towers—of which 3 remain—joined by curtain walls or ranges of buildings to enclose a courtyard. Various improvements were made to it in the Elizabethan or Jacobean period by "Black Thomas", 10th Earl of Ormonde; and an extensive remodelling was carried out by the Great Duke of Ormonde after the Restoration, which was probably when 2 sides of the courtyard and the tower at their junction were demolished; presumably because they were in a bad state as a result of Cromwell's bombardment of the castle 1650. The Great Duke transformed the castle from a medieval fortress into a pleasant country house,

Kilkenny Castle

Kilkenny Castle, co Kilkenny (BUTLER, ORMONDE, M/PB). The ancestral castle of the Ormonde Butlers which, with its round towers and iron-grey walls, dominates the town of Kilkenny from a height above the River Nore. First built 1192 by Strongbow's son-in-law, William Marshall, Earl of Pembroke, whose eventual heir, Sir Hugh le Despenser, sold it to James Butler, 3rd Earl of Ormonde, 1391. By 1307 it seems to have been of much the same shape as it is today;

rather like the château or schloss of a contemporary European princeling; with high-pitched roofs and cupolas surmounted by vanes and gilded ducal coronets on the old round towers. Outworks gave place to gardens with terraces, a "waterhouse", a fountain probably carved by William de Keyser, and statues copied from those in Charles II's Privy Garden. The Duchess seems to have been the prime mover in the work, in which William (afterwards Sir William) Robinson,

Kilkenny Castle: Street Front and 2nd Duke of Ormonde's Gateway

Kilkenny Castle: Picture Gallery

Surveyor-General and architect of the Royal Hospital, Kilmainham, was probably involved; supervising the construction of the Presence Chamber 1679. Robinson is also believed to have designed the magnificent entrance gateway of Portland and Caen stone with a pediment, Corinthian pilasters and swags which the 2nd Duke erected on the street front of the castle *ca* 1709. Not much else was done to the castle in c18, for the Ormondes suffered a period of eclipse following the attainder and exile of the 2nd Duke, who became a Jacobite after the accession of George I. In 1766 Walter Butler went to live in the castle, which had stood empty for some years, and carried out various repairs; decorating some of the rooms with simple late c18 plasterwork. His son, John, who was recognized as 17th Earl of Ormonde 1791, was probably the builder of the castle stables, across the street from the 2nd Duke's gateway; they have a long pedimented and balustraded front with rusticated blind arches; a cupola which was formerly raised on a tall lantern; and a horseshoe-shaped court. *Ca* 1826, the Kilkenny architect, William Robertson, when walking in the castle courtyard with the Lady Ormonde of the day, noticed that a main wall was out of true and consequently unsafe. One suspects it may have been wishful thinking on his part, for it landed him the commission to rebuild the castle, which he did so thoroughly that virtually nothing now remains from before his time except for the 3 old towers, the outer walls and —fortunately—the 2nd Duke's gateway. Apart from the latter, the exterior of the castle became uncompromisingly c19 feudal; all the 1st Duke's charming features being swept away. Robertson also replaced one of 2 missing sides of the courtyard with a new wing containing an immense picture gallery; the original gallery, on the top floor of the principal range, having been divided by him into bedrooms. Robertson left the interior of the castle extremely dull, with plain or monotonously ribbed ceilings and unvarying Louis Quinze style chimneypieces. The rooms, however, gained much from the tapestries, the portraits and the display of the famous Ormonde gold plate. In 1859-62 the picture gallery was remodelled to the design of Benjamin Woodward, and given a high, partly glazed timbered roof, which was painted with trees, waterfalls, birds and strange beasts by John Hungerford Pollen, who also carved the great chimneypiece of white marble, which has medallions of different scenes in the history of the Ormondes. At the same time, Woodward and his senior partner, Sir Thomas Newenham Deane, gave the castle

Kilkenny Castle: Library

Kilkenny Castle: Staircase

Kilkenny Castle: King Edward VII leaving after paying a visit

some Ruskinian Gothic windows and a Ruskinian Gothic stone staircase. In 1909, the dining room chimneypiece was replaced with a large Elizabethan carved stone mantel from the Castle at Carrick-on-Suir (*qv*), to which it has since been returned. The interior was largely redecorated and woodcarvings in the manner of Grinling Gibbons were introduced into some of the family rooms in the South Tower after the castle had suffered damage 1922 during the Civil War, when, having been occupied by one side, it was attacked and captured by the other; the Earl of Ossory (afterwards 5th Marquess) and his wife being in residence at the time. Several monarchs have stayed at Kilkenny Castle during the course of its history, including Richard II, James II, William III, Edward VII and George V. In 1935 the Ormondes ceased to live in the castle, which for the next 30 years stood empty and deteriorating. In 1967, however, 6th Marquess presented it to a local committee and it is now being gradually restored as a national possession. The South Tower is eventually to become the headquarters of the Butler Society, a world-wide association of members of the Butler family, which was founded at the same time as the castle was handed over. Some of the rooms of the castle are now open to the public.

Kilkishen House, Sixmilebridge, co Clare (STUDDERT/IFR). A c18 house of 2 storeys over a basement. 7 bay front; door-

case with engaged Doric columns and fanlight extending over door and sidelights; parapeted roof. Good interiors, including an oval drawing room with neo-Classical plasterwork.

Killadeas, Ballinamallard, co Fermanagh (IRVINE/LGI1912). A 2 storey Victorian Italianate house, in a splendid position on the shores of Lough Erne. Entrance front with pediment and porch in the form of a 3 arched loggia, flanked by a square tower with a glazed belvedere and urns on its parapet. Now an hotel.

Killadoon, Celbridge, co Kildare (LUCAS-CLEMENTS/IFR; CLEMENTS/IFR). A 3 storey block of *ca* 1770, joined to a single 2 storey

Killadoon

wing by a curved sweep; if the original intention was to build a balancing wing and sweep, the idea must have been abandoned fairly soon; because there is now a 3 sided bow on the other side of the house which would have clashed with the sweep and which appears in a C18 view. Built for Rt Hon Nathaniel Clements, MP, the banker, politician and amateur architect; one would naturally assume that it was to his own design, yet apart from having the "pattern-book" tripartite doorway with a fanlight, a baseless pediment and engaged columns which he seems to have favoured, it lacks the characteristics of the houses known to be by him or convincingly attributed to him. Apart from the doorway, the 5 bay entrance front is quite plain, as is the 6 bay garden front, which now has some relief in the external shutters of the ground floor windows. The wing has a 6 bay front and there are oculi in the sweep. All this plainness, however, seems like deliberate understatement; for it is, in fact, a house of great quality. The interior is very well finished; the rooms, though few in number, are of noble proportions. The hall has a Doric frieze and a neo-Classical chimneypiece of stone, with fluted Doric columns. The staircase, in a separate hall to one side, is of good joinery. The dining room has a modillion cornice and doorcases with entablatures carved with acanthus; painted in shades of chocolate, red and oyster. The library, extending into the bow at the side of the house, has a cornice of mutules. The drawing room, which has a gilded modillion cornice, remains almost exactly as it was when redecorated *ca* 1820s by Nathaniel Clements's grandson, 2nd Earl of Leitrim; with a beautiful French wallpaper in faded green and gold, gilt pelmet boards and the original red curtains and flounces.

Killaghy Castle, Mullinahone, co Tipperary. An old tower-house of the Tobin family, with a 2 storey 5 bay C19 castellated wing attached. Doorway with segmental-pointed arch; mullioned windows with hood

Killakee

mouldings; bartizan. Forfeited by the Tobins 1653; passed to the Greene family, from whom it passed through marriage to the Despards; it was garrisoned by Lieut Despard 1798. It then passed by inheritance to the Wright family, by whom it was sold. Since then, it has been owned successively by the families of Watson, Fox, Naughton and Bradshaw.

Killakee, Rathfarnham, co Dublin (MASSY, B/PB). A 2 storey stucco-faced Victorian Italianate house of symmetrical aspect, with a curved bow in the centre of its principal front, and similar bows in the side elevations. Balustraded parapet to roof. Veranda with slender iron uprights and balcony above along the centre of the principal front, giving the house the air of a villa in the Mediterranean. Now demolished.

Killala Castle

Killala Castle, Killala, co Mayo (BOURKE/LGI1904). The Palace of the (C of I) Bishops of Killala, a tall, plain 3 storey "L"-shaped building with a gable-ended tower-like block at the end of one of its arms. The entrance door, near the angle of the 2 arms, was fanlighted, with some blocking, and flanked by two small side-lights. The castle was said to be ruinous 1787, but some repairs to it were carried out 1796 when, presumably, one of the arms was given its

Wyatt windows. Soon afterwards the scholarly Bishop Joseph Stock came into residence; and a few months later again (Aug 1798), the French landed at Killala. The castle was occupied by General Humbert and 300 French troops; but they treated the Bishop and his family with courtesy and consideration, leaving them undisturbed on the top floor, where the Bishop's library and 3 principal bedrooms were situated. When Bishop James Verschoyle died 1834, the See of Killala was joined to that of Tuam, and Killala Castle ceased to be the episcopal residence (for the present episcopal residence—*see* KNOCKGLASS, co Mayo). For a period, it was the seat of the Bourke family, of Heathfield (*qv*); it then became a warehouse, and was demolished 1950s to make room for a housing estate.

Killala Lodge

Killala Lodge, Killala, co Mayo (PERY-KNOX-GORE, *sub* LIMERICK, E/PB and *sub* KNOX/IFR). A 2 storey 3 bay late Georgian house, with a 1 bay breakfront, a central Wyatt window and a fanlighted doorway; enlarged *ca* 1820 by the addition of a 2 storey projecting wing with a curved bow. Pretty little staircase in hall. Windows framed by reeded half-columns with foliage capitals; reeded architraves, with ribbons of acanthus, round doors; presumably by a local craftsman, since there is similar wood-

Killadeas

work in other houses in Killala. In 1837 the residence of T. Kirkwood; afterwards for a period owned by the Pery-Knox-Gore family. Now the home of Mr & Mrs David Willis, who have restored it beautifully.

Killaloe, co Clare: Bishop's Palace (*see* CLARISFORD).

Killarney House, co Kerry, (*see* KENMARE HOUSE).

Killashalloe, co Tipperary (*see* RICHMOND).

Killashee

Killashee, Naas, co Kildare (MOORE, *sub* THOMSON-MOORE/IFR). A Victorian Jacobean house, with a strong resemblance to Kintullach Castle, co Antrim (*qv*) and to Tempo Manor, co Fermanagh (*qv*), which assumed its present form 1863 and has been attributed to Thomas Turner, of Belfast; clearly, the 3 houses are by the same hand. Curvilinear gables; rectangular and round headed plate glass windows, some of them having entablatures crowned with strapwork. Open porch with curvilinear gable supported on coupled piers. Square turret at one end, with open belvedere and ogee spire. Now a school.

Killeen Castle

Killeen Castle, Dunsany, co Meath (PLUNKETT, FINGALL, E/PB1970). A castle originally founded by Hugh de Lacy in 1181; and which passed by marriage, along with the neighbouring castle of Dunsany (*qv*), to Sir Christopher Plunkett 1403; who left it to his eldest son, Lord Killeen, ancestor of the Earls of Fingall; Dunsany going to his 2nd son, ancestor of the Barons of Dunsany. In 1780–81, 7th Earl of Fingall carried out repairs to Killeen, which had been unoccupied for a period; the castle was enlarged and altered *ca* 1804 by Francis Johnston for 8th Earl and further enlarged and embellished 1841 for 9th Earl to the design of James Shiel; so that it grew into a

Killeen Castle: Entrance Hall

tall and massive battlemented and turreted pile. An imposing castellated enclosed porch—one of Shiel's additions—extends beyond the mound on which the castle stands, so that the entrance is at a lower level; a flight of stone steps with Gothic balustrades of oak leads up to the level of the main ground floor rooms. At the top of the steps is a long and narrow hall with a splendid ceiling of plaster Gothic fan-vaulting and pendants by Johnston; some of the vaults spring from corbel heads of medieval knights and kings, and there is more Gothic ornament over the doors. The library and the dining room—formerly the drawing room—open off this hall. The dining room, an elongated octagon, extending into a battlemented 3 sided bow on the garden front, has a ceiling by Shiel, with rectangular panels of decoration. The library has a ceiling of elaborate and delicate plaster Gothic tracery of the Johnston period; it was given its bookcases *ca* 1900 by Daisy, Countess of Fingall, wife of 11th Earl, a prominent figure in the Irish Revival as well as in Edwardian fashionable society; they were made by Hicks, the famous Dublin cabinetmakers. The great staircase, of oak, with elaborate Gothic ornamentation, is in the main 1841 addition; it leads up to a plaster-vaulted gallery above the hall. In the grounds, close to the castle, is a ruined medieval chantry church containing the tombs of various Plunketts. Killeen Castle was sold *ca* 1953.

Killegar, Carrigallen, co Leitrim (GODLEY, KILBRACKEN, B/PB). A 2 storey late-Georgian house, with a principal front of 8 bays. Pedimented breakfront, with 3 windows in lower storey, emphasized by plain pilasters, which are also used to emphasize the slightly projecting end bays. End windows of facade, in lower storey, set in shallow arched recesses. Projecting porch in adjoining front; courtyard at back. Largely gutted by fire a few years ago; afterwards rebuilt, the architect of the rebuilding being Mr Austin Dunphy.

Killenure Castle, Dundrum, co Tipperary (COOPER/IFR). A large tower-house of the O'Dwyer family, burnt by the Cromwellians but still very well preserved, with a plain and unassuming C18 house of 2 storeys over a basement alongside it. Sold in recent years; now a private school.

Killester, co Dublin (NEWCOMEN, V/DEP). A single-storey early C18 house with a high dormered roof on a wooden bracket cornice, a central pediment and Venetian windows in the projecting ends. Owned later in C18 by Sir William Newcomen, 1st Bt. Demolished early in the present century, some of the stonework being used by Sir Edwin Lutyens in his additions to Howth Castle (*qv*).

Killinan

Killinan, Kilchreest, co Galway (MAHONY/IFR). A plain irregular C19 house of 2 storeys over a high basement. Round-headed entrance doorway with blocking, up flight of steps with solid parapets and urns. Wyatt windows in side of house.

Killinane

Killinane House, Leighlinbridge, co Carlow. A 2 storey house of mid-C18 appearance. 5 bay front; pedimented and fanlighted tripartite doorway. Curved end-bow. In 1814, the residence of Edward Groome.

Killincarrig, Greystones, co Wicklow (HAWKINS/IFR). A 2 storey C19 house of stucco, with a balustraded roof parapet. 3 bay entrance front; irregular adjoining front with single-storey curved bow. Inherited by Elizabeth Hawkins-Whitshed, wife of Lt-Col Frederick Burnaby, the well-known Victorian soldier, explorer, politician, sportsman and balloonist. Now an hotel.

Killineer House, Drogheda, co Louth (CARROLL/IFR). A dignified 2 storey stucco-faced house of late Georgian style, built 1836. Entrance front of 6 bays above, and 2 bays on either side of a single-storey Doric

Killineer House

Killoskehane Castle

portico below. 3 bay side, with entablatures over ground floor windows. Parapeted roof. Elaborate plasterwork friezes in all principal rooms. Octagonal entrance hall with niches and busts. Bifurcating staircase with handrails of wrought iron in inner hall. Drawing room and ante-room with panels of pink wallpaper surrounded by gilt mouldings; ante-room has large figures in high relief, including a figure of Justice, in the flat of the ceiling. Dining room has a very attractive bold circle of plasterwork in the centre of the ceiling. Reeded doorcases with corner blocks carved with rosettes in most rooms. Garden temple with porch of two columns containing cupboards with elegant astragals in the Chinese manner. Beautiful garden with pond.

Killiney Castle

Killiney Castle, Killiney, co Dublin (WARREN/LGI1912). A Georgian house of 2 storeys over a basement, castellated C19; with 2 not quite similar corner turrets and a central 3 sided bow, a storey higher than the rest of the front and with Irish battlements. Obelisk on hilltop above the castle, erected 1742 to give employment.

Killinure, Athlone, co Westmeath. A 2 storey double bow-fronted house with a 1 bay centre and a single-storey Doric portico; built *ca* 1780 by the Murray family. Passed in 1838 to a Mr Mansfield; from 1846 to 1881 the residence of a branch of the Maunsell family. In 1922 the residence of Mrs P. P. Medge; afterwards of Capt A. Smyth; then of the Reid family.

Killoskehane Castle

Killoskehane Castle, Borrisoleigh, co Tipperary (WILLINGTON/LGI1958). An old castle with a 2 storey early C18 wing; the latter has a projection with a very handsome predimented and rusticated doorcase. In the C19, the whole building was re-roofed; the old castle battlemented and C18 wing given roof-dormers. A gable was added to the projection with the doorcase, and mullions were put into all the windows. The other front was made more consciously Tudor, with a porch-oriel and tall chimney-stack.

Killoughter

Killoughter, Ashford, co Wicklow (RED-MOND/LGI1863). A late-Georgian house of a single storey over a high basement, a larger version of a type of late-Georgian villa which is particularly associated with the outskirts of Dublin. 7 bay front; wide entrance doorway at the head of a long flight of steps, with a shallow segmental pediment extending over the door and sidelights. Originally owned by a branch of the Redmonds; J. H. O'B. Redmond, of Killoughter, was created a Papal Count in 2nd half of C19; his son assumed the surname of De Raymond, from which Redmond was believed to derive. Killoughter is now the home of Mr & Mrs S. K. Davies.

Killowen House, New Ross, co Wexford (GLASCOTT/LGI1863). A 2 storey 5 bay Georgian house; quoins on either side of the end bays, which break forward. Wyatt window in lower storey of end bays. Plain projecting porch. In 1950s, the home of Mrs Josephine Forrestal, widow of James

V. Forrestal, Secretary of the US Navy 1944–47 and First Secretary of Defence 1947–49.

Killruddery: as it was; and as it is today from same aspect

Killruddery, Bray, co Wicklow (BRA-BAZON, MEATH, E/PB). The most successful Elizabethan-Revival mansion in Ireland, and also one of the earliest, having been started 1820; built for 10th Earl of Meath to the design of Sir Richard Morrison; incorporating a C17 house with plain C18 additions. Three principal fronts, with pointed and curvilinear gables, pinnacles and oriels. Symmetrical entrance front with central polygonal battlemented tower; forecourt with wrought-iron gates, flanked by gabled office range. Adjoining front, incorporating C17 front, also symmetrical and with recessed centre between two gabled projections. Irregular garden front, with at one end an impressive domed conservatory added 1852 to the design of William Burn, now containing a collection of sculpture and known as the Statue Gallery. Entrance hall with segmental-pointed plaster barrel-vaulted ceiling; straight flight of oak stairs up to level of principal rooms. Great hall 40 feet high with arches opening into corridor in upper storey; ceiling of carved beams and braces carried on corbels decorated with the Meath falcon, the spaces

Killruddery: former Entrance Hall

Killruddery: Great Hall

Killruddery: Large Drawing Room

between the beams being filled with ornate plasterwork. Staircase hall, lit by stained glass window, with massive bifurcating staircase of oak. Large and small drawing rooms *en suite*, forming enfilade with Statue Gallery; both drawing rooms having Classical decoration. Large drawing room with ceiling of elaborately coved and coffered plasterwork, grey scagliola Ionic columns and panels on walls framed by scalloped gilt mouldings. Small drawing room with shal-

Killruddery: ceiling of Small Drawing Room (now Dining Room)

Killruddery: one of long Canals

low domed ceiling of more delicate plasterwork in a pattern of foliage, flowers and trophies; plaster draperies in lunettes. Late C17 and early C18 formal garden on a grand scale, one of the very few surviving layouts of this kind in Ireland. Long double canal; alleys with hedges; miniature amphitheatre of grass banks. The garden has been embellished over the years with statues and fountains, and magnificent plantings of ornamental trees and shrubs. Impressive Classical entrance gates to demesne, similar to those at Ballyfin, co Leix and Fota, co Cork (*qqv*). In early 1950s, when the house was found to be badly infested with dry-rot the present Earl of Meath reduced it in size by demolishing the entrance front and all of the adjoining front except for one of the gabled projections. A new and simplified entrance front was built on the same axis as its predecessor, but standing further back; the entrance being by way of a vestibule with a curving stone stair directly into the staircase hall, where one of the upper ramps of the staircase was replaced by a gallery providing communication between 1st floor rooms on either side. The library, in the surviving projection of the adjoining front, which has handsome C18 bookcases recessed in alcoves, was given a new ceiling of Caroline style plasterwork. The smaller drawing room became the dining room, the original dining room, along with the entrance hall and great hall, being among the rooms demolished. This reconstruction of the house was to the design of Hon Claud Phillimore.

Killua Castle, Clonmellon, co Westmeath (CHAPMAN, Bt, *of Killua Castle*/ PB1917; FETHERSTONHAUGH/IFR). A large 3 storey house of 1780 with a curved bow in the centre of one front and a 3 sided bow in the centre of the other, transformed into a castle *ca* 1830 by the addition of battlements, a round tower and 2 polygonal

Killua Castle: C18 house before being castellated

Killua Castle

At Killua Castle

towers; and by refacing it with random ashlar; this remodelling being possibly by James Shiel. A single-storey castellated wing was also added at one side; but on the whole the house kept its Georgian symmetry, as well as many of its Georgian sashwindows; the entrance door, in 3 sided bow, kept its semi-circular fanlight, while being given a suitably Gothic surround. The entrance door opened into an octagon hall with delicate late-C18 plasterwork in lunettes over the doors. Beyond the hall was a round room in the middle of the garden front. Large and romantic demesne, with lake and follies, including an obelisk commemorating the alleged planting by Sir Walter Raleigh of the first potato in Ireland. The seat of the Chapman family, of whom Lawrence of Arabia was an illegitimate son. Inherited in the present century by a branch of the Fetherstonhaugh family; sold between the wars and afterwards dismantled; now a spectacular ruin.

Killyfaddy, Clogher, co Tyrone (ANCKETILL/IFR). A Georgian house with a pillared porch.

Killyleagh Castle, Killyleagh, co Down (CLANBRASSILL, E/DEP; ROWAN-HAMILTON/ IFR; HAMILTON-TEMPLE-BLACKWOOD, DUFFERIN AND AVA, M/PB). Basically a "Plantation Castle", built by James Hamilton *ca* 1610; but with 2 massive round corner-towers, one of them probably surviving from a Norman castle built late C12 by John de Courcy, and the other added 1666 by Henry Hamilton, 2nd Earl of Clanbrassill; a deliberate and perhaps romantic archaicism which has its counterpart in the romantic castles built in Elizabethan and Jacobean England. 2nd Earl also built or restored the immense bawn or fortified enclosure between the castle and the town of Killyleagh; which remains as the castle's most spectacular feature, its high walls still keeping their original battlements and gun-holes. The 2nd Earl of Clanbrassill appears to have been poisoned by his wife, after she had prevailed on him to make a Will leaving his estates to her instead of to his Hamilton cousins, who were the rightful heirs. The cousins contested the Will and the litigation continued for 2 generations; in the end, there was a judgment of Solomon dividing the estates equally between Gawn Hamilton and his cousin Anne, whose share eventually passed by inheritance to the Blackwood family; even Killyleagh Castle being divided, the castle itself going to Gawn and the gatehouse and bawn to Anne. This led to a feud between the two families, who for more than a century confronted each other from opposite ends of the bawn; the Hamiltons in the castle, the Blackwoods in the gatehouse, which they rebuilt as a tall Georgian block. In the early years of C19, when the castle was lived in by the United Irish leader, Archibald Hamilton Rowan, who had returned from his exile in America after being pardoned, it fell into decay; whereas the Blackwoods of the period, who had become the Lords Dufferin, kept the gatehouse in good order, adding to it 1830; though their principal seat was Clandeboye (*qv*), at the other end of the county. When 5th Lord Dufferin (afterwards 1st Marquess of Dufferin and Ava) came of age, he ended the feud by handing over the gatehouse and bawn to his kinsman at the castle, Archibald Rowan-Hamilton. Being a romantic young man, he demanded in return a quit-rent of a pair of silver spurs and a golden rose in alternate years; which subsequently, having

Killyleagh Castle: Staircase

accumulated, were used to adorn his ambassadorial and viceregal dinner tables. As a further gesture, he built a suitably Baronial gatehouse in place of the Georgian house at his own expense; to the design of the English architect, Benjamin Ferrey. To set the seal on the reconciliation, Lord Dufferin married Archibald Rowan-Hamilton's daughter, Hariot. Almost simultaneously with the rebuilding of the gatehouse, Archibald Rowan-Hamilton — doubtless encouraged by Lord Dufferin's generosity — employed Charles (afterwards Sir Charles) Lanyon to enlarge, modernize and embellish the castle; the work being carried out between 1847 and 1851. Lanyon extended the castle and gave it a highly romantic skyline of turrets and pointed roofs; so that, in the words of Sir Harold Nicolson, whose mother's home it was, "it pricks castellated ears above the smoke of its own village and provides a curiously exotic landmark, towering like some château of the Loire above the

gentle tides of Strangford Lough". He refaced the walls and added a stupendous Jacobean doorway with strapwork as well as rustications on the columns, incorporating an actual C17 coat-of-arms. And inside he devised a most wonderful Jacobean staircase, with a positive riot of columns and pilasters covered with strapwork, cleverly contrived to give his characteristic feeling of space within the limited confines of the old castle. In order to provide access to the upper floors, there are in fact 2 staircases in the one space, set at right angles to each other; both being equally massive, with scroll balustrades of oak. Lanyon also redecorated the principal reception rooms, giving them fretted ceilings with modillion cornices.

Killymoon Castle

Killymoon Castle, Cookstown, co Tyrone (STEWART/LGI1912; MOUTRAY/LGI 1912). One of John Nash's earliest castles, built *ca* 1803 for William Stewart, MP, incorporating part of the previous house which was burnt *ca* 1800. A building with a romantic silhouette in a glorious position above the Ballinderry river with a backdrop of sweeping woods and parkland. The principal front dominated by an almost central battlemented and machicolated round tower and turret; at one end, an octagonal battlemented and machicolated tower; at the other, the profile of the square tower in the adjoining front, the base of which is arched to form a porte-cochère. The latter tower has slender octagonal corner turrets, with cupolas. Pointed windows grouped together under segmental hood-mouldings, which were regarded by Nash and his contemporaries as Saxon. Good interior planning with square, circular and octagon rooms fitted together. Hall with double staircase, lit by Gothic lantern on plaster fan-vaulted ceiling. Drawing room with plain gilt plasterwork cornice of wreath and honeysuckle design. Library in form of Gothic chapel, with stained glass windows. Sold after William Stewart's death 1850. Subsequently the seat of a branch of the Moutray family.

Killyon Manor, Hill of Down, co Meath (LOFTUS, *sub* MAGAN/LGI1868; MAGAN/IFR; CAREW, Bt/PB). A 3 storey gable-ended early or mid-C18 house, to which a new facade, with a parapet and cornice, framing bands and a small single-storey Ionic portico, was added *ca* 1800. Unusual fenestration, the 2 upper storeys being 4 bay, the ground floor having 2 windows rather close together on either side of the portico. The house is flanked by screen walls of brick, with blind arches. Ballroom at rear.

Killyleagh Castle

Killyon Manor

Kiłmacoom, Doneraile, co Cork (LY-SAGHT/IFR). A house built *ca* 1910, replacing a much older house with a thatched roof known as Fort William, in which the skeletons of 2 brothers who had killed each other fighting a duel in the C18 were once discovered.

Kilmacurragh

Kilmacurragh (also known as **West Aston**), **Rathdrum, co Wicklow** (ACTON/IFR). A 2 storey 5 bay house built 1697 by Thomas Acton. 3 bay breakfront centre with large pediment containing triangular-headed attic window; good quoins; elaborately moulded doorcase of wood with a repetition of re-entrants, the entablature curving upwards in a Baroque way; high-pitched roof on wooden bracket cornice. Rooms with fielded panelling; good staircase with barley-sugar balusters. In 1848 Lt-Col William Acton, MP, added 2 single-storey 2 bay projecting and overlapping wings in the same style as the centre, so that they might pass as contemporary with it, or at any rate, as early C18 additions. One of them even contains fielded panelling, perhaps brought from another house. Noted arboretum, particularly famous for its conifers and calcifuges, planted during C19 by Thomas Acton in conjunction with David Moore and his son, Sir Frederick Moore, curators of Glasnevin Botanical Gardens. Sold 1944 by Mr Charles Acton to the Department of Lands, which maintains the arboretum; but the house is now derelict.

Kilmaloda House, Timoleague, co Cork (BEAMISH/IFR; MACCARTHY-MORROCH/IFR).

A 2 storey C19 house in late-Georgian manner; handsome fanlighted doorway; large drawing room and dining room on either side of hall. A seat of the Beamish family; owned for some years *post* World War II by the late Mr F. D. MacCarthy-Morrogh.

Kilmanahan Castle

Kilmanahan Castle, co Waterford (GREENE/IFR and LG1863; WATSON/AA; HELY-HUTCHINSON, DONOUGHMORE, E/PB). A 2 storey 5 bay late-Georgian house mildly castellated, with a battlemented round tower at one end of its front, and a battlemented square tower at the other. Georgian sash windows, or triple windows, under hood mouldings; pointed concentric arches over entrance door. The house adjoins a medieval keep which in the old days was a much-disputed frontier post between the territories of the Ormondes and the Desmonds. Kilmanahan has for many years belonged to the Earls of Donoughmore, whose seat, Knocklofty (*qv*), faces it from the co Tipperary bank of the River Suir.

Kilmanock, Arthurstown, co Wexford (KNOX/IFR). A 3 storey 5 bay Georgian house with a triple window in the centre of the middle storey. C19 projecting porch. 3 bay end.

Kilmony Abbey

Kilmony Abbey, Carrigaline, co Cork (ROBERTS/LG11958). A house which, from its appearance, could be early or mid-C18, but altered early C19. Of 2 storeys and on a "U"-plan, the wings extending back. 9 bay front, the 7 bays in the centre being framed by rusticated pilasters, one of which is now mostly missing; blocked quoins at the sides. Single-storey Doric portico with die. Hall with staircase of good C18 joinery at its inner end: scrolled ends to treads, solid newels, panelled dado reflecting the curve of the handrail. Plaster panelling on walls of staircase well and in landing over hall; ceiling in geometrical compartments. Early C19 reeded doorcases at foot of stairs. Venetian window on half-landing. Ruined abbey in grounds. Now the home of Mrs Sheila O'Riordan.

See House, Kilmore

Kilmore, co Cavan: See House. The palace of the (C of I) Bishops of Kilmore, near their cathedral, which stands on a wooded hill surrounded by meadow—one of those cathedrals in the country that are a feature of Ireland. A 3 storey Grecian block of the 1830s, built "on a more eligible site" than the earlier palace; from its resemblance to Rathkenny (*qv*), in the same county, it can fairly safely be attributed to William Farrell. 3 bay entrance front; wide strip-pilasters at corners and framing centre bay, which is pedimented. Enclosed pilastered porch with die between 2 tripartite windows. 4 bay side elevation with 2 bay breakfront; entablatures on console brackets over ground floor windows.

Kilmore House, Richhill, co Armagh (JOHNSTON/IFR). A 3 storey Georgian block, given 2 curvilinear Jacobean-style gables and mullioned oriels in C19, between which 3 bays of the original elevation remain as they always were, complete with the astragals in the sash windows; the adjoining elevation also remained Georgian. The interior was also remodelled, presumably at the same time; the hall has a screen of tapering wooden piers, incorporating the stairs, which have a handrail of carved wood panelling. The dining room has a Victorian Gothic chimneypiece of marble. The home of the Johnston family, of which Francis Johnston, the eminent architect, was a younger son.

Kilmorna, Listowel, co Kerry (GUN/LG11912; O'MAHONY, *sub* MAHONY/IFR). A Victorian Tudor house with gables, tall chimneys and a battlemented turret. Burnt 1921.

Kilmorna, Lismore, co Waterford (ALEXANDER, *sub* CALEDON, E/PB1970). A small Georgian house.

Kilmorony

Kilmorony, Athy, co Kildare (WELDON, Bt/PB). A 2 storey 5 bay Georgian house with a lower 2 storey wing. Balustraded roof parapet. Now demolished.

Kilmoyle

Kilmoyle, Limerick, co Limerick. A restrained 2 storey early C19 Classical house; eaved roof, 3 bay front with Doric porch, 4 bay side. The home of Mr & Mrs John Dinan 1919–46.

Kilmurry, co Cork

Kilmurry, Kilworth, co Cork (GRANT/ LGI1912). A house of late-Georgian appearance, of stucco, with cut-stone dressings; consisting of a 3 storey 5 bay centre with 2 storey wings projecting forwards and having 1 bay front-facing ends. Central Venetian window above single-storey portico with rusticated piers instead of columns; strip-pilasters framing wings. Roof more or less concealed by parapet with urns. Long hall from which rises a bifurcating staircase with a wrought-iron balustrade. The seat of the Grant family, who sold it *ca* 1930s; since when it has been an institution.

Kilmurry, Thomastown, co Kilkenny (BUSHE/LGI1912; BUTLER, *sub* MOUNTGARRET, V/PB; ARCHER HOUBLON/IFR). A house of many periods, part of it believed to date from C17 or earlier; but now predominantly C18 and early C19. The back of the main block is 3 storey, but it has a 2 storey front of mid-C18 appearance; 5 bay, the roof parapet being adorned with urns. This front is now flanked by single-storey 1 bay early C19 Classical wings, with Wyatt windows and dies surmounted by sphinxes; the left-hand one extending along the whole side of the house to form a single-storey entrance front, with a centrepiece of Doric pilasters and half-columns. The wings were added

At Kilmorony

Kilmurry, co Kilkenny

Kilmurry, co Kilkenny: Hall

between 1814 and 1830 by the great advocate and orator, Charles Kendal Bushe, Chief Justice of Ireland, known as "The Incorruptible", whose home this was. In 1788, when he came of age, he unwittingly signed a paper making himself responsible for the debts of his father, a squarson of extravagant habits; with the result that Kilmurry, which he loved, had to be sold. In 1814, when he was at the height of his career, he and his wife came to stay with the other branch of the Bushes at the neighbouring house, Kilfane (*qv*); riding over to Kilmurry, he found the place for sale again and the trees marked for felling; but to his great sorrow, he did not feel that he could afford to buy it back. However, when he told his wife, she sprung the pleasant surprise that she had saved up all the money which he had given her at various times to buy jewellery; and which now amounted to a sum large enough to enable him to buy back his old home. The wings added by Charles Kendal Bushe contain a hall with a recessed screen of fluted Ionic columns, a library with bookcases recessed under arches and a dining room which was adorned, later in C19, with elaborate wood-carving. A fine long drawing room occupies the whole of C18 front; it was formed out of the previous entrance hall and the rooms on either side of it; beyond this drawing room was another drawing room in one of the wings, which has been made into a loggia by the removal of the back wall. All the rooms have early C19 doorcases with rosettes and reeded mouldings. The children of Charles Kendal Bushe sold Kilmurry after

his death to Major Henry Butler, of the Mountgarret family; whose daughter, Miss Mildred Butler, the eminent water colour painter, bequeathed it to her cousin, Mrs Archer Houblon, the equestrian.

Kilnacrott, Mountnugent, co Cavan. An early C19 Tudor-Gothic house with gables, mullioned windows, a porte-cochère and tall octagonal and cylindrical chimneys. At the back is a pedimented house of *ca* 1800 facing the yard. Now owned by a religious order.

Kilnahard Castle, Mountnugent, co Cavan (WILSON/IFR; BOYD-ROCHFORT/IFR). A 2 storey C19 castle of *ca* 1860, with small square turrets. Entrance arch of rough blocks of water-worn stone. Now the home of Sir Cecil Boyd-Rochfort, formerly principal racehorse trainer to Queen Elizabeth II.

Kilpeacon House

Kilpeacon House, Crecora, co Limerick (GAVIN, *sub* WESTROPP/IFR). An early C19 villa undoubtedly by Sir Richard Morrison, though it is undocumented; having a strong likeness to Morrison's "show" villa, Bearforest, co Cork (*qv*); while its plan is, in Mr McParland's words, "an ingenious contraction of that of Castlegar" (*qv*), one of his larger houses in the villa manner. 2 storey; 3 bay front; central breakfront; curved balustraded porch with Ionic columns; Wyatt windows under semi-circular relieving arches on either side in lower storey. Eaved roof. 5 bay side elevation. Oval entrance hall. Small but impressively high central staircase hall lit by lantern and surrounded by arches lighting a barrel-vaulted bedroom corridor. The seat of the Gavin family.

Kilquaine House

Kilquaine House, Craughwell, co Galway (LAMBERT/IFR). A 2 storey 5 bay gable-ended C18 house with a round-headed doorway. Arch surmounted by belfry at side of house leading into yard.

Kilroan, Glanmire, co Cork (PUNCH/IFR). An early to mid-C19 house built as a Rectory, in a simple Tudor-Revival style. Entrance front with gabled projections joined by segmental-pointed arcade. Adjoining front with gable and 3 sided bow. Windows with timber mullions. The house was bought *post* World War 1 by J.F. Punch, who increased the number of bedrooms by building out over the adjoining stables; the doors and panelling in the new addition coming from the liner *Celtic*, which was wrecked near the entrance to Cork Harbour at about this time.

Kilronan Castle

Kilronan Castle

Kilronan Castle (formerly **Castle Tenison**), **Ballyfarnan, co Roscommon** (TENISON, *sub* HANBURY-TENISON/IFR; KINGTENISON, KINGSTON, E/PB). A C19 castle dating from 2 different periods; the earlier part consisting of a 3 storey 3 bay symmetrical castellated block with slender corner turrets, pinnacled buttresses and tracery windows; the later part of 2 storeys, irregular and of rubble; with a baronial tower, pointed and trefoil-headed plate glass windows, gables and a battlemented porte-cochère joined to the front by a Victorian-Gothic corridor. Inherited by Florence (*née* Tenison), wife of 8th Earl of Kingston, who assumed the additional surname of Tenison.

Kilrush House, Freshford, co Kilkenny (ST GEORGE/IFR). A handsome early C19 house, almost identical to Grove, co Tipperary (*qv*). Built by A.J. St George, whose family had hitherto lived in the old castle nearby, which originally belonged to the Shorthall family. Of 2 storeys over a basement, consisting of a main block and a wing. 3 bay entrance front; handsome stone doorway with Doric half-columns and pilasters and an entablature carved with swags, below a large leaded fanlight. Windows on either side in arched recesses. 5 bay side elevation. Eaved roof. Plain entrance hall. Long inner hall with slightly curving staircase of wood, divided by arch carried on small Doric columns and partly top-lit through circular well-gallery. Above this gallery is a rotunda of Doric columns and pilasters with an elegant glazed dome. Drawing room opening into smaller room with double doors and hung with what may be its original wallpaper, of a grey and white leaf pattern, trimmed with gilt beadings. Dining room of great beauty, with its original dull maroon and silvery grey wallpaper and a chimneypiece of fluted black marble.

Kilshannig

Kilshannig, Rathcormac, co Cork (FERMOY, B/PB; ROSE, Bt, *of Rayners*/PB). A Palladian house by Davis Duckart, built 1765–66 for Abraham Devonsher, MP, a Cork banker; consisting of a centre block of 2 storeys over a basement with a mezzanine on the entrance front, joined to "L"-shaped stable and office wings by curved quadrant walls with gateways on the entrance front and long straight corridors on the garden front; the plan being a much reduced and simplified version of Vanbrugh's plan for Castle Howard in Yorkshire. Entrance front of red brick with stone dressings; 7 bays, with a single-storey 3 bay Doric frontispiece of stone below a central niche which is now empty; but which a photograph taken *ca* 1940 shows to have formerly contained a statue or relief of a warrior or god. Camberheaded windows in lower storey. The wings on this side, which are the horizontal arms of the "L"'s, have forward-facing single-storey 5 bay fronts with round-headed windows, now mostly blocked up. 5 bay garden front of stone; 3 bay breakfront framed by straight-edged quoining; blocked quoins at sides; entablatures over windows in lower storey, shouldered architraves above; semi-circular basement windows with keystones, glazed as fanlights. The corridors joining the centre block to the wings on the garden front are faced with blind pilastered arcades, the arches of which were formerly painted to resemble windows; the wings, which on this side run at right-angles to the front, so that only their ends are visible, are treated as 2 storey 2 bay pavilions similar to those at Castletown, co Kilkenny (*qv*), with oculi above round-headed windows; originally they were domed, like the Castletown pavilions; but the copper of the domes was sold last century, allegedly to pay debts. The interior of Kilshannig contains rococo plasterwork by the Francini brothers as fine as anything they executed elsewhere in Ireland. The hall is surrounded by Corinthian columns supporting an entablature which curves across the corners so as to make the room appear to be elliptical; and from which springs the deep and richly-ornamented cove of the

Kilshannig: Saloon ceiling

Kilshannig: Staircase

elliptical-centred ceiling. The saloon, dining room and library in the garden front also have coved ceilings, decorated with ravishingly beautiful plasterwork; including gods and goddesses, *putti* and other figures, the modelling of which is rightly described by Mr Guinness as "a poem of delicacy and graceful movement." There is a less elaborate rococo ceiling, and wall panels with swags which are a simplified version of the panels in the dining room of the co Kilkenny Castletown, in the corridor which runs out of one side of the hall, leading to the splendid circular cantilevered staircase of Portland stone. Abraham Devonsher, who was childless, left Kilshannig to his sister's grandson John Newenham, who assumed the name of Devonsher. *Ante* 1837, however, Kilshannig was sold by A.J.N. Devonsher to Edward Roche, who used it as a winter residence, as did his son, 1st Lord Fermoy; their main family seat, Trabolgan (*qv*), being close to the sea and too much exposed to the south-easterly gales to be comfortable in winter. In the present century, Kilshannig was owned by the Myles family. More recently, it was the home of Mr & Mrs Paul Rose. Since 1962, it has been the home of Cmdr & Mrs Douglas Merry.

Kilsharvan, Julianstown, co Meath (MCDONNELL/IFR). An attractive 2 storey late C18 house with shallow bows and a Doric portico. Windows set in blank arches.

Kiltanon, Tulla, co Clare (MOLONY/IFR). A Georgian house of 3 storeys, the top storey being treated as an attic above a bold cornice. Odd fenestration; C19 addition on ground floor to enlarge the principal rooms; 2 storey wing set back. Burnt early 1930s.

Kilteelagh, nr Nenagh, co Tipperary (GASON/IFR). A house rebuilt in High Victorian style 1863 by Lt-Col W.C. Gason. 2 storey; steep gables with bargeboards; rectangular plate-glass windows and large 2

Kilteelagh

storey Perpendicular window in centre. High-pitched polychrome roof. Fine demesne along the shore of Lough Derg. Sold 1962 by Col A. W. Gason to Lt-Col J. A. Dene.

Kilteragh

Kilteragh, Foxrock, co Dublin (PLUNK-ETT, *sub* DUNSANY, B/PB1970). A house built 1905–07 for Sir Horace Plunkett, the great Irish agricultural reformer; to the design of a Swedish architect named Caroe, though rather under the influence of Norman Shaw, with gables and a gabled tower. It was fan-shaped, so as to catch the sun, with a *stoep* modelled on that which Plunkett had seen at Groote Schuur, Cecil Rhodes's house near Capetown; most of the windows being on the sunny side; so that the entrance front, which faced north, was largely blank. Inside, the principal room was a drawing room running the whole width of the house, with one bow window facing the sea and another the mountains; and a large open fireplace of ornamental brickwork. Here, during the years from 1907 to 1923, all manner of people foregathered; most of them concerned with the welfare of Ireland. There was also a large hall which had good acoustics; and though Plunkett himself was un-musical, his guests used to sing Irish songs here. Plunkett's own bedroom was on the roof, and open to the elements—like that of the 1st Viscount Leverhulme—with a mechanical device enabling him to turn his bed towards the sun and against the wind. Burnt 1923.

Kiltinane Castle, Fethard, co Tipperary (BUTLER, DUNBOYNE, B/PB; COOKE, *sub* COOKE-COLLIS/IFR; DE SALES LA TERRIERE/ LG1969). A castle of the Butlers, Lords Dunboyne, romantically situated on a rock high above the Clashawley River, originally with 4 square corner towers of which 3 remain; 2 of them having been altered and added to during C18 and C19 by the Cooke family, to form the present house.

Kiltra House, Wellingtonbridge, co Wexford (BOYD/IFR). Small 2 Storey Georgian house with high-pitched eaved roof. Came into the Boyd family *ca* 1850.

Kilwaughter Castle

Kilwaughter Castle, Larne, co Antrim. An early C19 castle by John Nash, built *ca* 1807 for E. J. Agnew. Wide round tower at one corner, polygonal tower at another. Windows with astragals and somewhat fanciful tracery. Now demolished.

Kindlestown House, Delgany, co Wicklow. A 2 storey C19 house with a central tower in the manner of Ancketill's Grove, or Gola (*qqv*). In 1837, the seat of Capt Morris.

King House

King House, Boyle, co Roscommon (KING, KINGSTON, E/PB). The original early C18 seat of the Kings, afterwards Earls of Kingston; situated not in the middle of a demesne but, like the Damer House at Roscrea (*qv*), in a town; in this case, Boyle. A large "U"-shaped mansion of 2 storeys over a basement with a partly gabled attic, probably by William Halfpenny, an assistant of Sir Edward Lovett Pearce; built for Sir Henry King, 3rd Bt, MP, who died 1739; possibly incorporating the walls of earlier C17 house here which was burnt. The main block is gable-ended; the wings, which are 2 bays wide, have hipped roofs; they project on the entrance front, on either side of a gabled centre with a plain massive doorway. Deep cornices over wings; round-headed ground floor windows with keystones and blocking. 11 bay garden front facing river; 3 bay pedimented breakfront, large central Venetian window in upper storey. Window surrounds with blocking and keystones; deep cornice; large pediment; triangular

gables above cornice. Superimposed Venetian windows in each side elevation, the top one being in a gable. As at Ballyhaise, co Cavan and King's Fort, co Meath (*qqv*), there is vaulting in other storeys than just the basement; in fact all 4 storeys are vaulted over. This was, according to Rev Daniel Beaufort, a fire precaution; Sir Henry King having naturally been fire-conscious after the fire in the earlier house. Long and narrow hall, like gallery. The house was abandoned by the family at the beginning of C19 when they moved out of the town to Rockingham (*qv*); it subsequently became a military barracks and is now empty and dilapidated.

Kingsborough, co Sligo (*see* BALLINDOON HOUSE).

King's Fort, Moynalty, co Meath (CHALONER/LG1912; and *sub* ENNISKILLEN, E/PB). A brick-built house of *ca* 1740, 2 storeys over a basement, in which the ground floor rooms are vaulted over and formerly had good mid C18 stucco decoration on the vaults. One room had plaster panelling. The house is now in ruins, though fragments of the stucco work remain.

Kinlough House, Kinlough, co Leitrim (JOHNSTON/LG1912). A 2 storey 5 bay early C19 house. Pedimented central bay with Wyatt window; ground floor windows set in shallow arched recess; Doric portico with wreathes on frieze. Now a ruin.

Kinnitty Castle, Offaly (*see* CASTLE BERNARD).

Kintullagh Castle, Ballymena, co Antrim. A Victorian Jacobean house, bearing a strong resemblance to Killashee, co Kildare (*qv*) and to Tempo Manor, co Fermanagh (*qv*), which assumed its present form 1863 and has been attributed to Thomas Turner, of Belfast; without doubt, the 3 houses are by the same hand. Curvilinear gables; rectangular and round headed plate glass windows, some of the former having

Kintullagh Castle

entablatures on which there is strapwork. Square corner turret with belfry and ogee spire.

Kinturk, co Westmeath (*see* CASTLE POLLARD).

Knapton, Abbeyleix, co Leix (PIGOTT, Bt/PB1970; VESEY, DE VESCI, V/PB). A small house of *ca* 1773 with good neo-Classical interior decoration built onto an older structure. Now demolished.

Knightstown, Portarlington, co Leix (CARDEN, Bt, *of Templemore*/PB). A 2 storey early to mid-C18 house. 5 bay front, with pedimented breakfront; pedimented doorcase with Venetian window over. High roof on bracket cornice. 3 bay side elevation.

Knock Abbey (also known as **Thomastown Castle**), **Tallanstown, co Louth** (O'REILLY/IFR). An old tower-house with a 3 storey 6 bay buttressed Georgian wing, and also an early C19 Gothic wing. The old tower has Georgian Gothic doorway. Famous library, which was burnt *ca* 1920.

Knockagh Castle

Knockagh Castle, Templemore, co Tipperary. A partly-curving keep, with a large house of late C17 or early C18 appearance built onto the front of it; the house being of 2 storeys over a basement, with a 3 bay centre recessed between 2 bay projecting wings. Tall chimney stacks. In ruins by the end of C19.

Knockan

Knockan, Feeny, co Derry (STEVENSON/IFR). A 2 storey 5 bay gable-ended C18 house, with short single-storey gable-ended wings.

Knockanally, Donadea, co Kildare. A mid-C19 Italianate house of 2 storeys with a central 1 bay balustraded attic rising above the roofs on either side. 3 bay entrance front; central Venetian window; 1st floor windows in outer bays with entablatures and balconies on console brackets; Venetian windows below. Single-storey balustraded portico. In recent years the home of Capt Sheppard.

Knockanemeele, co Cork (*see* MAYFIELD).

Knockballymore, nr Newtown Butler, co Fermanagh (CRICHTON, ERNE, E/PB; STACK/LGI1912). A small but handsome early to mid-C18 house, of 3 storeys over a basement; the top storey having no windows in the front elevation. 5 bay front; floating pediment with lunette window; fanlighted doorway with blocking in surround. Broad steps to entrance door; bold string courses; high-pitched roof and tall chimneystacks carried on side walls. Single storey 1 bay later wing, prolonged by lower range. Owned by the Earls of Erne, but tenanted at the beginning of the present century by Rt Rev C. M. Stack, Bishop of Clogher.

Knockdrin Castle

Knockdrin Castle, nr Mullingar, co Westmeath (LEVINGE, Bt/PB). An imposing Gothic Revival castle of *ca* 1830, by James Shiel, built for Sir Richard Levinge, 6th Bt. The main block, dominated by 2 square turrets, is joined to a gate tower by a lower range. Arcaded Gothic central hall. Oak carvings; Elizabethan style staircase. Sold, *ca* 1940, afterwards owned for some years by Mr P. Dunne-Cullinan.

Knockglass, Crossmolina, co Mayo (PAGET, *sub* KNOX/IFR). A 2 storey 5 bay Georgian house with a hood moulding over the entrance door. Formerly the seat of the Paget family; now the residence of the (C of I) Bishop of Tuam, Killala, and Achonry.

Knockgrafton Rectory

Knockgrafton Rectory, Newinn, co Tipperary. A charming little Georgian "doll's house" built *ca* 1784 by Rev Nicholas Herbert, father of the diarist and authoress Dorothea Herbert; who was Rector of Carrick-on-Suir, where he normally lived, as well as of Knockgrafton; but who was ordered by his Archbishop to spend 3 months of every year here. Dorothea thought that the new Glebe had the appearance of "a Neat English one", but found the surroundings "barren" after Carrick; the society, too, was not up to Carrick society; though it was here that she met and conceived her hopeless passion for a neighbouring young squire, John Roe, of

Rockwell. The house was originally of 2 storeys and 3 bays; pedimented doorcase with blocking flanked by sidelights. A 3rd storey was added in c19, and also a 2 storey 1 bay service wing at one side.

Knocklofty, Clonmel, co Tipperary
(HELY-HUTCHINSON, DONOUGHMORE, E/PB).
A c18 house consisting of a 3 storey centre block with 2 storey gable-ended wings projecting forward on the entrance front to form a 3 sided court. On the entrance front, the centre block is of 7 bays and the wings are of 2 bays in their gable-ends, which are treated as broken and baseless pediments and surmounted by busts and balls on pedestals. They also each have an extra bay in the ends of the 2 storey corridors which have been built along their inner faces and which are surmounted by eagles. In early c19, a single-storey corridor was built along the front of the centre block, joining the wings; it is adorned with Doric pilasters, wreathes and acroteria and has a 3 bay projection in the centre, roofed with a shallow dome. The ground floor windows of the wings are camber-headed. On the garden front, which faces across the River Suir, the centre block is of 5 bays and the front is extended at one side by a very long 2 storey service wing, which turns inwards at an obtuse angle. There is a small square entrance hall with a domed ceiling, opening with arches on either side into book-lined galleries. Beyond is a very large 2 storey library, surrounded on 3 sides by a wrought-iron gallery; the bookcases rising as high as the ceiling, which has a surround of delicate early c19 plasterwork. The drawing room has similar decoration; the dining room is panelled. The demesne extends across the River Suir into co Waterford, taking in the demesne of Kilmanahan Castle (*qv*) which was formerly a separate property. There is an octagonal domed Gothic octagon in the park near the house and the original set of elaborate gate piers to the house are very fine.

Knocklyon Castle, Tallaght, co Dublin.
A 3 storey house with simple mullioned windows and a round corner tower. In 1837, the seat of W. Dunne.

Knockmaroon, Castleknock, co Dublin
(GUINNESS, MOYNE, B/PB). A plain 2 storey late-Georgian house, with a long service wing.

Knocknatrina House, Durrow, co Leix.
A 2 storey c19 Tudor-Gothic house with gables, mullioned windows, a curved bow and tall chimneys. Burnt *ca* 1940; now a shell.

Knocklofty: Entrance Front

Knocklofty: Garden Front

Knocktopher Abbey

Knocktopher Abbey

Knocktopher Abbey, Knocktopher, co Kilkenny (LANGRISHE, Bt/PB). A house incorporating the remains of 1st Carmelite friary in Ireland, rebuilt in High Victorian Gothic to the design of John McCurdy *ca* 1866 after a fire. Gables and trefoil-headed mullioned windows; high roofs; pyramidal-roofed porch tower.

Knocktopher Hall, Knocktopher, co Kilkenny. A gable-ended battlemented Georgian house of 3 storeys over a basement and 3 bays. Fanlighted doorway approached up a flight of steps with iron railings. Return.

Knocklofty: Library

Kylemore Castle

Knoppogue Castle

Knoppogue Castle, Quin, co Clare (BUTLER, DUNBOYNE, B/PB). A large tower-house with a low C19 castellated range, possibly by James Pain, built onto it. Recently restored and now used for "medieval banquets" similar to those at Bunratty Castle, co Clare (*qv*).

Kylemore Castle, Letterfrack, co Galway (MONTAGU, MANCHESTER, D/PB). A much-photographed C19 castle at the foot of a wooded hillside by a lough in Connemara. Built 1860s for Mitchell Henry, MP, a wealthy Liverpool merchant, to the design of James Franklin Fuller; of fine stonework and with a romantic grouping of battlemented and machicolated towers and turrets. Large and regularly-disposed mullioned windows and oriels, more reminiscent of a castle of 1840s than of 1860s. Subsequently the Irish seat of 9th Duke of Manchester. From *post* World War I, a convent and school of the Irish Dames of Ypres.

L

Ladestown, co Westmeath (*see* LEDES-TOWN).

Lagore, Dunshaughlin, co Meath (THUN-DER/LGI1958). A single-storey house of 5 bays, with projecting end bays.

Lahana House, Drimoleague, co Cork (BEAMISH/IFR). A low 3 bay house of 1 storey with a dormered attic, built *ca* 1740 by Abraham Beamish, who used timbers of bog oak for the high-pitched roof.

Lakefield

Lakefield (formerly **Gambonstown**), **Fethard, co Tipperary** (HACKETT/IFR; PENNEFATHER, *sub* FREESE-PENNEFATHER/LGI-1958; O'BRIEN, Bt/PB; GOODBODY/IFR). A 2 storey 5 bay late-Georgian villa by William Tinsley, of Clonmel; built 1831-33 for William Pennefather, whose family are said to have won the estate at cards from its previous owners, the Hacketts. It occupies the site of the Hacketts' house, which was joined to wings by arcaded curved sweeps; the sweeps still remain, though their arches have been filled in, and have been extended by walls to form a circular walled garden at the back of the house. Centre bay slightly recessed, and further emphasized with framing bands; central Wyatt window above Doric portico.Eaved roof. Central staircase hall, lit by lantern. The staircase is unusual in having a double lower ramp and a flying run of steps from the half-landing to the main landing, like the staircase at Glin Castle, co Limerick (*qv*). It is of wood and curves gracefully with balusters of the very lightest; so well made that it has not been necessary to anchor it to the ground floor; it just stands, like a piece of furniture. Two drawing rooms *en suite*, with modillion cornices. Doorcases with reeded architraves and rosettes. Sold 1907 by W. V. Pennefather to Capt J. G. O'Brien. At one time let to Mr Hubert Hartigan, the trainer, who trained the champion high jumper of the world in the walled garden at the back of the house. Sold 1955 by Sir John O'Brien, 5th Bt, to Mr & Mrs Arthur Goodbody.

Lakeview, Midleton, co Cork (HALLINAN/IFR). A Georgian house consisting of a 2 storey 3 bay centre with single-storey 1 bay wings; one of the wings having an attic storey and a tripartite fanlighted entrance doorway below. The other wing is bow-ended. Stairs of good joinery. In 1837, the residence of S. Fleming.

Lakeview, Killarney, co Kerry (O'CONNELL, Bt/PB). A 2 storey, stucco-faced C19 house with an Ionic porte-cochère.

Lambay Castle: Entrance Gateway

Lambay Castle: Lutyens Wing

Lambay Castle, co Dublin (BARING, REVELSTOKE, B/PB). A small late C16 fort with battlemented gables, possibly incorporating a C15 blockhouse, on Lambay Island, 3 miles off the north co Dublin coast; transformed by Sir Edwin Lutyens into a romantic castle for Hon Cecil Baring, afterwards 3rd Lord Revelstoke, who bought the island 1904 as a place to escape to with his beautiful young wife, the daughter of Pierre Lorrilard, the first American to win the Derby; the story of their early life here inspired Julian Slade's musical, *Free as Air*.

Lambay Castle: Hall

Lutyens made the old fort habitable and built a quadrangle of offices and extra bedrooms adjoining it, with roofs of grey pantiles sweeping down almost to the ground. He also built a circular curtain wall, or enceinte, surrounding the castle and its garden, with an impressive bastioned gateway; this wall serves the practical purpose of a wind-break, enabling trees and plants to grow inside it which would not grow outside. Everything is of a silvery grey stone, bleached pale by sun and storm. The rooms in the castle have vaulted ceilings and stone fireplaces; there is a stone staircase with many attractive curves and an underground gallery in the new quadrangle which might have been conceived by Piranesi. Lutyens also designed the approach from the harbour, with curved step-like terraces reminiscent of the now-vanished Ripetta in Rome; characteristically, having ascended these Baroque steps, one has to cross an open field to come to the curtain wall, the entrance gateway not being at first visible; so that there is a wonderful sense of expectancy. Close to the harbour is the White House, a largely single-storey horseshoe-shaped house with high roofs and white harled walls, which Lutyens designed 1930s for Lord Revelstoke's daughter, Hon Mrs (Arthur) Pollen. On a hill is an old Catholic chapel, with a portico of tapering stone columns and a barrel-vaulted ceiling.

Lamberton Park, Stradbally, co Leix (TYDD, Bt/EDB; BUTLER, *sub* DUNBOYNE, B/PB). A plain 2 storey Georgian house. In 1837, the residence of Mr Justice Moore. Now demolished.

Landenstown

Landenstown, Sallins, co Kildare (DIG-BY, B/PB). A 2 storey mid-C18 house with a front of 9 bays and an open-bed pediment-gable, the 2 end bays on either side being advanced; rather similar to the front of Ballykilcavan, co Leix (*qv*). The house is linked by canted arches to large barn wings, in a wide-spreading and particularly attractive Palladian composition.

Landmore, Aghadowney, co Derry (WATNEY/LGI1965). A 2 storey gable-ended house built 1788. 5 bay front; central Wyatt window above fanlighted doorway.

Landsdown, Nenagh, co Tipperary (TRENCH, ASHTOWN, B/PB). A 2 storey weather-slated house built 1779 by William Parker, whose initials and the date are cut in one of the decorative lozenges in the weather-slating. 3 bay front, the window being attractively spaced; in the centre, a round-headed window flanked by detached sidelights to produce a countrified Venetian window, above a doorcase with a segmental pediment also flanked by sidelights. Eaved roof. For a period, *post* World War II, the home of 4th Lord Ashtown. Now the home of Col & Mrs White-Spunner.

Langford Lodge, nr Crumlin, co Antrim (ROWLEY, LANGFORD, B/PB; PAKENHAM, *sub* LONGFORD, E/PB). A 3 storey Georgian house on a headland jutting out into Lough Neagh. Entrance front of 3 bays between two deep curved bows; Doric portico; 2 storey wing at side. End elevation of 2 bays and a deep curved bow. Passed to the Pakenhams through the marriage of Catherine, daughter of Elizabeth, Viscountess Langford, to 2nd Lord Longford; the children of this marriage included Catherine ("Kitty") Pakenham, wife of the great Duke of Wellington, as well as the two Peninsular Generals, Sir Edward Pakenham—afterwards killed at New Orleans during the American War of 1812–14—and Sir Hercules Pakenham, from whom were descended the subsequent owners of Langford Lodge, which is now demolished.

Lansdowne Lodge, Kenmare, co Kerry (PETTY-FITZMAURICE, LANSDOWNE, M/PB). A 3 storey house on an unusual cruciform plan, built between 1764 and 1775 by 2nd Earl of Shelburne, the C18 statesman, afterwards 1st Marquess of Lansdowne. The arm projecting in the centre of the front is pedimented, and has a plain doorway with sidelights; the arms at either side end in semi-circular bows. Camber-headed windows. The house was originally flanked by outbuildings, which have since disappeared. In the Victorian period, the house was

Lansdowne Lodge

given a roof-line of dormer-gables, into which the top storey windows were raised; and the Georgian glazing of all the windows was replaced by plate-glass. The house was mainly occupied by the agent for the Lansdowne estate. It now stands forlorn at the back of a housing-estate.

Lara, co Kildare (BARNEWALL, TRIMLESTOWN, B/PB; GANNON/LGI1875). A 3 storey gabled house built early or mid-C18 by a Lord Trimlestown. The gables covered with plaster, decorated with *fleurs-de-lis* cut into it with a trowel. Subsequently owned by the O'Reilly, Hunt and Cusack families; bought *ca* 1815 by Nicholas Gannon, whose son, James Gannon, made various additions to the house.

Larchgrove, Clonmel, co Tipperary (*see* GLENCONNOR HOUSE).

Larch Hill, Coole, co Meath. A plain but pleasant house, with several follies in the grounds, notably a Gothic fox's earth surmounted by a rustic temple and a tower decorated with shells and Dutch tiles. A statue of Nimrod graces an island in the lake.

Laurel Hill

Laurel Hill, Coleraine, co Derry (KYLE/LGI1912). A house given a new Italianate front 1843 by Henry Kyle, to the design of Charles (afterwards Sir Charles) Lanyon. 2 storey, 5 bay; 1 bay pedimented breakfront centre with 3 narrow round-headed windows above and a single-storey Corinthian portico below. Simple pierced balustrade round roof and on portico. Rusticated and vermiculated quoins; entablatures on console brackets above ground floor windows. Hall with columns at back, disguising the join with the earlier house. Some good plasterwork in reception rooms.

Laurentinum, Doneraile, co Cork (CREAGH/IFR; MORROGH-BERNARD/IFR; MACCARTHY-MORROGH/IFR). A Georgian house of 2 storeys (originally 3) over a high basement. 6 bay front with pilastered porch. Eaved roof.

Lawderdale, Ballinamore, co Leitrim (LAWDER/LGI1912). A plain 2 storey 3 bay early C19 house.

Leades, Aghinagh, co Cork (WOODLEY/IFR). A 2 storey 4 bay late-Georgian house. Fanlighted doorway in not-quite-symmetrical end elevation.

Leamlara (with author in foreground)

Leamlara, Carrigtwohill, co Cork (BARRY/LGI1912). A 2 storey house on a "U"-plan, the wings extending back, built in mid-C18 by a branch of the Barry family; given an eaved roof and otherwise altered the late-Georgian period. 7 bay cut-stone front with 3 bay breakfront; shouldered doorcase with entablature and entablatures on console brackets over-ground floor windows. Side elevations of 7 and 5 bays, both plain; in the 7 bay elevation, which was the principal garden front, the lower storey had been given wider late-Georgian windows going down almost to the ground. C18 plasterwork in small room off entrance hall; other rooms plain, with low ceilings. Staircase hall with impressive wooden bifurcating staircase at back of entrance hall, filling part of the space between the two wings. The house was most romantically situated on the side of a deep wooded glen in which there were 2 small lakes spanned by a mid-C18 bridge of rough masonry. Gothic gate lodge; Georgian Catholic church at corner of demesne, built by the Barry family. Sold *ca* 1953 by the heirs of Henry Standish Barry; afterwards totally demolished and the demesne devastated.

Leap Castle

Leap Castle, Coolderry, Offaly (DARBY/IFR). A massive and menacing square keep of the O'Carrolls which passed to the Darbys through the marriage of John Darby, an English officer, to Finola O'Carroll, mid-C16; enlarged and modernized by Jonathan Darby mid-C18, when it was given balancing 2 storey 1 bay wings with battlements and Georgian Gothic windows, and a Gothicized Venetian doorway in the manner of Batty Langley. Other additions were made at various times, so that the left-hand wing was prolonged by a range overlooking a courtyard. The hall had a floor of black and white marble pavement, and a cornice of C18 plasterwork. Leap Castle shared with Gill Hall, co Down (*qv*), the dubious title of being the most haunted house in Ireland; its ghosts included a particularly terrifying elemental, known as "It". Burnt 1922; now a rather sinister ruin.

Learmount Castle, Park, co Derry (BERESFORD, *sub* WATERFORD, M/PB). An early to mid-C19 Tudor-Gothic house. Main block with gabled front, pointed finials on gables; battlemented porch. Battlemented wing set back, ending in slender round battlemented tower and turret.

Ledestown (also known as **Ladestown**), **Mullingar, co Westmeath** (LYONS/LGI 1912). A late-Georgian house of 1823; 2 storeys over a high basement, 5 bay bow-ended front. Single-storey portico at head of broad flight of steps with iron railings; wide window above. Entrance hall and staircase hall in middle of house; bifurcating staircase. There was a printing press here in late C19.

Ledwithstown

Ledwithstown, Ballymahon, co Longford. A very perfect small early C18 house of 2 storeys over a high basement, possibly by Richard Castle. 3 bay front, tripartite doorway with pediment extending over door and side-lights, on pilasters which stand on miniature rusticated basements; broad flight of steps to hall door. Solid roof parapet; windows surrounds with keystones; bold quoins. Symmetrical rear elevation, with blocking round windows and central basement door. Deep hall with chimneypiece of black Kilkenny marble. Plaster panelling in ground floor rooms, with occasional shell and other ornament; wood panelling upstairs. The seat of the Ledwith family; now derelict.

Leixlip Castle

Leixlip Castle

Leixlip Castle, Leixlip, co Kildare (WHYTE/IFR; CONOLLY/LGI1912 and *sub* LONGFORD, E/PB; DE LA POER BERESFORD, DECIES, B/PB; GUINNESS, *sub* MÒYNE, B/PB). A medieval castle on a rock above where the Rye Water flows into the River Liffey, partly rebuilt C18 and with a C18 interior. Founded in C12 by one of Strongbow's followers; the massive round tower, which is still the castle's dominant feature, dates from this period. Later it belonged to the Crown, but was granted 1569 to Sir Nicholas Whyte, Master of the Rolls. In 1731, it was sold by John Whyte to Rt Hon William Conolly, nephew and heir of Speaker Conolly, the builder of the nearby Castletown (*qv*), whose widow continued to live at Castletown after his death. William Conolly left Leixlip for Castletown after his aunt's death 1752; but it remained in the Conolly family until 1914, being let to a succession of tenants; including, in C18, Primate Stone, the most powerful man in the Ireland of his day, and 4th Viscount (afterwards 1st Marquess) Townshend, when he was Viceroy. The C18 remodelling of the castle would appear to date from when Conolly lived in it, and also perhaps from Stone's tenancy, which was from 1752 onwards. The wing which forms a projection on the entrance front, balancing the old round tower, was more or less rebuilt at this period; it has a regular 3 storey 4 bay front towards the river, the windows being pointed and having Gothic astragals. Similar windows were pierced in the thick old wall of the entrance front, and were glazed with diamond panes, in a delightful Batty Langley manner. Inside, a series of spacious reception rooms was formed, one of which, now the library, has some simple mid-C18 plasterwork. The staircase, which is of wood, with pear-shaped balusters, rather similar to those at Rathbeale Hall, co Dublin (*qv*), would appear to date from early C18; it rises impressively in a separate hall behind the entrance hall. The dining room, which is in the old tower, and many of the rooms upstairs, have C18 panelling. Some of the rooms are of unusual shape, being in the tower, or extending into the thickness of the old walls. In 1837 the then tenant, Hon George Cavendish (*see* WATERPARK, B/PB),

added unobtrusive battlements to the castle; but apart from this, C19 medievalism passed it by. During World War I, however, Lady Decies, whose husband, 5th Lord Decies, bought the castle from the Conollys 1914, replaced some of the Georgian-Gothic windows with Tudor-style mullions, and panelled one or two rooms in oak. From 1923 until 1945 the castle was once again let; at one period it served as the French Embassy. The 6th and present Lord Decies sold it 1945 and in 1958 it was re-sold to Hon Desmond Guinness, who, with Mrs Guinness, founded the Irish Georgian Society in that same year. Mr Guinness's ancestor, Richard Guinness, had a brewery in Leixlip in mid-C18, before Richard's son, Arthur, founded the Guinness brewery in Dublin. Mr & Mrs Guinness restored, decorated and furnished the castle in an admirable way. The Georgian-Gothic glazing has been replaced in the windows where it had been removed. One of the bedrooms in the tower has been decorated with panels of an early C19 paper by Dufour, *Vues d'Italie*. The headquarters of the Irish Georgian Society was at Leixlip Castle from 1958 until 1968, when it was moved to Castletown. Below the castle, where the two rivers meet, there is a C18 boathouse on which stands a charming domed polygonal gazebo of brick.

Leixlip House, Leixlip, co Kildare (NESBITT, *sub* BEAUMONT-NESBITT/LGI1958; WEST *sub* COLTHURST/PB; CARVILL, *sub* EUSTACE-DUCKETT/IFR). A 3 storey 5 bay mid-C18 house, with a 2 storey bow-fronted wing. The home of Gen Brady, whose daughter married J. D. Nesbitt 1800. In the present century, the home of A.W. West; and more recently, of Mr & Mrs Michael Carvill.

Lemaneagh Castle, Kilfenora, co Clare (INCHIQUIN, B/PB). A tower of *ca* 1480 to which a 4 storey high-gabled house with rows of mullioned and transomed windows was added 1643 by Conor O'Brien and his wife, the formidable Maire Ruadh, who, after her husband had been killed in a skirmish with Ludlow's men 1651, saved her son's lands by offering to marry a Crom-

Lemaneagh Castle

wellian officer of Ludlow's choosing. Her offer was taken up and she duly married an English cornet of horse; according to tradition, he died through receiving a savage kick from her. Her son, Sir Donough O'Brien, 1st Bt, abandoned Lemaneagh in favour of Dromoland (*qv*) towards the end of C17. Lemaneagh is now a ruin. The gateway of the bawn and a stone fireplace from one of the rooms were taken early this century to Dromoland, where they are now.

Lenaboy, co Galway (O'HARA/LGI1912). An early to mid-C19 Tudor-Gothic house. Battlemented tower, steep gables, mullioned windows.

Leslie Hill

Leslie Hill, Ballymoney, co Antrim (LESLIE/IFR). A very fine mid-C18 house, consisting originally of a double gable-ended main block of 3 storeys over a high basement, joined to 2 storey office wings by single-storey links. Built *ca* 1755 by James Leslie; Mrs Delany, who stayed here on her way to see the Giant's Causeway 1758, found the house "unfinished and full of company". The main block has a 7 bay front with a 3 bay pedimented breakfront; the doorway, with 2 Doric columns and a fanlight under a baseless pediment, is described by Dr Craig as "straight out of the pattern-books and without solecisms". Lunette window in pediment, lighting attic. The wings were of 3 bays, and the links of 2; the ground floor windows of the wings, and those of the links, were recessed within blind arches, which were, in effect, a blocked-up arcade, complete with imposts. Flagged hall with screen; principal rooms have modillion cornices and doors with shouldered archi-

traves. Attic room with convex-coved ceiling and central roundel containing a portrait—possibly of the James Leslie who built the house. The wings and connecting links were unfortunately demolished 1955.

Levington Park, Mullingar, co Westmeath (LEVINGE, Bt/PB; DEASE, *sub* BLAND/IFR). A 2 storey 9 bay gable-ended C18 house with a high roof, a pediment and a pillared porch. The seat of a branch of the Levinge family; afterwards of E. F. Dease, father of Maurice Dease, 1st VC of World War I.

Leyrath

Leyrath

Leyrath, nr Kilkenny, co Kilkenny (WHEELER-CUFFE, Bt/PB1934; TUPPER/LGI-1958). Originally a Tobin castle, acquired by the Wheeler family C17. By 1826, the house here consisted of a simple 2 storey 5 bay pedimented front facing west, with 2 wings running back from it to enclose a small 3 sided office court; the entrance door being on the south side, under a Regency veranda. In 1861, Sir Charles Wheeler-

Cuffe, 2nd Baronet, married Pauline Villiers-Stuart, daughter of Lord Stuart de Decies, whose parents did not regard his house as grand enough for her; so in that same year he rebuilt the main western block on a larger scale and in a rich Italianate style, while leaving the two wings more or less as they were; his architect being John McCurdy. The entrance was moved from the south side to the new west front, which is pedimented and of 5 bays like its predecessor, but not entirely symmetrical; having a pair of windows on the ground floor to the left of the centre, but a single window on the right. Entrance door framed by Ionic columns carrying a balustrade, above which is a Venetian window framed by an aedicule with a segmental pediment. All the ground-floor windows have semicircular heads, while the heads of the windows of the upper storey—apart from the central Venetian window—are cambered. The garden front to the north has two single-storey balustraded curved bows, the windows of which are treated as arcades supported by Romanesque columns of sandstone; there is another Romanesque column separating the pair of windows in the centre of the front. The windows in the bows are glazed with curved glass. The roof is carried on a deep bracket cornice and there are prominent string courses, which give the elevations a High Victorian character. Hall with imposing imperial staircase, the centre ramp of which rises between two fluted Corinthian columns. There is a similarity between the staircase here and that at Dromana, co Waterford (*qv*), Pauline Lady Wheeler-Cuffe's old home; except that the Dromana staircase was of stone, whereas that at Leyrath is of wood, with ornate cast-iron balustrades. On the centre ramp of the staircase there is still a chair with its back legs cut down to fit the steps; this was put there in 1880s for Pauline, Lady Wheeler-Cuffe when she became infirm. Hall has a ceiling cornice of typical C19 plasterwork in a design of foliage, and doors with entablatures which still have their original walnut graining. To the left of the hall, in the garden front, are the drawing room, ante-room and dining room, opening into each other with large double doors; they have ceiling cornices similar to that in the hall, and good C19 white marble chimneypieces, enriched with carving; the drawing room and ante-room keep their original white and gold wallpaper. In the southern wing there are smaller and lower rooms surviving from before the rebuilding; while 1st floor rooms in this wing have barrel ceilings throughout and contain some C18 chimneypieces of black marble.

Linfield, Pallasgreen, co Limerick (LLOYD/IFR). Originally a large 3 storey red brick house with a 3 sided bow incorporating a pedimented door. Remains of good plaster. Now half-demolished. Stables at rear on axis, as at Grange, in the same county (*qv*).

Linsfort Castle (also known as **Mount Paul**), **Inishowen, co Donegal.** A 2 storey house on an "H"-plan built 1720 by Capt Arthur Benson. Front of 5 bays recessed between 1 bay projections; round-headed doorway.

Lisagoan, co Cavan (HUMPHRYS/LGI1912). A Classical house of *ca* 1820, built as a dower house for Ballyhaise (*qv*). Diocletian window and doorcase recessed in tall arch; Wyatt windows. Bifurcating staircase extending into bow at rear, the two upper flights being cantilevered out of the back wall of the house. Now a ruin.

Lisard

Lisard, Edgeworthstown, co Longford (MORE O'FERRALL/IFR). A handsome late C18 block incorporating an earlier house. Of 3 storeys over a rusticated basement; but with only 2 storeys of windows in the entrance front, and a mezzanine of blind recessed panels between them. Entrance front of 7 bays with a 3 bay pedimented breakfront; lunette window in pediment; lintels with keystones and pediments over windows in lower storey on either side of centre; lintels with keystones and entablatures over windows on either side of entrance doorway, which had a segmental pediment and pilasters, but was obscured by a C19 glazed and pedimented porch; long flight of steps up to hall door. Keystones over basement windows. Prominent roof on bold, simple cornice. Side elevation of 3 storeys over basement and 5 bays; centre bay breaking forward with a Wyatt window in each storey, including the basement. Partly curving staircase. Sold *ca* 1952; afterwards demolished.

Liscarton Castle, Navan, co Meath (TALBOT, TYRCONNELL, D/DEP; CULLEN/IFR). A C15 and C16 castle on the River Blackwater originally consisting of 2 massive towers joined by a hall. In C17 it belonged to Sir William Talbot, 1st Bt, father of James II's Lord Deputy of Ireland, Richard Talbot, Duke of Tyrconnell. The hall subsequently became roofless and one of the towers was reduced in height and made into a dwelling-house, with a thatched roof. The other tower, which has 4 corner turrets, remained at its original height. Nearby is the ruin of the medieval manorial church, with C18 windows. The home of James Cullen, younger brother of Paul, Cardinal Cullen, the great C19 Irish churchman and 1st Irish Cardinal. Remained in the Cullen family until 1966, when it was sold.

Lisconnan, Dervock, co Antrim (ALLEN/IFR). A house built probably in 2nd half of C18, on the site of a C17 house. Originally 2 storey and 4 bay, with a single storey 3 bay wing prolonging its front, which was given an upper storey to make the front symmetrical 1886; so that it now has a 2 storey front of 7 bays. The work of 1886 was so well done that the house appears to have been built all of a piece in C18. A single

Lisconnan

storey porch, again very much in keeping, was added *ca* 1900; above it is a central Venetian window. Georgian doorcases in hall; well-detailed coved ceiling in upper hall.

Lisdonagh, Headford, co Galway. A 2 storey house, probably of 1790s, with a front of 2 bays on either side of a curved bow. Rusticated fanlighted doorway in bow; oval hall, walls painted with an Ionic order and figures in *grisaille* by J. Ryan. Staircase behind hall, partly in 3 sided projection. On one side of the house is a detached pyramidally-roofed Palladian pavilion with a Venetian window on one face and a niche on the other; Dr Craig is doubtful whether a balancing pavilion was ever built. The seat of the Palmer family.

Lisgoole Abbey, Enniskillen, co Fermanagh (JOHNSTON/LGI1958). A 2 storey 3 bay gable-ended Georgian house with a battlemented tower at one end. Fanlighted doorway; large window inserted subsequently in bay to right of doorway, and large Wyatt window in base of tower.

Lisheen, co Sligo

Lisheen (formerly known as **Seafield**), **Ballysadare, co Sligo** (PHIBBS/LGI1912). In 1798, William Phibbs built Seafield, overlooking Ballysadare Bay, as a dower house for his son, Owen. It was Gothic, but the stables and cowsheds were joined to it in the Palladian manner. Owen Phibbs, who lived mainly in Dublin, used Seafield only as a summer retreat; but his son, William, came to live permanently at Seafield 1842, and in that year began building a much larger house about 200 yards away from the old one, which was allowed to fall into ruin. The architect of the new house was the Sligo-born John Benson, who was afterwards knighted for designing the building for the Dublin Exhibition of 1853. It was Classical, square, of 2 storeys, with a roof carried on a cornice. Entrance front of 7 bays; framing bands at the corners of the front, on either side of the centre bay and above the first floor windows; continuous entablatures below the windows in each storey. Entrance door recessed behind a Grecian temple or tomb doorway with two Ionic columns. Entablatures on console brackets over ground

floor windows. Adjoining front of 5 bays, the 3 centre bays being recessed. Framing bands and entablatures under the windows as in the entrance front; triangular pediments on console brackets over the two outer ground floor windows. Cast-iron veranda filling the recess between the end bays. Large hall, ballroom and library. Long gallery on 1st floor, lit by sky-lights, which subsequently became known as the Museum, having been filled with objects ranging from Egyptian mummies to Syrian swords and daggers collected by Owen Phibbs, son of the builder of the house, an archaeologist of note. The house was infested by a particularly malicious poltergeist; which gave it such a bad reputation that Owen Phibbs, on succeeding to it 1904, changed its name from Seafield to Lisheen. Later in the present century, in an attempt to get rid of the poltergeist, the family handed over the house for some weeks to a party of Jesuits, who celebrated Mass in it each day during their stay. D.W. Phibbs sold the house 1940, and it was immediately afterwards demolished.

Lisheen Castle, co Tipperary

Lisheen Castle, Templemore, co Tipperary (LLOYD/IFR). A small castle of *ca* 1840, with plain stone mullioned windows and a central battlemented and machicolated turret with the entrance door set in a recess at its foot. Burnt 1900.

Lisheens, Carrickmines, co Dublin (ORPEN/IFR). An Edwardian Tudor house, built 1901–02 for Charles St George Orpen to the design of his brother, Richard Orpen, who also designed an addition of 1913. Sold 1950 to Mr & Mrs Shannon.

Lismacue, Tipperary, co Tipperary (BAKER/IFR). A late-Georgian house with battlements and other mild Gothic touches. 2 storeys; entrance front of 3 bays with Gothic porch, prolonged by lower wing ending in a gable with a tracery window. Side of 5 bays has a battlemented pediment with pinnacles. Another pediment on the rear facade.

Lismany, Ballinasloe, co Galway (POLLOK/LGI1958). A 2 storey hybrid house with an irregular facade of gables, Tudor-Revival windows, Georgian windows with rusticated surrounds and 3 sided bows.

Lismehane (formerly **Maryfort**), **O'Callaghan's Mills, co Clare** (WESTROPP/IFR; O'CALLAGHAN-WESTROPP, *sub* O'CALLAGHAN/IFR). An early C18 gable-ended house of 3 storeys over a high basement; tra-

Lismehane

ditionally built by John Westropp; enlarged, refaced and generally embellished at the end of C19 by Col John O'Callaghan. 6 bay front; originally a narrow flight of steps led up to the hall door, but in late C19 a terrace was formed in front of the house from which a broader flight of steps led up to the entrance, which was under a single-storey Ionic portico, added at the same time. Segmental pediments and entablatures over windows. Late C19 2 storey wing at back. Cornices of heavy Victorian plasterwork in hall and two principal reception rooms, picked out in colours. Staircase of wood, curving in two directions, at back of hall; extending into projection in rear elevation. Demolished by Mr C. J. O'Callaghan-Westropp 1967.

Lismore, Crossdoney, co Cavan (NESBITT, *sub* BURROWES/LGI1912; BURROWES/IFR; LUCAS-CLEMENTS/IFR). A house probably of *ca* 1730 and very likely by Sir Edward Lovett Pearce. Main block of 2 storeys over a high basement; pedimented breakfront centre with a rather widely spaced Venetian window in both storeys; 2 bays on either side of centre. Overlapping "tower" wings of 1 storey over basement and 1 bay. Detached 2 storey 6 bay office wings, joined to house by screen walls. These wings have gable-ends with curvilinear gables facing the sides of the house; the outermost bay of each, in the front elevation is also gabled; the gables here were probably originally curvilinear also, though they are now straight. Round-headed windows in lower storey and basement of house and in lower storey of office wings. House had solid roof parapet with urns. Oculi in upper storey of office wings. Originally the seat of the Nesbitts; passed to the Burrowes through the marriage of Mary Nesbitt to James Burrowes 1854; passed to the Lucas-Clementses through the marriage of Miss Rosamund Burrowes to the late Major Shuckburgh Lucas-Clements 1922. Having stood empty for many years, the house fell into ruin and was finally demolished, except for one of the "tower" wings, *ca* 1952. The office wings are now used as farm buildings, and the family now live in the former agent's house, an early house with a Victorian wing and other additions.

Lismore Castle, Lismore, co Waterford (BOYLE, CORK AND ORRERY, E/PB; CAVENDISH, DEVONSHIRE, D/PB). A castle familiar to everyone who has crossed the bridge over the Blackwater to the north of the town of Lismore; its fawn-grey towers rising high from a cliff covered with trees which seem

Lismore Castle, co Waterford

to float on the surface of the river. Now predominantly of early C17 and C19; but incorporating some of the towers of the medieval castle of the Bishops of Lismore which itself took the place of a castle built by King John where there had formerly been a famous monastery founded by St Carthagh and a university which was a great centre of civilization and learning in the Dark Ages. The first Protestant Bishop, the notorious Myler McGrath, granted the castle and its lands to Sir Walter Raleigh; who, however, seldom lived here, preferring his house at Youghal, now known as Myrtle Grove (*qv*). In 1602, Raleigh sold Lismore and all his Irish estates to Richard Boyle, afterwards 1st Earl of Cork, one of the most remarkable of the Elizabethan adventurers; who, having come to Ireland as a penniless young man, ended as one of the richest and most powerful nobles in the kingdom. From *ca* 1610 onwards, he rebuilt Lismore Castle as his home, surrounding the castle courtyard with 3 storey gabled ranges joining the old corner-towers, which were given Jacobean ogival roofs; the principal living rooms being on the side above the Blackwater, the parlour and dining-chamber in a wing projecting outwards to the very edge of the precipice, with an oriel window from which there is a sheer drop to the river far below. On the side furthest from the river Lord Cork built a gatehouse tower, incorporating an old Celtic-Romanesque arch which must have survived from Lismore's monastic days. He also built a fortified wall—so thick that there is a walk along the top of it—enclosing a garden on this side of the castle; and an outer gatehouse with gabled towers known as the Riding House because it originally sheltered a mounted guard. The garden walls served an important defensive purpose when the castle was besieged by the Confederates 1642, the year before the "Great Earl's" death. On this occasion the besiegers were repulsed; but in 1645 it fell to another Confederate Army and was sacked. It was made habitable again by the

2nd Earl of Cork—James II stayed a night here in 1689 and almost fainted when he looked out of the dining room window and saw the great drop—but it was neglected in C18 and became largely ruinous; the subsequent Earls of Cork, who were also Earls of Burlington, preferring to live on their estates in England. Through the marriage of the daughter and heiress of the architect Earl of Burlington and Cork to the 4th Duke of Devonshire, Lismore passed to the Cavendishes. The 4th and 5th Dukes took no more interest in the castle than the Earls of Burlington had done; but the 6th Duke—remembered as the "Bachelor Duke"—began work at Lismore as soon as he succeeded his father 1811. By 1812 the castle was habitable enough for him to entertain his cousin, Lady Caroline Lamb, her husband, William, and her mother, Lady Bessborough, here. Caroline, who had been brought to Ireland in the hope that it would make her forget Byron, was bitterly disappointed by the castle; she had expected "vast apartments full of tattered furniture and gloom"; instead, as Lady Bessborough reported, "Hart handed her into, not a Gothic hall, but two small dapper parlours neatly furnished, in the newest Inn fashion, much like a Cit's villa at Highgate". Hart—the Bachelor Duke—had in fact already commissioned the architect William Atkinson to restore the range above the river in a suitably medieval style, and the work actually began in that same year. Battlements replaced the Great Earl of Cork's gables and the principal rooms—including the dining room with the famous window, which became the drawing room—were given ceilings of simple plaster vaulting. The Bachelor Duke, who became increasingly attached to Lismore, began a 2nd and more ambitious phase of rebuilding 1850, towards the end of his life. This time his architect was Sir Joseph Paxton, that versatile genius who designed the Crystal Palace and who, having started as the Bachelor Duke's gardener, became his close friend and right-hand man. During the next few years, the 3 remaining sides of the courtyard were rebuilt in an impressive C19 castle style, with battlemented towers and turrets; all faced in cut-stone shipped over from Derbyshire. The Great Earl's gatehouse tower, with its pyramidal roof, was, however, left as it was, and also the Riding House. The ruined chapel of the Bishops, adjoining the range containing the Great Earl's living rooms, was restored as a banqueting-hall or ball-room of ecclesiastical character; with choir-stalls, a vast Perpendicular stained glass window at either end, and richly coloured Gothic stencilling on the walls and the timbers of the open roof. The decoration of the room was carried out by John Gregory Crace, some of it being designed by Pugin, including the chimneypiece, which was exhibited in the Medieval Court at the Great Exhibition. The banqueting hall is the only really large room in the castle, the interior of which is on a much more modest and homely scale than might be expected from the great extent of the building; but in fact one side of the courtyard was designed to be a separate house for the agent, and another side to be the estate office. Subsequent Dukes of Devonshire have loved Lismore as much as the Bachelor Duke did, though their English commitments have naturally prevented them from coming here for more than occasional visits. From 1932 until his death 1944, the castle was continually occupied by Lord Charles Cavendish, younger son of the 9th Duke, and his wife, the former Miss Adele Astaire, the dancer and actress, who still comes here every year. The present Duke and Duchess have carried out many improvements to the gardens, which consist of the original upper garden, surrounded by the Great Earl's fortified walls, and a more naturalistic garden below the approach to the castle; the 2 being linked in a charming and unexpected way by a staircase in the Riding House.

Lismullen, Tara, co Meath (DILLON, Bt/PB). A 3 storey 5 bay early to mid-C18 house. Good quoins; wall carried up to form roof parapet; buttresses on facade. Side elevation of 2 bays and then 3 bays set slightly back; prolonged by 2 storey office wing. Burnt 1923; afterwards rebuilt without the top storey.

Lisnabin, Killucan, co Westmeath (PURDON/IFR). A C18 house castellated *ca* 1840 for Edward Purdon with battlements and slender polygonal turrets at the corners and on either side of the entrance door. Circular stair hall.

Lisnabrin, Curraglass, co Cork. A 5 bay bow-ended C18 house with a Diocletian window above a Venetian doorway. The seat of the Crokers, descended from a Cromwellian Colonel to whom the estate was granted. By a happy coincidence, Col Croker had been given shelter at Lisnabrin by its Irish Catholic owner, Walter Coppinger, and nursed back to health by his two daughters, having been brought here gravely wounded in a battle nearby. So instead of turning Coppinger out, Croker asked him for the hand of one of his daughters, and became his son-in-law.

Lisnagree

Lisnagree, Charleville, co Cork (BROWNE, *sub* GROSVENOR/IFR). A 2 storey early C20 house with 3 sided bows, camber-headed Georgian-glazed windows, external shutters and a single-storey bow-fronted wing with a dormered attic in a mansard roof. A seat of 5th Earl of Kenmare.

Lisnamallard House

Lisnamallard House, Omagh, co Tyrone (BUCHANAN, *sub* HAMMOND-SMITH/IFR; SCOTT/IFR). A Georgian house believed to have been built in front of an earlier house of 1724, which subsequently became part of the stable yard. 2 storey; 3 bay front with canted ends. Formerly belonged to the Buchanan family, of which James Buchanan, 15th President of the United States (*see* PFUSA), was a cadet. Bought by Charles Scott *ca* 1880, after which various alterations were carried out; notably the addition of a glass porch, and overhanging windows on the side elevations.

Lisnavagh

Lisnavagh, Rathvilly, co Carlow (BUNBURY/LG1863; MCCLINTOCK-BUNBURY, RATHDONNELL, B/PB). A large and rambling Tudor-Revival house of grey stone, built 1847 for William McClintock-Bunbury, MP, brother of 1st Lord Rathdonnell, to the design of John McCurdy. Many gables and mullioned windows; some oriels; but all very restrained, with little or no ornament and hardly any Gothic or Baronial touches apart from a porte-cochère on the service wing, which was set back from the main entrance front, and a loggia of segmental-pointed arches at the other side of

the house. The porte-cochère served the luggage entrance; the hall door having no such protection. Staircase of wood, ascending round large staircase hall. Drawing room with ceiling of ribs and bosses and marble chimneypiece in Louis Quinze style, *en suite* with library; richly carved oak bookcases. The house was greatly reduced in size *ca* 1953 by 4th Lord Rathdonnell; that part which contained the principal rooms being demolished, and the service wing being adapted to provide all the required accommodation. The porte-cochère, which comes in the middle of the entrance front of the reduced house, is now the main entrance. Because of the irregular plan of the house as it originally was, the service wing only abutted on the main building at one corner, which has been made good with a gable and oriel from the demolished part; so that the surviving part of the house looks complete in itself; a pleasant Tudor-Revival house of medium size rather than the rump of a larger house. A large library has been formed out of several small rooms; it is lined with the bookcases from the original library, and with oak panelling and Cordova leather of blue–green and dull bronze–gold. Fine baronial gate arch.

Lisnegar, Rathcormack, co Cork (BARRY, *sub* BURY-BARRY/LG1958; TONSON, RIVERSDALE, B/DEP; STAWELL/LG1912; LUBBOCK, *sub* AVEBURY, B/PB1970; HALLINAN/IFR; MEADE/LG1972; GUBBINS/LG1937 Supp). An early C18 house of the branch of the Barry family whose head was styled M'Adam Barry; enlarged and remodelled in the Tudor-Gothic style early C19 by William Tonson, 2nd Lord Riversdale. Gables with finials; 2 storey battlemented porch with pinnacles; 3 sided bows with wooden mullions. At one end of the house a taller block, also in the Tudor-Gothic style, was added. The interior of the original part of the house contains some C18 panelling. On the death of 3rd and last Lord Riversdale 1861, Lisnegar passed to his nephew, W. T. J. Stawell, who assumed the additional surname of Riversdale. After being sold by the Alcock-Stawell-Riversdale family in the present century, the house was reduced in size by the removal of the taller block. In the years following the end of World War II, Lisnegar was the home of M. G. Lubbock. Subsequently the home of T. E. Hallinan; after that, of Capt John Meade; now of Mrs Hogan (*née* Maureen Gubbins).

Lisreaghan: Triumphal Arch

Lisreaghan, (also known as **Bellevue**), **Lawrencetown, co Galway** (LAWRENCE/LG1912). The house here, with its Doric portico, has disappeared; to tell of its former existence, there are 2 Gothic follies and the avenue, now a public road, at one end of which is a fine C18 triumphal arch flanked by pedimented lodges, which was erected by Walter Lawrence to commemorate the Irish Volunteers of 1782. In its day, the demesne was noted for its fine cedars of Lebanon and evergreen oaks.

Lissadell

Lissadell

Lissadell, Carney, co Sligo (GORE-BOOTH, Bt/PB). A large and austere Grecian-Revival house of grey limestone standing among luxuriant woods and glades on the northern shore of Sligo Bay. Built 1830–35 for Sir Robert Gore-Booth, 4th Bt, MP, to the design of Francis Goodwin, of London; replacing an earlier house nearer the shore which itself replaced an old castle. Of 2 storeys over a basement; 4 regular elevations, with very little ornament apart from some Doric pilasters and corner-pilasters. Entrance front with pedimented and pilastered 3 bay central projection, its lower storey having open sides so as to form a porte-cochère. Adjoining front with 5 bays

Lissadell: Porte-Cochère

recessed between 2 bay projections; central feature of 4 pilasters with plain entablature. Other front with 3 bays on either side of a curved central bow, the parapet of which is raised above the parapet on either side. Back elevation—adjoining the entrance front—with 4 bays projecting boldly on either side of a recessed centre. Lofty 2 storey hall, partly top-lit, with square Doric columns below and Ionic columns above and double staircase of Kilkenny marble. Vast apse-ended gallery beyond, lit by a clerestory and skylights; with engaged Doric piers along one side, and Ionic columns along the other. The rather monumental sequence of hall and gallery leads to a lighter and more intimate bow room with windows facing towards Sligo Bay—the windows Yeats had in mind when he wrote, in his poem on Eva Gore-Booth and her sister, Constance Markievicz:

> " The light of evening, Lissadell
> Great windows open to the South".

This room, and the other principal reception rooms, have massive marble chimneypieces in the Egyptian taste. The anteroom has a striped wallpaper of a lovely faded rose. The billiard room is hung with banners, one of which was presented to Sir Robert Gore-Booth, the builder of the house, in gratitude for what he did during the Famine, when he mortgaged his estate so as to be able to feed everyone for miles around. The dining room has a geometrical ceiling and pilasters which were painted, early this century, with a remarkable series of full-length portraits of members of the family, together with the gamekeeper, forester and butler, by Count Casimir Markievicz, the artist son-in-law of the 5th Bt and husband of Constance Markievicz, fighter for Irish freedom, member of the first Dáil and friend of the Dublin poor. She was also an artist, just as her sister, Eva Gore-Booth, was a poet of distinction. Lissadell is now open to the public.

Lissan, Cookstown, co Tyrone (STAPLES, Bt/PB). A plain 3 storey 9 bay Georgian house with later additions. At one end, a single-storey wing with a three-sided mullioned bow. At the other, a gable-ended office range. And in the middle of the entrance front, a single-storey protuberance of unusual depth, embodying a porch and a bow-fronted porte-cochère with windows. Some time *post* mid-C18, a garden was laid out here by the architect, Davis Duckart; with "an artificial sheet of water with cascades, and a picturesque bridge".

Lissan Rectory, Cookstown, co Tyrone (STAPLES, Bt/PB). An Italianate villa by John Nash, the only one in Ireland; built 1807 for the Rev J. M. Staples, whose 1st cousin and near neighbour, William Stewart, MP, had commissioned Nash to design Killymoon Castle (*qv*). It has a round tower, round-headed windows and an arcade with chamfered columns, surmounted by a veranda of graceful Regency ironwork; and derives from a rather grander Nash villa in England, Cronkhill in Shropshire.

Lissanoure Castle, Killagan, co Antrim (MACARTNEY/LGI1912). A house extending around 4 sides of a large rectangular courtyard; built in various stages from *ca* 1770

onwards by George Macartney, 1st and last Earl Macartney, the diplomatist and Indian and colonial governor. 2 storey; front of 5 bays between 2 3 sided bows. According to one drawing, this front was Georgian Gothic; according to another, it was plain C18 Classical, with a tripartite pedimented doorway; as the latter drawing would appear to be the later of the two, and to show the house as it actually was, one would imagine the Gothic view to be fanciful. Inside the 2 bows were an octagonal drawing room and dining room; between them were 2 other reception rooms on either side of a hall, behind which was a spacious double staircase in a projection jutting out at the back into the courtyard; the staircase appears to have had 2 lower ramps and a single flying return, as at Glin Castle, co Limerick (*qv*). At right angles to the front, 2 long ranges ran back on either side of the courtyard, containing offices and stables; they had windows only facing into the courtyard, their outer walls being blank and battlemented. The 4th side of the courtyard also had a blank wall on the outside and windows facing inwards; with an archway in its centre. The ranges facing into the courtyard had pointed Georgian Gothic windows and dormer-gables. On Lord Macartney's death, Lissanoure was inherited by his great-nephew, George Hume, who assumed the name of Macartney; and who, from 1829 onwards, began to rebuild the house; pulling down the old castle, which stood at one corner of it; putting up a Tudor archway leading into the courtyard, surmounted by an octagonal battlemented belfry and spire, very much in the manner of William Vitruvius Morrison. Not until 1847 did he tackle the front of the house, having in the meantime built himself "an elegant cottage in the later English style, richly embellished" by the side of the lake. In that same year, after the front wall had been taken down, with a view to rebuilding it, there was an explosion of gunpowder which killed Mrs Macartney and presumably also damaged the structure of the house; for all work on it ceased and it was allowed to fall into ruin. The "elegant cottage" continued to serve as the family residence, and was later rebuilt in a more rustic style, with dormer-gables and elaborate bargeboards; and an office wing at the back almost twice as large as the house itself.

Liss Ard, Skibbereen, co Cork (O'DONOVAN/IFR). A long 2 storey early-Victorian house, built *ca* 1840 by H. W. O'Donovan, who succeeded his brother as The O'Donovan 1870. Entrance at end; fine rooms. Sold *ca* 1924 by Col M. W. O'Donovan, The O'Donovan. In recent years the home of the late Capt & Mrs Richard Ansdell.

Lisselane, Clonakilty, co Cork (BENCE-JONES/IFR). A house in a simplified French château style built 1851–53 by William Bence-Jones to the design of Lewis Vulliamy. The house was built in an attractive situation facing down the valley of the Arigadeen River; there had been no house here before, for though the 2 previous generations of the family had owned the estate, they had not lived here. William Bence-Jones's 3 small daughters helped with the

Lisselane

marking out of the foundations; but only one of them lived to see the house completed, the other two being struck down by scarlet fever at the end of 1851. The house is square in plan, of 2 storeys over a basement with a dormered attic in the high-pitched roof, which is on a bracket cornice. At one corner is a 3 storey round tower with a pointed roof, which, like the roof of the main block, is pleasantly sprocketed. Later in the C19, a smoking room wing was added, probably to the design of Sir Thomas Newenham Deane, who also appears to have designed the front gate-lodge. A large glass conservatory, which had been made for the Cork Exhibition of 1902, was added at one corner of the house by Reginald Bence-Jones, who in 1907 made a large library-hall, lined from floor to ceiling with oak bookcases, out of the former library, another room and part of the original hall: "And what do you call this grand room?", asked the survivor of the three little girls who had marked out the foundations, now grown into a rather formidable elderly lady, when she saw it. Reginald Bence-Jones and his wife also greatly extended the high terrace below the house and made a notable garden on both sides of the river, which they widened into a lake. Lisselane was sold by Reginald Bence-Jones 1930 to Mr C.O. Stanley, who enlarged the hall by building a single-storey addition along the entrance front *ca* 1947.

Lissen Hall, Swords, co Dublin (HELY-HUTCHINSON, *sub* DONOUGHMORE, E/PB). A 3 storey C18 house which appears to have been remodelled and embellished later in C18 in emulation of Mantua (*qv*), which faced it across the Broadmeadow River. 5 bay front; triple window above Venetian window above pedimented tripartite doorway. 2 storey end bows. Wall carried up to be roof parapet and adorned with urns and eagles.

Lissen Hall, Nenagh, co Tipperary (OT-WAY-RUTHVEN/IFR; CARROL/LGI1912). A fine 2 storey mid-C18 house, which Dr Craig considers to have been designed by the same architect or builder as Castle Otway, co Tipperary (*qv*). 5 bay pedimented breakfront; elegant frontispiece of channelled ashlar, the impost-moulding binding the doorway to the windows on either side. High-pitched roof. Now ruined.

Lissrenny, Tallanstown, co Louth (FILGATE/IFR). A 3 storey 7 bay red brick house of 1788–98, built by William Filgate onto the end of an earlier house with panelled

Lissrenny

rooms, and at right angles to it; forming a house with a "T"-plan. The 1788–98 block had a pedimented and fanlighted tripartite doorway and a parapeted roof. It was demolished 1974, leaving the earlier house to serve as the family residence. 2 rooms have since been added to it.

Little Island House, Little Island, co Cork (BURY/IFR). A Palladian house built for the Bury family; stylistically of *ca* 1780, and from its plan, probably a late work by Davis Duckart. 3 storey 7 bay centre block joined to office wings, lying at right angles to it and projecting forwards, by quadrant walls on the entrance front and by straight corridors with round-headed niches surmounted by oculi on the garden front; the plan being roughly similar to that of Kilshannig (*qv*). 3 bay breakfront on both entrance and garden fronts of centre block. Large hall, with staircase in separate hall to the left. 3 large rooms in garden front. Now a ruin, having stood empty and derelict for many years.

Lixnaw, co Kerry (PETTY-FITZMAURICE, LANSDOWNE, M/PB). The once-magnificent seat of the Fitzmaurices, Earls of Kerry, an old castle much enlarged C18 with fine gardens. By the beginning of C19, the castle was "decayed"; by 1837 it was in ruins. Now, only a few shapeless walls remain. Nearby was the circular domed mausoleum of one of the Earls of Kerry, regrettably destroyed by the encroachment of a quarry.

Lizard Manor, Aghadowney, co Derry (STRONGE, Bt/PB). A 2 storey C19 house in the Georgian style. 5 bay front, centre breakfront with 2 narrow windows above and plain projecting porch below. 3 sided bow in side elevation. Eaved roof on plain cornice.

Lloydsboro'

Lloydsboro', Templemore, co Tipperary (LLOYD/IFR). A 2 storey late-Georgian house with an eaved roof. 3 bay entrance front; single-storey Ionic portico with acroteria; front prolonged by a 3 storey wing set a little back. 4 bay side, prolonged by an elegant polygonal conservatory with pilasters.

Lodge, Puckaun, co Tipperary (STUD-DERT/IFR). A plain and slightly irregular 2 storey 5 bay late C17 or early C18 house, enlarged mid-C18 by the addition of 2 1 bay wings rising above the centre to the height of an attic storey; one of them with a gable treated as a pediment and adorned with an eagle and urns; the other with a pediment to match. Each wing had a Diocletian or lunette window above 2 Venetian windows. The gable has now lost its embellishments and both of the semi-circular attic windows have been blocked up; the surround of one still shows, whereas the other is obliterated.

Lodge Park, co Kildare

Lodge Park, co Kildare

Lodge Park, Straffan, co Kildare (HENRY/LGI1912; GUINNESS/IFR). A Palladian house of 1775–77, unusual in consisting of a centre block with 4 wings or pavilions instead of the usual 2; it is said that the builder, Hugh Henry, whose wife was a daughter of 1st Earl of Milltown, wished his house to have a frontage as long as that of his father-in-law's house, Russborough (*qv*). Believed to be by the amateur architect, Nathaniel Clements. Centre block of 2 storeys over a high basement and 5 bays; tripartite fanlighted doorway with baseless pediment and engaged columns, triple window above; some blocking in surrounds of lower storey windows; broad flight of steps up to hall door. Pavilions of 2 storeys and 3 bays; the inner ones, which are slightly higher than the outer, being linked to the centre block by curved sweeps with round-headed rusticated doorways between round-headed windows; all of which, like the fanlight above the entrance doorway in the centre block, have Gothic astragals. Outer pavilions linked to the inner ones by gated walls. Staircase with slender uprights in hall to the left of entrance hall. Reception rooms with simple Adam style decoration. Bought, soon after World War II, by Mr Richard Guinness.

Loftus Hall, nr Fethard-on-Sea, co Wexford (REDMOND/LGI1863; LOFTUS, ELY, M/PB). A gaunt, 3 storey mansion of 1871, with rows of plate-glass windows and a balustraded parapet; incorporating parts of the previous house here, which was late C17 or early C18, gable-ended and of 2 storeys

Loftus Hall

and 9 bays, with a dormered roof and a steep pediment-gable; it was fronted by a fore-court with tall piers surmounted by ball finials and had a haunted tapestry room. The house stands near the tip of the Hook Head, and must have been one of the most wind-swept noblemen's seats in the British Isles; "No tree will grow above the shelter of the walls", Bishop Pococke observed of Loftus Hall in C18, and the same is true of the place today. The site was originally occupied by an old castle of the Redmonds, which was known in their day as The Hall; and of which a square turret remained near the old house, but was demolished when the present house was built. The present house, which was built soon after his coming-of-age by the 4th Marquess of Ely —who also planned to rebuild his other seat, Ely Lodge (*qv*)—contains an impressive staircase hall, with an oak stair in Jacobean style, richly decorated with carving and marquetry; the gallery being carried on fluted Corinthian columns of wood. The house is now a convent.

Lohort Castle, Cecilstown, co Cork (PERCEVAL, EGMONT, E/PB; O'BRIEN, Bt/PB). An exceptionally large C15 tower-house of the MacCarthys, damaged in the Cromwellian period when it was bombarded and captured by Sir Hardress Waller; restored *ca* 1750 by 2nd Earl of Egmont, who made several good rooms in it; one of them being a library, another an armoury, containing enough weapons to equip 100 horse. 2nd Earl was presumably also responsible for the lay-out of the demesne, in which the castle, with its surrounding moat and star-shaped Vaubanesque outworks, was ringed with woods planted in the form of an octagon, from which straight avenues were aligned on it like the spokes of a wheel. The castle was remodelled 1876, when an outer bawn-wall was built and also a castellated gate-house; which though detached from the castle and some way from it, contained additional bedroom accommodation. Lohort subsequently became the home of Sir Timothy O'Brien, 3rd Bt, a well-known cricketer. It was gutted by fire *ca* 1920.

Londonderry: Bishop's Palace (*see* DERRY).

Longfield, Goold's Cross, co Tipperary (LONG, *sub* FREESE-PENNEFATHER/LGI1958; O'CONNELL BIANCONI, *sub* O'CONNELL/IFR). A 3 storey late C18 house, built by the Long family; with a curved bow in the centre of its front and rear elevation and a 3 sided bow at either end. 1 bay on either side of the bow in the front; fanlighted rusticated doorway. Oval hall; curved staircase of

Longfield

wood, with slim balusters, extending into real bow. Bought C19 by Charles Bianconi, "King of the Irish Roads", an Italian who, having come to Ireland virtually penniless, made a fortune by running a fast and efficient system of horse-drawn transport with his famous "long cars". Passed to a branch of the O'Connells through the marriage of Bianconi's daughter to a nephew of Daniel O'Connell, "The Liberator"; bequeathed 1968 by Mrs Mary O'Connell Bianconi to the Irish Georgian Society. Now run as a guest house by Mr Kevin Byrne, under the auspices of the Society, in order to help meet the cost of upkeep.

Longford House

Longford House

Longford House, Beltra, co Sligo (CROFTON, Bt, *of Longford House*/PB). A house of 2 storeys over a high basement, built 1782, which was intended to be flanked by 2 large wings of which only one was built. Front with 3 sided bow and pedimented doorcase; other front with rusticated Venetian loggia in basement. Lime avenue; old castle in grounds, also ruined oratory; Elizabethan or Jacobean Crofton chimney-piece removed from Mote, co Roscommon (*qv*) near house. The main block of the house was gutted by fire early in C19; the windows, however, have been replaced and it has been given a flat roof and is used as a store. After the fire, the wing was remodelled to serve as a house.

Longraigue, Foulksmills, co Wexford (DEANE/LGI1912, GIBBON/IFR). An earlier

Lohort Castle

house given a mildly Tudor-Revival appearance in C19. Front with gable at one end, and hood mouldings over windows; projecting porch. More gables at side of house.

Longtown

Longtown, Clane, co Kildare (BURDETT/ IFR; SWEETMAN/IFR). A late-Georgian house built by Capt George Burdett; leased *ca* 1819 and sold *ca* 1829 to Michael Sweetman, who greatly enlarged it. 3 storey; 5 bay centre recessed between 2 bay projections; single-storey Ionic portico. Roof parapet with dentil ornamentation. Sold 1944 by Gerard Sweetman, TD, sometime Minister of Finance; subsequently demolished.

Longueville

Longueville, Mallow, co Cork (LONG-FIELD/IFR). A 3 storey 5 bay C18 block, enlarged by the addition of 2 storey 3 bay wings in the late-Georgian period, probably between 1800 and 1805 by John Longfield, MP; the centre being refaced and some of its windows altered at the same time so as to make the front uniform. 1 bay central breakfront, Wyatt windows in 2 upper storeys above a fanlighted doorway beneath a single-storey portico. One of the wings was extended at right angles to the front *ca* 1866; and a charming Victorian conservatory of curved ironwork was added, probably at the same time. The principal reception rooms, which have simple early C19 plasterwork and doors of inlaid mahogany, extend on either side of the entrance hall, which has a floor of Portland stone. Behind is the staircase hall, with a bifurcating staircase which is most unusual in rising to the top of the house; the central ramp and two returns being repeated in the storey above. Longueville was sold by the Longfields to the late Senator William O'Callaghan, whose son and daughter-in-law have opened it as a guest house.

Lota, Glanmire, co Cork (ROGERS/LG 1863). A fine Palladian house overlooking the Lee estuary just above the mouth of the Glanmire River; built 1765 for Robert Rogers to the design of Davis Duckart. 3 storey 9 bay centre block joined to pyramidal-roofed pavilions by wings with win-

Lota

Lota: Staircase

dows set in niches beneath oculi; central feature of pilasters and urns and delightful Baroque porch with banded columns, blocked pilasters and concave-curving entablature and wrought-iron balustrade. Richly carved and moulded mahogany bifurcating staircase at back of hall; gallery supported by arch with coffered barrel vault on Doric entablature and columns; fluted Corinthian columns above. Oval recesses with frames of simple rococo plasterwork on walls. The exterior of the house has been much altered but the porch remains as it was, as does the hall and staircase. The house is now owned by the Brothers of Charity.

Lota Beg, Glanmire, co Cork (KELLETT, Bt/PB; MAHONY/IFR). A square late-Georgian house overlooking the Lee estuary built *ca* 1800 for Sir Richard Kellett, 1st Bt, to the design of the elder Abraham Hargrave. Impressive cantilevered staircase. Ionic triumphal arch at entrance to demesne by George Richard Pain. In 1837 the residence of D. Callaghan. Passed to the Mahony family later in C19.

Lota Lodge, Glanmire, co Cork (SHAR-MAN-CRAWFORD/LGI1912). A 2 storey Regency house with circular projections and an iron veranda. Eaved roof. Partly destroyed by fire 1902, rebuilt 1903.

Lotamore, Glanmire, co Cork (MAHONY/ IFR). A 2 storey 7 bay late-Georgian house overlooking the Lee estuary, its front pro-

longed to great length by later 2 storey wings. Fanlighted doorway. Owned *ca* 1870 by the Perrier family; afterwards by the Mahony family. In recent years, the home of Mr Richard Cudmore.

Lota Park, Glanmire, co Cork (MURPHY/ IFR; BEAMISH/IFR; GUBBINS/LG1937 Supp; MAHONY/IFR). A 2 storey house built 1801 by John Power. 3 bay entrance front; Wyatt windows in outer bays; fanlighted doorway with Ionic columns. Garden front overlooking the Lee estuary. Afterwards owned by James Roche ("J.R." of the *Gentleman's Magazine*), who added single-storey wings, one of them containing a ballroom, which in recent years was decorated in the Louis Quinze style; the other originally containing a library. Afterwards owned by John Molony and then by William Ware; bought *ca* 1837 by J. J. Murphy, whose body was shipped back to Ireland inside an upright piano after his death in Italy 1851, because the Neapolitan sailors refused to carry his coffin, on the grounds that it would bring them bad luck. Lota Park was afterwards the home of Lt-Col N. L. Beamish, an officer in the Hanoverian Service and a Knight of the Royal Hanoverian Guelphic Order, who died 1872. In the early years of the present century, it was the home of Joseph Gubbins, a well-known yachtsman. More recently, it was the home of Mrs Francis Mahony. Now a Cheshire Home.

Loughanmore, Dunadry, co Antrim (ADAIR/LG1858). A C18 house enlarged and castellated in the Victorian period. The entrance front dominated by a remarkable 5 storey porch-tower, with a spire; rising high above the rest of the house. A lower tower, also with a spire, at the other end of the house. The Victorian additions include a chapel.

Lough Bawn, Rockcorry, co Monaghan (HANBURY-TENISON/IFR). A 2 storey house in the manner of Francis Johnston, rebuilt after the previous house was destroyed by fire 1795. 3 bay front, centre bay breaking slightly forward; eaved roof. Shallow porch with coupled Doric columns; fanlight over doorway and sidelights. On either side of the porch, a Wyatt window under a shallow relieving arch. Central dormer with oval Adamesque fan panel between 2 windows. 2 storey wings, set back. Stable yard behind house.

Loughbawn, Collinstown, co Westmeath (BATTERSBY, *sub* MAXWELL/IFR). A late-Georgian house of *ca* 1820.

Loughbrickland House, Loughbrickland, co Down (WHYTE/IFR). A 2 storey late-Georgian house, with a front of 3 bays

Lota Beg: Gate

Loughbrickland House

plus a 3 sided bow, to which a 2 storey wing was added in the Victorian period. In the end of the Victorian wing facing the front is a 3 sided bow, intended to balance the earlier bow, but not quite doing so, since it is taller and narrower; also the Victorian wing has an eaved roof with gables and bargeboards, whereas the roof of the earlier part of the house is parapeted. In the lower storey of the earlier building are 2 Wyatt windows, flanking a pilastered porch.

Loughcrew: 3 views after fire of 1888

Loughcrew, Oldcastle, co Meath (NAPER/IFR). A large and severe neo-Classical house by C. R. Cockerell, in which Dr Watkin detects the influence of Robert Smirke. Built 1823 for J. L. Naper, replacing an earlier house which in turn replaced an old Plunkett castle, the birthplace of St Oliver Plunkett. The entrance front had a giant Athenian Ionic portico, and double pilasters at the corners. The garden front had a pedimented attic storey; below that were 3 central windows set under relieving arches, with a single window on either side; below again were 3 windows in each of the side bays, with a pilastered projecting frontispiece in the centre. Square plan with central staircase. Long service wing added 1823–25, ending in conservatory with pavilions. Stable yard cantilevered

Lough Cutra Castle

out to form covered way round perimeter. Grecian Doric gate-lodge on opposite side of road to entrance gate; the road here being made into a piazza by being lined with curved railings. The house was said to have a curse on it, for it was burnt 3 times within a 100 years. On 1st 2 occasions it was rebuilt, the exterior remaining unchanged; but after 3rd fire, *ca* 1960, the ruin was demolished; the vast stones and fallen capitals are now strewn about the ground like the remains of some lost city of antiquity.

Lough Cutra Castle, Gort, co Galway (GORT, V/PB; GOUGH, V/PB). A castle by John Nash, in a romantic situation above a lough; built from 1811 onwards for Col Charles Vereker, afterwards 2nd Viscount Gort, who had seen and admired East Cowes Castle, Nash's own country house on the Isle of Wight, and asked for a castle similar to it. To supervise the work, Nash sent over his 2 pupils, the brothers James & George Richard Pain, who settled in Ireland and built up an extensive architectural practice of their own. The castle is a graceful and dramatic composition of octagonal and round towers joined by a low 2 storey range; it is faced in ashlar and well furnished with battlements and machicolations. The interior is spatially effective; with a long, plaster-vaulted hall, a circular staircase and attractive octagonal rooms. 3rd Viscount Gort was ruined by the Famine, when he refused to collect any rents and gave large sums to charity; with the result that Lough Cutra was sold up by the Encumbered Estates Court 1851. The Gorts moved to England and by a twist of fate subsequently acquired East Cowes Castle. Lough Cutra was bought 1854 by the great soldier, Field Marshal Viscount Gough, who added a wing with a clock tower 1856, and had the interior redecorated by Crace; with friezes of military emblems, mottoes and other decoration painted on the ceilings, and a wallpaper specially made by Cole in a design incorporating coronets and Union Jacks. In 1900, 3rd Viscount Gough added an extension to accommodate the family collection of military trophies, which has since been

demolished. Lough Cutra was sold by the Gough family later in the present century. It then stood empty for many years becoming almost derelict; but was bought back *post* World War II by 7th Viscount Gort, and subsequently became the home of his great-niece (*née* Hon Elizabeth Sidney—*see* DE L'ISLE, V/PB), who restored it; even to having Lord Gough's wallpaper reproduced by Cole from the original blocks. It has since been sold once again.

Lough Eske Castle

Lough Eske Castle, nr Donegal, co Donegal (BROOKE, *sub* BROOKEBOROUGH, V/PB; WHITE/LGI1912). A Tudor-Baronial castle of 1866 by FitzGibbon Louch, built for the Donegal branch of the Brookes whose progenitor built Donegal Castle (*qv*). Of ashlar; 2 storeys over high basement, with 4 storey square tower at one end. Imposing Gothic porch between 2 oriels; battlemented parapet with 2 curvilinear blind gables. Tower with machicolations, crow-step battlements and curved corbelled oriels. Lower 2 storey battlemented range with corner turret at other end of front. Sold 1894, after the death of Thomas Brooke, to Major-Gen H.G. White. Largely gutted by fire some years ago; but one wing is still occupied.

Lough Fea, Carrickmacross, co Monaghan (SHIRLEY, *sub* FERRERS, E/PB). A very large and unusual Tudor-Gothic house by Thomas Rickman, the English architect and architectural writer who invented the

Lough Fea

Lough Fea

terms "Early English", "Decorated" and "Perpendicular" to describe the different periods of Gothic architecture. Built *ca* 1827 for E. J. Shirley, whose family had owned the estate since the marriage of Sir Henry Shirley to the daughter of Elizabeth I's favourite, the Earl of Essex; but had lived entirely at their English seat, so that there was no previous house here. Unlike most houses of its period and style, Lough Fea has no battlements and few gables; but a solid parapet which conceals much of the roof. There are also hardly any projecting bows or oriels, but rather small mullioned windows under hood mouldings; so that the elevations, of pinkish-grey ashlar, have a solid effect. There are several slender square turrets with sprocketed pyramidal roofs; also a polygonal lantern and a small tower and polygonal turret at the end of one wing; but no major tower, so that the house seems low and wide-spreading. The entrance front, facing the lough from which the estate takes its name, is flanked on one side by the chapel, and on the other by a great hall; which together form a 3 sided court. The interior is of great complexity, with many corridors and ante-rooms. There is a hall divided by a stone arcade, its walls hung with an early C19 wallpaper. There is a large and handsome library with oak bookcases, which formerly contained the famous library of E. P. Shirley, the antiquary, son of the builder of the house. The chapel is on the scale of a sizeable church, with 2 pulpits and a gallery. The *clou* of the house is, however, the great hall: vast and baronial, with a lofty hammer-beam roof, a minstrels' gallery and an arcade at 1st floor level. It was added after the rest of the house was completed; according to the story, Mr Shirley and Lord Rossmore vied with one another as to which of them could build the bigger room; Lord Rossmore enlarged his drawing room at Rossmore Park (*qv*) five times; but in the end Mr Shirley won the contest by building his great hall

P

The garden front of the house faces along a vista to an immense Celtic cross, which was erected by the tenants of the estate in token of their gratitude to the Shirleys. The demesne is noted for its magnificent woodlands.

Loughgall, co Armagh: The Manor (COPE/LGI1912). A 2 storey, mildly Tudor-Revival house of *ca* 1840, with many gables, some of them with bargeboards. Windows with simple wooden mullions; hood-mouldings over ground floor windows of main block. Lower service wing at one side, also many-gabled, with pointed windows in upper storey.

Loughglinn House: with extra storey

Loughglinn House, Loughglinn, co Roscommon (DILLON, V/PB). Originally a C18 house of 2 storeys over a basement with a dormered attic in a high-pitched roof. Entrance front with centre and end bays breaking forward, and 2 bays in between on either side; round-headed window above fanlighted doorway, each flanked by 2 narrow windows. Garden front, facing the lough from which the estate takes its name, with 23 sided bows; centre window flanked by 2 narrow windows above pedimented tripartite doorcase; 1 bay on the outside of each bow. 6 bay side elevation with 2 bay pedimented breakfront; unusual Venetian window with round-headed sidelights in centre of lower storey. A 3rd storey was added *ca* 1830, to the design of James Bolger; it was treated as an attic, above the original cornice. The house was gutted by fire 1904 and rebuilt without the top storey and the end bays of the garden front; the end bays of the entrance front being reduced to 1 storey only. At the same time, the entrance front was given a pediment and a segmental-pedimented Doric doorcase. The entrance

Loughglinn House: reduced in size after fire of 1904—2 views

front is flanked by a free-standing wing or pavilion of 2 storeys with rusticated window surrounds. The house is now a convent, noted for its cheeses.

Loughlinstown House, Shankill, co Dublin (DOMVILE/IFR). A 2 storey Georgian house. 7 bay front with 1 bay breakfront, in which there is a Venetian window above a tripartite rusticated and fanlighted doorway. Afterwards the home of the Galvin family.

Loughmoe Court

Loughmoe Court, Templemore, co Tipperary (PURCELL/IFR). A C15 tower with a large early C17 semi-fortified house of 3 storeys over a basement added to it; the later house ending in a square tower which balances the older tower. Regularly disposed mullioned windows; small curved gables, similar to those at Portumna Castle, co Galway (*qv*); string courses. Armorial fireplace in first floor room. The seat of the Purcells; one of whom, Nicholas Purcell, Baron of Loughmoe, was a Jacobite signatory of the Treaty of Limerick 1691. Now a ruin maintained as a National Monument.

Lough Rynn, Mohill, co Leitrim (LUCAS-CLEMENTS/IFR; CLEMENTS/IFR). A simple 2 storey Tudor-Revival house of cut stone, with gently sloping gables, mullioned windows, hood-mouldings and tall chimneys; built 1833 for Robert, Viscount Clements, probably to the design of William Burn;

Lough Rynn: Entrance Front

Lough Rynn: Garden Front

to which a wing in the same style but higher, and on a grander scale, was added 1889 to the design of Sir Thomas Drew for Col H. T. Clements, who inherited the estate from his cousin, William Clements, 3rd Earl of Leitrim. The 1833 range contains pleasant rooms with simple late-Georgian cornices; the later wing contains an oak-panelled hall and a very large and impressive drawing room or ballroom in the Norman Shaw style; with oak panelling, a heavy plaster cornice, a fretted ceiling and a vast and ornate inglenook fireplace. Stables with high-pitched roofs in French Renaissance style also by Drew. Heavily wooded demesne extending round the lough from which the estate takes its name. Walled garden with terrace above the water's edge, the parapet adorned with urns and sculpture.

Loughton

Loughton, Moneygall, Offaly (PEPPER/LGI1912; BLOOMFIELD, B/DEP; TRENCH, *sub* ASHTOWN, B/PB; ATKINSON/IFR). A 3 storey house built 1777 for Major Thomas Pepper on the site of a C17 house, with additions of 1835 by James Pain. Of elegant and restrained late-Georgian character, the main front consisting of 2 wide and shallow 3 sided bows of 3 bays each, with a 2 bay centre between them. Single storey wing of 2 bays, adorned with pilasters. Pediments and entablatures on console brackets over ground floor and first floor windows. Parapeted roof. Very handsome Georgian stables. The seat of 2nd Lord Bloomfield, whose aunt was the wife of Major Thomas Pepper's son; subsequently passed to the descendants of 2nd Lord Bloomfield's

Lough Rynn: Drawing Room or Ballroom

sister, Georgiana, wife of Henry Trench. From the Trenchs, it was inherited 1970 by Mr G. N. Atkinson.

Loughveagh, Gartan, co Donegal (CHAMBERS/LGI1863). From its appearance, a C19 remodelling of a 2 storey C18 house. 5 bay gable-ended front, with small central pediment-gable. Side elevation extended to 5 bays by 3 bay return with small gable. Attic lit by windows in the gables.

Louth Hall, Ardee, co Louth (PLUNKETT, LOUTH, B/PB). The familiar Irish castle theme of an old tower-house with a later building attached; but in this case the 3 storey 9 bay 1760 addition is as high as the old tower, and there is a continuous skyline of early C19 battlements; the whole effect being one of vastness and a certain grimness. In the entrance front, which is plain except for a small C18 pedimented and fanlighted doorway, the old tower projects at one end, forming an obtuse angle with the later building; it is differentiated by having pointed Georgian Gothic windows whereas in the rest of the facade there are ordinary rectangular sashes; it also has slightly higher battlements, with Irish crow-stepped battlements at the corners, which are balanced by similar battlements at the opposite end of the front. In the garden front, there is a projection at one end with a shallow curved bow, giving the effect of another tower; the ground floor windows of the bow being Georgian Gothic. There is good plasterwork of *ca* 1800 in the principal rooms, the largest room being a ballroom in the bow of the garden front.

Louth Hall: Dining Room with delicate plasterwork; now used for storing grain

Louth Hall: Stairs and Plasterwork

Louth Hall

Low Rock Castle, Portstewart, co Derry.
A 2 storey late-Georgian seaside villa, with
a bow like a round tower at either end of its
front; originally battlemented. The bows
contain circular rooms. The birthplace of
Field Marshal Sir George White, VC, the
defender of Ladysmith. (*See also* ROCK
CASTLE.)

Luggala

Lucan House

Lucan House, Lucan, co Dublin (SARS-
FIELD, LUCAN, E/DEP; COLTHURST-VESEY/
LGI1912; COLTHURST, Bt/PB; O'CONOR DON/
IFR; TEELING (*formerly* BURKE)/LGI1958). A
Palladian villa built 1770s by Agmondisham
Vesey, MP, replacing an earlier house which
itself replaced the old castle which had belonged to Patrick Sarsfield, Earl of Lucan,
hero of the Siege of Limerick. The estate
came to Agmondisham Vesey's father
through his 1st marriage to the Sarsfield
heiress; but instead of leaving it to his
daughter by her, who was the ancestress of
the Binghams, Earls of Lucan, he left it to
Agmondisham, who was his son by his 2nd
marriage. Agmondisham Vesey acted as his
own architect, while consulting Sir William
Chambers, and also James Wyatt and
Michael Stapleton, with regard to the interior. Of 2 storeys over a basement; 7 bay
entrance front with a central feature of a
pediment raised on a 3 bay attic, and carried
on 4 engaged Ionic columns; the ground
floor beneath them being treated as a basement and rusticated. The central feature of
Charleville, co Wicklow (*qv*) is similar. 5
bay side elevation; garden front with
central curved bow containing oval room;
the plan resembling that of Mount Kennedy, co Wicklow (*qv*). The house is
entirely free-standing, the offices being
detached and connected to it by an underground passage. The interior has very fine
neo-classical decoration on the walls and
ceilings, some if not all of it by Stapleton.
The hall has a screen of columns marbled to
resemble yellow Siena. The Wedgwood
Room, the ceiling of which curves downwards at the corners giving the effect of
shallow dome, has roundels painted by
Peter de Gree. The small but attractive
demesne by the River Liffey contains a
Coade stone urn on a pedestal designed by
James Wyatt and erected as a monument to
the great Sarsfield, and a Gothic hermitage.
Inherited from the Colthurst-Vesey family
by Capt Richard Colthurst (afterwards 8th
Bt), who sold it 1932 to H E Charles
O'Conor, President of Irish Association of
the Order of Malta. Re-sold *post* World
War II by Charles O'Conor's son-in-law,
William (later Sir William) Teeling, MP,
to the Italian Government, for use as their
Embassy.

Ludford Park, Dundrum, co Dublin
(DILLON/IFR). An irregular 2 storey house,
with a 3 bay late-Georgian facade at one
end.

Luggala, Roundwood, co Wicklow (LA
TOUCHE/IFR; WINGFIELD, *sub* POWERSCOURT,
V/PB; GUINNESS, *sub* IVEAGH, E/PB). Having
continued his father's work in creating a

Lucan House: Hall

Lucan House: Oval Room

romantic landscape at Bellevue, co Wicklow
(*qv*), Peter La Touche, of the wealthy
Dublin banking family, discovered the
valley and lake of Luggala in the heart of the
Wicklow mountains; bought the land *ca*
1790 and built a charming little house here
in gingerbread Gothic, described at the
time as a "cottage mansion" in the "pointed
style". The Knight of Glin suggests that it
may be by Francis Sandys or Sands, who
constructed a Turkish tent for Peter La
Touche at Bellevue in 1793, and whose
father and namesake designed another of
the Bellevue follies, the Gothic "dining
room". Partly single storey and partly with
an attic of trefoil or quatrefoil windows, the
house is adorned with miniature battlements
and crockets; the windows of the main front
are rectangular, but have lancet-shaped
hood mouldings. Peter La Touche used the
house as a hunting lodge, and as a place for
picnics and other expeditions from Bellevue; he would also lend it to "persons of
respectability". His nephew and heir continued to give tickets for the use of the
house to "any gentle party", but never went
there himself. Luggala was sold to Viscount
Powerscourt some time before mid-C19. In
1937 it was bought by Hon Ernest Guinness, who gave it to his daughter, Oonagh,
Lady Oranmore and Browne. The house
was burnt 1956, but rebuilt immediately
afterwards exactly as it was: gleaming white
against its setting of wooded hills.

Luttrellstown Castle, (known for a period
as **Woodlands**), **Clonsilla, co Dublin**
(LUTTRELL, CARHAMPTON, E/DEP; WHITE,
ANNALY, B/PB; GUINNESS, *sub* IVEAGH E/PB).
An old castle of the Pale, originally the seat
of the Irish Luttrells; whose members,
during the course of C18, included the
notorious Col Henry Luttrell, murdered in
his sedan-chair in the streets of Dublin
1717; and 2 sisters, Anne, who married
George III's brother, the Duke of Cumber-
land, and Elizabeth, who is said to have
committed suicide in Augsburg after being
sentenced to sweep the streets chained to a
wheelbarrow, on a charge of picking
pockets. The brother of these 2 ladies, Gen
Henry Luttrell, 2nd Earl of Carhampton,
sold Luttrellstown *ca* 1800 to Luke White,
MP, a self-made millionaire who changed

Lyons: Hall

Luttrellstown Castle

the name of the property to Woodlands, and encased the old castle in romantic early C19 Gothic, with battlements and round and polygonal turrets; he also added to it, and remodelled and redecorated the interior; creating the octagonal entrance hall, with its ceiling of plaster Gothic vaulting, and giving the ballroom its magnificent and unusual ceiling of plaster vaulting with Adamesque ornamentation. The only major interior surviving from the Luttrells' time is the library, which in their day was the entrance hall; it has an unusual C18 ceiling with a bow and arrow in high relief. The 2 principal ranges of the castle are at an acute angle to each other, which makes for attractive vistas through the rooms in unexpected directions. An entrance tower and porch, and a Tudor-Revival banqueting hall, were added to the castle later in C19, probably in 1850s by Luke White's son, who afterwards became 1st Lord Annaly. 3rd Lord Annaly, who held various Court appointments under Edward VII and George V, went back to calling the castle by its old name of Luttrellstown. For some years, early this century, Luttrellstown was owned by Major E. C. Hamilton; then, *ca* 1927, it was bought by Hon Ernest Guinness, who gave it to his daughter, Hon Mrs Brinsley Plunket, on her wedding. During the years that Luttrellstown has been her home, Mrs Plunket has decorated and furnished the castle with palatial elegance, and has entertained in the grand manner. She has replaced C19 Tudor banqueting hall with a splendid dining room in early C18 style; with birds and swags and foliage of stucco in high relief on the walls, and a painted ceiling by de Wit. The room was designed by Mr Felix Harbord, who also designed an Adamesque drawing room decorated with *grisaille* paintings by Peter de Gree from Oriel Temple (*qv*), and transformed the staircase hall with a painted ceiling by Thornhill. The demesne of Luttrellstown is of great extent and beauty, with a large lake spanned by a many-arched bridge, a sham ruin and a Doric temple.

Lyons, Hazlehatch, co Kildare (AYLMER/IFR; LAWLESS, CLONCURRY, B/PB1929; WINN, *sub* ST OSWALDS, B/PB). Originally the seat of the Aylmers. Sold 1796 by Michael Aylmer to Nicholas Lawless, 1st Lord Cloncurry, son of a wealthy blanket manufacturer, who built a new house here in 1797, to the design of an architect named Grace; a 3 storey block with a curved bow on either side of its entrance front, joined to 2 storey wings by curved sweeps. *Ca* 1801, soon after his release from the Tower of London, where he had been imprisoned for 2 years on account of his advanced political views and friendship with some of the United Irishmen, 2nd Lord Cloncurry employed Richard Morrison to carry out improvements and alterations to his father's house, the work continuing until *ca* 1805. During much of this period, Lord Cloncurry was in Italy, collecting antique and modern sculpture for the house; he also acquired 3 antique columns of red Egyptian granite from the Golden House of Nero, afterwards at the Palazzo Farnese, which were used as 3 of the 4 columns in a single-storey portico at Lyons, with a triangular

pediment surmounted by a free-standing coat-of-arms. The other notable alteration made to the exterior of the house at this time was the substitution of straight colonnades for the curved sweeps linking the main block to the wings; a change similar to that which Morrison made a few years later at Carton (*qv*). Also the main block and wings were faced with rusticated ashlar up to the height of one storey on the entrance front. The hall was given a frieze of ox-skulls and tripods based on the Temple of Fortuna Virilis in Rome, doorcases with fluted entablatures and overdoor panels with classical reliefs; a pair of free-standing antique marble Corinthian columns were set against one wall, and various items from Lord Cloncurry's collection of sculpture disposed around the other walls. The walls of the dining room and music room were painted with romantic landscapes—including views of Irish waterfalls—and other enchanting decoration by Gaspare Gabrielli, an artist brought by Lord Cloncurry from Rome. The bow-ended dining room was also decorated with a wall painting, of Dublin Bay; and was adorned with reliefs of the story of Daedalus. The 7 bay garden front was left quite plain; but before it a vast formal garden was laid out, with many statues and urns and an antique column supporting a statue of Venus half way along the broad central walk leading from the house to what is the largest artificial lake in Ireland. Beyond the lake rises the wooded Hill of Lyons. The Grand Canal passes along one side of the demesne, and there is a handsome Georgian range of buildings beside it which would have been Lord Cloncurry's private canal station. A daughter of 3rd Lord Cloncurry was Emily

Lyons

Lyons: Drawing Room

Lyons: formal Garden

Lawless, the poet, a prominent figure in the Irish Revival of the early years of the present century. Her niece, Hon Kathleen Lawless, bequeathed Lyons to a cousin, Mr G. M. V. Winn, who sold it *ca* 1962 to University College, Dublin, which has re-erected a handsome pedimented arch from Browne's Hill, co Carlow (*qv*) at one of the entrances to the demesne.

Lyttleton, Athlone, co Westmeath (MAGILL/LGI1912). A single-storey house in the "cottage" style with shallow curved bows.

M

Macmine Castle, Enniscorthy, co Wexford (RICHARDS/LGI1912). A C19 castle incorporating an old tower-house. 2 storey, except for a very tall, square, 4 storey tower, which has a battlemented and buttressed entrance porch projecting from its base. Simple battlements and corbelled angle turrets on the tower and the main building. Rectangular windows with hood mouldings. Quoins. Now a ruin.

Macroom Castle, Macroom, co Cork (MACCARTHY, CLANCARTY, E/DEP; SHELSWELL-WHITE/IFR). A C15 castle of the MacCarthys of Muskerry on the bank of the River Sullane; partly destroyed by fire in the Civil War, after which it was confiscated and granted to the Parliamentary Admiral Sir William Penn, father of William Penn of Pennsylvania; recovered after the Restoration by the MacCarthys, Earls of Clancarty, who restored and modernized it. Having been confiscated again, along with the other Clancarty estates, after the Williamite War, it passed to the Hedges Eyres. It was much admired by Dean Swift, in his progress through the country, and was described (1750), as consisting of "two square towers, about 60 foot high, with a large modern building between them"; its rooms included "an handsome large gallery". Early in C19, Robert Hedges Eyre reconstructed the castle as a large and uniform block, in which the old towers were "so perfectly incorporated as to be scarcely distinguishable from the rest of the building"; it had many windows and a battlemented parapet. The front of the castle faced the main square of the town of Macroom, from which it was separated by a forecourt with a battlemented wall and a turreted gateway. Passed by inheritance in the C19 to Hon William White, (afterwards 3rd Earl of Bantry), who assumed the additional surname of Hedges. The castle was burnt ca 1920 and has since been a ruin, part of which collapsed a few years ago.

Maddenton, co Monaghan (*see* HILTON PARK).

Magheramena Castle, Belleek, co Fermanagh (JOHNSTON/LGI1912). An early to mid-C19 Tudor-Gothic house of ashlar. 2 storey; blind gables, slender polygonal turrets with finials; small square battlemented tower at one corner. Solid parapet; rectangular windows with mullions and astragals under hood-mouldings; single-storey partly canted projection with pinnacles, quatrefoil decoration on the parapet and tall Gothic windows; these windows

Macmine Castle

having simple tracery and Georgian Gothic astragals. Single-storey battlemented wing ending in low round turret at other end of house.

Magheramorne, nr Larne, co Antrim (HOGG, Bt/PB; MCGAREL-GROVES, *sub* GROVES/LGI1969). A gabled Victorian house with a pillared porch.

Magherintemple, Ballycastle, co Antrim (CASEMENT/IFR). A house of ca 1875, in Scottish baronial style. The seat of the Casement family, of which Sir Roger Casement was a cadet.

Magherymore (formerly known as **Sea Park**), **Wicklow, co Wicklow** (LESLIE-ELLIS/LGI1958). A 2 storey mid-Victorian

house faced in granite; with a pediment, a balustraded roof parapet and round-headed windows. Sold *ca* 1958; now a convent.

Maiden Hall, Bennettsbridge, co Kilkenny (*sub* SOLLY-FLOOD/LGI1912; BUTLER, *sub* DUNBOYNE, B/PB). A house of *ca* 1745, remodelled 1830 with a veranda along its front in the Regency style. Originally owned by the Flood family; owned later in C18 by Richard Griffith, who, like his wife, was a talented novelist and letter-writer; owned later again by Rev Ambrose Smith; bought in C19 by John Butler, of the Dunboyne family. A wing was added 1910.

Maine, Annagassan, co Louth (STAFFORD/LGI1912). A 2 storey house of *ca* 1770. 7 bay front, Ionic doorcase.

Malahide Castle, Malahide, co Dublin (TALBOT DE MALAHIDE, B/PB). The most distinguished of all Irish castles, probably in continuous occupation by the same family for longer than any other house in Ireland. It also contains the only surviving medieval great hall in Ireland to keep its original form and remain in domestic use—at any rate, until recently. The great hall, which continued as the dining room, dates from C15; it was re-roofed and given various features in C19; but its dimensions, its vaulted undercroft and its corbel heads of Edward IV are original. Adjoining the hall, in the early medieval core of the castle, is

Magheramena Castle

Malahide Castle

Malahide Castle: Oak Room

Malahide Castle: Drawing Room

the Oak Room, its walls covered with carved panelling of different periods and nationalities. According to tradition, the carving of the Coronation of the Virgin above the fireplace of this room miraculously disappeared when the castle was occupied by the regicide, Myles Corbet, during the Cromwellian period, and reappeared when the Talbots returned after the Restoration. The opposite side of the castle to the great hall, dating from C16 or early C17, originally contained 4 tapestry-hung rooms; but this range was gutted by fire 1760. It was rebuilt *ca* 1770, probably by the same architect or builder who designed C18 wing at Ballinlough Castle, co Westmeath (*qv*); the then owner, Richard Talbot, being married to Margaret, daughter of James O'Reilly of Ballinlough, who, after her husband's death, was created Baroness Talbot of Malahide. Externally, the rebuilt range was given a Georgian Gothic character, a slender round corner tower being added at each end of it. Inside, 2 magnificent drawing rooms were formed out of the space which had been previously occupied by the 4 smaller rooms; with ceilings of splendid rococo plaster work which can be attributed stylistically to Robert West. The doorway between the 2 rooms has on one side a doorcase with an entablature carried on Corinthian columns, and on the other a doorcase with a broken pediment on Ionic columns. The walls of the 2 drawing rooms are painted a subtle shade of orange, which makes a perfect background to the pictures in their gilt frames. Opening off each of the two drawing rooms is a charming little turret room. A 3rd round tower was subsequently added at the corner of the hall range, balancing one of C18 towers at the opposite side of the entrance front; and in early C19, an addition was built in the centre of this front, with 2 wide mullioned windows above an entrance door; forming an extension to the Oak Room and providing an entrance hall below it. The castle was noted for its splendid contents, which included a magnificent collection of ancestral portraits of the Talbots, and also of the Wogans and of other families to whom they were allied; including portraits of many prominent Irish Jacobites. 7th Baron, who succeeded 1948, made a notable garden here, with a collection of rare shrubs from Australasia and other parts of the world. Owing to death duties resulting from the death of 7th Baron 1973, Malahide has been sold; the Talbots' connexion with the place, which went back to

Malahide Castle: Great Hall

the reign of Henry II, has been brought to an end. The castle was acquired by Dublin County Council and has recently been opened to the public by Dublin Tourism, which bought some of the furniture. Some of the portraits are also still in the castle, having been bought by the National Gallery and lent to Dublin Tourism. Much of the contents, however, have been dispersed.

Malcolmville, co Carlow (*see* HOLLODEN).

Malin Hall, Clonca, co Donegal (HARVEY/LGI1912). A 2 storey early C18 house; 5 bay front, doorcase with pilasters and entablature. Range at back with curvilinear end gable. Burnt *ca* 1920.

Mallow Castle, Mallow, co Cork (JEPHSON/IFR). The old Desmond castle at Mallow was rebuilt towards the end of C16 by Sir Thomas Norreys, Lord President of Munster—a son of Elizabeth I's life-long friend, Lord Norreys of Rycote—as what

Mallow Castle: old castle and its successor

Mallow Castle: Staircase

Mallow Castle: Drawing Room

was described at the time as "a goodly, strong and sumptuous house"; a 3 storey gabled oblong with polygonal turrets and projections; it had large Elizabethan mullioned windows, yet was defensible; indeed, it was strong enough to hold out against the Confederates under Lord Mountgarret 1642. By that time it was the seat of Major-Gen William Jephson, whose mother, Elizabeth—a god-daughter of the old Queen—was the daughter and heiress of Sir Thomas Norreys. It was, however, captured by Lord Castlehaven 1645 and badly damaged; and in 1689 it was burnt by order of King James. Its ruin still stands, facing the present house, which is long, low and many-gabled, of rough-hewn stone and with the air of an English manor house of the Tudor or early-Stuart period. One end of it actually dates from c16, being Sir Thomas Norreys's stables, to which the family retreated after the burning of the Elizabethan house. Various additions were made during c18, and in 1837 the house was enlarged and rebuilt by Sir Denham Jephson-Norreys, MP, 1st (and last) Bt, who is said to have acted as his own architect, though he appears to have enlisted the help of Edward Blore. Sir Denham—or his architect—kept to the scale and simplicity of the old stable range, and produced what is, for its day, a remarkably convincing reproduction of vernacular late c16 or early c17 architecture; with none of the pretentious "Baronial" or "Elizabethan" features which most early-Victorians could not resist. The 3 storey battlemented tower in the centre of the long front is as unassuming as the gabled and mullioned ranges on either side of it. Sir Denham is also said to have designed the great Elizabethan staircase with its finials, and the carved oak chimneypieces and overmantels in the drawing room and dining room, which were made by his estate carpenter. The drawing room and dining room, which open into each other, are panelled from floor to ceiling in elm. The house was enlarged *ca* 1954 by late Brig & Mrs Maurice Jephson, who added the present entrance

front at right angles to the old building. This was part of Sir Denham Jephson-Norreys's plan, though he never carried it out; but he had the stonework cut and ready, which was used a century later. The new wing contains a delightful upstairs library with a deep oriel overlooking the River Blackwater and the park, in which there is a herd of white deer, said to be descended from 2 white harts which Elizabeth I gave to her god-child, Elizabeth Norreys.

Malton, co Wicklow (*see* COOLLATTIN).

Manch House, Ballineen, co Cork (CONNER/IFR). A late-Georgian house built 1826 by Daniel Conner to the design of James & George Richard Pain; consisting of a main block of 2 storeys with a 3 storey tower at one corner. Both the tower and the main block have eaved roofs; the tower has a window flanked by sidelights in its top and bottom storeys, with a single window in the middle storey. The house was gutted by fire 1963, but afterwards rebuilt.

Manor of St John, Waterford, co Waterford (BONAPARTE WYSE/IFR). A Tudor-Revival house by A. W. Pugin, built for Sir Thomas Wyse, MP, the politician, diplomat and author who married Napoleon's niece, Laetizia, daughter of Lucien Bonaparte (*see* RFW). The house, which replaced an earlier house on a different site, is of red brick with stone facings; it has mullioned windows and a segmental-pointed doorway. In the present century, the Bonaparte Wyses leased the house to Sir Henry Forde (*see* CRAWFORD, E/PB), and afterwards to Mr & Mrs Arthur Crosbie, who bought it 1947 and re-sold it to Waterford Corporation *ca* 1965.

Mantle Hill

Mantle Hill, Golden, co Tipperary (SCULLY/LGI1912). A house built *ca* 1815–20 by the lawyer, Denys Scully, consisting of a square main block of 2 storeys over a basement, with a lower 2 storey service wing at the back. 3 bay front; single-storey Ionic portico with die; ground floor windows in arched recesses. 3 bay side. Wide-eaved roof, chimneys gathered together in single central stack. Unusual polychrome voussoirs over all windows.

Mantua, Swords, co Dublin. A mid-c18 house of 3 storeys over a basement with curved end-bows of only 2 storeys; the silhouette of their roofs exactly prolonging that of the main roof. 5 bay front; Venetian window above rusticated and pedimented tripartite doorway. In 1814, the residence of Dr Daly; in 1837, of Mrs Daly. Now demolished.

Mantua House, Castlerea, co Roscommon (GRACE, *sub* BOWEN/LGI1912). A Palladian house attributed to Richard Castle and believed to have been built *ca* 1747 for Oliver Grace, who married the daughter and heiress of John Dowell, the former owner of the estate. Centre block of 3 storeys over a basement and 5 bays; roundel between niches in centre of top

Marble Hill, co Donegal

Mantua House, co Roscommon

storey, above pedimented niche between 2 narrow windows, above fanlighted doorway also between 2 narrow windows. Rusticated window surrounds. Single-storey corridors joining centre block to 2 storey 3 bay wings, each with a roundel above a Venetian window; the wings also having rusticated window surrounds.

Marble Hill, Dunfanaghy, co Donegal. An early C19 house of 2 storeys over a basement. 3 bay front, Wyatt window in centre above handsome pedimented Grecian porch, with 2 Ionic columns; 2 bay side. Eaved roof on bracket cornice. Lower wing at back. Garden laid out by Mr Lanning Roper. Now the home of Mrs Jobling-Purser.

Marble Hill, co Galway

Marble Hill, Loughrea, co Galway (BURKE, Bt/PB). A house built *ca* 1775 by John Burke, and enlarged *post* 1813 by Sir John Burke, 2nd Bt. Of 3 storeys over a high basement; entrance front with 1 bay on either side of a three-sided bow; doorcase with rusticated pilasters. Side elevation of 2 bays and a further 2 bays projecting forwards. Now a ruin.

Maretimo, Blackrock, co Dublin (LAWLESS, CLONCURRY, B/PB1929). A plain late-Georgian house, with good interior plasterwork, standing in a demesne by the shore of Dublin Bay containing various follies. Now demolished.

Marino, Cobh, co Cork (STUART-FRENCH/LGI1958). A pleasant and unassuming mid-Victorian house with an eaved roof and 3 sided bows, built on the foundations of an earlier house which may have dated back to C17 and which was burnt *ca* 1860s. Spacious hall, containing an imposing staircase with an iron balustrade. The house faces down the Passage, the narrows between Lough Mahon and Cork Harbour. Lt-Col Robert & Mrs Stuart-French made a delightful garden here, with many different enclosures leading from one to the other. Col Stuart-French sold Marino *ca* 1972.

Marino, co Dublin

Marino, Clontarf, co Dublin (CAULFEILD, CHARLEMONT, V/PB). A mid-C18 house, originally known as Donneycarney, bought 1755 by that great Irish patriot and patron of the arts, 1st "Volunteer" Earl of Charlemont; who commissioned Sir William Chambers to enlarge, improve and redecorate it. As completed, it consisted of a 3 storey 5 bay block, in which the ground floor was more like a basement, and 1st floor like a *piano nobile*; with a pillared porch at ground floor level, entablatures over the windows and urns on the roof parapet; flanked by lower wings which did not match each other and which extended back to form the two sides of a small open court behind the house. The front of the left-hand wing was single-storey, with a curved bow in the side elevation and contained a large reception room, entered by way of a pillared ante-room to the left of the hall, which was long, low and narrow, extending almost through the full depth of the ground floor of the main block; divided by a screen of columns. In the right-hand wing, there was an octagon room designed by Chambers in which some of Lord Charlemont's collection of sculpture was displayed. The house was not on a grand scale, Lord Charlemont preferring to spend his money on the Casino, a small pleasure-house in the grounds in the form of a Roman Doric temple, also by Chambers, and built over the years 1758–76. It is one of the most exquisite miniature C18 buildings in Europe; within an exterior that appears to be sculptured rather than built are a num-

Marino, co Cork

Casino, Marino

Casino, Marino: ceiling of Entrance Lobby

ber of little rooms, each of them perfectly proportioned and finished; with plasterwork ceilings, doorcases and inlaid floors. Sir Sacheverell Sitwell compares them to the little rooms in the Petit Trianon; and indeed the Casino shows considerable French influence, both inside and out. Among those who worked on the Casino was Simon Vierpyl, the sculptor and builder from Rome, and Joseph Wilton, the sculptor. The house has long been demolished; but the Casino is maintained as a National Monument and at present is being restored by Mr John O'Connell of O'Neill Flanagan & Partners.

Markree Castle, Collooney, co Sligo (COOPER/IFR). The original C17 house of the Coopers at Markree was rebuilt in C18 as a 3 storey block; it had a 5 bay front with a 3 bay breakfront, and a garden front with 1 bay on either side of a curved bow. In 1802,

Joshua Cooper commissioned Francis Johnston to enlarge this house and transform it into a castle of the early, symmetrical kind. Johnston extended the front of the house to more than twice its original length to form a new garden front with a central curved and Irish-battlemented tower; the end bay of the original front and the corresponding bay at the end of Johnston's addition being raised to give the impression of square corner-towers. The entrance was in the adjoining front, where Johnston added a porch; the garden front, with its bow, was not altered as far as its plan went; but an office wing was built at one side of it, joined to it by a canted link. In 1866, the castle was further enlarged and remodelled by Lt-Col E. H. Cooper, MP, to the design of Wardrop, of Edinburgh. The garden front bow was replaced by a massive battlemented and machicolated square tower, increasing the size of the dining room; a new entrance was made at this side of the castle, under a porte-cochère at the end of a 2 storey wing with Gothic windows which was built jutting out from this front. Johnston's porch was replaced by a 2 storey battlemented oriel, and mullioned windows to match were put in on this and the new entrance front. A Gothic chapel was built where Johnston's office wing had been. The interior of the castle mostly dates from after Johnston's time. A straight flight of stone stairs leads up the main floor from under the porte-cochère, beneath a vaulted ceiling. Beyond is a vast Victorian double staircase of oak, lit by a heraldic stained glass window illustrating the family tree with portraits of ancestors and monarchs. Where Johnston's staircase used to be, there is a great top-lit galleried hall with a timbered roof. A long library divided by pairs of grey marble Ionic columns has been formed out of Johnston's entrance hall and the rooms on either side of it. The large drawing room in Johnston's round-faced tower in the middle of the garden front, and the ante-room adjoining it, were redecorated between 1837 and 1863 by E. J. Cooper, MP, in an ornate Louis Quatorze style; with much gilding and well-fed *putti* in high relief supporting cartouches and trailing swags of flowers and fruit. E. J. Cooper was a traveller and astronomer of note and built what was described as "the most richly furnished of private observatories" at Markree. There are impressive castellated entrances to the demesne, built in early 1830s to the design of Francis Goodwin, of London; that on the main Boyle to Sligo road being one of the most spectacular Gothic entrances in Ireland, with turrets and posterns and curtain walls. Mrs Alexander, the hymnwriter, stayed at Markree, which is believed to have been the castle she had in mind when she sang of "The rich man in his castle" in *All Things Bright and Beautiful*. "The purple-headed mountain, The river running by" is a precise evocation of the view from the terrace by the entrance front.

Marlay (originally known as **The Grange**), **Rathfarnham, co Dublin** (LA TOUCHE/IFR). The original early C18 house here, known as the Grange and built by Thomas Taylor, was sold *ca* 1760 to the banker, David La Touche, MP, afterwards 1st

Markree Castle

Markree Castle

Markree Castle: Entrance Hall

Markree Castle: Drawing Room

Markree Castle: castellated Entrance Gateway

Markree Castle: perspective of Gateway in Goodwin's Rural Architecture

Marlay

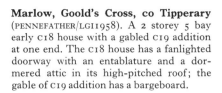

Marlay: Oval Room

Governor of the Bank of Ireland, who re-named it Marlay, having married a daughter of Rt Rev George Marlay, Bishop of Dromore; and who rebuilt the house later in C18. Of 2 storeys over a basement. 7 bay front, central window-door framed by frontispiece of coupled engaged Doric columns, entablature enriched with medallions and swags, and urns; window above it with entablature on console brackets; large central urn on plinth carved with swags in centre of roof parapet; smaller urns on either side. Side elevation of 2 bays on either side of a curved bow. Delicate interior plasterwork, said to be by Michael Stapleton. Hall with screen of Corinthian columns and frieze of tripods and winged sphinxes. Fine plasterwork ceilings in dining room and oval room, that in the dining room incorporating a painted medallion; husk ornamentation on dining room walls. Sold *ca* 1867 to one of the Tedcastle family, of the well-known firm of coal merchants. From *ca* 1925 to 1974 the home of the Love family; for a period, the stained glass artist, Evie Hone, occupied a house in the stable court. Now owned by the local authority and empty; used by Radio-Telefis Eireann as *Kilmore House* in their recent feature.

Marlay Grange, Rathfarnham, co Dublin (ROWLEY, *sub* LANGFORD, B/PB). A high-roofed Victorian Gothic house, with gables and dormer-gables, and a tower with a truncated pyramidal roof. *Post* World War II, the home of Mr & Mrs Louis Edge.

Marlborough House, co Dublin. A 2 storey 5 bay Georgian house. Pedimented breakfront centre, with Venetian window above pedimented and fanlighted tripartite doorway.

Marlfield, co Dublin (*see* CABINTEELY HOUSE).

Marlfield

Marlfield, Clonmel, co Tipperary (BAGWELL/IFR). A late C18 house built by Col John Bagwell, MP; consisting of a centre block of 3 storeys over a basement joined to single-storey wings by long, partly curving links. 7 bay entrance front, 3 bay breakfront, fanlighted doorway with side lights and 2 engaged columns. Links consisting of short 1 bay sections and curved sweeps with blind arcading and niches; wings each with a breakfront centre of blind arcading and niches, surmounted by a die and urn; and with 1 bay on either side. Garden front of centre block with 1 bay on either side of central curved bow; conservatory on one side, arcaded single-storey wing on the other. Handsome entrance gates, with twin Doric lodges, built 1833 for John Bagwell, MP, to the design of William Tinsley, of Clonmel. The centre block was burnt 1923, and rebuilt 1925 by Senator John Bagwell with a flat roof and a simple pedimented doorway with 2 columns instead of a doorway with a fanlight.

Marlow, Goold's Cross, co Tipperary (PENNEFATHER/LGI1958). A 2 storey 5 bay early C18 house with a gabled C19 addition at one end. The C18 house has a fanlighted doorway with an entablature and a dormered attic in its high-pitched roof; the gable of C19 addition has a bargeboard.

Martinstown House, Kilcullen, co Kildare (FITZGERALD, LEINSTER, D/PB; LONG, *sub* GUINNESS/IFR). A house in the Gothic cottage-ornée style, built *ca* 1830 as a shooting-box by 3rd Duke of Leinster, who is said to have also installed his mistress here. Of 2 stories, the upper storey being in fact an attic, with many steep gables and dormer-gables; tall chimneys. Pleasant simple Gothic detailing in rooms. Elegant staircase with wooden balusters and Gothic plasterwork; wood openwork arches in lobby. Large and lofty drawing room in single-storey wing, contrasting with the

Marlfield

lower rooms in the main part of the house; slightly coved ceiling with plain cornice. Subsequent owners included Major R. Turner, who sold it *ca* 1960. Now the home of Mr & Mrs T. F. Long.

Martinstown House

Martinstown House, Kilmallock, co Limerick (MCCALMONT/IFR). A modern house in the Classical style, built *ca* 1972 for Mrs Dermot McCalmont to the design of Mrs Baker-Baker; executed by Mr Christopher Jacob. 2 storey 7 bay main block with pedimented doorcase; single-storey wings. Generous roofs, on cornices; bold chimneystacks.

Maryborough, Douglas, co Cork (NEWENHAM/IFR; SHERRARD, *sub* MORROGH/IFR). A 3 storey 7 bay mid-C18 house with a lower late-Georgian bow-fronted addition. On the garden front, the house is weather-slated; and the main block is joined by a curving corridor to an office wing with a high-pitched sprocketed roof. Hall with ceiling of Adamesque plasterwork and floor of black and white pavement. Dining room with plasterwork frieze. Staircase of handsome C18 joinery, with Corinthian newels. Upper hall with ceiling of rococo plasterwork in the manner of Robert West. In the late-Georgian wing, there is an oval canti-levered stone staircase with an iron balustrade; the wing also formerly contained a ballroom and library; but these were destroyed by fire 1914 and rebuilt as kitchens. Originally the seat of a branch of the Newenham family; passed at the beginning of the present century to the Sherrard family.

Maryfort, co Clare (*see* LISMEHANE).

Marymount, co Kilkenny (*see* BORRIS-MORE HOUSE).

Marysborough, Glanmire, co Cork (WALLIS/IFR; MAHONY/IFR; DWYER, *sub* JAMESON/IFR). A Georgian house. A seat of the Wallises; sold 1843 by James Wallis to Henry Mannix. Subsequently bought by E. R. Mahony; then, in 1920s, by late Mr Walter Dwyer.

Maryville, Kilworth, co Cork (CORBAN-LUCAS, *sub* LUCAS/IFR). A house built *ca* 1830 by Laurence Corban, in early C19 villa style; of 2 storeys and 4 bays. Entrance door in 2 bay end of house with large semi-circular fanlight, pleasantly balanced by a blind arch of similar size in which the window alongside the door is set. Eaved roof. Lower service range at back. Elegant central staircase hall, top-lit through a glazed dome decorated with plasterwork; stairs rising round it of wood with slender turned balusters and carved scroll ornament on ends of treads, ending in gallery. Good plasterwork of 1830 period in drawing room and dining room; drawing room ceiling rose with surround of keyhole pattern. Passed by inheritance to the Corban-Lucas family and used for many years as the dower-house of Ballinacarriga (*qv*). Sold *ca* 1965 by Mr Desmond Corban-Lucas; now the home of Mr & Mrs N. Weale.

Maryville, Patrickswell, co Limerick (FINCH/LGI1912; DRING/IFR). Plain square house of 5 bays, the entrance recently removed to side. Spacious hall and neo-Classical plasterwork in dining room niche. Similar to Fort Etna (*qv*) nearby. Restored by the present owners, Mr & Mrs James Egan.

Masonbrook, Loughrea, co Galway (SMYTH/LGI1912). A handsome early C19 house with a portico and a curved staircase.

Massbrook House

Sold *post* World War II and then demolished.

Massbrook House, Crossmolina, co Mayo. A 2 storey gabled late-Victorian house on the shores of Lough Conn, with roofs sweeping down almost to the ground. Formerly the seat of the Walsh family; now of Mr de Ferranti.

Massy Lodge, Ballylanders, co Limerick (MASSY, B/PB). The summer residence of the Massy family in the Galtee Mountains; built *ca* 1800. 2 storey; 5 bay front; two three-sided bows on each of the side elevations. Now partly demolished.

Mayfield (formerly **Knockanemeele**), **Bandon, co Cork** (POOLE/LGI1958). A 3 storey 7 bay house of late C18 appearance, but which was, in fact, an earlier 2 storey house, said to have dated from C17, which was subsequently remodelled and given an extra storey. 1 bay breakfront centre; porch added 1872. 2 storey wing at side. Hall running the full depth of the house, with a curving staircase of wood behind an arch. Burnt 1921. Featured in *The Pooles of Mayfield* by Rosemary ffolliott, the genealogist, whose mother was a Poole.

Mayfield, Portlaw, co Waterford. An 1840s Italianate rebuilding of an earlier house by William Tinsley, of Clonmel, for a member of the Quaker family of Malcolmson who in early C19 founded the great cotton mills at Portlaw which brought great prosperity to the town. Of 3 storeys, with a tower projecting from the centre of the front; a composition which may have been inspired by the nearby Curraghmore (*qv*). After emigrating to USA 1851, Tinsley repeated the Mayfield theme in several American college buildings.

Mealiffe, co Tipperary (*see* MOYALIFFE CASTLE).

Meares Court, Mullingar, co Westmeath (MEARES/LGI1937Supp; WINTER, *sub*

PURDON/IFR; LISTER-KAYE, Bt/PB). A 3 storey early and late C18 house. 5 bay front, central Venetian window above doorway with pediment on 2 columns. Wall carried up to be roof parapets with urns.

Meenglas, Stranorlar, co Donegal (HEWITT, LIFFORD, V/PB). A Victorian house in a simple Tudor-Revival style. Steep roofs and gables; mullioned windows, rather small in relation to the area of wall. 3 sided bow; dormer window with tracery. Slender square turret at junction of main block and service wing, with sprocketed pyramidal roof.

Melcomb (also known as **Milcum**), **Newport, co Mayo** (O'DONNEL, Bt/PB1889). A 2 storey mid-C18 house with a central 3 sided bow. Entrance doorway in the bow, with blocking and pediment having neither architrave nor frieze; its tympanum containing a narrow fanlight. The house is flanked by detached wings standing at an angle of 45 degrees to it. Passed after the death of Sir George O'Donnel, 5th and last Bt, 1889, to his niece, Melicent Agnes (*née* O'Donnel), wife of Edwin Thomas, who assumed the additional surname of O'Donnel.

Mellon, Pallaskenry, co Limerick (WESTROPP/IFR). A house of 2 storeys over a basement built *ca* 1780 by John Westropp. Fanlighted doorway; 4 bay garden front facing across the Shannon. 2 bay side. A house with a delightful atmosphere.

Menlough Castle, co Galway (BLAKE, *of Menlough*/PB). A gabled C17 tower house with tall chimney stacks in the gables, on the bank of the Corrib River 2 miles above Galway; altered and enlarged at various periods. Some windows with Georgian sashes, other with C19 mullions. C19 battlements on the main tower and small Jacobean-revival curvilinear gables with ball finials, doubtless inspired by those at Portumna Castle (*qv*), along the roof-line of a later wing. Gatehouse. Menlough Castle

Menlough Castle

Menlough Castle

Menlough Castle: fire of 26 July 1910

was the scene of much high-living in c18 and early c19; Sir John Blake, 12th Bt, is said to have been made an MP to give him immunity from his creditors; according to the story, when he had been duly elected, his constituents came in a body to Menlough and called him ashore from the boat in which he was sitting in order to avoid 2 process-servers who were waiting for him on the river bank. In Victorian and Edwardian days, there were less extravagant festivities: regattas and parties on the lawns by the river. Then, on 26 July 1910, there was a disastrous fire at the castle, in which Eleanor Blake, daughter of 14th Bt, perished. The entire building was gutted, and has remained a ruin ever since.

Merlin Park

Merlin Park, nr Galway, co Galway (BLAKE/IFR; HODGSON/LGI1952; WAITHMAN/LGI1912). A long 2 storey house built *ca* 1807–1808 for Charles Blake. Of 6 bays and 2 3-sided bows. Given windows with mullions and transoms in c17 style later in c19. Sold in the Encumbered Estates Court by C.K. Blake, 1852; bought by Henry Hodgson. In 1912, the seat of W.S. Waithman.

Mervue

Mervue, nr Galway, co Galway (JOYCE/LGI1958). A 3 storey 5 bay late c18 house, to which single-storey 2 bay wings, with windows set in arched recesses, were added in c19. Probably later again in c19, the main block and wings were given roof parapets of fancy lattice-work, that on the main block being surmounted, at intervals, by the Joyce demi-griffin; and a vast 2 tier semi-circular glass conservatory was added as a lean-to in the middle of the front of the main block, so as to serve as a porch. One wing contained a large dining room with a plasterwork ceiling; the other, a large drawing room, *en suite* with a smaller one in the main block; both rooms having Victorian chimneypieces of green Connemara marble. From *ca* 1777 Mervue was the seat of the Joyces, who were originally merchants and bankers in Galway. In c19, Pierce Joyce kept a private pack of hounds here. His grandson, Lt-Col Pierce Joyce, sold Mervue 1953 to Royal Tara Ltd, who use part of the house as offices and for their china manufactory and part as a managing director's residence; the main block having been rebuilt and much altered after being gutted by fire 1957.

Middleton, Killashee, co Longford (HARMAN, *sub* KING-HARMAN/LG 1937 Supp; DE MONTFORT/IFR). A 2 storey mid-c18 house built by Wesley Harman. 3 bay front, with an additional bay added to the left. Doorcase with blocking. Bought 1764 by Henry Montfort; sold by a subsequent Henry Montfort *ca* 1837.

Middleton Park

Middleton Park, Mullingar, co Westmeath (BOYD-ROCHFORT/IFR). A mansion of *ca* 1850 in the late-Georgian style by George Papworth, built for George Augustus Boyd (afterwards Rochfort-Boyd). 2 storey 6 bay centre block with single-storey 1 bay wings; entrance front with 2 bay central breakfront and single-storey Ionic portico. Parapeted roof with modillion cornice; dies on parapets of wings. At one side of the front is a long, low service range with an archway and a pedimented clock tower. Impressive stone staircase with elaborate cast-iron balustrade of intertwined foliage. Sold *ca* 1958.

Milcum, co Mayo (*see* MELCOMB).

Milestown, Castlebellingham, co Louth (WOOLSEY, *sub* BARROW/IFR). A long, plain 2 storey house of late-Georgian aspect. The principal front has 2 wide 3 sided bows, joined by an iron veranda; there are 2 narrower 3 sided bows on the end of the house. Prominent eaved roof, on bracket cornice. Burnt 1923 but rebuilt 1925, using the old walls.

Milford, co Mayo

Milford, Hollymount, co Mayo (MILLER/ LGI1912; ORMSBY/IFR). A 2 storey early C18 gable-ended house, built to replace a late C17 house which was burnt. The lower storey of the front is 5 bay, with a fanlighted doorway in a single-storey 3 sided projection. The upper storey has 4 windows which are narrower than those below, and not in line with them. Milford passed by inheritance to the Ormsbys 1910, John Ormsby having married his cousin, Anne Bowen-Miller, 1851. A new wing was added, *ante* 1926, by C. C. Ormsby, who designed the addition himself. Richard Murphy, the poet, was born at Milford in the bedroom known as the "Bog Room"; his elegy, *The Woman of the House*, is in memory of his grandmother, Lucy, wife of Lt-Col Rev Thomas Ormsby, who lived at Milford until her death 1958.

Milford House, co Tipperary

Milford House, Borrisokane, co Tipperary (MURPHY/IFR). A house of mid to late C18 appearance, of 3 storeys over a basement. 5 bay front; 1 bay breakfront with a baseless pediment and, in each of the two upper storeys, a modified Venetian window in which the sidelights are exceptionally narrow and have wide spaces between them and the window in the centre. Fanlighted and pedimented doorcase with columns flanked by narrow sidelights. 2 bay end. Owned by Edmond Murphy, who died 1882, and afterwards by his nephew, until *ca* 1920. Recently restored.

Milford House, Milford, co Carlow (ALEXANDER/IFR). A dignified and well-proportioned 2 storey late-Georgian house, with a single-storey wing at one side. 5 bay entrance front, with single-storey Ionic portico. 4 bay garden front; 2 bay side. Parapeted roof. Chimneys all grouped into one long stack.

Milford, nr Armagh, co Armagh. A 2 storey vaguely Italianate C19 house. Camber-headed windows; 3 sided bow; pedimented 3 bay projection. Elaborate range of glasshouses running out at right angles from the middle of the front. The seat of the McCrums, of the firm of McCrum, Watson & Mercer, damask manufacturers, of Belfast.

Milford, Tuam, co Galway (ORMSBY/ IFR). A simple square Georgian house with a fanlighted doorway.

Milfort, Portlaw, co Waterford (MORLEY/ LGI1958). A 3 storey early to mid–C19 house, slightly Italianate in flavour, with a deep curved bow in the centre of one of its fronts and a pierced roof parapet. A seat of the Malcolmson family, who founded the great cotton mills at Portlaw in early C19, which brought great prosperity to the town. Passed through marriage to the Morleys; sold *post* death of Miss Violet Morley 1950.

Millbrook, Straffan, co Kildare (BAG-WELL/IFR). A 2 storey 3 bay house of *ca* 1830 with a fanlighted doorway. Curving staircase.

Millicent

Millicent, Sallins, co Kildare (KEATINGE/ IFR; GOULDING, Bt/PB; BOYLAN/IFR). A Georgian house of 2 storeys over a basement. 7 bay front with pedimented breakfront centre; small lunette window in pediment. Segmental pediment over central window in lower storey; entablatures over the two windows on either side. Roof on cornice set very close to the tops of the upper storey windows. Admirably restored by its present owner, Mr C. Gordon Falloon.

Millmount, Kilkenny, co Kilkenny. A house of 2 storeys over a basement built probably between 1760 and 1770 by William Colles, owner of the nearby Kilkenny Marble Works, which supplied the familiar black marble chimneypieces to houses all over Ireland. Of an unusual cruciform plan; one arm having a pedimented 1 bay end with a Venetian doorway; the 2 arms at right angles ending in curved bows.

Miltown Castle, Charleville, co Cork (EVANS-FREKE, *sub* CARBERY, B/PB; BRUCE/

Miltown Castle

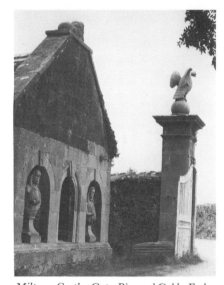

Miltown Castle: Gate-Pier and Gable-End with niches and busts

LGI1958). A 2 storey house of late C18 appearance; 3 bay entrance front, with 1 bay pedimented breakfront framed by straight-edged quoining; triple window above fanlighted doorway. 3 bay side. Splendid curved cantilevered central staircase. The entrance to the demesne could date from before the present house; it has impressive cut-stone piers, surmounted by balls and eagles; and a remarkable gate-lodge with a cut-stone gable-end in which there are niches sheltering busts of gentlemen in periwigs. The gable itself is surmounted by a lion. The stable court has further busts in niches.

Milverton Hall, Skerries, co Dublin (WOODS, *sub* WENTGES/LGI1958). A C19 house in the Italianate-French château style, of 2 storeys over a basement and with a dormered attic in the mansard roof. Entrance front with 3 centre bays recessed between 1 bay projections; deep single-storey balustraded Doric portico. 5 bay side elevation with 2 single-storey balustraded 3 sided bows.

Mitchellsfort (afterwards known as **Fellsfort**), **Watergrasshill, co Cork** (MITCHELL, *sub* BRASIER-CREAGH/IFR). A bow-fronted Georgian house. Exceptionally tall gate piers at entrance to demesne. The seat of the Mitchell family; subsequently owned by the Fell family, who changed its name to Fellsfort. Now demolished.

Mitchelstown Castle

the open side consisting of a number of towers linked by a terrace facing the Galtee mountains. The south front was plain and massive, with many windows and a square tower in the middle. The east front had a tall gate-tower, in the Tudor manner, at its southern end; it was known as the White Knight's Tower and was the main entrance. A hall led to a gallery 93 feet long, with a ceiling of plaster vaulting. At the far end of the gallery was the grand staircase, and opening off it in the south front were the drawing room, morning room, library and dining room. In the end, George IV never came; but Big George entertained as though he had a royal house-party the whole time. Even complete strangers were received with hospitality at the castle; there were sometimes as many as 100 people staying. All were dazzled by the splendour, by the display of plate and the army of servants.

Mitchelstown Castle

Mitchelstown Castle, co Cork (FITZGIBBON/IFR; KING, KINGSTON, E/PB; WEBBER/IFR). Originally the stronghold of that branch of the Geraldines which held the title of White Knight; passed to the Kings after the death of Maurice *Oge* FitzGibbon, 12th White Knight, whose niece married Sir John King, 1st Lord Kingston. By 1750, 4th Lord Kingston had a house here with a 2 storey hall, its upper storey surrounded by a "handsome corridor"; a "large and lightsome" staircase, its ceiling painted with the rape of Proserpine; and a long gallery. A new house was built by 2nd Earl of Kingston 1776; it was in this house that his daughter, Margaret, was taught revolutionary ideas by her governess, Mary Wollstonecraft; she afterwards married Lord Mount Cashell, who lived nearby at Moore Park (*qv*), but left him and settled in Italy, where she befriended Shelley, who wrote of her as "The Lady" in *The Sensitive Plant*. Margaret's sister, Mary, eloped 1797 with a cousin, who was a married man; her father afterwards shot him dead at an hotel near Mitchelstown and was consequently tried by his peers for murder, but acquitted, In 1823, 3rd Earl, known as "Big George" demolished his father's house and commissioned James and George Richard Pain to build him a castle which he stipulated should be bigger than any other house in Ireland; it had, moreover, to be ready to receive George IV on his next Irish visit; one of the towers was to be called the Royal Tower and contain a bedroom for the King. The castle was finished in two years, at a cost of £100,000; it did not quite manage to be larger than any other house in Ireland, but it was one of the largest and most successful of the earlier Gothic Revival castles. The buildings, of smooth, pale grey limestone ashlar, formed 3 sides of a court,

Mitchelstown Castle: Gallery

Mitchelstown Castle: Drawing Room

One of the under-cooks was a young man named Claridge, who later founded the hotel of that name. Then, in 1830, his tenants' failure to vote for the candidate of his choice in a by-election drove Big George out of his mind and he was taken to London, where he died 1839. His son, 4th Earl, continued to keep open house at Mitchelstown until 1844, when he suffered a financial crash. The Earl and his house party closed the doors of the castle against the bailiffs and stood siege for a fortnight; then the creditors took possession and much of the estate was sold up. Like his father, 4th Earl went mad. The castle and the reduced estate was eventually inherited by 5th Earl's widow, who married, as her 2nd husband, W. D. Webber. Henceforth, economy reigned at the castle; Elizabeth Bowen tells of how the scarcity of fruit in the Mitchelstown barm-bracks became a byword; so that once, when her grandfather was having tea here, another gentleman, who happened to get a slice of barmbrack with a currant in it, held it up for him to see; at which he remarked, in his best co Cork French, "*Vous avez raisong*". Elizabeth Bowen also describes the rather macabre garden party on, of all days, 5 August 1914, which was the castle's swan-song:

> "Wind raced round the castle terraces, naked under the Galtees; grit blew into the ices; the band clung with some trouble to its exposed place. The tremendous news certainly made that party, which might have been rather flat ... Ten years hence, it was all to seem like a dream— and the castle itself would be a few bleached stumps on the plateau".

The castle was burnt 1922, and the ruin was afterwards demolished; the ashlar having been bought by the monks of Mount Melleray for their new church.

Modreeny House, Cloughjordan, co Tipperary (DANCER, Bt/PB1933). A 2 storey Georgian house with a small central pediment; high polygonal addition to the left, low addition with Venetian window to the right. Doric gate-lodge.

Mohill Castle, Mohill, co Leitrim (CROFTON, Bt, *of Mohill*/PB; KANE/LGI1958). A simple early house with tall gable ends, close to the village street of Mohill. Occupied for a period in C19 by the Kane family.

Moira Castle, Moira, co Down (RAWDON, MOIRA, E/DEP). A large 3 storey C18 house with a 9 bay front, consisting of a 5 bay centre and a 2 bay extension, slightly higher than the centre, on either side. Only the roof of the centre section was visible; the roofs of the side bays were either flat, or concealed by the massive cornices with which these bays were surmounted. Pedimented and rusticated doorway; curved end bows. The front was prolonged by single-storey wings on either side, ending in piers with urns. Demolished at the beginning of C19.

Monart, Enniscorthy, co Wexford (COOKMAN/IFR). A 3 storey mid-C18 house of sandstone with limestone dressings. 5 bay front with breakfront centre; Venetian

Monart

window in centre of middle storey, with Diocletian window over it; modified Gibbsian doorcase. Later additions.

Monatrea House, Monatrea, co Waterford (SMYTH/IFR; PERCEVAL-MAXWELL/IFR). A 2 storey house of *ca* 1830 on the eastern side of Youghal Harbour; built by Rev Percy Smyth, of Headborough (*qv*), as a summer residence. 3 bay front, 4 bay side; both elevations plain except for quoins and a string course. The front is prolonged by a 2 storey 1 bay wing with a window in the upper storey and a blank wall below. Inherited by the Perceval-Maxwell family; sold *ca* 1964; now a country club.

Monasterboice House

Monasterboice House, Monasterboice, co Louth (DUNLOP, *sub* DELAP/LGI1912). A hybrid house, partly medieval, with a 3 light Perpendicular window, and partly Georgian Gothic; with a Regency bow front on the garden side, and Victorian ironwork and other Victorian features. Now semi-derelict. Folly tower and folly arch spanning public road.

Moneyglass House

Moneyglass House, Toome, co Antrim (HAMILTON-JONES/LGI1912). A handsome mid-C19 Italianate house of 2 storeys over a basement. Very much in the manner of Sir Charles Lanyon, and with a particular resemblance to Lanyon's rebuilding of Stradbally Hall, co Leix (*qv*), even to having round-headed windows on either side of the

entrance porch in the recessed centre of the front, and rectangular or camber-headed windows elsewhere in the facade. The centre of the front of 5 bays, with 2 bays projecting boldly on either side. Porch in the form of a 3 arched Italianate loggia, with Tuscan columns; surmounted by latticed balustrading, again very characteristic of Lanyon, and a heraldic achievement. Rock-faced rustication on the end piers of the porch, around the windows on either side of it and elsewhere. Roof parapet on bracket cornice; surprisingly, for a house of this style, the roof was low-pitched, and almost concealed. Now demolished, except for the porch.

Monivea Castle

Monivea Castle, nr Athenry, co Galway (O'KELLY/IFR; FFRENCH/IFR; BARNEWALL, TRIMLESTOWN, B/PB). An O'Kelly tower-house, acquired by the ffrenchs at the beginning of C17; confiscated under the Cromwellian Settlement 1658 and granted to 8th Lord Trimlestown, a "transplanted" peer from the Pale; regained from 11th Lord Trimlestown by Patrick ffrench, who added two new ranges to the old tower-house, 1713-15. One of these ranges was a very long single-storey front of 13 bays, with a 2 storey 3 bay pedimented centre, behind which rose the old tower. The other range ran back from the tower at right angles and was of 2 storeys with a dormered attic and irregular fenestration. It was intended to add a 2nd storey to the long front; but in the end the extra accommodation was obtained by giving the front a high roof with dormers, presumably in C19; perversely, the dormers were made a different shape on one side of the pedimented centre to what they were on the other. Mausoleum in grounds, in the form of a miniature tower house, with turret. In 1938 Monivea was bequeathed by Miss Kathleen ffrench to the Irish Nation as a "Home for Indigent Artists". The scheme came to nothing and the house, except for the old tower, was subsequently demolished.

Monksgrange

Monksgrange, Enniscorthy, co Wexford (RICHARDS/LGI1912; RICHARDS-ORPEN, *sub* ORPEN/IFR). A mid-C18 gable-ended house with curved sweeps and wings, built 1769 on the eastern side of Blackstairs

Mountain by Goddard Richards. Main block of 3 storeys over a basement; 5 bay front, with niches on either side of centre window in middle storey; doorway with pediment on console brackets, approached up broad flight of steps with railings of handsome ironwork; bold quoins and string-courses. Originally, only the right-hand wing was built: a coach-house in the form of a square pyramidal-roofed pavilion, linked to the main block by a curved sweep with rusticated doorways and little lunette windows. To the left, there was only a screen wall, which was taken down shortly *ante* 1798 so that a wing could be built; but the Rebellion—during which a bonfire was made of all the furniture—put an end to the work. Shortly *ante* 1914, E. R. Richards-Orpen, who inherited Monksgrange from his mother, began building a wing to the left of the house, according to his own design; with a curved sweep balancing that on the right, but ending in a much larger range than the right-hand pavilion. This range was to contain a new hall and other large rooms; and it was given an imposing end elevation, with a handsome rusticated arch and an entablature on console brackets; this was to be the new entrance front, a garden terrace being constructed along the original front of the house. Work on the new addition was interrupted by the Great War, but was resumed in 1920s; and the walls of the new building were completed by 1939; they are of local Blackstairs granite and Wicklow granite, some of the quoins being from Kilbryde, a demolished house in co Carlow, and from the burnt-out ruin of Castleboro (*qv*). With the outbreak of the Second World War, the work finally ceased, leaving the new building as a roofless shell, though the curved sweep had been completed; it has a dormered roof. The hall in the original block is low-ceilinged, with an arch opening to the stairs, which are of noble joinery and rise the full height of the house. The doors have shouldered architraves, and handsome C19 brass finger plates of cut scrollwork. Drawing room with small bookroom opening out of it to right of hall; dining room to left, with corner fireplace and chimneypiece inserted by Mr John Richards-Orpen. This room formerly opened into hall with arches, which have since been glazed, having been intended by E. R. Richards-Orpen to serve as an ante-room to the large rooms in his uncompleted wing. Opening off it is the only one of the new rooms to have been completed, behind the left-hand sweep; it is now the kitchen, but was intended as a 2nd ante-room, and has an armorial stained glass window.

Montalto

Monkstown Castle, Monkstown, co Cork (BOYLE, BLESINTON, V/DEP; SHAW, Bt/PB; NEWMAN/LGI1958). An early C17 semi-fortified house built 1636 by Anastasia (*née* Goold), wife of John Archdekin; according to the story, she intended it as a surprise for her husband, when he returned from serving with the Spanish Army; and she was also able to impress him with her economy, since it cost no more than 4*d*, the rest of the expenses having been covered by the profit she made supplying the workmen with provisions which she bought wholesale. Of 3 storeys over a basement, with a gabled attic; recessed centre between projecting gabled towers with corner-machicolations. Rusticated quoins and bold string-courses between the storeys. Central hall with stone chimneypiece dated 1636 but subsequently altered. Unlike most houses of its kind, Monkstown Castle survived the Civil Wars intact. Having been forfeited by the Archdekins, it was eventually granted 1685 to Michael Boyle, Archbishop of Armagh and Lord Chancellor of Ireland, father of 1st Viscount Blesinton of 1st creation. At the end of C18 it was acquired by Bernard Shaw (whose famous namesake was the grandson of his 1st cousin) and restored by him, though without having its original character altered. In mid-C19, it passed to the Newman family; and in 1908 it was bought by the Monkstown Golf Club, which used it until recently. It is now empty and in poor repair and its future is uncertain.

Montalto, Ballynahinch, co Down (RAWDON, MOIRA, E/DEP; KER/IFR; MEADE, CLANWILLIAM, E/PB). A large and dignified 3 storey house of late-Georgian aspect; which, in fact, was built mid-C18 as a 2 storey house by Sir John Rawdon, 1st Earl of Moira; who probably brought the stuccodore who was working for him at Moira House in Dublin to execute the plasterwork here; for the ceiling which survives in the room known as the Lady's Sitting Room is pre-1765 and of the very highest quality, closely resembling the work of Robert West; with birds, grapes, roses and arabesques in high relief. There is also a triple niche of plasterwork at one end of the room; though the central relief of a fox riding in a curricle drawn by a cock is much less sophisticated than the rest

Montalto: plasterwork in Lady's Sitting Room

of the plasterwork and was probably done by a local man. 2nd Earl, afterwards 1st Marquess of Hastings, who distinguished himself as a soldier in the American War of Independence and was subsequently Governor-General of India, sold Montalto 1802 to David Ker, who enlarged the windows of the house, in accordance with the prevailing fashion. In 1837, D. G. Ker enlarged the house by carrying out what one would imagine to be a most difficult, not to say hazardous operation; he excavated the rock under the house and round the foundations, thus forming a new lower ground floor; the structure being supported by numerous arches and pillars. It was more than just digging out a basement, as has been done at one or two other houses in Ulster; for the new ground floor is much higher than any basement would be; the operation made the house fully 3 storeyed. Entrance front of 2 bays on either side of a central 3 sided bow; the front also having end-bows. Shallow Doric porch at foot of centre bow. Ground floor windows round-headed; those above

Monkstown Castle

Q

rectangular, with plain entablatures over the windows of the original ground floor, now the *piano nobile*. Parapeted roof. The right-hand side of the house is of 10 bays, plus the end bow of the front; with a pilastered triple window immediately to the right of the bow in the *piano nobile*, balanced by another at the far end of the elevation. The left-hand side of the house is only of 3 bays and the bow, with a single triple window; the elevation being prolonged by a 2 storey wing with round-headed windows. Various additions were built at the back of the house and at the sides during the course of C19; a ballroom being added by D. S. Ker, grandson of the David Ker who bought the estate. In 1837 ground floor there is an imposing entrance hall, with 8 paired Doric columns, flanked by a library and a dining room. A double staircase leads up to the *piano nobile*, where there is a long gallery running the full width of the house, which may have been the original entrance hall. Also on the *piano nobile* is the sitting room with the splendid C18 plasterwork. Montalto was bought *ca* 1910 by 5th Earl of Clanwilliam, whose bride refused to live at Gill Hall (*qv*), the family seat a few miles to the west, because of the ghosts there. In 1952, the ballroom and a service wing at the back were demolished.

Moone Abbey, Moone, co Kildare (CARROLL/IFR). A distinguished small C18 Palladian house, standing near a C15 castle and a famous High Cross. Built for the Yates or Yeates family, who also built Colganstown, co Dublin (*qv*). The 5 bay gable-ended centre block was originally of 2 storeys, with a small floating baseless pediment containing a Diocletian window; in early C19 a 3rd storey was added; the front has also been given a plain projecting porch. The centre block is joined to the 2 storey 2 bay curvilinear-gabled wings by curved sweeps that are unusual in being convex, as at Beau Parc, co Meath (*qv*). In the sweeps are niches with keystones. Moone Abbey remained in the Yates family until *ca* mid-C19; it then passed to a branch of the Carroll family. It is now the home of Count Clemens Matuschka.

Moore Abbey: Hall

Moore Abbey: Dining Room

of which some fragments of carved stonework are built into a wall of the present house. Principal front consisting of a 7 bay centre block of 3 storeys over a basement, with 4 bay projecting wings of 2 storeys over a basement; all the windows in the centre and wings—including those in the basement—being uniform, with pointed heads and Gothic astragals; those in the 2 principal storeys having Gothic hood mouldings. The roof parapets of the centre and wings are battlemented. Small C19 projecting porch, with tracery windows; C19 Gothic balustrade on the broad flight of steps leading up to the porch, and along the area. Large single-storey hall, said to be basically C17 and where Adam, Viscount Loftus, Lord Chancellor of Ireland, held his Chancery Court 1641; but now wholly C19 Tudor-Gothic in character; with an elaborately fretted plasterwork ceiling, oak wainscot with trefoil-headed panels, a carved stone chimneypiece and a screen of pointed arches. Drawing room and dining room with frieze of delicate C18 Gothic

plasterwork, and similar Gothic ornament on the entablatures of the very handsome doorcases. Staircase with balustrade of simple uprights, lit by Perpendicular-style window. Gothic stable court behind house with battlemented tower. Impressive castellated entrance gateway to demesne. In later C19, Moore Abbey had the name for being a very cold house; once, when 4th Earl of Clonmell, a celebrated character of those times, came to stay, he brought an exceptionally heavy portmanteau with him in his luggage which, as the footmen were struggling to get it up the stairs, burst open and was found to be full of coal. During 1920s, the house was let to Count John McCormack, the singer, who sang *Song of my Heart* by the River Barrow in the demesne. At the end of Count McCormack's tenancy, 10th Earl of Drogheda sold Moore Abbey to a religious order. It is now a hospital run by the Sisters of Charity of Jesus and Mary.

Moore Fort, Ballymoney, co Antrim (MOORE/LGI1912). A gable-ended house of 2 storeys with an attic lit by windows in the gable ends, and with a 5 bay front; built 1833, but from its appearance could be C18. Porch in the form of a pilastered single-storey 3 sided bow, with fanlighted doorway in the angle wall. Inner door with Gothic astragals.

Moore Hall, Ballyglass, co Mayo (MOORE/LGI1912). A large late C18 house of 3 storeys over a basement on a peninsula in Lough Carra; built 1795 by George Moore, who had made a fortune in Malaga and whose radical son, John, was appointed President of the Provisional Government of Connaught by Gen Humbert, commander of the invading French force 1798. Entrance front with 2 bays on either side of a central breakfront rather similar to that at Tyrone House, co Galway (*qv*), with a triple window framed by short fluted pilasters on console brackets above a Venetian window above the entrance doorway; which here is beneath a shallow single-storey Doric portico, whereas at Tyrone there is a porch of 2

Moore Abbey

Moore Abbey, Monasterevin, co Kildare (LOFTUS, V/DEP and *sub* ELY, M/PB; MOORE, DROGHEDA, E/PB). One of the only 2 surviving examples of mid-C18 Gothic in major Irish country houses which are not old castles remodelled, the other being the Gothic front of Castleward, co Down (*qv*). A 1767 Gothic rebuilding, by Field Marshal Sir Charles Moore, 6th Earl and 1st Marquess of Drogheda, of a C17 house built on the site of a medieval abbey acquired in the reign of Elizabeth by the Loftuses, whose heiress married into the Moores 1699; and

Moore Hall, co Mayo

Ionic columns. The top of the portico was treated as a balcony, with an ironwork railing. Solid roof parapet; massive die in centre. The house and its surroundings feature in the writings of George Moore, whose home it was. It is now a gaunt ruin, having been burnt 1923; various plans to rebuild it on a smaller scale for George Moore's brother, Senator Col Maurice Moore, came to nothing. When George Moore died 1933, his ashes were buried on an island in the lough here; ferried across in a boat rowed by Oliver St John Gogarty, who soon regretted having volunteered as oarsman. "First off came my silk hat, the frock coat and . . .", Gogarty recalls. "I presume you will retain your braces", said Moore's sister, who sat in the stern of the boat, holding the urn.

Moore Hill, Tallow, co Waterford (PERCEVAL-MAXWELL/IFR). A fine late C18 house built by Hon William Moore, a younger son of 1st Viscount Mount Cashell. Of 3 storeys over a basement which is concealed on the entrance front, but which on the garden front, where the ground falls away steeply into the Bride valley, becomes more like a lower ground floor. This front is of 7 bays, prolonged by a service wing; in the centre is a handsome balustraded perron, with double flights of steps. Attractive wooden staircase in hall opening off entrance hall. 2 drawing rooms—now the dining room and kitchen—opening into each other with double doors. Inherited 1856 by Mrs Robert Perceval-Maxwell (*née* Moore).

Moore Lodge, Ballymoney, co Antrim (MOORE, Bt, *of Moore Lodge*/PB). A 2 storey house probably built 1759 by Samson Moore. 3 bay; shallow bows with tripartite windows; long service wing at back.

Moore Park, co Cork

Moore Park, Kilworth, co Cork (MOORE, *sub* PERCEVAL-MAXWELL/IFR; HOLROYD-SMYTH/IFR). A large and plain Georgian house, consisting of a 3 storey 9 bay centre block and 2 storey wings, each of 2 bays on either side of a curved central bow. The centre block had a pedimented doorcase with Corinthian columns and entablatures and a solid roof parapet; there was no parapet on the wings. One of the wings was extended by a further 3 bays in C19. The house had a large ballroom in one of the wings. The seat of the Earls Mount Cashell; the wife of 2nd Earl was the friend of Shelley (*see* MITCHELSTOWN CASTLE). Sold *ca* 1903 by Lady Harriette Holroyd-Smyth, daughter of 5th Earl, to the British War Office; burnt 1908.

Mooresfort, Lattin, co Tipperary (MOORE/IFR). Originally a 3 storey C18 house, seat of the Moores, which was sold

ca 1850 to Charles Moore, MP, a member of a different branch of the family, who completely remodelled it; making it 2 storeys instead of 3, in order to have higher rooms, and giving it a predominantly Victorian character. 5 bay entrance front with pediment and porte-cochère; 5 bay adjoining garden front with single-storey bow. Hall with floor of encaustic tiles open to Victorian staircase of wood. Drawing room with elaborate and graceful plasterwork on flat of ceiling and on frieze; which stylistically seems to belong more to 1820s or 1830s than to 1850s. Library with very large architectural bookcase which was probably in the house before it was remodelled, having on it the arms of the branch of the Moores who formerly owned the house. Charming little Victorian chapel, with altar supported by 4 Archangels. The house stands at one corner of a large and handsome office courtyard. The son of Charles Moore who remodelled the house was Count Arthur Moore, MP, who founded Mount St Joseph Cistercian Abbey at Mount Heaton (*qv*).

Morristown Lattin

Morristown Lattin, Naas, co Kildare (MANSFIELD/IFR). A house originally built 1692 by the Lattin family; of 2 storeys and a dormered attic, and with a deep 1 bay projection at either end of its front. By the beginning of C19, the house had undergone various alterations which gave it a somewhat freakish appearance. A 4 storey tower, crowned with a coat-of-arms, rose from the middle of the front, in a manner reminiscent of the towers at Gola and Ancketill's Grove, co Monaghan (*qqv*); the projections were joined by a single-storey balustraded corridor with Wyatt windows in the centre of which was a porch or frontispiece of fluted Doric columns. In 1845, G. P. L. Mansfield, whose mother was the heiress of the Lattins, remodelled the house in Tudor-Revival style, to the design of an architect named Butler. A new front was added, which, at the ends, is no more than a facade; but which fills the space between the 2 projections; with a symmetrical row of 3 steeply pointed and pinnacled gables, oriels and a Tudor-style porch. At the same time, the roof was raised; but it was still carried on the old walls; the new front serves no structural purpose, but is secured to the main building with metal ties running through to the back of the house. A tower was also built at one end of the front; and bow windows, with balconies over them, were added at the back. Tall Tudor-style chimneys. Library divided with columns. The front of the house faces along a straight avenue of trees, which continues on the far side of the public road.

Mosstown

Mosstown, Ballymahon, co Longford (NEWCOMEN, V/DEP). A double gable-ended C17 house, of 2 storeys with a dormered attic in the high-pitched roof. Long 11 bay entrance front; doorway with blocking not central; massive chimneystacks. Tower-like building at back. Tall octagon, probably a dovecote. Originally a seat of the Newcomen family; by 1798 it was owned by Alexander Crawford Kingstone. From the Kingstones it passed by inheritance to James Watson Murray, who owned it 1914. The property remained in the family until 1950s, but the house was abandoned 1930s; it was derelict by *ca* 1960 and afterwards demolished.

Mote Park

Mote Park

Mote Park, Ballymurray, co Roscommon (CROFTON, B/PB). A house of 3 storeys over a basement built 1777–87. 9 bay entrance front; 3 bay pedimented breakfront; single-storey Ionic portico. C19 roof on bracket cornice; 2 storey wing at one side and set back. Garden front with 3 bays on either side of central curved bow. Wyatt windows in bow, that on 1st floor being set under a relieving arch. Single-storey wing at side. Burnt *ca* 1880 and afterwards rebuilt with various modifications: an enclosed porch with engaged Doric columns replaced the portico; the base-moulding of the pediment was broken instead of continuous; and the front was prolonged by an extra 2 bays on one side, unbalancing it. And with plate-glass windows instead of the pre-fire astragals, the

Mote Park: Triumphal Arch

house acquired a Victorian heaviness. Magnificent Doric triumphal arch surmounted by lion at entrance to demesne. Sold by 5th Lord Crofton 1950s; now demolished.

Mountainstown

Mountainstown, Navan, co Meath (POLLOCK/LGI1958). An early C18 house of 2 storeys over a high plinth, with a charming air of bucolic Baroque. The 6 bay front is adorned with giant Ionic pilasters, 2 supporting the pediment and 1 at either side; but they have neither architrave nor frieze. The Venetian entrance doorway is enriched with Ionic pilasters, urns on the entablatures, a keystone and a finial which breaks through the string-course above; in front of it is a grand if somewhat rustic perron with a central balustrade and ironwork railings to the flights of steps. In the centre of the 4 bay side elevation—where the windows in the lower storey have been replaced by 2 Wyatt windows—is a little floating pediment; "mini-pediment" is perhaps the only word for it. This side of the house is prolonged by a 3 sided projection, with timber-mullioned windows in C17 style. There is a dormered attic in the high roof, which is also lit by a lunette window in the main pediment.

Mount Anville (also known as **Dargan Villa**), **Dundrum, co Dublin.** An early-Victorian Italianate villa, with an eaved roof on a bracket cornice; dominated by an unusually tall and massive campanile tower. The home of the railway contractor, William Dargan, the leading spirit of the Dublin Exhibition of 1853. Queen Victoria paid Dargan the exceptional honour of visiting him here when she came over to Dublin for the Exhibition; and she climbed to the top of the tower to see the "24 distinct views" which it afforded. Later in C19, the house became a well-known girls' convent school.

Mount Anville

Mount Armstrong, Donadea, co Kildare (RYND/LGI1912; BEATTY, *sub* WARWICK, E/PB; CONOLLY-CAREW, CAREW, B/PB). A 2 storey mid to late C18 house. 3 bay front; triple window in centre above tripartite pedimented doorway with baseless pediment. Hall with simple plasterwork frieze, separated from staircase hall by doorway with internal fanlight. Owned *ca* 1950 by Mr Alfred Chester Beatty, Jr. Bought *ca* 1965 by 6th and present Lord Carew.

Mount Bellew

Mount Bellew, Mount Bellew Bridge, co Galway (GRATTAN-BELLEW, Bt/PB). A house of predominantly late-Georgian appearance, remodelled *ante* 1820 by Sir Richard Morrison for C. D. Bellew. 3 storey centre block with entrance front of 1 bay between 2 3 sided bows, joined to 1 bay pedimented wings by 3 bay links. Venetian window in top storey of centre block; doorcase surmounted by urn. Triple windows under relieving arches in wings. Long hall divided by screens of Ionic columns, rather similar to Morrison's hall at Fota, co Cork (*qv*); leading by way of ante-rooms, to a large gallery on one side and a dining room on the other. Handsome library, which in its day contained one of the finest collections of books in Ireland. Sold *ca* 1938; afterwards demolished.

Mount Callan, Inagh, co Clare (SYNGE/IFR; TOTTENHAM/IFR). A Victorian house of 2 storeys over a basement built 1873 by Lt-Col G. C. Synge and his wife, Georgina, who was also his 1st cousin, being the daughter of Lt-Col Charles Synge, the previous owner of the estate. The estate was afterwards inherited by Georgina Synge's nephew, Lt-Col F. St L. Tottenham, who made a garden in which rhododendrons run riot and many rare and tender species flourish.

Mount Caulfeild, Bessbrook, co Armagh. A house of 2 storeys with a dormered attic, a gabled projection at one end of its front and a curvilinear gable at the other; probably a C19 rebuilding of a C18 house. 7 bay front, plus the gabled projection; window surrounds with blocking. Charming wooden porch, in the Chinese taste. In 1814, the residence of William Duff.

The Hall, Mount Charles

Mount Charles, co Donegal: The Hall (CONYNGHAM, M/PB). An early to mid-C18 double gable-ended house of 3 storeys and 5 bays, with bold quoins, a pedimented and shouldered doorcase and a solid parapet concealing the roof as well as the end gables. At one end of the house a rather elegant conservatory porch with round-headed windows and astragals.

Mount Caulfeild

Mount Colville, co Antrim (*see* GALGORM CASTLE).

Mount Congreve: Entrance Front

Mount Congreve: Garden Front

Mount Congreve: Gateway

Mount Congreve, Kilmeadan, co Waterford (CONGREVE/IFR). An c18 house consisting of a 3 storey 7 bay centre block with 2 storey, 3 bay overlapping wings; joined to pavilions by screen walls with arches on the entrance front and low ranges on the garden front, where the centre block has a 3 bay breakfront and an Ionic doorcase. The house was remodelled and embellished ca1965–69, when a deep bow was added in the centre of the entrance front, incorporating a rather Baroque Ionic doorcase; and the pavilions were adorned with cupolas and doorcases with broken pediments. Other new features include handsome gateways flanking the garden front at either end a fountain with a statue in one of the courtyards between the house and pavilions. The present owner has also laid out magnificent gardens along the bank of the River Suir which now extends to upwards of 100 acres; with large-scale plantings of rare trees and shrubs, notably rhododendrons and magnolias. The original walled garden contains an c18 greenhouse.

Mount Coote, Kilmallock, co Limerick (COOTE/LGI1912; LILLINGSTON, *sub* INGE-INNES-LILLINGSTON/LGI1965). A 3 storey Georgian house with an entrance front of 2 bays between 2 shallow curved bows; flanked by single-storey 1 bay wings with gables and bargeboards. Victorian porch. Demolished *ca* 1960 and a new house built in the Georgian style to the design of Mr Donal O'Neill Flanagan; of 2 storeys and 7

bays, with a pediment and a parapeted roof. The home of Mr Alan Lillingston, who won the Champion Hurdle as an amateur rider, and Lady Vivienne Lillingston.

Mount Corbett, co Wexford (*see* TALBOT HALL).

Mount Desert, Cork, co Cork (DUNS-COMBE/LGI1912). A 2 storey 7 bay early c18 house with slightly projecting end-bays, extended in the late-Georgian period by the addition of 2 storey wings running from the front of the house to the back, with forward-facing ends of 2 bays. The wings are of the same height as the centre, but of different fenestration; having a higher lower storey than that in the centre of the house, and a correspondingly lower one above. Fine early c19 entrance gateway: rusticated stone piers with pineapples and urns, elaborate wrought-iron gates incorporating 2 pike-heads used by the insurgents 1798. Now an institution.

Mount Druid

Mount Druid, Castlerea, co Roscommon (O'CONOR/LGI1912). A Georgian house consisting of a 3 storey 3 bay centre with 2 storey 1 bay wings extending back; one of them having 2 small curved bows in its side elevation. C19 enclosed porch with thin pilasters.

Mount Edwards, nr Cushendall, co Antrim (CUPPAGE/IFR). An old, plain 2 storey house, deep in relation to its length; described (1819) as "one of those old snug farm-houses that was built by gentlemen who got tracts of land, in former days, from the Antrim family". Many improvements were carried out at that period by Samuel Boyd; by 1835 Mount Edwards had been acquired by Gen Alexander Cuppage, who used it as a summer residence.

Mount Falcon, Ballina, co Mayo (KNOX/IFR). A Victorian Gothic house of rough-hewn stone, built 1876 for U.A. Knox, probably to the design of James Franklin Fuller. Of 2 storeys with a 3 storey block to which a tower was added. Plate-glass windows. There is a similarity between Mount Falcon and Errew Grange (*qv*). Mount Falcon is now an hotel.

Mount Falcon, Borrisokane, co Tipperary (FALKINER/LGI1912). An early c18 house of 2 storeys over a basement, built 1720 by Richard Falkiner. 5 bay front; small floating pediment with ball-finial on peak, round-headed window in tympanum. Partly balustraded roof parapet. Pedimented doorcase with blocking.

Mountfergus, co Clare (*see* FORTFERGUS).

Mountfin, Enniscorthy, co Wexford. A 3 storey 5 bay early to mid-c18 house, with projecting end bays. High solid parapet to roof; doorway with fanlight and baseless pediment. In 1814, the residence of Robert Edwards.

Mount Gordon, Castlebar, co Mayo. A mid-c18 house of 1 storey over a high basement; with a 3 sided central bow and a rusticated and round-headed doorway approached up a flight of steps. Single-storey 1 bay lean-to wings. Niches in the side-faces of the bow and in one of the wings.

Mount Hall, co Down (*see* NARROW WATER CASTLE).

Mount Hanover, Duleek, co Meath (MATHEWS/LGI1937Supp). A 3 storey house probably dating from the 1st half of c18. Windows with thick glazing-bars; fanlighted doorway at the head of a flight of steps with railings of particularly good iron-work.

Mount Hazel (with Pauline, Duchess de Stacpoole)

Mount Hazel, Ballymacward, co Galway (MACEVOY, *sub* DE STACPOOLE/IFR). A 3 storey Georgian house originally belonging to a branch of the Browne family. Projection in centre of one elevation with a Venetian window lighting the staircase; 2 bays on either side of it. 3 bay side. Eaved roof. Passed to the MacEvoys with the marriage of Teresa Browne to Edward MacEvoy 1850; their daughter and heiress, Pauline, married 4th Duke de Stacpoole. Demolished 1945.

Mount Heaton

Mount Heaton, Offaly (HEATON-ARM-STRONG/IFR). A castellated 2 storey Georgian house, rather similar in appearance to the nearby Busherstown (*qv*).Entrance front symmetrical except for the 2 corner towers, one of which is round and the other polygonal; 5 bay, the 2 end bays being stepped forward; porch with battlements and turrets, but with the traditional fanlight above the door. Windows given hood mouldings and thin mullions in place of the original sashes in C19. Plain interior, with a handsome late C18 or early C19 chimneypiece of inlaid marble in one of the principal rooms. Sold 1817 by W. H. Armstrong—according to local legend, he lost it at cards to the Prince Regent—and subsequently bought by Count Arthur Moore, of Mooresfort (*qv*), who founded Mount St Joseph Cistercian Abbey here. The house became the Abbey guest house; it was considerably altered *ca* 1950.

Mount Henry, Portarlington, co Leix (SMYTH/LGI1912). A late-Georgian house by Sir Richard Morrison, rather like a smaller version of Lyons, co Kildare (*qv*). 2 storey; entrance front with pedimented single-storey Ionic portico between two shallow curved bows, which have only a single window in each storey. 4 bay side elevation. Pediments and entablatures over windows. Hall lined with Ionic columns of scagliola; upper landing with circular well gallery and pairs of Doric columns under relieving arches. Now a Presentation Convent.

Mount Hevey, Hill of Down, co Meath. A house of *ca* 1810; 2 storeys over basement, 3 bays. The seat of the Hevey Langan family.

Mount Ievers Court

Mount Ievers Court

Mount Ievers Court, Sixmilebridge, co Clare (IEVERS/IFR). The most perfect and also probably the earliest of the tall Irish houses; built *ca* 1730–37 by Col Henry Ievers to the design of John Rothery,

whose son, Isaac, completed the work after his death and who appears to have also been assisted by another member of the Rothery family, Jemmy. The house, which replaced an old castle, is thought to have been inspired by Chevening, in Kent—now the country home of The Prince of Wales—with which Ievers could have been familiar not only through the illustration in *Vitruvius Britannicus*, but also because he may have been connected with the family which owned Chevening in C17. Mount Ievers, however, differs from Chevening both in detail and proportions; and it is as Irish as Chevening is English. Its two 3 storey 7 bay fronts—which are almost identical except that one is of faded pink brick with a high basement whereas the other is of silvery limestone ashlar with the basement hidden by a grass bank—have that dreamlike, melancholy air which all the best tall C18 Irish houses have. There is a nice balance between window and wall, and a subtle effect is produced by making each storey a few inches narrower than that below it. The high-pitched roof is on a bold cornice; there are quoins, string-courses and shouldered window surrounds; the doorcase on each front has an entablature on console brackets. The interior of the house is fairly simple. Some of the rooms have contemporary panelling; one of them has a delightful primitive overmantel painting showing the house as it was originally, with an elaborate formal layout which has largely disappeared. A staircase of fine joinery with alternate barley-sugar and fluted balusters leads up to a large bedroom landing, with a modillion cornice and a ceiling of geometrical panels. On the top floor is a long gallery, a feature which seems to hark back to the C17 or C16, for it is found in hardly any other C18 Irish country houses; the closest counterpart was the Long Room at Bowen's Court, co Cork (*qv*). The present owner, S/Ldr N. L. Ievers, has carried out much restoration work and

various improvements, including the replacement of the original thick glazing-bars in some of the windows which had been given thin late-Georgian astragals *ca* 1850; and the making of two ponds on the site of those in C18 layout. He and Mrs Ievers have recently opened the house to paying guests in order to meet the cost of upkeep.

Mount Jessop, Longford, co Longford. A plain 3 storey 6 bay gable-ended C18 house, the seat of a branch of the Jessop family. Now derelict.

Mountjoy Grange, co Tyrone (ELLISON-MACARTNEY/LGI1912). A long, low, irregular battlemented house, with hood mouldings over the windows and a small square tower at one end.

Mount Juliet, Thomastown, co Kilkenny (BUTLER, CARRICK, E/PB; MCCALMONT/IFR). A mid to late C18 house built by the 1st Earl of Carrick across the River Nore from the former family seat, Ballylinch Castle on an estate which he had bought *ca* 1750 from Rev Thomas Bushe, of Kilmurry (*qv*); traditionally named by him after his wife. Of 3 storeys over a basement; front of 7 bays between 2 shallow curved bows, each having 3 windows. 1 bay central breakfront, with Venetian windows in the 2 upper storeys above tripartite pedimented and fanlighted doorway. Centre window in 2 lower storeys of bows roundheaded. Perron and double steps in front of entrance door, with iron railings. Highpitched roof and massive stacks. Sold 1914 by 6th Earl of Carrick to the McCalmonts who had leased the house for some years. Major Dermot McCalmont made a new entrance in what had formerly been the back of the house, where the main block is flanked by 2 storey wings, extending at right angles from it to form a shallow 3 sided court, and joined to it by curved sweeps. The interior of the house was richly

Mount Juliet

decorated by 2nd Earl of Carrick 1780s with plasterwork in the manner of Michael Stapleton. The hall, which is long and narrow, is divided by an arcade carried on fluted Ionic columns, beyond which rises a bifurcating staircase with a balustrade of plain slender uprights; the present entrance being by way of a porch built out at the back of the staircase. The rooms on either side of the hall in what was formerly the entrance front and is now the garden front have plasterwork ceilings; one with a centre medallion of a hunting scene, another with a medallion of a man shooting. One of these rooms, the dining room, also has plaster-work on its walls, incorporating medallions with Classical reliefs. One of the wings flanking the present entrance front contains a ballroom made by Major Dermot McCalmont 1920s, with a frieze of late C18 style plasterwork; it is reached by way of a curving corridor. The demesne of Mount Juliet is one of the finest in Ireland, with magnificent hardwoods above the River Nore; it includes the Ballylinch demesne across the river. There is a series of large walled gardens near the house. Mount Juliet is famous for its stud, founded by Major Dermot McCalmont 1915, with *The Tetrarch* as 1st sire.

Mount Kennedy

Mount Kennedy, co Wicklow (CUNING-HAM, ROSSMORE, B/PB; GUN CUNINGHAME/IFR). An estate formerly belonging to the Kennedys—who built "a large Mansion House" here 1670 which was burnt during the Williamite War, and who became extinct in the male line with the death of Sir Richard Kennedy in a duel 1710—was eventually bought 1769 by Lt-Gen Robert Cuningham, afterwards C-inC in Ireland and 1st Lord Rossmore. *Ca* 1782, Gen Cuningham began building a new house here, which was finished by 1784; his architect was Thomas Cooley, who pro-duced a modified version of a design which Cuningham had obtained from James Wyatt ten years earlier. Cooley appears to have been assisted by Richard Johnston, elder brother of the more famous Francis. The house is of 2 storeys over a basement. Entrance front with 2 bays on either side of a single-storey Doric portico with a pedi-ment and coupled end columns, surmounted by a Diocletian window. Garden front with 2 bays on either side of a curved bow. 4 bay sides. The plan of the house re-sembles the plan of Cooley's block at Cale-don, co Tyrone (*qv*), which was built 1779; and also that of Lucan House, co Dublin (*qv*). A large hall, with a screen of Ionic columns at its inner end, opens into an oval drawing room extending into the garden front bow; to the left of the drawing room is the dining room, to the right, the boudoir

and other smaller rooms. The staircase, which is of stone, with a wrought iron hand-rail, is in a smaller hall to the left of the main hall. The principal rooms have beautiful and delicate plasterwork by Michael Stapleton on their walls and ceilings, in-corporating painted medallions in *grisaille* by Peter de Gree. Octangular upper hall, lit by circular domed lantern. Unusually fine vaulted basement; long underground passage. Lord Rossmore died 1801, when it is said that the banshee was heard at Mount Kennedy, crying "Rossmore, Rossmore!" His peerage, which had been given him largely on the strength of his wife's estates in co Monaghan, went by a special re-mainder to her nephew; but Mount Kennedy went to his niece, Mrs Gun Cuninghame, and remained in the Gun Cuninghame family until 1928. Ten years later, it was bought by Mr Ernest Hull, whose widow sold it *ca* 1971. It is now the home of Mr & Mrs Noel Griffin, having undergone a sympathetic restoration by Mr Donal O'Neill Flanagan and Mr Austin Dunphy.

Mount Leader, Millstreet, co Cork (LEADER/IFR). A 2 storey pedimented Geor-gian house with a single-storey Ionic portico and an eaved roof.

Mount Loftus, Goresbridge, co Kil-kenny (LOFTUS/IFR). Originally a house built 1750 by 1st Viscount Loftus of 2nd creation for his son, Edward, afterwards 1st Bt. Of 2 storeys over a basement and an attic lit in 3 bay entrance front by a single Diocletian window, and in the garden front by windows in 3 sided central bow. On the entrance front there was a pedimented door-way with Doric columns, which was sub-sequently re-erected on the front of an en-closed porch. The garden front was of 1 bay on either side of the bow. A 2 storey 3 bay office wing was subsequently added at one side of the house. A wide corridor-hall ran along the whole length of the entrance front on the ground floor, with the stairs at one end of it; the drawing room extended into the garden front bow. This house was demolished *ca* 1906 by Major J. E. B. Lof-tus and a much larger house built in its place; of local granite, irregular and ram-bling, with gables and bargeboards, a pyramidal-roofed tower, quoins and the porch of the previous house re-used. The greater part of the new house was destroyed by fire 1934, after which a house was made out of the surviving servants' wing, which had archway in it. This archway was made into a hall; one end of it being enclosed by the original porch, re-used yet again; the other end being glazed to form a small con-servatory. Charming enclosed knot-garden with old tower-like garden house.

Mount Long, Oyster Haven, co Cork. An early C17 semi-fortified house similar to Monkstown Castle (*qv*), romantically situ-ated on the side of Oyster Haven; built 1631 by Dr John Long, who was afterwards hanged for his part in the Rising of 1641. The principal room had a plasterwork frieze of Scriptural and hunting scenes. Now a ruin.

Mount Merrion

Mount Merrion, co Dublin (FITZ-WILLIAM, V/DEP; HERBERT, PEMBROKE, E/PB). An early C18 house which appears to have consisted of 3 rather similar blocks of more or less equal size arranged to form an open-fronted court. Only 1 block now sur-vives: it is square, rather low, of 2 storeys with a dormered attic. 5 bay front; 3 bay pedimented breakfront. Very high pedi-ment with fanlighted lunette window; cen-tral round-headed window below, longer than the windows on either side of it. 4 bay side elevation; round-headed windows in upper storey; 2 lunette windows and 2 rectangular sash windows below. The seat of the Viscounts Fitz-William, from whom it passed by inheritance early C19 to the Earls of Pembroke, together with the Fitzwilliam Dublin estate; which includes Merrion Square and Fitzwilliam Square.

Mount Morris

Mount Morris, Clonbur, co Galway. A Georgian house of 2 storeys over a base-ment with a high-pitched C19 roof on a bracket cornice. 3 bay front, the centre bay being slightly recessed; round-headed doorway; C19 entablature on console brackets over downstairs windows. 3 bay side. Bold string course.

Mount Odell, Whitechurch, co Water-ford (ODELL/LG1863). A gable-ended weather-slated house of *ca* 1678 built by Charles Odell. Gabled projection at rear.

Mount Long

Mount Oliver, Ballymascanlon, co Louth (*see* MOUNT PLEASANT).

Mount Panther, Dundrum, co Down (ANNESLEY, E/PB; MOORE/LGI1912). A noble house of *ca* 1770. Very fine room with Adamesque plasterwork on the walls and ceiling. Now ruinous.

Mount Patrick (formerly **Tower Hill**), **Glanmire, co Cork** (DRING/IFR). A C19 house of 1 storey over a high basement, with an eaved roof. In the grounds is a tall castellated round tower built 1843–45 by William O'Connell to the design of George Richard Pain in honour of Fr Theobald Mathew, "The Apostle of Temperance" (*see* THOMASTOWN CASTLE, co Tipperary), whose statue stands in front of it.

Mount Paul, co Donegal (*see* LINSFORT CASTLE).

Mount Pleasant (formerly **Curravordy**), **Bandon, co Cork** (BALDWIN/LGI1958). A Georgian house consisting of a 2 storey centre block with lower wings. Entrance front with 2 round-headed windows on either side of the centre, lighting the main and secondary stairs. Large hall with arch opening into staircase hall; staircase with elegant ironwork balustrade. A seat of the Baldwin family by whom it was sold in C19. The property was bought *ca* 1949 by Mr Gerald Allen, who did not, however, restore the house, which by that time was in bad repair; but used it to house refrigerating plant.

Mount Pleasant, Glenville, co Cork (*see* GLENVILLE PARK).

Mount Pleasant, Ballymascanlon, co Louth (MACNEILL, *sub* MCNEILE/LGI1972). A house enlarged 1830s and later by John (afterwards Sir John) MacNeill, an eminent civil engineer who was 1st Prof of Engineering at Trinity College, Dublin. His new addition, which he designed himself, has something of the air of one of the smaller Government Houses of the British Raj in India. The principal front is of 2 storeys in the centre, with a giant pedimented portico of 4 widely-spaced Tower of the Winds columns; and of 1 storey and 3 bays on either side. The side elevation is single-storey, with a 2 storey 1 bay centre between two curved bows. Balustraded roof parapets; entablatures over windows. To the right of the front is a Victorian tower. 2 storey galleried hall with bifurcating staircase. The house is now a Catechetical & Pastoral Centre and has been re-named Mount Oliver.

Mount Pleasant, Offaly (*see* GORTNAMONA).

Mount Plunkett, Athlone, co Roscommon. A house of unusual design built 1806 by George Plunkett. 2 storey 3 bay centre; end bays raised a storey higher to form pedimented roof-pavilions. Fanlighted doorway; ironwork balconies; curvilinear roof parapet over centre. Passed to the Grehan family *ca* 1850 and in 1876, to Robert Adamson. Later the residence of C. E. A. Cameron, Assistant Inspector-General of the RIC. Dismantled 1946; now a ruin.

Mount Prospect, Bandon, co Cork (DRAKE-BROCKMAN/LGI1972). A late-Georgian house of 2 storeys over a basement and 5 bays. Large and elegant fanlighted doorway, with diamond-glazed astragals. In 1837, the residence of Mrs Bradshaw; in late 1940s, of Mrs C. B. Drake-Brockman. Now owned by Mr & Mrs James Werner, who run a reproduction furniture business and a clothes boutique here.

Mount Rivers

Mount Rivers, Carrigaline, co Cork (ROBERTS/LGI1958). A 3 storey Georgian house which seems originally to have had a front consisting of a centre recessed between two projections with rounded corners. At a later date, the centre in the 2 upper storeys was filled in, making a front of 4 bays; on the ground floor there is still a central convex-sided recess, which is fronted by a single-storey portico with slender columns. The rounded outer corners of the front have curved windows and are framed by blocked quoins. Eaved roof. Staircase of good joinery behind entrance hall, rising to the top of the house. Drawing room and dining room with rounded corners. A seat of the Robertses; now being restored by Mr Leslie Roberts, having not been occupied by his family for some years.

Mount Shannon

Mount Shannon, Castleconnell, co Limerick (FITZGIBBON/IFR). A 2 storey C18 house, enlarged and magnificently furnished by John FitzGibbon, 1st Earl of Clare, Lord Chancellor of Ireland at the time of the Union and one of the most powerful men in the Ireland of his day; remodelled in neo-Classical style *post* 1813 by Byron's friend, 2nd Earl, to the design of Lewis Wyatt. James Pain also worked here for 2nd Earl, either supervising the remodelling according to Wyatt's design, or carrying out subsequent alterations. 7 bay entrance front with pedimented porte-cochère of 4 giant Ionic columns. Adjoining front of 5 bays, the end bays breaking for-

ward and having Wyatt windows under relieving arches in their lower storey. Lower service wing. Large rooms, but hardly any internal ornament; fine hall and library; French gilt furniture in the drawing room and morning room. 3rd and last Earl of Clare, who did not have the Government pension which 1st and 2nd Earls had enjoyed, and who was generous in giving financial help to emigrants after the Famine, left the estate impoverished; so that his daughter, who inherited it, was obliged to sell most of the valuable contents of the house 1888. The house itself was sold *ca* 1893 to the Nevin family; it is now a ruin.

Mount Stewart, Newtownards, co Down (VANE-TEMPEST-STEWART, LONDONDERRY, M/PB). A long, 2 storey Classical house of 1820s, one end of which is, in fact, a house built 1803–06 by 1st Marquess of Londonderry (father of the statesman, Castlereagh) to the design of George Dance. The 7 bay front of 1803–06 house survives as the end elevation of the present house; unchanged, except that its centre bay now breaks forward under a shallow pediment, similar to those on either side of the present entrance front, which are very much of 1820s. The 3 rooms at this end of the house keep their original ceilings of delicate plasterwork; the centre one, which was formerly the entrance hall, has a ceiling with pendentives, making it an octagon. Behind this former entrance hall is an imperial staircase with a balustrade of elegant ironwork, lit by a dome; this, too, is part of the earlier house. 3rd Marquess, Castlereagh's younger half-brother, who was far richer than either his father or brother had ever been, having married the wealthy Durham heiress, Frances Anne Vane Tempest, enlarged the house to its present form *ca* 1825–28, his architect being William Vitruvius Morrison. A new block was built onto what had been the back of the original house, as wide as the original house was long and long enough to make, with the end of the original house, a new entrance front of 11 bays, with a pedimented porte-cochère of 4 giant Ionic columns as its central feature; the 3 outer bays on either side being treated as pavilions, each with a 1 bay pedimented breakfront similar to that which was put onto the front of the original house. The outer bays have a balustraded roof parapet, which is carried round the end of the house and along the new garden front. The latter is as long as the entrance front, and has a boldly projecting centre with a pediment and a single-storey portico of coupled Ionic columns; and a curved bow at either end. The principal interior feature of the newer building is a vast central hall, consisting of an octagon, top-lit through a balustraded gallery from a dome filled with stained glass, with rectangular extensions so as to form a room much longer than it is wide; with screens of coupled painted marble Ionic columns between the octagon and the extensions. Morrison's reception rooms are spacious and simple; the drawing room has a screen of Ionic columns at either end. The interior of the house was done up *post* World War I by 7th Marquess, Secretary of State for Air in 1930s; the central room in the garden front being panelled as a

Mount Stewart

Mount Stewart: Central Hall

Mount Stewart: Temple of the Winds

smoking and living room. The 7th Marquess and his wife (the well-known political hostess and friend of Ramsay MacDonald) also laid out an elaborate garden, going down the hillside from the garden front of the house towards Strangford Lough. As well as this notable C20 garden, Mount Stewart boasts of one of the finest C18 garden buildings in Ireland: the Temple of the Winds, an octagonal banqueting house built 1780 to the design of "Athenian" Stuart, who based it on the Tower of the Winds in Athens. It has a porch on two of its faces, each with 2 columns of the same modified Corinthian order as that of the columns of the Tower of the Winds. Mount Stewart was given to the Northern Ireland National Trust by Lady Mairi Bury, daughter of 7th Marquess, *ca* 1977, and is now open to the public. The Temple of the Winds was given 1962 to the Trust, which has since restored it; the garden was given to the Trust 1955.

Mount Talbot

Mount Talbot

Mount Talbot, Athleague, co Roscommon (TALBOT, *sub* CROSBIE/IFR). Originally a C18 winged Palladian house, the wings being set at an angle of 45 degrees to the centre block and joined to it by curved open arcades with urn finials along their parapets. Then, *ca* 1820, the centre block was transformed into an impressive castellated and Gothic pile; the arcades and wings

Mount Talbot: Gateway

being left as they were, producing a somewhat hybrid effect. As transformed, the entrance front of the centre block was nearly symmetrical and had a massive square tower like a keep at one end, a pair of turrets in the centre, which resembled a Tudor gatehouse-tower; and a 3rd turret at the other end. The garden front was more ecclesiastical than military, and had a 3 bay projection with graceful pointed windows and Gothic pinnacles at the corners. Dining room with Gothic recess. Chaste and elegant Classical arch at entrance to demesne, with rusticated piers and urns on its entablature; flanked by 2 smaller arches for pedestrians. Mount Talbot was burnt 1922.

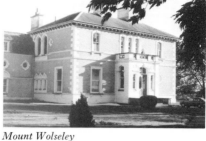

Mount Wolseley

storey slightly Italianate Victorian house. Camber-headed windows; ornate balustraded porch; roof on bracket cornice. Wing with pyramidal roof. Now a school.

but with unusual paired rectangular windows, set in shallow recesses rising through both storeys with relieving arches above them. In the centre, the entrance door was treated as though it were simply another window, flanked on either side by a window of similar shape and size. Towards the end of C19, 3rd Earl of Kilmorey added rectangular bows to this front; then, *ca* 1904, he built a single-storey wing at the back of the house containing a large room known as the Long Room, with a vaulted ceiling on timber supports. Between 1919 and 1921, 4th Earl built a wing to the left of the front, containing various rooms including a new large drawing room and a top-lit entrance hall; the entrance being moved round to this

Mount Trenchard

Mount Trenchard

Mount Trenchard, Foynes, co Limerick (SPRING RICE, MONTEAGLE OF BRANDON, B/PB). A late-Georgian house of 3 storeys over a basement, with 2 curved bows on its entrance front, which overlooks the estuary of the Shannon, and a wide curved bow in the centre of its garden front. At one side is a 2 storey Victorian wing almost as high as the main block; at the other side is 1 bay 3 storey addition and a lower 2 storey wing. Also in the Victorian period, a rather unusual porch was added, in the form of a short length of curving corridor, with an open arched end; it was placed not in the centre of the front, but to the left of the lefthand bow, growing out of the high 2 storey addition. This was subsequently removed and a more conventional entrance doorway made between the 2 bows with a pillared and pedimented doorcase. From the garden front, a straight walk between trees ascends the hillside. In recent years the home of Lt-Cmdr C. E. Hall; now owned by an order of teaching nuns.

Mount Usher, Ashford, co Wicklow. A simple double bow-fronted house in a famous river garden. Home of the Walpole family, by whom the garden has been created.

Mount Wolseley, Tullow, co Carlow (WOLSELEY, Bt, *of Mount Wolseley*/PB). A 2

Mourne Park

Mourne Park, Kilkeel, co Down (NEEDHAM, KILMOREY, E/PB). In 1806, Robert Needham, 11th Viscount Kilmorey, was left the Mourne estate by William Nedham, whom he had never met, and who may or may not have been a distant kinsman of his. Soon afterwards, he built a house among the glorious oak and beechwoods of his newly-inherited demesne—which lies on the southern slopes of the Mourne Mountains—in place of an earlier house. It was modest in scale; 2 storey, 3 bay, with Wyatt windows and a doorway with sidelights. Some time later, probably *post* 1820, a 3rd storey was added; then, *post* 1859, a new 2 storey front was built onto the house; so that the new front rooms had higher ceilings than the rooms in the older part of the house at the back. The new front, of granite ashlar, was of 3 bays, like the original front;

side of the house. At the same time, the principal staircase was remodelled to fit in with the new entrance.

Moyaliffe Castle, Thurles, co Tipperary (ARMSTRONG, *sub* KEMMIS/IFR). A rambling house of several periods and great character, incorporating some of the walls of an old Butler castle, remains of which can be seen on a mound immediately outside the windows of the garden front; a wing running in this direction is said to have been originally joined to it. The entrance front, on the opposite side to the castle, is now of C19 appearance; 2 storey, with plate glass windows, an overhanging gabled roof and a projecting 2 storey gabled porch; but the lower ranges extending at the back and side have windows with C18 astragals; they enclose a courtyard with an old well in the

Moyaliffe Castle

centre of it. Long hall with low panelling; C19 stair in separate hall at back. Panelled dining room, where one of the family portraits has a strange habit of coming down from the wall and depositing itself by the fireplace opposite at the time of the death of an important member of the family. Charming drawing room and morning room *en suite*; long upstairs corridor leading to the gallery of a 2 storey music room at the far end of one of the wings.

Moyclare

Moyclare, Ferbane, Offaly. A plain long and low C18 house with a range of similar height and style at right angles. Simple fanlighted doorway set in arched recess, flanked by 2 Wyatt windows. The seat of the Lawder family.

machicolated entrance tower with two slender polygonal turrets and a Perpendicular window above the front door; at one side was a single bay with another polygonal turret, at the other a lower and longer battlemented range. Burnt *ca* 1920.

Moyne, co Leix

voussoirs over the windows; enlarged late C19 by the addition of a 2 storey 2 bay wing at one side, and reconstructed after 2 successive fires 1888 and 1899. Enclosed porch with corner-pilasters and segmental pediment added to C18 facade; single-storey rectangular projections on the front and side of C19 wing. High-pitched roof with dormered attic. Long wing at back. Large hall with modillion cornice and panelling with stairs going out of it at one end. Large drawing room with good Adam-Revival ceiling. Dining room with frieze of plasterwork in late C18 style and carved wood chimneypiece in Elizabethan style.

Moydrum Castle

Moydrum Castle, Athlone, co Westmeath (HANDCOCK, CASTLEMAINE, B/PB). An early C19 castle by Richard (afterwards Sir Richard) Morrison, built 1812 for 1st Lord Castlemaine; incorporating an earlier house described at the time as "nothing more than an ordinary farm-house, contracted in its dimensions, mean in its external form, and inconvenient in its interior arrangements" in contrast to the "most finished and complete residence" which it became. As completed, the castle had a battlemented and

Moyglare House, Knocknatulla, co Meath. A 3 storey mid-C18 house with a 3 sided central bow and 1 bay on either side of it. Fanlighted doorway with baseless pediment. Fine plaster frieze in the hall. Recently the home of Dr & Mrs W. G. Fegan.

Moyne, Durrow, co Leix (HAMILTON STUBBER/IFR; HAMILTON/IFR). A 2 storey 5 bay early to mid-C18 house, with a baseless floating pediment containing an oculus, a central Venetian window and multiple

Moyne Park, co Galway

Moyne Park, Monivea, co Galway (BROWNE/LG1863; WAITHMAN/LG11912). An impressive 2 storey early C19 house of cut limestone. 7 bay entrance front; central feature of 4 giant Doric pilasters with partly broken entablature. Ground floor windows on either side of centre set in arched recesses; niches between 1st floor windows. Side elevation of 2 bays between two shallow

3 sided bows. For some years a college of the Sacred Heart Fathers; recently sold and now in private occupation once again.

Moyode Castle

Moyode Castle, Athenry, co Galway (PERSSE/IFR). An imposing C19 castle, with a 3 sided bow in the middle of its front, a storey higher than the bay on either side of it, and flanked by 2 little battlemented turrets, like rabbits' ears. A higher tower, and a very tall polygonal machicolated corner turret, at one end of the front. Now an ivy-smothered ruin.

Moyola Park, Castledawson, co Derry (DAWSON, *sub* CHICHESTER-CLARK/IFR). A handsome 2 storey C18 house, of coursed rubble with ashlar dressings. 5 bay entrance front, 3 bay pedimented breakfront; pedimented porch on Doric columns added later. 3 sided bow in side elevation. Solid roof parapet; flush quoins and window surrounds with blocking. The home of Lord Moyola (formerly Major James Chichester-Clark), Prime Minister of Northern Ireland 1969–71.

Moyriesk, Quin, co Clare (FOSTER-VESEY-FITZGERALD/IFR). A mid-C18 house of red brick consisting of a 2 storey main block joined by curved sweeps to single-storey wings at right angles to its front and facing each other across the forecourt. Altered mid-C19. Behind the house was a large C18 garden layout with a vista centring on Clooney, the Bindon seat. The Knight of Glin considers that Moyriesk and its layout therefore might have been designed by Francis Bindon. Bought by Rt Hon James FitzGerald, MP, Prime Serjeant of Ireland and a distinguished orator, towards the end of C18; sold by the Foster-Vesey-Fitz-Gerald family 1932. Now two-thirds demolished.

Muckridge, Youghal, co Cork. A 2 storey double bow-fronted Georgian house. The seat of a branch of the FitzGerald family.

Muckruss, Killarney, co Kerry (HERBERT/IFR; GUINNESS, Bt/PB; VINCENT/LG 1937Supp). A large cut-stone Elizabethan-Revival mansion by William Burn overlooking Muckruss Lake; built 1839–43 for Col Rt Hon H. A. Herbert, MP, replacing an earlier house. Stepped gables with pointed finials; mullioned windows; many oriels; tall chimneys. A porte-cochère was added *ca* 1870, to the design of William Atkins, of Cork. The interior of the house is

Muckruss

similar to that of most houses of its kind: there is a series of reception rooms with fretted ceilings *en suite* along the garden front, flanked by a large hall with a massive oak staircase. In the demesne, which is noted for its trees and shrubs, in particular for its azaleas, magnolias and palms, is a ruined medieval friary. Muckruss was sold about the turn of the century by Major H. A. Herbert, MP, to Arthur Guinness, 1st (and last) Lord Ardilaun, who re-sold it shortly before the outbreak of World War I to an American, Bowers Bourne. Mr & Mrs Bourne gave it to their daughter, Mrs Arthur Vincent; then, in 1932, after her death, they and their son-in-law, Senator Arthur Vincent, presented it to the Irish nation. The demesne is now known as the Bourne-Vincent Memorial Park; the house is open to the public, and contains pictures and objects of local historic interest.

Mullaboden, Naas, co Kildare (CRICHTON, *sub* ERNE, E/PB). An irregular 2 storey Victorian Italianate house, with highish roofs on bracket cornices and a campanile tower, with a balcony on consoles, over the centre of the entrance front.

Mullaghfin, Balrath, co Meath. A 2 storey 5 bay gable-ended house of *ca* 1770 with a pedimented Doric doorcase.

Mullagh House, Kells, co Meath. A 2 storey 5 bay Georgian house with a central pedimented projection. Fanlighted doorway in doorcase with entablature.

Mullinabro', Kilmacow, co Kilkenny (JONES/LGI1912). A bow-ended C18 house with a doorway rather similar to that at Woodstock, in the same co (*qv*): round-headed, rusticated and incorporating the flanking windows. Good mahogany doors. Now demolished.

Mulroy, Carrickart, co Donegal (LUCAS-CLEMENTS/IFR; STRUTT, *sub* RAYLEIGH, B/PB). A simple mid-C19 Tudor-Revival house of grey stone, probably by William Burn; rather steep gables and dormer-gables, mullioned windows. Hall divided by pointed arch; oak staircase. Spacious, pleasant rooms overlooking Mulroy Bay, along the shores of which is a woodland garden, particularly famous for its rhododendrons and azaleas. The planting was originally carried out by 5th and last Earl of Leitrim and has been continued since his death by his widow, the Countess of Leitrim. Mulroy is now the home of Lady Leitrim and of the late Lord Leitrim's nephew, Hon Hedley Strutt.

Mulroy

Murlough House, Dundrum, co Down
(HILL, DOWNSHIRE, M/PB). A 2 storey Victorian house in the Georgian manner, built 1860 for 4th Marquess of Downshire to the design of William Haywood, of London. 7 bay entrance front, prolonged by lower wing of 2 storeys over basement; 3 bay side; all faced in ashlar. Projecting porch with doors at sides and round-headed window with massive rusticated surround in its front face. Blocking round windows; continuous hood moulding over upper storey windows, which have cambered heads. Eaved roof on cornice. Now leased by the Church of Ireland for retreats, conferences and meetings.

Myra Castle, Strangford, co Down
(CRAIG-LAURIE, *sub* BIRNEY/LGI1952; WALLACE/LGI1912). A castle built *ca* 1850s by Rowland Craig-Laurie with plain, rendered walls and none of the pseudo-medieval detail which one would expect in a castellated house of its period; relying for its effect on the skilful grouping of its elements. Dominated by a tall, square 4 storey entrance tower, containing nothing but stairs, with a round turret at the other side of the front. Very simple battlements; rectangular windows, some with unobtrusive mullions.

Myross Wood

Myross Wood, Leap, co Cork (TOWNSHEND/IFR). A Georgian house consisting of a 2 storey 5 bay centre, with slightly lower 2 storey 2 bay wings. Fanlighted doorway with wooden Ionic porch built onto the front of it. Now owned by the Sacred Heart Fathers.

Myrtle Grove, Youghal, co Cork (BOYLE, CORK AND ORRERY, E/PB; ARBUTHNOT, Bt/ PB). Almost the only completely unfortified C16 Irish house to have survived intact and in anything like its original state; altered C18 and C19, but still unmistakably a Tudor

Murlough House

Myrtle Grove

Myrtle Grove: panelled Drawing Room

manor house with 3 steep gables in a row, a central porch-oriel and another oriel at one end; though the latter now have Georgian glazing, as do the other windows. Traditionally the Irish home of Sir Walter Raleigh; the oriel at the end of the house, which faces the old Collegiate Church and lights the large upstairs drawing room, being identified with what Raleigh referred to when he mentioned writing a letter in "my oriel window at Youghal". The room is in exactly the right position to have been Raleigh's great chamber, and it looks just as one would imagine it to have looked; panelled in dark oak, and with an elaborately carved chimneypiece and overmantel incorporating figures of Faith, Hope and Charity. The panelling and mantel do not appear to have been a C19 importation, for it is clear from an account of 1837 that they had then been here for longer than anyone could remember. Since it is most unlikely that they were installed in C18, they must have been in the room since at least C17;

and might possibly have even been here in Raleigh's time. Another upstairs room is similarly panelled; but the rest of the interior is Georgian, or later. By the front door is a yew tree under which Raleigh is believed to have smoked, and where he is supposed to have had a bucket of water thrown over him by a servant who thought he was on fire. A remnant of the old town wall of Youghal runs through the garden; it was doubtless on account of being within the wall that the house survived as it did. Together with the rest of Raleigh's Irish estates, the house was acquired by Richard Boyle, afterwards 1st Earl of Cork, 1602. In C18 it was acquired by the Hayman family, who let it *ca* 1830s and 1840s to Col Faunt. Later in C19, it was bought by the politician and colonial administrator, Sir John Pope-Hennessy (the original of Trollope's *Phineas Finn*), who sold it to another distinguished colonial administrator, Sir Henry Arthur Blake. It eventually passed to Sir Henry Arthur Blake's daughter, Mrs J. B. Arbuthnot, and then on to her son, Cmdr B. K. C. Arbuthnot; her eldest daughter is the wife of Claud Cockburn, the journalist, also living in Youghal.

N

Naas (The), co Kildare (*see* JIGGINSTOWN HOUSE).

Nadrid, Coachford, co Cork, (WOODLEY/ IFR; GALWAY/IFR; MATTHEWS, *sub* CLARKE/ IFR). A square late-Georgian house over-looking the River Lee. Fine garden, laid out by the present owner, Mrs H. L. Matthews and her late husband, Capt H. L. Matthews.

Nantenan, Ballinagrane, co Limerick (ROYSE/LGI1850–3; WHITE/IFR). A 2 storey mid-C19 house of the villa type, with an eaved roof on a bracket cornice. 3 bay front and side; porch with 2 Ionic columns and corner piers, flanked by Wyatt windows. Impressive C18 entrance gates: tall piers with ball finials, Gothic-arched wickets, flanking walls with niches.

Narrow Water Castle

Narrow Water Castle, Warrenpoint, co Down (HALL/IFR). A large and imposing Tudor-Revival mansion of *ca* 1836, by Thomas Duff of Newry, incorporating an earlier house known as Mount Hall. Many oriels and gables with finials; at one corner of the entrance front, a gatehouse tower with 4 cupolas, inspired by various English originals, such as the gatehouse at Tixall, Staffs. At the other side of the house is a tall polygonal battlemented tower with a round turret.

Neale (The), Ballinrobe, co Mayo (BROWNE, KILMAINE, B/PB). An early C18 house of 2 storeys over a basement which replaced an old castle. 7 bay entrance front; pedimented porch on 2 columns, up broad flight of steps. 5 bay side elevation. Small windows with thick glazing bars. Balus-traded roof parapet, which was removed when the house was re-roofed 1860s. Doors with shouldered architraves in hall. Oval of mid-C18 rococo plasterwork in centre of drawing room ceiling, surrounded by early C19 reeded mouldings entwined with foliage and fan decoration in corners. Mid-C18 plasterwork frieze in dining room, with *putti*, cornucopias, swags and fruit. After

The Neale

he succeeded 1907, 5th Lord Kilmaine en-larged the house by building a free-standing wing at an angle to it, so as not to take light from the windows; and joined to it by a curved bridge. Fine stables, built *ca* 1737 by Sir John Browne, 5th Bt, MP, father of 1st Lord Kilmaine. Well-planted park laid out by 1st Lord Kilmaine 1770s, divided by a large outcrop of rock (in Irish *aill*, hence the name, The Neale). The park contains a stepped pyramid designed by Lord Charle-mont, an octagonal Doric temple and another C18 folly, probably made up of frag-ments of medieval carving with a strange inscription, known as "The Gods of The Neale." 5th Lord Kilmaine sold The Neale to a former tenant of the estate 1925. The house was demolished *ca* 1939; the follies remain.

Necarne Castle, co Fermanagh (*see* CASTLE IRVINE).

Netley Park

Netley Park, Ballina, co Mayo (KNOX/ IFR). A compact late-Georgian house built *ante* 1816 by Capt H. W. Knox; more or less the twin of the nearby Greenwood Park (*qv*), which was built by his brother. Of 2 storeys over a basement; 3 bay entrance front, tripartite fanlighted doorway with blocking; 4 bay side. Hall with staircase at back of it. Drawing room wallpaper now at Williamsburg, USA. Passed eventually to Edith (*née* Knox), wife of J. E. F. Rowlette. Demolished 1962; now a ruin.

New Abbey

New Abbey, Kilcullen, co Kildare (BRERETON/IFR; DIXON, GLENTORAN, B/PB; URQUHART/LGI1958). A house of 2 storeys over a basement, built *ca* 1755 near the site of a Franciscan abbey founded 1486 and afterwards leased to Edmund Spenser, who probably wrote most of the six books of *The Faerie Queene* here. Entrance front with 1 bay on either side of a central 3 sided bow in which is a pedimented entrance doorway; 3 bay side elevation. Urns on roof parapet. Acquired 1779 by George Brere-ton, who was killed in a duel in Dublin 2 years later. The astragals of the windows removed during C19; and, *post* 1864, a partly-glazed Doric porch surmounted by a little glazed kiosk added on the entrance front by Major Robert Brereton, who also added a low wing to the right of the en-trance front 1901. Sold 1909, re-sold almost immediately to Capt Herbert Dixon, after-wards 1st Lord Glentoran, who added a 2 storey 2 bay wing to the left of the entrance front and set back from it, obscuring 1 bay of the side elevation; of the same height as the original block and in a similar Georgian style, with urns on the parapet and astragals in the windows; surprisingly, he did not at the same time put back the astragals in the original block. Subsequently sold again, and now the home of Mrs Kenneth Urquhart.

Newark (The), co Down (*see* ARDGLASS CASTLE).

Newbay, nr Wexford, co Wexford (FRENCH/IFR). A late-Georgian house by William Farrell and John Meason, built 1822 for Henry Halton; replacing a castle, the base of which is now incorporated in the stable-yard buildings. Bought 1869 by Thomas Jeffries, who added a wing 1886–87 to the design of W. E. Fitzsimons and car-ried out major alterations to the house. Passed to the Frenchs through the marriage of Annie, daughter of Thomas Jeffries, to George French 1899.

Newberry Hall

Newberry Hall, Carbury, co Kildare

(POMEROY, HARBERTON, V/PB). A Palladian house of red brick with stone facings, built during 1760s for Arthur Pomeroy, afterwards 1st Viscount Harberton; probably to the design of the amateur architect, Nathaniel Clements. Centre block of 2 storeys over basement with an attic storey above the cornice which has windows in the garden front, but not in the entrance front. Entrance front of 3 bays; pedimented breakfront with Diocletian window above tripartite fanlighted doorway with baseless pediment; the facade being similar to that of Colganstown, co Dublin (*qv*). Solid roof parapet with urns. The centre block is linked to 2 storey wings or pavilions, each with 1 bay on either side of a 3 sided bow, by curved sweeps with round-headed rusticated doors and windows. The garden front of the centre block is of 1 bay on either side of a curved central bow. Frieze of rococo plasterwork with birds and flowers in dining room. Doors with shouldered architraves. Sold *ca* 1840; subsequently owned by Edward Woolstenholme and then by William Pilkington, a Dublin publisher; bought by the Robinson family 1911.

Newberry Manor, Mallow, co Cork

(BRAMSTON-NEWMAN/LGI1958). A large plain rectangular 3 storey Georgian house. 9 bay front with breakfront centre; 4 bay side. Now demolished.

Newbridge House, Donabate, co Dublin

(COBBE/IFR). A house probably by Richard Castle, built 1737 for Dr Charles Cobbe, afterwards Archbishop of Dublin. Of 2 storeys over a high basement; ashlar-faced entrance front of 6 bays, with a pedimented tripartite doorcase. Broad flight of steps with ironwork railings up to hall door; shouldered window architraves; solid roof parapet with urns and eagles at corners. Hall with modillion cornice and large pedimented chimneypiece. Soon after the Archbishop's death 1765, his son, Col Thomas Cobbe, MP, who had a fashionable wife, a sister of 1st Marquess of Waterford, added a wing at the back of the house con-

Newbridge House

Newbliss House, Clones, co Monaghan

(MURRAY-KER/LGI1912). A 2 storey early C19 Classical house with an eaved roof on a bracket cornice. 5 bay entrance front; breakfront centre with Wyatt window in upper storey and enclosed Grecian porch with 2 Ionic columns and acroteria. 7 bay garden front, the 3 outer bays on either side forming shallow curved bows.

taining a very large drawing room, with a ceiling of rococo plasterwork by Robert West, who also decorated the family pew in the Protestant church at Donabate. This great room, which is now hung with a scarlet wallpaper, is entered by way of a corridor and through a monumental doorway with a pediment and fluted engaged Corinthian columns.

Newbliss House

Newbrook

Newbrook, Claremorris, co Mayo

(BINGHAM, CLANMORRIS, B/PB). A mid to late C18 house of 2 storeys over a basement, possibly by William Leeson. 7 bay entrance front; doorcase with blocked engaged Doric columns and pediment; broad flight of steps up to door. Adjoining front of 7 bays, with 3 bay breakfront; centre windows in lower storey longer than those at the sides. The rooms are said to have been spacious but not very lofty. Irish-battlemented tower in grounds. In 1837 the house was gutted by a fire which is said to have burnt for 8 days; it was not rebuilt.

Newcastle, Ballymahon, co Longford (HARMAN, *sub* KING-HARMAN/LGI1937Supp; PARSONS-HARMAN, ROSSE E/PB; KING-HARMAN, *sub* KINGSTON, E/PB). A large 3 storey 7 bay early C18 gable-ended house, with lower asymmetrical wings. Small central curvilinear gable on entrance front, which might be original; it has been repeated on the C19 projecting porch. High pitched roof. Drawing room ceiling of painted plasterwork in low relief, with musical emblems in the corners. Originally the seat of the Sheppard family, whose heiress married Wentworth Harman 1691; inherited 1784 by Lawrence Parsons-Harman, afterwards 1st Earl of Rosse, and eventually by his grandson, Hon Laurence King-Harman. Sold *ca* 1950 by Capt Robert Douglas King-Harman. For some years a convent; now an hotel.

Newcastle West, co Limerick: The Castle (FITZGERALD, DESMOND, E/DEP; COURTENAY, DEVON, E/PB). Originally one of the chief castles of the FitzGeralds, Earls of Desmond, with 2 C15 great halls, one of them raised on a vaulted basement. After the forfeiture of the Desmond lands in the reign of Elizabeth I, the castle was granted to the Courtenay family, ancestors of the subsequent Earls of Devon. During the centuries that followed, parts of the castle fell into ruin, while other parts remained intact, including the 2 C15 halls; though the latter ceased to be used for domestic purposes. Eventually, when the Devons came here, they occupied a long, irregular house of 2 storeys with an attic and 9 bays in the castle precincts.

New Court, Skibbereen, co Cork (FLEMING/LGI1958). A Georgian house, now demolished.

New Forest, Tyrrellspass, co Westmeath (DANIELL/IFR; GAIRDNER/LGI1958). A mid to late C18 house of 3 storeys over a basement. Entrance front with 2 bays on either side of central breakfront, in which there is a central window flanked by 2 narrower windows in each of 2 upper storeys, and a tripartite fanlighted doorway of a familiar "pattern book" design, similar to those at Colganstown and Newberry Hall, co Kildare (*qqv*) and numerous other houses; with columns, an entablature and a baseless pediment. Large drawing room and dining room on either side of hall; narrow library. Sold *ca* 1950 to Lt-Gen Sir Charles Gairdner, who was subsequently appointed Governor of W Australia and resold New Forest *ca* 1954 to Mr H. Hannevig.

Newgrove, Kells, co Meath. A 5 bay gable-ended C18 house with a pediment, containing an oculus, above a Venetian window, above a pedimented and fanlighted tripartite doorway. Buttresses at back. In 1814, the residence of Philip Reilly. Now a ruin.

New Hall

New Hall: cupboard in the form of an organ case

New Hall, Ennis, co Clare (MACDONNELL/LGI1912; ARMSTRONG-MACDONNELL, *sub* ARMSTRONG/IFR). A 2 storey house of pink brick built onto the end of an earlier house *ca* 1764 by Charles MacDonnell, MP; probably to the design of Francis Bindon. Front with 2 bays on either side of a central 3 sided bow surmounted by a balustrade and urns; curved end bows. High-pitched roof on eaved cornice. Pedimented doorcase in central bow; windows with keystones, those in the upper storey being of the original rather small proportions; those below having been enlarged at a later date. The octagonal hall, which has a Doric cornice and frieze with grinning masks, bucrania and crests in the metopes, contains the most remarkable feature of the interior: a cupboard in the form of an impressive and elegant Baroque organ case. There is fine plasterwork in the drawing room. New Hall was sold early in the present century to the Joyce family.

New Hamburgh, co Tyrone (*see* TULLY-LAGAN).

Newlands, Tallaght, co Dublin (WOLFE/IFR). A 2 storey Georgian house of 9 bays, the end bays breaking forward and framed by quoins. Ionic porch; single-storey wings with triple windows. The seat of Arthur Wolfe, MP, afterwards Lord Chief Justice of King's Bench and 1st Viscount Kilwarden, who helped save Wolfe Tone from the gallows 1794; the Tone family being freehold tenants on the estate of his cousin, Theobald Wolfe, of Blackhall, co Kildare (*qv*). In 1837, Newlands was the residence of J. Crotty.

Newmarket Court

Newmarket Court, Newmarket, co Cork (ALDWORTH/IFR). A fine early C18 house built for Richard Aldworth, MP, who married Hon Elizabeth St Leger, the woman Freemason (*see* DONERAILE COURT); possibly to the design of one of the Rothery family of architects. The house was described (1750) as having "two regular fronts of hewn stone", which it still has; they adjoin each other, and are each of 7 bays. The entrance front has a 3 bay recessed centre and a pedimented doorcase. The adjoining front has a 3 bay breakfront with superimposed pilasters, niches and an entablature between the two storeys which curves upwards in a Baroque manner. High pitched roof with solid parapet. For many years after being sold by the Aldworths, the house was owned by a religious order. At some period, the parapet was removed and the house re-roofed.

New Park, co Kilkenny (NEWPORT, Bt/PB1862; BLOOMFIELD/LGI1912). A late C18 house with rounded ends, on the opposite bank of the River Suir to the City of Waterford. Built by the rich and powerful C18 Waterford banking family of Newport, in whose day the house was noted for its picture collection. Subsequently passed to the Bloomfield family. Burnt 1932.

New Park, co Tipperary (*see* BALLYOWEN).

Newpark, Athlone, co Westmeath (SMYTHE, *sub* SMYTH/IFR). A 3 storey 3 bay C18 block joined on one side to a gabled wing with a round-headed window in an

arched recess by a screen wall with niches; probably there was originally a similar wing and screen wall on the other side. Diocletian window in centre of top storey, above Wyatt window. The seat of a branch of the Lyster family; passed through marriage to the Smythe family. Now an hotel.

Newport House, Newport, co Mayo (O'DONEL, Bt/PB1889). A 2 storey house of different periods of Georgian; with a front of 5 bays between 2 3 sided bows and a higher wing at right angles which has an elevation of 4 bays and a shallow curved bow. Handsome staircase hall with wide arches and plasterwork of 1820s; stairs of wood, with balustrade of plain slender uprights; curving gallery. Passed after the death of Sir George Clendinning O'Donel, 5th and last Bt, 1889, to his niece, Melicent Agnes (*née* O'Donel), wife of Edwin Thomas, who assumed the additional surname of O'Donel. Now an hotel.

Newstown, Tullow, co Carlow (EUSTACE-DUCKETT/IFR). A late-Georgian house with a pillared porch, built 1824–28 to the design of Thomas Alfred Cobden, of Carlow and James Sands, of London; incorporating an earlier house said to date from C17. Sold 1973.

Newtown, co Leix (*see* EDMONDSBURY).

Newtownbarry

Newtownbarry, co Wexford (BARRY/IFR; MAXWELL, FARNHAM, B/PB; HALL-DARE/IFR). The estate of Newtonbarry originally belonged to a branch of the Barrys; passed to the Farnhams with the marriage of Judith Barry to John Maxwell, afterwards 1st Lord Farnham, 1719. Subsequently acquired by the Hall-Dare family, who built the present house 1860s, to the design of Sir Charles Lanyon. It is in a rather restrained Classical style, of rough ashlar; the windows have surrounds of smooth ashlar, with blocking. 2 storey; asymmetrical entrance front, with 2 bays projecting at one end; against this projection is set a balustraded open porch. Lower 2 storey service wing. Eaved roof on plain cornice. Impressive staircase.

Newtown Anner

Newtown Anner, Clonmel, co Tipperary (OSBORNE, Bt/PB; OSBORNE/LGI1863; BEAUCLERK, ST ALBANS, D/PB). A 2 storey late-Georgian house with a front of 9 bays, the 3 outer bays on either side breaking forwards and rising an extra storey above the centre to form rather wide roof pavilions. Doorway with engaged columns and large semi-circular fanlight over door and sidelights. 2 storey curved bow at side. Fine saloon. The seat of the Osborne family; inherited by Catharine (*née* Osborne), wife of Ralph Bernal, MP, the C19 Radical politician, who assumed the name of Osborne; passed eventually to their grandson, 12th Duke of St Albans.

Newtown Bond, nr Edgeworthstown, co Longford (BOND/LGI1958). An early or mid-C18 gable-ended house of 3 storeys and 5 bays. Window surrounds with keystones in all three storeys. Fanlighted doorway with sidelights and baseless pediment carried on engaged columns.

Newtown Hill, Leixlip, co Kildare. A C18 house in the Palladian style consisting of a 2 storey 3 bay pedimented centre block joined by curved sweeps to wings with Gothic-glazed Venetian windows. The doorcase and other features are modern but appropriate. In 1814, the residence of Thomas Hind.

R

Newtown House, Termonfeckin, co Louth (MCCLINTOCK/IFR; SMYTH/IFR). A Victorian house in a mixture of Italianate and late-Georgian styles. 2 storey; 3 bay front with 3 light Romanesque window in centre above Ionic portico with latticed balustrade. Adjoining front of 7 bays, with pediment above central Wyatt window and pilastered enclosed porch with latticed balustrade. High-pitched eaved roof on bracket cornice. Hall divided by screen of Ionic columns; rooms with modillion cornices and friezes of plasterwork. Now owned by the Irish Countrywomen's Association.

Newtown House, Tramore, co Waterford (POWER/IFR). A mid-C18 block with the wall carried up to be the roof parapet, to which 2 storey wings with eaved roofs were added C19. Fanlighted doorway with pillars; C19 porch. The house is partly weather-slated. Wide friezes of plasterwork in drawing room and dining room. Bought *ca* 1790 by Joseph Power; sold 1858 to Pierce Power, who was of another branch of the same family. Sold 1913 after the death of Patrick Power, MP, a member of the Irish Nationalist Party, to the father of the present owner, Miss N. Hynes.

Newtown Park, Blackrock, co Dublin (CLOSE/LG1937Supp; MAINWARING-BURTON/IFR; MCGUIRE, *sub* CORBALLIS/IFR). A late C18 bow-ended house of 2 storeys over a basement. Entrance front of 3 bays, centre bay breaking forward with later single-storey portico of coupled Corinthian columns. 5 bay garden front, centre bay breaking forward with Wyatt windows. Very sophisticated plan; circular entrance hall, oval central room with Adamesque ceiling incorporating painted oval. Possibly designed under the influence of James Gandon; Ralph Ward, Surveyor-General of Ordnance, who lived here before his death 1788, having been the patron of Gandon's friend William Ashford, 1st President of the Royal Hibernian Academy. It could equally well, however, be an early work of Richard (afterwards Sir Richard) Morrison, having a likeness to several of his villas. In 1792, Alexander Crookshank, the Judge, was living here; in 1805 it was the home of John Armit, a wealthy Army agent and banker who was Sec of the Ordnance Board. Sold 1839 to H.S. Close; passed by inheritance from the Closes to the Burton family. Bought 1946 by Senator Edward McGuire, who had a notable collection of C17 and C18 European paintings here; and who sold it 1976.

Northland House

Noan, Thurles, co Tipperary (TAYLOR/LGI1912; ARMITAGE/IFR). A 2 storey 5 bay late-Georgian house. Doorway with large fanlight above 4 engaged Doric columns of stone.

Norman's Grove

Norman's Grove, Clonee, co Meath (WARD/IFR). A 2 storey C18 house with a high roof, incorporating what is said to be part of an earlier house. Long front with irregular fenestration; 2 storey gabled porch with round-headed window above entrance doorway. Underground passage leading from beneath the stairs to a field some distance from the house. In 1814, the residence of Luke Eiffe; in 1837, of J. Shanley. Owned *ca* 1849 by Capt Armit, who sold it *ca* that time to Christopher Ward. Now owned by Mr L.J. Ward.

Northesk, Glanmire, co Cork. An early C19 castellated house with several slender round towers. In 1837, it was the seat of J. Carnegie, who presumably built it, or at any rate gave it its name, being, or imagining himself to be, a cadet of the Carnegies, Earls of Northesk (*see* PB).

Northland House, Dungannon, co Tyrone (KNOX, RANFURLY, E/PB). A large, 3 storey, irregular classical mansion, probably of more than one date but in its final form *ca* 1840. Principal front consisting of 5 bays between 2 projecting pedimented end bays, extended to the left by a 9 bay wing of the same height and style, but set a little back. At the junction of the main block and the wing, a single-storey projecting porch of 3 bays, fronted by a portico of 4 Ionic columns. Along the adjoining front, an Ionic colonnade with a central pediment, running into an orangery at one end. Jutting out from the orangery, a conservatory of graceful curving glass, in the Crystal Palace manner. Rising from the corner of the main body of the house, behind the orangery, a belfry with Ionic columns. The house is now completely demolished. One of the Classical gate lodges survives.

Northlands, Shercock, co Cavan (ADAMS/IFR). A simple 2 storey 3 bay late-Georgian house with a projecting porch. Built 1822 by Very Rev Samuel Adams, Dean of Cashel.

O

Oakgrove, Killinardrish, co Cork (BOWEN-COLTHURST/IFR). A 2 storey Georgian house with a lower castellated wing; the main block having a front of 2 bays on either side of a fanlighted doorway below 2 windows close together. The house was burnt *ca* 1920; it has been rebuilt as a square modern house attached to the castellated wing.

Oakley Park, Kells, co Meath (BOMFORD/IFR). Originally a square c18 house, with a 3 bay front and a long hall with an apse at its inner end where a doorway led to the inner hall, containing a partly curving staircase. Bought by the Bomfords during the minority of George Bomford, and enlarged; stylistically, and from an unsigned and undated plan in existence, it would appear that the work was done soon after George Bomford came of age 1832. The house was almost doubled in size by adding a new block to its front; of the same length as the original block, and nearly as deep. The new front, of stucco with stone facings, is of 2 storeys and 3 bays, with a tripartite window above a single-storey portico of fluted Doric columns. Inside, the addition provided a new entrance hall behind which was an impressive staircase hall at right angles to it, with a bifurcating staircase behind a screen of columns. At the top of the stairs was a an upper hall lit by a glass dome and surrounded by fluted columns and pilasters. To the left of the hall and staircase hall was a large drawing room *en suite* with the somewhat smaller drawing room of the original block. The original dining room, entered from the staircase hall, continued to serve as such; but the original entrance hall, deprived of its light, became a back lobby and the original stairs the back stairs. A small 2 storey addition was made later at the back of the original block. Sold 1955 by Lt-Col George Bomford to Mr Laurence McGuinness, who has reduced the size of the house by demolishing the original block and the 2nd addition, leaving only the main c19 addition, which he has remodelled internally, to provide more rooms.

Oakly Park, Celbridge, co Kildare (NAPIER, *sub* NAPIER AND ETTRICK, B/PB; MAUNSELL/IFR). A fine 3 storey ashlar-faced house of 1724, built for Arthur Price, Vicar of Celbridge—who proposed to Swift's "Vanessa", and who later became Bishop of Meath and Archbishop of Cashel—possibly to the design of Thomas Burgh, MP, Engineer and Surveyor-General for Ireland. 7 bay front, 3 bay central breakfront; doorway with segmental pediment, solid roof

Oakly Park, co Kildare

parapet, bold string courses. Various subsequent alterations. Later in c18, it was the home of Lady Sarah Napier, sister of Lady Louisa Conolly, of Castletown (*qv*), and of Emily, Duchess of Leinster, mother of the United Irish leader, Lord Edward Fitz-Gerald. Lady Sarah, born Lady Sarah Lennox, daughter of 2nd Duke of Richmond, was the love of the young George III, who, according to a legend, wrote the song, *The Lass of Richmond Hill*, about her. Oakly afterwards became the seat of a branch of the Maunsell family; it now belongs to a religious order.

Oak Park, Carlow, co Carlow (BRUEN/IFR). A large early c19 Classical mansion by William Vitruvius Morrison. 2 storey; entrance front consisting of 5 bay centre block with pedimented portico of 4 giant Ionic columns, prolonged by wings of the same height, at first set back behind short colonnades of coupled columns and then returning forwards with pedimented Wyatt windows in their ends. Rather dull and amorphous 13 bay garden front, inadequately relieved by having 4 separate bays breaking forward with Wyatt win-

Oak Park, co Carlow

Oak Park, co Carlow: ceiling with key-hole pattern

Oak Park, co Carlow: Hall

dows, and by a pair of somewhat paltry single-storey balustraded curved bows. Rich interior plasterwork in Morrison's characteristic style. Hall with Ionic columns, free-standing, coupled and engaged; frieze of swags; ceiling of geometrical ribs. Damaged by fire *ca* 1910 and afterwards restored; sold *ca* 1957; now an agricultural research centre.

Oak Park, co Kerry

Oak Park, Tralee, co Kerry (BATEMAN/ LGI1912; SANDES and COLLIS-SANDES/LGI-1912). A High Victorian Ruskinian-Gothic house of polychrome brick; built 1857–60 by M. F. Sandes, a younger son of the Sandes family of Sallow Glen (*qv*), presumably with money which he had made as a lawyer in India. Designed by William Atkins, of Cork; who, as Mr Jeremy Williams has pointed out, was so proud of it that he put his initials over the door. Large trefoil-arched porch, on square piers; windows combining trefoil and ogee arches. Similar arches in the hall, on Gothic columns with polished marble shafts, screening the staircase, which is of wood, its balustrade decorated with brass flowers. The stables of the old Bateman house stand by the drive up to the later house. Oak Park is now the headquarters of the County Committee of Agriculture.

Oakport, Boyle, co Roscommon (GOFF/ LGI1912; KING, KINGSTON, E/PB). A 2 storey house with two adjoining 5 bay fronts; one having a large round-headed window in both storeys at one end.

Odell Ville, Ballingarry, co Limerick (MORONY/LGI1937Supp; LLOYD/IFR). A 2 storey 5 bay house built *ca* 1780 by John Odell. High roof; door with sidelights. Gothic gate-lodge. Passed by inheritance to the Morony family and then to the Lloyds; now the home of Mrs Allott (*née* Lloyd).

O'Harabrook, Ballymoney, co Antrim (O'HARA/LGI1912; CRAMSIE/IFR). A 2 storey 4 bay mid-C18 block, possibly built as a coaching inn, with 2 storey 4 bay wings added later, set a little back. Continuous parapet with ball finials running along roofline of both centre block and wings. Drawing room ceiling with unusual ovolo mouldings, clearly part of the original decoration.

Oldbridge

Oldbridge, nr Slane, co Meath (COD-DINGTON/IFR). A 3 storey C18 block, close to where the Battle of the Boyne was fought, enlarged *ca* 1832 to the design of Frederick Darley, who added 2 storeys to each of the existing single-storey wings, so that the original house became the central break-front of a much longer 3 storey facade.

Old Conna Hill

Old Conna Hill, Shankill, co Dublin (RIALL/LGI1958). A High Victorian Tudor-Gothic house by Sir Charles Lanyon and William Henry Lynn, built *ca* 1860 for Phineas Riall. The house, which has steeply-pointed gables and rectangular mullioned windows with trefoil-headed lights, is more Gothic than Tudor, with a decidedly ecclesiastical air; in fact the grouping of elements—the rather squashed church porch, the fleche, the odd little buttresses—is rather reminiscent of Lanyon's and Lynn's Unitarian Church on Stephen's Green, in Dublin. The interior of the house is sombrely rich: panelling, carved woodwork, elaborately moulded ceilings and stained glass.

Old Connaught House, Shankill, co Dublin (PLUNKET, B/PB). A plain early C19 Classical house.

Old Court, Douglas, co Cork (GOOLD, Bt/PB; GLASGOW/LGI1863). A double bow-fronted Georgian house. Owned in recent years by a religious order.

Old Court, co Down

Old Court, Strangford, co Down (FITZ-GERALD, LEINSTER, D/PB; DE ROS, B/PB). A low, rambling 2 storey house of mid-C19 aspect, with many gables, some of them set on 3 sided bows, the angle walls of which curved outwards under the eaves, so that some of the upstairs windows were bent in a vertical plane, like the windows in the stern of an old man-of-war. Bargeboards on the gables, hood mouldings over the windows. In a magnificent setting at the entrance to Strangford harbour. Burnt *ca* 1920; the family now live in a simple 2 storey 8 bay house with astragals. In the grounds, in a glade on the edge of the sea, is a delightful chapel, originally built 1629 by 16th Earl of Kildare's agent, Valentine Payne, and greatly enlarged and altered C19. Old Court went to a junior branch of the Leinsters, descended from Lord Henry FitzGerald, (a younger son of 1st Duke of Leinster and a brother of the patriot, Lord Edward), who married Charlotte, Baroness de Ros in her own right.

Old Dromore, Mallow, co Cork (DEANE, MUSKERRY, B/PB; WILLIAMSON, *sub* HEARD/ LGI1969). Originally a house built *ca* 1750 by Sir Matthew Deane, 4th Bt, MP; of stucco with cut-stone facings, and with a Venetian window and door in one of its fronts. A new and larger house was built by Sir Robert Deane, 6th Bt, *ca* 1781, the year in which he became 1st Lord Muskerry; but dismantled almost immediately afterwards. According to the story, he was so horrified by its cost that he ordered it to be dismantled and the materials sold after he had inhabited it for only 1 night. A plain square 2 storey late-Georgian house with a 5 bay front was subsequently built here. In C19, Old Dromore became the seat of the Williamson family.

Old Head, Kinsale, co Cork (DE COURCY, KINGSALE, B/PB). A house with a pediment and a balustraded roof crowned with a spire, built towards the end of C17 by 23rd Lord Kingsale near the old castle of his family on the Old Head of Kinsale; a site as windswept as that of Loftus Hall, co Wexford (*qv*). The house was abandoned by the family after the death of 24th Baron 1759; it has long disappeared, though there is a ruin on the Old Head which may possibly be a remnant of it.

Oldtown

Oldtown, Naas, co Kildare, (DE BURGH/
IFR). One of Ireland's 1st Palladian winged
houses, built *ca* 1709 by Thomas Burgh,
MP, Engineer and Surveyor-General for
Ireland, to his own design. 2 storey centre
block with 2 storey wings; centre block
adorned with pairs of Ionic pilasters, rising
to just below the 1st floor windows; each
pair carrying its own short section of
entablature; wings also adorned with pairs
of Ionic pilasters carrying massive entablatures. The centre block was burnt 1950s; a
house has now been made out of one of the
wings.

Oranmore Castle

**Oranmore Castle, Oranmore, co Gal-
way** (BLAKE/IFR; LESLIE-KING/IFR). A tall
and massive C14 and C15 castle on the shore
of Galway Bay, lapped on 2 sides by the sea
at high tide. Originally the seat of a branch
of the Blakes, who built a large house
attached to the castle; where, from 1773 to
1784, Xaverius & Isabella Blake lived and
squandered away their inheritance. After
the Blakes left Oranmore, the house was
demolished and the stone used to build pig-
sties; and the castle was unroofed, remaining in this state until 1947, when it was
bought by Lady Leslie, wife of Sir Shane
Leslie, the writer; who re-roofed it and
made it habitable and gave it to her
daughter, Mrs Leslie-King, who is also
well-known as a writer under the name of
Anita Leslie. Between 1950 and 1960, Mrs
Leslie-King and her husband, Cmdr Bill
Leslie-King (also a writer, who sailed solo
round the world 1973), added a 2 storey
wing joined to the castle by a single-storey
range; these additions being of cut-stone.
The castle contains 2 very large vaulted
halls.

Oriel Temple

Oriel Temple, Collon, co Louth (FOSTER,
sub MASSEREENE AND FERRARD, V/PB; FOSTER-
VESEY-FITZGERALD/IFR). A house which
seems to have started literally as a temple or
garden pavilion, built 1780s by John Foster
(afterwards 1st Lord Oriel), the last
Speaker of the Irish House of Commons
before the Union; who presumably then
lived in the earlier house, known simply as
Collon, where Arthur Young had visited his
father, Chief Baron Anthony Foster,
describing him as "this prince of im-
provers". The temple had a pedimented
portico and a room painted by Peter de
Gree (paintings now at Luttrellstown
Castle, co Dublin—*qv*), who was at work on
it when Rev Daniel Beaufort came here
1788, and remarked on how the artist
seemed "in bad health". At this period, the
demesne, which was noted for its beauty,
contained several ornamental buildings,
including a rustic cottage, where John
Foster's wife and daughter put on stuff
gowns and played at being cottagers, in the
manner of Marie-Antoinette; and a grotto
which his wife and daughter decorated with
shells, stones and coloured glass. *Ca* 1812
the Speaker—then over 70 though he was to
live to be nearly 88—added to the temple,
so that it became a somewhat amorphous 2
storey house, with the entrance doorway in
a bow, under a pedimented porch with 2
fluted Doric columns. The temple portico
was at the end of one of its fronts, and
looked unrelated to the rest. Now Mellifont
Cistercian Abbey and very much altered.

Ormeau

Ormeau, co Down (CHICHESTER, DONE-
GALL, M/PB). A rambling Tudor-Revival
house by William Vitruvius Morrison in
the south-eastern outskirts of Belfast. Many
gables; a tall polygonal turret with a cupola
at one corner, a smaller turret with a
pyramidal roof at the back of the house. The
seat of 2nd & 3rd Marquesses of Donegall;
the original seat of their family, Belfast
Castle (*qv*), having been destroyed by fire
1708 and not rebuilt. 3rd Marquess found
Ormeau inconvenient and badly constructed, and abandoned it towards the end
of 1860s in favour of the new Belfast Castle
(*qv*).

Ounavarra

**Ounavarra, Courtown Harbour, co
Wexford** (RICHARDS/LGI1912; HOWARD,
sub WICKLOW, E/PB). A pleasant early C19
house in a mild Tudor-Revival style
romantically situated above the Ounavarra
River. Of 2 storeys; entrance front with a
gabled projection at either side. Low-
pitched gables with wavy bargeboards;
mullioned and latticed windows; gabled
porch not centrally placed, alongside a large
rectangular mullioned and gabled window
lighting the staircase, which has the appearance of the window of a great hall. Elegant
bow-fronted conservatory. Garden front
with gabled projection and shallow curved
bow. C19 interior plasterwork; foliage ornament in hall and staircase hall; decorated
cornice in drawing room. Spacious staircase
hall with staircase of polished wood. Drawing room running the whole depth of the
house, extending into garden front bow and
divided by an arch. Originally owned by the
Richards family, of Ardamine (*qv*); leased
early in the present century to Mr & Mrs
M. W. Shuldham (*see* LGI1912). Subsequently the home of Mr William Words-
worth, and later of Miss Katharine Howard.
Now the home of Mr & Mrs Kenneth
O'Reilly-Hyland, who have decorated the
house most attractively, and laid out a fine
woodland garden above the river.

Owenmore

Owenmore, Crossmolina, co Mayo
(ORME/LGI1912; MCCAUSLAND/IFR). An early
C19 house of 2 storeys over a high basement.
Entrance front of 5 bays; single-storey
Doric portico with die up broad flight of
steps. Entablatures on console brackets
over windows of lower storey. Side elevation of 1 bay with a curved bow; at the
other side is a 2 storey bowed wing of the
same height and style as the main block, set
back from it and joined to it by a canted
bay. Eaved roof on cornice. 2 drawing
rooms *en suite* with decoration of *ca* 1830;
ceilings with plasterwork in compartments;
pediment over double doors. Dining room
ceiling with delicate plasterwork in centre
surrounded by rectangular frame with
similar decoration.

P

Pakenham Hall, co Westmeath (*see* TULLYNALLY CASTLE).

Palace Anne: the ruin of the house some years ago

Palace Anne: the surviving wing

Palace Anne, Ballineen, co Cork (BEAMISH-BERNARD, *sub* BEAMISH/IFR). A very distinguished early C18 house of red brick with stone dressings, built 1714 by Arthur Bernard, whose brother, Francis, Judge of the Court of Common Pleas, was the ancestor of the Earls of Bandon; named in honour of Arthur Bernard's wife, Anne Power or Le Poer. The house consisted of a centre block of 3 storeys over a high basement and 7 bays, with 3 curvilinear "Dutch" gables surmounted by segmental and triangular pediments, joined by short 1 bay links to 2 bay wings, also with curvilinear gables. The centre block had a doorcase with a pediment on console brackets up a long flight of steps; window surrounds with keystones and blocking; and bold quoins and string courses. There were elliptical windows in the gables. The wings had round-headed windows and their gables were adorned with pilasters and triangular pediments. Panelled hall and impressive staircase; oak-panelled dining room; room known as the Bullock's Hall which had the head of a bullock carved in oak over the fireplace, the model of which is said to have been the head of the enormous bullock killed for the house-warming after the house was built. In front of the house was a large formal layout with parterres and clipped yews and hollies. Arthur Bernard, the builder of the house, though very much a member of the ruling Protestant establishment of Bandon, was tolerant— not to say humanitarian—enough to construct a hiding-hole behind the dining room panelling in which Catholic priests who were in trouble with the authorities could be concealed. The house was lived in by the family until after the death of Arthur Beamish-Bernard 1855, though by 1842 it wore "a desolate and poverty-stricken aspect". Arthur Beamish-Bernard's nephew and heir, another Arthur, who went to America, sold the last remnants of the estate 1875, by which time the house had fallen into ruin. The walls of the centre block were still standing 1956, but were demolished soon afterwards; now only the right-hand wing remains, which though dilapidated still has its roof and some of its windows.

Pallas, Loughrea, co Galway (NUGENT, WESTMEATH, E/PB). A late-Georgian block of *ca* 1797 by William Leeson, built for Anthony Nugent, 4th Lord Riverston in the Jacobite Peerage, close to the old castle of this branch of the Nugents, which had a gable-ended house attached to it and remained partly roofed. Of 3 storeys over a high basement. 5 bay front with plain doorway and flight of steps up to it; blocking round windows. 5 bay side. Balustraded roof parapet and area parapet, probably C19, when the house appears to have been refaced. The grandson of the builder of the house succeeded as 9th Earl of Westmeath when the senior branch of the family became extinct 1871. 12th Earl sold Pallas *ca* 1934; it was subsequently demolished.

Pallastown, Belgooly, co Cork (HEARD/ LGI1969; CATTELL, *sub* MAHONY/IFR). A 2 storey early C19 house in a mild Tudor-Revival style, but with a Classical portico. The seat of the Heard family. Now the home of Mr & Mrs P. A. G. Cattell.

Palmerstown, Naas, co Kildare, (BOURKE, MAYO, E/PB). A house rebuilt in late-Victorian "Queen Anne" style by public subscription as a tribute to the memory of 6th Earl of Mayo, who was Chief Secretary for Ireland and then Viceroy of India, where he was assassinated by an escaped convict in the Andaman Isalnds 1872. One front with recessed centre and 3 bay projections joined by colonnade of coupled Ionic columns; other front with pediment

Palmerstown, co Kildare

raised on a 3 bay attic, between 2 3 sided bows. Mansard roof with pedimented dormers. Burnt 1923, afterwards rebuilt with a flat roof and balustraded parapet. Subsequently owned by Mr W. J. Kelly and then by Mrs Anne Biddle. The well-known caterer Mrs B. Lawlor, owner of the popular hotel in Naas, began her career as cook to 7th Earl and Countess of Mayo at Palmerstown.

Palmerstown House, Killala, co Mayo (KNOX/IFR). A 2 storey house of *ca* 1800, incorporating part of the buildings of Palmerstown Manor Court, which was burnt in the Rebellion of 1798. 3 bay front; Gibbsian doorcase, rusticated window surrounds with triple keystones and other mid-C18 features probably re-used from the earlier building.

Paradise Hill

Paradise Hill, Ennis, co Clare (HENN/ IFR). A 2 storey slightly Gothic Georgian house, with two curved bows and a Gothicized Venetian window in the Batty Langley manner as its doorway, given high-pitched roofs and pointed dormer gables in the Victorian period; also iron balconies. Burnt 1970.

Parkanaur, Castlecaulfeild, co Tyrone (BURGES/IFR). A large and romantic Tudor-Revival house, dating from various periods in 1st half of C19. A small, 3 gabled, 2

Parkanaur

Perryville

storey house, known as the "farm at Edenfield" was built here 1802–04 by J. H. Burges, who leased the estate from his cousin, Lady Poulett, daughter of Ynyr Burges who bought it 1771. Then a "cottage wing" extension of rubble with a hipped roof, identified as the present south wing, was added 1820–21. Finally in 1839, J. H. Burges's son, J. Y. Burges, having inherited money from Lady Poulett, who died in the previous year, enabling him to buy the freehold of the estate, embarked on the building of a higher and much larger wing, to the design of Thomas Duff, of Newry, which was completed 1848. Its cost was specified as not to exceed £5,000. The 3 gabled house of 1802–04, which now has an arched porch, can be seen to the left of the 1839–48 wing with its pinnacled and gabled projection and 2 further gables. The latter wing, and that of 1820–21, have mullioned windows with leaded lights; whereas the windows of the 1802–04 house have mullions and Georgian astragals. Impressive courtyard at back of house, with coachhouse and a tower intended for hanging meat. Rich Elizabethan or Jacobean interiors: long gallery with imported English carved wooden mantel dated 1641 and arched screen at one end; another C17 carved wooden chimneypiece with overmantel in inner hall; lofty Jacobean ceilings in sitting room, octagonal room and drawing room. The latter, which has a strapwork mantel, was not completed until 1854. Sold by Major Y. A. Burges *ca* 1958; now the Thomas Doran Training Centre for handicapped children.

Parkes Castle

Parkes Castle, Dromahair, co Leitrim. A Plantation house on the shore of Lough Gill, protected by a bawn with 2 round flanking towers and a gatehouse. Built by a member of the Parke family; figured prominently in mid-C17 wars; now a ruin maintained as a National Monument.

Parkmount, nr Belfast, co Antrim (MCNEILE/LG1972; ANDERSON/LG11958). A 2 storey Georgian house with a 3 storey return. 6 bay front; single-storey Ionic portico with coupled columns added later, and also Ionic loggia at end of house; the portico subsequently glazed and the loggia filled in with a single-storey projection. High solid parapet to roof. Large and elaborate Victorian conservatory parallel with front of house, but set back; concealing lower service wing behind.

Parknamore, Ballincollig, co Cork. A 2 storey High Victorian house with roundheaded windows and a steep crested roof on a heavy bracket cornice. The home of the late Major W. J. Green, and Mrs Green.

Parkstown, Ballivor, co Meath. A 3 storey 5 bay gable-ended house of *ca* 1770, with a pedimented doorcase and niches in the centre of each floor.

Partry, Claremorris, co Mayo (BLOSSE LYNCH/IFR). A plain 2 storey 5 bay Georgian house with a central Wyatt window above a porch. Eaved roof.

Pavilion (The), co Armagh (ARMAGHDALE, B/PB1924). A single-storey house with unusually wide Georgian-glazed windows, a remarkable portico of 4 Gothic columns supporting a Classical entablature and a doorway surmounted by segmental pointed fanlight. A Regency iron veranda on one side of the portico; a wood and glass conservatory, with Georgian astragals, on the other, obscuring the range behind it. The seat of John Lonsdale, 1st (and last) Lord Armaghdale, a prominent Unionist politician.

Perryville, Kinsale, co Cork (WARRENPERRY, *sub* LUCAS/IFR). 2 houses on the waterfront east of the town of Kinsale turned into a 3 storey art-nouveau mansion with a sinuous cast-iron veranda and an extraordinary horseshoe-shaped arch of plasterwork over the front door by Capt Adam Warren-Perry 1890s. The house boasted a ballroom and a drawing room in the French style, for Capt Warren-Perry hoped to entertain; but somehow he never did; his house was in too grand a manner for late-Victorian Kinsale.

Peterfield, co Tipperary (*see* JOHNSTOWN).

Phillpottstown, Navan, co Meath. A 2 storey early C18 house of 7 bays, with 2 bay projecting ends joined by an open porch. High-pitched roof. The seat of the Phillpott family.

Phoenix Lodge, Dublin (*see* ÁRAS AN UACHTARÁIN).

Pickering Forest, Celbridge, co Kildare (BROOKE, Bt *of Summerton*/PB). A 3 storey Georgian house with a front consisting of 3 bays and a 2 bay projection. In the angle of the projection, an enclosed porch with engaged Doric columns. The front prolonged by a single-storey 2 bay bow-ended wing.

Piltown House

Piltown House, Julianstown, co Meath (BRODIGAN, *sub* BURGES/IFR). A 2 storey ashlar-faced house of *ca* 1830, consisting of a main block of 5 bays with a 1 bay pedimented breakfront prolonged by a 3 bay wing of similar height set back. Wyatt window beneath pediment of main block, above single-storey curved bow with simple pilasters. Framing bands on main block and wing; double windows in 2 outer bays of

Piltown House: Domed Rotunda

wing. Domed rotunda with pictorial panels of Classical scenes, *trompe-l'oeil* balustrades and niches with statues. The seat of the Brodigan family.

Plassey House, Castletroy, co Limerick (MAUNSELL/IFR; CLIVE, *sub* POWIS, E/PB; RUSSELL/IFR). A rambling 2 storey Victorian Italianate house built by the Russells, whose prosperous milling firm of J. N. Russell & Sons was centred on the nearby Plassey Mills. Pedimented 3 bay front at one end of the long facade, with 2 light window above single-storey portico supported by square Corinthian pillars. Aedicules with Corinthian pilasters framing ground floor windows, which are glazed in an unusual way, each with 2 round-headed lights. Pediments and entablatures on console brackets above 1st floor windows. Eaved roof on heavy bracket cornice. The house is said to incorporate a late C18 house of the Maunsell family. Earlier in C18, the estate, which was originally known as Ballykilty, was owned by the great Robert Clive, who renamed it Plassey after his famous victory. He was thus able to take the title of Baron Clive of Plassey, co Limerick, when he was made an Irish peer; neatly commemorating the battle in the territorial designation of his peerage, which had to be a place in Ireland. Plassey House is now the National Institute for Higher Education.

Platten Hall

Platten Hall, Donore, co Meath (D'ARCY/IFR; REEVES/LGI1912; GRADWELL/LGI1958). A very handsome red brick house with stone facings probably built *ca* 1700 by Alderman John Graham on an estate which, before the Williamite War, had belonged to a branch of the family D'Arcy; considered by Dr Craig as a possible work of Sir William Robinson. Originally of 3 storeys; 9 bay front, 3 bay breakfront; splendid Baroque doorcase with segmental pediment, engaged Ionic columns and camber-headed fanlight. Camber-headed ground-floor windows with scroll keystones. Long side elevations which in later years were largely blind; in the centre of one side, however, was a pedimented doorcase. Large 2 storey panelled

Platten Hall: Hall

Platten Hall: Dining Room

hall with stairs and gallery of fine joinery; engaged fluted Corinthian columns superimposed on fluted Ionic columns. Carved frieze below gallery; fluted Corinthian newels and fluted balusters; ceiling with modillion cornice; floor of marble pavement. Oak panelling in dining room enriched with fluted Corinthian pilasters and elaborately carved segmental pediment over door. Pedimented stables at back of house. The house was originally set in a formal lay-out of elm avenues. Mrs Delany (then Mrs Pendarves) came to a ball here 1731. A later John Graham left the estate 1777 to a friend, Graves Chamney; it was sold *post* 1800 to Robert Reeves, whose son, S. S. Reeves, removed the top storey, giving the house a rather truncated appearance. In later years, too, part of the house was derelict; which would explain why the side windows were bricked up. Platten Hall was sold *post* 1863 to J. J. Gradwell; it was demolished *ca* 1950.

Pollacton

Pollacton, Carlow, co Carlow (BURTON, *sub* MAINWARING-BURTON/IFR; DENYS, Bt/PB1959). A 3 storey late-Georgian house, said to have been designed 1803 by Richard (afterwards Sir Richard) Morrison for Sir

Pollacton: Hall

Charles Burton, 2nd Bt; but more likely remodelled by Morrison at that date, having been built earlier. Entrance front with 3 bays on either side of a breakfront with 1 window flanked by small sidelights. Single-storey portico of Tower of the Winds columns. Similar columns, fluted, recessed in the hall, which had a coved ceiling, a modillion cornice and a frieze of rosettes and medallions with crests. Door to staircase hall beyond with interior fanlight. Handsome curving staircase of wood, with turned balusters. Inherited by Grace Ellen, Lady Denys-Burton (*née* Burton), whose son, Sir Charles Denys, 4th and last Bt, left it to his nephew, Mr Jasper Tubbs, who demolished it and is building a modern house in the Georgian style on the property.

Pomeroy House

Pomeroy House, Pomeroy, co Tyrone (LOWRY/IFR; ALEXANDER/IFR). A house built during 2nd half of C18 by Robert Lowry. 3 storey over concealed basement, the top storey being treated as an attic, above the cornice. Entrance front with central 3 sided bow, 1 bay on either side of it; later projecting porch added to bow, with Ionic corner-pilasters. 3 bay side; 5 bay garden front, prolonged by single-storey dining room wing of 1815, with Wyatt window in 3 sided bow and polygonal lantern rising out of its roof. Plaster swags in ceiling cornices of hall and reception rooms in garden front. Inherited by Major C. A. M. Alexander, whose mother was Mary Lowry; sold 1959 to Forestry Commission. Now demolished.

Popefield, Ballylinan, co Leix (REDMOND/LGI1937Supp). A single-storey Georgian house with a curved bow.

Portaferry House, Portaferry, co Down (NUGENT, *sub* DOUGLAS-NUGENT/IFR). A dignified house of 1821, by William Farrell, who apparently worked on a plan produced by Charles Lilley 1790; the 3 storey centre of the house being very possibly a 3 storey block of 1770s. The centre of the entrance front is of 5 bays, with a central Wyatt

Portaferry House

window in each of 2 upper storeys; and a porch with paired Ionic columns and Ionic end piers. On either side of the centre there is a wide, three-sided bow, of only 2 storeys but as high as the rest of the front. Ionic columns in hall and some good plasterwork. The house stands in beautiful parkland overlooking the entrance to Strangford Lough.

Portavo, Donaghadee, co Down (KER/ IFR). A house extensively altered in the early years of C19 by David Ker, who bought Montalto (*qv*) from Earl of Moira. Burnt 1844, rebuilt 1880.

Portglenone House

Portglenone House, Portglenone, co Antrim (ALEXANDER/IFR). A square late-Georgian block of 3 storeys over a basement, built 1823 by Nathaniel Alexander, Bishop of Meath. 3 bay front, the centre bay being slightly recessed; while the downstairs windows on either side of the centre are set within shallow blind arches. Fine classical hall, with screen of columns dividing it from the corridor and stairs. The columns, of a delicate mushroom pink marble, with carved stone capitals of Adam's "Diocletian" order, were originally at Ballyscullion (*qv*), as were some of the chimney-pieces in the house. In 1850 a wing was added by Nathaniel Alexander, MP, containing a new staircase lit by a delicate stained glass dome. At the same time, the entrance front was given a massive porch and Ionic porte-cochère; and the principal rooms were enriched with mid-C19 cornices and heavy moulded doorcases in the form of aedicules. Sold by Major R. C. Alexander 1948; now part of Our Lady of Bethlehem Abbey.

Port Hall, Lifford, co Donegal (FRIERE MARRECO/LG1952). A house by Michael Priestley, built 1746 for John Vaughan, of Buncrana Castle (*qv*). Of 5 bays; the entrance front of 2 storeys over a concealed basement with an attic above the cornice; the garden front, facing the River Foyle, of

3 storeys and an attic; the basement on this side constituting a full storey owing to the ground falling away. The attic, on both fronts, is blind except for a Diocletian window in the central pediment-gable; which, on the entrance front, is carried on a 3 bay breakfront; but on the garden front is floating. The entrance front has a fanlighted doorway with a rusticated surround; there are also rustications round the windows and rusticated quoins. The garden front is quite plain; it is flanked by low, gable-ended buildings running back towards the river and forming a deep court; these were used by Vaughan—who was a merchant—as offices and warehouses. Port Hall is now the home of Mr Anthony Marreco, long associated with Amnesty International.

Portland Park

Portland Park, Lorrha, co Tipperary (BUTLER-STONEY, *sub* STONEY/IFR). A 2 storey late-Georgian house. Front with a 1 bay projection at either end, joined by a balustraded Ionic colonnade. Side elevation of 2 bays and a shallow curved bow. Parapeted roof. Burnt *ca* 1920; now a ruin.

Portleman, Mullingar, co Westmeath (DE BLAQUIERE, B/PB1917). A 3 storey 6 bay C18 house on rising ground above Lough Owel. Entrance door was in pillared recess; elaborate curved staircase. Its name is perhaps an allusion to the fact that Lt-Col John Blaquiere, 1st Lord de Blaquiere, who acquired it towards the end of C18, was the son of a Swiss immigrant. Now demolished.

Portlick Castle, Athlone, co Westmeath. An old keep with a battlemented later wing. In C19, the seat of Robert Ralph Smyth, and then of his nephew, Robert Wolfe Smyth.

Portumna Castle, Portumna, co Galway (BURKE, *sub* SLIGO, M/PB; LASCELLES, HAREWOOD, E/PB). A large semi-fortified Jacobean house, probably the finest and most sophisticated house of its period in Ireland; built 1618 by Richard Burke, 4th Earl of Clanricarde, who was in close touch with the fashions of the English Court, his wife being the widow of Sir Philip Sidney and of Elizabeth's unfortunate favourite, the Earl of Essex; and who built the great Jacobean mansion of Somerhill, Kent, on his wife's estate. Portumna is a symmetrical oblong house 2 rooms deep, of 3 storeys over a basement; with square projecting corner-towers of the same height as the rest of the building. Skyline of battlements and small curved gables with pedestals and balls; 4 bay centre with an additional bay in each of the towers; mullioned windows. Doorcase with obelisks and strapwork, the entrance front being approached by way of two walled forecourts, one with a fine Tuscan gateway surmounted by strapwork. The garden

Portumna Castle: Gateway

Portumna Castle

Portumna Castle: C19 castle

front, which is similar to the entrance front, faces down the length of Lough Derg; it was very unusual for a house of its period in Ireland to have such a wonderful view. The exterior was not altered in C18 or early C19, except for the addition of a curved porch of Jacobean style in the middle of the garden front; but the interior was to a certain extent redecorated in C18. A long single-storey hall extended the full length of the centre on the entrance front, with a drawing room of similar size above it; the dining room was in the garden front, on the same floor as the hall. The principal stairs were of dark oak. The approach to the house was made more than ever effective by the building of elegant Georgian-Gothic entrance gates, from which a straight avenue ran to the gateway of the first forecourt. In 1826, the house was gutted by fire; unfortunately it was not rebuilt, but was left as a ruin, which it remains to this day. The offices were fitted up as a temporary residence for the family, who made do with this until 1862, when a Ruskinian Gothic mansion by Sir Thomas Newenham Deane was built at the opposite end of the park. It was of 2 storeys, with a high-pitched roof and an attic of steep gables and dormer-gables; faced in random ashlar, with banded masonry of a different coloured stone; there were small towers with pointed roofs and arcaded ogee- and trefoil-headed windows in the centre of the elevations, which were of the High Victorian "near symmetrical" kind. At one corner was a slender polygonal tower with a truncated roof. This house was not much lived in by the family; for 2nd and last Marquess of Clanricarde, who succeeded 1874, was the notorious miser and eccentric who spent his life in squalid rooms in London and dressed like a tramp. 2nd Marquess, who died 1916, left Portumna to his great-nephew, Viscount Lascelles, afterwards 6th Earl of Harewood and husband of Princess Mary; because, it was said, he was the only member of his family who ever went to see him. The 1862 house was burnt 1922; after which Lord Harewood, when he came here, occupied a small house on the place. Princess Mary (later Princess Royal) paid a visit to Portumna 1928, which was 1st time a member of the British Royal Family came to the Free State after Independence. Portumna was sold after Lord Harewood's death 1947.

Pouldrew House, Kilmeadan, co Waterford. A 2 storey house of 1814 with a 6 bay front and a pillared porch. Plain but imposing rooms. A seat of the Malcolmson family, who in early C19 founded the great cotton mills at Portlaw, which brought great prosperity to the town.

Poul-na-Curra, Glanmire, co Cork (COLTHURST, *sub* BOWEN-COLTHURST/IFR; MACKENZIE, *sub* GODFREY, Bt/PB). A 2 storey 7 bay Georgian house with an eaved roof. Early in the present century, the home of C.J. Colthurst; more recently, of Col F.W. (*not* "C.M.") Mackenzie & Mrs Mackenzie.

Power Hall (formerly **Snowhill**), **co Kilkenny.** (POWER/IFR). A house overlooking Waterford Harbour from the co Kilkenny side, just above where the Suir estuary is joined by that of the Nore and Barrow. Built *ca* 1765 by the Snow family; a massive 3 storey Georgian block. 5 bay front; doorway with very large fanlight. Impressive hall with columns; splendid oval stone staircase with balustrade of brass uprights. Subsequently owned by the O'Neill Power family, who changed the name of the house from Snowhill to Power Hall, and converted a room into a chapel, designed by Pugin. Demolished *ca* 1955.

Powerscourt: Entrance Front

Powerscourt: Garden Front

Powerscourt, Enniskerry, co Wicklow (WINGFIELD, (and SLAZENGER, *sub*) POWERSCOURT, V/PB). Probably the most famous of all Irish country houses, built 1731–40 for Richard Wingfield, MP, afterwards 1st Viscount Powerscourt of 3rd creation, to the design of Richard Castle; consisting basically of a 3 storey centre block joined by single-storey links to 2 storey wings, in the Palladian manner. The long silvery granite entrance front is of palatial splendour, yet not at all overwhelming. The 9 bay centre has a 5 bay breakfront with a pediment on 6

Ionic pilasters standing on the bottom storey, which is treated as a basement and rusticated; above the pediment is a central attic with scrolled ends. Between the pilasters, in the top storey, are roundels containing busts of Roman Emperors. The links are of 4 bays and also rusticated, with balustraded parapets, like the centre block; the wings are of 4 bays, and the facade is prolonged beyond them by quadrant walls, each interrupted by a pedimented Doric arch and ending in an obelisk carrying an eagle, the Wingfield crest. The garden front, which is of 7 bays between 2 curved bows surmounted by copper ogee domes, prolonged by a 2 storey wing at one side, was refaced in rusticated granite ashlar C19. The garden front is not quite symmetrical and the 2 fronts are not quite central to each other owing to the fact that the house incorporates an old castle, which was of a "U"-plan with 2 wings projecting forwards, on either side of an open court. The present front wall was built across this court, the

space of which was occupied by a large hall with a saloon or ballroom above it. The hall, though long and wide, with an arcade on either side, was low, like all the ground floor rooms; it had a coffered ceiling thickly encrusted with scallop and cockle shells in stucco; so that the room was somewhat reminiscent of the "grotto halls" in German Baroque palaces. The saloon, above the hall, which rose to the very top of the house, was the grandest country house interior in Ireland; an adaptation of the Vitruvian "Egyptian Hall"; with colon-

Powerscourt: Saloon

andes of fluted Ionic columns marbled Siena supporting an upper order of fluted Corinthian pilasters. Between the pilasters in the upper storey were aedicules with engaged Ionic columns and segmental pediments, pedimented recesses and clerestory windows. The richly ornamented compartmented ceiling, which was picked out in gilt, like the capitals of the columns and pilasters and some of the mouldings, was reflected in the pattern of the walnut parquetry floor. The principal reception rooms formed an enfilade along the garden front on 1st floor, opening off the saloon; but apart from the panelling and domed and coffered ceiling of the little octagon room at one end, their decoration was C19; the interior having been left unfinished for many years after the house was built. The C19 plasterwork ceilings, however, were of excellent quality, possibly designed by Sir Richard Morrison; and the rooms contained fine C18 chimneypieces, brought from houses in Dublin. The chimneypiece in the saloon, like that in the dining room downstairs, was brought from Italy by 7th Viscount, a man of great taste who also acquired the splendid Italian Baroque gilt furniture and chandeliers, mostly from a palace in Bologna, which gave the saloon an added magnificence. The ground below

the garden front of the house, sloping down to a pool beyond which rises the Sugarloaf Mountain, was made by Castle into an amphitheatre of grass terraces similar to those which he formed going up the hill behind Russborough (*qv*). From 1842 onwards, 6th Viscount employed Daniel Robertson, of Kilkenny, to transform Castle's unadorned terraces into an Italian garden in the grand manner, with balustrades and statues, broad flights of steps and inlaid paving. The statuary includes a pair of pegasi rearing up against the pool at the bottom of the great descent, and a pair of C17 bronze figures of Eolus in the fountain below the perron of the main terrace which came from the Palais Royale in Paris, having been sold by Prince Napoléon 1872 to 7th Viscount, who completed the garden. The demesne, which is of vast extent, with luxuriant trees and wonderful mountain scenery, provides a worthy setting for the garden and house. Its best-known feature is the waterfall, the highest in the British Isles, which, when George IV came to Powerscourt 1821, was dammed up in order that the monarch might have an even more exciting spectacle; the idea being to open the sluice while the Royal party watched from a specially-constructed bridge. The King took too long over his dinner and never got to the waterfall, which was fortunate; for when eventually the water was released, the bridge was swept away. Powerscourt was sold by 9th Viscount to Mr Ralph Slazenger, who also bought the contents, so that the house remained as it was; and a family link was maintained through the marriage of Mr & Mrs Slazenger's daughter to the present Viscount 1962. In 1974, however, the centre block of the house was gutted by a calamitous fire in which all the contents perished; a fearful loss to Ireland's heritage. The garden and demesne are open to the public.

Prehen, nr Derry, co Derry (TOMPKINS/ LG1869; KNOX/IFR). A very handsome mid-C18 house, probably by Michael Priestley, on an estate which originally belonged to the Tompkins family but came to a branch of the Knoxs with the marriage of Honoria, heiress of Alexander Tompkins, of Prehen, to Andrew Knox, MP; their daughter, Mary, was shot dead at the age of 15 by John Macnaghten, of Benvarden (*qv*), 1760. The house at Prehen is of 2 storeys, over a basement of brick vaulting; it is of rubble, with ashlar dressings. Entrance front with pedimented breakfront centre; pediment has acroteria. 4 bays in upper storey; lower storey has 1 bay on either side of the centre, in which the door and the 2 flanking windows are grouped into a single composition, as at Woodstock, co Kilkenny (*qv*); the door having a pediment over it. All the windows of the front and the doorway have handsome rusticated surrounds, and the windows have keystones. High roof, with high solid parapet. 4 bay side. The back of the house is "U"-shaped. Prehen was inherited 1910 by G. C. O. L. von Schleffer, whose maternal grandfather was Lt-Col George Knox. Herr von Schleffer assumed the additional surname of Knox and planned to take up residence at Prehen, which he loved intensely. Though paternally German, he thought of himself as an Irishman and regarded Ireland as his real home. But being a serving officer in the Prussian Guards, he was still a German subject after the outbreak of the Great War; with the result that Prehen was seized as enemy property and auctioned. He continued to regard Ireland as his home, though he had lost Prehen; and when he died, *Come Back to Erin* was played at his cremation in Hamburg, at his own request; and his ashes were brought to Derry and interred alongside the Knox vault. Prehen has recently become the home of Mr & Mrs Julian Peck; Mr Peck is maternally descended from another branch of the Ulster Knox family, being a grandson of Bishop Edward Arbuthnott Knox, and a nephew of E. G. V. ("Evoe") Knox, Editor of *Punch*, Monsignor Ronald Knox and Rev Wilfred Knox.

Prior Park, Borrisokane, co Tipperary (OTWAY, *sub* OTWAY-RUTHVEN/IFR; WALLER/ IFR). A 3 storey late C18 house built 1779– 86 for James Otway to the design of William Leeson. 5 bay front, very similar to that of the nearby Johnstown (*qv*), the 3 centre windows being grouped closely together. Pedimented and fanlighted doorcase; keystones over windows; good cornice. Owing to his extravagance and lavish hospitality, James Otway was obliged to sell the house, *ca* 1820, to George Waller. The interior was much altered *ca* 1850.

Priorswood, Coolock, co Dublin. A 2 storey 5 bay gable-ended C18 house, extended on one side by a single-storey 2 bay wing with windows set in arched recesses, and on the other by a much higher single-storey addition, having a curved bow in the side elevation. The main block has a pedimented breakfront with a Diocletian window above a fanlighted tripartite doorway. In 1837, the residence of T. Cosgrave.

Powerscourt: Garden

Q

Quarrymount

Quarrymount (also known as **Kilclooney**), **Milltown, co Galway.** A 2 storey house of *ca* 1840, on the borderline between late-Georgian and Victorian. 5 bay entrance front; 1 bay central breakfront with fanlighted doorway beneath single-storey Doric portico. Roof parapet of thin lattice-work; entablatures on console brackets over ground floor windows. Bow at end. Earlier wing at back. Built by J. J. Bodkin, MP, whose grandson was Fr William Bodkin, SJ, Rector of Stonyhurst and Beaumont Colleges and English Provincial of the Society of Jesus.

Quinsborough, Ardnacrusha, co Clare (QUIN, *sub* DUNRAVEN, E/PB; and HEADFORT, M/PB). A Georgian house consisting of a 2 storey double bow-fronted centre joined to 2 storey 2 bay wings by screen walls with niches. 3 sided bows on front, with 2 bays above a plain doorway and sidelights between them. Parapeted roof; lunette windows in wings. The seat of George Quin,

Quivey Lodge

uncle of 1st Earl of Dunraven and father-in-law of 1st Marquess of Headfort; whose 2nd son inherited Quinsborough and assumed the surname of Quin.

Quintin Castle, Portaferry, co Down (ANCKETILL/IFR). A romantic early C19 castle, part of which dates from C17, surrounded by battlemented walls and outworks and rising spectacularly from among the rocks on the sea coast.

Quinville Abbey, Quin, co Clare (SINGLETON/LGI1912). A C19 Tudor-Gothic house with gables, pointed dormers and oriels.

Quivey Lodge, co Fermanagh. A 2 storey C19 Tudor-Revival house, consisting of a main block and a lower 2 storey service wing. Gables, mullioned windows with hood mouldings; and a corbelled oriel.

Quintin Castle

R

Racecourse Hall, Cashel, co Tipperary.
A 2 storey early C19 villa with an eaved roof. 3 bay front; central Wyatt window above porch with pilasters and fanlighted doorway. Ground floor windows set in arched recesses. In 1837, the residence of Avary Jordan.

Rademon, Crossgar, co Down (SHAR-MAN-CRAWFORD/LGI1912). Originally a 5 bay early to mid-C18 house of 3 storeys over a basement, with single-storey wings; built by the Johnson family, whose heiress married James Crawford later in C18. Enlarged and embellished mid-C19; gutted by fire 1950s. Rebuilt very successfully to the design of Hon Claud Phillimore, who lowered the centre block by a storey, and added a storey to the wings, so as to produce a 2 storey 9bay front; the 5 bays of the original main block being pleasantly emphasized by having taller ground floor windows than those in the end bays, which were formerly the wings; and by the extra spacing between the 5 central windows and those on the outside. Eaved roof on plain cornice; curved end bow. In the demesne, there is a handsome hill-top obelisk, erected by the tenants of the estate *ca* 1864 in memory of William Sharman-Crawford, MP, the radical politician.

Raford, Athenry, co Galway (DALY/IFR and *sub* BLAKE/IFR). A 3 storey house built in late 1750s and attributed by the Knight of Glin to Francis Bindon. Breakfront centre with oculus flanked by two small windows above Diocletian window above pedimented and fanlighted tripartite doorway. C19 eaved roof. Hall with staircase and gallery; turned wooden balusters, plasterwork ceiling of a style characteristic of co Galway, with foliage and trophies; rather similar to the plasterwork at Castle ffrench (*qv*). Now the home of Mr Charles Bishop.

Rahanna, Ardee, co Louth (RUXTON, *sub* FITZHERBERT/IFR). A square 2 storey house of *ca* 1820, with a wide-eaved roof and a recessed central bay.

Raheen Manor

Raheen Manor, Tuamgraney, co Clare (LYSAGHT/IFR). A 2 storey castellated house with buttresses along its front and a square tower at one end. A home of the writer and poet, S. R. Lysaght, and of his son, Dr Edward MacLysaght, the historian, genealogist, and former Chief Herald.

Rahinston, Enfield, co Meath (BOMFORD/IFR; FOWLER/IFR). An Italianate house of *ca* 1875, attributed stylistically to Sir Charles Lanyon. 3 bay front, faced in Roman cement with sandstone dressings; pediments over windows, porch with engaged columns. Roof carried on bracket cornice. Bow window at side with curved glass.

Raleigh's House, co Cork (*see* MYRTLE GROVE).

Ramore, Ballinasloe, co Galway (MAC-DERMOTT/LGI1958). A Georgian house consisting of a centre of 3 storeys and 3 bays, between 2 3 sided bows of only 2 storeys but of the same height as the centre. Pedimented doorcase. Eaved roof.

style showing the influence of Norman Shaw; with stepped and curvilinear gables, mullioned windows, an arcade carried on piers and columns along the ground floor and a corner turret with a spire and a belvedere of timber open-work. Small Romanesque and Italianate chapel with campanile tower in grounds by lake. Now a school.

Randlestown, Navan, co Meath (EVER-ARD, Bt(PB). An important early C18 house, begun *ca* 1710 by Lt-Col Mathias Everard, who, though he had fought for James II, recovered the estate under the Articles of

Randlestown

Ramsfort

Ramsfort, Gorey, co Wexford (RAM/IFR; ERRINGTON, Bt, *of Lackham Manor*/PB1917). The splendid mansion built by Col Abel Ram 1751 to the design of George Semple was bombarded and then burnt during the Rebellion of 1798. It was replaced by a modest early C19 2 storey house with an eaved roof and two three-sided bows, built on a different site. Later in C19, a wing was added in Francois Premier style; later again, by which time Ramsfort had become the seat of Sir George Errington, MP, 1st (and last) Bt, a further addition was made in a

Limerick; completed by his brother Christopher. 2 storey; 7 bay entrance front with 3 bay breakfront and bolection doorcase; garden front also of 7 bays with 3 bay breakfront. A 3rd storey was added *ca* 1780, treated as an attic above the cornice; and, at the same time, the former garden front because the entrance front, being given a pillared Doric doorcase. Most imaginative late-Georgian interior plasterwork, with trophies roped swags, etc, on the domed staircase. Future in considerable doubt owing to neighbouring mine.

The Ranelagh

Ranelagh (The), Roscommon, co Roscommon. A mid to late C18 house by George Ensor, built as one of 4 charter schools in this part of Ireland endowed by a bequest from Richard Jones, 1st and last Earl of Ranelagh. 2 storey, 5 bay; 3 bay pedimented breakfront. Large and wide pediment with the Ranelagh coat-of-arms; pedimented doorcase; bold quoins; window surrounds with keystones and blocking. Subsequently became a private house; now the home of Miss S. E. Clarke.

Raphoe, co Donegal: Bishop's Palace. The Palace of the (C of I) Bishops of Raphoe. An unusually late example of C17 semi-fortified house with square corner towers; built *ca* 1661 by Bishop Robert Leslie. Originally of 2 storeys over a basement; 3 bay front, with an additional bay in each of the towers. Early C18 pedimented and rusticated doorcase. 3rd storey, with battlements and bartizans, probably added in late C18. The Palace was still occupied by the Bishops 1830s; it is now a ruin.

Rapla, Nenagh, co Tipperary (WILLINGTON/LGI1958). A C18 house of 3 storeys over a basement and 5 bays. Pediment; central Diocletian window in top storey above 3 bays in storey below. Pedimented doorcase. Now a ruin.

Rappa Castle

Rappa Castle, nr Ballina, co Mayo (KNOX/IFR). An early or mid-C18 house, consisting of a 3 storey centre block of 4 bays, with 2 storey, 2 bay wings. Centre block and also wings had high-pitched, gable-ended roofs, with tall chimney stacks in the gable ends. Demolished 1937, now a ruin.

Rath House, Ballybrittas, co Leix (DEASE, *sub* BLAND/IFR). A C19 Classical house of 2 storeys over a basement, on an estate which originally belonged to the Bagot family, but passed by inheritance to the Dease family 1836. Semi-circular pillared porch. Attractive Victorian domed conservatory at end of house, facing onto a formal garden. The other end of the front is

prolonged by a range containing a domestic chapel in simple Gothic and an archway leading into the yard. Circular entrance hall; handsome library.

Rath House, Termonfeckin, co Louth (BRABAZON, *sub* MEATH, E/PB; MCCLINTOCK/IFR; DILLON, V/PB). A mid-C18 gable-ended house of 2 storeys over a basement. 5 bay front with pedimented breakfront. Lunette window in pediment; Venetian window in upper storey; round-headed doorway with sidelights below. Long flight of steps to entrance door.

Rathaldron Castle, Navan, co Meath. A tall C15 castle with a 2 storey castellated wing. Pedimented doorcase. Gothic gateway. At the beginning of the present century, it was the seat of Capt F. L. H. de la P. O'Reilly.

Rathaspick

Rathaspick, nr Wexford, co Wexford. 2 storey late C17 or early C18 house; 7 bay front, the 3 centre bays being recessed; doorway with segmental pediment; high pitched roof on cornice. Slightly lower 2 storey 1 bay wings. Now the home of Mrs M. Cuddihy.

built by Sir Walter Plunkett, son-in-law of Moyses Hill, MP, of Hillsborough (*see* DOWNSHIRE, M/PB); the subsequent additions and remodelling were carried out for Hamilton Gorges, who bought it 1751 and who was the son, by her 2nd husband, of Nichola Beresford (*née* Hamilton), the subject of the famous ghost story (*see* GILL HALL); they are in the manner of Richard Castle, who died 1751, so would be by one of his followers. The main block is of 3 storeys over a basement, with a 5 bay front; segmental headed doorcase; balustraded roof parapet. The curved sweeps are very wide and have pedimented doorways between niches. The front elevations of the wings are 2 storey; but in their ends, facing each other across the forecourt, are single Venetian windows. The main block is of brick, but the facade was plastered over in mid-C18 remodelling; at some period it was painted Venetian red, of which only a suggestion remains; so that, in the words of Mr Cornforth, "the house has a marvellously faded, weathered look" reminiscent of the villas of the Veneto. The hall, which keeps its old colouring of faded blue, which

Rathbeale Hall: Staircase Hall

Rathbeale Hall

Rathbeale Hall, Swords, co Dublin (GORGES/LG1965; MEREDITH, Bt *of St Catherine's Grove*/EDB; SOMERVILLE, Bt/PB; CORBALLY/LGI1912). A house of late 1680s, incorporating an old tower-house, given a Palladian front, curved sweeps and wings *ca* 1751. The house was originally

Mr Guinness describes as "magic", has a chimneypiece and overmantel and a Doric frieze dating from mid-C18; but the staircase, which rises at the back of the hall, and is of wood, with pear-shaped balusters, rather like those at Leixlip Castle, co Kildare (*qv*), appears to be late C17, as is the

Rathbeale Hall: Boudoir

woodwork in the boudoir and the bedroom above it, which are among the very few surviving C17 interiors in Ireland. Both rooms are panelled; the boudoir has an elaborately carved Baroque chimneypiece and overmantel, with pairs of fluted Corinthian columns supporting an entablature ornamented with foliage, and a monumental doorcase with more carved foliage; the bedroom has panelling with scrolled mouldings and a chimneypiece framed by 2 tiers of carved pilasters. The drawing room has a ceiling of simple rococo plasterwork which would have been put in during mid-C18 remodelling. Hamilton Gorges's son married the heiress of the Meredith family of Dollardstown (*qv*) and assumed the name of Meredith, being subsequently created a Bt; through his daughter, Rathbeale passed to the Somerville family, by whom it was sold in 1832 to the Corbally family, who sold it 1958. After that, it became almost derelict; but was then bought by Mr & Mrs Julian Peck, who restored and furnished it most sympathetically. A few years later, however, it was sold once again.

Rathcoffey, Maynooth, co Kildare (WOGAN, *sub* WOGAN-BROWNE/LGI1912; TALBOT, TALBOT DE MALAHIDE, B/PB; ROWAN-HAMILTON/IFR). Only the gatehouse tower remains of the castle of that important Irish Jacobite family, the Wogans, which passed by inheritance to the Talbots of Malahide and was sold *ca* 1785 by Richard Talbot, afterwards 2nd Lord Talbot de Malahide, to Archibald Hamilton Rowan, the future United Irish leader; who pulled down the castle and built what was described as "a less austere residence" on its site, close to the gatehouse tower. It is of 3 storeys and has a front consisting of 3 bays recessed between 2 bay projections, which are joined at ground floor level by an arcade. As at Ballyhaise House, co Cavan, and King's Fort, co Meath (*qqv*), the ground floor is vaulted over. Now a ruin.

Rathellen

Rathellen, co Sligo. A plain 2 storey C19 house with gables and bargeboards. The seat of the Lyons family.

Rathescar

Rathescar, Dunleer, co Louth (FOSTER-VESEY-FITZGERALD/IFR). A house originally built soon after mid-C18 by the Fosters, and greatly enlarged and altered early C19 by J.L. Foster, MP, afterwards Judge of Common Pleas. The C18 house forms the centre of the principal front: a 3 storey 3 bay gable-ended block with the top storey treated as an attic above the cornice. On either side of it are 2 storey 1 bay overlapping wings. In the lower storey of the wings there are Wyatt windows, set in arched recesses going down to the ground; there are similar arched recesses in the 3 bays of the centre, rising through the 2 lower storeys; presumably these date from an early C19 refacing. The centre block has a deep open Doric porch, a Wyatt window on either side of it and a central die on the roof parapet; all of which would also be early C19. The left-hand wing extends back to form a 2 storey adjoining front of 8 bays with a 2 bay central breakfront and a trellised porch. From the centre of the house sprouts an odd round tower, rather like the top of a lighthouse; with rectangular windows all round it, a frill of pierced battlements and a conical roof. This might be thought to be a Victorian eccentricity, but in fact it dates from early C19, and could derive from the C18 central attic-towers at Ancketill's Grove and Gola (*qqv*) in the neighbouring county of Monaghan. Sold 1850s to the Henry family.

Rathfarnham Castle

Rathfarnham Castle, Rathfarnham, co Dublin (LOFTUS, ELY, M/PB; BLACKBURNE/LGI1958). A C16 castle with square corner towers, refaced C18 and given regular elevations, of 3 storeys over a basement, with Georgian sash windows; also given a straight roof parapet with urns. Entrance front of 3 bays between the towers, which are of 1 bay each; the 3 centre windows in the middle storey being round-headed and

Rathfarnham Castle: Hall

Rathfarnham Castle: Ceiling

that over the doorway, which is now obscured by a later pillared porch, Venetian. Adjoining elevation with central bowed projection; garden front with curving perron ascending to door in centre. Interior of 1770–71, designed by James Stewart for Henry Loftus, 1st (and last) Earl of Ely of 2nd creation. Low-ceilinged hall with Doric columns and entablature, cornice of mutules and pedimented Doric doorcases; formerly adorned with busts on marble pedestals. Principal reception rooms on floor above, which is treated as a *piano nobile*. The gallery or drawing room has a ceiling with a central compartment of circles and semi-circles, surrounded by a border of plaster reliefs which formerly incorporated painted panels, possibly by Cipriani. Another room has a ceiling of painted medallions and delicate plasterwork in square, rectangular and circular compartments. Roman triumphal arch at one entrance to demesne, Gothic gateway at another. By 1837 the castle had been emptied of its furniture and pictures, and its then owner, 2nd Marquess of Ely, was planning to demolish it "and to divide the demesne into a number of small plots for the erection of villas". It was, however, spared and became the seat of Rt Hon Francis Blackburne, Lord Chancellor of Ireland. It is now owned by the Society of Jesus.

Rathkenny, Cootehill, co Cavan (LUCAS-CLEMENTS/IFR). A 2 storey Classical block of 1820s by William Farrell, built for Theophilus Lucas-Clements with money given to him by his cousin, Harriet, whose father, Capt John Clements, made a considerable fortune commanding a ship in the East India Company service. Pedimented entrance front; 4 bay side elevation; 3 bay garden front, facing the river. Strippilasters between windows and at corners; entablatures on console brackets over ground floor windows; roof largely concealed by parapet. The house was originally prolonged by an office wing and conservatory, which were demolished 1920. High, well-proportioned rooms, compactly arranged; simple cornices; drawing room

Rathkenny

Rathkenny: "Tea House"

opening into library with double doors. Across the river from the house is a delightful early C18 garden, full of yew and box, with walls of faded red brick and a Georgian Gothic "tea house". The garden, laid out by Elizabeth (*née* Sandford), widow of Robert Clements, MP, was aligned on the previous house, which stood on the opposite bank of the river a short distance from the present one. Now, as at various times in the past, there is a bridge; but it is said that at one time in C18, the only way to get from the house to the garden was by boat; enabling the men to make merry in the tea house, in sight of their womenfolk but out of their reach. Percy French wrote *Ballyjamesduff* while staying here.

Manor House, Rathlin Island

Rathlin Island, co Antrim: The Manor House (GAGE/IFR). A long, low range of buildings on the waterfront of Church Bay; incorporating workrooms for weavers built 1760s by Robert Gage, former cottages and a 2 storey 6 bay late-Georgian house. The latter is entered by a porch at one end—and at the extreme left-hand end of the whole

long range—with a doorway of rusticated quoins surmounted by an oculus. Various additions were made 1816; a stone archway built 1819; and still further additions 1831. Some of the rooms have Victorian marble chimneypieces.

Rathmore House, Tullow, co Carlow. A 2 storey house of mid-C19 appearance. 7 bay front with die; keystones over windows; balustraded enclosed porch.

Rathmoyle, Castlerea, co Roscommon (IRWIN/IFR). A 3 storey 3 bay late-Georgian house with 2 storey gabled and bargeboarded Victorian wings. Irregular side elevation, larger than the front would suggest.

Rathmullan House, Rathmullan, co Donegal (BATT/LGI1912). A 2 storey mid- to late-C19 house, with a front of 3 3 sided bows, and 1 bay and a doorway under a projecting canopy on either side of the central bow. 4 bay side elevation. Eaved roof; downstairs windows have entablatures on console brackets over them. Now an hotel.

Rathnally, Trim, co Meath (SHAEN CARTER/IFR; THOMPSON/LGI1958). A 2 storey early C18 house built for Rt Hon Thomas Carter, MP, Master of the Rolls and Secretary of State; attributed to Sir Edward Lovett Pearce, though somewhat altered. 3 sided bow; blocking round windows; high-pitched roof. Room with good cornice of mutules and pedimented doorcase.

Rathrobin, Tullamore, Offaly (BIDDULPH/IFR). A house originally built 1694 by Nicholas Biddulph, near an old castle. Rebuilt C19 in irregular Tudor-Revival style; numerous gables, with ball finials; dormers; gabled single-storey porch; mullioned windows. Burnt *ca* 1920, now a ruin.

Rathurles House

Rathurles House, Nenagh, co Tipperary (BRERETON/IFR). A 2 storey Georgian house, 6 bay front with pedimented and fanlighted doorway flanked by 2 narrow windows. Windows with external shutters.

Rathvinden, Leighlinbridge, co Carlow (MCCLINTOCK/IFR). A plain 2 storey Georgian house. Attractive little polygonal gatelodge.

Rathwade, Nurney, co Carlow (FORBES-GORDON, *sub* SEMPILL, B/PB). A gabled house at the end of a long straight avenue. The home of Capt A. N. Forbes-Gordon.

Rattoo House, Lixnaw, co Kerry (GUN/LGI1912). A High Victorian house with trefoil-shaped recesses over the windows and some Ruskinian Gothic dormer-gables.

Ravensdale Park

Ravensdale Park, Dundalk, co Louth (FORTESCUE, *sub* FORTESCUE-BRICKDALE/LG-1972; and CARLINGFORD, B/PB1898; DIXON, GLENTORAN, B/PB; GORE, ARRAN, E/PB). A large and somewhat severe early Victorian mansion of granite, of plain but irregular aspect, dominated by a tall Italianate campanile with an open belvedere at the top. Built for Thomas Fortescue, 1st Lord Clermont of the later creation, the architect being Thomas Duff, of Newry. Partly 2 storey and partly 3, but mostly of the same height; eaved roof. Entrance front with a deep central recess enclosed by a screen of arches and Ionic pilasters and columns; the tower being at one side of the recess. Very long and austere 2 storey 10 bay garden front adjoining. Another front of 5 bays with a domed octagon at one corner. Imposing if slightly hotel-like partly top-lit hall, with screens of fluted Corinthian

Ravensdale Park: Hall

Ravensdale Park: Dining Room

columns and pilasters on two sides; staircase with wrought-iron handrail rising from one end. Dining room with scroll pediments over doors, supporting medallions; elaborate plasterwork frieze and cornice of foliage, and oval-shaped plasterwork surround in flat of ceiling; similar ceiling in ballroom. Library with rather Soanian flat arched recesses, containing bookcases. Domed 1st floor landing with Ionic columns. Became the home of Lord Clermont's younger brother and successor, the poli-

Ravensdale Park: Library

tician Chichester Fortescue, 1st (and last) Lord Carlingford; who married the celebrated Frances, Countess Waldegrave, subject of Osbert Wyndham Hewett's biography, *Strawberry Fair*. Sold to Sir Daniel Dixon, Mayor and subsequently Lord Mayor of Belfast, father of 1st Lord Glentoran; later sold to the Earl of Arran. Finally sold 1920, and burnt soon afterwards.

Red Castle, Moville, co Donegal (COCHRANE, *sub* DUNDONALD, E/PB). An early C18 house of 2 storeys over a basement and 9 bays, with a high-pitched roof and dormered attic; standing behind a protective wall on the shore of Lough Foyle. Piers with ball and pineapple finials built into the wall in front of the house; suggesting that there was formerly a water-gate and railings here. The seat of the Doherty family; passed to a branch of the Dundonald Cochranes with the marriage 1866 of Elizabeth Doherty to Capt Hon Ernest Cochrane.

Red Hall, Ballycarry, co Antrim (EDMONSTONE, Bt/PB; KER/IFR; MACAULAY/LGI1912; MCCLINTOCK/IFR). A C17 tower-house, enlarged by the addition of two wings containing large reception rooms *ca* 1790 and remodelled C19. In the older part of the house there are ceilings of primitive but vigorous plasterwork, which might have been presumed to date from the 1st half of C17 except that two figures in high relief, probably representing the owner of the house and his wife, are dressed in the fashions of *ca* 1735. Originally a seat of the Edmonstones; sold *ca* 1790 by Sir Archibald Edmonstone, 1st Bt, to Richard Gervas Ker; subsequently owned by the Macaulay family; bought 1927 by Vice-Adm J.W.L. McClintock.

Red House, Ardee, co Louth (RUXTON/LGI1912; FORTESCUE, *sub* FORTESCUE-BRICKDALE/LGI1972; and CARLINGFORD, B/PB-1898). A 3 storey late C18 house of red brick, built for the Parkinson family. Front with 2 bay centre and end bays breaking slightly forward; end bays with Wyatt windows in their upper storeys and large tripartite windows below; on one side a single storey C19 bow. C19 eaved roof. Inherited at the beginning of C19 by W. P. Ruxton, MP, whose mother was Elizabeth, daughter and heiress of Robert Parkinson; and by whom it was devised to his wife's nephew, the politician Chichester Fortescue, 1st (and last) Lord Carlingford, of Ravensdale Park, in the same co (*qv*).

The Reeks

Reeks (The), Beaufort, co Kerry (MCGILLYCUDDY OF THE REEKS/IFR). A 2 storey, 5 bay late Georgian house with an eaved roof and a pilastered porch, doubled in length with an addition of the same height and in the same style, so as to form a continuous front of 10 bays, in which the original porch, now no longer central, remains as the entrance. The end 2 bays of the addition project slightly.

Renville Hall, Oranmore, co Galway (ATHY/LGI1912; BLAKE/IFR; HEMPHILL, B/PB). A simple 2 storey late-Georgian house close to the ruin of Renville Castle; built or remodelled 1819 by P. E. L. Athy. 3 bay front; fanlighted doorway; windows with unusually small panes for their period. Single-storey curved bow at side. In 1820s, Renville was occupied by 3rd Lord Wallscourt and his wife, while their nearby family seat, Ardfry (*qv*), was being restored. Later it became the property of 4th Lord Wallscourt. In recent years it was owned by 5th and present Lord Hemphill.

Renvyle, Letterfrack, co Galway (BLAKE/IFR; GOGARTY/IFR). A house of the Blake family overlooking the Atlantic at the western end of Connemara; originally single-storey, but with an extra storey added mid-C19 at the same time as 2 wings were built, so as to form a 3 sided quadrangle. The timber used for the additions is said to have been shipwrecked in the Bay, the Blakes having the right of flotsam. The house was quite plain, with low, horizontal windows; it was weather-slated on the outside and panelled in oak within. In the present century it was bought by Oliver St John Gogarty, the surgeon, poet, novelist, classicist and wit, who entertained here in great style. The house was burnt 1923 and rebuilt by Gogarty 1930s as an hotel; with a higher roof, to provide more bedroom accommodation, and with weather-slating only on its upper storey; the lower storey being whitewashed. It was afterwards sold by the Gogartys, but is still an hotel, having been extended.

Retreat (The), Clonakilty, co Cork (GILLMAN/LGI1912). A single-storey Victorian house in an ornate Gothic style, with an eaved roof and polychrome walls. Demesne bordered on three sides by Clonakilty Bay, well planted with ornamental trees and shrubs.

Reynella, Delvin, co Westmeath (REYNELL/LGI1912; MOUNT, Bt/PB). A 2 storey house built 1793 by Richard Reynell. Front of 2 bays on either side of a 3 sided bow incorporating a doorway with an entablature. C19 eaved roof on bracket cornice. *Ca* 1953, the home of Sir William Mount, Bt, and Lady Mount; more recently, of Mr & Mrs John Roberts.

Rhone Hill

Rhone Hill, Moy, co Tyrone (GREER/IFR). A 2 storey gable-ended house of 1724, with a pediment in which there is a round-headed window lighting the attic. The front is not quite symmetrical; there are 3 bays to the left of the pediment, only 2 to the right. C20 porch.

Richardstown Castle, Ardee, co Louth. An old tower-house with a 3 bay 3 storey house of *ca* 1860 on one side of it. The seat of the Henry family.

Rich Hill

Rich Hill, co Armagh (RICHARDSON/IFR). An important C17 house, built between 1664 and 1690 by Major Edward Richardson, MP. 2 storey with gabled attic in high-pitched roof. "U"-plan, entrance front with projecting wings to form a shallow 3 sided court. 5 bay centre range, 1 bay in the end of each wing; 1 bay on inner face of each wing. Pedimented curvilinear "Dutch" gables on ends of wings; also 2 similar but smaller gables in centre range, and one on the inner face of each wing. Tall brick chimneystacks with arched recessed panels. C18 doorway with Doric columns, entablature and pediment. Magnificent wrought-iron gates, made 1745, perhaps by the Thornberry brothers, of Armagh, now at Hillsborough Castle, co Down (*qv*), where they were taken 1936.

Richmond, Fermoy, co Cork (FURLONG, *sub* HODDER/IFR). A 2 storey Victorian Italianate house, with a not quite regular 8 bay front. Windows with entablatures on console brackets in lower storey, camber-headed windows above; projecting porch, not central, with round-headed doorway and side window; bracket cornice. The seat of the Furlong family.

Richmond (formerly Killashalloe), Nenagh, co Tipperary (GASON/IFR). A fortified house onto which a house of 3 storeys over a high basement was built 1733; long flight of steps up to hall door. In the late-Georgian period the house was doubled in size, turned to face the other way and given a fine bifurcating staircase. The house was partly demolished 1956.

Richmond House, co Waterford

Richmond House, Cappoquin, co Waterford (VILLIERS-STUART/IFR). A 3 storey late Georgian block. 5 bay front with Doric porch; 3 bay side. Eaved roof on bracket cornice. In 1814, the residence of Michael Keane; in 1914, of Gerald Villiers-Stuart. Now a guest house.

Riddlestown Park

Riddlestown Park, Rathkeale, co Limerick (BLENNERHASSETT/IFR; FITZGERALD, KNIGHT OF GLIN/IFR). A house of 1730, probably by one of the Rothery family of architects. 3 storeys over basement; doorway with entablature on console brackets; moderately high-pitched roof. Interior panelling, now removed. Passed by inheritance from the Blennerhassett family to D. F. L. FitzGerald, 27th Knight of Glin, who sold it.

Ringabella House, Minane Bridge, co Cork (HODDER/IFR). An attractive late-Georgian house with a large fanlight over the entrance door and a side facing across the entrance to Cork Harbour and out to sea. Well-proportioned rooms with pleasant early C19 cornices and ceiling rosettes. Now the home of Mr & Mrs Albert F. Clark, who have made a loggia facing over the walled garden at the back of the house.

Ringlestown House, Kilmessan, co Meath (LANGRISHE, Bt/PB). A pleasant Victorian house in the late-Georgian manner, its front improved in recent years by the introduction of a leaded fanlight. Small and elegant bifurcating staircase. The house overlooks a small lake with a grotto. The seat of the Pringle family; sold 1956 to Capt H.R.H. Langrishe (now Sir Hercules Langrishe, 7th and present Bt).

Ringmahon, Blackrock, co Cork (MURPHY/IFR). A plain early C19 house of 2 storeys over a basement. Entrance front with large and elaborate Victorian enclosed

porch of 3 bays, pedimented and decorated with branching fluted pilasters, strapwork and swags. Eaved roof. Plain 4 bay garden front; 2 bay end. Lower 2 storey wing. Old gate-tower in grounds; handsome entrance to demesne with pineapples on piers.

Ripley House, Caragh Lake, co Kerry (FITZMAURICE/IFR). Gable-ended C19 house with eaved roof and 3 sided bow.

Riverstown House, co Cork

Riverstown House, Riverstown, co Cork (BROWNE/LGI1912). An early C18 house, enlarged and remodelled 1730s by Dr Jemmett Browne, Dean of Ross and afterwards Bishop of Cork. The house consists of a double gable-ended block of 2 storeys over a basement which is concealed on the entrance front, but which forms an extra storey on the garden front, where the ground falls away steeply; and a 3 storey 1 bay tower-like addition at one end, which has 2 bows on its side elevation. The main block has a 4 bay entrance front, with a doorway flanked by narrow windows not

Riverstown House, co Cork: Dining Room

centrally placed. The hall, though of modest proportions, is made elegant and interesting by columns, a plasterwork frieze and a curved inner wall, in which there is a doorway giving directly onto an enclosed staircase of good joinery. To the left of the hall, in the 3 storey addition, are 2 bow-ended drawing rooms back to back. Straight ahead, in the middle of the garden front, is the dining room, the chief glory of Rivers-

town, the walls and ceiling of which are decorated with plasterwork by the Francini brothers, probably their earliest work in Ireland and dating from *ca* 1734. The decoration of the ceiling incorporates an oval of allegorical figures representing *Time rescuing Truth from the assaults of Discord and Envy*, based on a painting by Poussin now at the Louvre. The walls are surrounded by panels with large Classical figures in high relief. The spaces between the windows are covered with exuberantly rococo decoration of flowers and foliage incorporating mirrors, which still have their original glass. The house was owned by Bishop Browne's descendants until the present century. In 1950s, it was empty and deteriorating; so that at one stage there was a plan to remove the dining room plasterwork, for fear that it would otherwise perish. It could not, however, be removed from the walls; so moulds were taken from it, from which were made the copies now at Áras an Uachtaráin (*qv*). It was indeed fortunate that the Riverstown dining room was left intact; since, from 1965 onwards, the house was sympathetically restored by its present owner, Mr John Dooley, with the help of the Irish Georgian Society. The rooms have been suitably and most attractively furnished, and the house is now open to the public.

Riverstown House, Monasterevin, co Kildare (DE RYTHER/LGI1863). A C18 house of which all that now remains is what appears to have been a service block, with triple niches on its ends.

Rochfort, co Westmeath (*see* TUDENHAM PARK).

Rockbarton, Bruff, co Limerick (O' GRADY, GUILLAMORE, V/PB1953). A 3 storey house with a 3 bay front, C19 in its facing but basically late C18. Centre bay breaking forward; single-storey Ionic portico; heavy triangular and segmental pediments on console brackets over windows. Curved bow at side. It originally had a spacious 3 flight cantilevered stone staircase in the centre. Now a ruin.

Rockbrook House, Rathfarnham, co Dublin (CAMPBELL, GLENAVY, B/PB). A 2 storey 5 bay Georgian house, with a lower 2 storey wing extending forwards at right angles to its front. The home of 2nd Lord Glenavy, father of the journalist and broadcaster Patrick Campbell (now 3rd Baron).

Rock Castle, Portstewart, co Derry (O'HARA/LGI1912; MONTAGU, *sub* MANCHESTER, D/PB). Originally a charming little Georgian Gothic cliff top "toy fort", with square corner turrets; of 3 storeys over a basement, with pointed windows and oculi in the top storey. Built 1834 by Henry O'Hara; described by Thackeray, who saw it a few years later, as "a hideous new castle". Enlarged after the death of Henry O'Hara, without losing the character of a Georgian castle; passed to the Cromie family, from whom it passed by inheritance to the Montagu family. Sold 1917 to the Dominican Sisters. (*See also* LOW ROCK CASTLE).

Rockdale, Tullyhogue, co Tyrone (LOWRY/IFR). A 3 storey 4 bay house built *ca* 1800. No longer owned by the Lowry family.

Rockenham

Rockenham, Passage West, co Cork (JOHNSON/LGI1912). A very attractive 2 storey Regency house on the edge of a cliff above Lough Mahon. Entrance front consisting of a 3 sided bow separated by 1 bay from a 1 bay rectangular projection framed by strip-pilasters, and a single-storey bow-fronted wing. Round-headed windows in lower storey of main block and wing; round-headed entrance doorway, with hood-moulding on female head corbels. Eaved roof on well-moulded cornice. Garden front, facing the water, with 3 bay pedimented projection and 3 sided bow. Hall with early C19 ceiling rosette, separated by a screen of grey marble Ionic columns from an elliptical staircase hall, in which there is a slightly curving stair with an iron balustrade. Octagon room with

views up and down river. Drawing room with early C19 cornice and ceiling rosette painted in the original colouring of greens, greys and reds; recess at one end with yellow scagliola columns; doors with unusual round-headed panels. Library in single-storey wing; curved wall, recessed bookcases with scroll pediments and Gothic-shaped openings. Originally the seat of the Johnson family; afterwards sold to the Abbott family. Subsequent owners included Col Lindsay & Mrs Doreen Walmsley. Now owned by Mrs Mary Kenneally.

Rockfield, co Meath

Rockfield, Kells, co Meath (ROTHWELL/ LGI1912). An impressive 3 storey 9 bay late C18 house, with an elevation almost identical to that of the nearby Williamston (*qv*), so that it can safely be assumed that both houses are by the same architect. Ground floor treated as a basement, with channelling. Entrance front with 3 bay breakfront; small single-storey Doric portico with die and coupled columns; entablatures over 1st floor windows, pediment over window in centre. Handsome late-Georgian interior. Library with Ionic columns. Curving staircase with ironwork balustrade behind screen of columns, leading up to drawing room and dining room *en suite* on 1st floor, which is thus treated as a *piano nobile*.

Rockfield, Cappagh, co Waterford

Rockfield, Cappagh, co Waterford (GROVE-WHITE/IFR). A 3 storey Georgian house, with various additions: on the entrance front, an unusual 2 storey lean-to, lower than the main block of the house and running for its full length, with a 2 storey projecting porch in the centre. At the back of the house, which is of 3 bays, 2 lower wings at right angles to each other. Unusual 2 storey canopies over the outer windows in the rear elevation; roof of main block on bracket cornice. Belonged to a branch of the Hely family; inherited by Colonel James Grove-White, of Kilbyrne, co Cork (*qv*), 1891. Sold 1932.

Rockfield, Tramore, co Waterford (GALLWEY/IFR). A pleasant stucco-faced mid-C19 house with a pillared porch on its entrance front and a bow on its garden front overlooking Tramore Bay; built *ca* 1863 by Abraham Denny. Fine drawing room extending into the garden front bow. Bought 1892 by W. J. Gallwey who added a wing at one side containing an attractive and unusual long room, with a ceiling of Edwardian plasterwork; it was originally a winter garden.

Rockfleet, Newport, co Mayo. A 2 storey late-Georgian house on an inlet of Clew Bay close to an old castle of the celebrated C16 chieftain, Grannuaile or Grace O'Malley; enlarged and remodelled from 1939 onwards by the British diplomat, Sir Owen O'Malley, and Lady O'Malley (better known as the writer and traveller, Ann Bridge). An extra storey, with a flat roof, was added to the house; and a new 2 bay block built to the right of the original 3 bay front and projecting forwards from it. The new additions are of random ashlar with the joints raked out and well pointed to resist the weather; the windows are small Georgian sashes. The whole effect is that an old castle enlarged and modernized in C18. The principal rooms are arranged round an oval staircase hall, which is original to the house but was raised and surmounted by a lantern when the extra storey was added. One of the rooms is an octagon. The library bookcases and some of the chimneypieces are of macacauba, a Portuguese colonial timber, which Sir Owen, who was Ambassador in Lisbon, sent to Ireland in the form of containers for his furniture.

Rockforest, Mallow, co Cork (COTTER, Bt/PB). A 2 storey late C18 house with a very long front, at either end of which was a projection with a curved bow. Moderately high-pitched roof. Side elevation with curved bow, rectangular projection with Venetian window lighting staircase, and 3 bays. Large rooms, some with curving walls; simple dentil cornices; doors with interior fanlights; double staircase. Sold *ca* 1917; subsequently reduced in size by the demolition of more than half the front.

Rockgrove, Glounthaune, co Cork (DRING/IFR). A 3 storey house of mid to late-C18 appearance. 5 bay front with Venetian window above tripartite fanlighted doorcase with 2 Doric columns and central baseless pediment. The seat of the Dring family, who sold it early in the present century. Having been in poor repair for many years, it has recently been restored.

Rock Hill

Rock Hill, Letterkenny, co Donegal (STEWART/LGI1912). From its appearance, a

3 storey Georgian house of 3 bays on either side of a curved central bow, with a new 2 storey 5 bay bow-ended front added at one end of it towards mid-C19; the new building being of the same height as the old, which was given an eaved roof on a bracket cornice similar to that of the addition. The balustraded porch with Doric columns in the middle of the new front seems to have been added later again. The architect of the new front was probably John Hargrave, of Cork.

Rockingham

Rockingham, Boyle, co Roscommon

(KING and KING-HARMAN, *sub* KINGSTON, E/ PB; STAFFORD-KING-HARMAN, Bt/PB). A large Classical mansion by John Nash in a splendid situation on the shores of Lough Key; built 1810 for Gen Robert King, 1st Viscount Lorton, a younger son of 2nd Earl of Kingston to whom this part of the King estates had passed. Originally of 2 storeys with a curved central bow fronted by a semicircular Ionic colonnade and surmounted by a dome; the facade projecting slightly on either side with recessed Ionic columns framing the 3 ground floor windows, which were flanked by niches with statues; on the skyline of these two projections were coronets on pedestals flanked by sphinxes. The entrance was in the adjoining front which was of 3 bays with a recessed centre and an Ionic porch. 12 years after the house was completed an extra storey was added to provide more bedrooms; at the cost of sacrificing the dome and making the house ungainly, where it had previously been of graceful proportions. With the extra storey, the house had an air of Nash's larger London houses, such as Carlton House Terrace. Either 1822 or 1863, when the house was restored after a serious fire, the porch on the entrance front was replaced by a balustraded Ionic porte-cochère, continued on either side by a short colonnade. The sphinxes and coronets were not re-erected on top of the new third storey; or if they were, they perished in the fire; for the house in recent years had a plain balustraded roof parapet. The recessed Ionic columns in the principal front and the statues in the niches likewise disappeared; and the elevations were not improved by having plate-glass windows instead of the original astragals. At some period, a pilastered orangery was built at the opposite end of the house to the entrance. The house had no "back," the offices being all underground and entered through a tunnel which passed under the formal garden before the other front, a rather ponderous composition with a central breakfront, a fanlighted doorway, Wyatt windows and a mezzanine. Entrance hall with coved and

Rockingham: Central Hall

Rockingham: Round Drawing Room

Rockingham: Gate House over avenue

voluted ceiling. Large top-lit single-storey inner hall with coved ceiling and modillion cornice, open on one side to a very grand imperial staircase, from which it was divided by a screen of Corinthian columns. The staircase had an iron balustrade and partly curving upper ramps. Round room in garden front bow, beneath where the dome was formerly; flanked by drawing room and dining room. Magnificent demesne; wooded peninsulas and islands in Lough Key, one island, opposite the house, having an old castle of the MacDermots on it, to which was added an early C19 folly castle. Straight beech avenue three-quarters of a mile long passing beneath Gothic gatehouse; 70 or 80 miles of drives. 2nd Viscount Lorton succeeded his cousin as 6th Earl of Kingston; but Rockingham passed to his younger brother, Hon Laurence King-Harman, from whom it passed eventually to the

Rockingham: MacDermots Castle

Stafford-King-Harman family. The house was gutted by a 2nd and more disastrous fire 1957; the then owner, Sir Cecil Stafford-King-Harman, 2nd and present Bt, at first considered rebuilding it as it was originally, with 2 storeys and a dome; but finding that this would cost too much he sold the estate to the Department of Lands, which has made the demesne into a "forest park" and demolished the ruin of the house.

Rockport

Rockport, Cushendun, co Antrim

(DE LA CHEROIS-CROMMELIN, *sub* STONE/IFR). A 2 storey sea-side house of *ca* 1815; 4 bay entrance front with recessed doorway; adjoining front consisting of 3 3 sided bows under the wide eaves of the roof, with triangular recesses between them. The 2 outside bows have only 1 window in each storey; the centre bow has 3 windows below and one window and 2 oculi above.

Rockshire House, co Kilkenny

(NEW-PORT, Bt/PB1862). A fine 2 storey house overlooking the city of Waterford from the Kilkenny side of the River Suir, built 1780s by a member of the rich and powerful C18 Waterford banking family of Newport. Long facade with 2 3 sided bows. Pillared hall; magnificent drawing room or ballroom, higher than the other principal rooms; with a ceiling of fine late C18 plasterwork and good doorcases. The house was saved from destruction by Mr Donal O'Neill Flanagan, the architect, who bought it and restored it sympathetically as the offices of his firm.

Rockville, Elphin, co Roscommon

(LLOYD/LGI1958). A long, low and irregular early to mid-C19 house, with Wyatt windows and hood mouldings. Demolished *post* Second World War.

Roebuck Castle, Dundrum, co Dublin

(BARNEWALL, TRIMLESTOWN, B/PB; WESTBY/ IFR). A castle probably built in 2nd half of C16 by 5th Lord Trimlestown; badly damaged during the upheavals of C17 and in ruins for most of C18; rebuilt *ca* 1790 by

Roebuck Castle

Roe Park

having a large early C17 stone fireplace carved with coats-of-arms, the monogram of Christ and an inscription recording that the house was built by John Ronayne 1624. In early C19, Ronayne's Court was the residence of Charles Evanson; in recent years, of Lt-Col John Lucy.

Rookwood, Ballygar, co Galway. A 3 storey 3 bay C18 house. 1 bay pedimented breakfront centre; blocking round windows; single-storey Ionic portico. 3 sided end bow. The seat of the Thewles family; acquired in 1st half of C19 by Edmond Kelly; passed to a nephew, Robert Bayley; sold after the death of E.K. Bayley 1898. Demolished *ca* 1950.

Roscrea, co Tipperary (*see* DAMER HOUSE).

A drawing room was added by Sir Francis Macnaghten, 1st Bt, 1826. The 2 main exterior features are a 3 sided end bow and a curved central bow with a curved pedimented and pillared doorcase. Victorian Classical plasterwork in drawing room and dining room. Large and imposing pedimented stable-yard. Roe Park is now an old peoples' home.

Roebuck Castle: Hall Chimneypiece

13th Lord Trimlestown; sold to a branch of the Crofton family, and re-sold 1856 to the trustees of E. P. Westby, who remodelled the castle 1874; giving it an elaborate 3 storey High Victorian Gothic porch crowned with a steep battlemented gable, and plate-glass windows with pointed or segmental-pointed heads, some of them set in rectangular surrounds with carving in the spandrels. In the hall, he installed a large and ornate Victorian Gothic chimneypiece of carved stone and marble. The castle remained in the Westby family until 1943, when it was sold to the Little Sisters of the Poor.

Roebuck Hall, Dundrum, co Dublin (KING/LGI1958). A compact late-Georgian 2 storey house of 3 bays; recessed centre with Wyatt window and recessed Grecian Doric porch. Wing at rear. The family home of Mr Cecil King, the diarist and former Chairman of *Daily Mirror* Newspapers.

Roe Park, (formerly **Daisy Hill**), **Limavady, co Derry** (CONOLLY/LGI1912; MCCAUSLAND/IFR; MACNAGHTEN, Bt/PB; ALEXANDER/IFR). A long, irregular 2 storey house of several different periods of Georgian; of which the nucleus appears to be a 5 bay house originally known as Daisy Hill, built at the beginning of C18 by Rt Hon William Conolly, Speaker of the Irish House of Commons and builder of Castletown, co Kildare (*qv*). Additions were subsequently built by Marcus McCausland, whose son, Dominick, added a dining room *post* 1782.

Rokeby Hall

Rokeby Hall, Dunleer, co Louth (ROKEBY, B/DEP; ROBINSON, Bt, *of Rokeby*/PB1910; MONTGOMERY, *sub* WADDINGTON/IFR). A house built in later 1780s for Richard Robinson, Archbishop of Armagh and 1st Lord Rokeby. It was formerly believed to be by Francis Johnston; but Mr McParland has shown that Johnston carried out a design probably by Thomas Cooley, and in which other architects as well may have had a hand; and that the design bears a relationship to Lucan House, co Dublin (*qv*); having the same central feature of a pedimented Ionic order in its upper story; though at Rokeby the pediment is not raised on an attic, as at Lucan, and there are pilasters rather than engaged columns. There are 2 bays on either side of the central feature, which is of 3 bays; the house is of 2 storeys over a rusticated basement and has a bold dentil cornice and a high roof parapet. The front is of beautifully crisp ashlar; the steps up to the hall door curve gracefully, and are rusticated at the sides. Staircase of wood, with slender balusters on fluted bases and with delicately-carved scrolls on ends of steps; drawing room with chaste plasterwork frieze.

Ronayne's Court, Douglas, co Cork. A house built 1624 by John Ronayne, altered and refaced C18 and later. Front with many windows and pilastered doorcase. Low-ceilinged downstairs rooms, thick walls; good staircase at one end of the house. Drawing room occupying the whole centre of the house on 1st floor, which must have been the original hall or great chamber,

Rosegarland: Staircase Bow

Rosegarland: Old Tower House with C19 Turrets

Rosegarland, Wellingtonbridge, co Wexford (SYNNOTT/IFR; LEIGH/IFR). An early C18 house of 2 storeys over a high basement was built by the Leigh family close to an old tower house of the Synnotts, the original owners of the estate. Later in the C18, a larger 2 storey gable-ended range was added at right angles to the earlier building, giving the house a new 7 bay front, with a very elegant columned and fanlighted doorway, in which the delicately leaded fanlight extends over the door and the sidelights. There is a resemblance between this doorway and that of William Morris's town house in Waterford (now the Chamber of Commerce) which is attributed to the Waterford architect, John

Roberts; the fact that it is also possible to see a resemblance between the gracefully curving and cantilevered top-lit staircase at Rosegarland—which is separated from the entrance hall by a doorway with an internal fanlight—and the staircase of the Morris house, would suggest that the newer range at Rosegarland and the Morris house are by the same architect. At the back of the house, the 2 ranges form a corner of a large and impressive office courtyard, one side of which has a pediment and a Venetian window. In another corner of the courtyard stands the old Synnott tower house, which, in C19, was decorated with little battlemented turrets and a tall and slender turret like a folly tower, with battlements and rectangular and pointed openings; this fantasy rises above the front of the house. The early C18 range contains a contemporary stair of good joinery, with panelling curved to reflect the curve of the handrail. The drawing room, in the later range, has a cornice of early C19 plasterwork and an elaborately carved chimneypiece of white marble. The dining room, also in this range, was redecorated *ca* 1874, and given a timber ceiling and a carved oak chimneypiece. Rosegarland was the scene of the World Ploughing Championships 1973.

Rosemount, Grey Abbey, co Down (*see* GREY ABBEY).

Rosemount, Moate, co Westmeath (NAGLE, Bt/PB1850; NUGENT, *sub* CLIBBORN/LG1937Supp). A 2 storey house built 1773 by Owen Geoghegan. 3 bay front with a slightly scaled-down Venetian window above a pedimented and fanlighted tripartite doorway. Good surrounds to windows; wall carried up to be roof parapet, with slight demarcation, and adorned with eagles. 2 bay side. Inherited by Lady Nagle (*née* Geoghegan), wife of Sir Richard Nagle, Bt, of Jamestown; afterwards passed to a branch of the Nugent family.

Rosemount, New Ross, co Wexford. An elegant C18 house of 2 storeys over a basement and 5 bays. Fanlighted doorway with diamond astragals; impressive perron with double stairs and ironwork railings in front of it. The seat of the Rossiter family, afterwards of the Byrne family, from whom it passed by inheritance to the Place family.

Rosetown, co Kildare (BATEMAN/LGI 1912). A 3 storey house with irregular fenestration and a pedimented doorway not centrally placed. Long irregularly fenestrated 2 storey wing. Room with plasterwork frieze. In 1814, the residence of John Bateman.

Roseville, Lismore, co Waterford. A house of mid-C19 appearance in the "Cottage Gothic" style, with gables, overhanging eaves and serrated bargeboards. Gothic mullioned windows, some of them Georgian-glazed; glazed Gothic porch; large and elaborately ornamented conservatory with Gothic tracery, lattice-windows and Gothic blaustrade.

Roslea Manor, co Fermanagh (*see* ROSSLEA MANOR).

Roslyn Park (also known as **Sandymount Park**), **Sandymount, co Dublin.** A late C18 villa designed by James Gandon for William Ashford, 1st President of the Royal Hibernian Academy; afterwards the seat of Capt W. Dillon. Now a school.

Rosmead Gate

Rosmead, Delvin, co Westmeath. A large 3 story Georgian block, once the seat of the Wood family, now a ruin; columns from it were used in the rebuilding of Balrath Burry (*qv*). 7 bay front, with 3 bay breakfront centre. At the entrance to the demesne is an elegant triumphal arch with Corinthian pilasters and large urns on the flanking walls; this was brought here from Glananea (*qv*).

Ross, Moycullen, co Galway (MARTIN/IFR). A tall 3 storey late C18 house, with a 3 bay front and 2 bays deep. Venetian window in centre of front above pedimented and fanlighted tripartite doorway. Good quoins; balustraded roof parapet. Lower wing at back. The home of Violet Martin, "Martin Ross" of the literary partnership of Somerville and Ross (*see* DRISHANE HOUSE, CO Cork). Sold by Mrs Mascie-Taylor (*née* Martin) 1924.

Ross Ferry House, co Fermanagh. A house of mixed C19 aspect; Wyatt windows with Georgian astragals; pointed gables, some with bargeboards; and a tall tower capped with fancily-bargeboarded gables.

Ross House, Newport, co Mayo (O'-MALLEY/IFR). A house of different periods, consisting of a plain front of *ca* 1800 and a long rambling range at the back, of which the furthest part is very old. The house stands at the end of a narrow peninsula jutting out into Clew Bay.

Rossanagh

Rossanagh: carved Chimneypiece

Rossanagh (or **Rossana**), **Ashford, co Wicklow** (TIGHE/IFR; CORBALLIS/IFR). A 3 storey early C18 house of red brick, enlarged a little later in C18 by the additon of 2 wings.

Roseville

Rossanagh: Dining Room

3 sided bow and 1 bay projections with slightly curved corners. At a later date again, the parapet was battlemented. Magnificent and very ornate panelled room, with modillion cornice, fluted Corinthian pilasters and elaborate Baroque doorcase. Carved chimneypiece with female terms; carved birds, foliage and flowers round overmantel. Sold *ca* 1940 to the Corballis family, who re-sold it 1950s. The house is now somewhat truncated, having been reduced in size; the panelled room is now in the USA.

Rossenarra, Kilmaganny, co Kilkenny (READE/LGI1958). An early C19 house in the Palladian manner, consisting of a 3 storey 5 bay centre block joined by open arcades to 2 storey office wings running back, their ends facing the front being of 2 bays with pediment-gables. The centre block has a 1 bay breakfront and a central Wyatt window above a Doric porch with acroteria. Entablatures over ground floor and first floor windows; eaved roof on bracket cornice. 3 bay side. The seat of the Reade (afterwards Morris-Reade) family; more recently of the McEnerys. Sold *ca* 1961 by Mrs John McEnery (daughter by her 1st husband of Hazel Martyn, Lady Lavery, whose portrait as an Irish colleen by her 2nd husband, Sir John Lavery, RA, has appeared regularly on Irish banknotes since 1922), afterwards Mrs Denis Gwynn (*see that family*/IFR). Now the home of Mr Richard Condon, the American novelist and playwright, who bought it after it had stood empty for some years and restored it admirably.

Rosslea Manor

Rosslea Manor (also known as **Roslea Manor**, and formerly **Spring Grove**), **Rosslea, co Fermanagh** (MADDEN/IFR). A Georgian house of 2 storeys over a basement, enlarged and altered mid-C19 by John Madden, when a 3rd storey was added, as well as a large single-storey wing; also a pedimented and pilastered porch, not centrally placed, and a 2 storey curved bow on the entrance front; and a pedimented projection of full height on each of the two other fronts. Both the main block and the

single-storey wing—which contained a dining hall *cum* ballroom 90 feet long—had eaved roofs on bracket cornices. Stables with cupola at side of house. The house was largely gutted by fire in 1885, and the parts that suffered were demolished *ca* 1914; the rest being converted for the use of the Forestry Commission. The estate remained in the family until 1930s, when part of it was sold; further sales taking place from 1942 onwards.

Rossmore Park

Rossmore Park: in ruins

Rossmore Park, Monaghan, co Monaghan (WESTENRA, ROSSMORE, B/PB). A C19 castle of great size and complexity; partly Tudor-Gothic, of 1827, by William Vitruvius Morrison; and partly Scottish Baronial, of 1858, by William Henry Lynn. The 1827 range, built for 2nd Lord Rossmore, dominated by a square tower and turret with crow-step battlements; and having a line of gables and oriels. Various small additions were made at one end, in order to enlarge the drawing room; according to the story, Lord Rossmore vied with Mr Shirley of Lough Fea (*qv*) as to which of them could build the bigger room. The 1858 range dominated by a taller and more massive tower with a polygonal turret and cupola, a balustraded parapet and other Scottish Renaissance touches; also by a slender square tower with a spire. Eventually the combined ranges boasted of at least 117 windows, of 53 different shapes and sizes. The 3 towers together produced a romantic silhouette, particularly as the castle was magnificently situated on a hilltop, overlooking a landscape of woods and lakes. In the later Victorian and Edwardian days, Rossmore was noted for its gaiety; the then (5th) Lord Rossmore, known as "Derry", being one of the brighter sparks of the Prince of Wales's set, and author of some lively memoirs called *Things I Can Tell*. *Post* World War II, the castle became severely infested with dry-rot, and was abandoned by 6th Lord Rossmore in favour of Camla Vale (*qv*). Now demolished.

Rosstrevor, co Down (ROSS-OF-BLADENS-BURG/LGI1912). An early C19 Tudor-Revival house, with a long, irregular front of large and small gables, and with many tall chimneys. The seat of the Ross family, who were granted the hereditary distinction "of Bladensburg" by the Prince Regent in recognition of the victory won by Major-Gen Robert Ross in the American War of 1812–14.

Rosstrevor

Rostellan Castle

Roundwood, co Leix

CI8 black marble chimneypiece with keystone. Study with dentil cornice and corner fireplace. After Roundwood was sold by the Hamilton family some years ago, its future

Rostellan Castle, Rostellan, co Cork

(INCHIQUIN, B/PB; WISE/LGI886). A CI8 house at the end of a broad peninsula jutting into Cork Harbour; built on the site of an old castle and possibly incorporating parts of it. The castle, which originally belonged to the FitzGeralds, was captured in 1645 by Morrogh O'Brien, 6th Lord and afterwards 1st Earl of Inchiquin—the notorious "Morrogh of the Burnings"—to whom it was afterwards granted. It was rebuilt as a house some time *ante* 1750, probably by 4th Earl of Inchiquin, a prominent member of the "water club" founded 1720, which grew into the Royal Cork, the oldest yacht club in the British Isles. There is a legend that the building of the house disturbed an old graveyard, and that a woman cursed the Inchiquins for removing the gravestone of her family, predicting that they would never have a direct heir; and indeed, neither 4th Earl nor his 3 immediate successors had sons; after which the male line of Morrogh of the Burnings became extinct. In 1777, 5th Earl, afterwards 1st Marquess of Thomond, enlarged and remodelled the house, to which further additions and alterations were carried out early CI9 by his nephew, 2nd Marquess. In its final form, it was of 3 storeys with a front of 5 bays between 2 3 sided bows; and it had a side elevation of a 3 sided bow and 4 bays. There were prominent string courses on the front, and quoins at the angles of the bows; some of the windows had blocked surrounds. Originally the hall was adorned with weapons and armour, and the rooms contained a splendid collection of portraits. In CI9 a Gothic porch was added, and also a long and low Gothic chapel wing flanking the front, with pinnacles and a Perpendicular window and ending in a squat battlemented round tower. Along the waterfront near the house was a castellated terrace with canon mounted on it, giving it the appearance of a battery. The 5th Earl and 1st Marquess built a tower in honour of Mrs Siddons, whom he entertained here. After the death of 3rd and last Marquess of Thomond 1855, Rostellan was bought by Dr T. A. Wise. It was subsequently bought by the politician and colonial administrator, Sir John Hope-Hennessy, sometime owner of Myrtle Grove (*qv*). It was finally owned by C. J. Engledow, MP. After standing empty for some years, it was demolished 1944.

Rosturk Castle

Rosturk Castle, Mulrany, co Mayo

(STONEY/IFR). A CI8 house on the shore of Clew Bay, rebuilt as a rather austere CI9 castle of rubble and random ashlar. Of 2 and 3 storeys; round and square corner towers of different sizes; a few turrets and corbelled bartizans. Small, simple battlements and rudimentary machicolations; plain walls with few, and in many cases, rather narrow, windows, of the ordinary rectangular Victorian plate-glass type. At one side is a very extensive castellated office quadrangle; which, with its small battlements, its squat towers and its narrow window-openings is reminiscent of an Arab fort.

Roundwood, Mountrath, co Leix

(HAMILTON/IFR). A 3 storey house of *ca* 1750; 5 bay entrance front with pedimented breakfront; rusticated Venetian window above doorway with pediment and blocking flanked by 2 narrow windows; the doorway being of limestone, whereas the rest of the front is of sandstone. Bold quoins at corners of elevation and at sides of breakfront. Window surrounds with fluted keystones. 2 storeyed hall with curving gallery and rectangular opening to staircase; the handrails of the staircase and gallery are in the Chinese taste, with uprights, horizontals and curving diamonds of wood. Doors in hall and elsewhere have shouldered architraves. Dining room with plain cornice and

Roundwood, co Leix: Staircase Hall

was in doubt; but it was acquired *ca* 1970 by the Irish Georgian Society and has since been sympathetically restored and furnished by Mr Brian Molloy, who runs it as a guest house.

Roundwood, co Wicklow. An early CI9 castellated house with turrets and a sym-

metrical facade. The home of Sean T. O'Kelly, 2nd President of Ireland. Rebuilt on a slightly reduced scale after a fire *ca* 1957. Now the home of Mr Galen Weston.

Rowallane, Saintfield, co Down (MOORE/LGI1912). A long, plain, low house of 2 storeys, with a higher block at one end; built 1861 by J. R. Moore. Irregular fenestration, some of 1st floor windows having pleasant little iron balconies. Famous garden, mostly laid out by H. A. Moore—whose sister was 1st wife of the artist, songwriter and entertainer, Percy French—between 1903 and 1955, now owned by Northern Ireland National Trust. The garden contains various turrets, an obelisk made of spherical stones from the river bed, and other C20 follies.

Roxborough, Loughrea, co Galway (PERSSE/IFR). A C18 house of 2 storeys over a basement, with a gable-ended front and a gable-ended return. Front of 5 bays, with fanlighted doorway. The girlhood home of Lady Gregory (*née* Persse), the playwright (*see* COOLE PARK). Burnt 1922.

Roxborough Castle

Roxborough Castle, Moy, co Tyrone (CAULFEILD, CHARLEMONT, V/PB). In 1602, Charles Blount, Lord Mountjoy, built a fort on the co Armagh bank of the River Blackwater, which was subsequently enlarged and given the name of Charlemont. Inside the fort was the charming little C17 governor's house, which resembled one of those hunting lodges built in the castle style in Elizabethan or Jacobean England; with symmetrical bows and clusters of chimneys rising like turrets from its 4 corners. This became the home of the Caulfeild family, who, when raised to the peerage, took the title of Charlemont. The famous C18 "Volunteer" Earl of Charlemont lived mostly at Charlemont House in Dublin and at Marino (*qv*), the seat which he acquired just outside the capital; but some time in C18, a new house, called Roxborough, was built facing Charlemont Fort from the co Tyrone side of the river; and

this became the principal seat of the Volunteer Earl's descendants. This house, a plain 5 bay block of 3 storeys over a high basement, was enlarged and remodelled from 1842 onwards by 2nd Earl; his architect being William Murray. Wings were added of 1 bay and 2 storeys over a basement, running the full depth of the original block; these were in Murray's rather restrained Italianate style; the original block being given triangular window pediments and similar features so as to match them. The entrance was moved round to the side of one of these wings, which became the new entrance front; of 3 bays with a low portico. At the other side of the house, a large office court was built; a feature of which was a row of 4 little octagons with pyramidal roofs, described in the plan as "larders". The entrance door under the portico opened into a hall at basement level, from which a flight of steps led up to a vestibule in the main block of the house, with the staircase opening off it at one side. The space saved by moving the entrance to the wing enabled a new large drawing room to be formed in the original block; but the

Roxborough Castle

proportions of the other 2 principal rooms, the dining room and library, remained unchanged. Some time in C19, the rooms were adorned with chimneypieces and doors brought from Charlemont House in Dublin. *Ca* 1864, soon after 3rd Earl inherited, the house was radically transformed by the

Charlemont Fort

young "eclectic" Belfast architect, William J. Barre. Murray's wings were rebuilt on a much larger scale, so that they became 3 storeys high and projected on either side of the original block. The ends of the wings were treated as corner towers or pavilions, and given high Mansard roofs in the French château manner, crowned with decorative ironwork; but in a typically Victorian way, one of these roofs was made a little different from the other 3. The skyline was further enlivened with pointed and pinnacled dormers, tall chimneystacks with segmental caps, and a row of steep little pediments like saw teeth along the roof cornice. There were similar but larger pediments over the downstairs windows, some of them interlocking and with tympana containing carved heads representing members of the Charlemont family, their ancestors and several of the leading political personages of the day. Barre's exterior ornamentation of his new wings defies description; his biographer, writing 1868, a year after his untimely death, describes it as "the very extensive use of Classic and Gothic detail indiscriminately, in immediate connection with each other". All this ornament was confined to the wings, the original block remaining much as Murray left it; except for the addition of a porch, not centrally placed, on one of its fronts; the entrance having been moved here from the wing. The whole effect was spectacular, if somewhat reminiscent of the Grand Hotel at a fashionable Victorian resort. Both Roxborough and the house in Charlemont Fort were burnt 1922.

Rubane House, co Down (*see* ECHLINVILLE).

Runkerry

Runkerry, Bushmills, co Antrim (MACNAGHTEN, Bt/PB). A slightly Baronial Victorian mansion of sandstone, in bare and treeless surroundings on the edge of the Atlantic. Built 1883, to the design of S. P. Close, for Edward Macnaghten, MP, afterwards a Lord of Appeal and Lord Macnaghten, who later inherited the nearby family seat, Dunderave (*qv*) from his elder brother. Crow-stepped gables; a turret with a pointed roof; pedimented 3 sided bows. Now an old peoples' home.

Russborough

Runnamoat

Shooting at Runnamoat 1893: members of the Chichester and Tempest families with (right), *Denis Charles O'Conor, afterwards O'Conor Don* (see CLONALIS)

Runnamoat (also known as **Runny-meade**), **Ballymoe, co Roscommon** (BALFE/IFR; CHICHESTER-CONSTABLE/LG 1952). A 3 storey house of late C18 appearance; 5 bay front, 1 bay central breakfront, doorway with sidelights and very shallow segmental fanlight. The seat of the Balfe family; passed through marriage to the Chichester family, who assumed the additional surname of Constable on inheriting Burton Constable, Yorks. Burnt 1933.

Russborough, Blessington, co Wicklow (LEESON, MILLTOWN, E/PB; TURTON/LG1965; DALY/IFR; BEIT, Bt/PB). Arguably the most beautiful house in Ireland; described 1748 when it was nearing completion, as "a noble new house forming into perfection"; a perfection which it achieved and keeps to this day, having suffered hardly at all from subsequent alterations or the depredations of time. Built for Joseph Leeson, afterwards 1st Earl of Milltown, a great collector who bought many important pictures; designed by Richard Castle, and begun 1741. Entrance front extending for 700 feet, consisting of a 7 bay centre block of 2 storeys over

Russborough: Stairs and Rococo plasterwork

a basement, joined by curving Doric colonnades to wings of 2 storeys and 7 bays which are themselves linked to outbuildings by walls with rusticated arches surmounted by cupolas. The whole facade is of silvery-grey granite, the detail wonderfully crisp. The main block has a central feature of a pediment on 4 engaged Corinthian columns, with swags between their capitals; the columns rising only through the principal storey, the upper storey being treated as an attic, above the cornice. The roofline of the main block, colonnades and wings is crowned with urns. The wings have

3 bay breakfront centres with Ionic pilasters; the arches in the walls beyond have segmental pediments. The garden front of the centre block is plain except for the cornice and the urns on the parapet; and the pair of Corinthian columns with an entablature framing the centre window in the lower storey. All the principal rooms, which lead from one to the other in splendid succession round the centre block, have ceilings of magnificent baroque plasterwork, some of which are probably by the Francini brothers; they keep their original doorcases and mid-C18 marble chimneypieces and

Russborough: Saloon

also their original floors of inlaid parquetry. In the saloon, in the middle of the garden front, the walls are hung with crimson cut velvet and the doorcases and dado are of mahogany. The drawing room, as well as its richly decorated coved ceiling, has ovals of baroque plasterwork on the walls, which were designed to frame a series of oval paintings by Vernet; these were sold and lost sight of earlier this century, but were recently tracked down by the present owner and restored to the room. The entrance hall has a Doric frieze and a ceiling of restrained, geometrical design; whereas the staircase hall, adjoining it to one side, is in complete contrast, with a riot of the most exuberant rococo plasterwork covering the walls above the stairs, which are of mahogany, with balusters in the form of columns. The slope behind the house was made by Castle into a series of grass terraces, with a pool half way up; it is possible that this layout was meant to culminate in an obelisk or temple, but in the event, nothing was built and the terraces remain unadorned. Castle made similar grass terraces, but going down from the house instead of up, at Powerscourt (*qv*) which were transformed into an

Italian garden c19. The entrance to the demesne is through a triumphal arch, from which the avenue approaches at right angles to the long entrance front, so that the composition gradually unfolds. Having passed to the widow of 6th Earl of Milltown, who presented the majority of the pictures to the National Gallery of Ireland 1902, Russborough eventually went to 6th Earl's nephew, Sir Edmund Turton, 1st (and last) Bt, MP. It was sold 1931 to Capt Denis Daly, and re-sold 1951 to Sir Alfred Beit, Bt, who has made the house a setting for the famous Beit collection of pictures, furniture and objects.

Russellstown Park, Carlow, co Carlow (DUCKETT, *sub* EUSTACE-DUCKETT/IFR). A 2 storey Classical house of 1824 by Thomas Alfred Cobden, consisting of a square main block 3 bays by 3, with a lower service wing terminated by a higher 1 bay block. Singlestorey Grecian Doric portico on entrance front of main block; plain entablatures over downstairs windows; parapeted roof.

Rye Court, Farnanes, co Cork (TONSON-RYE/IFR). A plain 3 storey 8 bay c18 house. Later porch with columns at corners. Burnt 1921. A small house has since been built in what used to be the flower garden.

Rye Hill, Athenry, co Galway (REDINGTON/LGI1899; ROCHE/LGI1912). A late-Georgian house of 2 storeys over a basement. Front of 2 bays on either side of a shallow curved bow, incorporating a doorway; the 2 inner bays and the bow constituting a breakfront. Wyatt windows in lower storey of outer bays, segmental pediments over lower storey windows in inner bays. Parapeted roof. Bowed projection at side of house.

Rye Hill

Ryevale, Leixlip, co Kildare (OTWAY, *sub* OTWAY-RUTHVEN/IFR; DALGETY/LG 1972). A c18 house in Palladian style consisting of a 2 storey 3 bay pedimented centre block with a pedimented and fanlighted doorway, joined to pavilions with Venetian windows by 3 sided links with pyramidal roofs. In 1814, the residence of Rev Cæsar Otway; in 1837, of Daniel P. Ryan. Afterwards the home of Mr & Mrs A. T. Dalgety.

Rynn, Rosenallis, co Leix (CROASDAILE/IFR). A house of 1855 in the Georgian style, with a portico; built to replace an earlier house on the same site which had been burnt. Sold 1935 and subsequently demolished.

Rynskaheen, Nenagh, co Tipperary (WALLER/IFR). A fishing lodge on Lough Derg, built towards the end of c19 by Rev W.R. Quinlan on the site of an older house or cottage; extensively altered and modernized 1968–69 by Brig Hardress Waller, to the design of Mr Desmond Staehli, of Limerick.

S

St Anne's

St Anne's: Ballroom

St Anne's: Staircase

St Anne's: Drawing Room

St Anne's: Lakeside Temple

St Anne's, Clontarf, co Dublin (GUIN-
NESS, Bt/PB; PLUNKET, B/PB). The most
palatial house to be built in Ireland during
2nd half of C19; on the northern shore of
Dublin Bay, approached by a long, straight
avenue which crossed over a public road on
its way. The original Georgian house here,
known as Thornhill, was pulled down *ca*
1850 by Benjamin Guinness, afterwards the
1st Bt, head of the Guinness Brewery, and
an Italianate house by Millard of Dublin
built in its stead. Then, *ca* 1880, Sir Benjamin Guinness's son, Arthur, 1st and last
Lord Ardilaun, doubled the house in size
and made it into a palace comparable to the
best of the mansions that were being built
at that period in the USA by people like the
Vanderbilts, in taste no less than in grandeur; for both Lord and Lady Ardilaun
were patrons of the arts and of scholarship.
The architect of the rebuilding was James
Franklin Fuller, the work being completed
by George Ashlin. The exterior of the
house, which was carried out in Bath and
Portland stone brought over from England,
kept its Italianate character; it was of 2
storeys, with a heavy balustraded roof
parapet carried on a cornice of dentils and
modillions. Entrance front of 11 bays, with
a pedimented breakfront and a single-storey
Ionic porte-cochère; the pediment, which
had elaborate armorials in its tympanum,
being supported by Corinthian pilaster
superimposed on Ionic half-columns. Pediments over all the windows on either side of
the centre; those in the upper storey being
segmental, those below, triangular. Along
one of the other fronts was an arcade with
pilasters; and there was also a great conservatory. Rich *Beaux-Arts* interiors. Ballroom with gallery supported by Ionic
columns, their shafts being of different Irish
marbles—one wonders whether Lord Ardilaun had heard of Sir John Perceval's advice
to William Conolly, the builder of Castletown (*qv*), a century and a half earlier, to
make use of "all the marbles he can get of
the production of Ireland", so that his
house might be "the epitome of the Kingdom". Vast double staircase of marble in
the Renaissance style. Dining room with
wooden pilasters and carved wooden
chimneypiece and overmantel with scroll
pediment, in the Caroline style. Saloon
with Corinthian pilasters and compartmented ceiling. Drawing room with ornate
plasterwork in coved ceiling, and organ in
apse. Palm court. In the gardens, which were
regarded as beautiful even by those who,
like Lennox Robinson, thought the house
too pretentious, there was a lakeside temple
and a long clipped alley lined with statues.
Lady Gregory has left us a picture of the
widowed Lady Ardilaun living at St Anne's
in 1920s, "a lonely figure in her wealth,
childless and feeling the old life shattered
around her". The grand entertainments for
which the house had been intended to be a
background had come to an end with the
passing of Viceregal society; instead, Lady
Ardilaun devoted herself to supporting the
Abbey Theatre and to good works; she
would give tea parties for poor women from
the tenements, and present each of them
with a geranium in a pot to take away. When
she died, 1925, St Anne's was inherited by

her husband's nephew, the Most Rev Hon Benjamin Plunket, former Bishop of Meath. Lady Gregory noted how Mrs Plunket was "very anxious to do what is right for Ireland by keeping up the place, 17 labourers paid every Saturday". In 1939, however, St Anne's was acquired by Dublin Corporation; and in 1943, when it was being used as an ARP store—wits said as a store for fire-fighting equipment—the house was partially gutted by fire. It stood derelict until 1968, when it was completely demolished.

St Austin's, Inch, co Wexford (LESLIE-ELLIS/LGI1958). A late-Georgian house of 2 storeys over a basement; 3 bay front with projecting porch; 3 bay side. Roof somewhat concealed.

St Catherine's Park, Leixlip, co Kildare (STAFFORD-KING-HARMAN, Bt/PB). A house in the Palladian style, consisting of a small centre block with pavilions joined to it by curved sweeps. Bought by Sir Cecil Stafford-King-Harman, 2nd and present Bt, after the destruction by fire of his family seat, Rockingham, co Roscommon (*qv*), 1957.

St Clerans, co Galway (*see* ISSERCLERAN).

St Columb's, Churchhill, co Donegal (HILL, *sub* MAHONY/IFR). A simple 2 storey 3 bay red colourwashed Georgian house with a fanlighted doorway, wonderfully situated on a gentle slope between 3 loughs; bought 1954 by Mr Derek Hill, the artist, and decorated and furnished by him in a most imaginative way; with Morris wallpapers and fabrics, de Morgan tiles, Eastern stuffs and an assemblage of attractive objects from all over the world. Iron veranda at rear.

St Columba's, co Dublin (*see* HOLLY PARK).

St David's Castle, Naas, co Kildare. An old castle with Georgian sash windows and quatrefoil openings and C19 battlements. Formerly the glebe-house of St David's Church, Naas.

St Edmundsbury, Lucan, co Dublin. Originally a plain 2 storey early C19 house; Doric porch with coupled columns. The seat of Thomas Needham. Acquired mid-C19 by William Moran, who had made money in jute in Bengal, and who added 2 storey wings in a slightly Oriental style. Probably at the same time, the original block was given a balustraded roof parapet and pediments on console brackets over the ground floor windows. Sold *ca* 1900; now an old peoples' home. At some period after the sale of the house by the Morans, the Hindu-Gothic decoration was removed from the wings.

St Ernan's, nr Donegal, co Donegal (HAMILTON/LGI1937Supp; FOSTER, *sub* FOSTER-VESEY-FITZGERALD/IFR; STUBBS/LGI1937 Supp; FITZMAURICE-DEANE-MORGAN, MUSKERRY, B/PB). A house on an island in the estuary of the River Eske, built early C19 by John Hamilton, of Brownhall (*qv*); then passed to John Hamilton's daughter, Arabella, wife of A.H. Foster. Subsequently owned by Henry Stubbs, who largely re-built the house, so that it became late-Victorian in character, with gables and ornate bargeboards; but with a pillared porch, which was probably a surviving early C19 feature. In the present century, it was the seat of Hon M.C.C. Fitzmaurice-Deane-Morgan, afterwards 6th Lord Muskerry.

Saintfield House

Saintfield House, Saintfield, co Down (PERCEVAL-PRICE/IFR). A tall double gable-ended house, built *ca* 1750 by Francis Price. Of 3 storeys over basement; 5 bay front with pilastered doorcase. The house was occupied for 3 days by the insurgents after the Battle of Saintfield June 1798. Single-storey 3 bay wings, ending in 2 storey 2 bay pavilions with high pyramidal roofs and central chimneys—one of which has since been demolished—were added *ca* 1800 when Nicholas Price, Black Rod to the Irish Parliament, sold his Dublin house. The interior has been altered at various times; the hall was given a ceiling of Adamesque plasterwork *ca* 1900.

St Helen's, Booterstown, co Dublin (NUTTING, Bt/PB). An opulent C19 Classical house consisting of a 2 storey 5 bay centre block, with a pediment on coupled Corinthian pilasters and a balustraded single-storey portico, and single-storey wings. Balustraded roof parapets. The front prolonged on one side by a lower wing with mullioned windows and on the other by an elegant glass conservatory with a curving roof.

St John's Manor, Enniscorthy, co Wexford. A 2 storey Georgian house with 2 curved bows and a fanlighted doorway between them.

St Mary's Abbey (also known as **Talbot Castle**), **Trim, co Meath** (TALBOT, SHREWSBURY, E/PB). A C15 tower house, built by Sir John Talbot, 1st Earl of Shrewsbury, for his own occupation when Lord-Lieutenant of Ireland; given gables in C17, by which time it had become a "Latin School", one of the pupils in the following century being Arthur Wellesley, the future Duke of Wellington; given Georgian-Gothic windows and a long 2 storey Georgian-Gothic wing added to it early C19. When, a little later in C19, the school closed down, the building was bought by the last schoolmaster, Rev James Hamilton, and was occupied as a private house by him and his descendants until 1909, when it was bought by Mr Archibald Montgomery, who carried out various improvements to it and panelled the principal rooms. The original tower-house was built out of a ruined section of the old St Mary's Abbey, and incorporated part of the cloister, which forms a vaulted recess on one side of the drawing room.

St Raphael's, Montenotte, Cork, co Cork. A large and imposing mid to late C19 Italianate block, of 2 storeys over a high basement. 7 bay front; single-storey Corinthian portico with fluted columns; pediments and entablatures over windows; roof on bracket cornice. The home of the O'Shaughnessy family.

St Wolstans, Celbridge, co Kildare (ALEN/LGI1833-37; CANE/LGI1937Supp). A house originally belonging to the Alen family and said to have been built early C17 by John Allen, the architect of Strafford's great palace at Naas (*qv*). Subsequently much altered and now of C18 aspect. 3 storey 5 bay gable-ended centre block with 2 storey overlapping wings of the same height as the centre and with the same solid roof parapet. The wings, which extend back to form side elevations, are of 1 bay towards the front; the ground floor windows being set in recessed arches. The centre block has a pilastered doorcase with a baseless pediment. Interior remodelled 1830s.

St Wolstans

Salisbury

Salisbury, Clonmel, co Tipperary (BAG-WELL/IFR; CLEEVE/IFR; O'BRIEN, Bt/PB). An unusually tall late-Georgian house of 3 storeys over a basement. Weather-slated garden front of 1 bay on either side of a curved central bow. Owned by the Bagwell family of Marlfield (*qv*); leased in the present century to J. W. Cleeve; and from *ca* 1928 onwards to Sir David O'Brien, 6th and present Bt.

Sallow Glen

Sallow Glen, Tarbert, co Kerry (SANDES/LGI1912). A gable-ended 3 storey early or mid-C18 house with a later porch; to the back of which a 2 storey wing was added at right angles later in C18; the wing being of 3 bays with a 3 sided bow, and having bold string courses. From 1917–42, Sallow Glen was the home of Mr & Mrs John Dinan. Now demolished.

Sallymount

Sallymount, Brannockstown, co Kildare (CRAMER-ROBERTS/LGI1958; CLOSE/LGI1937Supp). A Georgian block of 3 storeys over a basement, 6 bays long and 5 bays deep, with a parapeted roof and a string-course under the top storey windows giving them the effect of an attic. In the Victorian period, 2 single-storey 3 sided pilastered bows were added on one front, with a pilastered rectangular projection between them; and single-storey pilastered rectangular projections were added on the adjoining fronts, one of them having a pierced parapet and running the full depth

of the house. Stylistically, these additions seem likely to have been to the design of George Ashlin. On the death of M.W.C. Cramer-Roberts 1939, Sallymount passed to his daughter, Mrs Maxwell Close, by whom it was sold.

Salruck

Salruck, Derrynaclough, co Galway. A 2 storey gabled house of mid-C19 appearance. Fancy bargeboards and pointed wooden finials; windows with wooden mullions and astragals. The seat of the Thomson family.

Salterbridge

Salterbridge, Cappoquin, co Waterford (CHEARNLEY/LGI1912; WINGFIELD, *sub* POWERSCOURT, V/PB). A 2 storey house of 1849 built onto the front of an earlier house extending round 3 sides of a courtyard, enclosed on 4th side by a screen wall with an arch. The 1849 front consists of a 3 bay projecting centre, with a parapet and plain pilasters between the bays; and 2 storey 1 bay wings with eaved roofs and single-storey 3 sided bows. Wyatt windows, some of them with wooden mullions inserted later C19. Glazed Classical porch. Many Georgian-glazed windows in courtyard. Hall with bifurcating oak staircase behind a screen of dark wood Corinthian columns. Drawing room with ceiling decoration of scrolls and shields.

Sanders Park, co Cork (*see* CHARLEVILLE PARK).

Sandford House, co Kerry. A gable-ended C18 house of 2 storeys over a basement. 5 bay front with pedimented breakfront; Venetian window above tripartite doorway. In 1814, the residence of Rev Nicholas Neilan. Now demolished.

Sandymount Park, co Dublin (*see* ROSLYN PARK).

Santry Court

Santry Court

Santry Court, Santry, co Dublin (BARRY/IFR; DOMVILE/IFR; POË-DOMVILE, *sub* POË/IFR). A very important early C18 house of red brick with stone facings, built 1703 by 3rd Lord Barry of Santry, commonly called Lord Santry. Of 2 storeys over an exceptionally high basement, and with a dormered attic behind the roof parapet. 9 bay entrance front with pedimented breakfront; doorway with segmental pediment and Corinthian columns at the head of a great flight of steps. Partly balustraded roof parapet, with urns. Curved sweeps and wings added later, probably *ca* 1740–50 by the notorious 4th and last Lord Barry of Santry, commonly called Lord Santry, a leading member of the Irish Hell Fire Club who was tried and convicted before his peers for the murder of a porter at an inn at Palmerstown 1739, but saved from the death penalty on a recommendation for mercy; his estates were restored to him but his peerage was forfeited for life. The house had a fine interior; a large hall, a staircase of wood with barley-sugar balusters, Corinthian newels and carved acanthus decoration; a dining room with plaster-panelled walls and a ceiling in low relief; a panelled study. Domed temple (now at Luggala, co Wicklow—*qv*) and bridge with balustrades and lions in demesne. Santry was inherited by the Domviles after the death of the last Lord Barry of Santry 1751. On the death of Sir Compton Domvile, 4th and last Bt, 1935, it passed to his nephew, Sir Hugo Poë, 2nd and last Bt, who assumed the additional surname of Domvile. The house was gutted by fire in the present century; and after standing as a ruin for many years, has recently been demolished. The doorcase from the entrance front is to be re-erected in Dublin Castle.

Saunders Grove

Saunders Grove: view from top of Cascade

Saunders Grove, Baltinglass, co Wicklow (SAUNDERS/LGI1912; TYNTE-IRVINE/IFR). A very fine early C18 house built 1716 by Morley Saunders, MP, 2nd Serjeant-at-Law, who bought the estate. Of 3 storeys over a basement and with 2 fronts, each of 9 bays. Entrance front with pedimented breakfront and pedimented doorcase with blocked columns. Garden front of brick with stone dressings; 3 bay breakfront, solid roof parapet with eagles and urns. The garden front faced along a formal canal in the grand manner, with steps and cascades, now mostly bulldozed. Gate piers with exceptionally large balls at entrance to demesne. The house was burnt 1923 and replaced by a modern house built 1925; of 2 storeys with an attic in the high-pitched roof and 7 bays; incorporating the doorcase from the entrance door of the original house.

Scart

Scart, Castlecove, co Kerry. A house of late-Georgian appearance with gables, but without any Gothic or Tudor-Revival touches. Of 1 storey over a high basement and with an attic. Entrance front with recessed centre between 1 bay gabled projections; fanlighted entrance door under the eaves of the roof. In the C19, the home of the Jermyn family.

Scarteen, Knocklong, co Limerick (RYAN/IFR). A 2 storey gabled C19 house of mildly Tudor-Revival character. Mullioned windows with hood mouldings; single-storey shallow battlemented bows. Overhanging roofs with bargeboards; Victorian glazed porch. Seat of the Ryan family, whose famous pack of foxhounds, the Scarteen Black & Tans, is kennelled here.

Scarvagh House

Scarvagh House, Scarva, co Down (REILLY/LGI1912). A 2 storey house with 2 storey wings extending forwards, to form a 3 sided entrance court. Built *ca* 1717 by Miles Reilly, originally intended as offices, the idea being to build a house in front of it. Altered towards mid-C19 by J. T. Reilly. The elevations are plain, except for a 2 storey Jacobean-style porch with a curvilinear gable in the centre range, flanked by 2 shallow oriels surmounted by segmental-headed dormer-gables; while the wings end in square battlemented towers. The porch is of a golden stone, contrasting attractively with the rest of the house, which is rendered. Some of the rooms have C19 fretted plaster ceilings, and heavily carved Jacobean-style chimneypieces and overmantels of wood.

Scregg

Scregg, Knockcroghery, co Roscommon. A 3 storey 5 bay mid-C18 house. Blocked Diocletian window in centre of front above Venetian window above pedimented tripartite doorway with columns standing forward from the entablature and carrying nothing. Rusticated window surrounds. The seat of the Kelly family.

Sea Court, Lislee, co Cork (LONGFIELD/IFR). A 2 storey 6 bay Georgian house with a fanlighted doorway beneath a pillared porch. An Edwardian wing containing a large reception room was added by Mountifort Longfield and his wife, Geraldine Spencer (*née* Edwards), who sold Sea Court *ca* 1920. Now the home of Mr & Mrs A. S. Marquart.

Seafield, co Cork (*see* BANTRY HOUSE).

Seafield, Castletownshend, co Cork (TOWNSHEND/IFR; CHAVASSE/IFR). An irregular 2 storey house with shallow bows in 2 adjoining fronts, the nucleus of which is a Georgian house with a fanlighted doorway, built by a contractor named Bailey for himself. Enlarged mid-C19 by Judge J. F. Townshend, and a wing containing a drawing room and dining room added 1913-14 by Major Henry Chavasse, to the design of Henry Hill, of Cork. Though the roof of the house, which is eaved, is level, the level of the ground floor goes down, in 3 stages, towards the harbour; so that the rooms get higher as the floors descend. Massive stone terrace round 2 sides. Let during 1950s to Capt & Mrs. F. Harrison Maynard. Sold 1960.

Seafield, co Dublin

Seafield, Donabate, co Dublin (HELY-HUTCHINSON, *sub* DONOUGHMORE, E/PB). A Palladian villa of Sir Edward Lovett Pearce's school, probably a remodelling of an earlier house, carried out soon *post* 1737 for Benedict Arthur. Of 3 storeys over a basement, the top storey being an attic of narrow windows with 3 small hip-roofs above them on the entrance front and 3 gables of late C17 style above them on the garden front. Entrance and garden fronts of 7 bays, the entrance front having a 2 storey pedimented Doric portico *in antis*, with a broad flight of steps leading up to it. Balustraded roof parapet on entrance front; ground floor windows with rusticated surrounds. The chief—and unusual—feature of the interior is the impressive 2 storey hall, which runs through the full depth of the house, with windows at each end; crossed by a gallery to provide communication between 1st floor rooms on either side. The walls are decorated with superimposed fluted Ionic and Corinthian pilasters; with, between them, *grisaille* paintings of Classical figures which were probably added later C18. Some of the other rooms are panelled; the dining room has a carved cornice and frieze and fluted Corinthian pilasters. At one side of the house is a Victorian wing with an Italianate tower. Bought by John Hely-Hutchinson in 2nd half of C19. Now the home of Mr G. R. Dawes.

Seafield, co Sligo (*see* LISHEEN).

Seafield, Gorey, co Wexford HORE/LGI1863). A 2 storey Georgian house; 3 bay front with Doric portico; curved bow at side; eaved roof on bracket cornice.

Seaforde

Transformation Scene: Col Rt Hon W. B. Forde at reins of his coach outside Seaforde before and after the advent of plate-glass windows and porch

Seaforde, co Down (FORDE/IFR). A severe but impressive early C19 block, faced in cream-coloured ashlar. Built 1816–20 by Col Mathew Forde, replacing an earlier house burnt 1816; thought to be by the English architect, Peter Frederick Robinson. Of 3 storeys over a basement, the top storey being treated as an attic above a dentil cornice. 5 bay entrance front; entablatures on console brackets over downstairs windows. The fanlighted entrance door was originally under a gracefully-curving single-storey portico with coupled Ionic columns; but in 2nd half of C19, this gave place to a large enclosed pilastered porch, added by Col Rt Hon W. B. Forde, MP, who also added to the austerity of the facades by putting in plate glass windows. 5 bay side elevation; garden front with 1 bay on either side of a wide curved bow; the windows in the side bays, and also the centre windows of the bow, being tripartite, except in the attic storey, those in the side bays being set in shallow recesses beneath relieving arches. Magnificent Grecian-Revival interior. Large and deep hall, with a fireplace on either side and a screen of stone columns, of the Tower of the Winds order. Staircase with handsome brass balusters in separate hall at side. Bow-fronted saloon, flanked by dining room and library. The library is a room of rare beauty, its decoration com-

pletely unaltered; the architecturally-treated bookcases keep their original graining, of a delightful faded brown; above them are Grecian friezes of figures in low relief, made of cut paper, like the friezes in the oval drawing room at Caledon (*qv*), in their original colouring of grey-green on a biscuit ground. The house stands in a wonderful position between an artificial lake and a natural lough, surrounded by glorious parkland and woods with the Mourne Mountains as a backdrop. At the entrance to the demesne is a Grecian triumphal arch, with a pediment and acroteria.

Sea Park, co Wicklow (*see* MAGHERY-MORE).

Seaport Lodge

Seaport Lodge, Portballintrae, co Antrim (LESLIE/IFR; STEWART MOORE/IFR). A 2 storey bow-fronted house, built *ca* 1770 by James Leslie, of Leslie Hill (*qv*) as a marine residence, or "bathing lodge". Round-headed entrance door in bow; other ground floor windows also round-headed, those on either side of the bow being tripartite. Originally the windows had Gothic astragals, but these were subsequently removed and plate glass put in. Single-storey bows in the end elevations, with similar windows. Balustraded roof parapet. Oval hall with Classical plasterwork ceiling.

Seskinore, Omagh, co Tyrone (PERRY, *sub* MCCLINTOCK/LGI1912; MCCLINTOCK/IFR). A 2 storey house of mid-C19 aspect. Entrance front of 2 bays on either side of a pedimented breakfront, with 3 narrow round-headed windows above and a balustraded Ionic portico below; the outside columns of the portico being coupled. Curved end bow. The estate originally belonged to the Perry family, and passed by inheritance to this branch of the McClintock family early C19.

Shaen

Shaen, Port Laoise, co Leix (KEMMIS, *sub* WALSH-KEMMIS/IFR). A house of late-Georgian appearance, of 2 storeys over a

Shaen: Gateway

basement. Entrance front with 2 3 sided bows and pedimented 1 bay projection in centre; Grecian Ionic porch with acroteria. Castellated gateway at entrance to demesne. Now a home for the elderly.

Shanaganagh Castle

Shanaganagh Castle, Shankill, co Dublin (ROWAN-HAMILTON/IFR; HEYMAN/LGI-1958). A house or castle formerly belonging to the Walshe family; bought *ca* 1800 by Gen Sir George Cockburn, a soldier, an ardent Whig politician and an avid collector of antiquities, who greatly enlarged it, to the design of one or both of the Morrisons; so that it became a somewhat haphazard mixture of plain late-Georgian and castellated; with a curved bow and a slender battlemented round tower. The Morrison additions included a large ballroom, a dining room and a room called the "Monumental Room" containing Cockburn's collection of Greek and Roman relics. Having acquired 4 circular Greek altars and a large Corinthian capital which were too large to display indoors, Cockburn had them erected one on top of another to form a column in front of the house with an inscription commemorating the passing of the Great Reform Bill 1832; but, in 1838, Whig though he was, he put another inscription on the back of the monument which read: "Alas To this day a Hum Bug". Shanaganagh passed to the Rowan-Hamiltons through the marriage of Cockburn's daughter, Catherine, to Cdre G.W. R. Rowan-Hamilton. It was sold 1919. Sir Harold Nicolson, whose mother was a Rowan-Hamilton, subsequently bought Cockburn's Reform Bill monument and disposed its components about the garden at Sissinghurst Castle, Kent. As a child, he had stayed frequently at Shanaganagh with his grandmother, who once took him to a fête or horse-show in the neighbourhood where she suddenly told him to look at a lady sitting in a high dog-cart; when he asked who the lady was, his grandmother replied: "Never mind, remember only that you have seen Mrs O'Shea".

Shanbally Castle: Porch Tower

Shanbally Castle: Garden Front

Shanbally Castle: ceiling of Staircase

Shanbally Castle, Clogheen, co Tipperary (O'CALLAGHAN, LISMORE, V/PB1898; BUTLER, *sub* ORMONDE, M/PB; POLE-CAREW, *sub* POLE, Bt/PB). The largest of John Nash's Irish castles, built *ca* 1812 for Cornelius O'Callaghan, 1st Viscount Lismore. Long and irregular, of smooth, silver-grey ashlar; with round and octagon towers, battlements and machicolations. Rectangular and pointed windows with wooden tracery. Entrance front with pointed-arched and vaulted porte-cochère under porch-tower; low projecting wing at one side, ending in an octagon tower, enclosing a cloistered office court. Garden front with round tower at one end, octagon tower at the other and central feature with 2 square turrets; graceful Gothic veranda. Long top-lit hall occupying the lower part of an inner court, with ceiling of plaster fanvaulting; and, at one end, a bifurcating staircase of oak with carved pendants under the soffits. Ceiling of delicate plaster fan vaulting above staircase. Octagonal dining room with cornice of half-vaults. Round and square drawing rooms and library

Shanbally Castle: Bedroom corridor

forming an enfilade along the garden front through double doors; library with gently arched ribbed ceiling. Horseshoe-shaped bedroom corridor with plaster vaulting running round the inner court from one arm of the staircase to the other. The castle stood in a suitably Reptonian landscape bounded to the north and south by 2 mountain ranges, the Galtees and the Knockmealdowns. Nash's original plans for the castle are recorded as having been in the possession of Repton, who probably advised on improvements to the demesne, if not on the castle itself. Indeed, Shanbally had a strong likeness to Repton's and Nash's most notable joint creation, Luscombe Castle, Devon. Though very much larger than Luscombe, and more massively built, it had the same sense of being a picturesque and comfortable retreat rather than a medieval fantasy. 2nd and last Viscount Lismore left Shanbally to his cousins, Lady Beatrice Pole-Carew and Lady Constance Butler, daughters of 3rd Marquess of Ormonde; it was sold by Major Patrick Pole-Carew 1954. After a valiant but unsuccessful attempt by Hon Edward Sackville-West (5th Lord Sackville), the author and music critic, to rescue it, the castle was demolished 1957 and its ruin dynamited.

Shanbolard

Shanbolard, Moyard, co Galway (ARMSTRONG-LUSHINGTON-TULLOCH/LGI1958). A long, low castellated house, mostly of 1 storey, with a 2 storey tower at one end, in which is situated the entrance door. Very large billiard room. Office wing now demolished.

Shandy Hall, Dripsey, co Cork. A plain 2 storey 5 bay Georgian house with an eaved roof. The home of Surgeon-Major Philip

Cross, who was put on trial 1887, for poisoning his wife in order to marry his children's governess; he was found guilty, and hanged early in the following year.

Shanemullagh House, Castledawson, co Derry (GAUSSEN/LGI1912). A 2 storey C18 house of coursed rubble; ashlar window surrounds with blocking.

Shane's Castle, Randalstown, co Antrim (O'NEILL, B/PB). The original C17 castle here, by the side of Antrim Bay at the north-eastern corner of Lough Neagh, took its name from Shane McBrian O'Neill, a scion of the ancient Irish Royal House, who was allowed to keep 120,000 acres of his lands after the Plantation of Ulster. It grew into a large C18 castellated house, of 3 storeys over a basement, with a battlemented parapet, projecting end bays and curved bows; its principal front being at right angles to the water's edge. A lakeside terrace and a conservatory or orangery was built across the end of the castle some time *ante* 1784, when Mrs Siddons stayed at Shane's and wrote of how she and her fellow-guests would pluck their dessert in the conservatory while the waves splashed outside and "the cool and pleasant wind came to murmur in concert" with the musicians playing in the adjoining corridor. In a storm, however, the wind and waves must have drowned all else, for it is recorded that the spray would beat into the very attics of the castle. Mrs Siddons was particularly impressed by the luxury of the O'Neills' establishment, comparing it to "an Arabian Nights entertainment". Rev Daniel Beaufort, who came to Shane's 1787, was no less impressed, and described it as follows: "Drawing room adorned with magnificent mirrors, off breakfast room is rotunda coffee room, where in recesses are great quantities of china, a cistern with a cock and water, a boiler with another, all apparently for making breakfast; a letter box and round table with four sets of pen and ink let in for everybody to write. Conservatory joins house, fine apartment along lough, at end alcove for meals, from it a way to h & c bathing apartments with painted windows. On other side of house, pretty and large theatre and magnificent ballroom 60 × 30, all of wood and canvas painted, and so sent ready made from London". At the beginning of C19, 1st (and last) Earl O'Neill commissioned John Nash to enlarge Shane's in the castle style. Work began 1815 and in that year a very much larger lakeside terrace and conservatory were built; the terrace broad and battlemented, with a watch-tower at one end and a look-out at the other; the conservatory also battlemented, but with round-headed windows. But in 1816, when the walls of Nash's main addition were only just showing above the ground, the castle was burnt down; allegedly by the family banshee, which was annoyed at having its room invaded during a particularly large house-party. After the fire, all work was abandoned, and the family retreated to the fine 3 sided Georgian stable court, which stands a little further back from the shore of the lake; the centre range below the cupola being remodelled, with Wyatt windows. In 1860s, a new castle was built at one corner of the stables by 1st

Shane's Castle: as it was 1780

Shane's Castle: ruin of Castle, Orangery, Terrace and Battery

bay to the left, so as to provide a new drawing room running from the front of the house to the back; and by a castellated office wing to the right. The back of the house, which is more irregular, is treated in much the same way, and adorned with a delightful Gothic conservatory on the level of the half-landing of the stairs, carried on a stone arcade. The interior of the house keeps much of its early c18 character. Hall with grained panelling and handsome c18 chimneypiece of black marble, flanked by 2 smaller rooms with corner fireplaces. Late-Georgian staircase hall with graceful wooden stairs and walls marbled Siena 1894. Dining room with Gothic plasterwork in ceiling and Gothic pelmet. The drawing room is charmingly Victorian, with flowered paper and curtains of faded gold dating from 1894 and an Italian white marble chimneypiece brought back from Milan *ca* 1860 by James Aylward. It formerly opened into a conservatory built 1861 to the design of Sir Joseph Paxton; but this was removed 1961. The entrance front faces along an avenue of trees to a *claire-voie* with rusticated stone piers which was part of c18 layout. Impressive castellated entrance to demesne, said to have been designed by Daniel Robertson and originally intended for Dunleckney Manor, co Carlow (*qv*).

Shannon Grove, Pallaskenry, co Limerick (BURY/IFR; WALLER/IFR; ARMITAGE/LG1969). A very distinguished small early c18 house by the side of the Shannon estuary; begun *ca* 1709 by John Bury and completed *ca* 1723 by his son, William; the

Lord O'Neill of the present creation, to the design of Sir Charles Lanyon and William Henry Lynn; not Scottish-Baronial, like most of Lynn's other castles, but plain gabled High Victorian, with a square tower at one end; the tower and its turret had straight parapets, with no battlements. Lynn added a billiard room to the castle for 2nd Lord O'Neill 1901. In 1922, the Victorian castle was burnt; its ruin was subsequently cleared away, and for the next 40 or so years the family lived once again in the stables. Then a new house was built for the present Lord O'Neill at the opposite corner of the stables to where the Victorian castle had stood; it is in the Classical style, and has well-proportioned elevations, each with a recessed centre; and a handsome fanlighted doorway. Nash's conservatory by the ruins of the old castle is maintained as a camellia house, and the great castellated terrace remains as the most spectacular feature of the grounds, with a formidable battery of c18 cannon pointing across the water.

Shankill Castle, Paulstown, co Kilkenny (TOLER-AYLWARD/IFR). A castellated house incorporating a house built or remodelled 1713 by Peter Aylward, who came into the estate, which had previously belonged to the Butlers of Paulstown Castle, through his marriage to Elizabeth Butler. This early c18 house appears to have had a recessed centre and projecting end bays. Some time *ante* 1828, the end bays were crenellated, one of them being raised to look like a tower; and they were joined by a Gothic porch. The front was extended by 1

Shannon Grove

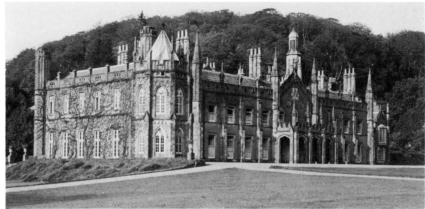

Shelton Abbey

Shannon Grove: Staircase

Shelton Abbey: Drawing Room

Shelton Abbey: Library

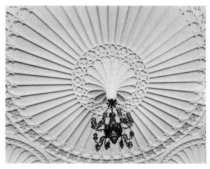

Shelton Abbey: ceiling

architect seems likely to have been one of the Rothery family. Of 2 storeys over a basement, with a dormered attic in the high pitched roof. The entrance front and the front facing the river are both of 5 bays; but whereas the entrance front has a fairly simple doorcase with a segmental pediment (dated 1709), the river front doorcase (dated 1723) is splendidly baroque and incorporates a cartouche of arms; and it stands at the head of a much more impressive flight of steps than the entrance door does, owing to the basement being much higher on this side; doubtless a precaution against flooding. The roof is crowned by 2 tall and massive chimneystacks of patterned brickwork. All the main rooms have fielded panelling and there is a staircase of fine joinery with alternate barley-sugar balusters. The house is flanked by two "L"-shaped detached wings, with mullion-and-transom windows. Originally these wings had curvilinear gables on the entrance front. Shannon Grove was, for some years *post* World War II, the home of Mr & Mrs R. W. Armitage. It is now the home of Mr & Mrs John W. Griffith.

Sheen Falls, Kenmare, co Kerry (WAR-RENDER, BRUNTISFIELD, B/PB). A gabled house, largely rebuilt *ca* 1950, above the Falls of the River Sheen which give the property its name. Owned by Lord Bruntisfield, who sold it *ca* 1962.

Sheephill, co Dublin (*see* ABBOTSTOWN).

Shelton Abbey, Arklow, co Wicklow (FORWARD-HOWARD, WICKLOW, E/PB). A 2 storey house with an 11 bay front, built 1770 by Rt Hon Ralph Howard, MP, afterwards 1st Viscount Wicklow; transformed into a Gothic Revival abbey *ca* 1819 by 4th Earl of Wicklow to the design of Sir Richard Morrison; the "abbey style" being regarded as particularly suited to its "sequestered situation" in the Vale of Avoca, surrounded by thick woods. The front of the house was lavishly adorned with buttresses and pinnacles; the roof parapet and pediment were crenellated, and a

single-storey Gothic portico was added in the centre. A new wing of 2 storeys and 5 bays was built at right angles to the front, joined to it by a polygonal corner tower with a pointed copper roof. The entrance hall kept its handsome C18 chimneypiece with a scroll pediment, and its Classical niches; but was given a ceiling of elaborately moulded beams and braces of oak, with gilt pendants; in later years, these beams were painted white. Behind the entrance hall was the lofty "Prayer Hall", with stained glass windows and a ceiling of plaster fan-vaulting. A cloistered corridor led to the Grand Staircase of oak, its landing carried on a slender Gothic arcade; and to the large and small drawing rooms, both with ceilings of plaster Gothic pendants. The dining room and library provided a contrast, being in Morrison's most restrained Classical style; the dining room having a ceiling in shallow compartments and a frieze of swags; the library having a frieze of wreathes and bookcases with acroteria. The front of the house was prolonged by a gabled office wing set a little back; and *ca* 1840 4th Earl added to the picturesque effect by building a wing further back again and on higher ground, with a clock-tower and a tall and slender belfry and copper

cupola. This wing was known as the Nunnery and accommodated 4th Earl's unmarried daughters; such is the power of suggestion that they became Catholics and nuns. A stable building behind the Nunnery is believed by the present Earl of Wicklow to have been the earlier house, built C17; where, according to tradition, James II paused on his flight after the Battle of the Boyne; he had one of his nose-bleeds in the hall, and his blood spattered the door-post, which was afterwards cut out and preserved as a relic for many years until a servant unwittingly used it for firewood. The demesne had some magnificent trees and a sub-tropical garden laid out early in the present century by 7th Earl and his 1st wife. The main avenue was almost straight and 2 miles long, bordered on each side by a high wall of rhododendrons; a seemingly unending passage which heightened the sense of expectancy until at last, emerging into a glade, one saw the grey pinnacles and green copper roofs of the abbey backed by trees. In 1947, the present Earl of Wicklow opened Shelton as an hotel in an attempt to meet the cost of upkeep; but he was obliged to sell it 1951, owing to taxation. The house is now a school; the demesne is largely spoilt by industrial development.

Shepperton Park, Leap, co Cork (TOWNS-HEND/IFR). A plain 3 storey 4 bay C18 house.

Sherlockstown, Sallins, co Kildare (SMITH, *sub* GRANARD, E/PB). A long, irregular, slightly castellated house. Tower-like centre, with a battlemented gable, flanked by square projecting turrets joined by a battlemented cloister of 2 segmental pointed arches; above which is a tall, round-headed window. Wings of the same height as the centre, and more or less equal

Sherlockstown

in length; but one of 3 storeys and the other of 2 storeys; both irregularly fenestrated. At each end of the facade, a rather thin corbelled bartizan. The seat of the Sherlock family. Subsequently owned by Mr & Mrs A. Edward Smith; now by Mrs S. O'Flaherty.

Shrigley Hall, Killyleagh, co Down. A Victorian Italianate house, with a balustraded roof parapet and an impressive iron and glass conservatory standing on a basement. The home of the Martin family, who owned the cotton and subsequently flax-spinning mill at Shrigley, where they built a village and created one of those small, flourishing, paternalistic Victorian industrial communities; the people showed their gratitude to John Martin 1871 by erecting a stupendous High Victorian clock-tower and drinking-fountain in his honour in the centre of the village outside the mill gate; it is by Timothy Hevey, of Belfast. The village was swept away between 1968 and 1972, in favour of a new housing-estate on the opposite hillside; the monument now stands isolated and derelict.

Silverspring, co Tipperary. A 2 storey 8 bay early c18 house, the 2 end bays at either side of the front projecting. Good window surrounds; high-pitched roof.

Sion House

Sion House, Sion Mills, co Tyrone (HERDMAN/IFR). A house of 1840, rebuilt 1883 in the half-timbered style by E. T. Herdman; the architect being his brother-in-law, William Unsworth, of Petersfield, Hants. Various buildings in the "model village" of Sion Mills, where the family flax spinning mill is situated, are in the same style. Sion House was sold 1966.

Skevanish, Innishannon, co Cork (PEA-COCKE/LGI1912). A gabled Victorian Tudor house, romantically situated on a wooded hillside above the Bandon River. Burnt *ca* 1920. The house stood as a ruin for more than 50 years; but a modern house has recently been built on the site by Mr Barry O'Driscoll, incorporating part of the old wall.

Skryne Castle, co Meath. An old tower-house with a plain 3 storey 3 bay gable-ended c18 wing. Battlemented porch.

Slane Castle

Slane Castle, Slane, co Meath (CONYNG-HAM, M/PB). A large and very early Gothic Revival castle in an incomparable situation above the River Boyne; begun 1785 by 2nd Lord Conyngham to the design of James Wyatt; completed by Francis Johnston for his son, afterwards 1st Marquess Conyngham; built on the foundations of a medieval castle of the Fleming family and replacing an earlier house. "Capability" Brown, James Gandon, Thomas Hopper and other architects were at various times consulted about the building and may have had a hand in it. Of 3 storeys over a basement, which becomes a lower ground floor on the river side where the ground falls away steeply. Completely symmetrical in its elevations; its plan being in fact a larger and modified version of the plan of several Classical Irish houses of this period, notably Caledon, Mount Kennedy and Lucan House (*qqv*); with a bow in the centre of the river front which is raised above the rest of the building to form an impressive round tower. Apart from this round tower, and a small square tower at each corner—only very slightly raised above the level of the main parapet—the house is, to all intents and purposes, a large Georgian block with battlements and a few other medieval touches, such as a machicolated gallery above the entrance front. The interior, too, is Classical, with the exception of what is the finest room. The hall has a cornice of mutules and 4 fluted Tuscan columns supporting the ceiling; the drawing room has a frieze of typical late-Georgian plasterwork and a Classical apse on one side; the fact that this is partly pierced with Gothic arches, form-

ing a charming little alcove in one corner of the room, is more of a Georgian-Gothic frivolity rather than a serious attempt at medievalism. The exception is the great circular ballroom or library which rises through 2 storeys of the round tower and is undoubtedly the finest Gothic Revival room in Ireland; with a ceiling of Gothic plasterwork so delicate and elaborate that it looks like filigree. Yet this, too, is basically a Classical room; the Gothic ceiling is, in fact a dome; the deep apses on either side of the fireplace are such as one finds in many of

Wyatt's Classical interiors, except that the arches leading into them are pointed; they are decorated with plasterwork that can be recognized as a very slightly Gothicized version of the familiar Adam and Wyatt fan pattern. There are some charming little rooms in the corner towers, that off the drawing room being hung with yellow brocade. The upper storey of the round tower is divided into 3 elliptical bedrooms. The 2 grandest bedrooms, however, are on the floor below: the Lord Lieutenant's, and George IV's. George IV stayed here as Prince of Wales, and again as King 1821; the wife of 1st Marquess being the Lady Conyngham who was his favourite. The dead-straight road from Dublin to Slane is said to have been made specially for him. This road forms a fitting prelude to the castle, as do the fine Gothic entrance gates to the demesne. The approach from the north, through the village of Slane, is, however, even more impressive; the village cross-roads being transformed into a *place* worthy of the capital of a European princeling by having 4 elegant matching Georgian houses at the 4 corners, facing each other diagonally.

Slaney Park, Baltinglass, co Wicklow (GROGAN/LGI1958). A Georgian house with a front of 2 wide curved bows and a pillared porch; originally of 3 storeys, but rebuilt with only 2 after a fire 1939.

Slevyre

Slevyre, Borrisokane, co Tipperary (HICKIE/IFR). A large Victorian-Italianate mansion on the shores of Lough Derg, built *ca* 1870 by Lt-Col J. F. Hickie. 2 storey; irregular front. Entrance door at the foot of an unusually tall 4 storey campanile tower. Balustraded roof parapet; tripartite and Venetian windows; windows with entablatures or pediments over them. Sold *ca* 1950; now a convent. A very attractive modern house in the Classical style, rather like a pavilion, has been built elsewhere in the demesne by Brig & Mrs W. S. F. Hickie.

Smarmore Castle, Ardee, co Louth (TAAFFE/IFR). A medieval castle, inhabited by the Taaffes since 1320, which now forms the centre of a long and not quite symmetrical front, having a plain C18 addition on either side of it; both additions being 3 bay, but whereas that to the left is 2 storey, that to the right is 2 storey over a high basement. The left hand addition is in fact the side of a range which extends back at right angles to the old castle. This consists of a 3 bay centre, with an entrance doorway surrounded by blocking, recessed between 2

Smarmore Castle

projecting gable-ended wings; both gables being crowned with chimney-stacks. The right hand gable end is 2 bay; that to the left has a single long central window above 2 small windows at ground level. Also in C18, the old castle was given a skyline of battlements, as well as pointed sash windows, regularly disposed. Library and drawing room upstairs; dining room and a 2nd drawing room on ground floor.

Snowhill, co Kilkenny (*see* POWER HALL).

Somerset, Coleraine, co Derry (TORRENS/LGI1912). A C19 villa deriving from the villas of Sir Richard Morrison. 2 storey; 3 bay, bow-ended front; 3 sided bow in centre incorporating entrance door. The seat of the Richardson family; passed through marriage to the Torrens family.

Somerton, co Dublin (*see* SUMMERTON).

Somerville, Balrath, co Meath (SOMERVILLE, Bt/PB; AGNEW-SOMERVILLE, *sub* AGNEW, Bt, *of Clendry*/PB). A Georgian house altered and greatly embellished in a later period, probably *ca* 1830. The alterations included moving the entrance to what had been the back of the house, which became the new entrance front; of 3 storeys and 5 bays, with a single-storey Ionic portico. The former entrance front became the garden front; though it is the same height as the rest of the house, it only has 2 storeys, so that the rooms on this side are much higher. It is of 5 bays with a central pedimented breakfront and a single-storey curved bow which is balustraded, like the main roof parapet. The principal reception rooms, with their high coved ceilings, have a palatial air; the ceiling plasterwork in the saloon and library is in the manner of Michael Stapleton and could be taken for late C18; but is more likely C19. The draw-

Somerville

Somerville: ceiling

ing room has a domed ceiling rather in the manner of Sir Richard or William Vitruvius Morrison. Impressive stable yard, with battlemented octagon tower above pedimented archway. Somerville was inherited by Mr Quentin Agnew, nephew by marriage of Sir James Somerville, 6th Bt and 2nd (and last) Lord Athlumney. He consequently assumed the additional surname of Somerville; but has since sold the Somerville estate.

Sonna, Ballynacarrigy, co Westmeath (TUITE, Bt/PB). A C18 house consisting of a plain 3 storey 7 bay centre block joined to 3 bay single-storey wings by 1 bay links. Centre block with segmental-pedimented doorcase and wall carried up to be roof parapet. On a February night 1783, Sir George Tuite, 7th Bt, was found murdered in his study here, his brains having been beaten out. His King Charles spaniel, which was with him, had likewise been battered to death. There was no robbery, nor had any papers been disturbed; the murderer was never discovered. Sonna is now demolished.

Sopwell Hall: Hall

Sopwell Hall

Sopwell Hall, Cloughjordan, co Tipperary (TRENCH/IFR). A house of 2 storeys over a basement, built 1745 by Col Francis Sadlier, who used to climb the scaffolding during the building and read accounts of that year's Jacobite rising to the workmen. Attributed by the Knight of Glin to Francis Bindon, stylistically as well as on account of Col Sadleir's connexion to Bindon and to Bindon's chief patron, Lord Bessborough. 7 bay entrance front, all the windows and the round-headed doorway having block architraves and large keystones which in the upper storey, break into the frieze of the entablature. Bold cornice. Archway to yard, flanked by walls with niches, at one side of

front. 3 bay side elevation, also with block architraves. Plain 7 bay garden front. Interior much altered 1866–68. Wide and deep hall, lined with rather unusual fluted Doric pilasters and square columns of oak and divided by screen of arches. Staircase of good C18 joinery in staircase hall at side, leading up to large top-lit domed landing, with shallow arches and marbled halfcolumns; rather Soanian in character but presumably dating from 1866–68 remodelling. Room on right of hall with C18 panelling and ceiling with oval garland. Drawing room with Victorian plasterwork cornice. The old castle where the family originally lived stands a short distance away from the

house; it is still roofed and has glass in its windows. It is unusually long for its height; with tall chimneys and *machicoulis*. Sopwell passed to the Trenchs through the marriage of Mary Sadleir, daughter of the builder of the house, to Frederick Trench, MP.

South Hill, Milltown, co Dublin (FITZGERALD-LOMBARD/LGI1958). A double bowfronted Georgian house, the bows being curved and set close together. Acquired *ca* 1860 by J. F. Lombard, who enlarged it considerably; sold *ca* 1914 by Major R. E. Fitzgerald-Lombard; demolished *ca* 1939.

South Hill, Delvin, co Westmeath (TIGHE/IFR; CHAPMAN, Bt, *of Killua Castle*/ PB1917). A plain 3 storey 7 bay early C19 house with interior plasterwork of theMorrison school. Passed by inheritance from a branch of the Tighe family to the Chapmans. The home of Sir Thomas Chapman, 7th and last Bt, of whom Lawrence of Arabia was the illegitimate son.

Spiddal House, Spiddal, co Galway (MORRIS, KILLANIN, B/PB). Originally a small Georgian house, which was replaced by a large house of 2 and 3 storeys with irregular elevations built in 1910 by 2nd Lord Killanin, to the design of William A. Scott. Plain rectangular plate-glass windows and features in a Romanesque style; at one end a square tower surmounted by an open belvedere with Romanesque columns and a dome; alongside the tower, a 2 storey veranda with Romanesque columns and arches. At the other end, a Romanesque loggia joined to the house by a short colonnade surmounted by an iron balcony; sculptures by Michael Shorthall, of Loughrea, above the capitals of the columns. In the centre of the principal front, a single-storey projection with an iron balcony and a Regency-style veranda above it. The house was rebuilt 1931, following a fire 1923; the architect of the rebuilding being M. Byrne. The principal front of the house, as rebuilt, is basically similar to what it was previously, and the Romanesque loggia and 2 storey Romanesque veranda remain as they were; but the tower is no longer surmounted by a belvedere, the single-storey projection in the middle of the front has been removed and the windows now have astragals. Sold *ca* 1960 by 3rd and present Lord Killanin.

Springfield Castle

Springfield Castle: Dining Room

Springfield Castle, Dromcolliher, co Limerick (PETTY-FITZMAURICE, *sub* LANS-DOWNE, M/PB; DEANE, MUSKERRY, B/PB). A 3 storey C18 house adjoining a large C16 tower-house of the FitzGeralds, later bought by the Fitzmaurices, whose heiress married Sir Robert Deane, 6th Bt, afterwards 1st Lord Muskerry, 1775. Front with 5 bay centre between 2 slightly projecting end bays; high-pitched roof. Room with Bossi chimneypiece and delicate and elaborate Adamesque plasterwork on walls: medallions with Classical reliefs surrounded by husk and ribbon ornament. A 2 storey C19 Gothic wing with pinnacled buttresses was added at one end of C18 block, extending along one side of the old castle bawn, which had the tower-house at one corner and a smaller tower at another and outbuildings along two of the remaining sides to form a courtyard. C20 entrance gates and lodge in the New Zealand Maori style. C18 house was burnt 1923 and a new house was afterwards made out of C19 Gothic wing, which was extended in the same style.

Springfield House, Buttevant, co Cork (DAVISON/LG1972). A double gable-ended early C18 house onto which a new 2 storey

bow-ended front was built in the late-Georgian period. The new front is of 3 bays with a pillared and fanlighted doorcase; the end bows are curved. Bowed drawing room with cornice of simple plasterwork; dining room of similar proportions on opposite side of hall.

Springfield Manor, Fanad, co Donegal (DILL/IFR). A 2 storey stone house with single-storey wings, built *ca* 1695 by Henry Patton, of the same family as Mary Patton who married Thomas Keyes and was the grandmother of Adm of the Fleet Lord Keyes (*see* PB). The house was approached by a long and broad elm avenue. Acquired towards end of C18 by the brothers John & Mark Dill, whose descendants lived here until 1891. The house was partially demolished 1911–12 and finally demolished 1968.

Springfort Hall, Mallow, co Cork (FOOTT/LG11912; GROVE-WHITE/IFR; CLARKE/IFR). A 2 storey early C19 house with 2 deep curved bows on each of its 2 principal fronts. Open porch with square piers on entrance front, between the 2 bows and below a central Wyatt window; large triple windows in lower storey of bows. Service wing at side. Spacious bow-ended reception rooms; ceilings with surrounds of early C19 plasterwork. Plaster Gothic vaulting in staircase hall.

Spring Grove, co Fermanagh (*see* ROSS-LEA MANOR).

Springhill, Moneymore, co Derry (LENOX-CONYNGHAM/IFR). A low, white-washed, high roofed house with a sense of great age and peace; its nucleus late C17, built *ca* 1680 by "Good Will" Conyngham who afterwards played a leading part in the defence of Derry during the Siege. Altered and enlarged at various times; the defensive enclosure or bawn with which it was originally surrounded was taken down, and 2 single-storey free-standing office wings of stone with curvilinear end-gables were built early C18 flanking the entrance front, forming a deep forecourt. Col William Conyngham, MP, added 2 single-storey wings to the house *ca* 1765, which was when the entrance front assumed its present appearance: of 7 bays, the windows on either side of the centre being narrower

Springhill: Staircase

Springhill: Drawing Room

than the rest, and with a 3 sided bow in each of the wings. In the high roof, a single central dormer lighting the attic. The hall has C18 panelling; behind the hall is an early C18 staircase of oak and yew with alternate straight and spiral twisted balusters. The Gun Room has bolection-moulded oak panelling which could be late C17 or early C18, though it cannot have been put into this room until much later, for there are remains of C18 wallpaper behind it. The large and lofty drawing room in the right-hand wing is a great contrast after the small, low-ceilinged rooms in the centre of the house; it has a modillion cornice and a handsome black marble chimneypiece. Though essentially a Georgian room, it has been given a Victorian character with a grey and green wallpaper of Victorian pattern. Next to the drawing room, in the garden front, is the dining room, added *ca* 1850 by William Lenox-Conyngham; a large simple room of Georgian character, with a red flock paper and a chimneypiece of yellow marble brought from Herculaneum

Springhill

by the Earl of Bristol Bishop of Derry and presented by him to the family. The garden front, which is irregular, going in and out, faces along an old beech avenue to a ruined tower which may originally have been a windmill. Transferred to the Northern Ireland National Trust by W. L. Lenox-Conyngham, HML, shortly before his death 1957. Springhill is featured in his mother, Mina's book *An Old Ulster Home*; and is open to the public.

Spur Royal

Spur Royal (also known as **Augher Castle**), **Augher, co Tyrone** (RICHARDSON-BUNBURY, Bt/PB; CARMICHAEL-FERRALL/LGI-1912). A square 3 storey "Plantation castle" with an unusual triangular tower in the centre of each of its sides; built *ca* 1615 by Sir Thomas Ridgeway, afterwards Earl of Londonderry; burnt 1689, and restored *ca* 1832 by Sir James Richardson-Bunbury, 2nd Bt, who added two castellated wings to the design of William Warren; producing what is one of the most original of all late-Georgian Irish Castles. Now the home of Mr John Leckey.

Stackallan House (formerly **Boyne House**), **Navan, co Meath** (HAMILTON-RUSSELL, BOYNE, V/PB; BURKE/LGI1965). One of the few surviving grand Irish country houses of the beginning of c18; built *ca* 1716 for Gustavus Hamilton, 1st Viscount Boyne, one of William III's generals. Of 3 storeys, with 2 adjoining pedimented fronts, one of 9 bays and one of 7 bays. Good quoins and window surrounds; continuous entablatures over windows; bold string-courses; high-pitched and wide-eaved sprocketed roof on modillion cornice. The home of Mrs Anthony Burke, whose late husband was the grandson of Sir Henry Farnham Burke, Garter Principal King of Arms, and the great-grandson of Sir Bernard Burke, Ulster King of Arms: 2 generations of the dynasty that edited *Burke's* series of genealogical publications.

Stacumny House, Celbridge, co Kildare (BRADSTREET, Bt/PB1924; NUGENT, *sub* WEST-MEATH, E/PB). A plain 3 storey Georgian house to which a wing in the Classical style, containing a ballroom, was added *ca* 1910. The wing has since been demolished. Originally the seat of the Bradstreet family; bought *ca* 1890 by Hon R. A. Nugent; sold *ca* 1963 by his daughter Mrs Michel Popoff. Now the home of Mr & Mrs Vincent Poklewski-Koziell.

Stameen, Mornington, co Meath (CAIRNES/IFR). A 2 storey Victorian house with a central pediment-gable on one front, and a similar gable on a projection at the end of the side elevation. The pediment-gables have broken base-mouldings; below them are triple windows. At one side of the central feature in the front is a single-storey projection. The front is prolonged by a bay slightly set back, and then by a lower 2 storey service wing. Eaved roof on bracket cornice.

Stedalt, Stamullin, co Meath (MA-CARTNEY-FILGATE, *sub* FILGATE/IFR). A 2 storey Victorian house with camber-headed windows, a single-storey 3 sided bow decorated with Romanesque pilasters at either end of its front, and a high roof on a bracket cornice. The seat of the Tunstall-Moores; Lucy, sister and heiress of G. B. Tunstall-Moore, married C. H. R. Macart-ney-Filgate 1910.

Steeple (The), Antrim, co Antrim. An elegant 2 storey early C19 house with an eaved roof on a deep cornice. Entrance front with 2 curved bows and a Tuscan porch which may have been added later; 5 bay side. Plaster-vaulted hall, divided by screen of 3 fluted Doric columns with entablature from curving staircase. Formerly the seat of the Clarke family; now the offices of Antrim RDC.

Stephenstown, Dundalk, co Louth (FORTESCUE, *sub* HAMILTON/IFR). A square Georgian house of 2 storeys over a basement, 5 bays long and 5 bays deep, enlarged *ca* 1820 by the addition of 2 wings of 1 storey over a basement, running the full depth of the house and prolonging the front and rear elevations by 2 bays on either side. One of these wings was demolished *ca* mid-C19; that which survives has large tripartite fanlighted windows in both its elevations.

Stephenstown

Stackallan House

The entrance front has a fanlighted and rusticated doorway, now obscured by a porch with engaged Doric columns. Some time in the earlier part of C19, the windows were given Tudor-Revival hood mouldings; but late C19 the house was refaced with cement, and the hood-mouldings were replaced by Classical pediments and entablatures. Parapeted roof. Long central axial hall with a pair of columns at the far end. Drawing room with broad plasterwork frieze of foliage and C19 decorative plasterwork panels on walls. After the death of Mrs Pyke-Fortescue 1966, Stephenstown was inherited by her nephew, Major Digby Hamilton, who sold it *ca* 1974.

Stewart's Lodge (or **Steuart's Lodge**), **Leighlinbridge, co Carlow** (STEUART/ LGI1863; DUCKETT-STEUART, *sub* EUSTACE-DUCKETT/IFR). A house of late-Georgian appearance, of 2 storeys with a deep curved bow in the centre of one of its fronts rising a third storey. 1 bay on either side of the bow.

Stillorgan House

Stillorgan House, Stillorgan, co Dublin (ALLEN, v/DEP). A house begun 1695 by John Allen, MP, afterwards 1st Viscount Allen; consisting of a 2 storey 7 bay centre block and single-storey 7 bay wings. Both the centre and wings had high-pitched roofs with dormered attics; the centre had 4 very tall and slender chimneys, 2 at each end. Formal gardens; obelisk and grotto by Sir Edward Lovett Pearce. Mrs Delany, who visited Stillorgan 1731, described the house as "like one made of cards". The house was demolished 1860; the obelisk and grotto remain.

Stokestown, New Ross, co Wexford (DRAKE/LGI1958). A 2 storey 3 bay Georgian house with Wyatt windows. Eaved roof; projecting porch.

Stone House, Dunleer, co Louth (McCLINTOCK/IFR). A 3 storey 5 bay gable-ended mid-C18 house with a pedimented Doric doorcase. In 1814, the residence of William McClintock.

Stoneville, Rathkeale, co Limerick (SOUTHWELL, v/PB; MASSY/IFR). A 2 storey 5 bay gable-ended early C18 house, originally a hunting lodge owned by Hon Henry Southwell, MP; bought by the Massys after

his death 1758. Tripartite doorway. At the back of the house is a wing said to be earlier and also a fine stable range added 1802 by J. F. Massy, enclosing a courtyard.

Stormont Castle, Dundonald, co Down (CLELAND/LGI1912). An earlier house rebuilt as a large Scottish Baronial castle 1858 by the Belfast architect, Thomas Turner, with a tall tower reminiscent of the Prince Consort's tower at Balmoral Castle. Classical interior. Subsequently the official residence of the Prime Minister of Northern Ireland; the Northern Ireland Parliament house having been built in its grounds.

Stradbally Hall: Entrance Front

Stradbally Hall: Garden Front

Stradbally Hall, Stradbally, co Leix (COSBY/IFR). The original Stradbally Hall, on low-lying ground close to the town of Stradbally, was 1st built 1699 by Lt-Col Dudley Cosby, probably incorporating part of an earlier house; for in a painting of 1740s a gabled C17 tower can be seen at one corner of what had by then grown into a sizeable mansion. The house was enlarged 1714, also by Col Cosby, and a new, rather Gibbsian front added *ante* 1740s view was painted; presumably by his son, Pole Cosby, and perhaps to the design of the Irish architect, John Aheron. In the picture, the new front appears to have been added at one end of the earlier house, so that they stand side by side, each with its own door, like 2 houses in a street; both 3 storey, the new front pedimented with projecting end bays and Venetian windows. The house had

a formal approach, with a bridge across the river and a partly walled forecourt; and was surrounded by an elaborate formal layout of parterres, groves and avenues, with a rectangular pool or canal and numerous statues and garden buildings. In 1768, Dudley Cosby, 1st (and last) Lord Sydney and Stradbally, a diplomatist who was Minister to the Court of Denmark, demolished the house; and, in 1772, he built a new house on a different—and what was regarded as a healthier—site; of 2 storeys over a high basement and 9 bays; his overseer being Arthur Roberts. C19 views show it to have had a shallow pediment or gable

over the 3 outer bays on either side; this would have been rather unusual in a house of 1772, but the gables may have been part of an early C19 Gothic remodelling, for these views also show hood-mouldings over the windows. The garden front had a recessed centre, between 2 3 sided bows, of 1 storey and basement. In 1866–69, R. A. Cosby employed Sir Charles Lanyon to enlarge the house and remodel it in his characteristic Italianate style. Lanyon added a new entrance front, which was advanced from the old front wall so that the house became 3 rooms deep instead of 2. This new front has a 2 bay projection at either side, and a large single-storey balustraded Doric portico. On either side of the portico, in the recessed centre, is a group of 3 round-headed windows; a mannerism which appears in other Lanyon houses,

Stradbally Hall: Gallery

notably Moneyglass, co Antrim (*qv*). The upper storey windows are camber-headed; the lower ones, at the sides, rectangular with entablatures on console-brackets over them. On the garden front, Lanyon left the 2 3 sided bows, but filled in the recessed centre with a giant pedimented 3 arch loggia. The house was given a high-pitched eaved roof on a bracket cornice, and a deep curved bow in the centre of the end elevation. At the other end, a slightly lower 2 storey over basement bachelors' wing was built. The portico leads into an entrance hall with a vaulted ceiling and a flight of steps up to the level of the principal storey. The former entrance hall—which still keeps its C18 chimneypiece—has been made by Lanyon into a central top-lit staircase hall. The staircase, of Victorian oak turnery, leads up to a very impressive top-lit gallery, with a screen of pink marble Corinthian columns at either end and an elaborately coffered and ornamented barrel-vaulted ceiling. The 3 reception rooms in the garden front remain much as they were before the Lanyon rebuilding, with simple late-Georgian plasterwork; though the walls of the drawing room are decorated with panels of a charming Victorian paper in a gilt diaper pattern. The ballroom, one of the additional rooms formed 1866–69, extending into the bow at the end of the house, has a ceiling decorated with panels of early C19 pictorial paper in *grisaille*.

Stradbrook House, Blackrock, co Dublin (ACTON/IFR). A 2 storey bow-ended house of *ca* 1820.

Stradone House, Stradone, co Cavan (BURROWES/IFR). A late-Georgian house by John B. Keane, with a 2 storey front and a large return with an extra mezzanine storey. The front of 5 bays, the centre bay being recessed under a giant arch, beneath a pediment. The ground-floor windows on either side of the centre set in shallow arched recesses. Eaved roof on bracket cornice. The house is now demolished, but a Grecian gate lodge survives.

Straffan House, Straffan, co Kildare (BARTON/IFR). An imposing C19 house in a style combining Italianate and French château. Main block of 2 storeys with an attic of pedimented dormers in a mansard roof; 7 bay entrance front, the centre bay breaking forward and having a tripartite window above a single-storey balustraded Corinthian portico. Entablatures on console brackets over ground-floor windows; tri-

Straffan House

angular pediments over windows above and segmental pediment over central window. Decorated band between storeys; balustraded roof parapet; chimneystacks with recessed panels and tooth decoration. The main block prolonged at one side by a lower 2 storey wing, from which rises a tall and slender campanile tower, with 2 tiers of open belvederes. Formal garden with elaborate Victorian fountain. The house was reduced in size *ca* 1937 by Capt F. B. Barton, the 4 bays of the main block furthest from the wing being demolished. It was sold by him *ca* 1949 to Mr John Ellis, and re-sold *ca* 1960. It is now the home of Mr Kevin McClory, the film producer.

Straffan Lodge, Straffan, co Kildare (GUINNESS/IFR). A Georgian house of 2 storeys over a basement and 5 bays, described (1837) as "the neat residence of Mrs Whitelaw". Later single-storey wing with mullioned bow. Dining room decorated in Tudor style with oak panelling late C19 or early C20. Now the home of Mr & Mrs Robert Guinness, who have built a garden temple flanking the end of the house.

Strancally Castle, Knockanore, co Waterford (KEILY, *sub* USSHER/IFR; LLOYD/LGI1912; PARKES, *sub* CAREW/IFR and BECK-WITH-SMITH/LGI1969). A castle by James and George Richard Pain, built *ca* 1830 for John Keily in a romantic situation above the Blackwater, close to the remains of an old

Desmond castle notorious for its "Murdering Hole", a hole in the rock through which the bodies of its lord's victims were cast into the river. The interior of the castle is rather plain, with Gothic chimneypieces of marble; that in the dining room having battlements and miniature turrets. Sold to the Lloyd family C19; sold *ca* 1946 to S.E. Parkes. Subsequently resold.

Strangford House

Strangford House, Strangford, co Down (NUGENT, *sub* DOUGLAS-NUGENT/IFR). An elegant 3 storey late C18 house, built 1789 by a customs-collector named Norris. 3 bay front, the centre bay breaking forward; fanlighted doorway with sidelights, the lintel of the door being decorated with carved swags. The top storey has no windows in the front, but there is a rectangular blind panel above each window. Good interior plasterwork and joinery.

Strancally Castle

Stream Hill, Doneraile, co Cork (DILL/ IFR). A gabled late-Victorian or Edwardian house built of a pleasant pink sandstone, quarried on the spot. Attractive garden.

Strokestown Park

Strokestown Park: Library

Strokestown Park, Strokestown, co Roscommon (HALES PAKENHAM MAHON/IFR). A house with a centre block and wings, in the Palladian manner, of which the centre block is basically C17, completed 1696; but altered and refaced in the late-Georgian period; probably 1819, when J. Lynn is recorded as having carried out additions and alterations here for Lt-Gen Thomas Mahon, 2nd Lord Hartland. Of 3 storeys over a basement and 7 bays; the 3 centre bays and the sides being emphasized by framing-bands. Fanlighted doorway under single-storey balustraded Ionic portico; balustraded roof parapet with central die. The wings, which are of 2 storeys and 4 bays and joined to the centre block by curved sweeps as high as they are themselves, seem likely to have been added *ca* 1730, to the design of Richard Castle. The curved sweeps have niches flanked by oculi above Gibbsian doorcases, a composition characteristic of Castle; the wings are prolonged by screen-walls with niches and pedimented archways. One wing contains a magnificent

stable with vaulting carried on a row of Tuscan columns. Some of the principal rooms in the centre of the house have C18 panelling. In a late-Georgian addition at the back of the house there is a splended library with a coved ceiling and an original early C19 wallpaper of great beauty, in yellow and brown, which gives the effect of faded gold. The entrance to the demesne is a tall Georgian-Gothic arch at the end of the tree-lined main street of the town of Strokestown, one of the widest main streets in any country town in Ireland; it is said that 2nd Lord Hartland, who laid it out, wanted to have a street wider even than the Ringstrasse in Vienna.

Stuart Hall, Stewartstown, co Tyrone (STUART, CASTLE STEWART, E/PB). A 3 storey Georgian block with a pillared porch, joined to an old tower house by a C19 Gothic wing. In recent years, the top 2 storeys of the main block were removed, giving it the appearance of a Georgian bungalow. The house was bombed *ca* 1974 and subsequently demolished.

Suirvale, Cahir, co Tipperary (SMITH/ IFR; GARDNER/IFR). A 2 storey 3 bay gable-ended house, of C18 appearance but said to incorporate an earlier priest's house, joined by a 2 bay dormer-gabled link to a projecting 2 storey wing containing a large drawing room. External shutters; hood moulding over centre 1st floor window of original house.

Summer Grove, Mountmellick, co Leix. A very distinguished medium-sized house of *ca* 1760, built for a family of Huguenot origin named Sabatier, who were still living in the house 1837. The front of the house is of 2 storeys on a high plinth; but at the back 3 storeys have been fitted into the same height. The entrance front, of small squared stones which look like bricks, is of 5 bays, with a 1 bay pedimented breakfront. Diocletian window in pediment, above Venetian window, above pedimented and rusticated tripartite doorway; elaborate wrought-iron lamp bracket over door such as is found frequently in Dublin houses, but which is rare, if not unique, in the country. High and slightly sprocketed roof. Small square entrance hall with rococo decoration in ceiling and in an arch incorporating 3 smaller arches over doors on the inner wall. Drawing room with coved ceiling of rococo plasterwork in the manner of Robert West, though a little provincial. Shouldered and pedimented doorcases. Summer Grove has been unusually fortunate among smaller Irish country houses in having been consistently well maintained by successive owners. It is now the home of Mr & Mrs Barrie Whelan.

Suirvale

Summer Hill, co Mayo

Summer Hill, co Mayo: ceiling

Summer Hill, Killala, co Mayo (PALMER/ LGI875). A distinguished gable-ended mid-C18 house of 2 storeys over a basement; with a resemblance to the nearly homonymous Summer Grove, co Leix (*qv*). 5 bay front with 1 bay pedimented breakfront centre. Pediment with oculus and broken base-moulding; central Venetian window above shouldered doorcase with entablature flanked by small windows. Rectangular light above door with curving diamond glazing. Interior plasterwork in a simple and somewhat primitive rococo, complete with the odd rather amateurishly-moulded bird. Originally the seat of a branch of the Bourke family; subsequently passed to the Palmer family. Now falling into ruin.

Summerhill, Enfield, co Meath (LANGFORD, Bt/EDB; ROWLEY, LANGFORD, B/PB). The most dramatic of the great Irish Palladian houses, probably by Sir Edward Lovett Pearce in collaboration with Richard

Castle. Built 1731 for Hercules Rowley, MP, who inherited the estate from his mother, the daughter of Sir Hercules Langford. Crowning a hill, on the lower slopes of which stood C17 house of the Langfords, the house consisted of a 2 storey 7 bay main block, with a central feature of 4 giant recessed Corinthian columns, joined by 2 storey curving wings to end pavilions with towers and shallow domes. The skyline was further diversified by 2 massive square towers rising boldly at either end of the main block; one of several features reminiscent of Vanbrugh, who was, incidentally, Pearce's 1st cousin once removed. The front was prolonged by walls of rusticated stonework ending in rusticated arches. All the stonework of the front was beautifully crisp and sharp. The garden front was less spectacular, but elegant, with two storeys of engaged columns as its central feature; it faced along a tree-lined gorge. Large 2 storey hall. Staircase hall with plasterwork on its walls. Fine rococo ceiling in drawing room, with busts in circular frames and *putti* in clouds. Small dining room ceiling also rococo, with *putti* in clouds in centre. Adjoining room with coved ceiling springing from Doric order; this room and the small dining room were eventually thrown together to make a larger dining room. The house was damaged by fire C19; it was restored, but the original decoration of the hall was lost, as well as the original staircase. In 1879 and 1880, the Empress Elisabeth of Austria took Summerhill for the hunting season; it is said that her unquiet spirit found more happiness here than in any of the other numerous palaces and houses which she inhabited. After being burnt *ca* 1922, the house stood for 35 years or so as a ruin. Even in its ruinous state, Summerhill was one of the wonders of Ireland; in fact like Vanbrugh's Seaton Delaval, it gained added drama from being a burnt-out shell. The calcining of the central feature of the garden front looked like more fantastic rustication; the stonework of the side arches

Summerhill: Garden Front

was more beautiful than ever mottled with red lichen; and as the entrance front came into sight, one first became aware that it was a ruin by noticing daylight showing through the front door. But *ca* 1957 the ruin was demolished; an act of destruction, which, at the time, passed almost unnoticed.

Summerseat, Clonee, co Meath (GARNETT/LGI1912). A Georgian house of 2 storeys over a basement and 3 bays, with single-storey wings. Large round-headed windows.

Summerton (or **Somerton**), **Castleknock, co Dublin** (BROOKE, Bt, *of Summerton*/PB; LAIDLAW/LGI1958). A 2 storey late-Georgian house with an entrance front consisting of a recessed centre between 1 bay projections joined by an Ionic colonnade. 4 bay side. Heavy quoins; parapeted roof. Room with ceiling of Adamesque plasterwork. In the days of Sir George Brooke, 1st Bt, Summerton was the scene of lavish Edwardian hospitality; with the result that it had to be sold 1911, the buyer being T.K. Laidlaw.

Summerville, co Tipperary (*see* BALLINGARRANE).

Summerville, co Waterford (*see* CORBALLYMORE).

Sutton House, Sutton, co Dublin (JAMESON/IFR). A Victorian Tudor pile, with gables, mullions and immense chimneys; one end being in the nature of a gabled tower, 4 storeys high. Owned for a period *post* World War II by Mrs van der Elst, the campaigner for the abolition of capital punishment. Now an hotel.

Swainston, Kilmessan, co Meath (PRESTON/IFR). A fine C18 house consisting of a 2 storey 7 bay centre block joined to wings by curved sweeps with Ionic pilasters. The centre block has a breakfront, a segmental pediment over the doorway and a parapeted roof.

Summerhill, co Meath: Entrance Front and as a ruin

Swiftes Heath

Swiftes Heath, Jenkinstown, co Kilkenny (SWIFTE/IFR). A 2 storey early C18 or perhaps late C17 house, refaced in stucco C19. Both the front and side elevations are adorned with giant Corinthian pilasters which are of brick, like those at Bantry House (*qv*), but plastered over; presumably they are C19 embellishments, though they could possibly be earlier. Pedimented entrance front of 7 bays, the end bay on either side projecting boldly; balustraded C19 porch with clusters of Corinthian

columns at the corners. 7 bay side elevation. Low rooms; modillion cornice in the hall and the drawing room, which has a small closet opening off it at one corner. The boyhood home of Dean Swift, who was brought up here by his uncle, Godwin Swift, Attorney-General to the Duke of Ormonde for the County Palatine of Tipperary. Sold 1970.

Sybil Hill, Raheny, co Dublin (PLUNKET, B/PB). A plain late-Georgian house, built 1808 for James Barlow to the design of Frederick Darley. Of 2 storeys; entrance front with 1 bay on either side of a central bow; adjoining front with curved bow and 5 bays. In the present century, it became the home of Most Rev and Hon Benjamin Plunket, former Bishop of Meath, after he left the nearby St Anne's (*qv*). Sold *ca* 1950 by Mr Benjamin Plunket.

Sylvan Park, Kells, co Meath (ROWLEY/LGI863; AUSTIN, Bt/PB). A 3 storey pedimented house with a roof on a bracket cornice. Bought *post* World War II by Mr W. R. Austin. Subsequently sold and now demolished.

Syngefield

Syngefield, Birr, Offaly (SYNGE, Bt/PB). A mid-C18 house of 2 storeys over a basement; originally of 7 bays; with a Gothic-glazed Venetian window in both storeys of the 2 end bays of the front, and another in the middle, above a Venetian doorway. Diocletian windows in the end bays of the basement; round-headed windows in the basement on either side of the balustraded entrance steps. After a fire, one of the end bays was removed, so that the front ceased to be symmetrical. (For the seat of that branch of the Synge family of which the poet and playwright, J. M. Synge, was a cadet—*see* GLANMORE CASTLE, co Wicklow.)

T

Talbot Castle, co Meath (*see* ST MARY'S ABBEY).

Talbot Hall (formerly **Mount Corbett**) **New Ross, co Wexford** (TALBOT, *sub* O'REILLY/IFR; REDINGTON/LGI1899). A 3 storey 3 bay double gable-ended early to mid-C18 house, with a fanlighted doorway and a curved wing wall on one side linking the house to outbuildings. C19 hood mouldings over windows. Georgian Gothic entrance arch on avenue. Occupied 1798 by the insurgents, who planned their attack on New Ross in the dining room. Passed by inheritance from the Talbot family to the Redington family. Now the home of the Misses Roche.

Tanavalla, Listowel, co Kerry. A late-Georgian house of 2 storeys over a basement. 3 bay front, with fanlighted doorway; 4 bay side. Wide-eaved roof.

Tanderagee Castle, Tanderagee, co Armagh (MONTAGU, MANCHESTER, D/PB). A rather restrained C19 Baronial castle, built *ca* 1837 by 6th Duke of Manchester, as Viscount Mandeville, on the site of an ancient castle of the O'Hanlons. At one end, a sturdy machicolated tower; at the other, a gabled block rather reminiscent of a Tudor manor house; with a strange corbelled look-out turret at one corner. Now a potato-crisp factory.

Tanavalla

Tanderagee Castle

Taney House

Taney House, Dundrum, co Dublin (JAMESON/IFR). A gable-ended Georgian house of 2 storeys over a basement with a 3 bay front, enlarged by the addition of a block of 2 storeys over a basement at one end and set back. Enclosed porch fronted with pillars in centre of original house.

Tankardstown, Slane, co Meath (BLACKBURNE, *sub* TOWNSHEND/LGI1958). A 2 storey late-Georgian house. Entrance front consisting of 3 bays and an end bay breaking forward; the lower storey of this bay being rusticated, and having an entrance doorway, with a pediment on consoles, not in line with the window above. 3 bay side elevation; ground floor windows set in arched recesses with blocking; blocking round 1st floor windows also. Parapeted roof.

Tanrego House, Ballysadare, co Sligo (VERSCHOYLE/IFR). A plain 2 storey "L"-shaped Georgian house. The home of the father of Derek Verschoyle, poet, Literary Editor of the *Spectator* and reputed model for Peter Beste-Chetwynde in Evelyn Waugh's novel, *Decline and Fall*.

Tanrego House

Tara House (formerly **Hyde Park**), **Inch, co Wexford** (BEAUMAN/LGI1886; KELLY/LGI1958). A compact 2 storey villa by Richard Morrison, built *ca* 1807 for J. C. Beauman. 3 bay front, with slightly recessed centre; single-storey Doric portico, Wyatt window under relieving arch on either side. Wide-eaved roof. Very good interior plasterwork by James Talbot. Impressive domed staircase hall with oval oculus; the dome being without pendentives, but resting directly on the cornice. Keyhole pattern in plasterwork on soffit of stairs. For some years the home of Sir David Kelly, former British Ambassador to Russia, and his wife, the writer on travel, architecture and gardens, Marie-Noele Kelly.

Tarbert House, Tarbert, co Kerry (LESLIE/IFR). A plain 2 storey 7 bay Georgian house with a 3rd storey added mid-C19. Glazed porch also C19. The interior has a fine panelled room with Ionic pilasters.

Templemore Abbey

Temple House

Temple House, Ballymote, co Sligo (PERCEVAL/IFR). Originally a 2 storey house of *ca* 1820, built by the Perceval family when they moved from the original castle here; with a 5 bay front, the centre bay being recessed and having a Wyatt window over an enclosed Ionic porch. The house was greatly enlarged and embellished 1860 by Alexander Perceval, who added a higher 2 storey block of 7 bays at right angles to its back, forming a new and more impressive entrance front; the original front becoming the side elevation. The new front, which is of limestone ashlar, has a 1 bay pedimented breakfront framed by coupled Ionic pilasters in the upper story; and a large arched porte-cochère with coupled engaged Doric columns at its corners. The end of the original house prolongs the front of 1860 block by 1 bay set back; at the other end of the new block there is a single-storey 2 bay wing. Central triple window; entablatures and triangular and segmental pediments over windows in both new and original front; balustraded roof parapets on both the original house and 1860 block. The house is reputed to contain more than 90 rooms. Fine stable building; lodge with Ionic porch.

Templemore Abbey (also known as **Templemore Priory**), **co Tipperary** (CARDEN, Bt, *of Templemore*/PB). Templemore Castle, the original seat of this branch of the Carden family, was destroyed by fire towards mid-C18; after which a handsome 9 bay house with a pediment carried on 4 giant engaged Roman Doric columns, pilasters at the corners, a balustraded roof and windows with cambered heads was built elsewhere in the demesne. This house was demolished early C19 and a new house built on a more elevated site in a demesne adjoining the original park to the west; it was originally known as Templemore Priory, but afterwards called Templemore Abbey. In 1819, this house was no more than a single-storey Gothic cottage with a very tall round tower and a crocketed square tower; but it was subsequently greatly enlarged by William Vitruvius Morrison, in the Tudor-Gothic style. As completed, the house had a symmetrical 2 storey entrance front, with oriels, gables with finials and a battlemented parapet; and a long, irregular side elevation, partly of 3 storeys; also adorned with gables, finials, battlements and crockets. Templemore Abbey was burnt 1922; now demolished.

Tempo Manor, nr Enniskillen, co Fermanagh (MAGUIRE/VF; EMERSON-TENNENT, Bt/PB1876; LANGHAM, Bt/PB). An old castle of the Maguires; sold early C19 by Constantine Maguire, whose younger brother, Captain Bryan Maguire, a celebrated duellist and eccentric, succeeded him as chief of his race and died destitute in Dublin 1835, leaving an only surviving son, the last of the line, who went to sea and was never heard of again. Tempo was acquired by William Tennent, a Belfast banker, whose daughter and heiress was the wife of Sir James Emerson-Tennent, MP, a distinguished politician, colonial administrator and writer. A new house, incorporating part of the old castle, was built 1863; it has been attributed by Mr Dixon and Dr Rowan to Thomas Turner, of Belfast. It is in a rather unusual Victorian-Jacobean style, with a strong resemblance to Kintullagh Castle, co Antrim (*qv*) and Killashee, co Kildare (*qv*). Curvilinear gables; rectangular and round-headed plate glass windows, some of them having entablatures crowned with strapwork. Of 2 storeys, the upper storey being in fact an attic in the high-pitched roof. At one end is a turret with a belfry and spire. Tempo subsequently passed by marriage to the Langham family. The park here is said to be the scene of Maria Edgeworth's novel, *Castle Rackrent*.

Terenure

Terenure, co Dublin (DEANE/LGI1912; SHAW, Bt/PB). A handsome 2 storey C18 house, originally the seat of the Deane family. Front of 5 bays between 2 curved bows, with a 3 bay pedimented breakfront and a pillared porch. Urns on pediment and roof parapet. Towards the end of C18, the house was leased by Robert Shaw, Accountant-General of the Post Office, a great-great uncle of George Bernard Shaw. His son, Sir Robert Shaw, 1st Bt, MP and Lord Mayor of Dublin, acquired the property, which was bought for him by his father-in-law, Abraham Wilkinson, who lived nearby at Bushy Park (*qv*). Later, when the demesne of Terenure had been cut in half by a new road, Sir Robert abandoned it in favour of Bushy Park, which his wife had inherited. Terenure, having been let for a period to a member of the Taaffe family, was eventually sold to Frederick Bourne. It is now a Carmelite college.

Termon

Termon, Carrickmore, co Tyrone
(BERESFORD, *sub* WATERFORD, M/PB; ALEX-ANDER/IFR). A 3 storey late-Georgian house built 1815 as a rectory by Rev C.C. Beresford, whose crest appears in the dining room ceiling. 3 bay front, with projecting porch; 4 bay rear elevation, with large windows on ground floor. After Disestablishment, it became the property of Rev C.C. Beresford's daughter, Charlotte, wife of Rev Samuel Alexander.

Tervoe: Entrance Front

Tervoe, Clarina, co Limerick (DE LA POER MONSELL/IFR). A 3 storey block of 1776, built by Col W. T. Monsell, MP, on the site of a house dating from *ca* 1690; to which single-storey wings, running from the front of the house to the back, were added *ca* 1830. A single-storey Ionic portico was added on the entrance front probably at the same time. The entrance front was of 7 bays, with a 3 bay breakfront centre; the centre window on 1st floor had a pediment over it. The ends of the wings on the entrance front were pedimented, and each had a single Wyatt window surmounted by a blind panel. Parapeted roof. In the garden front, facing the Shannon, the wings were

Tervoe: Garden Front

bow-ended. Square hall with plasterwork frieze; plain and elegant stone staircase in room to left of hall. Oval music room in one of the wings, with Classical figures painted on walls. The family ceased to live here 1951, and the house was demolished 1953.

Thomastown Castle, co Louth (*see* KNOCK ABBEY).

Thomastown Castle, co Tipperary

Thomastown Castle, co Tipperary: Garden Front

Thomastown Castle, Golden, co Tipperary (MATHEW/IFR; DALY/IFR). Originally a long 2 storey house of pink brick built from 1670 onwards by George Mathew, half-brother of the Great Duke of Ormonde; with a centre 1 room deep consisting of a great chamber or gallery above a rusticated arcade, and projecting wings; a massive oak staircase led up from the arcade to the first floor. It was probably by the same builders who worked for the Duchess of Ormonde at Dunmore House (*qv*), near Kilkenny; while Dr Loeber suggests that the arcade may have been designed by Sir William Robinson. The Mathews grew richer through heiress marriages, and the grandson of the builder of the house, another George, who inherited 1711, carried out various additions and improvements; it was probably he who filled in the centre of the garden front, between the 2 projecting wings, to provide a dining room 50 feet long, facing across the park to the Galtee Mountains. On this side of the house he made a great formal garden

with terraces "studded with busts and statues"; the park was laid out in avenues and geometrical enclosures. This George Mathew was known as "Grand George" and renowned for his hospitality; people could come uninvited to Thomastown and use it as though it were an inn; many legends have grown up about him, though he has become somewhat confused, in local folklore, with "Big George", Earl of Kingston (*see* MITCHELSTOWN CASTLE). In 1812, Francis Mathew, 2nd Earl of Llandaff, called in Richard (afterwards Sir Richard) Morrison to enlarge the house and transform it into a castle. Morrison's transformation was literally no more than skin-deep: he refaced the house in cement, which was originally painted the rather surprising shade of pale blue; a mask of Gothic openings was applied to the front of C17 arcade which was glazed and turned into a "Gothic Hall" with a Gothic chimneypiece of plaster and other Gothic plasterwork. Slender turrets, square and polygonal, were added to the entrance and garden fronts, which remained symmetrical; the 2 on either side of the entrance have pinnacles like rockets or darts growing out of them; from a distance they look like rabbits' ears. The office wing to the right of the entrance front was enlarged into a vast Gothic kitchen court and stables; a detached entrance tower was also built. The great upstairs room became a Gothic library; the drawing room remained Classical and was adorned with scagliola columns. Fr Theobald Mathew, the "Apostle of Temperance", grew up here, his father having been a cousin of 1st Earl of Llandaff who more or less adopted him and made him his agent. Lady Elizabeth Mathew, sister of 2nd Earl, left Thomastown to her cousin on her mother's side, the Vicomte de Rohan Chabot, son of the Comte de Jarnac. It eventually passed to the Daly family; but from *ca* 1872 onwards it was allowed to fall into disrepair; it is now one of the most spectacular of all the many ruined Gothic castles in Ireland, much of it submerged beneath the ivy which grows here with an unbelievable luxuriance. In 1938, the ruin was bought by the late Archbishop David Mathew, the historian, in order to keep it in the family and save it from destruction.

Thomastown Park, Birr, Offaly (BENNETT/LGI1904; RYAN/IFR). A house built *ca* mid-C18 by a Mr Leggat. Old castle in demesne. Sold by G/Capt R.S. Ryan 1951.

Thomastown Park, Athlone, co Roscommon. A 3 storey 7 bay Georgian house with a pillared porch.

Thornhill, co Dublin (*see* ST ANNE'S).

Thorn Park, Oranmore, co Galway (BUTLER/IFR). A Victorian house of 1 storey and a gabled attic. Pointed gables; battlemented single-storey 3 sided bows.

Tibradden, Rathfarnham, co Dublin (GUINNESS/IFR). A house built *ca* 1860.

Timoleague House, Timoleague, co Cork (TRAVERS/IFR). A square late-Georgian house, built *ca* 1830 by Col Robert Travers. Burnt 1920; a new house built on a different

Timoleague House

site 1924 by S. E. Travers, to the design of W. Henry Hill, of Cork. The new house is of stone, with a high eaved roof and a 5 bay symmetrical front, with modern casement windows; the ground floor windows having pleasantly cambered heads. Ruins of old Barry castle in grounds. Gardens with notable collection of trees and shrubs from all over the world.

Glebe House, Timoleague

Timoleague, co Cork: Glebe House (WESTBY/IFR). An Attractive late-Georgian Glebe House of 2 storeys over a basement, possibly based on a design by Richard (afterwards Sir Richard) Morrison. 3 bay front, with simple entablature over doorcase, joined by screen wall with archway to outbuilding; 3 bay side, with Wyatt windows on either side of the centre in the lower storey. Eaved roof on simple bracket cornice. Earlier this century, when it was still a Rectory, the house was occupied for many years by Rev Canon L. R. Fleming (*see* LGI1958), father of the writer and journalist Lionel Fleming, who describes it in *Head or Harp*.

Timoney Park, co Tipperary. A C19 Tudor-Gothic house with battlements and turrets.

Timpany, Ballynahinch, co Down (ROBB/IFR). A gable-ended house with a thatched roof, of 1 storey and an attic, with curved dormers. Built 1780 by Capt James Robb. The house was enlarged and improved 1858 by Alexander Robb, who raised the walls so that the attic became a 2nd storey; and re-roofed the house with slates; he also added a return at the back.

Tinerana, Killaloe, co Clare (PURDON/IFR). A Victorian house beautifully situated on the shores of Lough Derg, in a demesne with fine trees.

Tinnakill, Abbeyleix, co Leix. A 3 bay C18 house with a pedimented breakfront and a high roof.

u

Tinnehinch, Enniskerry, co Wicklow (GRATTAN/IFR; GRATTAN-BELLEW, Bt/PB). A C18 house in a beautiful situation by the Dargle River, which, together with an estate, was presented by the Irish Parliament to Henry Grattan, the great orator, statesman and Irish patriot, in gratitude for the part he played in obtaining its freedom from British control 1782. The house was formerly an inn, the best in co Wicklow, and much frequented by Grattan himself. It consisted of a 3 storey 5 bay centre, with 1 bay overlapping wings of the same height but containing only 2 storeys, so that the rooms in the wings were higher than those in the centre of the house. 1 bay pedimented breakfront centre; round-headed doorway with blocking. Triple windows in wings, those on the ground floor being set under relieving arches. The house was destroyed by fire this century; one storey of the ruin still stands, and has been made into a feature of the garden of the present house, which is in the former stables.

Tinode, Blessington, co Wicklow (COGAN/LGI1899). A Victorian house of granite, built 1864 to the design of W. F. Caldbeck, of Dublin. Entrance door under elaborately moulded hood on red marble pillars.

Tintern Abbey

Tintern Abbey, Ballycullane, co Wexford (COLCLOUGH/IFR). A medieval abbey, a daughter house of Tintern Abbey, Monmouthshire, in a romantic situation by the side of a creek on the western side of Bannow Bay; granted after the Dissolution to Sir Anthony Colclough, an Elizabethan soldier, who turned the abbey church into a dwelling house where his descendants lived until 1958. It was unusual among country houses in keeping the appearance of a medieval abbey church, dominated by its massive C15 tower; probably unique in Ireland, though it has at least one English counterpart, Buckland Abbey, Devon. Eventually, it was given pointed Georgian-Gothic windows, set in the blocked-up nave arches, and a Gothicized Venetian doorway in the Batty Langley manner. A wing was also added resembling a transept, with a large Decorated window. The interior was

churchwarden Gothic. Presented to the Nation by Miss Lucy Colclough 1958; now being restored by the Office of Works as a monastic ruin, though some of its Tudor and Georgian-Gothic features are to be preserved.

Tivoli, Cork, co Cork (MURPHY/IFR). A mid to late C18 house in the Palladian manner and probably designed under the influence of Davis Duckart, consisting of a bow-fronted centre block of 2 storeys over a basement joined to wings or pavilions by straight open arcades. Built by James Morrison, a rich Cork merchant and Mayor of Cork, who named it Tivoli because of its steep and romantically-wooded grounds going down to the Lee estuary, which he adorned with a reproduction of the Temple of Vesta, as well as with a larger and more elaborate temple in the Gothic taste. Tivoli was eventually acquired by James Morrison's grandson, James Morgan, a member of another wealthy Cork merchant family, who bought it from a cousin who was also his sister-in-law. Some time *ca* 1820s the house was largely gutted by a fire caused by James Morgan's children playing with fireworks. In the early years of the present century, Tivoli was the home of A. St J. Murphy. The house was demolished a few years ago, the follies having long disappeared. The estate was ideally depicted in Nathaniel Grogan's large painting of the Lee estuary in the National Gallery of Ireland.

Tober, Dunlavin, co Wicklow. A 3 storey 5 bay early C18 house with its windows close together, away from the corners. Shouldered doorcase with entablature. The seat of the Powell family. Now a ruin.

Tobertynan, Enfield, co Meath (MACEVOY, *sub* DE STACPOOLE/IFR). A small castellated house of 2 storeys over a basement and 3 bays, with battlements and cylindrical corner turrets; and with a 3 storey battlemented addition at one side. Mainly built *ca* 1810 by Francis MacEvoy, a distinguished surgeon, afterwards the home of his brother, James, the father-in-law of Sir

Tobertynan

Bernard Burke, Ulster King of Arms and Editor of the *Burke's* series of genealogical publications. Passed to the de Stacpooles with the marriage of Pauline MacEvoy to 4th Duke de Stacpoole. Sold 1962.

Tollymore Park: Gateway

Tollymore Park: C18

Tollymore Park: same Front C19

Tollymore Park: later Entrance Front

Tollymore Park, Bryansford, co Down (HAMILTON, CLANBRASSILL, E/DEP; JOCELYN, RODEN, E/PB). A C18 and C19 house extending round 4 sides of a courtyard; of which the earliest part was built mid-C18 by James Hamilton, Viscount Limerick and 1st Earl of Clanbrassill of 2nd creation; whose grandmother was the heiress of the Magennis family, the original owners of the estate. As 1st built, the house consisted of a 2 storey block with 1 bay on either side of a central 3 sided bow, and single-storey 3 bay wings; the entrance door being not in the middle of the bow, but in the bay to the left of it. The architect of this original range is likely to have been Thomas Wright, of Durham, probably very much in collaboration with 1st Earl. By 1787 the 3 other sides of the courtyard had been built, all single-storey; the entrance had been moved from its original position to the centre of the adjoining front, and the house already had the long corridors with windows containing roundels of Flemish stained glass, for which it was noted in later years. Towards mid-C19—by which time Tollymore had passed by inheritance to the Earls of Roden—an extra storey was added to all those parts of the house which had formerly

been of 1 storey only. The entrance front became a typical late-Georgian composition of 9 bays with a pedimented breakfront centre and a single-storey Doric portico; the corresponding front on the other side of the courtyard being also of 9 bays and pedimented. A little later in the century, but *ante* 1859, the house was further enlarged and the original C18 2 storey block was given high roofs in the French château manner; which, rising to the left of the entrance front, made it seem lop-sided. Probably at this time, too, the upstairs windows of the central bow of C18 block were given segmental pediments; the appearance of this side of the house having already been slightly changed some time before by the insertion of a Venetian window in an arched recess on either side of the bow in the lower storey, in place of the original entrance doorway and the corresponding window. The Victorian writer and political thinker, W. H. Mallock, an inveterate stayer in country houses, preferred Tollymore to all the other Irish houses which he frequented. The demesne of Tollymore is famous for its picturesque scenery and its numerous follies. It is one of the earliest examples in Ireland of a naturalistic landscape park in the manner of William Kent, having been laid out by 1st Earl of Clanbrassill (then Viscount Limerick) in mid-C18. The follies, gateways and bridges, mostly erected by 2nd and last Earl of Clanbrassill and some of them probably designed by Thomas Wright, include a barn made to look like a Gothic church, with a tower and spire, gate piers with spires, an obelisk, a grotto or hermitage, an

elegant Gothic arch with crocketed pinnacles and flying buttresses, and a castellated gateway known as the Barbican Gate. The Tollymore estate was bought by the Northern Ireland Ministry of Agriculture in 2 portions 1930 and 1941. The house was demolished 1952; but the demesne is maintained as a forest park and open to the public.

Tottenham Green

Tottenham Green, Taghmon, co Wexford (TOTTENHAM/IFR; and *sub* ELY, M/PB). A house of late C17 or early C18 appearance, but said to incorporate a much older structure. Of 1 storey over a very high basement, which was more like a ground floor, and with an attic in the high-pitched roof which was lit by dormers and by a Venetian window in the large pediment which was the chief feature of the 5 bay entrance front. Below the pediment was a pedimented doorway flanked by narrow windows and approached up a long flight of steps. At one end of the front was a projecting wing of the same height added *ca* 1712, with 2 long windows at right angles to the front. Though not large, the house possessed a ballroom. The Venetian window in the pediment lit a bedroom known as the "Bishop's Room", which was associated with the story of the ghost of the unhappy Anne Tottenham, who died 1775. Earlier in C18, Tottenham Green was the seat of Charles Tottenham, MP, known as "Tottenham in his Boots" from having appeared in the Irish House of Commons in riding-boots after an historic ride from co Wexford to vote in a crucial division. (He is not to be confused with

"Boots" Carew—*see* BALLINAMONA PARK.)
Sir Charles Tottenham, 2nd Bt, inherited
the estates of the Loftus family and became
1st Marquess of Ely; Tottenham Green
went to his younger son, Lord Robert
Tottenham, Bishop of Clogher. It was sold
ca 1873 to a Mr Bell; re-sold 1913 to James
Cullen; sold once again 1945 and demolished *ca* 1950.

Tourin, Cappoquin, co Waterford (MUS-
GRAVE, Bt, *of Tourin*/PB; JAMESON/IFR).
Originally an "E"-shaped late C17 house
with a pediment, wide eaves and tall
chimneys, built onto an old castle; replaced
post 1844 by a square 2 storey mid-C19
Italianate house with an eaved roof on an
unusually deep and elaborately moulded
bracket cornice, which is echoed by a wide
string-course. Entrance front of 3 bays between 2 end bays; porch at one side
balanced by single-storey projection with
fanlighted window. 4 bay garden front
with triple windows in both storeys of
outer bays; single-storey curved bow in
centre, with elegant ironwork veranda. The
house stands close to the Blackwater a little
upstream of Dromana (*qv*), and on the
opposite bank. The seat of the Musgraves;
inherited by Mrs T. O. Jameson (*née* Mus-
grave).

Tower Hill, co Cork (*see* MOUNT PATRICK).

Towerhill, Ballyglass, co Mayo (BLAKE,
Bt, *of Menlough*/PB). A 2 storey house of *ca*
1790. Entrance front of 6 bays with pedimented breakfront centre and round-
headed rusticated doorway. Adamesque
interior plasterwork. Sold *post* World War
II by Lt-Col A. J. Blake; subsequently demolished.

Tourin

Townley Hall

Townley Hall, Drogheda, co Louth
(BALFOUR/LGI1912; CRICHTON, ERNE, E/PB).
Francis Johnston's Classical masterpiece,
just as Charleville Forest (*qv*) is his masterpiece in Gothic; a house "of singular and
impressive austerity", in the words of
Christopher Hussey. Designed 1794 for
Blayney Balfour. Of 2 storeys over a basement, with 3 7 bay fronts that are identical
except that the entrance front has a single-
storey Grecian Doric portico with coupled
columns; and devoid of all ornament except
for a string-course and a bold cornice;
deriving their beauty from perfect proportions. Parapeted roof. Entrance hall
with coffered ceiling and arched recesses in
the manner of Soane. Superb central rotunda, lit by glazed dome, with a wonderfully light and graceful staircase curving up
inside it. Around the upper storey of this
rotunda are apses, niches and arched recesses, producing an "endlessly curving
movement" and an infinite variety of

Townley Hall: Central Rotunda and Staircase

spatial effects; Mrs Townley Balfour, the widow of the grandson of the builder, said, after living in the house for more than 40 years, that it gave her pleasure every time she passed up and down the staircase. Large, simple rooms arranged round the central rotunda; library with lightly coffered ceiling *en suite* with drawing room hung with jade-green Chinese wallpaper. Kitchen wing extending along one side of yard at basement level, with windows set in deep arches and Grecian Doric columns supporting plain and massive entablatures under relieving arches. Inherited, after the death of Mrs Townley Balfour 1954, by Mr David Crichton; who sold it to Trinity College, Dublin 1956.

Trabolgan

Trabolgan, Whitegate, co Cork (ROCHE, FERMOY, B/PB; CLARKE/IFR). A Georgian house, of 2 storeys at the front, and 3 storeys at the back; to which single-storey wings were added C19 making a facade of exceptional length; consisting of a 2 storey 8 bay centre with wings of 5 bays on either side, beyond which are shallow curved bows each with 3 windows. The centre block has a parapeted roof and a single-storey Doric portico; the wings have round-headed windows. This, the principal front of the house, faces out to sea; so that in a south-easterly gale it is hard to open the hall door. The 3 storey rear elevation was thus also an entrance front, which was used in stormy weather. The reception rooms form a long enfilade in the principal front, extending on either side of the entrance hall. The 1st room in the right-hand wing is an orangery or winter garden, beyond which is a bow-fronted ballroom. Corresponding with the orangery in the left-hand wing is a large drawing room with an Adamesque—or Adam-Revival—ceiling. The staircase, which has a blustrade of plain metal uprights, is in a separate hall behind the entrance hall. The house is approached by avenue of more than a mile in length, which having been closely hemmed in by trees and shrubs for most of its way, emerges spectacularly into the open by the sea and sweeps round to the long front of the house. Half-way up the avenue is a triumphal arch; and there is a tower on the headland between the house and Roche's Point at the entrance to Cork Harbour. The seat of the Roche family, Lords Fermoy. Sold *ca* 1880 to William Clarke; sold by the Clarkes *ca* 1947; for some years after that a holiday-camp; subsequently a college.

Trafalgar House, Montenotte, Cork, co Cork. A house of 2 storeys over a basement built early C19 by an admirer of Nelson, who as well as naming it after the great naval victory, had a magnificent marble chimney piece made for the principal reception room decorated with reliefs of Nelson's head, HMS *Victory* and Britannia. The house was refaced in mid-Victorian period and a porch with Romanesque columns added at one end. 5 bay front with triangular and segmental pediments on console brackets over windows; roof on modillion cornice. Graceful curving staircase with thin turned balusters. In 1837, the residence of T. Lyons; in the present century, of Rt Hon Sir Stanley Harrington, who built a pleasant bow-ended conservatory at one end of the house as a 21st birthday present for one of his daughters. After being sold by the Harringtons, the house suffered various vicissitudes, in which the Nelson chimney-piece was most unfortunately destroyed. It has now been admirably restored as the offices of Henley & Kavanagh, Chartered Quantity Surveyors.

Trimlestown Castle, Kildalkey, co Meath (BARNEWALL, TRIMLESTOWN, B/PB). A medieval tower-house with a C18 house attached. Here lived 12th Lord Trimlestown, a celebrated figure in mid-C18 Ireland; he kept a large eagle chained up by the front door and he had a magnificent coach which had been presented to him by Marshal Saxe; for, as a Catholic, he had spent much of his life abroad, where he had acquired a skill in medicine, so that he would treat the poor of the neighbourhood gratuitously; he also treated a fashionable lady for the vapours by getting 4 assistants to threaten her with rods in a darkened room. In his time, the castle had a fine formal garden; there was an aviary of rare birds and a greenhouse full of exotic plants; there was also a long straight avenue. Early in C19, the castle was adorned with what a contemporary described as "ornamental towers, an embattled parapet and other marks of the style which prevailed in the latter part of the sixteenth century". Soon afterwards, however, it was abandoned by the family, and fell into ruin.

Tuam Palace, Tuam, co Galway. The Palace of the (C of I) Archbishops (afterwards Bishops) of Tuam; built between 1716 and 1741 by Archbishop Edward Synge. Described 1787 by Rev Daniel Beaufort as old-fashioned and ill-contrived. Improvements carried out early C19, completed 1823; so that the Palace was described (1837) as "large and handsomely built, though not possessing much architectural embellishment".

Tudenham Park

Tudenham Park (formerly **Rochfort**), **Mullingar, co Westmeath** (ROCHFORT, *sub* BELVEDERE, E/DEP; HOPKINS, Bt, *of Athboy*/PB1860; TOTTENHAM/IFR). A large 3 storey block of *ca* 1742 by the side of Lough Ennell; attributed by the Knight of Glin to Richard Castle. Built for George Rochfort, brother of 1st Earl of Belvedere, who lived alongside him at Belvedere (*qv*); and who, having quarrelled with him, built a large sham ruin to shut out the view of his brother's house. Faced with ashlar which appears to have been re-pointed mid-C19. Entrance front with central niche and oculus above a Doric columned doorcase. Side elevations with central curved bows. Large hall with a fireplace on either side; large and lofty reception rooms, some with coved cornices in the style of Robert West. 2 storey upper hall with well gallery and glass dome which, like the staircase window, was re-glazed with stained glass C19. Good early wallpapers in some bedrooms. Terrace near house overlooking the water. Immense Victorian entrance gates, railings and lodge. Sold *ca* 1836 to Sir Francis Hopkins, 2nd Bt, who left it to his sister, Anna Maria, wife of N. L. Tottenham; its name was subsequently changed from Rochfort to Tudenham Park. Used as a hospital during World War I, and occupied by the military in World War II. Stood empty and derelict for some years; demolished *ca* 1957; now a shell.

Tudor Hall, Holywood, co Down (DUNN/IFR1976). A Tudor-Revival house of 1840.

Tulfarris, Blessington, co Wicklow (HORNIDGE/IFR). A 2 storey late-Georgian house with a 5 bay front, the centre bay breaking forward; Victorian porch with glazed arches. 2 bay end, with a Wyatt window set under a relieving arch on the ground floor.

Tulira Castle, Ardrahan, co Galway (MARTYN/LGI1912; MARTYN-HEMPHILL, HEMPHILL, B/PB). An old tower-house, onto which a castellated house by George Ashlin was built from 1882 onwards for Edward Martyn, a leading figure in the Irish literary and artistic revival, who started a studio for making Irish stained glass and founded the Palestrina Choir at the Pro-Cathedral, Dublin. The castellated house is of 2 storeys, with a porch-tower and turret in the centre of its entrance front, and with polygonal corner-turrets, the battlements of which are slightly higher than those of the main roof-parapet. Symmetrical garden front with oriel surmounted by gable and coat-of-arms in centre. Large and regularly disposed mullioned windows. Prominent gargoyle-spouts. Fine Gothic hall where Edward Martyn, whose bedroom and study were rooms of monastic simplicity in the old tower, would play polyphonic music on the organ after dinner. Staircase with stained glass and other decoration of 1891 by John Dibblee Crace. Passed after Edward Martyn's death to his cousin, Mary, wife of 3rd Lord Hemphill.

Tullagreine House, Carrigtwohill, co Cork. A 2 storey 5 bay early C19 house with a 1 bay breakfront centre. Eaved roof. Porch at side and projecting ranges at rear. Imposing stables on opposite side of main road to house. The seat of a branch of the Martin family; more recently, of the late Major W. J. Green. Now an hotel.

Tullamaine Castle

Tullamaine Castle, Fethard, co Tipperary (MAHER/IFR; JACKSON, *sub* REDESDALE, B/PB). A C19 castle by William Tinsley, of Clonmel, built 1835–38 for John Maher, MP, on the site of an earlier house. Dominated by a square battlemented and machicolated tower; a lower tower with bartizans at the other end of the principal front. Battlemented screen wall with turrets. Long hall. In recent years the home of Hon Mrs Jackson, one of the famous Mitford sisters. Afterwards the home of Mr William Albertini.

Tullig House, Millstreet, co Cork. A plain 2 storey 5 bay Georgian house with an eaved roof and a Victorian glass porch.

Tullig House

Tully, Louisburgh, co Mayo. A small house of *ca* 1800. In 1814, the residence of Nicholas Garvey; now of Sir Charles & Lady Harman.

Tullydoey

Tullydoey, Dungannon, co Tyrone (PROCTOR/LGI1958). A 2 storey gable-ended early or mid-C18 house, with roof dormers, built near what is believed to be the remains of an old priory. 7 bay front; later gabled porch, with a fanlight in the form of a shallow segmental pointed arch above the door and sidelights.

Tullylagan: before and after excavation

Tullylagan (sometimes known as **Tullylagan Manor**, formerly **New Hamburgh**), **Cookstown, co Tyrone** (GREER/IFR). Built

ca 1830; 2 storeys over a basement, which was subsequently excavated, so that it became in effect a ground floor. 3 bay front; 2 storey projecting porch, with coupled pilasters on both storeys and large window with entablature in upper storey. Eaved roof on bracket cornice. Wing at side, originally 1 storey over basement, which became a ground floor as in the main block.

Tullymore Lodge

Tullymore Lodge, Ballymena, co Antrim (O'NEILL, B/PB). A 2 storey late-Georgian house. 5 bay front, 3 sided end-bows. 3 bay projecting porch with Wyatt window in centre. Eaved roof. All the chimneys grouped together in one long stack; but while the stack has a continuous base and a continuous coping along the top, there are gaps between the individual chimneys.

Tullymore Park, co Down (*see* TOLLYMORE PARK).

Tullynally Castle: Entrance Front

Tullynally Castle (formerly **Pakenham Hall**), **Castlepollard, co Westmeath** (PAKENHAM, LONGFORD, E/PB). With its long, picturesque skyline of towers, turrets, battlements and gateways stretching among the trees of its rolling park, Tullynally covers a greater area than any other castellated country house in Ireland; it looks not so much like a castle as a small fortified town; a Camelot of the Gothic Revival. Its vast extent is due to the fact that castellated out-offices are joined to the house, which is basically a compact C18 block, its Georgian sash-windows clearly visible at one end of the great complex. Originally, C18 house was of 2 storeys, as appears in a drawing done 1738 by G. E. Pakenham, younger brother of the then owner; which also shows the great formal layout of basins, cascades and canals which existed in those days and which was subsequently made into a naturalistic landscape. The house was enlarged 1780 to the design of Graham Myers; presumably 3rd storey was added at this time. Then, between 1801 and 1806, 2nd Earl of Longford (who was the brother of the two Peninsular War generals, Sir Edward Pakenham, who afterwards fell at New Orleans, and Sir Hercules Pakenham, as well as of Catherine, the wife of the great Duke of Wellington) employed Francis Johnston to make the plain Geor-

Tullynally Castle: Garden Front

Turlough Park

Tullynally Castle: Hall

gian house gently Gothic. Johnston gave the house a battlemented parapet and slim round corner turrets; by the time he had finished, the name on the builder's bills had changed from Pakenham Hall House to Pakenham Hall Castle. 2nd Earl enlarged the house and made it more Gothic in 1820s, his architect this time being James Shiel; whose work included the addition of a 3 sided bow on the garden front and alterations to the hall. Then, between 1839 and 1842, the trustees of the young bachelor 3rd Earl employed Sir Richard Morrison to alter and enlarge the house yet again. Morrison added a 2 storey battlemented range on the entrance front, containing a private apartment for the family and linked to the house by a tall octagonal tower with a turret, which successfully ties together the whole composition. On the garden front, he added a kitchen wing with battlemented gables. Morrison's 2 wings form 2 sides of a court, and join the house to the stable court beyond, which is entered by a castellated gateway. A tower was added at one corner of the stable court 1860, to the design of J. Rawson Carroll. The chief feature of the interior is the vast hall, which rises through 2 storeys and has no gallery to take away from the effect of space. It has a ceiling of plaster Gothic vaulting, Gothic niches containing family crests, simple early C19 oak panelling and a built-in organ. The dining room dates in its present form from Shiel's remodelling; it is an octagon, extending into his 3 sided bow; with a ceiling of plaster half-vaults and oak panelling similar to that in the hall. The drawing room has a curved

end with a Gothic alcove and a ceiling of simple geometrical design. The library is everything that a library should be; spacious and comfortable, with oak bookcases going up to the ceiling and windows facing south over idyllic parkland. Opening off it, in one of Johnston's corner turrets, is a delightful little round room with a vaulted ceiling and pointed windows. The house was one of 1st in the British Isles to be centrally heated, the original system having been designed by Richard Lovell Edgeworth (father of the novelist, Maria Edgeworth), the inventor; who lived a few miles away at Edgeworthstown (*qv*) and was a friend of 2nd Earl. Subsequent Earls of Longford continued to equip the house with all the latest in modern comforts and labour-saving gadgets; so that its back regions are now a veritable museum of fascinating C19 domestic appliances. 6th Earl of Longford, the playwright and founder of the Gate Theatre, was succeeded here by his nephew, the writer, Mr Thomas Pakenham, son of the present Earl of Longford; who has restored the original Irish name of Tullynally and who opens the house to the public.

Tullynisk Park, Birr, Offaly (PARSONS, ROSSE, E/PB). A 2 storey 5 bay late-Georgian house, with a giant arch beneath which the fanlighted doorway and the triple window above it are recessed. The dining room has a niche which encloses the Rosse arms in plaster relief.

Tullyveery, Killyleagh, co Down (HERON/IFR). A mid-C18 house with later additions.

Turbotston, Castlepollard, co Westmeath (DEASE, *sub* BLAND/IFR). A 2 storey late-Georgian house of the school of Francis Johnston. 3 bay entrance front, centre bay breaking forward with Wyatt window above single-storey Ionic portico. Roof with slightly overhanging eaves. Lower 2 storey service wing at one side. 4 bay side elevation. Now demolished.

Turlough Park, Castlebar, co Mayo (FITZGERALD/IFR). The original bow-fronted C18 house here, which had been the home of the notorious G.R. ("Fighting") Fitz-Gerald—whose eccentric and cruel behaviour, which included tying his father to a pet bear, brought him in the end to the gallows—was abandoned by the family in favour of a High Victorian Ruskinian Gothic

house built 1865 for C. L. FitzGerald to the design of Sir Thomas Newenham Deane. It is of 2 storeys, with a dormered attic in the high-pitched roof; of grey stone, with banding of the same coloured stone as the rest; the only polychromy being provided by the pink marble shafts of the great triple window in the centre of the symmetrical entrance front. Below this window, which has trefoil-headed lights with quatrefoil lights above them, is an open Gothic porch. Lower service wing at one side joining up with extensive office ranges. The ruin of the earlier house is near the avenue, just inside the entrance gate.

Turret (The), co Limerick (*see* BALLIN-GARRY).

Turvey

Turvey, Donabate, co Dublin (BARNE-WALL, KINGSLAND, V/DEP; and TRIMLES-TOWN, B/PB). A late C17 house of 2 storeys and a gabled attic which became an attic storey with a parapet and 3 lunette windows when the house was altered *ca* 1725-50. Front of 9 bays with tall narrow windows grouped together in threes. Doorcase with baroque semi-circular pediment and urns. Rooms with C18 panelling; staircase of good joinery. Rococo plasterwork in library. The seat of that branch of the Barnewall family who held the now dormant or extinct Viscountcy of Kingsland. Towards the end of C18, when there was a false rumour of the death of the bachelor 5th Viscount Kingsland, who lived abroad, a Dublin tavern waiter named Mathew Barnewall, believing himself to be the heir, took possession of Turvey with a party of his friends and dispensed "rude hospitality" there to the local populace; cutting down trees and lighting bonfires. After a short while he was evicted and committed to prison for contempt; but in 1814, thanks to the researches of a friendly lawyer, he was actually recognized as 6th Viscount. He did not, however, succeed in claiming Turvey or any of the other estates which formerly went with the title, since they had been bequeathed by 5th Viscount, who died 1800, to his kinsman, 13th Lord Trimlestown.

Twyford, Athlone, co Westmeath
(HANDCOCK, CASTLEMAINE, B/PB). A 2 storey
5 bay C18 house with single-storey 1 bay
wings. The windows on either side of the
centre in the main block are grouped together. Originally owned by the Handcock
family, from whom were descended the
Lords Castlemaine; passed 1790s to the
Hodson family, who owned it until *ca* 1960.

Tykillan, Kyle, co Wexford (WALKER/
LG1937Supp). A 3 storey 5 bay C18 house,
with a Venetian window in the centre of the
middle storey and a C19 porch below. Wing
set back.

Tynan Abbey

Tynan Abbey, Tynan, co Armagh
(STRONGE, Bt/PB). A house built 1750 by Rev
James Stronge; remodelled and enlarged in
Tudor-Gothic *ca* 1820–30 by Sir James
Stronge, 2nd Bt. Imposing 2 storey entrance front, battlemented and pinnacled;
battlemented central tower with entrance
doorway below corbelled oriel. Pointed
Gothic windows; end of front canted, with
vast Gothic tracery windows of Perpendicular style rising through both storeys in the
end and angle walls. Long side elevation;
range with many steep dormer-gables recessed between the end of the entrance
front, and a balancing, but not similar,
projection; which ends with a church-like
tower and spire. The 2 projections are
joined at ground level by a cloister of segmental-pointed arches, interrupted in the
centre by a 3 sided battlemented and gabled
bow. Some alterations and extensions were
carried out later in C19, to the design of
William J. Barre. The seat of Sir Norman
Stronge, 8th Bt, former Speaker of the
Northern Ireland House of Commons.

Tynte Lodge, Tullaghan, co Leitrim
(TYNTE, *sub* TYNTE-IRVINE/IFR). A 2 storey
double bow-fronted Georgian house, with a
single-storey bow in the centre, which was
probably the original entrance. 2 folly
towers.

Tynte Park, Dunlavin, co Wicklow
(TYNTE-IRVINE/IFR; ABERCROMBY, Bt/PB).
A restrained Classical house of *ca* 1820. 2
storey; 5 bay front; the windows in the 2
outer bays being set in panels breaking forward. Single-storey Grecian Doric portico.
Oval staircase. Sold *ca* 1974 by Mrs Tynte-

Tyrone House

Tyrone House : as a ruin

Tyrone House : ceiling

Irvine; now the home of Sir Ian Abercromby, 10th and present Bt.

**Tyrone House, Clarinbridge, co Gal-
way** (ST GEORGE, *sub* FRENCH/IFR). A large
square cut-stone house by an inlet of Galway Bay; built 1779 for Christopher St
George, reputedly to the design of John
Roberts, of Waterford. Entrance front with
2 bays on either side of a central breakfront

rather similar to that of Moore Hall, co
Mayo (*qv*) with a triple window framed by
short fluted pilasters on console brackets
above an enriched Venetian window above a
tripartite doorway with Ionic pilasters, a
balustraded entablature and a balustraded
porch supported by 2 Ionic columns. Bold
quoins; alternate triangular and segmental
pediments over ground floor windows;
entablatures over windows above; shouldered window surrounds. Balustraded roof
parapet and area; also balustrades on either
side of the broad steps up to the hall door.
In contrast to all this display, the 6 bay
garden front and the 4 bay side elevations
were severely plain. Hall with ceiling of
Adamesque plasterwork incorporating
paintings of the four seasons; tripods and
husks above the doorcases, which were
richly moulded with Classical decoration.
Life-size marble statue of one of the Lords
St George in niche surmounted by coronet
and festoon. Coloured Adamesque ceilings
in drawing room, dining room and other
rooms with central medallions of Classical
groups; also some medallions and plasterwork on walls. After enjoying his magnificent house for about 20 years, Christopher
St George handed it over to his son and
retired to Kilcolgan Castle (*qv*), nearby,
where he lived with a "*chère amie*", turning
Catholic to please her. In 1808, the great
house was described as standing stark on
its eminence, "without a tree, bush or
offices in sight"; later, woods grew up
around it. Christopher St George's son and
grandson were both very fashionable; but
by the end of C19, life at Tyrone was not
quite what it had been; the grandson's
widow and other members of the family
inhabited various corners of the house, the
cooking was done over an open fire in a
room on the top floor, and the drawing
room and dining room were most of the
time kept locked. However, the family had
not come down in the world nearly as much
as Violet Martin ("Martin Ross") imagined
it had when she visited Tyrone 1912, which
gave her the inspiration for *The Big House
of Inver*, written after her death by Edith
Somerville. When she saw it, the house
stood empty, having been abandoned by the
family 1905, though they continued to own
it. From then until 1920, when it was burnt,
it was a favourite haunt of trippers from the
neighbouring towns, who were allowed to
dance in the dining room. It is now a gaunt
and rather sinister ruin which can be seen
for miles around, the woods having all gone.
Facing the house is a medieval church and
the crumbling St George family mausoleum, which inspired a well-known poem
by Sir John Betjeman:

"There in pinnacled protection,
One extinguished family waits
A Church of Ireland resurrection
By the broken, rusty gates".

U

United States Embassy (formerly **Chief Secretary's Lodge**), **Phoenix Park, Dublin** (DE BLAQUIERE, B/PB1917). A house originally built 1776 by Sir John Blaquiere, MP, (afterwards 1st Lord de Blaquiere), Secretary to the Lord Lieutenant and one of the leading figures in the political life of Ireland during later C18; in a demesne carved out of Phoenix Park which he obtained on the strength of being the Park's Bailiff. In 1782, he was asked to surrender the house and grounds in return for compensation, and the house became the official residence of the Chief Secretary, the principal executive of the government of Ireland under British rule. The house was enlarged and altered at various times, but has a predominantly late-Georgian character; of 2 storeys, with a bowed projection at either end of its principal front. Along this front is a fine enfilade of reception rooms. A large glass conservatory was added at one end 1852 by Lord Naas (afterwards 6th Earl of Mayo and Viceroy of India—*see* PB), while he was Chief Secretary. Later in the century, probably 1865 during the Chief Secretaryship of Chichester Fortescue (afterwards Lord Carlingford—*see* FORTESCUE-BRICKDALE/LG1972), the 2 bowed projections were joined by a single-storey corridor, into which were thrown the centre rooms, making them much deeper; the main wall of the house being carried by Ionic columns. The house became the United States Legation 1927; afterwards the Embassy.

Uppercourt

Uppercourt

Uppercourt (formerly **Upperwood**), **Freshford, co Kilkenny** (DE MONTMORENCY, Bt/PB; EYRE, *sub* EYRE-HUDDLESTON/LG1952). A 3 storey 5 bay late C18 block with a 3 storey 2 bay later addition of the same height and in the same style at one side of it; beyond which is a 2 storey 3 bay wing. The late C18 block has a 3 bay pedimented breakfront and a single-storey balustraded Ionic portico; there are urns on the pediment and roof parapet. The top storey is treated as an attic, above the cornice; as is the top storey of the later addition. Elaborate early C19 Italian plasterwork. The seat of the Ryves family, whose co-heiress married Sir William Morres, 1st Bt; the 3rd and last Bt reverted to his family's original surname of de Montmorency. Acquired C19 by the Eyre family, who gave the house its ornate oratory. Sold *ca* 1929; now owned by a religious order. In the village of Freshford, there is a small house which was magnificently decorated on the small scale by the Italian plasterers for their landlady.

V

Velvetstown, Buttevant, co Cork (CROFTS/IFR). A large High Victorian house of polychrome brick, built 1875 by Christopher Crofts; replacing an earlier house nearby, which remained intact. Triangular-headed windows; roof on bracket cornice. The house was burnt 1895 and was left as a ruin, the family returning to the earlier house.

Vernon Mount, Douglas, co Cork (HAYES, *sub* HOLROYD-SMYTH/IFR). A delightful little "Petit Trianon" built *ca* 1784 by Henry Hayes; described by Mr Guinness as "a study in curves", being oval in shape, with curved end-bows to give ripples to its curving 2 storey 3 bay front; while inside the ceilings, however small, are curved and domed and the stone staircase, with its delicate ironwork balustrade, rises in a most graceful curve. Entrance doorway with very large fanlight extending over door and sidelights and with Composite columns and pilasters. The hall, in which the staircase rises, has columns and a c18 stove in the form of an urn. The drawing room and dining room open into each other with double doors, one leaf of which opens automatically when the other is opened; the drawing room ceiling, a domed octagon, has a centre panel painted by Nathaniel Grogan, surrounded by Adamesque ornament. There are 2 other ceilings painted in this style, one of them in the oval landing at the head of the stairs, which has a domed rotunda of marbled Corinthian columns and overdoors painted in *grisaille*. Hayes, who was knighted 1790, was sentenced to transportation 1801 for attempting to abduct a rich heiress, whom he held captive here for one night; though he does not appear to have been in need of money. He travelled to Botany Bay in comfort, with his valet and a mountain of luggage; and returned to Vernon Mount 1812, his daughter having persuaded the Prince Regent to grant him a free pardon. Vernon Mount was in recent years the home of Mr & Mrs Peter Coste; it is now the headquarters of the Munster Motor Cycle & Car Club.

Viceregal Lodge, Dublin (*see* ÁRAS AN UACHTARÁIN).

Victoria Castle, co Dublin (*see* AYESHA CASTLE).

Virginia Park, Virginia, co Cavan (TAYLOUR, HEADFORT, M/PB). A plain 2 storey house with a 3 bay centre and single-storey 3 bay wings.

Vosterburg, Montenotte, Cork, co Cork (LEYCESTER/LGI952; REEVES/LGI1912; MURPHY/IFR). A house overlooking the Lee estuary which was originally built towards mid-c18 by Daniel Vorster, a Dutchman who settled in Cork and "educated" many of the merchants of the city in "writing, arithmetic and the most regular method of book-keeping". As well as building the house, Vorster laid out a garden "with fountains, statues and canals". Vosterburg was subsequently rebuilt, so that it is now a house of late-Georgian appearance. Of 2 storeys over a basement and with a Victorian dormered attic in the roof. 5 bay entrance front; wide central window above doorcase with semi-circular fanlight and coupled engaged Doric columns; fanlight with curved astragals. Garden front of 2 bays on either side of a central curved bow. Subsequently owned by the Leycester family; in 1st half of c19, the residence of W. M. Reeves; later, the residence of a branch of the Murphy family.

W

Wardstown, co Donegal. A 3 storey Georgian house with curved end bows and also a curved bow in the centre of its front. Blocking round doorway; camber-headed windows. Now a ruin.

Waringstown House

Waringstown House, Waringstown, co Down (WARING LGI1958). One of the earliest surviving unfortified Irish houses, built 1667 by William Waring, who also built the nearby church; the architect of both the house and the church is said to have been James Robb, chief mason of the King's Works in Ireland. Originally, the house appears to have been of 2 storeys and an attic, with pedimented curvilinear gables along the front such as still exist at the sides; but the front was fairly soon afterwards raised so that it became 3 full storeys, probably at the same time as 2 storey 1 bay overlapping wings were added; giving the house a facade of late C17 or early C18 appearance, with 6 bays in the centre block and a pedimented doorcase flanked by 2 narrow windows. The 2 centre bays are framed with rusticated quoins, similar to those at the sides of the centre block and on the wings. The front is prolonged by 2 short C18 curved sweeps, ending in piers with finials. Tall C19 Tudor-Revival chimneys. Surprisingly, for so large a house, the walls are of rammed earth. Since the death of Mrs D. G. Waring 1968, the house has stood empty; its future is uncertain.

Warren's Court

Warren's Court, Lissarda, co Cork (WARREN, Bt/PB). A 2 storey Georgian house. 6 bay pedimented front with single-storey Ionic portico. Urns at corners of roofline, eagle on peak of pediment. 4 bay side. Fine demesne with lakes.

Waterfoot (The), Letter, co Fermanagh (BARTON/IFR; LOANE/IFR). 2 plain 2 storey late-Georgian ranges with eaved roofs, at right angles to each other. Built by Lt-Gen Charles Barton, completed by his son, H. W. Barton. Passed to Mr R. B. Loane, whose mother was a daughter of Capt C. R. Barton, of The Waterfoot.

Waterfoot House, Newcastle, co Down (BYERS/IFR). A pleasant Victorian "marine residence" attractively situated by the water's edge.

Waterford, co Waterford: Bishop's Palace. The Palace of the (C of I) Bishops of Waterford; one of the largest and—externally—finest episcopal residences in Ireland. Begun 1741 by Bishop Charles Este to the design of Richard Castle. The garden front, which faces over the Mall and now forms a magnificent architectural group with the tower and spire of later C18 Cathedral, by John Roberts, is of 3 storeys; the ground floor being treated as a basement and rusticated. The centre of the ground floor breaks forward with 3 arches, forming the base of the pedimented Doric centrepiece of the storey above, which incorporates 3 windows. In the centre of the top storey is a circular niche, flanked by 2 windows. On either side of the centre are 3 bays. Bishop Este died 1745 before the Palace was finished, which probably ex-

plains why the interior is rather disappointing. The Palace ceased to be the episcopal residence early in the present century, and from then until *ca* 1965 it was occupied by Bishop Foy School. It has since been sold.

Waterloo, Mallow, co Cork (LONGFIELD/IFR; HOPE-JOHNSTONE, *sub* LINLITHGOW, M/PB). A 2 storey 5 bay late-Georgian house with a low pediment, a pillared porch and urns on the roof parapet. Projection with 3 sided bow at side and other additions. Castellated tower by entrance gates. A seat of the Longfield family, by whom it was sold *ca* 1946. Subsequent owners have included Mr E. W. Hope-Johnstone and Mr & Mrs E. Nelson.

Waterston, Athlone, co Westmeath (HARRIS-TEMPLE, *sub* HARRIS, B/PB). A very handsome 3 storey 7 bay house by Richard Castle, with a solid roof parapet, rusticated window surrounds on the ground floor and a pedimented and rusticated doorway. Built *ca* 1749 for Gustavus Handcock, MP, ancestor of the Temple family who subsequently owned it; and whose heiress was the 2nd wife of 2nd Lord Harris. Brick gateway; hermitage; dovecot. The house is now in ruins.

Waterview, Loughrea, co Galway (MAHONY/IFR). A small Regency house.

Waterville House, Waterville, co Kerry (BUTLER, *sub* DUNBOYNE, B/PB). A plain 2 storey 5 bay late C18 or early C19 house, with an irregular wing at the back incorporating part of an earlier house.

Waterville House

Wells

Wells, Gorey, co Wexford (DOYNE/IFR). A Tudor-Gothic house of *ca* 1840 by Daniel Robertson, of Kilkenny; built for Robert Doyne, replacing an earlier house which, for nearly 3 years after the Rebellion of 1798, was used as a military barracks. Gabled front, symmetrical except that there is a 3 sided oriel at one end of the facade and not at the other, facing along straight avenue of trees to entrance gate. Sold *ca* 1964.

West Aston, co Wicklow (*see* KILMA-CURRAGH).

Westbourne House

Westbourne House, Ennis, co Clare. A 2 storey gabled C19 house with a pillared porch. Eaved roof.

West Cove House

West Cove House, Castlecove, co Kerry (BARTON/IFR). A 2 storey 5 bay late-Georgian house with a fanlighted doorway, its front prolonged by a slightly lower 2 storey 1 bay gable-ended wing. Owned in C19 by a branch of the O'Sullivan family; now the home of Lt-Col & Mrs H. D. M. Barton.

Westfield, Mountrath, co Leix (FRANKS/IFR). A Georgian house rebuilt after being burnt *ca* 1920, and given a decidedly "Twenties" flavour. Windows with small panes; prominent roof; small pediment on entrance front. Porch with 2 recessed Grecian Doric columns.

Westport House, Westport, co Mayo (BROWNE, SLIGO, M/PB). A large square C18

Westport House: Front with Terraces

house extending round 4 sides of an inner court which has since been roofed over; one side of it consisting of a house of *ca* 1730 by Richard Castle; the other 3 sides having been added 1778, probably to the design of Thomas Ivory. The 1730 house, which was built for John Browne, afterwards 1st Earl of Altamont, on the site of an earlier house and possibly incorporating the cellars of the castle of his O'Malley forebears, remains as the entrance front; it is of 2 storeys over a basement, with a 3 bay central voluted attic, and 7 bays. The central 1st floor window is flanked by roundels which formerly sheltered busts; below is a rusticated tripartite doorway with a wide pediment extending over the door and flanking windows; its tympanum now containing the arms of 1st Earl, which must date from *post* 1771, when he received his earldom. Below the pediment are vigorously carved satyrs' masks. At either end of the roof parapet is an eagle. The 1778 ranges were added by the 2nd Earl, whose marriage to the heiress of great sugar plantations in Jamaica made his family one of the richest in Ireland during later C18 and early C19; so that they were model landlords and were able to lay out the town of Westport in the grand manner and develop it as a port. One of 2nd Earl's fronts has a pedimented breakfront with Tuscan pilasters; the other 2 are plain, except that one of them—of 8 bays—has a Venetian window beneath a Diocletian window at either end. 3rd Earl, afterwards 1st Marquess of Sligo, employed James Wyatt to complete the interior of the house 1781. 2nd Marquess, in 1816 and 1819, added 2 large terraces on either side of the house, containing additional rooms at basement level; the lie of the land being such that, on all sides except the entrance front, the basement is in fact a ground floor of full height. One of 2nd Marquess's additions contained a large library by Benjamin Dean Wyatt, which was destroyed by fire 1826 owing to an overambitious heating system. A new library was subsequently made by roofing in the

Westport House: Entrance Front

Westport House: Hall

inner court; the burnt addition being rebuilt *post* 1845. It is now fronted by replicas of two columns from the Treasury of Atreus at Mycenae, which 2nd Marquess brought back after travelling in Greece as a young man 1810, with his friend, Byron. During that trip, he bribed two sailors from a British warship to help sail his yacht; for which, on his return to England, he was fined £5,000 and sentenced to 4 months imprisonment. The entrance hall is the only surviving interior by Castle; it has

Westport House: ceiling of secondary Staircase

Westport House: Chinese wallpaper

a Doric frieze and a coffered barrel vaulted ceiling. Its inner end is now open with arches to an imperial staircase of Sicilian marble which in 1857–59 took the place of the library in the roofed-in court; it was designed for 3rd Marquess by George Wilkinson and has a metalwork balustrade by Skidmore. A small staircase hall in one of the 1778 ranges has an oval domed ceiling on pendentives with delicate contemporary plasterwork. The dining room is by Wyatt and has plasterwork characteristic of him, on ceiling and walls; incorporating medallions of Classical figures. The adjoining gallery is said to have originally had Wyatt decoration, which 2nd Marquess commissioned Benjamin Dean Wyatt to remove after it had gone out of fashion. The house stands in a magnificent setting close to the shore of Clew Bay, by the side of a river which has been widened into a lake and is spanned by a 4 arched c18 bridge connecting the house with the stables. Balustraded terraces in the grand manner were laid out by 6th Marquess 1913, descending from the garden front of the house to the water's edge. The present (10th) Marquess, faced with the crippling burden of the rates on the house, contemplated selling or demolishing it. Instead, his son and daughter-in-law, the Earl and Countess of Altamont, have endeavoured to meet the outgoings by opening the house to the public and developing it as a tourist attraction.

Whigsborough, Birr, Offaly (DROUGHT/LGI1958). A 2 storey 3 bay gable-ended c18 house with a 1 bay extension of the same height on the left and a slightly lower 1 bay extension on the right. Round-headed doorway. Gothic tower, probably late c18, on front of stables. Fine Classical gate piers with swag friezes.

White Castle, Moville, co Donegal. A late c18 house of 2 storeys with a low attic storey lit by a fanlighted lunette in 3 sided central bow, and by 2 very low windows in

the curved end bows. On either side of the central bow is 1 bay with Wyatt windows in each of the 2 storeys; but with no attic windows. There is also a 3 sided bow at the back of the house. The seat of the Carey family.

Whitechurch House

Whitechurch House, Cappagh, co Waterford (ALLEN/LGI1958). A 2 storey early c19 house built round a courtyard. 5 bay front; central Wyatt window above single-storey Ionic portico with paired columns; fanlighted doorway. Eaved roof. Staircase with wrought-iron balustrade rising round main hall. In 1837, the residence of R. Power; in 1914, of Richard William Forsayeth. Until his recent death, the home of the late Mr William Allen, the well-known authority on Georgia and the Middle East; whose celebrated library was here.

Whitegate House, Whitegate, co Cork (FITZGERALD, *sub* UNIACKE/IFR; STEWART/LGI1912). A plain 2 storey house with a bow at the end of its front. Passed from the FitzGeralds to the Stewarts through the marriage. 1855, of Anne, daughter of James Penrose, by his wife, Louisa Pettitot (*née* FitzGerald), to Thomas Stewart.

White Hall, co Antrim

White Hall, Ballymena, co Antrim (WHITE/LGI1912). A gable-ended Georgian house of 3 storeys over a basement. 3 bay front with Wyatt windows in both storeys, as well as in the basement; fanlighted doorway. Steps with good ironwork railings up to entrance door; an eagle at each end of the roofline. The home of Field Marshal Sir George White, VC, the defender of Ladysmith.

White Hall, Aghadown, co Cork (TOWNSHEND/IFR; ALLEYNE/LGI1958). A 2 storey 4 bay late-Georgian house.

White Hill, Edgeworthstown, co Longford (WILSON-SLATOR, *sub* WALSH/LGI1958). A 2 storey gabled Victorian house with a 3 sided bow and some battlements and pinnacles. Imposing castellated gatehouse. Demolished and devastated *ca* 1961.

White House, co Kilkenny (*see* BALLYLINE HOUSE).

Whitfield Court

Whitfield Court, Kilmeadan, co Waterford (CHRISTMAS/LGI1863; CHAVASSE/IFR; DAWNAY, *sub* DOWNE, V/PB). Originally the seat of the Christmas family who were among the richest of the Waterford merchants by the beginning of c18; and who, by 1746, when Charles Smith published his *History of Waterford*, had a "well-built" house here, its hall "painted in Clara Oscura with several of the heathen deities" and containing "two statues of Neptune and Amphitrite". Around it was a garden with a "large and beautiful canal", a "*jet d'eau*", a wilderness and a shell-house; the latter no doubt similar to that at Curraghmore (*qv*). In 1830s the course of the road from Waterford to Cork was altered and the new road cut off the house from its walled garden; so William Christmas built himself a new house *ca* 1841, on higher ground to the south of the new road; the old house being allowed to fall into ruin. His architect was Abraham Denny, of Dublin, who produced a delightful villa in the Greco-Italian style, well suited to its picturesque setting. The 2 outer bays of its 2 storey 3 bay entrance front are raised a storey higher than the centre to form 2 sturdy Italianate towers with shallow pyramidal roofs; their top storeys being in the form of 3 arched belvederes but with the arches glazed as windows. The roof parapet between the 2 towers is balustraded; below is a single-storey Ionic portico. The entrance front is prolonged beyond the right-hand tower by 2 more bays, set a little back, and then by a lower service wing. The adjoining front is of 5 bays and made lop-sided by the fact that it has a tower on one side but not on the other; but this adds to its "picturesqueness". The 3 centre bays are recessed, with a single-storey curved bow fronted with a curved Ionic colonnade. The other front is of 6 bays. Apart from in the centre of the entrance front, the roof is eaved, on a plain cornice. Most of the windows have entablatures or pediments over them. The principal rooms are arranged round an impressive staircase hall with an imperial staircase; the gallery of which is supported by Corinthian columns and pilasters; there being more Corinthian pilasters framing the upstairs corridor openings. The reception rooms have ceilings of shallow coffering, in a simple geometrical design reminiscent of Soane. Romantic cliff-top garden with terraces. Leased 1897–1913 to the Chavasse family. Sold 1916 to Lady Susan Dawnay, who built a pleasant loggia at one end of the house and carried out various improvements to the garden. During the Civil War, after

Whitfield had been occupied successively by units of the Republican and Free State armies, who fought a battle on the lawn, the gardener wrote to Lady Susan, who was away at the time: "Both sides greatly admired your Ladyship's antirrhinums".

Williamston, Carbury, co Kildare. A 2 storey C18 house flanked by wings and yards in the Palladian manner; related by the Knight of Glin to Colganstown (*qv*) and other houses attributed to the amateur architect, Nathaniel Clements. 3 bay front, Venetian window above tripartite doorway; wall carried up to form parapet, urns at corners. The seat of the Williams family.

Williamston, Kells, co Meath (GARNETT/ LGI1912). An impressive 3 storey 9 bay late C18 house, with an elevation almost identical to that of the nearby Rockfield (*qv*), except that, here, there is no breakfront; it can safely be assumed that the 2 houses are by the same architect. Ground floor treated as a basement, with channelling; Doric porch; pediment over central 1st floor window.

Williamstown House, Castlebellingham, co Louth (WALSH/IFR). A mid-C19 Italianate house of 2 storeys over a rusticated and vermiculated basement. 5 bay front, with broken pediment above central Wyatt window and portico with Ionic columns and Doric corner piers. Entablatures on console brackets over some windows. Windows with straight-arched heads in upper storey; rectangular windows below and camber-headed windows in basement. Eaved roof on bracket cornice.

Willowfield, Ballinamore, co Leitrim. A 2 storey 5 bay gable-ended mid-C18 house. A seat of the Percy family.

Wilmont, Dunmurry, co Antrim (READE/ LGI1958). A plain 2 storey Victorian house, built 1859. 3 bay front, with balustraded porch; lower wing, ending with wing as high as main block. Adjoining front with central curved bow and 1 bay on either side. Camber-headed windows in upper storey of main block. Eaved roof on bracket cornice.

Wilton, Urlingford, co Kilkenny (BUTLER/IFR). A double bow-fronted house of *ca* 1780. Now derelict.

Wilton Castle: as a ruin

main block, 2 storey wing. Dominated by a tall square tower at one end, and with a tall polygonal tower and turret at the other. Porch with oriel over. Burnt 1923; the ruin, with its dramatic silhouette, is a prominent landmark.

Windsor, Douglas, co Cork (BERNARD, BANDON, E/PB). From its appearance, a 3 storey 5 bay late-Georgian house with a 1 bay breakfront, refaced in the Victorian period, when it was given a porch with fancy columns and an elaborate bracket cornice. Originally owned by the Earls of Bandon; let to G. Cooke *ca* 1837. Sold at the beginning of the present century to Sir Abraham Sutton.

Woburn House

Woburn House, Millisle, co Down (DUNBAR, afterwards DUNBAR-BULLER, *sub* PACK-BERESFORD/IFR). A large and imposing 2 storey C19 Italianate mansion. Entrance front with curved bow at one end, projecting wing at the other and central 3 storey tower incorporating porte-cochère. Superimposed Ionic and Corinthian corner-pilasters on tower above rusticated Doric piers; entablatures on console brackets over ground-floor windows, segmental pediments over windows in upper storey, tri-

angular pediments over windows in 3rd storey of tower. Balustraded roof parapet; shallow pyramidal roof on tower, on cornice with pediments at front and sides. Adjoining symmetrical 7 bay garden front, prolonged by single-storey wing ending in pedimented pavilion; central balustraded single-storey bow; entablatures and segmental pediments over windows as in entrance front; dormered attic in roof behind balustraded parapet.

Woodbine Hill, Ardmore, co Waterford (ROCH/LGI1958). A plain late-Georgian house built 1846 by George Roch, replacing an earlier house on a lower site which was "spared for old affection's sake". The house is in a fine position overlooking the mouth of the River Blackwater. Now the home of Mr & Mrs W. G. Roch-Perks, who run it as a riding stables.

Woodbrook, Portarlington, co Leix (WILMOT-CHETWODE/LGI1912). A 2 storey 5 bay late-Georgian house with a fanlighted doorway; extended at the back by a lower wing linking it to a 3 storey bow-ended block with a 4 storey polygonal tower. Recently the home of Mr & Mrs Denis Quirke.

Woodbrook, Killane, co Wexford (BLACKER/IFR). A square late C18 house with Wyatt windows. Tripartite fanlighted doorway under single-storey Ionic portico. Hall with rather Soanian vaulted ceiling. Very spectacular spiral flying staircase, of wood, with wrought-iron balustrades; a remarkable and brilliant piece of design and construction. Very large drawing room.

Woodbrook, Bray, co Wicklow (COCHRANE, Bt/PB). A 3 storey 5 bay stucco-faced block of *ca* 1840, incorporating a simple 2 storey Georgian house, joined by single-storey wings to end pavilions. The centre block has an entrance front with a small pediment, a balustraded roof parapet, an Ionic porch and entablatures and segmental pediments on console brackets over the windows. The wings originally contained offices and were fronted by arcades; but in the present century they were remodelled to contain a ballroom and a large dining room, and the arcades were replaced by colonnades. The ballroom has a coved ceiling painted in *grisaille*; the dining room is

Wilton Castle

Wilton Castle, Enniscorthy, co Wexford (ALCOCK/IFR). A spectacular C19 castle by Daniel Robertson, of Kilkenny, built on a moated platform surrounded by parapet walls and sham fortifications. Heavily battlemented and machicolated; 3 storey

Woodbrook, co Wicklow

divided by pillars and has wall paintings by Zucharelli. The hall has a *boiserie* in the French manner. The library was decorated early in present century in the Elizabethan style, with oak panelling and a fretted ceiling. The garden front was originally irregular; but was made symmetrical *ca* 1966 and given a pediment and pilasters. At about the same time, the pedimented upper storey of the facade of the Royal College of Physicians in Dublin, which was being renewed, was brought here and re-erected to form a charming "gloriette" facing the garden front; its 3 arched windows framing the sea.

Woodbrook, Boyle, co Roscommon (KIRKWOOD/LGI1958). The seat of the Kirkwoods, featured in David Thomson's widely acclaimed evocation of Anglo-Irish life, *Woodbrook*. No longer owned by the family.

Woodfort

Woodfort, Mallow, co Cork (CARROLL-LEAHY/LGI1958). An imposing C19 house in the Georgian style of 2 storey over a basement and 7 bays, with a 3 bay pedimented breakfront flanked in the lower storey by a single Wyatt window on either.side; extended by 2 bays on either side—with a large pedimented triple window in their lower storey—*ca* 1906 by T. J. Carroll-Leahy, and, at the same time, given a mansard roof with an attic of Wyatt window dormers. Now a hospital.

Woodhouse

Woodhouse, Bessbrook, co Armagh. A many-gabled late-Victorian house with eaved roofs and elaborate bargeboards.

Woodhouse, Stradbally, co Waterford (UNIACKE/IFR; BERESFORD, WATERFORD, M/PB). A 2 storey house of early C19 appearance, probably incorporating an earlier house. 6 bay front with pillared and fanlighted doorway at one end; eaved roof. The seat of a branch of the Uniacke family passed by inheritance to the Beresfords. Sold by Lord William Beresford *ca* 1970; now the home of Mr John Rohan.

Woodlands (formerly **Clinshogh**), **Santry, co Dublin.** A square early C18 house of brick, of 2 storeys over a high basement, with a pyramidal roof from the centre of which rises a gazebo or lantern. Regarded by Dr Craig as "perhaps the most interesting small house of the early C18 in the whole of Ireland" and attributed by him with certainty to Sir Edward Lovett Pearce. Built *ante* 1735 by Rev John Jackson, Vicar of Santry, a friend of Swift. The house has 4 regular fronts and 4 sturdy, regularly-disposed chimneystacks; the 5 bay entrance front now having a slightly discordant late C18 fanlighted doorway. Dr Craig considers the gazebo here to be the precursor of the central attic-towers at Gola, co Monaghan (*qv*) and other houses; but the Woodlands gazebo has none of the freakishness of those other towers; it is the natural termination of the roof. The interior is divided by a long vaulted corridor-hall running from front to back. In 1837, the residence of Col A. Thomson.

Woodlands, Clonsilla, co Dublin (*see* LUTTRELLSTOWN CASTLE).

Woodlands

Woodlands, Faithlegg, co Waterford (POWER/IFR; GALLWEY/IFR). A 2 storey house of *ca* 1840, built by Michael Dobbin, Barrister-at-law, on land leased from the Bolton family, the former owners of the nearby Faithlegg House (*qv*). 4 bay front; single-storey Doric portico of wood, now glazed to form a porch. Eaved roof. 2 bay side elevation. Fine large drawing room and dining room. Subsequently acquired by the Powers who had bought Faithlegg 1819, and used by them as a dower house. The Powers added a wing at the back of the house enclosing a courtyard, which has now been made into an attractive patio. The house is magnificently situated high above the estuary of the Suir, with views up both channels of the river on either side of the Island. Inherited by Mrs H.W. D. Gallwey (*née* Power), along with Faithlegg; became the family seat after Faithlegg was sold 1936. Now the home of her son Lt-Col Hubert Gallwey, Editor of *The Irish Genealogist*, and Mrs Gallwey.

Woodlawn, Kilconnell, co Galway (TRENCH, ASHTOWN, B/PB). A 3 storey house refaced and much embellished in an Italianate style and enlarged by the addition of single-storey wings *ca* 1860 for 2nd Lord Ashtown; probably to the design of James F. Kempster, of Ballinasloe. The main block has a recessed centre and projecting outer bays with triple windows, joined by a single-storey balustraded Ionic portico;

Woodlawn

the roof parapet is also balustraded, with tall finials; there is a modillion cornice and much channelling; the downstairs windows are surmounted by segmental pediments. The wings each consist of 3 bays and a projecting pedimented end pavilion with a triple window. Georgian Gothic arch at one of the entrances to the demesne. Sold *ca* 1947 by 4th Lord Ashtown to the late Mr Derek Le Poer Trench; who re-sold it *ca* 1973.

Woodlock

Woodlock, Portlaw, co Waterford. A 2 storey house of mid-C19 appearance; 6 bay entrance front with single-storey Ionic portico; unusual entablatures on brackets over ground-floor windows, and projections like rudimentary balconies beneath the windows above; deep cornice and heavy roof parapet with recessed panels; corner-pilasters; single-storey balustraded and pilastered wing on one side, 2 storey wing on the other. The 2 wings have similar elevations on the garden front, where the main block is of 8 bays with a single-storey curved balustraded bow in the centre; the 2 storey wing being joined to the main block by a short arcaded loggia. A seat of the Malcolmson family, who in the early C19 founded the great cotton mills at Portlaw, which brought great prosperity to the town. Now a convent.

Woodrooff, Clonmel, co Tipperary (PERRY/IFR). A C18 house flanked by square courts with cupolas, niches and oculi, added later C18 possibly to the design of Davis Duckart. Now mostly demolished.

Woodsgift, Urlingford, co Kilkenny (ST GEORGE, Bt/PB; KEATINGE/IFR). A large 3 storey Georgian block with a lower wing. 7 bay front with breakfront centre; later porch. Roof parapet with finials. 5 bay side elevation. Burnt *ante* 1914 and the ruin afterwards demolished.

Woodstock, Inistioge, co Kilkenny (FOWNES, Bt/EDB; TIGHE/IFR). A house by Francis Bindon, probably dating from 1740s, which is unusual in being built round a small inner court, or light-shaft. 3 storeys; handsomely rusticated entrance front of 6 bays with a central niche and statue above the entrance doorway, and an oculus above that again. Elaborate door-

Woodstock, co Kilkenny: Entrance Front

Woodstock, co Kilkenny: statue of Mary Tighe

Woodstock, co Kilkenny: Garden Front

Woodstock, co Wicklow

way, formed by grouping the door itself and the 2 flanking windows into a single composition; the lunette above the door breaking through the entablature. Single-storey wings, with pedimented centre-pieces, added later; but with the same rusticated window surrounds as the main block. 5 bay garden front, plainer than the entrance front, with triple keystones above the ground floor and 1st floor windows. In 1770s, Sarah Ponsonby lived here with her cousins, Sir William and Lady Betty Fownes; her friend, Eleanor Butler, having escaped from Borris, co Carlow (*qv*), where she was being kept in disgrace, was let into Woodstock through a window, hiding herself in Sarah's room for 24 hours before being discovered; shortly afterwards, the 2 friends left for Wales, where they subsequently became famous as the "Ladies of Llangollen". Woodstock passed to the Tighes with the marriage of the daughter and heiress of Sir William Fownes to William Tighe, whose daughter-in-law was Mary Tighe, the poetess, author of *Psyche*; she died at Woodstock 1810 aged 37, and Flaxman's monument to her is in a small neo-Classical mausoleum behind the Protestant church in the village of Inistioge, at the gates of the demesne. There was also a statue of her in one of the rooms in the house. Woodstock was burnt *ca* 1920 and is now a ruin; but the demesne, with its magnificent beechwoods, still belongs to the Tighes.

Woodstock, Newtownmountkennedy, co Wicklow (TOTTENHAM, *sub* ELY, M/PB). A 3 storey 5 bay block of *ca* 1770, with single-storey 3 bay wings and pedimented end pavilions added *ca* 1840 by Rt Rev Lord Robert Tottenham, Bishop of Clogher, who bought the property 1827; it had previously been rented for a period by the Lord-Lieutenant, Marquess Wellesley (*see* WELLINGTON, D/PB). The centre block has a 1 bay breakfront and a die which was probably added by Bishop Tottenham at the same time as the single-storey Ionic portico, which is by Sir Richard Morrison. Giant blind arches in end pavilions; balustraded parapets on wings. Garden front with curved bow in central breakfront; now asymmetrical because of projecting C19 wing on one side and other additions. Hall running through the full depth of the house, divided by a screen of columns from the staircase, which is of fine solid C18 joinery; rococo plasterwork in the manner of Robert West in panels on the walls above the staircase, and curving round the apse at the back of the hall in the bow of the garden front; similar plasterwork on the ceiling of the staircase and landing. Dining room with rococo plasterwork in centre of ceiling. Large and lofty drawing room in right hand wing with frieze and cornice of elaborate C19 plasterwork, rather in the manner of Sir Richard Morrison. Handsome C19 room with bold cornice and ceiling medallion in wing flanking garden front. Sold 1947; afterwards the home of Mr & Mrs G. Van den Bergh. It is now the home of Mr & Mrs William Forwood, who have carried out a most sympathetic restoration

of the house, with the help of Mr Jeremy Benson.

Woodstown, co Waterford (CAREW, B/PB; BARRON/IFR; CHOLMELEY-HARRISON/IFR). An elegant Regency villa overlooking Waterford Harbour, attributed to George Richard Pain; built 1823 onto an earlier house by Robert Carew, afterwards 1st Lord Carew, as a present for his wife. Of 2 storeys and square in plan, with a graceful iron veranda running all round the ground floor; each front being of 3 bays, with Wyatt windows. Eaved roof. 1st Lady Carew, who lived here during her widowhood, died 1901 at the age of 103, having, as a girl, attended the Duchess of Richmond's celebrated ball before Waterloo. In 1905, Woodstown was sold to E. A. W. Barron. The Barrons sold it 1944 and in 1945 it was bought by Mr C. D. Cholmeley-Harrison, who let it during the summer of 1967 to Mrs Jacqueline Kennedy, and who sold it 1971, having acquired Emo Court, co Leix (*qv*).

Woodville, Glanmire, co Cork (MANNIX, Bt/EDB; CUMMINS/IFR). A Georgian house, originally the seat of the Mannix family; leased from 1803 by the Cummins family, who were connected to the Mannixs by marriage; and who bought it later in C19. The house is believed to have been largely rebuilt by N. M. Cummins some time *ante* 1838 and made 3 storeys high having formerly been only 2; if so, the top storey was subsequently removed, for the house is now of only 2 storeys. It has a plain front of 6 bays, prolonged by a wing set back.

Woodville, Lucan, co Dublin (HAMILTON/IFR). A rambling house, consisting of a symmetrical mid-C18 block with a fanlighted doorway in its entrance front, and a large late-Georgian wing. Garden front joined to stables by curved sweeps with pineapples; and with curved bow. Small hall with stone staircase; enfilade of reception rooms along garden front, including large bow-fronted drawing room with C19 wallpaper in white and gold; and room with plasterwork frieze of fruit. In 1837 the seat of Major-Gen Sir H. S. Scott. In the present century, the house stood empty for 40 years; but from *ca* 1950 until their death it was the home of the Misses Eva & Letitia Hamilton, both of them distinguished painters, and their younger sisters. It has since been demolished.

Woodville, Gortalea, co Kerry (LOMBARD, *sub* FITZGERALD-LOMBARD/LGI1958; HICKSON/LGI1912). A 2 storey 3 bay Georgian house with a lower 2 storey wing. Enclosed porch with engaged Ionic columns.

Woodville, Templemore, co Tipperary (WEBB/LGI1958). A 2 storey house of late-Georgian appearance, with a 3 bay front and a 1 bay wing set back. Single-storey pedimented portico; external shutters; eaved roof on bracket cornice; Gothic glazed window in wing.

Wykeham House, Bagenalstown, co Carlow (BAYLISS, *sub* LOFTUS/IFR). A gabled Victorian house of stone. The home of Miss M. B. Bayliss.

Y

Yeomanstown, Naas, co Kildare (MANS-FIELD/IFR; MOORE, *sub* MCCALMONT/IFR). An early C18 double gable-ended house of exceptional quality, originally belonging to a branch of the Eustace family. Of 2 storeys, with an attic in the high-pitched roof lit by windows in the gable-ends. 5 bay entrance front with large floating pediment containing an oculus; the windows being grouped closely together leaving wide solid corners. Heads of windows in upper storey have undulating arrises. Round-headed doorway with blocking; deep wooden bracket cornice under roof; partly curvilinear end-gables. Plain and asymmetrical garden front. The house is built of brick, but has been rendered. Both the entrance and garden fronts face along straight avenues of trees. Inherited by John Mansfield later C18. Subsequently sold to the Gill family; now the home of Mr A. L. Moore and Mrs Moore (*née* Gill).

Yeomanstown Lodge, Naas, co Kildare (MANSFIELD/IFR; USSHER/IFR). A Georgian farmhouse with a fanlighted doorway, enlarged early in C19 by the addition of a higher block at the back of it; so that it now has a 4 bay garden front, containing a spacious drawing room and dining room *en suite*, with cornices of simple plasterwork. The staircase, in its own hall to the left of the entrance hall, has elaborate but unsophisticated plasterwork on its soffits. Formerly owned by the Mansfield family, of Morristown Lattin and Yeomanstown (*qqv*). Now the home of Mr & Mrs Patrick Ussher.

Yeomanstown

Author's Addenda and Corrigenda

IN SUGGESTING (INTRODUCTION, p xxvii) that the total number of Irish country houses burnt during the period 1919–23 did not exceed 70, I fear I underestimated; basing my calculations on a contemporary list which is incomplete; though it appears to exaggerate the number of burnings since it includes some houses that were not in fact burnt. One would be safe in putting the total number at something between 150 and 200, which is still very much less than what it is popularly believed to be.

The "mood of unrelieved pessimism" (INTRODUCTION, p xxviii) regarding the future of country houses in the Irish Republic was somewhat dispelled early in 1978 (after this book had gone to press) by the abolition of the Wealth Tax and the bringing in of a tax concession specifically for "Heritage Houses"—a concession which, though small in itself, established a valuable precedent.

Owing to the very limited time I had in writing this book, I tended to rely on memory or on existing printed descriptions when dealing with castles and other buildings dating from before 1700 which had long been ruinous or at any rate uninhabited; and I did not attempt to investigate the present state of the majority of these buildings. Consequently, I did less than justice to the National Parks and Monuments Branch of the Irish Republic's Office of Public Works, which now cares for many more of these buildings than my text would imply. Buildings mentioned in this book which are now vested in the Office of Public Works but are not credited as such in the text include the old castle and friary at Adare; Athcarne Castle; the old tower house adjoining Buncrana Castle; Burntcourt Castle; Cahir Castle; the old castle at Carrigaholt; Doe Castle; Donegal Castle; the old keep and round tower at Drishane Castle; Dromaneen Castle; the ruined church near Dunsany Castle; Dunsoghly Castle; Jigginstown House; Kanturk Castle; Lemaneagh Castle; MacDermots Castle near Rockingham; the old Mallow Castle; the old castle at Roscrea in which Damer House is situated; Ross Castle (*see* KENMARE HOUSE); and St Mary's Abbey.

The Office of Public Works has carried out, or is in the process of carrying out, extensive conservation and restoration works on many of the buildings mentioned in this book which are in its care; so that the photographs of some of them in the text, which were taken half-a-century or more ago and show them as neglected if picturesque ruins, are now happily out of date. Among the buildings restored or being restored by the Office of Public Works are Burntcourt Castle; Cahir Castle, where a great deal of work has been done and a permanent exhibition set up; the old buildings at Drishane Castle, one of which has been reroofed; Kanturk Castle, where the Jacobean doorway—which has detached columns and not pilasters, as stated in the text—has been re-erected; Parkes Castle; Portumna Castle, where a very ambitious scheme for the restoration of the castle and Jacobean gardens, which will eventually entail the reroofing of the building, is now in progress; and Ross Castle. In addition to the buildings actually vested in the Office of Public Works, two others mentioned in this book are in its "guardianship"; namely Bunratty Castle—where the actual restoration work was carried out by the Office of Public Works under the supervision of Mr Percy Le Clerc and where the Office of Public Works continues to maintain the building—and the old castle at Kilbolane.

I would like to thank Mr D. Newman Johnson, Inspector of National Monuments, Mr John Kenworthy-Browne and Mr Frederick O'Dwyer for some of the corrections and additional information in the pages that follow.

Aghadoe, Killeagh, co Cork (DE CAPELL BROOKE, Bt/PB 1967) A plain early C19 house in the villa style, standing above a romantic wooded glen on an estate which was granted to Philip de Capell 1172, and continued to be owned by his descendants until the present century; it was known by the local inhabitants as "the Maiden Estate" to distinguish it from the other large properties in the neighbourhood, all of which had, at some period in their history, been forfeited. By C16, the family name had become corrupted to Supple; 1797 Richard Brooke Supple of Aghadoe changed his name to de Capell Brooke on inheriting the estate of the Brookes in Northamptonshire. There is a design of *ca* 1700, probably by a French architect, for an elaborate Palladian mansion at Aghadoe, which was never carried out.

Annaghmakerrig, Newbliss, co Monaghan (POWER/LGI 1912). A house of Victorian appearance, in watered-down Tudor-Jacobean. Entrance front with central porch-gable; adjoining front with 2 curvilinear gables, single-storey 3 sided bows, windows with blocked surrounds. Finials on gables. The seat of the Moorhead family; inherited by Martha (*née* Moorhead), wife of Sir William James Tyrone Power—whose father was the early C19 Irish actor, Tyrone Power, ancestor of the film actor of that name—and in recent years the home of her grandson, Sir Tyrone Guthrie, the producer, who bequeathed it to the Irish nation as a centre for artists and writers.

Archerstown. The house incorporates parts of the medieval castle of the Archer family. A section of the castle bawn wall is incorporated in the wall of a small deer park, which still contains deer believed to be descended from the deer that were here in the Archers' time.

Ashburn. For Ashburn, read Ashbourne.

Ballinterry House, Rathcormac, co Cork (BARRY/IFR). An early C18 house built on the site of a castle which in 1699 belonged to Andrew Morrogh or Murragh, an attainted Jacobite; the house was, until comparatively recently surrounded by old fortifications including 4 round towers, of which one and the fragments of another survive. Gable-ended main block of 2 storeys with attic lit by windows in gable-ends; 5 bay front, originally 7 bay, the windows on either side of the centre having been blocked up; presumably in the late-Georgian period, when the other windows of the front appear to have been reduced in size and the interior walls rearranged. Simple fanlighted doorway. Original grass terrace with flagged pavement along front. 2 storey return wing; central projection at rear of main block containing late-Georgian stairs with balustrade of plain sturdy wooden uprights. Stairs now open to hall; formerly separated from it by screen of C18 panelling with Gothic fanlight, now removed to 1st floor lobby of wing. Bought 1703 by 4th Earl of Barrymore; afterwards passed to the Ross family and then by marriage and descent to the Ryders and Henleys successively. From 1821 to 1862 the home of Archdeacon ("Black Billy") Ryder, remembered for his part in the "Gortroe Massacre" 1834, a tragic episode of the Tithe War. Ballinterry is now the home of Mr Hurd Maguire Hatfield, the stage and screen actor, who has carried out a sympathetic restoration of the house.

Ballyellis, Buttevant, co Cork (HAROLD-BARRY/IFR; ESMONDE, Bt/PB). A 2 storey 5 bay Georgian house with a pillared doorway. Hall with stairs through arch; cornices of simple early C19 plasterwork in principal rooms. A seat of the Harold-Barry family; now the home of Capt Witham Esmonde and Mrs Esmonde (*née* Harold-Barry).

Ballyknockane Lodge. Built 1867 to the design of Sir Thomas Newenham Deane, on the lands of Kilcash Castle (*qv*).

Barnane. Work was carried out here 1863, to the design of Sir Thomas Newenham Deane.

Barons Court. The main C19 remodelling of the house was carried out between 1836 and 1840 by 2nd Marquess (afterwards 1st Duke) of Abercorn; Sir Richard Morrison was involved in the work as well as William Vitruvius Morrison, who died 1838 while it was in progress. The projecting wings flanking the entrance porte-cochère were foreshortened and other alterations carried out 1946–47, to the design of Sir Albert Richardson.

Blarney Castle. The keep was actually built in two different periods.

Brittas Castle, Thurles, co Tipperary. Brittas was bequeathed by Capt John Frederick Knox to Miss Mabel Anna Langley; so it is now back in the Langley family once again.

Burntcourt Castle. It is said of Burntcourt, "Seven years building, seven years lived in, seven days burning".

Cahir. The inner ward and the base of the keep of the castle are C13.

Castlestrange, Athleague, co Roscommon (MITCHELL/LG 1875). A square house, now ruined. Imposing "U"-shaped stables; long medieval bridge over river Suck near gate. Ornamental ritual stone in demesne.

Daly's Grove, Ahascragh, co Galway (DALY/IFR). Originally a plain 3 storey C18 house; 3 bay front, windows spaced very widely apart; fanlighted doorway with sidelights beneath shallow relieving arch. Irregular 2 bay side. The house was increased in depth *ca* 1830 by the building of a 3 storey battlemented addition at the back; so that the side elevation was extended by another 2 bays; the stone of the new building contrasting with the stucco of the old. Private chapel. The original seat of the Dalys of Castle Daly (*qv*); Dermot O'Daly, grandson of Dermot O'Daly of Killimer, having been transplanted here 1656. Passed C19 to a junior branch of the Castle Daly family; sold 1928.

Dollardstown. In 1920s, Dollardstown, by then somewhat decayed, was the home of Mrs Hannah Laffan, mother of Brendan Bracken (afterwards Viscount Bracken), who spoke of the house as "that old barracks".

Donahies (The). The house was faced with particularly attractive brick.

Dromdihy House, Killeagh, co Cork. A handsome Classical house of 1833 built by Roger Green Davis, consisting of a centre with wings; the wings being ornamented with Doric columns. Entrance at one end, under a portico. Now a ruin.

Drummin, Carbury, co Kildare. A square 2 storey house of late-Georgian appearance with an eaved roof on a bracket cornice. Entrance front with round-headed doorway; 5 bay garden front. The entrance was subsequently moved to one side of the house, where a 2 storey projection was built; a corresponding projection being built at the other side. The original hall became a dining room, the former entrance doorway a window. The seat of a branch of the Grattan family, descended from a cousin of Henry Grattan, the orator, statesman and Irish patriot; inherited 1915 from Miss Anne Grattan by R. C. de Courcy-Wheeler (*see* IFR).

Dunsoghly Castle. The tower is of 4 storeys rather than 3. The roof of the castle is the best surviving example of a medieval trussed roof in Ireland.

Flood Hall. Though it was the home of his father, Chief Justice Warden Flood, and of his cousin and heir, John Flood, Flood Hall was not in fact the home of Henry Flood, the statesman, who lived at Farmley, a short distance away.

Fortwilliam, Milford, co Cork (SHEEHY/IFR). A house of mid-C19 appearance in the cottage style, with gables and ornamented bargeboards.

French Park. The house incorporated a mid-C17 house, built by Patrick French, a burgess of Galway who acquired the estate and other lands, and who died 1669.

Glenshelane House, Cappoquin, co Waterford (KEANE, Bt/PB; FITZ GERALD, *sub* LEINSTER, D/PB). A house in the simple late-Georgian "cottage" style, romantically situated far up a wooded glen in the Knockmealdown foothills. Originally built *ca* 1820 as a shooting-lodge by the Keane family of Cappoquin House (*qv*); subsequently enlarged and occupied by the sisters of Sir Richard Francis Keane, 4th Bt. 2 storeys, partly over basement; upper storey partly in attic with dormer-gables. Entrance front with gable and 3 sided bow. Large single-storey curved bow on end of house, containing semi-circular drawing room. Now the home of Brig Denis FitzGerald, who has made a very attractive garden on the slopes above the house.

Glinsk Castle. Not so much a house with a recessed centre, as a main block with large projecting corner towers.

Holestone. Owned by the Hamilton family for the past 50 years.

Jigginstown House. As well as the extensive walls and vaulted basement of the main block, other buildings survive; notably the 2 corner pavilions.

Kilcash Castle, Ballypatrick, co Tipperary (BUTLER, ORMONDE, M/PB). One of the chief strongholds of the Ormonde Butlers, a large tower house with a hall wing on the southern slopes of Slievenaman. Kilcash was the seat of a junior branch of the family from 1639 until 1758, when John Butler, of Kilcash, became *de jure* 15th Earl of Ormonde. The castle afterwards fell into decay, but is still owned by the Ormonde family, who in 1867 built Ballyknockane Lodge (*qv*) on their lands here. Kilcash gives its name to a well-known C18 Irish song (translated into English by Frank O'Connor), which mourns the death of Margaret, wife of Colonel Thomas Butler and of the *de jure* 15th Earl.

Killora Lodge, Glounthaune, co Cork (MAHONY/IFR). A 2 storey 5 bay late-Georgian house with an eaved roof. Fanlighted doorway, now inside later porch with doors at sides and modillion cornice. Cornices of early to mid-C19 plasterwork in principal rooms. The home of Mrs Francis Mahony.

Killoskehane Castle. Remodelled 1867, to the design of Sir Thomas Newenham Deane.

Killoughter. For "shallow segmental pediment" read "shallow segmental fanlight". Bought by Captain Halpin, who commanded the steamship *Great Eastern* when she laid the first Atlantic cable.

Killynether House, Newtownards, co Down (VANE-TEMPEST-STEWART, LONDONDERRY, M/PB). A house enlarged and remodelled 1875–76 by 5th Marquess of Londonderry to the design of Henry Chappell, of Newtownards, in a mixture of Gothic and Tudor with many slender turrets. On the hill above the demesne is the Scottish Baronial Scrabo Tower, erected 1858 as a memorial to 3rd Marquess, a distinguished soldier and diplomatist, to the design of Sir Charles Lanyon and William Henry Lynn. Part of the demesne is now in the care of the National Trust.

Kilmacoom. The older family house here, Fort William, still stands some distance from the present house. The story about the skeletons appears to be apocryphal.

Knockagh Castle. The ruined C17 house which appears in the photograph has now been completely destroyed; and only the round medieval tower remains.

Knockgrafton Rectory. For Knockgrafton read Knockgraffon.

Knocklyon Castle. The house has a medieval core.

Lemaneagh Castle. The stone fireplace is not at Dromoland, but at the Old Ground Hotel, Ennis.

Levington Park. Now the home of Mr J. P. Donleavy, the novelist.

Lisfinny Castle, Tallow, co Waterford. A 2 storey house of late-Georgian appearance, built in front of an old Desmond castle, which rises above it. 5 bay front, round-headed doorway not central; eaved roof. In 1837, the home of Capt Edwards Croker; recently, of Col L. P. Barrington.

Loughananna House, Kilbehenny, co Limerick (KENNEDY, Bt/PB). A 2 storey house with a 3 bay Victorian front which was added to an earlier range by Abel Buckley, MP, builder of the nearby Galtee Castle (*qv*). The Victorian front has quoins and wide, camber-headed windows surrounded by stone blocking. The older range was once the home of Col John O'Mahony, the Fenian. Since 1963, Loughananna has been the home of Mr and Mrs Robert Kennedy.

Loughmoe Court. Not a National Monument.

Marino, Clontarf, co Dublin. The present very extensive work of restoration on the Casino is being carried out by Mr Austin Dunphy of O'Neill Flanagan and Partners in conjunction with Mr D. Newman Johnson of the Office of Public Works.

New Park, Moville, co Donegal (MONTGOMERY OF ALAMEIN, V/FB). A house on the northern shore of Lough Foyle, built *ca* 1773 by Samuel Montgomery, a prosperous Derry merchant in wines and spirits. The home of Sir Robert Montgomery, one of the founders of British rule in the Punjab; also of Bishop Montgomery, father of FM Viscount Montgomery of Alamein. Sold by "Monty's" eldest brother, Harold Robert Montgomery.

Newpark, Ballymote, co Sligo (DUKE/LGI1912). A late C18 house. The seat of the Duke family; now of the Kitchin family.

Newtown, Waterford, co Waterford (BONAPARTE WYSE/IFR). A handsome 3 storey late C18 block, probably built by Thomas Wyse of the Manor of St John (*qv*), the leading Catholic merchant of contemporary Waterford. 3 bay pedimented breakfront; central Venetian window over semi-circular pillared porch beneath tripartite window. Sold by Thomas Wyse 1797, since when it has been a well-known Quaker (now non-denominational) school.

Parkes Castle. Not, strictly speaking, a Plantation house; but an earlier castle remodelled during the Plantation period.

Portumna Castle. The hall did not extend the full length of the centre, but was on one side of a central passage, in the more usual Tudor or Jacobean manner. The stairs were situated in the spine of the building, between the 2 ranges of rooms. Much of the interior appears to have been laid out in sets of state apartments, in the French style. There was a long gallery on the top floor, facing south down Lough Derg. Early in the present century, after Portumna had been inherited by Viscount Lascelles, there was a plan to restore the Jacobean castle to the designs of Dr John Bilson; but this came to nothing.

Rathcoffey. The gatehouse is not the only part of the old castle to have survived; the C18 house is in fact a remodelling of a C13 hall house.

Rath House, Ballybrittas, co Leix. The estate did not originally belong to the Bagot family.

Redwood Castle, co Tipperary. A tower house of the Egans, said to have been built *ca* 1580 but probably C15; now being restored by Mr Michael Egan. The Egans were hereditary lawyers, and in former times had a law school here.

Rochestown, Cahir, co Tipperary (WISE, *sub* MCCLINTOCK/IFR). A house altered 1867 for a member of the Wise family, to the design of Sir Thomas Newenham Deane. Inherited by Mrs James McClintock, *née* Wise.

St Austin's Abbey, Tullow, co Carlow (DOYNE/IFR). A High Victorian house, rather similar to Derrylahan Park (*qv*), built *ca* 1858 by Charles Henry Doyne, younger son of Robert Doyne, of Wells (*qv*), to the design of Sir Thomas Newenham Deane and Benjamin Woodward. Burnt *ca* 1920.

Turbotston. The house is not demolished, but still stands intact and is being cared for by its present owner, Mr John Donohoe.

Turvey. The late C17 building incorporates an earlier tower house.

Woodbrook, Bray, co Wicklow. The panelling in the hall is English, with carving in the manner of Grinling Gibbons.

Woodstock, Inistioge, co Kilkenny. The statue of Mary Tighe, illustrated on p 287, has been established by Mr John Kenworthy-Browne as a work of the Florentine sculptor, Bartolini.

Index

NOTE. *This Index covers families, architects, historical personages, etc. Families connected with the houses are listed under their surname alone; the names of individual members of the families are only listed in full in the case of personages of special historical or other interest. Full names are also used in the case of persons mentioned incidentally in the text, as distinct from persons actually connected with the houses in question. Architects who worked on the houses or influenced their style have "arch" after their names; the names of other artists and craftsmen who worked on the houses are followed by "painter", "sculptor", or whatever may apply. Double and treble-barrelled names are listed, according to Burke's practice, under the last name.*